Digital Jim Crow: Empowering yourself against the visual Diet of Escapism, racism, and abuse contributing to the erosion of our spirits and decay of the well-being of marginalized peoples.

Neither the publisher nor the author is engaged in rendering professional advice or services to the individual reader. The ideas, procedures, and suggestions contained in this book are not intended as a substitute for consulting with your physician or mental health provider. All matters regarding your health require medical supervision. Neither the author nor the publisher shall be liable for or responsible for any loss or damage allegedly arising from any information or suggestion in this book.

Table of Contents

Forward 5

Introduction 7

Part I: Brief Overview 12

Chapter One: The Benefits of Screens 13

Chapter Two: History of Visual Media 21

Chapter Three: How Our Brain Interprets Visual Data 30

Part II: The Many Reasons We Should Have a Balanced Visual Diet 35

Chapter Four: ADHD, Dyslexia, Dyspraxia, and Dyscalculia and Visual Media 36

Chapter Five: Autism, Tourette's Synestheisa, Sensory Processing Conditions, Highly Sensitive People and Visual Media 50

Chapter Six: The Traumatized Brain 66

Chapter Seven: How we Learn 83

Chapter Eight: Children's Brains on Screens 92

Chapter Nine: Dopamine's Role 110

Chapter Ten Doom Scrolling 119

Chapter Eleven: Video Games and Gaming Disorder 127

Chapter Twelve: Smartphones 139

Chapter Thirteen: Toxic Positivity 147

Chapter Fourteen: How Women and Girls are Portrayed in Visuel Media 161

Chapter Fifteen: Dating in a World of Swipe Culture 170

Chapter Sixteen: Sex and Sexuality 183

Chapter Seventeen: How Racial Identities are Portrayed on Screens 192

Chapter Eighteen: Poor Visual Diets of Healthcare Professionals Affecting Marginalized Populations 217

Chapter Nineteen: Data Broking 229

Chapter Twenty: Anger and Rage Cycles 246

Chapter Twenty-One: Artificial Intelligence (AI) 263

Part III: Planning for success in your digital detox 285
Chapter Twenty-Two: Planning for your Digital Wellness 286
Chapter Twenty-Three: Goal-Oriented Planning.......................................298
Chapter Twenty-Four: Ideal Visual Diets for Neurodivergent Folks 320

Part IV: Action Phase..339
Chapter Twenty-Five: BIPOC Folk's Needs 340
Chapter Twenty-Six: Evidenced-Based Ways for Healthy Relationships with Screens 353
Chapter Twenty-Seven: Science of Mindfulness..388
Chapter Twenty-Eight: Practical Mindfulness..397
Chapter Twenty-Nine: Regulate your Body 427
Chapter Thirty: Reparenting Unmet Needs..438
Chapter Thirty-One: Using Art and Creativity to Tend to Your Needs....459
Chapter Thirty-Two: Interventions to Tend to Your Needs.......................468

Part V: Potential Options for a Successful Digital Detox and Sustainable Goals 491
Chapter Thirty-Three: How an Ideal Visual Diet Can Appear 492
Chapter Thirty-Four: Managing your New Visual Diet.............................511

Key Takeaways 528
Appendix 532
Index...550

Forward

For years, marginalized communities have been targeted by content designed to capture our attention, shape our behaviors, and limit our agency. This book is not about rejecting technology, it's about understanding how to regain control over our visual consumption.

The creators of screen-based content have perfected a formula that cultivates compulsive behaviors, especially amongst marginalized populations. They've made billions by producing content that is difficult to walk away from, limiting our ability to self-regulate. This has profound implications for how we see ourselves, how we function in the world, and how we're perceived by others. These dynamics aren't always easy to recognize, let alone unpack.

When I began writing this in 2022, I became acutely aware of the stimuli constantly influencing me in real time. My intention is to offer a grounded, research-based framework that helps us understand how certain types of content affect our bodies, minds, and spirits, and how we can fall into cycles that feel hard to escape.

Just as important, the effects of others' poor visual diets ripple outward. Harmful and stereotypical imagery can shape how marginalized people are treated, further reinforcing inequities and weakening trust between those in power and those fighting for justice.

Technology itself is not to blame. It is a tool, just like the laptop I'm using to write this book or the phone I bring to my face throughout the day. But the systems driving our attention, the software coded to manipulate us into staying engaged, are to blame. The engineers who design these features, and the companies who profit from mass dependency, deserve our scrutiny. While technology can be empowering and connective, it can also erode our well-being. We'll explore that more deeply throughout this book.

My aim is to provide objective, accessible research on how a visually saturated environment, especially one dominated by harmful or one-dimensional narratives, can disrupt our relationship with ourselves and each other. I focus in particular on the experiences of BIPOC communities, especially Black and Brown folks, as well as neurodivergent individuals, whose relationships with visual content are often shaped by unique and underexplored dynamics.

Too much of anything can harm us. Just as someone who eats fast food daily shouldn't expect to feel their best, a poor visual diet can flood our systems with negative inputs that affect our emotional, physical, and spiritual health. This book isn't about shaming what we consume, it's about giving us the tools to understand it, reclaim it, and move with greater intention.

My goal isn't to tell you what not to watch or consume visually, but to illuminate how the things we do consume can affect us. This book isn't about shame or judgment; it's about understanding our complex relationship with digital media and developing tools for more intentional engagement. If we choose to indulge in something that excites us, we might also need a plan to help bring ourselves back to center.

Inside these pages, you'll find meta-analyses and evidence-based methods that reveal how our visual diets can harm us, often without our conscious awareness. I speak not just from research, but from personal experience. Since childhood, I've consumed visual media in excess. I know firsthand the long-term effects.

Writing this book has been profoundly therapeutic. It's given me a chance to reflect on and unpack the layers of my own experience, on how I learned to soothe, to numb, and eventually, to heal. In many ways, it's helped me reparent my inner child and acknowledge the moments when I wasn't protected or guided in the ways I needed most.

I want to express my deep gratitude to my friends and family for their continued support. To those who listened patiently as I went on passionate rants about the latest studies or insights. To those who shared articles, clips, or simply asked thoughtful questions that pushed my thinking forward, you were all part of this journey.

The more I researched how visual media affects us, the more I felt seen. That's the part I want to emphasize **in excess**, visual content can have serious effects, but I'm not advocating for a no-screen lifestyle. While I respect those who choose that path, it's not realistic for many of us, including myself. What *is* realistic, and necessary, is learning how to manage our expectations and relationships with media.

My hope is that this book offers tools, insights, and compassion for anyone who has struggled, or still struggles, with a poor visual diet. You're not alone. And you can take your power back.

Introduction

"I'm opposed to a lot of the time that we as a civilization have come to spend looking at screens. For my money, life is much delicious damn near everyplace but inside that screen." -Nick Offerman

Do you ever find yourself overstimulated, so much so that you have to look away from the screen, leave the room, or just shut everything off? Are there certain places you avoid, television shows you won't watch, or visual triggers that bring you to the brink of tears?

On the flip side, do you actively seek out high-stimulation environments, intense shows, rapid-fire content, high-drama scenarios, because they make you feel alive, or because they distract you from something else? Have your loved ones commented that what you watch feels overwhelming, even chaotic? Do you instinctively reach for your phone, needing to "see what's going on," even in moments of silence or peace? Does being away from screens make you feel anxious or like something's missing?

Are you finding yourself disconnected from the joy of things that once brought you peace? Reaching instead for a device to fill that void? And what about your anger, have you noticed it growing? Do you find yourself engaged in digital battles with strangers, trying to make your point to people who just don't seem to *get it*?

This is not a judgment. This is recognition.

Many of us are swept up by our visual environments, pulled into a current of constant stimulation. We float in this sea of screens, unanchored and reactive, letting our attention be shaped and reshaped by every swipe, scroll, and stream.

Each of us is affected, whether subtly or significantly, by what we consume. What we see has the power to shape how we think, how we feel, and how we relate to others. It influences our culture, our biases (implicit and explicit), our view of the world, and how we show up in it. These effects ripple outward, into our families, our communities, and the systems we operate in.

So, what *is* a visual diet?

Simply put, it's what we absorb visually. Just like food affects our physical bodies, visual content impacts our mental, emotional, and even spiritual states.

Let me offer an example from my own life. I am an alcoholic and cannabis addict, currently in active recovery. When I was actively using, the substances I ingested left me depleted, sluggish, and disconnected from myself the next day. And similarly, when I overconsume digital content, when I binge-watch, doomscroll, or immerse myself in emotionally intense media, I don't feel like myself the next day either. I may be wired, irritable, or emotionally overwhelmed.

I've struggled immensely to maintain a visual diet that supports a sense of balance. My nervous system, shaped by developmental trauma, racialized stress, and systemic inequities, is already working overtime. Add in a chaotic visual diet, and it's a recipe for dysregulation.

As a BIPOC individual raised in an environment that offered limited support, for me and for others who looked like me, it's no surprise I turned to screens to escape. Many of us do. They offer alternate realities that feel safer, more predictable, or simply easier to endure than the real world. But there's a cost.

In a society full of perceived threats, both external and internal, we can lose connection with others and with ourselves. This disconnection can stifle oxytocin, the neurochemical responsible for attachment and bonding. Without those healthy social ties and emotional touchpoints, many of us feel isolated. Screens become our substitute, but they don't feed our deeper needs.

Trauma Bond

It's fascinating, and concerning, how the human brain can experience a flood of dopamine and immense fatigue *at the same time*. Few things evoke this kind of internal contradiction, but our relationship with visual media is one of them.

A visual diet is, in a reductive sense, much like a food-based diet. What we see, read, play, and interact with stimulates our brains in complex ways. Some effects are short-term, others long-lasting. Some are harmless. Others can quietly wire us into trauma bonds.

I'll unpack this relationship between trauma bonding and visual diets more deeply in Chapter Seven, but for now, consider this: many of us are unconsciously forming emotional ties to the very stimuli that dysregulate us, because the cycle of tension, reward, and relief mirrors patterns we've known elsewhere in life.

We live in a world saturated with stimulation. Every app, screen, and platform are designed to capture our gaze and keep us locked in. Given our evolutional wiring and the stress of navigating systemic, generational, and personal traumas, it's no wonder we find ourselves so easily hooked.

In fact, some of this content is designed to be irresistible.

The documentary *The Social Dilemma* highlights the sophisticated nature of this system. Algorithms, UX design, and behavioral science converge to engineer platforms that feed directly into our nervous systems. These technologies weren't just *made* to capture our attention; they were *refined* for it.

While I'm not here to, just vilify tech companies, I *am* here to raise awareness. These creators are not blameless, especially when their content disproportionately targets children and marginalized communities. They know what they're doing.

It's easy to say, "Just unplug," or "People should be more disciplined," but that oversimplifies the problem. We're not just consuming content, we're engaging with highly engineered, deeply immersive experiences that trigger compulsive behaviors.

Take the news, for instance. It's rarely just reporting, it's flashing graphics, dramatic headlines, scrolling tickers, urgent music. It's dopamine on demand. Or consider video games and streaming services, deliberately designed to keep us bingeing, one hit after another. Our phones? They've become portable dopamine regulators, buzzing with endless cues to "check in."

We're already past the point of no return. The technologies are here. They're not going away.

So, what do we do?

We get smarter.

We learn how these systems affect us. We examine our relationship with visual media. We explore how to come back to our bodies, to be more embodied, more intentional, more aware.

To be clear: correlation doesn't mean causation. Visual overstimulation isn't the sole cause of today's mental health crises. Human well-being is shaped by genetics, environment, trauma, systems of oppression, and so much more. Mental health is *epigenetic*, *systemic*, and deeply interwoven with the world we live in.

But the influence of our visual diet shouldn't be ignored. It plays a role, especially when unexamined.

Generations of trauma echo forward, making some of us more susceptible to these traps. These content streams don't just entertain, they condition. They shape how we think, how we feel, and what we believe. They keep us locked into emotional loops, echo chambers that feel familiar but keep us small.

Distraction has its place, especially for those navigating harsh realities. But where is the off switch?

Right now, there isn't one.

And that's what makes awareness and regulation so critical. We may not be able to shut the whole system down, but we *can* start choosing how, when, and why we engage.

As a clinician, I'm acutely aware that no single factor can define an individual's experience or serve as the sole focus of treatment. Instead, healing and understanding emerge from the *synthesis* of many dynamic influences, biological, psychological, social, cultural, and environmental. These forces intertwine to shape the perspectives, or "realities," that each person carries with them through life.

When I use the term *realities*, I do so synonymously with *perspectives*. Each of us lives through a lens shaped by our unique experiences, past and present, as well as our culture, environment, and, importantly, what we choose to give our attention to. Based on these individual factors, it becomes clear: differing realities among individuals aren't just expected, they're inevitable.

Technology has only deepened this divide.

Rather than offering a diverse buffet of perspectives or exposing us to a range of viewpoints over time, our current technological ecosystem increasingly funnels us into isolated sound chambers, echo chambers of confirmation and repetition. The days of delayed access to information, where opinions were formed after digesting data over time, have been replaced by the immediacy of algorithmic gratification. We now consume content that is fast, filtered, and persistently aligned with what we've already shown interest in.

I'll explore the historical evolution of media consumption in the following chapter. But for now, let me say this: the concept of an influential visual diet is nothing new. What *has* changed is the speed, intensity, and personalization of that diet, and how it reinforces tunnel vision rather than inviting nuanced or divergent thought.

This is the danger of an echo chamber.

When we're only exposed to perspectives that mirror our own, we lose the opportunity to grow. To shift. To challenge assumptions. Over time, our worldviews can become rigid and incomplete filtered through a singular lens, rather than reflecting the complexity of a shared, ever-changing world.

We now live in a reality that has been irrevocably shaped, and augmented, by the constant availability of screens. These devices are incredible tools of innovation and connection, but their effects are still unfolding in real time. Researchers are only beginning to understand the depth of their influence on human development, cognition, and interpersonal connection.

We cannot, nor should we, seek to fully eliminate screens from our lives. That's not realistic, nor is it necessary. But we *can* be more intentional. We *can* take greater responsibility for our visual diets and how they shape our inner and outer worlds.

This book wasn't written to criticize technological advancement. Far from it. I believe in the potential of these tools when used thoughtfully. Every innovation has a spectrum of outcomes, just like coffee. In moderation, it can boost energy, sharpen focus, and support productivity. But in excess, it can lead to anxiety, jitteriness, and dependency. It can disrupt our nervous systems and create a cycle of craving that masks deeper imbalances.

Visual content functions the same way.

I've lived on both ends of the spectrum. And my hope in sharing this is not to tell readers what to avoid, but to offer awareness, and more importantly, *agency*. Because when we understand what we're consuming and how it's influencing us, we can start making choices that support rather than sabotage our growth.

My personal visual diet has also augmented my view of the world and my proclivities in terms of those who I bring into my personal life. Compounded by my own traumas, visual media has been a constant companion in my life. With the great work my therapist and I have accomplished, together, I feel closer to narrowing that hold that visual media has upon me.

Although there is a consistent theme and message that flows throughout the book. I encourage readers to jump around to different chapters. This book is made to be read from start to finish or bouncing around. Feel out which works for you and challenge your visual diet.

Part I: Brief Overview

Chapter One

"I'm bored way too easily. I'm staring at screens half the day. I need to be overstimulated. And how will that express itself artistically?" -Bo Burnham

The Benefits of Screens

There are very few… just kidding. The benefits of screens and screen time have been heavily researched and are worth serious discussion. These technological marvels, much like any invention, can span a spectrum of behavioral outcomes, ranging from helpful to harmful.

While a myriad of studies highlights the potential detriments of screen time, it's important to note that some of these findings are contested and not easily replicable. The same can be said about the studies presenting positive findings for screens time. Despite these concerns, when used thoughtfully and within a supportive framework, screen time can foster child development and provide individuals with accessible ways to hone their skills and intellect.

Limitations in Early Childhood

For children under two years old, screen time offers limited benefits. According to the American Academy of Pediatrics (AAP):

> *"Recommendations to discourage media exposure for children younger than 2 years were based on research on TV and videos, which showed that in-person interactions with parents are much more effective than video for learning of new verbal or nonverbal problem-solving skills... The video deficit is thought to be attributable to infants' and young toddlers' lack of symbolic thinking, immature attentional controls, and the memory flexibility required to effectively transfer knowledge from a 2-dimensional platform to a 3-dimensional world."*
> — Reid et al., 2016

In short, infants and toddlers benefit most from hands-on exploration and direct interaction with trusted caregivers as they develop cognitive, language, sensorimotor, and social-emotional skills.

Parent Interaction Matters

A 2010 study by DeLoache et al. found that children using "baby media" alone did not show significant gains in word learning. In fact, the most successful learning outcomes were observed in children whose parents taught them new words through everyday interaction, without the aid of media.

> *"Infants between 12 and 18 months learned very little from a highly popular media product... but performance was highest in the parent teaching group. Even with the substantial amount of exposure that they had to the video, the infants learned only a few of the words featured on it but the performance was highest in the parent teaching group, those children who had no exposure to the video, but whose parents had attempted to teach them new words during everyday interactions"*

This trend is echoed in another study (Richert et al., 2010) where children aged 12–24 months only demonstrated notable learning gains when parents modeled the words and directly interacted with them, even when a learning DVD was used.

Screen Time with Social Support

A longitudinal study involving 253 low-income families (Mendelsohn, 2010) found that screen time could be beneficial—if caregivers were present and engaged in conversation during the experience. The study concluded:

> *"Media verbal interactions moderated adverse impacts of media exposure... with adverse associations found only in the absence of these interactions. Media verbal interactions... were predictive of 14-month language development independently of overall level of cognitive stimulation in the home."*

So, it's not just the content, it's the context. Media becomes a learning tool when used as a springboard for real, meaningful interaction.

Interactive Learning and Parasocial Relationships

Dayanim et al. (2015) further emphasized the power of interactive support: in their 4-week experiment, 15–24-month-olds showed a strong learning curve from instructional videos, but only when parents supported the experience.

Children may also form *parasocial relationships*, one-sided emotional bonds, with screen characters like Dora the Explorer, or Sesame Street figures. Research by Brunick et al. (2016) suggests that repetition, relatable voices, and childlike characters encourage attachment, which in turn can support learning. As we'll explore later, secure attachments, whether with real people or characters, can enhance a child's capacity to learn.

Building Digital Literacy

We live in a digital world. Teaching children to use age-appropriate devices responsibly fosters digital literacy, an essential skill. Whether through touchscreens, e-books, or educational apps, screens can support development when paired with guided, age-appropriate use. Additionally, the World Health Organization's recommendations for age-appropriate use should be considered at home, play dates, friend's homes, socializing outside of home, daycare and preschool.

Later in this book, we'll discuss what "age-appropriate" actually means, acknowledging the challenges faced by marginalized communities that may lack access to ideal learning environments due to systemic inequities.

High-Quality TV Programs as an Indicator of Positive Brain Health

According to the American Academy of Pediatrics (AAP):

> *"High-quality TV programs (e.g., Public Broadcasting Service [PBS] programs, such as Sesame Street and Mister Rogers' Neighborhood) can demonstrably improve cognitive, linguistic, and social outcomes for children 3 to 5 years of age. Choosing PBS content has been found to be protective of poor executive function outcomes observed in children who start consuming media in early infancy. For families who find it difficult to modify the overall amount of media use in their homes, changing to high-quality content may be a more actionable alternative; to make these changes, pediatric providers can direct them toward curation services, such as Common Sense Media, for reviews of videos, apps, TV shows, and movies."*
> — *AAP, 2016*

This highlights an essential shift in mindset: when screen use is unavoidable or hard to scale back, upgrading the *quality* of the content may offer real developmental advantages.

Equally important is the need for high-quality media to reflect diverse representation. Children's programming must be inclusive of different races, cultures, abilities, and gender identities to support cognitive and emotional development in a way that fosters equity and inclusion. A diverse media landscape helps young viewers develop empathy, recognize their own value in society, and appreciate the value of others. These concepts will be explored more thoroughly later in the book.

Benefits to Adolescents

Adolescents experience a unique developmental period, particularly in terms of identity formation and peer connection. During the COVID-19 pandemic, digital media played an unexpectedly vital role in sustaining these connections:

> *"Media has filled the gaps in social interaction created by distancing guidelines, serving as an important avenue of engagement."*
> — *Fry, 2021*

This adaptive use of screens offered adolescents a lifeline, supporting mental health through ongoing access to friends, social networks, and even support groups. While post-pandemic conditions shift the conversation around screen use, the social-emotional benefits remain relevant and cannot be dismissed. The adolescent need for community, connection, and a sense of belonging is powerful—and digital tools can be a meaningful part of that.

The Power of Community Across Lifespans

This benefit is not exclusive to children or teens. Adults, especially older individuals experiencing isolation, can also benefit from digital platforms that allow for parasocial or virtual social relationships. These interactions can mitigate the negative effects of loneliness and provide a sense of belonging and engagement.

Likewise, individuals with accessibility concerns or limitations, whether physical, cognitive, or environmental, often find in screens a powerful gateway to connection, creativity, and advocacy. Online spaces allow people to find others who share their identities or experiences, helping foster community in ways that physical spaces sometimes cannot.

The ability of screens to bridge geographic, social, and emotional distances is both remarkable and vital in our increasingly connected world.

A Note on Further Resources

While this book is not specifically intended as a guide for raising children in the digital age or increasing digital literacy specifically for children, parents and caregivers seeking practical advice may benefit from Julianna Miner's book *Raising a Screen-Smart Kid: Embrace the Good and Avoid the Bad in the Digital Age* (2019). Miner offers clear, grounded, and realistic strategies for navigating screen time while preserving a child's emotional, social, and intellectual development.

1. Set Boundaries and Rules

- **Establish screen-free zones and times** (e.g., bedrooms, mealtimes, family gatherings)
- Set limits on screen time (e.g., 1-2 hours per day for children under 12)

- Encourage physical activity and outdoor play

2. Monitor and Control Screen Use

- **Use parental control software to restrict access to inappropriate content and set limits on screen time**
- Set up screen-free accounts for young children (under 2 years old)
- Supervise and participate in online activities with your child

3. Foster Healthy Online Habits

- **Teach your child to critically evaluate online information and identify biases**
- Encourage online etiquette (e.g., respectful comments, no cyberbullying)
- Discuss online safety and privacy with your child

4. Promote Balance and Variety

- **Encourage a mix of screen-based and non-screen activities** (e.g., reading, drawing, sports)
- Support your child's interests and passions, even if they don't involve screens

5. Model Healthy Screen Use Yourself

- **Demonstrate responsible screen use yourself** (e.g., no screens during meals, limit your own screen time)
- Engage in activities with your child that don't involve screens (e.g., board games, outdoor activities)

6. Educate Yourself

- Stay informed about the latest online trends and risks
- Attend workshops or online courses on digital parenting and online safety

7. Encourage Open Communication

- Talk to your child about their online experiences and concerns
- Listen actively and offer guidance and support

8. Teach Digital Citizenship

- Discuss online etiquette, cyberbullying, and digital rights with your child
- Encourage your child to respect others' online privacy and personal space

9. Foster Empathy and Critical Thinking

- **Encourage your child to consider the perspectives of others online**
- Teach critical thinking skills to evaluate online information and identify biases

10. Be Patient and Flexible

- Recognize that screen use is a normal part of modern life
- Be willing to adapt your approach as your child grows and changes

By following these guidelines, you can help your child develop healthy screen habits and become a responsible digital citizen. Remember to stay informed, communicate openly, and model healthy screen use yourself.

Another fantastic book detailing the ways children can benefit from a screen detox is 'Reset your Child's Brain: A Four-Week Plan to End Meltdowns, Raise Grades, and Boost Social Skills by Reversing the Effects of Electronic Screen-Time' by Dr. Victoria L. Dunckley. Since the book is a bit older, I recommend taking what you can gain from it as much as possible. Especially the plan to set your child up for success.

TIPS FROM "RESET YOUR CHILD'S BRAIN by Victoria Dunckley (Reset Your Child's Brain, 2015)

Adjusting Your Child's Environment

1. **Go Wired** - easier to enforce house rules, and less convenient when only in certain locations.

2. **Reduce artificial brightness** - check devices and lower screen brightness to more closely match surrounding environment

3. **Use red tones or warm screens** in your screens and use the bedtime feature available on most smartphones which reduces brightness as night falls

4. **Use smaller screens and view from farther away**

5. **Maintain a sleep sanctuary** - bedroom free of electronics, and optimize bedroom lighting, including pitch-back during sleep time

6. **Minimize Screen**-Time after sundown

Additionally, the entire household is represented as an important focus for success.

House Rules: Everyday Screen-Time Guidelines and Boundaries

1. Keep bedrooms screen-free
2. Create a family workstation
3. Match Screen-time with Exercise time
4. Screen-Time is a privilege not a right
5. Ban media multitasking
6. Designate Screen-free Times and Zones
7. Walk the talk
8. Use timers and checkouts

Promoting Brain Health

1. Greenery, nature and sunlight
2. Movement, exercise and free play
3. Deep sleep and clean diet
4. Creativity
5. Mindfulness and meditation
6. Bonding: Human touch, Empathy and Love

You may be wondering why it is even important to "raise a screen smart child" or limit their digital footprint/accessibility to screens. For that, I bring you to recent news:

> *On March 24, 2025, in Houston, Texas, three teenage sisters, ages 14, 15, and 16, were arrested for allegedly attempting to stab their mother after she turned off the home's Wi-Fi. According to Harris County Sheriff Ed Gonzalez, the girls coordinated a plan to kill their mother, chasing her with kitchen knives through the house and into the street. During the incident, one of the girls threw a brick that struck their 39-year-old mother in the ankle, and their 70-year-old grandmother was knocked over while trying to protect her. Fortunately, neither the mother nor the grandmother sustained serious injuries. The three sisters were charged with aggravated assault with a deadly weapon and were booked into the Harris County Juvenile Detention Center.* (ABC News, 2025)

Many people may wonder, *What is happening? This would never have happened in their home. Those children deserve the punishment they get,* etc.

Whatever the specifics are in the case, this is clearly a disproportionate reaction to simply turning off Wi-Fi. We may not get the specifics for quite some time or at all. However, many people may want to get in front of this in their own homes. This isn't an isolated incident. In the book, 'Reset Your Child's Brain', Dr. Dunckley identifies other cases where children have attacked their family members when screens were limited. This is clearly addiction behavior. The underdeveloped brains of our youth are no match for the power of screens and neither are adults.

Summary

- While excessive screen time has been criticized, research shows that, when used appropriately, screens can support skill development, learning, and social engagement.

- For children under two years old, screens have limited benefits as in-person interactions are far more effective for cognitive and language development. Studies indicate that infants learn best through parental interaction rather than passive media exposure. However, when parents actively engage with children during screen time, such as co-viewing educational content and reinforcing lessons, it can enhance learning outcomes.

- High-quality TV programs, such as those from PBS, have been shown to improve cognitive, linguistic, and social development in children aged 3-5. The presence of diverse representation in media is also emphasized as important for fostering inclusivity.

- For adolescents, screens played a crucial role in maintaining social connections, especially during the COVID-19 pandemic. Beyond social engagement, screens can also help mitigate isolation for older adults and individuals with accessibility challenges.
- Strategies for parents to manage children's screen use, including setting limits, fostering online etiquette, encouraging offline activities, and modeling healthy screen habits. Books like *Raising a Screen-Smart Kid* by Julianna Miner and *Reset Your Child's Brain* by Victoria Dunckley are recommended for further guidance.

- Ultimately, screens can be beneficial when used in moderation, with parental guidance, and with a focus on high-quality content.

Chapter Two

"I find television very educating. Every time somebody turns on the set, I go into the other room and read a book." Groucho Marx.

The History of the Screen

Before images inundated our daily lives, the written word dominated our visual diets. However, this medium was not universally accessible. Widespread illiteracy limited the public's ability to engage with written content. According to Tyrel C. Eskelson of Hokkaido University in Sapporo, Japan (2021), literacy rates in Western Europe were below 20% during the Middle Ages, only rising to around 50% by the mid-17th century.

As highlighted by Getty Museum medievalists Erin Migdol, Elizabeth Morrison, and Larisa Grollemond (2021), literacy during this period was largely concentrated among the wealthy and privileged, particularly nobles and religious figures like nuns. Those in power held sway over the dissemination of knowledge, using literacy as a gatekeeping tool. For the rest of the population, the ability to read, and thus access knowledge, was out of reach.

Visual media was not a primary concern for most individuals of the time. Life expectancy hovered around a mere 33 years (Carrieri & Serraino, 2005), and survival, not art or balanced "visual diets", took priority. This historical reality remains relevant today in many impoverished parts of the world, where concerns about screen time are far overshadowed by issues of accessibility, survival, and equity.

The Printing Press and Visual Expansion

A turning point in the democratization of knowledge came with the invention of the printing press by Johannes Gutenberg around 1436. This technological advancement enabled the mass production of books and newspapers, significantly lowering costs and expanding access to information.

The press catalyzed a dramatic shift in the public's "visual diet." For the first time, readers from various social strata could explore new perspectives and stories through mass-distributed texts. While some written content included simple illustrations, most information still required readers to conjure vivid images using only their imagination.

The Birth of Photography

The transition from text to image took a major leap forward with the evolution of the camera, which can be traced back over 2,000 years to the camera obscura, a dark chamber where images from outside were projected onto a wall through a small hole or lens (Grundberg et al., 2022).

Later, in the 18th century, German anatomy professor Johann Heinrich Schulze demonstrated that light could darken silver salts, laying the foundation for photographic development. This experimentation culminated in Nicéphore Niépce's first successful photograph in 1826 or 1827 (Grundberg et al., 2022).

Imagine the astonishment of those early viewers: to see real-world imagery captured and displayed for the first time, rather than relying solely on imagination or eyewitness accounts. This development allowed individuals to witness scenes and places they might never experience in person.

Photography and the Democratization of Vision

Photography rapidly evolved into a powerful storytelling and documentation tool. It enabled historical preservation, family portraiture, and visual journalism. The advent of smaller, handheld cameras in the late 19th century made image-capturing more accessible to everyday people, not just artists or the elite.

This shift paralleled what the printing press had done centuries earlier. Now, visual expressions, whether creative, personal, social, or political, was no longer proprietary to the wealthy. The average individual could capture and share their worldview, using photography to document their lives and speak to larger social realities.

Much like artists past and present, early photographers filtered their lived experience through the lens—literally and metaphorically. This medium became an extension of human expression, a form of connection, and a tool for both personal identity and public change.

From Portraits to Moving Pictures: The Evolution of Screen-Based Media

Portraits slowly gave way to moving pictures, which dazzled the minds of many. These moving images opened an entirely new realm of expression, previously unimaginable to everyday people. The way we perceive and interact with our world has, for some time now, been irrevocably shaped by images pulsing through our screens.

On September 7, 1927, Philo Taylor Farnsworth invented the first working television, and by the mid-1940s, televisions began appearing in homes across the United States—albeit in limited numbers and with primitive capabilities compared to today. As Mitchell Stephens (1998) notes, editing, sound quality, and the quantity of content were rudimentary by modern standards.

The Era Before Television: The Golden Age of Radio

Before television, the radio reigned supreme. Families would gather around the set to hear news, dramatic stories, or presidential addresses. Alongside newspapers, this defined the public's "visual diet", or more accurately, their auditory and imaginative diet. Visual overstimulation was rare. Still, this era did not exclude art entirely; rather, access to it was highly stratified.

Artistic experiences were largely limited to the privileged. As Sgourev (2015) explains, social and economic privilege was intricately tied to artistic patronage during the late 19th and early 20th centuries. Museums, galleries, and private collections were often inaccessible to the working class. Consequently, many lived their lives without exposure to the fine arts, unless mediated by religious iconography or mass-produced reproductions.

The Rise of Televised Media and the Dawn of Constant Stimulation

In the early days of television, the flickering light from screens was a novelty, not a constant. News broadcasts were scheduled events, and once programming ended for the night, a network might display a test pattern or high-pitched tone, signaling viewers to turn off their sets.

But as televisions became more affordable and widespread, media companies began to develop strategies to extend programming hours, meeting a growing appetite for news and entertainment that, until then, many hadn't realized they had.

The introduction of 24-hour news changed everything.

On June 1, 1980, Ted Turner launched CNN, the first television channel to offer round-the-clock news coverage. For the first time, viewers could tune in at any hour and catch up on regional, national, or global events. Shortly after CNN's debut, other networks followed suit, fueling a cultural and neurological shift.

What began as a convenience quickly evolved into a new normal: the visual dopamine flood. The continuous stream of stimulation began to rewire how people consumed information, and how often they sought it.

Information Overload and the Modern Screen Experience

Prior to 24-hour television, dopamine floods were typically associated with more tangible or experiential sources, emotional highs from events, achievements, or personal interaction. With the rise of constant visual input, however, our brains began responding to screens as consistent sources of novelty, pleasure, and alertness.

With the introduction of reruns, cable channels, and eventually handheld devices, content became not just accessible, but inescapable. Suddenly, anyone with a television or a phone could engage with an endless flow of stimuli, whether informational, entertaining, or anxiety-inducing.

Information overload, once a rare phenomenon, became a chronic condition. For some, insomnia followed, and for others, increased anxiety and attention fragmentation. Yet this era also brought unparalleled access to knowledge, diverse voices, and global awareness.

Like many other tools in human history, screens are both liberating and overwhelming, depending on how, when, and why they are used.

Information Overload and Media Representation

A 2018 study examining information overload (IO) in the context of online news exposure surveyed 419 individuals aged 15 to 90, with a median age of 38. The results revealed a compelling pattern:

> *"The younger the individuals were, the more they suffered from IO by using online news... The current media and information landscape may be overwhelming and quite challenging to understand, especially for the younger—mostly less experienced in terms of news consumption—users."*
> — *Schmitt et al., 2018*

Interestingly, the study found no significant correlation between gender or specific information sources and IO. However, when lowering the alpha level of significance to 10%, a slight tendency emerged: users who relied more heavily on e-readers were more likely to feel overwhelmed. This could be attributed to the sheer volume of textual content available through that medium.

Additionally, researchers suggest that younger users, often engaging in media and information multitasking, may devote less focused attention to what they consume, leading to a heightened perception of overload.

But information overload isn't limited to the realm of news consumption.

Technological Overload

In the workplace, a related phenomenon, technology overload, is increasingly recognized. According to Karr-Wisniewski & Lu (2010):

> *"More information technology (IT) usage in the workplace can, at times, lead to productivity losses... Technology-based productivity*

> *losses arise from three main sources: information overload, communication overload, and system feature overload."*

This triad can significantly impact efficiency, clarity, and emotional well-being, highlighting that "more tools" does not always equate to "more productivity."

Accessibility, Choice, and Cognitive Overwhelm

Today's hyper-accessibility to visual and informational content, especially via screens, can lead to cognitive paralysis. Take the example of car shopping: imagine being presented with 40 different models, all with varying features, reliability ratings, and price points. Without prior knowledge or guidance, the abundance of options can feel overwhelming, delaying decision-making and increasing stress.

This phenomenon aligns with behavioral economics research showing that humans often perform better with fewer choices. Limited options help narrow focus and reduce decision fatigue. At the same time, excessive limitations can make life feel monotonous, or trigger entitlement, frustration, or even rage, especially when perceived freedoms are restricted.

It's a double-edged sword: more access brings more opportunity but also more complexity, confusion, and, for some, emotional exhaustion.

Representation and Systemic Media Inequity

Beyond the cognitive strain of excess information, what we see, and what we don't see, on screens has a powerful impact.

Historically, black and brown communities were largely excluded from the evolution of visual and print media. Whether due to systemic educational barriers, economic exclusion, or lack of access to early media technologies, these communities were marginalized in both production and representation.

Early film and television portrayals of black and brown individuals were often deeply racist and dehumanizing, featuring grotesque caricatures, "blackface," and infantilized depictions, often portrayed by white actors. These representations embedded harmful stereotypes that reverberate even today.

In the current media landscape, negative portrayals still persist. A 2023 Pew Research survey found that:

> *"63% of respondents said news about Black people is often more negative than news about other racial or ethnic groups... About half (51%) attributed this to media outlets pushing agendas, while others cited uninformed journalists (45%), racist views within*

newsrooms (42%), the speed of the news cycle (37%), and a lack of Black staff (36%)."

These findings reflect ongoing systemic biases in the industry. A 2020 expert panel hosted by the University of Nevada, Las Vegas, summarized the issue clearly:

> *"Structural racism in modern media is pernicious, and resolving it will require honest discussions, a more diverse workforce, and a confrontation of its roots in an ugly and discriminatory history."*
> *— UNLV, 2020*

A Takeaway on Choice and Representation

As this chapter has explored, too many choices can be paralyzing. But within that wide array of choices, many people remain underrepresented or misrepresented. Screens offer connection, education, and inspiration, but they also reflect and perpetuate societal inequalities.

The lack of equitable representation across visual media not only continues the marginalization of BIPOC communities but also limits the full potential of screens as tools for unity, empathy, and transformation.

In future chapters, I'll further explore the long-standing issue of underrepresentation in media and its psychological, cultural, and systemic implications. For now, the key takeaway is this:

We are drowning in choices, but too many voices are still left out.

Emotional Storytelling and the Power of Persuasion

In today's media landscape, emotional storytelling plays a critical role in shaping public perception and behavior. Visual media content creators intentionally craft emotion-focused content to elicit strong emotional responses from viewers, whether it's joy, fear, outrage, or empathy.

Why? Because feelings drive engagement.

When individuals feel something deeply, they're more likely to share content, watch longer, or return for more, making emotional arousal a key tool for increasing viewership. This engagement can then be monetized through advertising, product placement, or brand loyalty.

But this isn't a new tactic. Throughout history, emotional media has been used to mobilize movements, challenge injustice, and inspire hope. However, it has also been used to manipulate, scapegoat, and mislead.

Today, emotion-driven content has evolved into a double-edged sword. On one side, it can awaken empathy and action. On the other, it can fuel pseudoscience, conspiracy theories, and targeted propaganda, which are especially dangerous in a media ecosystem where "reality" has become subjective, and facts are often bent to fit narratives.

This creates new avenues of harm for marginalized groups, who may be subjected to misrepresentation or denied access to factual resources due to biased, emotionally manipulative content that reinforces systemic inequities.

The Environmental Toll of LCD Screens

The emotional cost of screens is one side of the story. The environmental impact is another, and it's staggering.

LCD (liquid crystal display) technology, developed in 1968 by George Heilmeier and his team, became mainstream when Sharp introduced the first LCD TV in 1988. By 2007, LCDs had overtaken plasma and CRT TVs, becoming the dominant form of screen technology worldwide (NPR, 2008).

But this dominance comes at a devastating cost.

> *"The production process of LCD screens involves the use of toxic chemicals and rare earth metals. Many LCD screens contain materials such as lead, mercury, and cadmium, which can leach into the soil and water supply if not properly disposed of... E-waste is often shipped to developing countries, where it is dismantled and recycled in hazardous ways."*
> — *Votechnik, 2023*

While it's important to recognize that Votechnik is an e-waste recycling company with a vested interest in framing e-waste as toxic, their concerns are supported by independent scientific studies.

A 2019 study from the University of Saskatchewan examined over 300 chemicals used in LCD screens:

> *"Nearly 100 of the tested chemicals showed significant potential to cause toxicity. Ninety percent of the monomers exhibited concerning traits: they either accumulate in organisms, resist degradation, or travel long distances in the atmosphere. A quarter of the chemicals showed all three characteristics."*
> — *USASK, 2019*

These substances aren't just harmful during production or disposal—they linger in ecosystems and bodies; with consequences we may not fully understand for decades.

The Hidden Human Cost of Screen Production

Beyond chemical toxicity, LCD production and the widespread use of lithium-ion batteries, essential for smartphones, laptops, and tablets, have a human cost that's often invisible to end users.

Numerous investigations have revealed exploitative mining practices, including:

- **Child labor** in cobalt and lithium mines

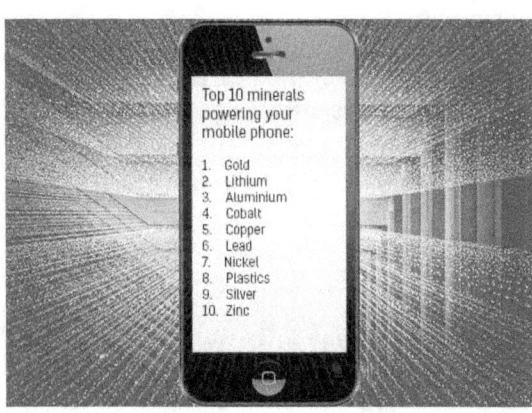

- **Environmental contamination** of air, water, and soil

- **Health problems** among miners and surrounding communities

- **Soil erosion**, **deforestation**, and **soil salinization**, which reduce agricultural productivity and disrupt local ecosystems

(Amnesty International, 2021; Mining & Mining, 2021; Washington Post, 2016) (Mec Mining, 2018)

These issues are disproportionately felt in developing countries, where regulatory frameworks and worker protections are often weak or nonexistent. The result is a global system of environmental injustice: wealthy consumers in the Global North benefit from technology that directly harms vulnerable populations in the Global South.

When you are due for an upgrade on your device, consider the cost of purchasing a new device when your current device is still functional. The hidden cost of screens and tech usage is devastating to countries and people outside of the US and other developed countries. Our addiction to tech is immediately damaging to the world, the lives of the labor involved and our future. Less is more.

Summary

- The historical evolution of screens and their impact on society, literacy, media, and the environment are still evolving. The rise of television, particularly with 24-hour news cycles, contributed to information overload, further exacerbated by the digital age. As companies continued to utilize a 24-hour cycle with their own business, the inevitable avalanche of overstimulation continue to develop until where we are now.

- Regarding the concerns of racial representation in media, noting how systemic oppression has historically excluded Black and Brown individuals from visual content while perpetuating negative stereotypes. Additionally, emotional manipulation in modern media that can drive misinformation and widen societal gaps is commonplace.

- The environmental toll of LCD screens isn't one to ignore. There is a costly and hidden consequence for the proliferation of screens. Toxic chemicals, e-waste issues, and exploitative mining practices are associated with screen production. Please reconsider frequent tech upgrades due to their hidden costs on both people and the planet.

Chapter Three

"The infinite wonders of the universe are revealed to us in exact measure as we are capable of receiving them. The keenness of our vision depends not on how much we can see, but on how much we feel." Helen Keller

Visual Processing and Encoding

Before diving into the core theme of this book, the visual diet, it's important to understand how our brains interpret visual data. Whether you're reading these words on a page or listening while doing another activity, your brain is hard at work. It's adapting to the environment, interpreting what it sees and hears, and filtering that data for meaning based on your unique experiences.

This incredible interplay between our visual receptor cells (in the eyes) and the brain's processing centers is both automatic and astonishing. It happens within nanoseconds, and we rarely notice it.

Take a moment to consider this: your brain is constantly scanning the world around you and formulating a plan of action based on what it sees. This is not just convenience, it's evolution at work. Our ancestors relied on this rapid visual analysis to survive, and we still use those same biological tools to distinguish between what is safe, threatening, or important.

When you take in visual stimuli, your eyes act as the collectors, gathering light, shapes, colors, and movement. This raw data is then sent to your brain, where a rapid interpretive process begins. Based on past experiences and associations, your brain assesses whether what you're seeing is familiar or unfamiliar.

If the information is known and trusted, your nervous system remains calm, allowing you to integrate the data without triggering any stress responses. Think of the nervous system as a gatekeeper: it decides whether the input is safe or whether it requires a more serious reaction—like fight, flight, freeze, or fawn.

Once the input is deemed "safe," it connects with various regions of the brain, activating neural pathways and potentially triggering emotional or physiological responses. This might include the release of pleasure-inducing chemicals like dopamine, the balancing effects of mood stabilizers like serotonin, or perhaps no noticeable reaction at all.

Whether the visual input is retained or forgotten depends on how meaningful it is to you. If it registers as important, your brain may commit it to long-term memory. If not, it might remain in short-term memory for a brief moment before fading into what we might call *mental oblivion*.

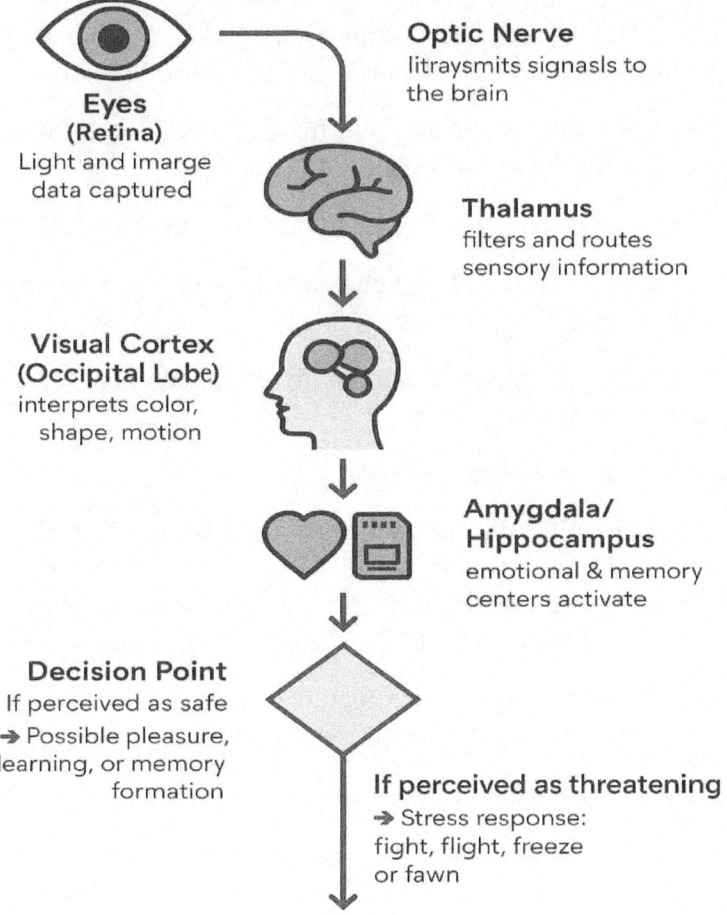

Visual Processing and Encoding: A Deeper Dive

Let's explore how our brains interpret visual information at a deeper, biological level.

Whether you're reading these words or listening to them while multitasking, your brain is constantly receiving, filtering, and interpreting visual data at lightning speed. This interplay between your eyes and your brain is not just automatic, it's evolutionary, incredibly complex, and deeply tied to how we experience and respond to the world.

Let's get a bit more technical.

The Journey of Light Through the Eye

Light enters through the pupil, which dilates or contracts depending on brightness. It then passes through the lens, projecting the image onto the retina. Within the retina, light stimulates layers of specialized cells, ganglion cells, bipolar cells, and photoreceptors (rods and cones), that begin processing the data.

Interestingly, photoreceptors can become fatigued after prolonged exposure to bright or intense colors, which is why we sometimes see afterimages.

As the information travels, the axons of the ganglion cells form the optic nerve, which carries the visual signal to two main areas:

- The thalamus (specifically, the lateral geniculate nucleus, or LGN)
- The superior colliculus, which is involved in reflexive eye movements and orientation

From the thalamus, signals are routed to the visual cortex at the back of the brain, where interpretation begins.

A Hierarchy of Visual Interpretation

The visual cortex isn't a single structure, it's a network of specialized regions. At the base of this hierarchy is V1 (primary visual cortex), which handles the most basic visual information, like the orientation of a line or the direction something is moving. As the signal moves up the chain:

- V2 processes more complex features, such as contours, textures, and foreground/background differentiation.
- Beyond V2, information splits into two major pathways:
    - The "What" pathway (ventral stream) leads to the inferior temporal cortex (IT), where we recognize objects.
    - The fusiform face area, within IT, specializes in identifying faces.

"More than 50% of the neocortex is devoted to processing visual information."
— *William G. Allyn, University of Rochester*

Vision is not passive, it's a massive, coordinated brain function involving half of our cerebral cortex.

Color, Emotion, and the Blue Light Spectrum

The connection between color and emotion is well documented. A 2007 study at Chiba University examined participants' physiological and psychological responses to red, green, and blue paper using EEG and blood pressure monitors.

Participants reported their emotional states on scales such as:

- Relaxed ↔ Agitated
- Comfortable ↔ Uncomfortable
- Tired ↔ Not tired
- Sleepy ↔ Alert

Key findings:

- Blue evoked calmness, lightness, alertness, and coolness.
- Red induced feelings of heaviness, excitement, warmth, and increased arousal.
- Green remained emotionally neutral.

(Yoto et al., 2007)

This matters because the blue light spectrum, heavily present in most screens, is intentionally used to keep us engaged and alert. While switching to warmer colors can help mitigate the stimulating effects, it won't eliminate the emotional or neurological impact of activating content designed to provoke a response.

Sensory Response and Reaction Time

Our response to visual stimuli varies by individual and situation. A 2015 study of 120 medical students found that, on average, auditory reaction time is faster than visual reaction time—likely because sound travels and is processed more quickly than light. (Jain et al., 2015)

Additionally, multitasking and environmental distractions reduce responsiveness. A 1999 study showed that visual reaction time declines significantly during physical activity compared to auditory reaction time. (Yagi et al., 1999)

These findings support a simple truth: Mindless consumption leads to diminished awareness. And in some cases, this can create real danger—particularly when we are so engrossed in visual media that we fail to notice what's happening around us.

Visual Media Hijacks Our Neurobiology

When we are exposed to intense or emotionally triggering content, our bodies often shift from a parasympathetic (relaxed) state to a sympathetic (aroused) state. This "hijacking" of our nervous system can cause:

- Increased heart rate
- Heightened stress
- Altered perception of safety and danger

Over time, constant exposure to high-intensity screen content can reshape our worldview, making our internal environments feel just as chaotic as the media we consume.

And if we possess visual acuity—whether natural or aided—our brains are highly susceptible to these patterns. Visual media shapes our understanding of ourselves and the world.

A Sociodynamic, Not Just Neurological, Concern

This book is not just for the neurotypical or neurodivergent reader. The visual diet we consume is a sociodynamic dilemma—a product of screen saturation, media design, systemic inequality, and evolving neurobiology.

We live in a visually overwhelming world. And while we cannot stop the flood of visual content, we can make more conscious decisions about what we engage with and how.

Summary

- The brain processes visual information in profound ways while screens impact perception and cognitive function. The speed and complexity of the process of the neurological pathways involved in visual encoding are neurologically lit up while processing visual data.

- Different colors affect emotions and physiological responses, particularly the stimulating effects of blue light from screens. Studies on reaction times highlight the brain's prioritization of visual and auditory stimuli.

- Overstimulation caused by screen content, which can trigger stress responses and alter perceptions of reality, reinforcing the importance of mindful media consumption is widely known and our use of this media type should continually be scrutinized.

Part II: The Many Reasons We Should Have a Balanced Visual Diet

Chapter Four

"It is not our differences that divide us. It is our inability to recognize, accept, and celebrate those differences." Audre Lorde

Neurodiversity and Visual Processing

Given how rapidly and powerfully visual media can influence our perception and prime us for action, it's crucial to explore how neurodiverse individuals experience and process visual stimuli. This population, with its diverse cognitive presentations, is increasingly gaining attention in the research community, not only in terms of how neurodivergent people *respond* to stimuli, but also how they *interact* with, *interpret*, and even *reshape* their environments.

The nuanced ways in which neurodivergent individuals process visual input provide a valuable framework, not only for understanding their lived experiences, but for broadening how we think about human cognition and response as a whole. Neurodivergence can highlight alternative neuropathways formed through consistent exposure to visual stimulation. If we are to develop a responsible visual diet, we must do more than acknowledge neurodivergence, we must center it.

This isn't simply about inclusion. It's about understanding that the visual world affects people differently, and for neurodivergent individuals, often described metaphorically as "sponges for stimuli", those effects can be intensified. The overload we discuss throughout this book is frequently amplified in neurodivergent bodies and minds.

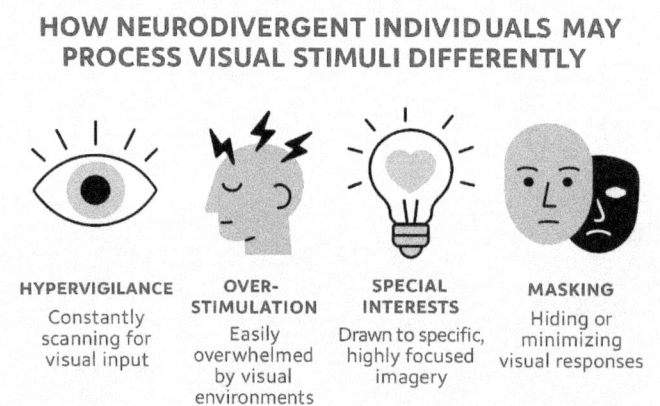

This Is Not About Pathology

Let me be clear: my goal here is not to pathologize neurodivergence.

As someone who belongs to this community, I know all too well the exhausting, ongoing pressure to mask, to "pass," and to adapt ourselves to neurotypical expectations. The pathology-based framing of neurodivergence remains deeply embedded in medical and educational research, and later in this book, I explore the damage that framework has caused.

But for now, I want to highlight something often overlooked: neurodivergent individuals are not "broken" versions of a norm. They are variations within the spectrum of human cognition, and often, they are innovators, empathizers, and creative thinkers who see the world from angles others cannot.

Neurodivergence and the Workplace

Despite their talents, an estimated 80% of neurodivergent individuals are unemployed or underemployed due to inflexible hiring and workplace practices (Houdek, 2022). However, when workplaces are willing to adapt, they often gain access to incredible insight, skill, and creative problem-solving.

For instance, highly sensitive individuals may thrive in environments where sensory regulation is prioritized, where lighting is softer, sounds are minimized, and fragrances are controlled. These environmental changes don't just benefit neurodivergent individuals, they can positively affect the entire organization.

> *"Civil service and public organizations may prosper if they recruit neurologically atypical individuals. Their unique perspectives, thinking styles, coping strategies, and life experiences can lead to service innovation and better organizational outcomes."*
> — Houdek, 2022

The Role of Telework

The COVID-19 pandemic sparked a revolution in remote work, and for many neurodivergent people, it provided much-needed flexibility.

According to Canonico & Lup (2020):

> *"Teleworking may actually suit workers with (Autism) better than their neurotypical counterparts... Virtual communication tends to be more formal and specific, requiring clear planning and explicitness, something that benefits individuals who interpret language literally. It also removes the pressure of interpreting nonverbal cues such as eye contact or informal social rituals."*

For many neurodivergent individuals, virtual environments reduce the barriers and burdens of social masking, spontaneous conversation, and overstimulating office dynamics. Additionally, telework platforms often use concrete performance metrics, which many neurodiverse minds respond to more effectively than vague or abstract feedback. When expectations are clearly defined, and individuals are given autonomy over how and when they meet them, they can thrive in ways traditional work structures do not allow.

Bringing It Back to Visual Diet

Neurodivergent individuals are not immune to the overstimulating visual environments of our world, in fact, they may be more *deeply* affected by them. From screen content and lighting to messaging and interface design, the visual world can be overwhelming, disorienting, or even harmful without conscious regulation.

That's why a visual diet, one that's intentional, informed, and empathetic, matters for everyone. Neurodivergence isn't an exception to being accommodated. It's a valid, essential way of existing, and one that should be accounted for from the very beginning of any conversation about perception, cognition, or content design.

The Neurodivergent Mind's Visual Processing

Returning to how neurodivergent individuals relate to and process visual stimuli, it's worth noting that much of the previously referenced research does not specify whether participants were neurodivergent. If such demographic information was included and I missed it, I sincerely apologize for not crediting the researchers accordingly.

The term neurodiverse was first coined by sociologist Judy Singer, who described it as the "neurological variation central to the success of the human species" (McGee, 2012). Since then, the term, and its sister term, neurodivergent, has come to refer broadly to individuals whose neurological development diverges from what is considered "typical."

This includes (but is not limited to) those diagnosed with:

- Attention-Deficit/Hyperactivity Disorder (ADHD)
- Autism
- Dyspraxia
- Tourette's Syndrome
- Dyscalculia
- Dyslexia

(ADHD Aware, 2021)

Current estimates suggest that 30–40% of the population falls under this umbrella. However, these numbers are based on formal diagnoses, and they don't account for the vast number of people who go undiagnosed or misdiagnosed, particularly among BIPOC and low-income populations.

The path to diagnosis is often:

- Expensive
- Time-consuming
- Gatekept by outdated diagnostic criteria
- Biased toward white, cisgender, and middle/upper-class individuals

For many marginalized individuals, access to culturally competent mental healthcare is limited. Services are frequently underfunded, and the tools used to evaluate neurodivergence are often not designed with diverse lived experiences in mind. As a result, many neurodivergent people go unseen, unsupported, and underserved, despite having the same needs and challenges as those with formal diagnoses.

Why This Matters for Visual Media

Given this large and likely underestimated portion of the population, it's vital to understand how visual content affects neurodivergent minds.

Neurodivergent individuals often experience:

- Heightened sensitivity to visual input (colors, movement, brightness)
- Different thresholds for overstimulation
- Unique patterns of attention (e.g., hyperfocus vs. distractibility)
- Nonlinear processing styles

So, when we talk about building a responsible visual diet, we're not just discussing aesthetics or screen time, we're addressing a core need for accessibility, safety, and wellbeing for a large segment of the population.

Up next: we'll begin with a focus on ADHD, a condition often misunderstood yet deeply intertwined with visual processing challenges and strengths.

ADHD and Visual Processing

Attention-Deficit/Hyperactivity Disorder (ADHD) is one of the most common neurodevelopmental conditions, affecting approximately 3–5% of school-aged children (Fried et al., 2014). These figures only account for those diagnosed early, often through educational systems that have the resources, or biases, to recognize such traits. Many individuals go undiagnosed well into adulthood, though they carry the same cognitive signatures. ADHD is a globally prevalent neurodivergent condition.

Between 2007 and 2012, researchers observed a 24.6% increase in ADHD diagnoses among adults aged 18 to 64, rising from 3.41% to 4.25%. Notably, the gender gap also narrowed by 31.1%, though these findings were based on binary, cisgender data and did not address the broader gender spectrum (London & Landes, 2012).

Understanding ADHD Through a Neuropsychological Lens

According to the *DSM-5 (2015)*, a diagnosis of ADHD requires that symptoms persist for more than six months, significantly impair academic, occupational, or social functioning, and fall into two categories:

1. Inattention
2. Hyperactivity/Impulsivity

Symptoms cannot be better explained by another psychiatric condition. However, diagnostic overlap and misinterpretation of symptoms often lead to misdiagnosis, especially when inattentiveness is mistaken for mood disorders or cognitive deficits.

From a neuropsychological perspective, ADHD is associated with deficits in:

- **Sustained attention**
- **Executive functioning**
- **Response inhibition**
- **Working memory**
- **Encoding**
- **Automaticity**

In ADHD, the controlled processes (those requiring attention and flexibility) are frequently overtaxed, while automatic processes (those done with ease and speed after practice) struggle to take root. As Fabio et al. (2012) describe, this imbalance compromises cognitive efficiency, particularly in environments that rely heavily on repetitive, linear instruction.

Visual Encoding and Engagement

The way the ADHD brain encodes information, especially visual information, is unique. Visual content that is emotionally engaging or rapid in pace may capture attention effortlessly, while slower or less stimulating material may be difficult to sustain attention on, even if it's relevant or necessary.

A compelling example of this comes from a University of Central Florida study (Schleub, 2017), where a child with ADHD is shown two 10-minute clips:

- One, a math lesson video
- The other, a clip from *Star Wars*

While watching the math lesson, the child stims, rocks, twirls, doing everything possible to remain in their chair. But when the *Star Wars* clip begins, the child becomes still, engaged, and visibly attentive.

This doesn't mean *Star Wars* should replace curriculum (definitely not, considering Disney's problematic history), but it does reveal a deeper truth: ADHD learners are capable of deep engagement when content is crafted in a way that stimulates without overwhelming. Educational systems built on neurotypical norms miss this opportunity entirely.

Visual Response, Arousal, and the ADHD Brain

A 2014 study by Fried et al. examined eye movement and blink patterns in unmedicated ADHD participants. They found:

- Increased blink rates
- More frequent microsaccades (small, involuntary eye movements)
- The effect was especially pronounced right before and during tasks requiring focus

These findings matter because blink rate is associated with cognitive arousal and mental effort. In ADHD, the visual system is not disengaged, it's hyper-engaged, but in a scattered or inefficient way. The data suggests these individuals are *trying* to regulate focus but are constantly redirected by the very stimuli they are trying to process.

Fabio et al. (2015) further found that ADHD individuals often struggle with encoding learning material, making them more vulnerable to attention drift when information isn't delivered in a stimulating or relatable way. When combined with modern screen culture, flooded with fast, emotionally charged content, the ADHD brain can be drawn toward stimulus-heavy material and away from slower, evidence-based content.

This is where visual diet matters most. A catchy, color-saturated, emotionally manipulative news clip might "stick" in the mind more than a balanced, evidence-backed journal article, not because of intellectual preference, but because of neurological processing patterns. And this opens the door to echo chambers and misinformation ecosystems that prey on emotional reaction rather than critical engagement.

ADHD, Trauma, and Sleep: Hidden Variables

The conversation doesn't stop at attention.

Research shows a notable intersection between ADHD and trauma. In an Australian study of 6–8-year-olds, children with ADHD were significantly more likely to have experienced traumatic events than their neurotypical peers (Schilpzand et al., 2017). Whether trauma contributes to ADHD-like symptoms or exacerbating existing ones remains a complex, ongoing question, but the connection is real and deserves more focus.

Additionally, disordered sleep is a major factor. A 2019 study by Bijilenga et al. reported that 73–78% of individuals with ADHD experience a delayed circadian rhythm. This disrupts regulation, attention, and mood. Could improved sleep hygiene enhance executive functioning and emotional regulation? Likely, yes, but longitudinal studies are needed across diverse populations to fully understand this relationship.

Final Thoughts on ADHD and Visual Engagement

The ADHD brain is not deficit; it's a different operating system. One that interacts with the visual world intensely, emotionally, and sometimes unpredictably. Visual media that overwhelms, over-stimulates, or bypasses critical thinking will be absorbed into the ADHD brain faster, and more deeply, than slow, nuanced, evidence-based material.

This is why inclusive education, thoughtful content design, and individualized learning strategies aren't luxuries, they're necessities.

And if you're someone with ADHD or love someone who is, know this:
You're not broken.
You're built differently.
And that difference can be a superpower, when the world learns how to meet you where you are.

Dyslexia and the Visual Brain

Dyslexia is a neurodivergent way of experiencing the world that, admittedly, I had very little direct clinical experience with prior to writing this book. Whether that's due to limitations in my intake or assessment process, or perhaps the guilt and shame often surrounding this diagnosis preventing disclosure, I can't say for certain. What I can say is that the research conducted for this book has reshaped my clinical lens, and I hope it brings greater understanding to you as well.

Dyslexia is typically defined as a difficulty with word-level reading and spelling, caused by phonological processing deficits (Adlof, 2019).

Because dyslexia involves both visual and sound-based processing, it's a crucial inclusion in this exploration of visual processing and neurodivergence.

What's particularly fascinating is that dyslexic individuals can actually absorb and encode visual data effectively, and this ability isn't confined to linguistic content. McLean, Stuart, Coltheart, and Castles (2011) showed that individuals with dyslexia could rapidly process visual information unrelated to language or sound. This creates an interesting relationship with screen content, especially highly visual and non-verbal media.

The Role of Genetics and Environment

There's also a strong hereditary component to dyslexia. Heritability estimates range from about 50% in young children to 80% in older children, once the influence of instruction evens out across the population (Olson et al., 2014). The literacy of caregivers and the quality of instructional environments heavily shape how dyslexia emerges and is supported, or not.

The emotional and social toll of dyslexia can be heavy. Livingston et al. (2017) reported increased risk of educational, occupational, emotional, and social challenges among individuals with developmental dyslexia. And still, the neurotypical world offers little structural support for this population, often leaving them vulnerable to harmful narratives.

Educators may mistake a student's reading difficulty for low intelligence, when what's needed is targeted instruction. Employers, too, may dismiss accommodations or remain unaware of dyslexic presentations, causing alienation or professional stagnation.

The stigma remains powerful. Dyslexia is often misunderstood, mischaracterized, or hidden altogether due to fear of judgment. But it is not a weakness. It's a different neural architecture, requiring a different way of engaging with the world, particularly in our visually saturated society.

Dyspraxia and Visuospatial Processing

Dyspraxia, and its often-overlapping sibling, Dyscalculia, were areas I knew little about before researching this book. What I found was a rich body of research, offering valuable insight into how these brains interact with motor coordination and visual stimuli.

Gibbs, Appleton, and Appleton (2007) describe dyspraxia as an impairment in the organization, planning, and execution of physical movement, with developmental rather than acquired origins. This often manifests as motor clumsiness, uncoordinated posture, or delayed fine motor skills. Importantly, dyspraxia exists on a spectrum, and the frequency or intensity of these motor challenges varies between individuals.

Though it's often labeled as Developmental Coordination Disorder (DCD) in medical literature, I will continue to use the term *dyspraxia* to avoid further pathologizing of neurodivergent bodies.

Dyspraxia has important sociocultural consequences. In societies that value athleticism, grace, and fluid movement, those with dyspraxia are frequently seen as "clumsy," "awkward," or "slow." These terms are more than labels, they are forms of exclusion that have real effects on self-worth and opportunity.

Prevalence is estimated at around 10% of the population (Gibbs et al., 2007), with AMAB individuals being diagnosed at four times the rate of AFAB individuals. And yet, clinical and public awareness remains low, leading many children to be overlooked or mischaracterized until much later in life.

Visual Processing and Learning in Dyspraxia

Motor coordination isn't the only domain impacted by dyspraxia. Visual perception and spatial orientation are also deeply affected. Research has shown that vision is a foundational tool in developing postural control and coordination (Chokron, 2021).

The subset known as visuospatial dyspraxia specifically affects the brain's ability to process visual fields, spatial organization, and visual attention (Mazeau, 2005). I conceptualize it as a kind of visual veil, a filter that limits how much sensory data is actually perceived or meaningfully interpreted.

This can lead to difficulty with nonverbal stimuli like facial cues, posture, or subtle social gestures, particularly depending on where someone falls on the spectrum. But it's not all deficit. In fact, individuals with dyspraxia have shown strengths in recognizing object shapes, speed, and direction (Chung & Khuu, 2014).

Hands-on, kinesthetic approaches are especially effective. A 2018 study using the ATHYNOS game found that children with dyspraxia showed faster improvements in motor coordination and hand-eye integration when engaged through physical interaction rather than visual explanation (D'Avila-Pesantez, 2018). Experiential or hands-on training or learning can help bridge the gap between neurotypical training or education models. Additionally, the hands-on experience of visual media can further leave individuals with this type of brain, further, susceptible to harm of a poor visual diet.

Dyscalculia and the Visual-Numerical Brain

Dyscalculia is a specific learning disability that affects the development of numerical and arithmetic skills. Castaldi et al. (2022) describe its origin as linked to the suboptimal functioning of key regions in the dorsal visual stream, particularly the parietal cortex.

Given that dyscalculia is inherently visual in nature, affecting how individuals interpret numerical symbols and their relationships, it is essential to explore its role within the broader context of visual processing and neurodivergence.

Dyscalculia affects approximately 3–7% of the population (Rubinsten & Henik, 2009), with some estimates placing the figure as high as 10% of children (Butterworth & Kovas, 2013). Despite its prevalence, it remains under-identified and under-supported, particularly in educational environments.

The Approximate Number System (ANS)

One of the primary cognitive systems affected in dyscalculia is the Approximate Number System (ANS), a rapid, intuitive system responsible for our subconscious understanding of quantities, patterns, and numerical relationships.

The ANS operates beneath conscious awareness, activating whenever we see or engage with numbers, quantities, or numerical comparisons. It helps us make quick judgments, like estimating how many apples are on a table or how far we are from another car while driving. These abilities are not innate but develop over time through learning and environmental interaction.

In children with dyscalculia, development of the ANS is delayed or atypical. Skagerlund & Träff (2014) reported that 10-year-old children with dyscalculia demonstrated number acuity equivalent to that of 5-year-olds, a gap that has major implications for how these children experience early education and self-worth.

Visual Processing in Dyscalculia

A study by Cheng et al. (2018) found that children with dyscalculia exhibit deficits in:

- General processing speed (measured via reaction time tasks)
- Spatial processing (assessed using mental rotation tasks)
- Visual attention (using visual tracing tasks)

These findings support the connection between dyscalculia and impaired dorsal visual stream development. However, this isn't a universal finding.

Decarli et al. (2020) challenged these claims, noting that when unrestricted visual stimuli are presented, children with dyscalculia may simply adopt different problem-solving strategies. For example, they may choose to count individual dots rather than estimate, even in small sets, leading to slower reaction times but not necessarily reduced accuracy. This speaks to the adaptive flexibility of the dyscalculic mind, finding ways to work around numerical uncertainty. As stated earlier, neurotypical brains generally see the world differently. That means problem solving in a different but not deficient manner.

Spectrum, Not Stereotype

As with other forms of neurodivergence, no two individuals with dyscalculia are the same. Some show clear symptoms early on; others develop coping strategies that mask their struggles until later in life.

This variability makes rigid diagnostic models problematic. A one-size-fits-all approach to screening and support can exclude and marginalize individuals who do not meet neatly defined criteria.

One former neurodivergent client once said to me:

> *"I felt so stupid. People didn't know what was going on around me, and I was too scared to say anything."*

This heartbreaking statement highlights the urgent need to reform educational systems with:

- Dynamic, individualized assessments
- Teacher training in neurodivergence
- Wider access to screening tools
- Classroom strategies designed for all brains, not just neurotypical ones

Visual-Numerical Training as Intervention

Fortunately, there is promising research showing that visual training can strengthen numerical understanding in dyscalculic children.

In a 2019 study by Cheng et al., a game-based learning intervention was tested in which children played a computer game involving collecting apples with a pig avatar. The goal was to choose the largest bunch of apples, regardless of apple size, reinforcing the relationship between numerosity and value.

The study found that this non-symbolic numerosity training improved the children's performance in traditional arithmetic tasks, suggesting a causal link between visual numerosity processing and symbolic arithmetic ability (Cheng et al., 2019).

Final Thoughts on Dyscalculia and Visual Engagement

Dyscalculia is not a matter of "bad at math." It is a fundamental difference in how the brain processes numerical and visual data, especially in high-pressure, fast-paced environments.

Understanding these differences is essential to dismantling the stigma and building systems that celebrate and support diverse cognitive styles. The burden should never fall solely on the child to adapt, it is the responsibility of schools, educators, and society to meet these learners where they are.

As with all neurodivergent minds, those with dyscalculia carry great capacity, for strategy, creativity, pattern recognition, and adaptive thinking. They deserve tools that help unlock that potential, not systems that punish them for differences they cannot control.

Visual Processing in Neurodivergent Conditions

ADHD

- Easily distracted by visual stimuli
- Difficulty filtering visual input
- High rates of eye movements (e.g. saccades, blinks)

DYSLEXIA

- Difficulty with visual recognition of letters/words
- Rapid visual processing of non-linguistic stimuli

DYSPRAXIA

- Impaired visual-motor coordination
- Difficulty judging distances
- Issues with spatial awareness

DYSCALCULIA

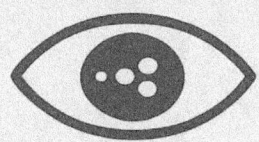

- Impaired perception of quantities
- Difficulty recognizing symbols and numbers

Abscotsistock

Summary

- **Neurodiversity in Visual Processing** – Neurodivergent individuals, including those with ADHD, autism, dyslexia, and dyspraxia, process visual information differently. Their heightened sensitivity to stimuli can shape their perception and learning.

- **Workplace Challenges and Opportunities** – Many neurodivergent individuals struggle with traditional work environments, with high unemployment rates. However, businesses can benefit from their unique skills if they offer flexible work arrangements, such as remote work, which has proven beneficial for many.

- **ADHD and Visual Stimuli** – Individuals with ADHD have distinct attention mechanisms that influence how they engage with visual content. Research shows that their brains respond differently to engaging versus non-engaging stimuli, which has implications for education and media consumption.

- **Dyslexia and Visual Perception** – Dyslexia affects word processing but not necessarily visual comprehension. Stigma and misunderstanding around dyslexia contribute to educational and workplace challenges.

- **Dyspraxia and Visual-Motor Skills** – Dyspraxia affects motor coordination and, in some cases, visual-spatial perception, influencing how individuals interact with their environment and learn motor-based skills.

- **Dyscalculia** -diverse and complex learning disability, requiring personalized educational strategies. More dynamic assessments and teacher training are needed to support neurodivergent students early on. Innovative visual learning techniques could play a crucial role in improving numerical comprehension and reducing the stigma associated with dyscalculia.

Chapter Five

"The most interesting people you'll find are ones that don't fit into your average cardboard box. They'll make what they need. They'll make their own boxes." Dr Temple Grandin

Autism Spectrum Conditions and Visual Processing

When the term *neurodivergence* is mentioned, many people's minds immediately go to autism. Media portrayals have strongly linked the concept of neurodiversity to autism, often reducing the full spectrum of neurodivergence to one presentation. For this reason, I've intentionally placed Autism Spectrum Conditions (ASC) later in this exploration, to avoid reinforcing stereotypes and to make space for the full breadth of neurodivergent experience.

Because of the wide variability of autism presentations, and the limited space available in this book, I acknowledge that what follows will not be exhaustive. The research on ASC is vast, and while I've done my best to represent key elements, some perspectives and studies may be unintentionally omitted.

Core Characteristics of Autism and Visual Interpretation

Autism is not a monolith. It encompasses a wide range of traits and presentations, often overlapping with sensory sensitivities, social communication differences, and unique patterns of visual processing. As Chokron et al. (2021) describe, some common visual and behavioral traits in individuals with ASC may include:

- Limited or inconsistent eye contact
- Fragmented visual perception
- Difficulty tracking rapid movement
- Challenges appreciating distance and depth
- Fear of collision with people or objects
- Tendency to become disoriented in familiar spaces
- Misuse of objects or difficulty with autonomy

These traits suggest deep involvement of cerebral visual systems in ASC, contributing to how autistic individuals navigate and interpret the world.

Hyperactivation of Visual Cortices

Research by Damarla et al. (2010) found that individuals with autism demonstrate hyperactive responses in the occipital lobes during visual detection tasks, suggesting a heightened and more intense level of visual sensory input.

This overactivation may explain why screen-based content becomes compelling, comforting, and even regulating for many autistic individuals. I use the word *compulsory* not in a pathological sense, but to describe the strong intrinsic pull some autistic individuals experience toward highly visual, structured, and predictable stimuli, such as digital media or gaming environments.

Digital Media and Virtual Connection

Many autistic individuals feel more comfortable in digital or virtual environments than in traditional in-person social settings. Studies show that some prefer virtual social interactions, which allow for greater control, less ambiguity, and clearer boundaries.

Lahiri et al. (2013) observed that autistic participants often fixate longer on virtual representations of social interaction than on live human faces. This could be interpreted not as avoidance, but as a preference for controlled environments where visual information can be processed more manageably.

Similarly, online gaming communities offer spaces where autistic individuals can connect with others on shared interests, communicate at their own pace, and regulate social input, all within a visually structured format.

The N170 and Face Processing

The N170 event-related potential (ERP) is an important neural marker used to assess early facial recognition and categorization. This negative waveform peaks around 130–200 milliseconds after stimulus onset, primarily at occipitotemporal electrodes.

In neurotypical individuals, the N170 is consistently larger in response to human faces than to objects, and more pronounced when faces display emotion (Bechor et al., 2019; Bentin et al., 1996). However, in individuals with autism, the N170 amplitude is often reduced or delayed when viewing real human faces (Marco et al., 2011).

What's especially interesting is that this effect may be stimulus-specific: some studies show no significant N170 differences when autistic individuals view animated characters, video game avatars, or non-human stimuli (e.g., furniture or landscapes). This suggests that the context and nature of

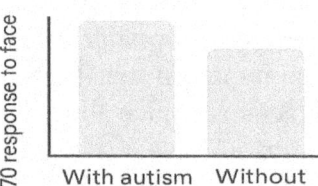

AUTISM SPECTRUM CONDITIONS AND VISUAL PROCESSING

VISUAL PROCESSING TRAITS
- Limited eye contact
- Fragmented vision
- Fear of collision or disorientiation
- Fixation on artificial stimuli such as screens

Autistic individuals often show a reducel brain response to human faces, but not other stimuli

N170 response to face — With autism / Without autism

N170 response to faces
- Preference for structured virtual environments
- Comfort with digital social interaction

SCREEN ENGAGEMENT
- Preference for structured virtual environments
- Comfort with digital social interaction

Hyperactive occipital lobes may drive compulsory engagement

Marco et aL, 2011; Lahiri et aL, 2013

visual stimuli matter greatly, not just the category (face vs. object), but its emotional resonance, familiarity, and processing load.

Rethinking Visual "Preference"

Autistic individuals are often portrayed as "face-avoidant" or socially disconnected. But emerging research complicates that narrative. These studies suggest that differences in visual engagement may not indicate a *lack* of interest or capacity, but rather a different method of processing, one that prefers predictable, structured, and less overwhelming visuals.

Screens, in this sense, become not just a refuge, but a source of empowerment, learning, and even social bonding.

Tourette's and Visual Processing: The Power of Association

Gilles de la Tourette Syndrome (GTS) is a childhood-onset, multifaceted neuropsychiatric condition characterized by the presence of multiple motor tics and at least one vocal (phonic) tic, lasting for a minimum of one year.

Symptoms typically begin around age 6, often with motor tics involving the face, head, and neck. Phonic tics, such as throat clearing, grunting, or sniffing, tend to appear several years later. While these tics can fluctuate over time, they often remain stable in type for short periods. Tics may range from simple movements or sounds to complex gestures or vocalizations, which in rare cases can include obscene language.

Tics are involuntary yet patterned, appearing out of place in timing or context, which distinguishes them from spontaneous gestures in neurotypical individuals.

(Kleimaker et al., 2020)

Comorbidities and Developmental Trajectory

Tourette's is commonly comorbid with other neurodevelopmental conditions:

- Around 60% of individuals also meet criteria for ADHD
- Approximately 40% present with Obsessive-Compulsive Disorder (OCD)

While symptoms often peak around ages 10–11, many individuals experience improvement or full remission in adolescence or early adulthood. However, for about 20%, tics persist and may significantly impact quality of life. In most cases, counseling and environmental accommodations are more beneficial than aggressive clinical interventions.

Perception–Action Binding and Visual Stimulation

An especially compelling insight comes from Petruo et al. (2019), who studied 35 adolescents with Tourette's and 39 neurotypical controls using EEG data during a Go/NoGo task.

The study found that individuals with Tourette's demonstrated a heightened tendency for:

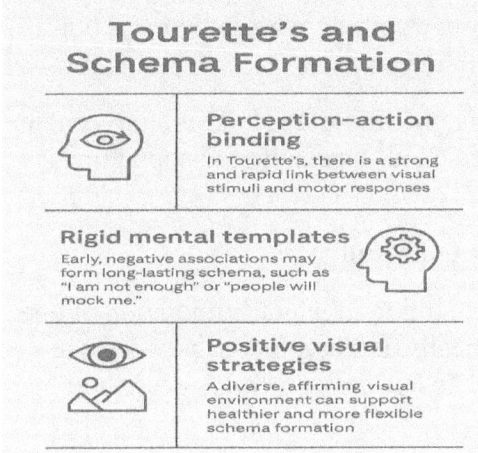

"Perception–action binding" – the automatic and rapid formation of associations between stimuli and motor responses.

This suggests that individuals with Tourette's may form stronger and faster cognitive links between what they see and how they physically react. While this mechanism may enhance learning or adaptability in some contexts, it may also contribute to:

- Rapid acquisition of maladaptive associations (e.g., tying specific environments to anxiety or fear)
- Greater sensitivity to visually charged or emotionally intense stimuli
- A tendency toward pattern rigidity, especially in response to repetition or trauma

The Role of Visual Diet and Schema Development

This heightened perception–action binding opens a compelling discussion around visual diet. For individuals with Tourette's, early and consistent exposure to a diverse range of visual experiences, including inclusive, affirming, and culturally expansive content, could be profoundly beneficial.

A poor visual diet, on the other hand, marked by repetitive, fear-based, or isolating stimuli, could foster narrow schema development. These early-formed mental templates might shape how individuals view themselves, others, and the world in a way that reinforces attachment wounds or a sense of *otherness*.

As one example: if a child with Tourette's repeatedly experiences social exclusion or mockery in environments they associate with their tics, they may build a long-lasting belief that they are "not enough." Because of their strong stimulus–response wiring, even subtle cues can resonate deeply, leading to emotional imprints that are harder to shift without intentional, supportive intervention.

Not Stubborn, Just Wired Differently

This does not mean that individuals with Tourette's are inflexible or resistant to growth. It means that intentional exposure to rich, varied, and affirming visual content, particularly early in life, can help develop broader neurological flexibility. This is not about changing who someone is but rather supporting how they engage with the world.

In a society saturated with visual media, the importance of curating content that nurtures and uplifts cannot be overstated, especially for populations with increased sensitivity to perception–action links.

Synesthesia and the Visually Connected Mind

Synesthesia is a unique neurological condition in which stimulation of one sensory or cognitive pathway automatically and involuntarily triggers a second, unrelated sensory experience. As *Psychology Today* describes:

> *"Synesthesia is a neurological condition in which stimulation of one sensory or cognitive pathway (for example, hearing) leads to automatic, involuntary experiences in a second sensory or cognitive pathway (such as vision). Simply put, when one sense is activated, another unrelated sense is activated at the same time."*
> — Psychology Today, 2022

This might manifest as hearing music and simultaneously seeing swirling colors or feeling a physical sensation in response to a sound. Synesthesia is not one single experience, but a constellation of presentations, each deeply personal and intricately wired.

Types of Synesthesia

Here are some of the most documented forms of synesthesia:

- **Auditory–Tactile Synesthesia:** Sounds produce physical sensations, like tingling or warmth.

- **Chromesthesia:** Sounds trigger visual colors or patterns.

- **Grapheme–Color Synesthesia:** Letters or numbers are linked to specific colors.

- **Lexical–Gustatory Synesthesia:** Words trigger distinct tastes (e.g., the word "justice" tasting like peanut butter).

- **Mirror–Touch Synesthesia:** Feeling a touch on your body when witnessing someone else being touched—like an amplified form of empathy.

- **Number Form:** Numbers automatically evoke spatial maps in the mind.

- **Ordinal Linguistic Personification:** Ordered sequences (like days of the week) are associated with personalities or genders.

- **Spatial Sequence Synesthesia:** Numerical or temporal sequences are visualized in specific spatial layouts.

These experiences can be fascinating, overwhelming, or both. What links them all is the visual cortex activation in response to non-visual stimuli, a kind of sensory crosstalk that reveals just how interconnected our perceptual systems really are.

Memory, Perception, and Sensory Strength

Research by Fresa et al. (2021) and Rothen et al. (2018) has shown that synesthetes often exhibit enhanced sensory processing and memory performance, particularly in visual perception and recall. These findings suggest a stronger link between sensory input and memory encoding, possibly because of how multi-sensory experiences create richer, more durable impressions in the brain.

In other words: synesthetes don't just *see more*, they may *remember more* as a result of how they process.

Inducing Synesthesia in Non-Synesthetes

Remarkably, some forms of synesthesia can be induced temporarily in individuals without the condition. A 2019 study by Nair and Brang (University of Michigan) demonstrated that short-term visual deprivation could produce sound-induced visual phenomena. In the absence of visual input, participants reported seeing color and shape in response to auditory cues, indicating that the visual cortex is still active, even without sight.

This opens fascinating questions about the plasticity of the brain and the latent potential for sensory crossover in all of us.

As someone who experiences color deficiency, I find synesthesia particularly beautiful. The idea of seeing a world in vivid color, pattern, and movement as sound or texture shifts, of linking taste to word, or emotion to shape, is deeply profound.

Synesthesia and the Visual Diet

So, what happens when a synesthete encounters overstimulating visual content?

If sensory experiences are cross-linked, then emotionally intense, disturbing, or overwhelming media may leave a deeper imprint than it would in someone without synesthesia. For example, someone who associates sound with shape might find violent media not just emotionally triggering, but visually intrusive in ways that are difficult to explain to others.

Likewise, someone who experiences gustatory responses to words might have visceral reactions to distressing language, while a chromesthetic person might be flooded with unwanted color patterns during noisy, chaotic screen time.

The implications for a visual diet are clear: synesthetes may need to be extra discerning in how they curate their visual and multisensory input. They may also benefit from using their unique neural pathways as a strength, leveraging those associations to deepen learning, enhance memory, and build more meaningful connections with the world.

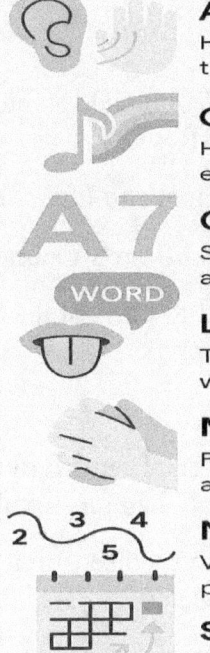

Types of Synesthesia

Synesthesia is a condition in which stimulation of one sense automatically triggers another sense. The following are some of the many reported types:

Auditory-tactile
Hearing sounds causes the sensation of touch

Chromesthesia
Hearing sounds evokes experiences of color

Grapheme-color
Seeing letters or numbers as specific colors

Lexical-gustatory
Tasting specific flavors when hearing words

Mirror-touch
Feeling the same sensation as another person

Number form
Visualizing numbers as points in space

Spatial sequence
Visualizing sequences of items in spatial patterns

Sensory Processing Conditions (SPC) and Visual Diet

Sensory Processing Conditions (SPC), sometimes referred to as Sensory Processing Disorder (SPD), describe a neurodivergent experience where the brain has difficulty detecting, modulating, or interpreting sensory input. These inputs can include touch, sound, smell, taste, vision, proprioception (body awareness), vestibular (balance and spatial orientation), and interoception (internal bodily cues like hunger or heartbeat).

Jessica Wood, writing in *The Journal for Nurse Practitioners* (2020), defines SPD as:

"A neurological disorder in which the brain has a difficult time processing (detecting, modulating, interpreting) input from one's senses... When there are persistent atypical response patterns to sensory stimuli that also cause dysfunction in everyday life activities, the condition is considered SPD."

However, in keeping with a non-pathologizing framework, I will use the term Sensory Processing (SP) rather than SPD, acknowledging the diversity of sensory experiences without labeling them as dysfunctional.

Current Recognition and Diagnostic Challenges

As of 2022, SP is not recognized in the DSM-5, ICD-10, or ICD-11, though its traits are commonly folded into other diagnoses such as Autism Spectrum Conditions, ADHD, and anxiety disorders. This lack of standalone recognition complicates access to support, especially given that up to 90% of individuals with autism present co-occurring SP traits (Galiana-Simal et al., 2020).

SP is, however, recognized by:

- The Diagnostic Classification of Mental Health and Developmental Disorders of Infancy and Early Childhood-Revised
- The Interdisciplinary Council of Development and Early Disorders

Subtypes of Sensory Processing (Dr. Lucy Jane Miller's Framework)

Dr. Lucy Jane Miller, a pioneer in SP research and founder of the SPD Foundation, has categorized SP into three main subtypes:

1. Sensory Modulation Conditions

- Sensory Over-Responsivity (SOR): Heightened sensitivity; may trigger fight-or-flight responses to seemingly benign stimuli.
- Sensory Under-Responsivity (SUR): Diminished sensitivity; may appear inattentive, underreactive, or dissociated.
- Sensory Craving: An intense, seemingly insatiable need for sensory input that may lead to boundary violations or risky behavior.

2. Sensory-Based Motor Conditions

- Postural Disorder: Difficulty maintaining body control and balance during everyday tasks.
- Dyspraxia: Challenges with motor planning and coordination (discussed earlier in this book).

3. Sensory Discrimination Conditions

- Difficulty identifying and interpreting specific sensory inputs (e.g., not noticing someone calling your name or misjudging distances).

Alternate Classification Model (Dr. Roseann Schaaf)

Dr. Schaaf's model offers another lens for understanding SP through five domains:

1. Poor Sensory Perception
2. Vestibular and Bilateral Integration Deficits (VBID)
3. Somatodyspraxia – tied to body coordination and spatial processing
4. Sensory Reactivity – aligned with over-/under-responsivity
5. Visuodyspraxia – specific difficulty in visual–motor integration

Lane et al. (2019) reinforce the deep interconnection between tactile, vestibular, and visual systems in the brain. These inputs are integrated across the CNS (e.g., thalamus, cortex, vestibular nuclei) and are critical for postural control, spatial orientation, and sensory regulation.

SP and the Modern Visual Landscape

Given SP's core involvement with sensory arousal, it's no surprise that individuals with SP may be especially susceptible to visual overstimulation. When our screens are designed to be emotionally addictive, via color, animation, sound, and fast transitions, they can become either:

- Overwhelming, causing shutdown or avoidance
- Or compulsively soothing, becoming a crutch for regulation

For individuals with Sensory Craving traits, content like fast-paced video games, highly stimulating cartoons, or looping social media videos can feed a dopamine-driven cycle. For those with Over-Responsivity, even "normal" screen content might cause anxiety, stress, or dysregulation.

SENSORY PROCESSING (SP) CLASSIFICATIONS

Dr. Lucy Jane Miller's Framework	Dr. Roseann Schaaf's Framework
Sensory Modulation Conditions • Sensory Over-Responsivity • Sensory Under-Responsivity • Sensory Craving	Poor Sensory Perception
Sensory-Based Motor Conditions • Postural Disorder • Dyspraxia	Vestibular and Bilateral Integration Deficits (VBID)
	Somatodyspraxia
	Sensory Reactivity
Sensory Discrimination Conditions	Visuodyspraxia

Why This Matters

When technology becomes a primary source of comfort, regulation, or identity, it can also become a dependency. This doesn't mean screens are evil, it means we need to use them intentionally, especially when supporting neurodivergent individuals with unique sensory processing needs.

Developers, content creators, and designers hold a moral responsibility to consider these needs. Products that ignore sensory diversity in favor of engagement metrics may exacerbate compulsive behavior or lead to sensory burnout in vulnerable users.

A Note on Regulation and Resilience

Because of SP's influence on dopaminergic reward systems (discussed further in Chapter 9), many individuals with SP may experience:

- A heightened need for regulation tools
- More intense emotional highs/lows
- Greater difficulty disengaging from stimulating content

This isn't a failure of willpower, it's neurology. And it's why building healthy, affirming, and diverse visual diets is essential for sensory wellbeing.

Highly Sensitive People (HSP) and the Sensory World

Highly Sensitive People (HSP) represent a neurodivergent presentation often defined by heightened emotional attunement, deep sensory awareness, and a powerful capacity for empathy and processing nuance. Though sometimes misunderstood as fragile or overly emotional, HSPs possess a richly developed system for integrating and responding to stimuli, particularly in social and emotional contexts.

In a groundbreaking study from UC Santa Barbara and Albert Einstein College of Medicine, researchers examined 18 HSP participants using fMRI scans while they viewed photos of loved ones and strangers expressing a range of emotional expressions (Acevedo et al., 2014). Participants completed the task twice, one year apart, and their brain activity was monitored for consistent patterns.

What They Found

The researchers observed increased activation in brain regions involved in:

- **Sensory integration**
- **Empathy**
- **Awareness**
- **Action planning**

Interestingly, the limbic system, particularly the amygdala, often associated with emotional reactivity, was not activated. This implies that HSPs do not process emotion through impulsive or reactive pathways, but instead engage in deliberate, thoughtful preparation for response.

Additionally, during the viewing of positive social stimuli, researchers observed activity in the Ventral Tegmental Area (VTA), a dopamine-rich brain structure associated with reward and pleasure. This means that connection, attunement, and social empathy are inherently rewarding for HSPs at the neurological level.

"These results suggest that... sensory-processing sensitivity does not necessarily engage limbic emotional processes but rather influences preparations to act via higher-order systems involved in awareness, integration of sensory information, and action planning."
— Acevedo et al., 2014

Health Implications

The connection between sensory-processing sensitivity and physical health has also been studied. In a sample of 383 college students, researchers from the University of Texas found that individuals who scored high on the HSP scale reported:

- Higher levels of perceived stress

- More frequent physical health symptoms

- A stronger link between sensitivity and somatic awareness than between general stress and health outcomes
  (Benham, 2006)

These findings suggest that heightened awareness of internal and external sensations may lead HSPs to experience:

- Genuine chronic physiological arousal

- Or an increased attunement to subtle bodily cues others might ignore

While these outcomes vary by person, they underscore the mind-body sensitivity of HSPs, and the importance of balancing stimulation and recovery.

THE HIGHLY SENSITIVE BRAIN

Brain Activation
- Premotor areas
- Empathy centers
- Sensory integration regions
- Ventral tegmental area (VTA)

Differences vs. Neurotypical Processing
Processing does not engage emotion-related regions such as the amygdala. Instead, HSPs demonstrate preparation for deliberate, thoughtful responses.

Research Findings
- Sensitivity linked to greater perceived stress and somatic symptom awareness
- Focus of attention more sustained, increasing likelihood of empathic or sensory overload

Visual Stimulation
Overstimulation may lead to compulsive consumption and difficulty disengaging from content

Focus and the Power of Attention

A study by Dimulescu, Schreier, and Godde (2020) revealed another striking trait of HSPs: the ability to direct and maintain attention more effectively than non-HSPs.

Using EEG data, researchers found that HSPs demonstrated:

"Better control over the focus of their attention."

This suggests that when visual stimulation is present—whether on screens, in nature, or in human interaction, HSPs may process it more deeply and with greater neurological investment. However, if their attention isn't redirected, they may become overwhelmed by emotional or sensory content, triggering a flood of empathic or physiological responses.

The HSP and the Visual Diet

So, what happens when an HSP engages with visually overstimulating media, especially in a society saturated with screen time, marketing psychology, and emotionally manipulative design?

They may experience:

- Overarousal from emotional storylines or imagery
- Compulsive consumption due to dopamine-driven reward systems
- A form of empathic saturation where the nervous system begins mirroring the emotional experiences onscreen

This is not escapism—it's the creation of an alternate, immersive emotional reality. For some, this can lead to deeper emotional insight. For others, it may blur boundaries between self and screen, making recovery and regulation more difficult.

A Reflection for the Reader

If you're neurotypical, take a moment to reflect:

- How many hours a day are you visually stimulated by technology?
- How often do you check your phone, scroll social media, or binge shows?
- How might your brain respond differently if your neurochemistry primed you to absorb stimuli deeply and empathize with it fully?

Now imagine being an HSP in that world.

Final Thoughts

We began this book by exploring neurodivergent responses to visual stimuli because these minds reveal the spectrum of experience that often goes ignored. The HSP brain, much like the autistic, ADHD, dyspraxic, dyslexic, or Tourettic brain, reminds us that there is no one way to process or relate to the world.

As the field of neurodiversity grows, so too must our willingness to design systems, content, and environments that honor, not erase, these differences. The future of mental health, education, and human connection depends on our ability to not only tolerate variation, but to celebrate and support it.

Summary

Autism Spectrum Conditions (ASC)

Autistic individuals often experience heightened visual sensitivity, leading to increased engagement with screens and artificial stimuli over real-world social interactions. Their face-processing deficits (N170 wave response) indicate weaker recognition of human faces but not necessarily artificial visuals. This hypersensitivity may contribute to compulsive screen use, though not always negatively.

Tourette's Syndrome (TS)

TS is characterized by motor and vocal tics, often linked to ADHD and OCD. Research suggests individuals with TS form stronger associations between stimuli and actions (perception-action binding), making them more reactive to repetitive visual patterns. Exposure to diverse visual stimuli early in life may help broaden cognitive flexibility and emotional resilience.

Synesthesia

Synesthesia involves cross-wired sensory experiences, such as seeing colors when hearing sounds. Studies indicate synesthetes have enhanced sensory integration and memory, with some forms of synesthesia being inducible in non-synesthetes through temporary visual deprivation. Their unique sensory processing can intensify emotional and cognitive responses to visual stimuli, influencing how they interact with the world.

These findings emphasize the need for personalized approaches in education and support systems to accommodate diverse neurodivergent experiences.

Sensory Processing Conditions (SPC)

SPC, often referred to as Sensory Processing Disorder (SPD) in older literature, is a neurological condition where the brain struggles to process sensory information, affecting responses to tactile, auditory, visual, gustatory, olfactory, proprioceptive, vestibular, and interoceptive stimuli (Wood, 2020). Despite its high comorbidity with Autism Spectrum Conditions (ASC), SPC is not currently recognized in the DSM-5, ICD-10, or ICD-11.

Dr. Lucy Jane Miller identified three main subtypes of SPC:

1. Sensory Modulation Conditions – Includes sensory over-responsivity (hypersensitivity), under-responsivity (diminished awareness), and sensory craving (excessive need for stimulation).
2. Sensory-Based Motor Conditions – Includes postural disorder (difficulty maintaining stability) and dyspraxia (issues with coordinated movement).
3. Sensory Discrimination Conditions – Involves difficulty identifying and processing sensory input.

Dr. Roseann Schaaf proposed an alternative five-domain model for SPC, including poor sensory perception, vestibular and bilateral integration deficits (VBID), somatodyspraxia, sensory reactivity, and visuodyspraxia.

SPC individuals often experience heightened responses to visual stimuli, which can lead to compulsive screen use and an unhealthy reliance on digital media. Given the dopamine-driven nature of digital interaction, SPC individuals may struggle with self-regulation and overstimulation, making them susceptible to technology dependence.

Highly Sensitive People (HSP)

Research by Acevedo et al. (2014) showed that HSP individuals display heightened brain activation when processing emotional stimuli, especially images of loved ones. However, unlike other emotional responses, their amygdala (fear/emotional center) is not activated, instead, brain regions associated with awareness, sensory integration, and action planning are engaged.

- HSP individuals show greater dopamine responses to positive social stimuli.
- They are more attuned to external stimuli, which can enhance empathy but also contribute to overstimulation.
- A study by Benham (2006) found that HSP individuals report higher stress levels and more frequent health symptoms, possibly due to chronic sensory arousal.
- EEG research by Dimulescu et al. (2020) revealed that HSP individuals have better control over their attentional focus, which

may amplify the impact of screen-based stimulation on their nervous systems.

Considerations

- How does excessive visual stimulation shape neurodivergent experiences?
- Does technology create an alternate reality for individuals highly sensitive to visual input?
- What responsibilities do developers have in creating products that can lead to compulsive screen use?

As our dependence on technology grows, it is crucial to study its impact on neurodivergent individuals, ensuring ethical and responsible development while acknowledging diverse neurological realities.

Chapter Six

"Trauma by nature drives us to the edge of comprehension, cutting us off from language based on common experience or an imaginable past." Dr. Bessel Van Der Kolk

The Traumatized Brain and Visual Processing

> *"Trauma is not the event that happens. It is how you respond to it. It changes your brain... Telling you long after it's over how to react to things, long after the event is over."*
> — Dr. Bessel van der Kolk, *Big Think*, 2021

As a trauma therapist, it would be an oversight not to address how trauma reshapes the brain, especially in relation to visual processing. Trauma is not a single event, it is a protracted relationship between the nervous system, the body, and the environment. It lingers, looping through neural pathways and disrupting our sense of safety, identity, and belonging.

When a traumatic experience overwhelms the system, whether it's a single, acute event or a series of chronic micro-aggressions, the brain adapts. But these adaptations often hijack our internal sense of time, self, and perception.

Visual Pathways and Trauma Memory

The visual cortex, located at the back of the brain in the occipital lobe, works in tandem with several other brain regions to encode, associate, and interpret what we see. However, in trauma, this system can become hyper-sensitized or disrupted.

Here's how trauma changes visual processing:

- The amygdala, which assesses threat, can become overactive, interpreting neutral visual stimuli as dangerous.

- The hippocampus, responsible for contextual memory, can become disorganized, making it hard to distinguish between past and present.

- The prefrontal cortex, the "rational" brain, may go offline, limiting one's ability to override fear-based reactions.

- The visual cortex itself can store "flashbulb memories", vivid, often involuntary images that become part of the trauma imprint.

This is why a traumatized individual might overreact to a familiar face, a flickering light, a certain color, or a particular shape. The brain is not "wrong", it's trying to protect, even if that protection is based on an outdated signal.

The Lingering Lens of Trauma

Trauma often changes what we see, and how we see it.

- Faces may feel unreadable.
- Environments may feel unsafe.
- Pleasure may feel unreachable.
- The world may appear hostile, even when it's not.

As a result, people may develop visual scanning behaviors: hypervigilance, avoiding eye contact, difficulty making sense of facial expressions, or even dissociation, where they mentally "leave" a scene while physically remaining present.

These visual shifts are not due to brokenness. They are signs of a brain doing its best to survive.

I added the criterion for diagnosis of PTSD and CPTSD for the purposes of identifying the components, which can affect an individual's visual diet. If you're familiar with the diagnostic criterion, feel free to jump ahead. The World Health Organization's current (at the time of writing this book) ICD-11 code for Post Traumatic Syndrome Disorder (WHO, 2022) states that for an individual to qualify for this diagnosis, they need to have:

> *"Exposure to an event or situation (either short- or long-lasting) of an extremely threatening or horrific nature. Such events include, but are not limited to, directly experiencing natural or human-made disasters, combat, serious accidents, torture, sexual violence, terrorism, assault or acute life-threatening illness (e.g., a heart attack); witnessing the threatened or actual injury or death of others in a sudden, unexpected, or violent manner; and learning about the sudden, unexpected or violent death of a loved one."*

Furthermore, they go on to state that there are behavioral considerations post exposure such as re-experiencing the event, avoidance of stimuli, which reminds individuals of the event/s, ongoing and often occurring experiences of threats, which can affect relationships

> *"Following the traumatic event or situation, the development of a characteristic syndrome lasting for at least several weeks, consisting of all three core elements:*

How Trauma Impacts the Brain

source: https://www.nicabm.com/trauma-polyvagal-theory-and-how-trauma-impacts-the-body/dy text

Trauma has long last impacts and creates changes in areas of the brain. These structural changes result in behavioral changes:

1. **Fear Driven** - we become a FEAR driven and are heightened neuroception of danger and threat (cues of danger/life threat)
2. **Avoidance Connection** - As there is more difficulty to engage with ordinary situations (cue of safety) and we are filtering out system disruption more continually; social connection feel overwhelming
3. **Dissociation** - Internal disconnection with the sensory centers of the body, lessened ability and a dampening of the self-sensing system

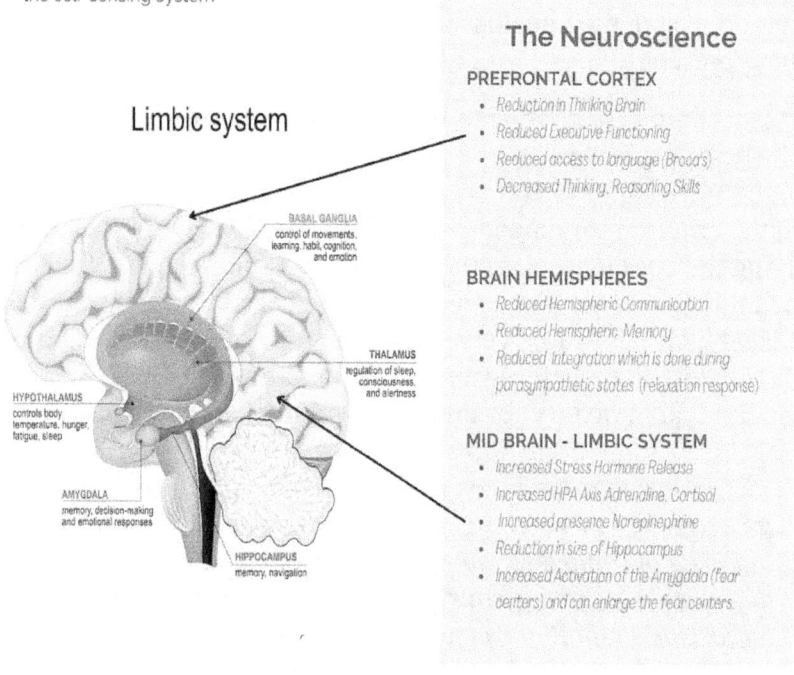

Julie Cardoza, LMFT, EMDRIA Approved Consultant @juliecardoza.com

- o Re-experiencing the traumatic event in the present, in which the event(s) is not just remembered but is experienced as occurring again in the here and now. This typically occurs in the form of vivid intrusive memories or images; flashbacks, which can vary from mild (there is a transient sense of the event occurring again in the present) to severe (there is a complete loss of awareness of present surroundings), or repetitive dreams or nightmares that are thematically related to the traumatic event(s). Re-

experiencing is typically accompanied by strong or overwhelming emotions, such as fear or horror, and strong physical sensations. Re-experiencing in the present can also involve feelings of being overwhelmed or immersed in the same intense emotions that were experienced during the traumatic event, without a prominent cognitive aspect, and may occur in response to reminders of the event. Reflecting on or ruminating about the event(s) and remembering the feelings that one experienced at that time are not sufficient to meet the re-experiencing requirement.

- *Deliberate avoidance of reminders is likely to produce re-experiencing of the traumatic event(s). This may take the form either of active internal avoidance of thoughts and memories related to the event(s), or external avoidance of people, conversations, activities, or situations reminiscent of the event(s). In extreme cases the person may change their environment (e.g., move to a different city or change jobs) to avoid reminders.*

- *Persistent perceptions of heightened current threat, for example as indicated by hypervigilance or an enhanced startle reaction to stimuli such as unexpected noises. Hypervigilant people constantly guard themselves against danger and feel themselves or others close to them to be under immediate threat either in specific situations or more generally. They may adopt new behaviors designed to ensure safety (e.g., not sitting with one's back to the door, repeated checking in vehicles' rear-view mirrors).*

• *The disturbance results in significant impairment in personal, family, social, educational, occupational or other important areas of functioning. If functioning is maintained, it is only through significant additional effort.*

Additional Clinical Features:

• *Common symptomatic presentations of Post-Traumatic Stress Disorder may also include general dysphoria, dissociative symptoms, somatic complaints, suicidal ideation and behavior, social withdrawal, excessive alcohol or drug use to avoid re-experiencing or manage emotional reactions, anxiety symptoms including panic, and obsessions or compulsions in response to memories or reminders of the trauma.*

- *The emotional experience of individuals with Post-Traumatic Stress Disorder commonly includes anger, shame, sadness, humiliation, or guilt, including survivor guilt."*

The criteria for CPTSD in the ICD-11 Code (WHO,2022),

Whereas the diagnostic requirements for Complex Post-Traumatic Stress Disorder include all Essential Features of Post-Traumatic Stress Disorder, the diagnosis of Complex Post-Traumatic Stress Disorder also requires the additional Essential Features of severe problems in affect regulation, persistent negative beliefs about oneself, and persistent difficulties in sustaining relationships:

- *Severe and pervasive problems in affect regulation. Examples include heightened emotional reactivity to minor stressors, violent outbursts, reckless or self-destructive behavior, dissociative symptoms when under stress, and emotional numbing, particularly the inability to experience pleasure or positive emotions.*

- *Persistent beliefs about oneself as diminished, defeated or worthless, accompanied by deep and pervasive feelings of shame, guilt or failure related to the stressor. For example, the individual may feel guilty about not having escaped from or succumbing to the adverse circumstance or not having been able to prevent the suffering of others.*

- *Persistent difficulties in sustaining relationships and in feeling close to others. The person may consistently avoid, deride or have little interest in relationships and social engagement more generally. Alternatively, there may be occasional intense relationships, but the person has difficulty sustaining them.*

- *The disturbance results in significant impairment in personal, family, social, educational, occupational or other important areas of functioning. If functioning is maintained, it is only through significant additional effort.*

Additional Clinical Features:

- *Suicidal ideation and behavior, substance abuse, depressive symptoms, psychotic symptoms, and somatic complaints may be present.*

Boundary with Normality (Threshold):

- *A history of exposure to a stressor of extreme and prolonged or repetitive nature from which escape is difficult or impossible does not in itself indicate the presence of Complex Post-Traumatic Stress*

Disorder. Many people experience such stressors without developing any disorder. Rather, the presentation must meet all diagnostic requirements for the disorder.

Course Features:

- *The onset of Complex Post-Traumatic Stress Disorder symptoms can occur across the lifespan, typically after exposure to chronic, repeated traumatic events and/or victimization that have continued for a period of months or years at a time.*

- *Symptoms of Complex Post-Traumatic Stress Disorder are generally more severe and persistent in comparison to Post-Traumatic Stress Disorder.*

- *Exposure to repeated traumas, especially in early development, is associated with a greater risk of developing Complex Post-Traumatic Stress Disorder rather than Post-Traumatic Stress Disorder.*

Developmental Presentations:

- *Complex Post-Traumatic Stress Disorder can occur at all ages, but responses to a traumatic event, that is, the core elements of the characteristic syndrome, can manifest differently depending on age and developmental stage. Because Complex Post-Traumatic Stress Disorder and Post-Traumatic Stress Disorder both share these same core elements, information provided in the Developmental Presentations section for Post-Traumatic Stress Disorder also applies to children and adolescents affected by Complex Post-Traumatic Stress Disorder.*

- *Children and adolescents are more vulnerable than adults to developing Complex Post-Traumatic Stress Disorder when exposed to severe, prolonged trauma such as chronic child abuse or participation in drug trafficking or as child soldiers. Many children and adolescents exposed to trauma have been exposed to multiple traumas, which increases the risk for developing Complex Post-Traumatic Stress Disorder.*

- *Children and adolescents with Complex Post-Traumatic Stress Disorder are more likely than their peers to demonstrate cognitive difficulties (e.g., problems with attention, planning, organizing) that may in turn interfere with academic and occupational functioning.*

- *In children, pervasive problems of affect regulation and persistent difficulties in sustaining relationships may manifest as regression, reckless behavior, or aggressive behaviors towards self or others, and in difficulties relating to peers. Furthermore, problems of affect regulation may manifest as dissociation, suppression of emotional experience and expression, as well as avoidance of situations or experiences that may elicit emotions, including positive emotions.*

- *In adolescence, substance use, risk-taking behaviors (e.g., unsafe sex, unsafe driving, non-suicidal self-harm), and aggressive behaviors may be particularly evident as expressions of problems of affect dysregulation and interpersonal difficulties.*

- *When parents or caregivers are the source of the trauma (e.g., sexual abuse), children and adolescents often develop a disorganized attachment style that can manifest as unpredictable behaviors towards these individuals (e.g., alternating between neediness, rejection, and aggression). In children less than 5 years old, attachment disturbances related to maltreatment may also include Reactive Attachment Disorder or Disinhibited Social Engagement Disorder, which can co-occur with Complex Post-Traumatic Stress Disorder.*

- *Children and adolescents with Complex Post-Traumatic Stress Disorder often report symptoms consistent with Depressive Disorders, Eating and Feeding Disorders, Sleep-Wake Disorders, Attention Deficit Hyperactivity Disorder, Oppositional Defiant Disorder, Conduct-Dissocial Disorder, and Separation Anxiety Disorder. The relationship of traumatic experiences to the onset of symptoms can be useful in establishing a differential diagnosis. At the same time, other mental disorders can also develop following extremely stressful or traumatic experiences. Additional co-occurring diagnoses should only be made if the symptoms are not fully accounted for by Complex Post-Traumatic Stress Disorder and all diagnostic requirements for each disorder are met.*

- *In older adults, Complex Post-Traumatic Stress Disorder may be dominated by anxious avoidance of thoughts, feelings, memories, and persons as well as physiological symptoms of anxiety (e.g., enhanced startle reaction, autonomic hyperreactivity). Affected individuals may experience intense regret related to the impact of traumatic experiences on their lives.*

Culture-Related Features:

- *Cultural variation exists in the expression of symptoms of Complex Post-Traumatic Stress Disorder. For example, somatic or dissociative symptoms may be more prominent in certain groups attributable to cultural interpretations of the psychological, physiological, and spiritual etiology of these symptoms and of high levels of arousal.*
- *Given the severe, prolonged, or recurrent nature of the traumatic events that precipitate Complex Post-Traumatic Stress Disorder, collective suffering and the destruction of social bonds, networks and communities may present as a focal concern or as important related features of the disorder.*
- *For migrant communities, especially refugees or asylum seekers, Complex Post-Traumatic Stress Disorder may be exacerbated by acculturative stressors and the social environment in the host country.*

Sex- and/or Gender-Related Features:

- *Females are at greater risk for developing Complex Post-Traumatic Stress Disorder than males.*
- *Females with Complex Post-Traumatic Stress Disorder are more likely to exhibit a greater level of psychological distress and functional impairment in comparison to males.*

The Traumatized Brain and Visual Saturation

First and foremost, if you or someone you care about is struggling with symptoms of trauma, please know that you are not alone, and help is available.
Trauma-informed therapists are trained to support individuals navigating these experiences, and many offer sliding scale options or work through community organizations for those without insurance. Please do not suffer in silence. Trauma changes the brain, especially the way it processes reality, and healing requires more than just "resilience" or willpower.

One of the most important messages to understand about trauma is this:

Trauma is not what happened, it's what happens inside you as a result. It's how your mind and body adapt in the aftermath, how your nervous system responds, and how your perception of the world shifts to survive.

If you're uncertain, I highly recommend Dr. Bessel van der Kolk's book, *The Body Keeps the Score*. It offers not just compelling research and case studies, but also a variety of treatment approaches, because trauma therapy is not one-size-fits-all. Finding the right therapist is like finding a trusted partner, it may take time and trial, but you are worth the search.

Trauma Alters the Visual Diet

Following trauma, your internal visual world, your thoughts, memories, flashbacks, dreams, can become the site of the poor visual diet. This doesn't mean you're "making it up." It means that your brain, in trying to keep you safe, has rewired its relationship with imagery and sensation.

This rewiring may show up as:

- Intrusive visual flashbacks
- Hypervigilance toward visual cues (e.g., noticing every face, every shift in body language)
- Avoidance of triggering visual content (even joyful things that now feel dangerous)
- Emotional detachment or dissociation when visually overwhelmed

Reexperiencing and Avoidance

One of trauma's cruelest paradoxes is the loop between reexperiencing and avoidance.

A person might be flooded with traumatic images from the past, reliving pain they never asked for. In response, they might seek escape in visual distractions, screens, shows, games, or social media, that activate dopamine and bring momentary relief. Over time, this coping can spiral into:

- Overreliance on stimulating media
- Shallow or compulsive media consumption
- Difficulty feeling presence or connection in real-world interactions

This isn't weakness. It's survival.

But when that survival pattern replaces our ability to engage, trust, and connect, it becomes a new layer of the trauma, what some might call a trauma bond with the media or device that distracts us.

The Barking Dog: A Metaphor for PTSD

If you've never experienced PTSD, consider this:

Your neighbor gets a new puppy.
At first, it's something that happened around you, until it won't stop barking.
All night. Every day.
You start to hear it even when it's not there, on the bus, in your car, in your

dreams.
No matter where you go, it's like the barking has followed you.

You try everything to silence it, white noise, earplugs, sleeping pills.
Nothing works for long.

Eventually, you avoid anything that might remind you of barking.
Cartoons. Dogs. Parks. Even certain sounds in music.
This is a glimpse of what PTSD can feel like.

Now imagine your internal visual field, your thoughts and memories, is the barking.
And you can't look away.

Of course, it makes sense that someone might seek comfort in screens, videos, or games, anything that promises a different world. And while dopamine-inducing content can bring short-term relief, it may also:

- Disrupt relationships
- Reinforce trauma bonds
- Displace opportunities for deeper healing

Hope Through Understanding

The truth is: trauma *does* alter the way we attach, to people, to content, to reality itself. But understanding how it operates opens the door to healing.

As you've explored throughout this book, the visual diet we consume, on screens, in our minds, and through our relationships, has profound effects on our nervous systems. For trauma survivors, that diet needs to be nourishing, grounding, and intentional.

The work of healing is not about "forgetting the barking." It's about rewiring the nervous system so that you no longer hear it everywhere you go, and when you do, you know how to respond with care.

Trauma Bonds and the Visual Diet

A trauma bond is a relationship, often with a person, but sometimes with an organization, community, or even a behavior, that persists despite causing harm, coercion, or emotional damage.

"Trauma bonds are emotional attachments between victims and their abusers or captors… marked by paradoxical complexities of abuse, control and dependency, and deep feelings of love, admiration, and gratitude in the victim for the abuser."
— Casassa et al., 2022

Another definition expands on this:

"A powerful emotional dependency on the abusive partner and a shift in world- and self-view... which can result in denial or minimization of the coercion and abuse... This attachment can continue even after the relationship has ended."
— Chambers et al., 2024

But trauma bonds don't just occur between people. They can form:

- With groups (e.g., cults, religious organizations)
- With systems (e.g., institutions that exploit loyalty)
- Or even with technology, behaviors, or screen-based content that repeatedly dysregulate or numb us, while making us feel temporarily safe, seen, or distracted.

Screens, Pandemic Isolation, and Trauma Loops

The COVID-19 pandemic amplified many people's relationships with screen-based content, often turning them into coping tools, and for some, trauma bonds.

In a study of 143 women aged 17–73, researchers found a significant relationship between increased social media use during the pandemic and rising body image dissatisfaction, which led to disordered eating behaviors (Gobin et al., 2021).

Similarly, a study of 2,441 participants reported increased binge drinking behaviors, often as a coping mechanism for stress, isolation, and screen-related burnout (Weerakoon et al., 2020).

A separate study involving 102 participants in Germany and Austria found:

- Work-related confinement was associated with increased social media use and gaming (especially in males)
- Social isolation led to more TV consumption in younger participants
- The less structured someone's day was, the more screen time they consumed (Arend et al., 2021)

Global Reflections: From Minneapolis to the Middle East to South Asia

A University of Minnesota study (2021) examined 720 individuals from a range of demographics:

- 43% increase in TV and streaming consumption
- 37% increase in social media use

- 20% increase in smartphone screen time
- 17% increase in gaming

Participants cited a range of motivations: boredom, anxiety, isolation, staying informed, and seeking connection.

In another profound example, a longitudinal study of Israeli ex-POWs from the 1973 Yom Kippur War showed that increased TV news consumption during the COVID-19 outbreak correlated with worsening PTSD symptoms. For individuals with delayed trauma responses, this kind of repetitive media exposure acted as a pathogenic reactivation of their nervous system (Solomon et al., 2021).

A multi-nation study of 548 participants across India, Nepal, Bangladesh, and Indonesia also reported:

- Higher rates of compulsive screen use
- Increased sleep disturbances
- Conflict with loved ones due to binge-watching
- A staggering 73.7% increase in media use for "escaping boredom, relieving stress, or overcoming loneliness" (Ayushi, 2020)

When Content Becomes a Captor

The concept of trauma bonding helps us understand how screen time and visual content can move from coping mechanism to compulsion, or even emotional dependence. For individuals with trauma histories, this relationship may mirror:

- Attachment to harmful sources of validation
- Seeking dopamine to escape dysregulation
- Numbing emotions while reinforcing disconnection

This is especially true when screen content provides fleeting emotional relief or a false sense of connection, before reinforcing shame, isolation, or burnout.

Binge-Watching, Visual Saturation, and the Long Arm of Trauma

Binge-watching has become a ubiquitous coping strategy, particularly during and after the COVID-19 pandemic. But its implications are more complex, and more potentially harmful, than many realize.

Research from Zhang et al. (2017) found that binge-watching is associated with:

- Mood disturbances

- Sleep disruption
- Fatigability
- Impairment in self-regulation

In Ayushi's 2020 study, binge-watching was identified not only as a symptom but potentially a cause of dysregulation, though more longitudinal research is needed to understand its long-term effects, especially in a post-COVID world.

Pandemic Media Use: Soothing or Saturating?

During lockdowns, streaming platforms soared. Netflix alone gained 25 million new subscribers in 2020, rising to over 193 million globally (Netflix, 2020). That doesn't even account for the millions more who accessed content through shared accounts, an access model that has since changed, forcing many to re-evaluate their digital consumption.

But beyond convenience or boredom, this increase in visual content brought something darker.

Holman et al. (2019) uncovered evidence linking exposure to graphic, traumatic media with worsened mental health outcomes, especially when that exposure involved bloody or emotionally charged imagery. The researchers wrote:

"Graphic content may trigger fear and anxiety… amplify emotional responses… promote intrusive thoughts, and activate attentional biases toward threat-related stimuli."

In short: the more disturbing the visual content, the more our brains may fixate on it, especially in those already anxious or traumatized.

The Digital Sponge Effect

Now pair that insight with the accessibility of modern visual media:

- On-demand video streaming
- Social media feeds
- Breaking news apps
- Short-form, high-stimulus content like TikTok and Instagram Reels

Suddenly, we see a world where individuals, particularly those cut off from prior routines or relational anchors, soak in content not as entertainment, but as a survival mechanism. For many, this level of consumption is unprecedented and unnatural, and our nervous systems are struggling to keep up.

The Global Climate of Fear and Disconnection

The pandemic created a global climate of fear, grief, uncertainty, and collective trauma. But trauma doesn't just cause fear, it also disrupts reward systems, especially those tied to pleasure, connection, and joy.

As trauma takes hold, it can sever us from:

- Dopamine-producing activities that once brought comfort
- Meaningful relationships
- Sensory anchors to safety and embodiment

Instead, we may seek out low-effort, high-dopamine inputs, media, alcohol, food, scrolling, or gaming, not to thrive, but to numb. And when that becomes habitual, it can foster dependency, avoidance, and eventually, dysfunction.

Neurobiological Toll of Trauma and Neglect

The damage of trauma, especially when experienced early or chronically, goes far beyond mental health. It restructures the very architecture of the brain.

Cassiers et al. (2018), analyzing 25 studies, found:

- Sexual abuse linked to structural deficits in the reward circuit, genitosensory cortex, and amygdala hyperreactivity
- Emotional maltreatment tied to abnormalities in fronto-limbic socioemotional networks
- Neglect resulted in disturbed white matter connectivity, impairing cognitive and emotional function
- Frontal cortical volume reduction was common across all maltreatment types

These findings highlight what many trauma survivors already know:

The world may not feel safe, and even when it is, your body doesn't believe it.

The Role of Attachment in Prevention

Fortunately, trauma does not guarantee a lifetime of suffering.

A powerful study by McLaughlin, Sheridan, and Nelson (Harvard Medical School) showed that responsive caregiving can act as a neurobiological shield. Their research found:

- Poverty and adverse childhood experiences (ACEs) can result in cortical thinning, especially in areas involved in survival processing
- Secure attachment, attunement, and unconditional support, however, negate cortical thinning

In other words:

Love, safe, responsive, validating love, protects the developing brain.

This is why parenting, community, and social environments are critical to prevention and healing. These aren't just psychological strategies, they're neuroprotective interventions.

We are still climbing out of a collective crisis, and for many, the binge-watching, doomscrolling, and media flooding that got us through those years has not been replaced with something more nourishing.

But we now know:

- The traumatized brain is more vulnerable to compulsive media use
- The visual diet we consume can shape our nervous system's ongoing sense of safety, or lack thereof
- And intentional support, connection, and attunement can prevent or even reverse damage over time

This chapter isn't about shaming survival behaviors. It's about understanding how we got here and offering tools to help us find our way out, together.

Dissociation and the Visual Dynamic of Shifting Brain Chemistry

Dissociation can be one of the most unsettling and disorienting psychological experiences, especially for those encountering it for the first time. It's not simply "zoning out" or being forgetful. It is the brain's adaptive response to threat, often triggered by sensory cues, most notably, visual stimuli.

At its core, dissociation is the brain's way of disconnecting from overwhelming pain, emotion, or fear. It occurs when the limbic system, our survival circuitry, is activated by something the brain perceives as dangerous, even if the danger is no longer present.

The Limbic System and Dissociation

According to the Queensland Brain Institute:

"The limbic system is the part of the brain involved in behavioral and emotional responses, especially those needed for survival: feeding, reproduction, caring for young, and fight-or-flight responses."

It includes:

- The amygdala – our brain's threat detector
- The hippocampus – central to memory and context
- The hypothalamus – regulating hunger, mood, and hormones
- The thalamus and basal ganglia – involved in processing sensory input and habit formation

When triggered by a visual cue, a color, a shadow, a gesture, even a flicker of light, the brain may initiate a dissociative response to protect the individual. In trauma-impacted brains, this visual input doesn't just pass through unnoticed. It can rekindle old neural firestorms, prompting what's known as trauma reenactment or repetition compulsion, where the individual unconsciously re-lives or re-creates aspects of their trauma.

The Visual Weight of Dissociation

Because of the brain's heavy reliance on visual processing, many dissociative episodes are *visually informed*. Individuals might:

- "See" past events play out like hallucinated memories
- Lose awareness of current surroundings
- Experience fragmented perception, as if viewing the world through a movie screen, fog, or tunnel
- Disengage entirely from their body (depersonalization) or the environment (derealization)

In these moments, the nervous system protects the psyche by displacing it.

And in today's world, saturated by visual overstimulation, the risk of this displacement becomes more frequent, especially for individuals with trauma histories.

Fractionating and Parts of Self

For some individuals, particularly those with complex or developmental trauma, dissociation may come with fragmentation of identity or ego states. This can look like:

- A "younger self" taking over during stress
- Shifting between emotional states with little memory or context
- Speaking, acting, or reacting as if from a different time or developmental stage

This is not dramatization or attention-seeking. It is the brain's way of compartmentalizing distress to survive. And when a person is exposed to poor visual diets, doomscrolling, trauma porn, violent media, chaotic timelines, it can reignite these fragmented states, often without warning.

The Screen as a Mirror

In this visual world, screens often act as mirrors and magnifiers. For the dissociative brain, the stream of content can become both:

- A trigger (activating unresolved trauma)
- And an escape (offering numbness from internal chaos)

But this feedback loop can make healing harder. If someone dissociates frequently while watching media, scrolling, or gaming, they may lose time, relationships, and a sense of self, all while retraining the brain to disconnect even further.

Summary

- **Seeking Trauma-Informed Care**: Trauma affects neurochemistry, making self-reliance insufficient for healing.
- **Visual Diet & PTSD**: Trauma survivors often experience intrusive visual memories and avoidance behaviors, impacting their perception and screen habits.
- **Trauma Bonds**: Emotional dependencies can form with not just people but also organizations, social media, and entertainment.
- **COVID-19's Role**: Increased media consumption during the pandemic exacerbated stress, trauma responses, and unhealthy coping strategies.
- **Research on Media & Trauma**: Studies link increased screen time to PTSD symptoms, compulsive behaviors, and mood disturbances.
- **Dissociation & Visual Stimuli**: The limbic system's response to trauma can trigger dissociative episodes, where visual triggers may cause emotional distress or reenactment.

Chapter Seven

"Education is the passport to the future, for tomorrow belongs to those who prepare for it today." Malcolm X

How We Learn

Our capacity to learn is central to this book, because it is directly tied to how we absorb and respond to visual media. What we see, hear, and experience doesn't just pass through us, it shapes our behavior, our relationships, and our sense of self.

If we're learning how to interact with others based solely on comment sections or video game lobbies, we're on a trajectory that may lead to more misunderstanding, division, or even harm. This chapter will explore just how susceptible our minds are to outside stimuli, especially when it is constant, visual, and unregulated.

Learning is a Continuous Experience

Researchers comparing human and machine learning point out a key difference:

> *"Learning is an inherently continuous phenomenon. We learn further about tasks we have already learned and can adapt to new environments by interacting in them... There is no hard boundary between training and testing phases, we learn as we perform."*
> — Wortsmann, M., 2019

In other words: humans learn in real time. We don't wait for a test. We don't freeze during "inference." We integrate knowledge every moment, especially through repeated experience.

And that's the core message:
When we're constantly consuming visual content, we are learning from it. Whether that content is helpful, harmful, or neutral, it's building associations in our brain. Those associations become automatic over time, reinforced by the repetition of stimuli. Even if the content is fictional, exaggerated, or distorted, our nervous system doesn't always distinguish fact from frequency.

The Brain Learns Through Relationships, Not Just Data

Harvard researchers Pamela Cantor et al. (2019) offer a robust and compassionate model of how human development works. Their framework includes:

- Neural malleability and plasticity
- Attachment and relationships
- Resilience, motivation, and meaning-making
- Contextual influences like trauma, adversity, and cultural narratives

They write:

> *"Human development occurs through reciprocal interactions between the individual and their contexts and culture, with relationships as the key drivers... Contexts, and how children interpret them, can be risks or assets for learning."*

In short:
We learn in relationship, with others, with our environments, with our culture, and with ourselves.

This also means that poor relationships, or hostile environments, can deeply undermine the learning process.

The Visual Diet as an Educational Force

What happens when a child learns more from YouTube than from their caregiver? What lessons are absorbed when TikTok becomes the primary social reference point? How do memes, influencers, or algorithms become unintentional teachers? The visual diet isn't just entertainment, it's a curriculum.

That's why what we consume matters. If it replaces human connection, safe relationships, or developmental support, it doesn't just "distract", it rewires.

Cortical Thinning and the Biology of Learning

Let's return to the brain. As mentioned in an earlier chapter, cortical thinning is a biological process that impacts learning capacity. While normal during aging, it can be accelerated by:

- Trauma
- PTSD
- Adverse childhood experiences (ACEs)
- Neurodegenerative conditions like Alzheimer's or MS

"Cortical thinning occurs throughout the entire life and extends to late-life neurodegeneration."
— *Vidal-Piñeiro, et al., 2020*

This matters because when a child's environment is chaotic, unsupported, or filled with stress and overexposure (including to visual media), their brain may reallocate resources just to survive, leaving less capacity for higher-order thinking, memory, and flexibility.

Global and Cultural Views of Learning

In Indonesia, Basri H. (2020) identified six core principles of learning, including:

1. Physical and mental maturity
2. Readiness and motivation
3. Understanding the goal of learning
4. Internal ability and self-efficacy
5. Repetition and reinforcement
6. Environmental influences

These principles reflect both internal and external contributors to learning, and show how visual repetition plays a powerful role.

Meanwhile, in China, researcher Jiaosheng Qiu (2019) explored constructivist and mobile learning models. He emphasizes:

> *"Constructivist learning theory advocates teacher-guided, student-centered learning, through context, collaboration, conversation, and meaning construction."*

This form of learning is interactive, guided, and relational, not passive. Compare that to many screen-based learning environments, where the learner is isolated, stimulated, but not always engaged in meaningful collaboration.

So, What Are We Actually Learning?

If we believe that humans are always learning, then the question becomes:

> *What are we learning from our screens?*
> *What patterns, behaviors, or beliefs are being reinforced by repetition?*
> *What does our environment, digital and real, teach us about how to live, relate, and grow?*

Learning is not neutral. It is constructed through experience.

If our experiences are mostly virtual, algorithm-driven, or emotionally triggering, we must pause to ask:
Are we learning how to live, or just how to react?

Final Takeaway

The micro (internal capacity) and macro (cultural, technological, environmental) dimensions of learning are inseparable. A secure, supported child in a rich interpersonal environment can thrive. But in a high-stress, overstimulated, underconnected world, even the most curious mind can struggle to learn well.

This chapter sets the stage for what comes next:
How screen-based visual input doesn't just inform, it forms us. And how mindful, intentional visual diets can restore our capacity to learn, connect, and grow.

Reinforcement Learning: Not Just About Rewards

Reinforcement learning is a fundamental way we learn from experience. When something good happens (a reward), our brain strengthens the connection. When something goes wrong (a prediction error), the brain recalculates.

Surprisingly, this same mechanism is at play in social situations, especially when we're faced with group disagreement or social pressure.

Research shows that social conformity and reinforcement learning share a common neural pathway.
— *(Klucharev et al., 2009; Levorsen et al., 2021; Zhang et al., 2020)*

The Brain's Response to Social Conflict

When you disagree with a group, your brain doesn't just note the difference, it reacts as if it made a mistake.

Functional MRI studies show that conflict with group opinion activates areas like the:

- Rostral cingulate zone
- Ventral striatum

These regions are also involved in prediction error signals in reinforcement learning, those moments when your brain says, *"Something unexpected just happened. Update the plan."*

This "conflict-related signal" predicts whether someone will conform to group norms in future behavior.
— *(Klucharev et al., 2009)*

Why It Matters: Conformity Is Learned

Social conformity isn't just about peer pressure or fear of rejection. It's reinforced, like any habit. Every time we adjust our behavior to align with the group, especially when rewarded or validated, the brain stores it as a lesson.

The more intense the conflict-related signal in the ventral striatum, the more likely a person is to conform. This isn't just a theory, it's visible in brain scans.

> *"The amplitude of the signal correlates with conforming behavior."*
> — *(Levorsen et al., 2021)*

Digital Implications: When Algorithms Teach Us Who to Be

This research has urgent implications in a world governed by digital feedback loops:

- Likes, shares, retweets, upvotes, all act as digital reinforcers
- AI bots and misinformation campaigns simulate group consensus
- Viral content, even when false, influences what we believe to be "normal" or "popular"

In the 2016 U.S. election, social media became a breeding ground for manipulated conformity. False claims weren't just persuasive, they reprogrammed reality for many users.

Marginalized Communities and the Risk of Reinforced Oppression

Reinforcement learning + digital conformity is especially dangerous for marginalized groups.

When platforms amplify biased content or harmful narratives, conformity mechanisms can:

- Normalize internalized oppression
- Reinforce harmful societal norms
- Create echo chambers that shape identity and limit autonomy

Without digital literacy and critical reflection, we may unconsciously conform to realities that were never ours to choose.

Key Takeaways

- Social conflict activates a "prediction error" signal, pushing us toward conformity.
- This signal arises in brain regions tied to reward learning: the rostral cingulate zone and ventral striatum.
- The stronger the signal, the more likely a person is to conform.

- Brain areas involved in social conformity (e.g., pMFC, anterior insula) overlap with those used in reinforcement learning.
- In the digital world, conformity is shaped algorithmically, not organically.
- Misinformation, AI-generated groupthink, and platform design all exploit this mechanism.
- For marginalized communities, the cost of unconscious digital conformity can be even more severe.

Addictions and the Visual Diet

> *"Addiction is defined as not having control over doing, taking, or using something to the point that it can be harmful to you."*
> *— Yale Medicine, 2022*

Our understanding of addiction has expanded beyond substances like drugs or alcohol. Today, researchers and medical professionals recognize that people can form compulsive relationships with behaviors, technologies, and even screen-based media.

And when it comes to visual content, the design is often not neutral, it's crafted to keep us engaged, immersed, and returning for more.

Beyond Substances: Addiction as Behavior

Addiction isn't always about a chemical. It's about compulsion, dysregulation, and the biopsychosocial interplay that traps us in behavior loops, sometimes without realizing it.

One widely recognized framework, the *Components Model of Addiction*, outlines six key traits that can help identify addictive patterns (Griffiths, 2013):

The Six Core Components of Behavioral Addiction

1. Salience
   The activity dominates your thoughts, feelings, and behaviors, even when you're not doing it.

2. Mood Modification
   You use the activity to cope, seeking a high, a buzz, or emotional escape.

3. Tolerance
   You need more time or intensity to get the same emotional payoff.

4. **Withdrawal**
   Irritability, restlessness, or discomfort when you can't engage in the behavior.

5. **Conflict**
   The behavior causes tension with others or interferes with work, relationships, or daily functioning.

6. **Relapse**
   After attempts to cut back, the behavior returns, sometimes worse than before.

Screens, Dopamine, and the Digital Trap

Screens have been engineered to trigger reinforcement cycles, clicks, likes, shares, scrolls. These interactions aren't passive; they're behaviorally conditioned responses.

As visual consumers, we're learning behaviors that resemble addiction. The cues are built into the design: colors, sounds, endless feeds, intermittent rewards. We are learning to stay hooked.

A Complex Web: The Biopsychosocial Model

> *"Addiction can be viewed as a chronically evolving biopsychosocial disorder, encompassing dimensions both internal and external to the individual."*
> — Smith, 2021

Understanding addiction requires zooming out.

According to the biopsychosocial model, addiction arises from:

- Personal factors (e.g., trauma, genetics, self-esteem)
- Environmental context (e.g., culture, stress, social norms)
- Behavior itself (e.g., the reward or relief it brings)

Interventions, then, must be just as layered: targeting not only the compulsive behavior, but the person's history, environment, and underlying needs.

Why This Matters for the Visual Diet

You weren't born addicted to your screen.

But slowly, through conditioning, culture, and repetition, you may have developed a relationship with it that mirrors addiction. Especially if:

- You work online
- You cope through bingeing or scrolling

- Your social connections depend on apps or media

It's not your fault, but it's also not neutral. Understanding how addiction develops is the first step toward healing, boundaries, and intentionality.

Lingering effect of visual stimuli

One could probably ask, what is the harm in binging for a few hours a day? It's just a short amount of time in that day. That is true but add it up and it compounds over time. If someone were to just spend 3 hours a day watching screens, that equals 1,134 hours in a year. That is 47.25 days out of the year just spent watching content. These are bound to have lingering effects upon our mind.

In a longitudinal study spanning 20 years, 599 participants were examined based on their TV viewing patterns and given Structural MRI scans. The results were striking.

> *"Over the 20 years, participants reported viewing an average of 2.5 plus or minus 1.7 hours of television per day. The range spanned 0–10 hours. Among middle-aged adults, greater television viewing in early to mid-adulthood was associated with lower gray matter volume. Sedentariness or other facets of television viewing may be important for brain aging even in middle age."* (Dougherty, et al, 2021).

Our brains are learning to be less and less engaged and atrophying. The screens are shifting our brain chemistry. This longitudinal study was related to television, and other studies are being conducted related to our handheld devices. However, due to their proliferation throughout our globe, one can only image how 20 years of handheld devices augment our minds.

Summary

- **Learning as a Continuous Process:**
    - Humans learn through continuous interaction with their environment, forming neural associations that reinforce behaviors.
    - Excessive exposure to visual media can deeply embed information, whether true or false, into one's cognitive framework.
- **Developmental Influences on Learning:**

- o Learning is influenced by epigenetics, neural plasticity, relationships, and socio-cultural contexts.
- o Secure attachments and supportive environments can prevent issues like cortical thinning, which impairs cognitive function.

- **Social Conformity and Reinforcement Learning:**
  - o Brain regions linked to reinforcement learning also drive social conformity.
  - o Exposure to digital content influences behavior in ways similar to reward and punishment mechanisms, making individuals more susceptible to misinformation and social pressures.

- **Addiction and Media Consumption:**
  - o Addiction is not limited to substances but extends to compulsive behaviors like excessive screen use.
  - o Screens are designed to capture and retain attention, reinforcing addictive behaviors that impact mental and social well-being.

- **Long-Term Cognitive Effects of Screen Exposure:**
  - o Prolonged screen time contributes to reduced gray matter volume, affecting cognitive function and brain aging.
  - o A 20-year study found that excessive television watching in early adulthood correlated with cognitive decline, raising concerns about modern digital consumption.

- **Conclusion:**

Unrestricted exposure to visual media can shape learning, influence social behaviors, and even contribute to addiction. A better understanding of how media affects cognition is crucial for fostering digital wellness and mitigating negative effects on brain development.

Chapter Eight

"It's not just about limiting screen time; it's about teaching kids to develop good habits in real life as well as managing their screen time."

– Cynthia Crossley, Co-Founder of Habyts

How Children's and Adolescents' Brains Are Affected by Visual Stimuli

Children have long been fascinated by the colorful lights and motion of screens. Just take a glance around any public space and you'll likely spot a child fully immersed in a glowing device, so captivated they may even walk into an obstacle while watching. But what is actually happening in their developing brains as these black mirrors flash with stimulation?

Early Brain Development and Screens

The World Health Organization (WHO) has raised concerns about early screen exposure, and for good reason. The first few years of life are a critical window for brain development, where the quality and type of stimulation shape long-term cognitive, emotional, and motor growth.

Dr. Tedros Adhanom Ghebreyesus, WHO Director General, puts it plainly:

> *"Achieving health for all means doing what is best for health right from the beginning of people's lives."*

Their latest guidelines emphasize the importance of active, human-centered engagement, not screen time, for optimal development.

WHO Recommendations on Screen Use for Young Children

Infants (Under 1 Year Old)

- Physical activity: Several times daily, especially through floor-based play (including at least 30 minutes of tummy time for non-mobile babies).
- No screen time recommended.
- Reading and storytelling with a caregiver encouraged when sedentary.
- Sleep: 14–17 hours (0–3 months), or 12–16 hours (4–11 months), including naps.

Children 1–2 Years Old

- At least 180 minutes of various physical activities, spread throughout the day.
- No more than 1 hour of being restrained at a time (e.g., stroller, high chair).
- Screen time:
  - For 1-year-olds: *Not recommended at all.*
  - For 2-year-olds: *Maximum of 1 hour per day; less is better.*
- Reading and storytelling encouraged instead of screens.
- Sleep: 11–14 hours including naps, with consistent wake/sleep routines.

Children 3–4 Years Old

- At least 180 minutes of physical activity per day, including 60+ minutes of moderate-to-vigorous intensity.
- Limit screen time to no more than 1 hour/day; again, *less is better.*
- Storytelling and reading should replace passive screen exposure when sedentary.
- Sleep: 10–13 hours, including naps if needed, with regular bedtimes.

(WHO Guidelines, 2022)

Why These Guidelines Matter

Children's brains are especially plastic, meaning they're constantly wiring and rewiring in response to their environment. Visual media, particularly screens that are fast-paced, emotionally charged, or high in stimulus, can shape attention patterns, delay language acquisition, and limit real-world social development, especially when it replaces caregiver interaction.

When screens supplement human connection, they can serve a purpose (like interactive reading apps or calls with family). But when screens replace those interactions, they can disrupt essential neural development, especially in the early years.

An infant's mind is a sponge, especially to visual stimuli. Through exposure and repetition, infants begin to perceive and form associations that help them make sense of their world. These associations are essential for understanding how to survive and interact within an increasingly visually dependent society.

Of course, this process assumes typical visual development without neurodivergent presentations or other sensory impairments. But for many children, especially those exposed early and frequently to screens, the picture gets more complicated.

Sleep and Screen Time: A Hidden Cost

Recent research by Ribner et al. (2019), examining 429 infants at four months old, found a negative association between screen time and sleep: for every additional hour of screen-based media, infants lost an average of 13 minutes of night sleep.

HOW CHILDREN'S AND ADOLESCENTS' BRAINS ARE AFFECTED BY VISUAL STIMULI

Recommendations on Screen Use
WHO GUIDELINES (2022)

INFANTS (LESS THAN 1 YEAR
- No screen time
- Encouraged: reading and storytelling
- Several times a day: physical activity

CHILDREN 1–2 YEARS
- Encouraged: reading and storytelling
- At least 180 min./day: physical activity
- 1 year: no screen time
- 2 years: ≤ 1 hour/day

CHILDREN 3–4 YEARS
- Encouraged: reading and storytelling
- At least 180 min./day: physical activity
- ≤ 1 hour/day: screen time

Now, 13 minutes might not sound like much, but small losses add up. Over weeks and months, this accumulated sleep deprivation can contribute to developmental concerns. Hyperstimulation from media doesn't just delay bedtime, it may also reduce sleep quality by dysregulating circadian rhythms and delaying melatonin production.

Why It Matters

Poor sleep in early development can have cascading effects, not only for the child but for their caregivers as well.

Studies by Fjell et al. (2021) show that chronic sleep disturbances in children are associated with faster cortical thinning, particularly in the right lateral temporal cortex, a region linked to language, memory, and social processing. Ribner and colleagues also noted the powerful relationship between maternal and infant sleep.

If caregivers use screens during nighttime feedings or care routines, they might inadvertently disrupt both their own and their child's sleep cycles by increasing exposure to stimulating blue light.

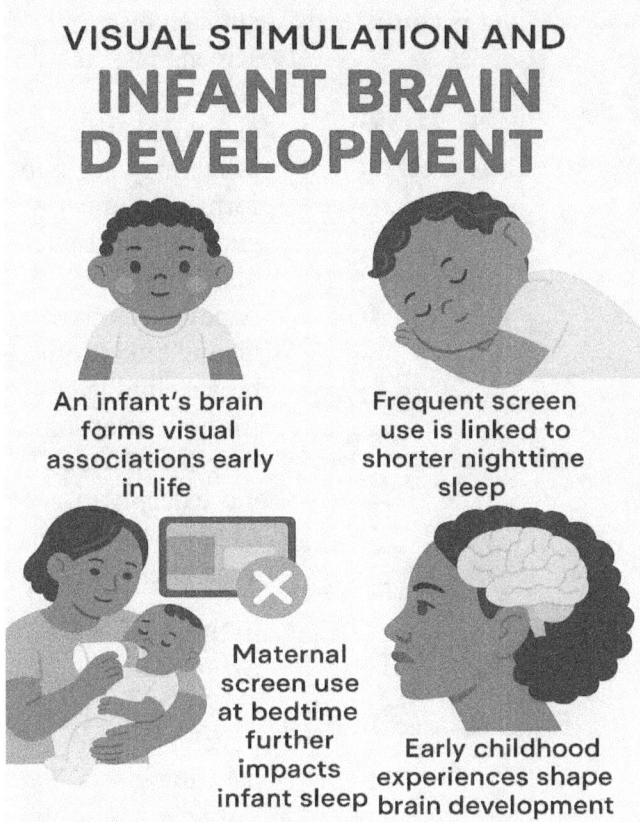

Key Takeaway

Early screen exposure isn't just a question of entertainment, it may directly influence a child's biological rhythms, sleep quality, and even brain structure. What begins as a tool for soothing or distracting can subtly, but powerfully, shape how both children and caregivers rest, recover, and grow.

A longitudinal study of 416 newborns across multiple countries, conducted by McHarg et al. (2020), found a significant connection between early screen exposure and later cognitive development. Specifically, screen use as early as four months was negatively associated with inhibition skills by 14 months of age.

Why does this matter? Inhibition is a core part of executive functioning (EF) the brain's ability to regulate attention, behavior, and emotions. The researchers offered two key explanations:

1. **Distraction** – Screens may pull parents' attention away from their children, reducing crucial face-to-face interactions.

2. **Parental self-regulation** – Parents with lower impulse control might use screens more often themselves, creating both environmental and possibly genetic influences on their child's development.

Further research supports the idea that even very young infants are learning rapidly from their environments. A 2018 study by Ferguson et al. showed that infants as young as 3 to 4 months can recognize and learn abstract rules using both visual and auditory stimuli, even when those cues are unfamiliar. In other words, it only takes a few exposures for a child to form associations, which begin shaping their understanding of the world.

If, in those early moments, a caregiver is consistently distracted by a screen, missing eye contact or emotional cues, the infant may begin to form attachment gaps. These subtle disruptions in bonding can have lasting effects on how a child later forms relationships. (We'll explore this more deeply in Chapter Thirty on attachment theory.)

How children's brains are affected by visual stimuli

Many infants are exposed early and frequently to screens

For every additional hour of screen time, infants lose an average of 13 minutes of sleep a night

Sleep disturbances in children are linked to faster cortical thinning

Poor sleep can harm both children and caregivers

In the documentary *Brain Matters* (2020), developmental psychologist Alicia F. Lieberman from the University of California, San Francisco, says:

> *"The first three years of life are the magical years for intervention because the changes we facilitate then can last for the rest of the child's life and the parent's life and create a new way of relating."*

Similarly, Patricia Kuhl of the University of Washington explains:

> *"It's experience-expectant. The brain is sitting there with all of its neuromachinery, for language, for culture, for values. It sets up routines to predict the future. The brain tends to settle on things that happen most frequently."*

The key takeaway: what children see most often becomes the blueprint their brain uses to understand the world.

Brain Growth, the Neocortex, and the Impact of Visual Stimuli

The neocortex, the front third of the brain visible from a side view, is responsible for forming associations, integrating sensory input, and preparing us for action. It plays a critical role in emotional regulation, executive functioning, and decision-making (Zull, J., 2006).

Importantly, the brain doesn't reach full maturity until around age 25, when the prefrontal cortex, the center for reasoning and impulse control, fully develops (Arain, M., et al., 2013). That means from birth through early adulthood, our brains remain highly plastic, constantly shaped by experience.

During infancy and early childhood (especially from birth to age 5), the brain is wired to absorb, process, and adapt to environmental stimuli at an extraordinary rate. The type and frequency of stimuli, especially visual stimuli, can influence which neural connections are strengthened or eliminated.

As Extension Human Development Specialist Judith Graham from the University of Maine explains:

> *"At birth, a baby's brain contains 100 billion neurons, roughly as many nerve cells as there are stars in the Milky Way, and almost all the neurons the brain will ever have. The brain starts forming prenatally, about three weeks after conception."*

She continues:

> *"During the first years of life, the brain undergoes a series of extraordinary changes. At birth, the number of synapses per neuron is 2,500.*
> *By age two or three, that number grows to about 15,000 synapses per neuron."*

This dramatic growth is then followed by synaptic pruning, the brain's way of eliminating connections that are rarely or never used. It's a natural and necessary part of development, helping the brain become more efficient.

Why This Matters

If a child's primary source of stimulation involves high-speed, high-contrast, low-interaction visual input (like screens), their brain may begin to prioritize these types of experiences. This early wiring sets the foundation for how they:

- Focus attention
- Regulate emotions

- Build social connections
- Engage in learning and play

These patterns are not easily reversed. That's why the early years are often referred to as "critical" or "sensitive" periods of development. What happens most often during these years tends to shape a child's reality and can follow them into adolescence and adulthood.

During early childhood, the brain is developing at an extraordinary rate. In fact, infants can form over a million new neural connections every second in their first year of life (Harvard, 2019). These connections lay the foundation for how a child perceives, relates to, and survives within their environment. This means that every experience, every interaction, shapes their understanding of the world around them.

When screens replace human interaction during these critical developmental windows, a host of challenges can arise.

A comprehensive systematic review and meta-analysis from Chao L. et al. (2020), covering 80 international studies, paints a concerning picture. Conducted by Central South University in Changsha, China, and Xiangya Hospital, the findings reveal significant negative effects of excessive screen use in early childhood. These include:

- Increased risk of overweight and obesity
- Shorter sleep duration and more sleep disturbances
- Higher levels of aggression and behavioral issues
- Greater risk of musculoskeletal pain and bullying
- Reduced executive functioning and motor development
- Poorer dietary behaviors and less physical activity

In short, too much screen time is associated with lower quality of physical, cognitive, and emotional health outcomes.

The Role of Human Connection in Early Development

David Lawrence, founder of *The Children's Movement of Florida*, puts it plainly:

> *"Television is a lousy babysitter because humans need interactivity. They need relationships."*

This sentiment is echoed in the findings of the *Abecedarian Project*, one of the most well-respected early childhood development studies in the world. This five-decade longitudinal study tracked low-income children born between 1972 and 1977. From infancy through age five, children in the intervention group received full-time, high-quality educational care that prioritized individualized games and activities designed to strengthen social, emotional, and cognitive development, especially in language

The outcomes were powerful and long-lasting:

1. IQ gains persisted through age 12, with stronger effects seen at 12 than at age 8.

2. Reading, writing, and general knowledge scores remained higher for those who had received the intervention.

3. Students were less likely to be held back a grade.

4. Parents of children in the intervention group reported higher perceptions of school success, in line with actual performance.

5. Interestingly, children's self-perceptions of cognitive ability were not tied to intervention, highlighting the complex relationship between self-esteem and achievement.

These results underscore a profound truth: Children thrive when provided with consistent, responsive, and enriching relationships, especially in the earliest years.

When screens replace these human connections, especially during moments of critical brain development, we risk impeding a child's ability to regulate emotions, build language, develop empathy, and establish healthy learning habits. What's learned early is often learned deeply, and what's missed may take years to recover.

Emotional Regulation and Impulse Control

Emotional regulation and impulse control are cornerstones of healthy neurodevelopment, and both are being challenged in our visually saturated world. Increasingly, research points to the impact of screen use on a child's ability to manage impulses, delay gratification, and regulate emotion. These findings don't serve as judgment for parents or caregivers, but rather as a call to consider a more balanced, developmentally supportive visual environment.

Let me be clear: I'm not a parent, and I say this with deep empathy. Implementing WHO recommendations for screen use isn't always feasible, especially when caregiving resources are limited. But understanding how visual media affects impulse control is essential if we hope to support children's growth holistically.

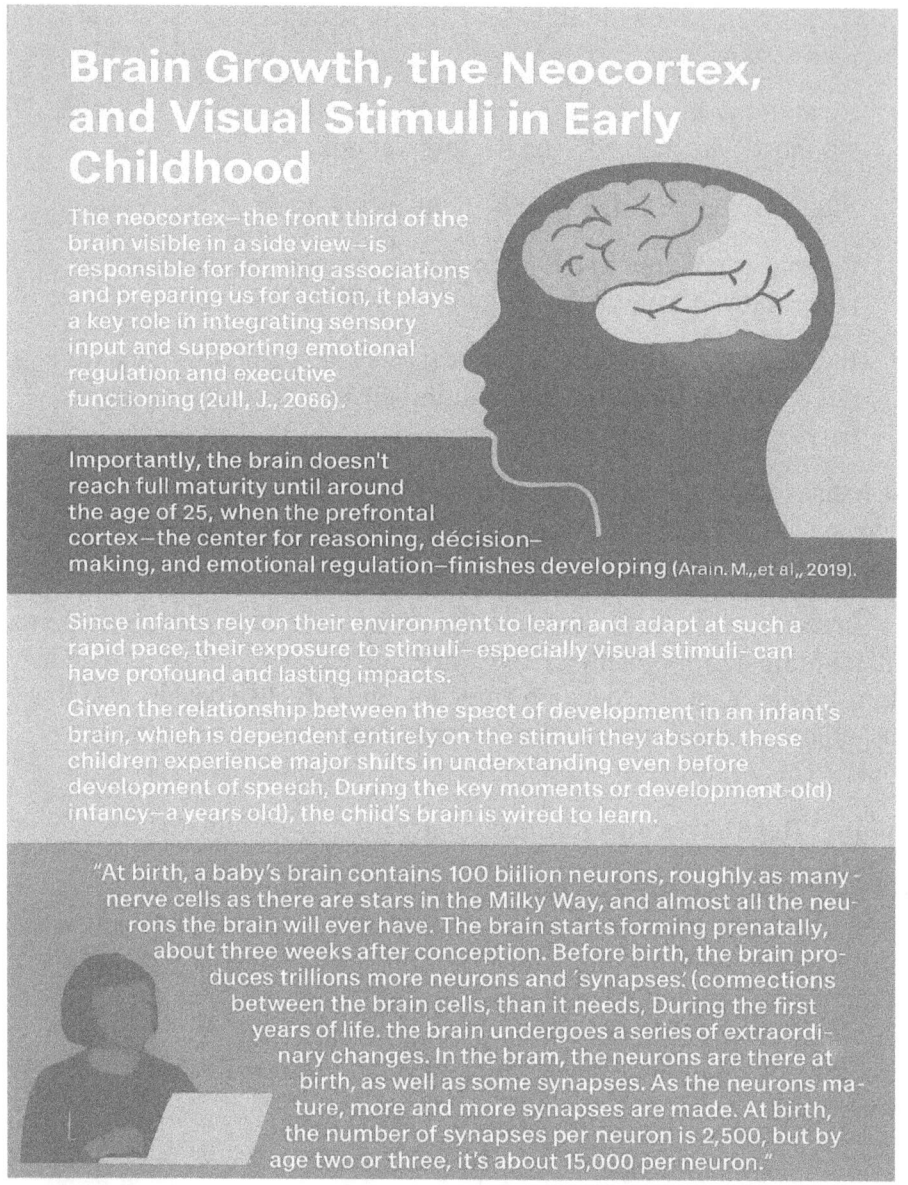

Brain Growth, the Neocortex, and Visual Stimuli in Early Childhood

The neocortex—the front third of the brain visible in a side view—is responsible for forming associations and preparing us for action, it plays a key role in integrating sensory input and supporting emotional regulation and executive functioning (Zull, J., 2066).

Importantly, the brain doesn't reach full maturity until around the age of 25, when the prefrontal cortex—the center for reasoning, decision-making, and emotional regulation—finishes developing (Arain. M., et al., 2019).

Since infants rely on their environment to learn and adapt at such a rapid pace, their exposure to stimuli—especially visual stimuli—can have profound and lasting impacts.

Given the relationship between the spect of development in an infant's brain, which is dependent entirely on the stimuli they absorb, these children experience major shifts in understanding, even before development of speech. During the key moments or development-old) infancy—a years old), the child's brain is wired to learn.

"At birth, a baby's brain contains 100 billion neurons, roughly as many nerve cells as there are stars in the Milky Way, and almost all the neurons the brain will ever have. The brain starts forming prenatally, about three weeks after conception. Before birth, the brain produces trillions more neurons and 'synapses' (connections between the brain cells, than it needs. During the first years of life, the brain undergoes a series of extraordinary changes. In the brain, the neurons are there at birth, as well as some synapses. As the neurons mature, more and more synapses are made. At birth, the number of synapses per neuron is 2,500, but by age two or three, it's about 15,000 per neuron."

Delayed Gratification: The Marshmallow Test and Beyond

One of the most well-known studies on impulse control is the Stanford Marshmallow Experiment, originally conducted in the 1970s. In this study, children were offered a choice: they could eat one marshmallow now or wait to receive two marshmallows later. The amount of time a child waited was considered a measure of their ability to delay gratification (Simple Psychology, 2023).

The original findings suggested that children who waited longer tended to have better life outcomes, academically, socially, and emotionally. However, a 2018 replication study found that while there was still a correlation between delay time and later outcomes, the effect size was much smaller and often not statistically significant (Watts, et al., 2018). In short: delay of gratification is important, but it's not the sole predictor of a child's future success.

The Impact of Screen-Based Rewards

More recent studies, however, suggest that modern screen-based interactions may significantly hinder a child's ability to delay gratification.

In a study led by Dr. Dimitri Christakis, 15 toddlers were given three different toys to interact with:

1. A plastic guitar
2. An iPad that played simple musical notes
3. An iPad app with flashing lights, sounds, and colors

When asked to hand each item back, 60% of children willingly gave back the guitar, but only 45% gave back the iPad with the engaging app (CBS News, 2018). The findings suggest that highly stimulating digital content can activate the brain's reward circuit in ways that make it harder for young children to disengage, even when asked directly.

Another study involving 28 preschoolers examined their ability to delay gratification across different contexts, including screen time. Not surprisingly, children who were regular mobile media users were less able to delay gratification, showing diminished impulse control compared to their peers (Tom, et al, 2017).

What This Means for Development

Impulse control is a developmental skill that unfolds over time, guided by relationships, modeling, and experiences that allow for challenge and recovery. When screens consistently provide instant gratification, they may short-circuit this learning process.

When children are immersed in a visual diet that consistently offers fast rewards and immediate dopamine hits, they are less likely to build the patience, frustration tolerance, and regulation skills necessary for real-life challenges.

This isn't about banning screens. It's about reintroducing balance, through presence, play, and opportunities for kids to practice waiting, reflecting, and choosing.

Many studies have explored how the brain, especially the prefrontal cortex, supports delayed gratification and impulse control. In particular, the right hemisphere of the prefrontal cortex plays a central role in helping us pause, reflect, and choose long-term rewards over immediate gratification (Moriguchi et al., 2018; Kluwe-Schiavon et al., 2020; Jiang et al., 2018).

Recent findings also point to the right temporoparietal junction (TPJ) as another key player in impulse regulation, expanding our understanding beyond the prefrontal cortex alone (Soutschek et al., 2020). While this level of detail may feel more academic, it's included here to emphasize an important point: *impulse control isn't housed in just one part of the brain, it's a complex, interconnected process.*

That complexity matters when we talk about children and screens. Many digital platforms are designed to override impulse control by triggering a dopamine response, the brain's reward signal. For developing brains that aren't yet ready to navigate this flood of stimulation, it's like handing a child the keys to a car and expecting them to drive safely. They're not developmentally equipped to manage those sensory and emotional demands, yet.

We must set children up for success by creating realistic boundaries that respect both their development and the digital world they live in.

A multi-method, cross-sectional study in the western U.S. (n = 72 racially diverse children and caregivers) found that:

> *"The amounts of children's mobile media use, television use, and dysregulation negatively predict their self-regulation, and mobile media use is a stronger predictor than television use."*
> (Choe, et al., 2022)

This highlights a key concern: the earlier children are exposed to mobile media, the more likely they are to develop challenges with self-regulation, a core component of executive functioning.

To be clear, correlation is not causation. Many factors, including socioeconomic status, parenting style, and systemic inequities, contribute to a child's behavior and development. But the pattern is strong enough to call for mindful use, especially for marginalized children, including BIPOC communities who may already face disproportionate stress and fewer resources for digital literacy.

And no, this doesn't mean children should quit screens cold turkey. Abrupt removal can create new tensions and emotional upheaval. Instead, a gentle, gradual shift, focused on supplementing unmet needs (connection, stimulation, rest) can be far more effective.

Likewise, raising children without any digital literacy can have its own long-term risks. The goal is balance, developing media-savvy children who can self-regulate, engage critically, and enjoy the benefits of technology without becoming overwhelmed by it.

Executive functioning

If you're a parent, caregiver, or someone who works closely with children, you've likely heard the term executive functioning. It's commonly referenced in conversations about a child's ability to manage behavior, regulate emotions, and adapt to everyday challenges. But executive functioning isn't just a buzzword, it's a cornerstone of healthy cognitive and emotional development.

Executive functions are higher-order brain processes that help us regulate thoughts and actions in pursuit of goals. They involve planning, working memory, impulse control, emotional regulation, and flexible thinking. In children, these abilities begin to form in early childhood and shape everything from social relationships to academic success.

As Soto et al. (2020) summarize:

> *"Executive functions are higher-order neurocognitive processes associated with regulating thoughts and behaviors by maintaining problem sets to attain future goals… Deficits in executive functions are theorized to be etiologically important for a broad range of psychopathologies… [and] play a critical role in many important functional outcomes beginning as early as young childhood."*

Executive functioning affects:

- Social and family relationships (Clark et al., 2002; Gewirtz et al., 2009)
- Organizational skills (Kofler et al., 2018)
- Academic achievement (Best et al., 2009)
- Occupational success (Barkley et al., 2008)
- And broader mental health concerns like ADHD, depression, and schizophrenia

Given its critical role, it's important to explore how screen time influences the development of executive function in young children.

What the Research Says

A longitudinal study of 179 children between 24–36 months old found that:

> *"There was a linear relation between screen time at 24 months and executive functioning one year later. Increased screen time was associated with worse executive functions."*
> *(McHarg et al., 2020)*

This matters because many key activities that support cognitive development, like imaginative play, social interaction, and physical manipulation of objects, are often displaced by screens. When screens become the dominant form of engagement, the child's brain may not get the stimulation it needs to develop essential skills.

In another study using MRI scans of 47 preschoolers, researchers discovered physical evidence of this impact:

> *"Increased use of screen-based media… was associated with lower microstructural integrity of brain white matter tracts that support language, executive functions, and emergent literacy skills… Screen use was also associated with lower behavioral scores."*
> *(Hutton et al., 2020)*

These findings reveal something powerful: excessive screen use doesn't just change how kids behave; it can actually change how their brains are built.

As screens increasingly replace play, face-to-face connection, and exploration, the implications are profound. While the long-term outcomes remain to be seen, it's clear that early and excessive exposure to visual media can significantly alter a child's developmental trajectory.

The takeaway here is not to shame or alarm, but to inform. As a community, we have the opportunity to approach children's digital environments with care, curiosity, and caution, ensuring that technology supports their development rather than shaping it in unpredictable ways.

Adolescents

The adolescent brain is in a critical phase of growth and change, and how it's shaped during this time can impact everything from identity formation to emotional regulation and cognitive flexibility.

One of the most ambitious efforts to study this developmental window is the Adolescent Brain and Cognitive Development (ABCD) Study, a multi-site, longitudinal neuroimaging project that tracks over 11,000 youths from age 9–10 into early adulthood. In one wave of data involving 4,524 participants, researchers collected self-reported and parent-reported mental health data, administered neurocognitive assessments, and conducted structural brain imaging to examine how behavior and brain structure evolve over time, particularly in relation to screen media activity (Paulus, et al., 2018).

What They Found

The ABCD study revealed that extensive screen media use is associated with measurable changes in adolescent brain structure. However, not all changes were negative. Some adaptations might help adolescents navigate a visually saturated digital environment, while others raise concerns about underdeveloped areas crucial for long-term well-being. This nuance is key: visual stimuli isn't inherently bad, but unbalanced exposure, particularly at the expense of physical and social engagement, can lead to developmental gaps.

What Adolescents May Be Missing

As Dr. Lynn Wagner of Integrative Lifestyle Medicine explains:

> *"The physical part of doing projects, such as building with blocks, uses a whole different part of your brain and a whole different skill set, which they need for the rest of their life. So, screen time just robs them of that."* (NBC, 2019)

She continues:

> *"Engaging with peers, going out and doing stuff, talking with your family, that is what naturally grows your brain the way it's supposed to."*

In other words, digital experiences are not equal substitutes for real-world interaction, movement, or creative problem-solving. When these developmentally essential behaviors are replaced by passive consumption or dopamine-driven media, the brain may grow in lopsided ways, overdeveloping some circuits while undernourishing others.

The Risks of a Screen-Heavy Adolescence

According to the Mayo Clinic (2022), excessive screen time in youth has been associated with:

- Obesity
- Inadequate sleep schedules and poor sleep quality
- Behavioral challenges
- Delays in language and social development
- Increased exposure to violent content
- Attention issues
- Reduced time spent on learning activities

Each of these outcomes, obesity, poor sleep, attention challenges, and more, can have long-lasting effects on mental health, academic achievement, and emotional resilience. But while it's tempting to blame screens entirely, they're usually just one piece of a much larger puzzle: environment, stress, access to resources, and the quality of human connection all play vital roles. It's easy to focus on changing children's screen habits without looking at our own. If we reduce kids' screen time, it naturally calls for more interaction, structure, and engagement from the adults in their lives. And that requires us to reevaluate how **we**, as adults and caregivers, use screens and what's pulling our attention away from connection.

That's not a simple ask.

For many caregivers, especially those working long hours or multiple jobs, screen time becomes a lifeline. It offers peace, quiet, and space to catch up on rest or complete other tasks. In that moment, handing a child a device may feel like the best option available. But this can quietly evolve into a cycle: kids rely on screens for stimulation and regulation, while adults use screens for escape, rest, or distraction. Both parties begin struggling to reengage with each other.

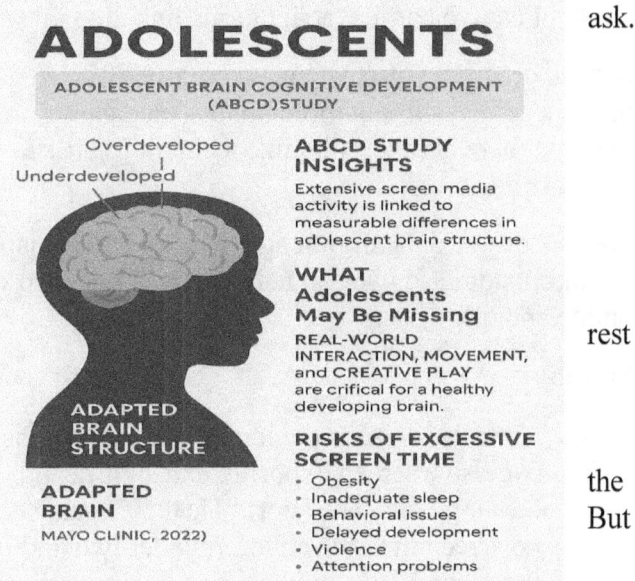

And here's the hard truth: in our modern world, the idea of limiting screen time to ideal recommendations (such as those from the Mayo Clinic or WHO) just isn't realistic for most families. Reaching those goals would require near-constant supervision, structured activities, and emotional availability, things that are incredibly difficult to maintain in a household where both caregivers work, or where time, energy, and resources are already stretched thin.

The solution isn't about blame or perfection. It's about being intentional.

It's about recognizing when screens have shifted from being a helpful tool to a default setting. And it's about making small, sustainable changes that allow for more presence, more connection, and more regulation, for both kids and adults.

Also, it's important to note: not all screen time is detrimental. There's evidence that specific types of screen interaction, particularly video games, can lead to cognitive benefits. A large case-control study, drawing on the ABCD cohort, found that regular video game players exhibited:

- Improvements in both bottom-up and top-down attention
- Enhanced attentional and sensorimotor integration
- Better selective and peripheral visual attention
- Gains in response inhibition and working memory

- Positive cortical adaptations linked to these improvements

It's important to note that excessive use of video games can undermine these benefits. I'll talk more about video games in Chapter 11. So again, the point here isn't to villainize technology. It's to examine how we use it, and how it uses us.

We can't rewind the digital age. But we can reshape our relationship with it. And in doing so, we can help children grow up with the tools to thrive, online and off.

Summary

- Children's brains are highly sensitive to visual stimuli, and excessive screen exposure can significantly impact their development. The World Health Organization (WHO) recommends no screen time for children under two and limited screen time for those aged 2–4, emphasizing the importance of physical activity, interactive play, and adequate sleep.

- Studies show that screen exposure can negatively affect sleep, executive functioning, and emotional regulation. Infants who experience high screen exposure may develop weaker inhibitory control, and screen time has been linked to cortical thinning, which can impact cognitive and emotional development. Research also suggests that parental screen use can disrupt attachment and interaction, further influencing a child's ability to self-regulate.

- Brain development in early childhood is rapid, with neurons forming millions of new connections per second. If screens replace human interaction during this crucial period, children may develop difficulties with impulse control, emotional regulation, and executive functioning. Longitudinal studies, such as the Abecedarian project, demonstrate that early childhood interactions and structured learning environments positively impact cognitive and emotional development well into adulthood.

- Children's ability to delay gratification, a key marker of impulse control, is also affected by screen exposure. Studies indicate that mobile media use is a stronger predictor of self-regulation difficulties than television. Because digital media is designed to stimulate dopamine responses, children are ill-equipped to manage its effects, increasing the risk of dependency.

- The research highlights the importance of balance, setting realistic screen boundaries while promoting interactive, engaging activities to foster healthier cognitive and emotional development.

- Executive functioning refers to higher-order cognitive processes that regulate thoughts and behaviors, playing a crucial role in emotional regulation, social skills, and academic success. Deficits in executive functioning are linked to various mental health conditions, including ADHD, depression, and schizophrenia.

- Recent research highlights concerns about the impact of screen time on executive functioning, particularly in young children. A longitudinal study found that increased screen exposure in toddlers negatively affects cognitive development, reducing engagement in critical activities like imaginative play. MRI studies further suggest that excessive screen use alters brain structure, particularly in areas supporting language, executive functions, and literacy skills.

- For adolescents, the **Adolescent Brain and Cognitive Development (ABCD) Study** has demonstrated significant neurological and behavioral changes due to extensive screen use. While screens can be beneficial, especially in improving certain cognitive abilities through video gaming, overuse is linked to issues such as obesity, sleep disturbances, attention deficits, and delays in social development.

- Managing screen time presents challenges, particularly for working caregivers who rely on screens for convenience. However, instead of villainizing technology, the focus should be on using it responsibly. Parents and caregivers must model healthy screen habits and balance digital media with real-world interactions to support children's development.

Chapter Nine

"You start doing the addictive behavior to feel good and then your receptors get overloaded with dopamine, then you stop doing the addictive thing and some of the receptors have shut down and you don't have enough dopamine to feel good. So, then you feel bad and go back to the addictive behavior to get more dopamine. The strange thing is that it works with what we think of as uppers and downers and whatever you call gambling" - Bill Nye

Visual Stimuli and Dopamine

Why talk about dopamine in a book about the visual diet?

A better question might be, how can we not?

Dopamine plays a central role in how we process visual stimuli, how we learn, how we form habits, and how we respond to the world around us, including how we connect with screens.

At its core, dopamine is the neurotransmitter most responsible for reward, motivation, and behavioral reinforcement. But its influence goes far beyond "feeling good."

What Researchers Say About Dopamine

- *"Dopamine, released by specific populations of dopaminergic neurons, is a key modulatory neurotransmitter in the CNS, mediating sensory adaptation, motor program initiation, and reward behaviors."* — Zhang, et al. (2007)

- *"Dopamine modulates cellular, synaptic and gap-junction signaling in various circuit elements, effectively changing how signals are processed by retinal circuits and altering retinal output."* — Roy & Field, 2019

- *"D1-type receptors energize behavior toward goals. D2-type receptors suppress inhibitory pathways, making it easier to act. Both types influence action selection and motivation."* — Soutschek, et al. (2022)

- *"Dopamine modifies a large variety of cellular and synaptic biophysical parameters in a seemingly paradoxical manner."* — Durstewitz, (2006)

Dopamine isn't just about pleasure. It's about learning, movement, emotional response, and sensory prioritization.

How Visual Input Activates Dopaminergic Systems

Our visual diet, especially the screen-based kind, is full of predictable, stimulating, emotionally charged imagery. This creates a cascade of dopamine-rich responses, especially when we engage with:

- TikToks and Reels
- Violent or sensational news
- High-action video games
- Pop-ups and notifications
- Streaming shows designed with cliffhangers

These responses reinforce dopaminergic behaviors, making us return for more, often unconsciously.

But that's not inherently bad. Dopamine is not the villain, it's the messenger. The problem arises when we overfeed this system with hyper-stimulating content and underfeed it with real-world connection, play, exploration, and rest.

Dopamine and the Visual Brain

Recent research connects dopamine directly to visual processing, especially in threat detection and sensorimotor responses:

> *"Dopamine is thought to have a dynamic effect on action and behavior selection at the earliest levels of sensory integration. The superior colliculus (SC), a subcortical structure receiving direct retinal input, detects stereotypical salient visual information... It relays this to emotional centers like the amygdala via pathways that influence fear, flight, and defensive behaviors."*
> — Montardy, et al., 2022

In other words, dopamine helps us react to the world, and in trauma-impacted or hyperstimulated systems, it can even prime us for danger, overwhelm, or chronic hypervigilance.

What This Means for Marginalized Communities

For individuals or communities already carrying intergenerational trauma, especially those facing systemic marginalization, this matters deeply. A brain that is already primed for threat doesn't need more input reinforcing danger, disconnection, or instability.

Excessive exposure to activating visual content can amplify:

- Anxiety

- Hyperarousal
- Fight/flight/freeze/fawn responses
- Negative self-image or hopelessness

In short, dopamine + poor visual diet = a recipe for dysregulation, especially when compounded by trauma.

Reframing the Relationship

Dopamine isn't the enemy.

It is part of the instruction manual for being human. It teaches us, guides us, and supports survival. The key is to nourish it, not flood it.

We can do this by:

- Balancing screen time with embodied experiences
- Prioritizing relational engagement over passive scrolling
- Choosing content intentionally, not habitually
- Creating digital boundaries that leave room for stillness and reflection

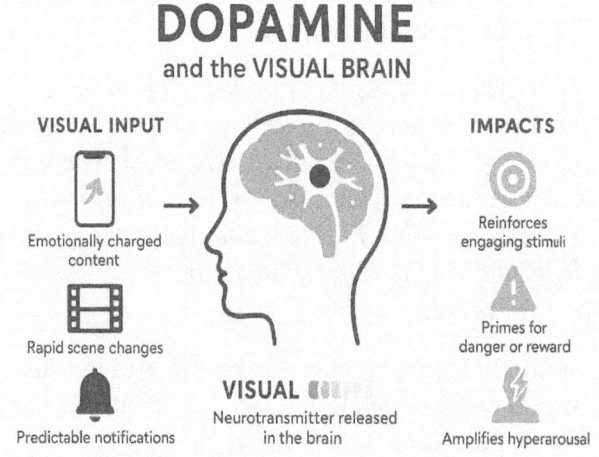

What does Dopaminergic mean?

Simply put, a dopaminergic relationship means a substance or action increases dopamine in the brain, which increases the relationship between stimuli and behavior. For example, the dopaminergic relationship with video games is heavily known to increase the use of that stimuli. I'll go more into video games, smartphones, social media and other dopaminergic relationships with visual media later in this book.

Dopamine is an integral neurotransmitter in the reward circuit, which motivates us for action, deploys pleasure chemicals to facilitate further consumption of the substance or action and allows us to formulate a schema or script of the behavior to return to. *"The best short answer to the question of what dopamine does in reward is that it causes 'wanting' for rewards but not learning or 'liking' for the same rewards."* (Berridge, 2007). Although the relationship of not liking the reward isn't strong, the desire for it is incredibly potent. That means that once we receive it, it may not be fulfilling and merely satiate a small level of desire. This keeps us coming back for more. A fix upon the next serving of dopamine until we attain it and then seek more. In essence, it can develop into a relationship where more is never enough.

Much akin to a warped version of mindfulness, dopamine only cares about the moment. Not the consequences of continuing in the behavior but the motivation of more. The books, Dopamine Nation by Dr. Anna Lembke and The Molecule of More by Dr. Lieberman and Michael Long are fantastic resources if you would like a deep dive into dopamine and its profound relationship with our behaviors and mind.

Recent researchers have identified the relationship of light amongst dopamine receptors. Turns out, our intrinsic relationship with light sources produces increased dopamine in the brain. Those of us living in the Pacific Northwest don't need to be taught this relationship as you can examine the increase in positive feelings directly on the faces of those passing by on gray and sunny days, respectively.

> *"Neuromodulators such as dopamine, enable context-dependent plasticity of neural circuit function throughout the central nervous system. For example, in the retina, dopamine tunes visual processing for daylight and nightlight conditions. Specifically, high levels of dopamine release in the retina tune vision for daylight (photopic) conditions, while low levels tune it for nightlight (scotopic) conditions."* Roy & Field, (2019).

Our brains are wired for dopaminergic responses in well-lit or daylight conditions. Screens trick our brains to release dopamine and cause us to chase pleasure and rewards, no matter how futile. Even in lowlight conditions, a quick jolt of dopamine can flood our system if we glance at our phones. If done habitually, and let's face it, who hasn't enacted this behavior habitually, we then develop the association of the neurochemical processes and the reward of that sweet dopamine hit.

Neuromodulation: How Our Brains Interact with Different Stimuli

Our brains are constantly processing and responding to the world around us, modulating between threat and safety, attention and distraction, stimulation and rest. This modulation happens through incredibly dynamic systems, including dopaminergic pathways and neuromodulatory circuits that help us adapt our behavior in real-time.

Researchers have begun to uncover how our brains regulate responses to visual stimuli, both threatening and non-threatening. One particularly fascinating study by Yao et al. (2016) explores how visual input is interpreted and translated into action:

> *"In response to non-threatening visual stimuli, hypothalamic dopaminergic neurons, and their positively regulated hindbrain inhibitory interneurons, increase activity, suppressing synaptic transmission from the visual center to the escape circuit. By contrast, threatening visual stimuli inactivate some of these neurons, resulting in disinhibition of the visuomotor transformation and escape generation."*

In short:

- Non-threatening visuals calm the system and suppress fight-or-flight responses.
- Threatening visuals lift that suppression and activate the brain's escape circuits.

This mechanism demonstrates that neuromodulation, our brain's ability to regulate itself, is influenced directly by what we see. The brain processes different visual patterns and cues and decides what type of behavioral response is most appropriate. Over time, this tuning of neural activity forms the foundation for our emotional, behavioral, and even survival responses.

But what happens when we're constantly exposed to overstimulating or negative visual input, when our visual diet is filled with violence, chaos, rapid scrolling, or content that provokes anxiety or comparison? We begin to live in a state of chronic dysregulation, with escape circuits constantly activated, even when no real threat exists. Over time, this shapes how we feel, think, and relate to others.

The Overlooked Role of Audio

Visual input is only half the story. Much of the screen-based content we consume is deeply entwined with sound, music, alerts, voiceovers, ambient noise, and these auditory elements dramatically shape how we interpret and respond to what we see.

When visual and auditory stimuli are combined, the brain engages in multisensory integration, a process that heightens emotional arousal, enhances memory encoding, and amplifies the perceived significance of the experience. That's why suspenseful music can make a horror movie unbearable, or why a whispered voiceover on TikTok can feel intimate and emotionally stirring.

However, when these dual stimuli are overwhelming, our neuromodulatory system, particularly dopamine-based circuits, may struggle to recalibrate. This can lead to:

- Heightened stress responses
- Poorer impulse control
- Difficulty distinguishing between real threats and safe, neutral environments

This impact is even more profound in children, adolescents, and individuals with trauma histories or neurodivergent processing styles, whose systems are already more reactive to sensory input.

The Brain and Sensory Overload

In a remarkable study, Yousef et al. (2016) used transcranial magnetic stimulation (TMS) to observe how the brain processes visual stimuli amidst background noise. Their findings offer insight into how distracting environments affect neural clarity:

> *"Our data may also have implications for human diseases with altered brain dopamine processing such as Parkinson's Disorder and schizophrenia... visual hallucinations are more likely in low light when there is high visual stimulus noise."*

In simpler terms: when our brains are overloaded with noisy input, especially in the dark, those with pre-existing dopamine dysregulation (e.g., Parkinson's, schizophrenia) can struggle to process what's real and what's not.

Even in the general population, overstimulation blurs perception. Auditory and visual "noise" don't just make it harder to focus, they literally interfere with how our brain forms decisions, emotional responses, and judgments.

ASMR vs. Misophonia: Two Sides of Neuromodulation

To highlight how sensitive and unique our neuromodulatory systems are, consider the polar opposites of ASMR and misophonia.

- ASMR (Autonomous Sensory Meridian Response) is a phenomenon where soft, specific audio-visual triggers, like whispering, tapping, or soft textures, elicit a sense of calm, pleasure, and even tingling. People actively seek it out for stress relief or emotional regulation. (Samermit & Davidenko, 2019)

- Misophonia, on the other hand, is a condition where certain sounds, like chewing or pen-clicking, trigger extreme irritation, anxiety, or even rage.

These contrasting experiences demonstrate how deeply individual our sensory processing is, and how easily a poor visual or auditory diet can lead to emotional dysregulation, depending on how each brain responds.

Screens, Dopamine, and Human Evolution

We're in the midst of a radical shift in how the human brain interacts with the world. And like any rapid evolution, we're feeling the growing pains.

We've had over a century to adapt to the rise of cars. The first gasoline-powered automobile patent was filed in 1885, but it wasn't until decades later that cars became integrated into everyday life.

Now compare that to the smartphone, introduced in 2007. In just over 15 years, it has saturated nearly every corner of the globe, without the time, tools, or research needed to understand how it's reshaping our minds, relationships, and attention spans.

We're all adjusting in real time.

While screens aren't inherently bad, they demand respect. Like a powerful tool or a fast-moving vehicle, they require intention, boundaries, and education.

The hope? That with research, reflection, and regulation, we'll find a healthy homeostasis, a way to integrate these tools into our lives without losing our grip on the very things that make us human.

Dopamine Detoxing?

When we talk about dopamine and its role in our visual diet, it's crucial to clarify:
We are not trying to eliminate dopamine.

Dopamine doesn't disappear from your brain if you avoid stimulating content. No matter how hard we try to "detox" from visual input, dopamine is still there, and it should be. Dopamine is a vital neurochemical. It fuels motivation, helps us connect, and allows us to feel pleasure.
Without it, life would feel flat, unfulfilling, and joyless. There are many misleading monikers discussing the ideal of fasting from dopamine or detoxing. What may be more appropriate is reimagining our relationship with dopamine. Creating new associations to prevent increased problematic and even maladaptive behaviors individuals are using to avoid or "diminish" dopamine in their brains.

Misconceptions About "Dopamine Fasting"

There's a lot of misinformation floating around the internet about "dopamine detoxing" or "dopamine fasting." These concepts often get warped into something extreme, where people avoid not just screens, but also food, music, talking, or social interaction.

As Dr. Peter Grinspoon, physician and educator at Harvard Medical School, wrote in a blog for *Harvard Health Publishing*:

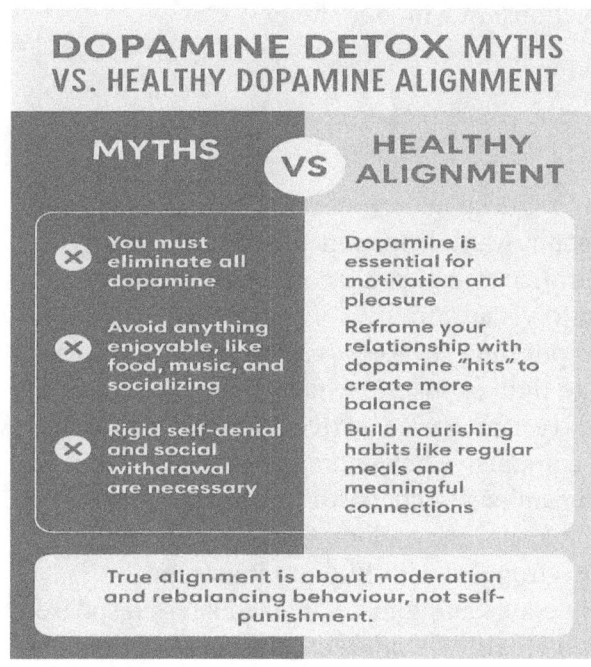

"People are adopting ever more extreme, ascetic, and unhealthy versions of this fasting, based on misconceptions about how dopamine works in our brains. They are not eating, exercising, listening to music, socializing, talking more than necessary, and not allowing themselves to be photographed if there's a flash." (Harvard, 2020)

This isn't detoxing, it's deprivation.

A Better Approach: Reimagining the Relationship

Rather than trying to eliminate dopamine, we should aim to reframe our relationship with it.

Instead of chasing constant, short-term dopamine hits from screens or compulsive behaviors, we can:

- Build new associations with healthier sources of joy
- Create intentional routines that include meaningful, low-stimulus pleasures (like nature walks, reading, or real conversations)
- Practice self-awareness around our triggers and compulsions, not to avoid all pleasure, but to understand it

This isn't about punishment. It's about realignment.

Replacing One Maladaptive Habit with Another?

Some people, in an effort to break free from screen addiction or overstimulation, swing to the other extreme: social withdrawal, rigid self-denial, or undereating. But this can backfire, creating more distress, more shame, and more disconnection.

If we isolate ourselves from others, our thoughts can turn against us. If we stop nourishing our body or engaging in joy, we undermine the very mental clarity we're trying to restore.

Dopamine isn't the enemy. It's a powerful teacher. When we listen to what it's trying to tell us, without letting it drive the car, we begin to build a more intentional and empowered relationship with our choices.

Summary

- **Dopamine's Role**: It is a crucial neurotransmitter involved in motivation, pleasure, and reward. Dopamine influences sensory processing, motor control, learning, and emotional responses, particularly in reaction to visual stimuli.
- **Visual Stimuli and Dopaminergic Responses**: The brain releases dopamine in response to light exposure, which is why screens can be so engaging. Excessive screen use can overstimulate dopamine pathways, reinforcing compulsive behaviors.
- **Neuromodulation**: Dopamine affects how the brain processes sensory input, including visual and auditory stimuli. When overwhelmed, the brain struggles with filtering important information, potentially contributing to heightened stress responses.
- **Screen Time & Mental Health**: Overuse of screens can prime the brain for heightened anxiety and hypervigilance, especially for individuals with intergenerational trauma. This can impact emotional regulation and cognitive function.
- **Dopamine Detoxing**: Contrary to popular belief, avoiding screens does not decrease dopamine production. Instead of "detoxing," it is more effective to reshape our relationship with dopamine by creating healthier associations with activities outside of screens.

Takeaway:

Decolonize screens and work towards mindful engagement, balancing digital consumption with real-world experiences to prevent overstimulation and dependency. More on that later in the book.

Chapter Ten

"I'd get a lot more sleep if I didn't insist on reading the entire internet before bed." -Unknown

Doomscrolling

"Doomscrolling" is a relatively new term, but one that has quickly become familiar to many. It refers to the compulsive act of scrolling through endless streams of negative or distressing content, often well beyond the point of usefulness or awareness.

As Pas (2023) puts it:

> "Doomscrolling is a vicious cycle of seeking negative information to conform with one's negative beliefs about a certain topic, decreasing one's mental well-being. Depression is an indicator for negative beliefs about oneself, the environment, and the future, where doomscrolling tends to be a way to confirm these beliefs, fueling the need to keep scrolling for more."

In other words, people may doomscroll to *reinforce* an already negative worldview, even though it worsens their mental state.

Researchers further describe doomscrolling as:

> "A vicious cycle in which users find themselves stuck in a pattern of seeking negative information, no matter how distressing the news is. Online platforms, using algorithmic systems that are tuned to maximize attention, serve content based on our previous interactions. Whether the motivation is a desire to stay informed, a loss of self-control, or the influence of algorithms serving endless feeds, the result is compulsive scrolling behavior."
> (Satici et al., 2023; Nguyen, 2020; Sharma et al., 2022)

It's a behavior shaped by both internal and external forces: emotional states like anxiety or depression, and systems designed to keep us engaged. As platforms continuously present us with emotionally charged content, our nervous systems may become trapped in cycles of hypervigilance, stress, and information overload.

The Trauma Bond of Doomscrolling

We've all likely known, or been, someone caught in the spiral of doomscrolling. That compulsive urge to keep digging deeper into troubling news, personal pain, or overwhelming world events. It's an experience that floods the body and mind with sensations, sometimes distress, sometimes numbness, and often a mixture of both.

I placed this chapter directly after discussing trauma for a reason: doomscrolling can easily become a trauma bond. With our near-limitless access to content, it's never been easier to lose ourselves in a vortex of pain, outrage, or hopelessness, all from the palm of our hand.

Consider this:

> *"In 2020, the amount of data on the internet hit 64 zettabytes. A zettabyte equals roughly a trillion gigabytes. By 2025, that number is expected to reach 175 ZB. Cisco estimates that two-thirds of the world population will have internet access by 2023, with 5.3 billion users, and more than three times as many internet-connected devices as people."*
> (Heath, 2023)

With that volume of content, and the speed and brevity of formats like 30-second videos, it's no surprise that people are exposed to dozens, even hundreds, of emotionally charged inputs in a single scroll session. And the more we engage, the more the algorithm feeds us what it believes we want to see, often reinforcing emotional states like fear, anger, or despair.

This isn't always a desire for negativity. Sometimes it's driven by a deep yearning to understand. When something feels unresolved or unjust, doomscrolling can feel like a search for meaning, context, or validation. But in the process, we often ignore the body's cues that we're becoming overstimulated or emotionally dysregulated.

> *"People often seek out information as a means of coping with challenging situations. Attuning to negative information can be adaptive, it alerts people to risks and prepares them for similar threats in the future."*
> (Buchanan et al., 2021)

But the survival system doesn't know we're sitting safely on a couch, it just registers the threat. Doomscrolling keeps our sympathetic nervous system activated, pushing us into fight, flight, freeze, or fawn. When prolonged, this can lead to emotional exhaustion, chronic anxiety, or a reenactment of trauma, replaying old wounds in new digital forms.

It's like feeding your nervous system a diet of visual junk food: high stimulation with little nourishment. There's a spike of emotional energy, but the crash is heavy. Just like an overtrained athlete pushed beyond their limits, we can't stay on the doomscroll treadmill without breaking down somewhere along the line.

And yet, it's not always about avoidance or self-harm. Sometimes, it starts with good intentions, a thirst for knowledge, a drive for justice, a need to stay informed. But without mindful boundaries, this quest for insight can override the internal warning signs that beg us to slow down, rest, and reset.

1. What Is Doomscrolling?

Definition: Compulsively consuming negative or distressing content, often online or through social media.

It feels like: Fear, outrage, numbness, helplessness

It's fueled by: Algorithms, novelty, emotional charge

2. Doomscrolling as a Trauma Bond

Trauma Bond: A psychological attachment to distressing stimuli, often tied to unresolved trauma.

Why we do it:

- Seeking control or understanding
- Searching for meaning or validation
- Habitual nervous system activation

3. The Numbers Behind the Scroll

The Data Avalanche (Heath, 2023)

- 2020: 64 Zettabytes of internet data
- 2025: Expected to hit 175 ZB

- Over 5.3B internet users
- 3x more internet-connected devices than people

Dozens to hundreds of emotionally charged inputs per session
Algorithmic loops reinforce distressing emotional states

4. What Happens to the Body & Mind

Sympathetic Nervous System Overdrive

- Fight / Flight / Freeze / Fawn responses
- Chronic stress, anxiety, emotional burnout
- Reenactment of trauma through digital exposure

Like a diet of visual junk food

- High stimulation
- Low nourishment
- Emotional spikes → crashes

5. The Good Intentions Trap

Many begin with:

- A desire for knowledge
- A sense of justice
- A need to stay informed

Without boundaries, these can override our ability to:

- Recognize overstimulation
- Rest and reset
- Regulate emotional well-being

What You Can Do

Mindful Scrolling: Pause, breathe, and notice how your body feels
Set Time Limits: Use tech tools or reminders
Break the Cycle: Engage with the physical world, walk, nature, art
Digital Hygiene: Curate your feed, unfollow distressing accounts
Talk It Out: Share emotions with trusted friends or therapists

A powerful global example of doomscrolling unfolded during the early stages of the COVID-19 pandemic. With uncertainty at an all-time high, many people found themselves compulsively consuming news updates, infection statistics, and emotionally charged stories, searching for answers, control, or simply reassurance in the face of the unknown.

But for many, especially those from marginalized communities, this habit came at a steep emotional cost.

A study examining BIPOC sexual and gender minority individuals assigned female at birth found a clear link between increased exposure to COVID-related news and negative mental health outcomes. Participants reported higher levels of anxiety, depression, and COVID-related worry, alongside an increased likelihood of turning to substance use as a coping mechanism.

> *"Results indicate that when sexual and gender minority individuals assigned female at birth were exposed to more COVID news, they felt more anxious and depressed, were more worried about COVID, and were more likely to turn to substances to cope. Many of these effects persisted into the next day."*
> — Dyar et al., 2022

The study's authors emphasized that while staying informed is important, there must be a balance. Overexposure to emotionally intense media can trigger a closed-loop cycle: the more one consumes, the worse one feels, and the more one seeks out similar content, often in search of relief or clarity that never comes.

This is what makes doomscrolling so seductive. It gives the illusion of control in moments of powerlessness or helplessness, even as it drains our emotional reserves and clouds our judgment.

Why Do People Get Accustomed to Doomscrolling?

The lure of falling down a dark digital rabbit hole is hard to resist, for most of us, at one point or another. Just as people slow down to stare at a car accident on the highway, the instinct to look, to understand, to make sense of chaos, pulls us in. Whether it's a natural disaster, a political scandal, or a personal crisis unfolding online, doomscrolling gives us something to hold onto.

Neurologically, doomscrolling activates the brain's dopaminergic reward system. Each new headline or post delivers a *potential* payoff, new information, new insight, or even just confirmation of our fears. That drip-feed of content keeps our motivation high and creates a loop of seeking, finding, and seeking again. Even if what we find is distressing, the act of searching itself is rewarding.

So, why do people get used to this behavior?

While the specific reasons vary from person to person, there's usually a common underlying need: the desire to regain a sense of control in an uncontrollable situation. In the midst of a crisis or catastrophe, information can feel like power. Doomscrolling becomes a way to *do something*, to stay informed, stay alert, or feel emotionally prepared. Unfortunately, that sense of control is often an illusion.

This is especially common with news consumption during global or local emergencies. Reading or watching endless updates can feel productive, but in reality, it can lead to increased anxiety, emotional fatigue, and even impaired decision-making.

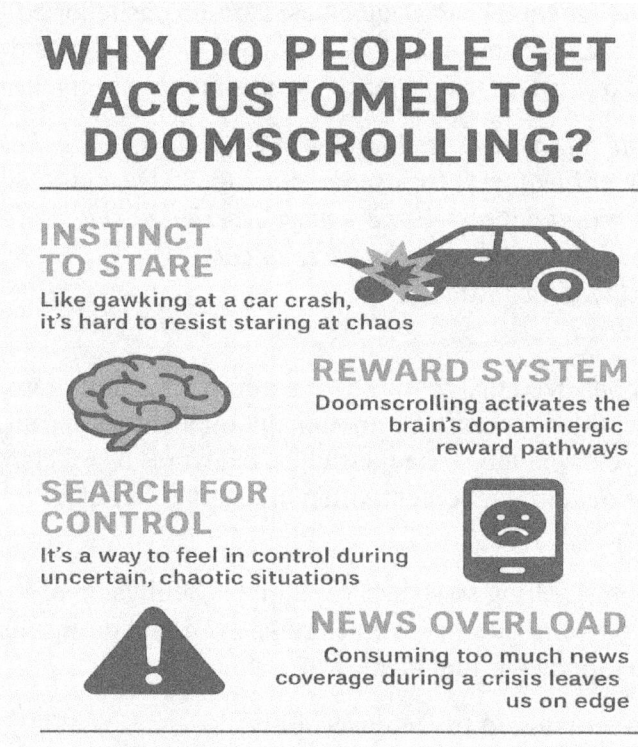

"Findings contribute to an emerging evidence base that points to the benefits of partial news avoidance. They also reiterate the value of public health advice that suggests limiting news during a crisis."
— Mannell & Meese, 2022

The key word here is limit, not eliminate. In many cases, staying completely uninformed isn't realistic or responsible. But knowing *when to stop* is crucial for maintaining emotional and cognitive wellness. Overexposure to crisis coverage can leave us hypervigilant, irrational, and overwhelmed, affecting not only our internal world, but also how we show up for others around us.

Doomscrolling may feel like a way to cope, but left unchecked, it can lead to intrapersonal distress and interpersonal disconnection, as we spiral into a cycle that promises safety and understanding, but only delivers more uncertainty.

Case Study

Antonio loves podcasts. So much so that he spends most of his free time listening to them while doing mundane activities in his home. However, the consequence of his particular adoration with podcasts is the time he spends after the show is finished. He would doom scroll the content he just listened to. Antonio's particular flavor of podcasts is true crime. As Antonio states, *"I try not to doom scroll. I listen to a podcast and I look it up and then I find myself going into the craziness."* Antonio would identify his angst over researching content. Scrolling and scrolling until his hyperfixation would be too much for his nervous system. Negatively affecting his sleep and consequently, his work and relationship, Antonio knew that this wasn't sustainable. With the help of other apps, Antonio started blocking access to his app that gave him a pathway to podcasts. YouTube, Pandora, and Spotify were at the top of his list of banned apps as he navigated a two-month detox. Antonio stated he had many instances of relapses as he used his laptop instead. Fortunately, a friend offered to hold it for him while he completed the detox. Despite, initially, having difficult feelings and mood swings, Antonio persevered and accomplished his two-month detox without a relapse. The Libby app (library app) became Antonio's saving grace as he found audiobooks to shift his focus while giving him better sleep habits.

Managing Doomscrolling with Kindness Scrolling

A simple way to begin managing doomscrolling is by asking yourself two key questions:

1. *How is this content affecting my mood?*
2. *How is my body reacting to this information?*

However, for individuals who are prone to dissociation or have a complex relationship with their bodies, for any number of reasons, checking in physically can feel overwhelming or even triggering. In those cases, consider an alternate question:
How am I behaving after engaging in this dopamine-rich habit of doomscrolling?

Recent research offers a compelling solution: kindness scrolling.

> *"We found that reading about COVID-related acts of kindness did not produce the same negative consequences as reading COVID news. Hearing about acts of kindness from a familiar YouTube creator even produced less negative effect than having no exposure at all. This suggests that people might benefit from balancing doomscrolling with 'kindness scrolling.'"*
> — Buchanan et al., 2021

In other words, consuming positive content, especially stories of people helping one another can serve as a balm for your nervous system. It has the potential to counterbalance the distress caused by consuming fear-based, high-arousal news. Not only does it ease emotional strain, but it also offers a subtle but powerful reminder: *hope still exists.*

The good news? There's no shortage of this kind of content. A quick search for "acts of kindness" online yields thousands of uplifting stories, videos, and social media threads. Unlike doomscrolling, which can heighten stress and reinforce helplessness, kindness scrolling can ground us, shift our perspective, and help rebuild a sense of connection and compassion, both for others and ourselves.

As the news cycle increasingly focuses on sensationalism and opinion-based commentary, intentionally engaging with kind, hopeful content helps us form new, healthier patterns of emotional engagement, and maybe even a little faith in the world around us.

Summary

- Doom scrolling refers to the compulsive act of consuming negative news and content, often reinforcing preexisting negative beliefs and worsening mental well-being. It creates a cycle where individuals continuously seek distressing information, driven by factors such as loss of self-control, algorithmic recommendations, and crises.

- With the vast amount of internet content available, people can easily find material that aligns with their emotions. While seeking information can be a coping mechanism, excessive doom scrolling can trigger stress responses like fight, flight, freeze or fawn, leading to heightened emotional distress and even trauma reenactment. This behavior was notably prevalent during the COVID-19 pandemic, where excessive exposure to negative news correlated with increased anxiety, depression, and unhealthy coping mechanisms.

- Doom scrolling is fueled by the brain's dopamine-driven reward system, making it difficult to stop. Many engage in this habit as a way to regain a sense of control in uncertain situations, but overconsumption of crisis-related news can lead to heightened stress and interpersonal strain. Researchers recommend limiting news intake rather than completely avoiding it to maintain digital wellness.

- One effective way to counter doom scrolling is through kindness scrolling, or consuming positive content that fosters hope and emotional balance. Studies suggest that engaging with uplifting stories and acts of kindness can mitigate the negative psychological effects of doom scrolling and contribute to overall well-being.

Chapter Eleven

"If Pac-Man had affected us as kids, we'd all be running around in dark rooms, munching pills and listening to repetitive electronic music."
— Marcus Brigstocke

Video Games

Let me start with full transparency: I'm an avid video game player. Even as I write this book, I continue to immerse myself in games. I've spent countless hours engaged in quests, strategy, storytelling, and exploration, completing challenges carefully crafted by developers. From heartwarming narratives to intense action-packed experiences, I've seen how video games can shift my mood and flood my system with dopamine. And still, I return to them, again and again.

Will I stop gaming? No.
Do I expect others to give up gaming? Also no.

But I do believe it's essential to talk about how video games affect our bodies, physiologically, emotionally, and neurologically. Writing this book and diving deep into the data has made me more aware of my gaming habits. While I am still playing, I've noticed the desire lessen, simply because I understand more about what's going on inside my brain when I do.

So, here's the invitation: play your video games. Enjoy them. But let's do so with mindfulness and balance, especially for those whose brains are still developing. For some kids and teens, the ability to "just stop" isn't fully formed yet. Their executive functioning isn't developed enough to moderate usage in the same way adults (hopefully) can. We'll unpack that later.

Gaming Disorder: A Recognized Diagnosis

According to the *World Health Organization's ICD-11 codes*, Gaming Disorder (predominantly online) is defined by a persistent or recurring pattern of gaming behavior, whether digital or video gaming that involves:

1. **Impaired control** over gaming (e.g., inability to regulate frequency, intensity, or duration)
2. **Increasing priority** given to gaming over other life interests and daily responsibilities
3. **Continuation or escalation** of gaming despite negative consequences

This pattern must cause significant impairment in personal, social, educational, or occupational functioning, and typically be present for at least 12 months, though a shorter duration may qualify in severe cases.

Now, let's be clear: long gaming sessions don't automatically mean someone has a disorder. Plenty of individuals binge-play games while still maintaining healthy relationships, work responsibilities, and overall balance. The distinction lies in whether gaming begins to replace or disrupt these core life functions.

If you or someone you care about meets these criteria, it may be worth seeking guidance from a professional experienced in gaming-related challenges. Support is available, and there's no shame in needing it.

Emotional Arousal and Video Games

When used excessively, video games can have a powerful effect on emotional regulation and arousal. Many research studies have explored the link between gaming and changes in mood, stress, and reward system activity. As you read, consider people you know, perhaps even yourself. Do some of the behaviors or symptoms resonate?

If so, this could be an opportunity to reflect on your current visual diet and consider how you might gently recalibrate it.

Gaming isn't inherently bad, far from it. It can build skills, foster community, and offer meaningful emotional experiences. But like anything powerful, it must be approached with intention and awareness.

The Effects of Video Games on the Brain

Playing video games for more than three hours a day has been linked to a range of physical and neurological concerns. According to Kim (2020), extended screen time can lead to Computer Vision Syndrome, which includes symptoms such as eye strain, difficulty focusing after play, and frequent headaches.

In addition to physical discomfort, researchers at Tohoku University have found that excessive gaming, particularly in children, may impact frontal lobe development (Kim 2020). This is significant because the frontal lobe is essential for executive functioning, including decision-making, emotional regulation, and impulse control. When this area of the brain is underdeveloped or overstimulated, impulsive behavior may increase, ironically fueling further gaming and creating a self-reinforcing feedback loop. The more one plays, the more one struggles to stop.

These findings don't even account for the sedentary lifestyle that often accompanies video gaming. Prolonged sitting reduced physical activity, and social isolation can all lead to compounded psychological and health concerns, which are discussed later in this chapter.

Gaming, Dopamine, and the Pursuit of Pleasure

A fascinating survey of 835 gamers by Walia et al. (2022) explored the psychological underpinnings of video game use, especially in individuals exhibiting symptoms of gaming addiction. They found a U-shaped relationship between hedonic experience (the pursuit of pleasure and avoidance of pain) and intensity of gameplay, but only in high-symptom users.

In short:

- Low-addiction symptom gamers showed no correlation between how long they played and how much pleasure they got.
- High-symptom gamers experienced less pleasure initially the longer they played—until they hit a point of excessive dopamine release, which then temporarily improved their experience.

This pattern aligns with both sensitization and tolerance theories:

- Sensitization: The brain becomes hypersensitive to the game's stimuli, creating a craving-like response.
- Tolerance: More time or intensity is needed to achieve the same level of satisfaction.

The takeaway? Gamers who show signs of dependency may need to play more to feel good, or to escape feeling bad.

Hedonic vs. Eudaimonic Gaming

Interestingly, many modern games don't offer quick rewards or instant gratification. Instead, they challenge players with long-term goals, intense difficulty, and often brutal in-game consequences. These experiences are often more eudaimonic, focused on meaning, perseverance, and growth, than simply hedonic.

In this light, video games can be:

- Hedonic when they offer constant stimulation and escapism.
- Eudaimonic when they cultivate mastery, emotional resilience, or community.

Some games walk the line between both, offering intermittent rewards that drive players to chase meaning while also stimulating the brain's dopamine-driven pleasure system.

Punishment, Persistence, and the Dark Allure of FromSoftware Games

Here, I'm referring to the *Soulsborne* lineage, Demon's Souls, Dark Souls, Bloodborne, Sekiro, and Elden Ring, as well as the growing number of games inspired by their legacy. These games influence the reward system of the brain not by offering constant gratification, but by doing the opposite: withholding.

They operate on deprivation and difficulty, punishing players for every misstep. You are meant to struggle. You are meant to fail, over and over, until you learn the mechanics, the timing, the world.

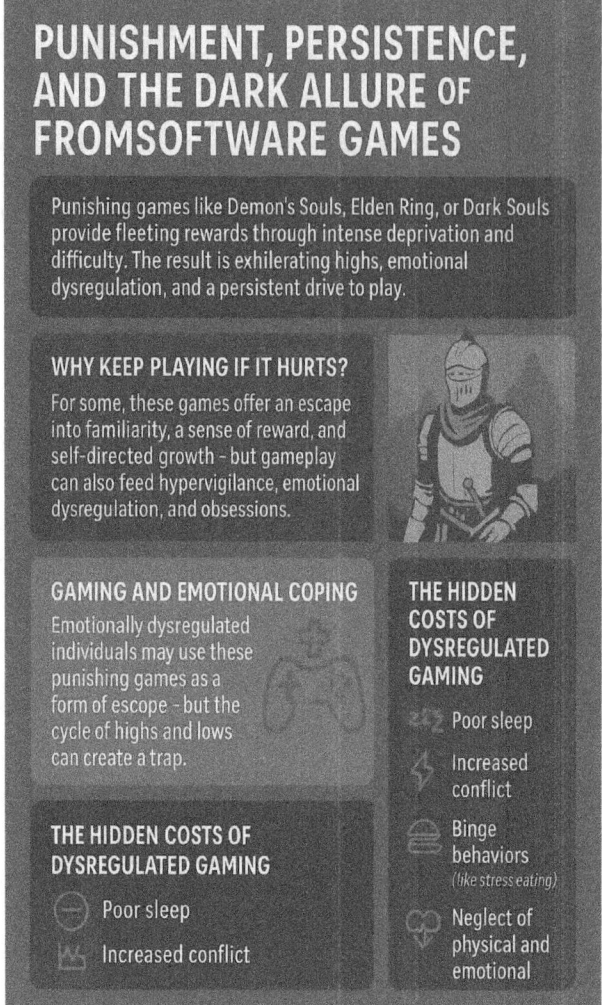

Only then, through repetition and adaptation, are you allowed a glimpse of victory. And even that victory is fleeting, before the next boss, the next trap, the next death.

Anyone who has seen a friend play one of these games has likely witnessed emotional dysregulation in action. From rage-quits to throwing controllers to walking away only to return later, it's all part of the journey. These moments have become legend, fueling both the genre's popularity and its notoriety.

I've walked that path as well. I've rage quit, I've returned, I've completed nearly all of the FromSoftware titles, except *Sekiro*, the elusive unicorn that still taunts me. And like many, I've experienced both the exhilaration and the emotional cost of these punishing titles.

Why Keep Playing If It Hurts?

That's the question: *Why subject yourself to something that causes stress, frustration, and emotional overload?* The answer is deeply personal. For me, it was an escape through familiarity. I'm no stranger to stress, and these games offered something I hadn't found elsewhere: a deeply earned reward. A triumph earned through persistence and growth. The story wasn't just unfolding on screen; it was happening in my nervous system.

But there was a cost. That same gameplay loop also fed hypervigilance, emotional dysregulation, and a kind of minor obsession. The effort was meaningful, but the toll was real.

Gaming and Emotional Coping: When Escape Becomes a Trap

Researchers like Maria Di Blasi et al. (2019) have explored how emotionally dysregulated individuals may use video games, especially difficult ones like these, as a form of coping:

> *"These video games can help gamers to reduce difficulties in identifying, describing, and processing their feelings... For individuals who struggle with emotion regulation, the video game environment may be the main domain where they can approach emotion regulation without negative consequences... escapism acts as an emotion-focused coping strategy to manage negative feelings. But for gamers with higher emotional dysregulation, this escape may offer only temporary relief while simultaneously pushing them deeper into the game to feel better, thereby increasing the risk of problematic gaming."*

In other words, games like these can be both a lifeline and a liability. They offer refuge and resilience but can also trap players in a loop, especially when emotional regulation skills are underdeveloped or compromised.

The Hidden Costs of Dysregulated Gaming

Emotional dysregulation during gameplay isn't just an in-game issue. It can spill into real life, manifesting as:

- Poor sleep
- Increased conflict
- Binge behaviors (like stress eating)
- Neglect of physical and emotional needs

The result? A system under pressure. A body and brain struggling to find equilibrium in a loop that offers high highs and deep lows.

And again, I want to emphasize this isn't a call to vilify gaming. It's a call to understand it. To reflect on what's driving our engagement. To ask ourselves whether our use is aligned with our values, our needs, and our well-being.

Because as with any powerful tool, the question is never *"Should we use it?"* but *"How do we use it well?"*

Anecdotally, when, briefly, interviewing a video game tester or "debugger", this individual stated the conditions, which these individuals experience such as unlimited access to caffeine to accomplish their rigorous work of play after play of the video games as well as the "heavy lunch crash" and subsequent video gaming, when arriving home. They reported a crash at home as well but stated it was minimal in comparison to the midday crash. This falls in line with some professionals in the field reporting on the effect of dopamine to our systems, namely video gaming.

Psychiatrist Dr. Anna Lembke, in her *Wall Street Journal* article, "Digital Addictions Are Drowning Us in Dopamine," explains:

> *"As soon as dopamine is released, the brain adapts by reducing, or downregulating, the number of dopamine receptors that are stimulated. This causes the brain to level out by tipping to the side of pain, which is why pleasure is usually followed by a hangover or comedown.*
>
> *If we wait long enough, that feeling passes and our system restores balance. But our instinct is to counteract it, to chase pleasure once more.*
>
> *If we keep repeating this cycle for hours every day, over weeks or months, the brain's set point for pleasure begins to shift. We no longer engage in the activity to feel good; we do it just to feel normal. As soon as we stop, we experience withdrawal symptoms: anxiety, irritability, insomnia, low mood, and intense cravings."*

In other words, what begins as pleasure-seeking can turn into dependency, particularly when the behavior involves high-dopamine activities like video games.

A large-scale study of 4,416 gamers (94% of whom were male) revealed that many struggled with *multiple* problematic online behaviors, not just gaming. In order of prevalence, researchers found challenges related to:

- Online gaming
- Social networking
- Gambling

- Pornography
  (Rozgonjuk et al., 2021)

But this study wasn't about where those behaviors started, it simply showed that they often *co-exist*. This points to an important truth: people rarely develop one compulsive digital behavior in isolation. These behaviors are typically part of a broader pattern.

That means recovery also has to be broad. Visual detoxes, for example, may help, but only if they're part of a more holistic approach that accounts for someone's full lifestyle, coping strategies, and underlying needs.

It's also worth mentioning the concept of functional addiction. Some individuals may appear to manage their daily responsibilities just fine, they work, socialize, pay bills, but still feel compelled to engage in a behavior to an unhealthy degree. They may *want* to stop but can't. Or they may never feel like they've had enough time for the activity. The issue isn't about whether they're "functioning", it's that their relationship with the behavior is compulsive and difficult to regulate.

Unlike substances, visual media doesn't pose an immediate overdose risk. But the long-term consequences, especially of a sedentary lifestyle, are significant. Over time, excessive screen-based behavior can contribute to health problems like:

- Weight gain
- Diabetes
- Reduced mobility
- Cardiovascular issues

The bottom line: not all screen use is inherently bad. But when it crosses the line into compulsion, the effects ripple into every part of a person's life, physically, emotionally, and socially. A compassionate, realistic, and comprehensive approach is essential.

The Online Video Game Environment

Let's shift focus to the experience of playing video games in online environments, particularly those that involve text or voice communication. While competition is a central feature of many multiplayer games, the social dynamics often cross the line into toxicity.

Researcher Ayushi Ghosh, from Maulana Abul Kalam Azad University of Technology in India, examined 13 popular online video games and found troubling patterns:

> *"The results of this research indicate racism and sexism truly intoxicate the gaming communities to a great extent. Racism is observed to be the highest in the FIFA community, while the Bloodstained community expresses strong negative emotions. Interestingly, the Sims community showed the highest frequency of sexist terms based on term frequency results, despite differing findings in empirical evaluations."* (Ghosh, 2021)

Ghosh also highlighted a well-known case of online harassment: Anita Sarkeesian, a Canadian-American feminist and media critic, became the target of a coordinated campaign of abuse after she launched a nonprofit to challenge sexism in media. She received an overwhelming number of rape and death threats, as well as messages urging her to commit suicide and bombarding her with racist and sexist slurs. Her experience is just one example of how hostile the online gaming world can be, especially for women and marginalized individuals.

This doesn't mean that every corner of the gaming community is toxic. Many gamers form supportive, inclusive online spaces. But it's important not to minimize how widespread the problems of sexism, racism, and queerphobia have become in digital gaming spaces.

These patterns of abuse can be particularly damaging for marginalized individuals who may already lack strong social support. Repeated exposure to hostile messages can lead to internalized oppression, where individuals begin to absorb and reflect the very hate they encounter in their visual and social environments.

This hostility isn't limited to in-game communication. It extends to forums, comment sections, and even game reviews. Researcher Melissa Corboz, for example, studied the online reception of the 2020 game *The Last of Us Part II* and found:

> *"Words referring to queer people appeared more frequently in negative than in positive reviews. In those negative reviews, 27.11% of references were overtly queerphobic, and at least 23.50% were covertly so. These figures rise further if you include critiques that target queer representation specifically in The Last of Us Part II (13.55%) and those that link queer representation to political agendas (16.57%)."* (Corboz, 2022)

In summary, the online gaming environment can serve as a powerful force, for connection or for harm. For those already struggling with self-worth, identity, or belonging, a toxic gaming space becomes more than just unpleasant, it can reinforce cycles of trauma, exclusion, and self-doubt.

Neurodivergent Video Game Usage

The neurodivergent brain is just as, if not more, susceptible to the powerful influence of video games. As discussed earlier, video games have evolved from simple entertainment to complex, reward-driven experiences. Designed to sustain engagement through intermittent reinforcement, modern games deliver potent dopaminergic responses, especially impactful for developing minds.

ADHD and Video Game Engagement

A quasi-systematic review of 128 peer-reviewed studies published between 1970 and 2021 revealed significant findings about the relationship between ADHD and video games:

> *"Patients with ADHD show greater problems with attention, motor control, and working memory. They struggle with response inhibition, take more risks, and perform worse when rewards are delayed. They are also more sensitive to both reward and punishment. A number of studies found a link between ADHD and increased video game use, particularly among males, and noted that playing more than one hour per day may worsen ADHD symptoms."*
> *(Rodrigo-Yanguas et al., 2022)*

A study conducted in Montreal (2016–2018) involving 280 children aged 4–12 examined three groups: children with ADHD, a clinical-control group, and a community-control group. Researchers found that:

> *"Children with ADHD showed an increase in video game play as they aged, while other groups did not. This suggests that early exposure may be a risk factor for increased usage, especially during puberty and adolescence—a high-risk period for addiction in youth with ADHD."*
> *(Masi et al., 2021)*

The study also highlighted how game type and reinforcement structure matter. Games like *Fortnite* and MMORPGs, with high-reward systems, are more likely to encourage excessive play.

Causality: Which Comes First?

Another study clarified the directionality between video game use and ADHD symptoms:

> *"Higher levels of video game engagement at age 12 predicted increased ADHD symptoms at age 13. However, the reverse was not true: ADHD symptoms at 12 did not predict more video game*

engagement at 13."
(Tiraboschi et al., 2022)

This finding suggests that video game use may be a contributing factor in the development or worsening of ADHD symptoms, not simply a result of them. Moreover, gender and socioeconomic status (SES) also played roles. Boys were more likely to engage in higher levels of gameplay, and lower SES was correlated with greater video game use.

Positive Effects of Video Gaming on the Brain

While much attention is given to the risks and potential harms of video gaming, especially with young or vulnerable populations, it's equally important to acknowledge its *positive* impacts. A growing body of research has shown that video games can support cognitive, behavioral, emotional, and even identity-related growth, depending on how they're used, and the type of games played.

Structural Brain Changes

Research has found that video games can enhance specific brain functions over time. In particular, studies of expert and professional gamers have revealed structural changes in the brain:

> *"By studying lifelong experts or professional gamers, some studies have detected structural grey matter changes that correlated with improved executive performance, involving the posterior parietal and prefrontal regions."*
> *(Palaus et al., 2017)*

These changes were associated with improved:

- Decision-making
- Cognitive flexibility
- Prospective memory
- Strategic planning

Behavioral Stability

In contrast to concerns about behavioral harm, some studies suggest no significant negative shifts in behavior over time. One study, for example, found that:

> *"Individuals who showed more symptoms of video game addiction at the start of the study did not report reduced social or physical activity levels by the end."*
> *(Weinstein, Przybylski, & Murayama, 2017)*

This challenges the assumption that video game use necessarily leads to social withdrawal or sedentary habits.

Benefits for ADHD and Cognitive Skills

For children with ADHD, serious video games (designed for education or health outcomes) have shown measurable benefits:

> *"Serious video games for health can produce significant improvements in attention, hyperactivity and impulsivity, executive functions, memory, reading and writing skills, emotional regulation, motor skills, and visual processing."*
> *(Rodrigo-Yanguas et al., 2022)*

These games may, in turn, boost academic performance and day-to-day emotional resilience.

Serious video games are defined as:

> *"Video games specifically designed for educational or health purposes, as opposed to commercial games meant solely for entertainment."*
> *(Rodrigo-Yanguas et al., 2022)*

Video Games as Tools for Gender Affirmation

For transgender and gender-diverse (TGD) youth, video games can offer affirming and empowering experiences. The ability to customize avatars provides a unique space for identity exploration:

> *"Participants shared that customizing avatars allowed them to present as their affirmed gender without fear of judgment. This freedom fostered both internal and external validation of their gender identity—something often missing in real life due to transphobia and discrimination."*
> *(McKenna et al., 2022)*

Summary

- The WHO classifies "gaming disorder" as a condition characterized by impaired control, prioritization of gaming over other activities, and continuation despite negative consequences. Research indicates that excessive gaming can lead to cognitive and physical issues, such as eye strain, frontal lobe development concerns in children, and sedentary lifestyle risks.

- Studies show that video games can reinforce hedonic pleasure-seeking behaviors, potentially leading to compulsive gaming. Some games, particularly challenging ones like those from FromSoftware, induce emotional dysregulation but also provide a sense of achievement. Gaming can serve as an emotional coping mechanism, especially for individuals struggling with regulation.

- Online gaming communities often foster toxic behaviors, including racism, sexism, and queerphobia, which can be detrimental to marginalized groups. Additionally, neurodivergent individuals, particularly those with ADHD, may be more susceptible to excessive gaming due to heightened reward sensitivity and difficulty with impulse control.

- Despite these concerns, video games also have positive effects, such as enhancing cognitive skills, problem-solving abilities, and social connections. Moderation to maximize benefits while minimizing risks can be an effective goal.

Chapter Twelve

"Smartphones are miracles, and they've turned us into gods. But in one simple respect, they're primitive: you can't slam down the receiver."
— Richard Powers

Smartphones

In season 5 episode titled "sex education" of Parks and Recreation, the character Tom Haverford was in a court proceeding after he was in a car accident due to live tweeting his driving. The judge ordered him to go for a week without looking at a screen. Tom stated immediately after the verdict, "Nooo! Send me to jail!" The character played by Aziz Ansari, presented with immense difficulty abiding by this court order and started creating a paper iPhone and homemade Pinterest board with office materials. He even goes to great lengths to not look at a screen by using a mirror over his shoulder to watch someone else engage in computer usage.

Finally, going to his boss, Ron Swanson played by the great Nick Offerman, he complains about his plight. Ron looks over the paper iPhone Tom tosses onto his desk and states, "This is the work of a lunatic." Seeing his employee in pain and concerned for his well-being, he states that he will take him to his cabin and immerse him in nature to help support Tom, the best way he knows how. Tom gets a splinter from attempting to chop wood and complains about the need to look up WebMD for sterilization techniques and Ron has an ideal about purging all of "the garbage from his system" by talking about things he uses on screens. After a full day of attempting to purge himself of his thoughts about screens, Tom presents a myriad of thoughts based on his interactions with screens much to Ron's quiet annoyance.

Tom, eager to return to screens, tricks Ron by presenting a half-hearted understanding of his problematic screen usage by citing overused statements from his extensive viewing knowledge of the show Intervention. He then asks to use Ron's car to purchase more steaks, which the nature and meat loving Ron agrees. Tom crashes Ron's car after tweeting with a burner phone. The show culminates with Tom apologizing to Ron about crashing his car. Ron calmly and determinedly inquires why Tom needs constant distraction. Tom honestly answers, "The truth is –I spend a lot of time looking at screens because recently, a lot of stuff in my real life isn't going so great." Ron holds the fate of Tom in his hands since the judge stated earlier in the episode that if Tom had any slip ups, he would have a month-long sentence of no screens. However, he compassionately provides wisdom, instead, by telling him to engage with people and not use technology as a crutch.

Many folks can relate to Tom's experience. Especially other BIPOC individuals. The distraction can help us defer a bit of time from our problems and concerns by going down the deep dark hole of the web. By engaging in content, at the level of Tom, some place others at risk and can alienate our relationships.

Since 2007, technology has put knowledge at our fingertips. The release of the first iPhone marked a turning point, ushering in the age of smartphones and paving the way for Android devices to further revolutionize our digital lives. I still remember when I first heard about smartphones. It felt like the future had arrived, and with it, dreams of flying cars or teleportation devices à la *Back to the Future*. While we haven't quite reached those sci-fi milestones, we've encountered something else entirely: the immense and measurable influence of technology on our sense of self, across nearly every domain of life.

Amidst the many problematic aspects of screen time, it's important to acknowledge the powerful tools that technology offers. Think about the handheld editing software that used to require expensive desktop suites, or the vast online marketplaces now accessible to artists and small business owners. For many, these tools transformed distant dreams into achievable goals.

Now consider the wellness space. Today, there's no shortage of meditation, mindfulness, or self-help apps. For people who may have grown up stigmatizing mental health support, these apps provide a private, accessible entry point to self-care. Innovation in this space is helping to normalize emotional wellness, and it's doing so by borrowing from the very playbook that makes screen time so addictive.

Recent research supports this. Certain wellness apps have been shown to enhance motivation in people experiencing depression by stimulating the same dopamine circuits that make phones so hard to put down (Mouchabac et al., 2021). These apps use features like reminders, streaks, and progress tracking, similar to language learning apps like Duolingo. (And if you've ever tangled with the guilt-tripping Duolingo owl, you know exactly how persistent those notifications can be.)

Each alert delivers a small hit of dopamine. Whether it's a cheerful ping or a nudge to keep a streak alive, this pattern of reward taps into the same neurological circuits that drive compulsive screen use, creating a feedback loop of both pleasure and pressure.

Still, for all the ways technology improves our quality of life, there are very real concerns about misuse. Much like the rise of fast food, we didn't fully understand the long-term health consequences until it was too widespread to ignore. And just like with fast food, the problem isn't the tool itself, it's how we use it.

When we engage with our devices in a *symbiotic* way, they can support our lives, enhance our creativity, and improve our well-being. But when that relationship turns *parasitic*, draining our time, energy, or self-worth, it's time to pause and reevaluate. Finding a healthy homeostasis with our tech isn't just possible. It's essential.

Dr. Ranjit Singh, a professor in the Department of Electronics and Communication Engineering at Ajay Kumar Garg Engineering College in India, offers a compelling perspective in his article *"Perils of Screen Addiction"* (2022):

> *"Screen addiction is similar to addiction to drugs, gambling, and alcoholism. It doesn't injure health like alcohol, nevertheless its 'toxicity' affects the subconscious and our relationship with the world."*

He elaborates on how dopamine, the brain's key neurotransmitter for reward and motivation, plays a central role in this cycle of dependence:

> *"Dopamine levels rise when we're just about to find a reward and diminish after we receive it. As a result, evolution uses this chemical process to induce anticipation, motivation, and pain alleviation."*

Tech giants like Apple and Google have capitalized on this biological mechanism. Over the years, they've fine-tuned addictive design strategies to capture, and commodify, our attention. Singh uses the randomness of a Facebook feed as a prime example: the "digital confetti" of unexpected likes, comments, and posts keeps users coming back, chasing another dopamine hit.

> *"The power of the dopamine system is well known among drug users and smokers. Habit-forming substances hijack this system by flooding it with dopamine beyond natural levels. Similarly, screen overuse becomes a compulsive loop, the more we seek pleasure from it, the more we need it just to feel normal."*

Much like any other addiction, many people chase increasingly intense dopamine highs as their tolerance grows. This can manifest in several ways, including relying on multiple screens simultaneously to get that next "fix", often without conscious intent. Realistically, there is no shortage of apps designed specifically to keep us transfixed. These platforms are engineered to sustain engagement through continuous user interaction. In fact, keeping people enthralled is a key strategy app developers and software engineers use to stay competitive.

In a saturated market, every app is fighting for attention. If it fails to capture users, it risks fading into obscurity. That's no easy job, and I don't mean to place blanket blame on developers, after all, not all users are negatively affected. Still, the impact on a significant portion of users, especially young people, is hard to ignore.

Many young individuals are already paying the price for compulsive relationships with smartphones and social media platforms like Instagram. An online survey conducted in Spain in 2020, involving 385 undergraduate students, found a significant age-related correlation between problematic smartphone use and high Instagram engagement. Not surprisingly, those who were 20 years old or younger, and often unemployed, reported higher usage levels. (Romero-Rodríguez, et al., 2020). Using the Smartphone Addiction Scale (SAS-SV), the researchers identified varying degrees of problematic use. Interestingly, the study found no gender differences in usage intensity. However, one key takeaway was this: self-esteem, a core component of psychological well-being, was negatively impacted by problematic smartphone use.

These findings align with earlier research exploring the relationship between internet use and self-esteem. A 2014 study involving 408 university students in Iran revealed that 40.7% met criteria for internet addiction. Significant correlations were found between depression, low self-esteem, and internet addiction (Bahrainian, 2014). Similarly, a 2015 study at Süleyman Demirel University in Turkey examined 319 university students and found that women scored significantly higher on the Smartphone Addiction Scale than men. Participants with high smartphone use also reported higher levels of depression, anxiety, and daytime dysfunction. Furthermore, positive correlations were identified between problematic phone use and poor sleep quality (Demirci, et al., 2015).

Another study conducted in 2018 by the Catholic University of Korea examined 5,003 adults aged 19–49 and found a strong link between both internet addiction (IA) and smartphone addiction (SA) with depression and anxiety. Interestingly, the study revealed that smartphone addiction had a stronger effect on mental health symptoms than general internet addiction. The researchers noted:

> *"Internet addiction (IA) and smartphone addiction (SA) exert significant effects on depression and anxiety... Another interesting finding was that SA exerted stronger effects on depression and anxiety than IA. This leads us to speculate that IA and SA have different influences on mental health problems."*
> (Kim, et al., 2018)

Smartphone Use, Self-Esteem, & Age

Study in Spain (2020)
385 undergraduate students were surveyed
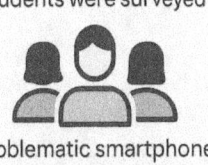
Problematic smartphone use correlated with high Instagram engagement

Negative relationship with self-esteem

Study in Iran (2014)
Of 408 students, 40.7% had internet addiction

Associated with low self-esteem and depression

Study in Turkey (2015)
319 university students were surveyed

Females had higher problematic use scores

Linked to depression, anxiety, daytime dysfunction

(Romero-Rodriguez et al., 202; Bahrainian, 2014; Demirci et al., 2015)

To further illustrate this point, a 2019 study conducted in Lebanon with 1,103 adolescents aged 13–17 found that 40% experienced occasional or frequent problems due to internet use, and 3.6% experienced significant problems. Using stepwise regression, researchers identified that higher levels of aggression, depression, impulsivity, and social fear were significantly associated with higher internet addiction. Conversely, having more siblings and a higher socioeconomic status appeared to be protective factors against internet addiction (Sahar et al, 2019).

The last finding is particularly compelling. It suggests that the number of social influences in a child's home, like siblings, can actually help buffer against internet addiction. While socioeconomic status may not be something families can easily change, the presence of supportive relationships and shared experiences appears to offer protection. In a world increasingly mediated by screens, these kinds of interactions may be more important than ever.

It's worth noting just how many individuals, according to previous research, fall into the moderate-to-high range of internet or smartphone addiction. I tend to use the terms interchangeably now, given that our smartphones today are significantly more powerful than they were when many of these studies were first published (between 2014 and 2019). The internet is no longer tethered to a desk, it's always in our pocket. And so is its influence.

Our brains are constantly being reshaped by our behaviors, especially in youth. As one study puts it:

> *"The more often young people consult their smartphone, the greater the risk of developing ADHD symptoms."*
> (Masi, et al., 2021)

That relationship was further clarified in a 2021 study of 360 athletes, which found that:

> *"Greater ADHD symptoms were indirectly associated with higher smartphone overuse scores via need frustration."*
> (Li, et al., 2021)

Another study of 487 school-aged children revealed that depression, ADHD, and even parenting style all played a role in predicting smartphone addiction, but one factor stood out:

> *"Interpersonal problems and stress were stronger predictors of smartphone addiction than even depression, ADHD, or parenting attitudes."*
> (Hong, et al., 2021)

Meanwhile, in a 2020 study of 333 college students, researchers uncovered a sobering reality:

> *"ADHD symptoms and smartphone addiction were both negatively associated with wellbeing. However, dispositional hope served as a protective factor."*
> (Hong, et al., 2020)

Dispositional hope, a concept involving both agency (motivation toward goals) and pathways (planning to meet them), has been described as:

> *"A stable predictor for subjective well-being."*
> (Wang, et al., 2020)

In short: hope matters. And so do the systems, relationships, and habits that support it.

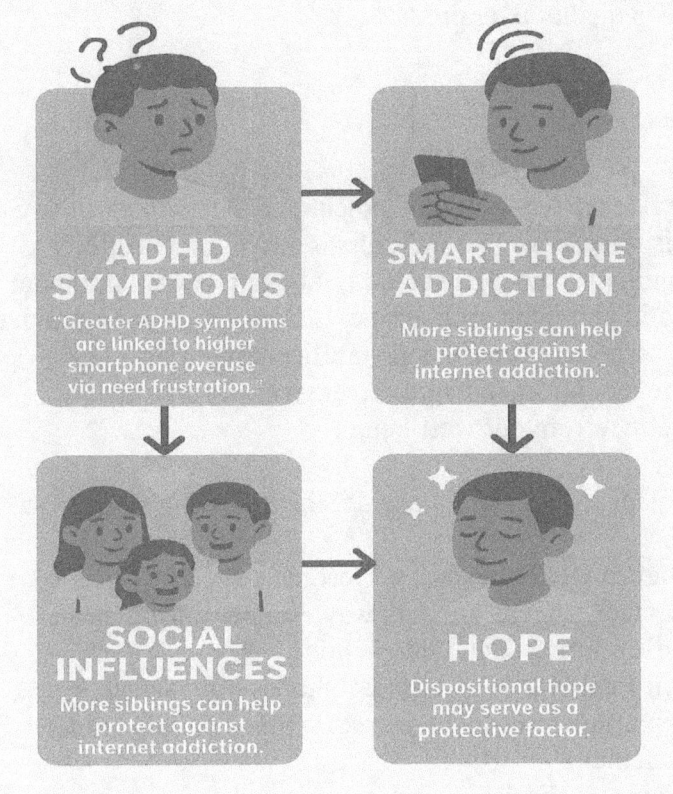

Sleep and Smartphone Use

Smartphone use has been shown to negatively impact both sleep and daytime productivity. While this may not surprise most, it's worth noting how widespread the behavior has become, many people use their phones right up until the moment they try to fall asleep.

"Late-night use of smartphones for work may interfere with sleep, thus leaving employees depleted in the morning and less engaged during the workday."
—Lanaj, Johnson, & Barnes, (2014)

This disruption to our natural sleep-wake cycle (circadian rhythm) has broader consequences for health and well-being.

> *"Light-at-night from electronics has been linked to depression and even suicide risk in numerous studies. In fact, animal studies show that exposure to screen-based light before or during sleep causes depression—even when the animal isn't looking directly at the screen. Sometimes parents hesitate to remove electronics from a child's bedroom out of concern for emotional distress, but doing so may actually be protective."*
> —Postdam, 2024

Although not everyone experiences the same intensity of disruption, no one is fully immune to the effects of artificial light at night. Even mild sleep disturbances can accumulate and harm long-term health.

General sleep hygiene guidelines also recommend that beds be used exclusively for sleep and sex. However, when people regularly use their phones in bed, it can rewire the brain's association between bed and rest.

On top of that, both the blue light emitted by screens and the stimulating content we consume keep our bodies and minds alert, delaying the onset of sleep and reducing sleep quality overall.

Summary

Finding Balance

Given the mounting evidence regarding the potential dangers of excessive smartphone usage, it is imperative that individuals strive for a healthier relationship with technology. The goal should not be to vilify smartphones but to encourage mindful and intentional usage. Like any tool, smartphones have the potential for both great benefit and significant harm. It is our responsibility to ensure that we are using these devices in ways that enhance rather than detract from our well-being.

To cultivate a more balanced approach, consider the following strategies:

1. **Implement Digital Detox Periods** – Designate specific times during the day when screens are put away, such as during meals, before bedtime, or during social interactions.
2. **Utilize Built-In Features** – Many smartphones offer screen time monitoring, app usage limits, and grayscale mode to help reduce excessive engagement.
3. **Engage in Offline Activities** – Find hobbies and activities that do not involve screens, such as reading physical books, exercising, or engaging in outdoor recreation.
4. **Prioritize Human Connection** – Make a conscious effort to engage in face-to-face interactions, strengthening relationships without the interference of screens.
5. **Improve Sleep Hygiene** – Establish screen-free bedtime routines, use blue light filters, and remove electronic devices from the bedroom to promote better sleep.

Final Thoughts

The smartphone era is still relatively new, and we are only beginning to understand its long-term effects. While these devices offer incredible benefits, we must remain vigilant about their impact on our mental health, relationships, and overall well-being. Like Tom Haverford in *Parks and Recreation*, many of us may struggle to step away from our screens, but with mindfulness and effort, we can learn to navigate the digital world in a way that enriches our lives rather than consumes them.

The challenge before us is not to eliminate smartphones from our lives but to master the art of using them wisely.

Chapter Thirteen

"Contrary to popular belief, there are no negative emotions. There are only emotions that are harder to experience or that cause more distress for certain people, and the more you suppress those emotions, the harder they are to manage."
— Whitney Goodman, Toxic Positivity: Keeping It Real in a World Obsessed with Being Happy

The Rise of Toxic Positivity

In the digital age, social media platforms have become spaces where users craft idealized versions of their lives, often filtered through an unrealistic lens of perpetual happiness. This phenomenon, known as toxic positivity, promotes the idea that positivity is the only acceptable emotional state, discouraging expressions of struggle, sadness, or frustration. While optimism can be valuable, the pressure to maintain an always-cheerful facade can lead to emotional suppression, self-doubt, and a distorted sense of reality.

Defining Toxic Positivity

Toxic positivity refers to the excessive and ineffective overgeneralization of a happy or optimistic state in all situations. It minimizes, invalidates, and often dismisses genuine human emotions that are not deemed "positive." Phrases such as "just stay positive," "good vibes only," and "everything happens for a reason" exemplify this mindset. While these statements may be well-intentioned, they discourage individuals from fully experiencing and processing complex emotions.

Social Media and the Curation of Happiness

Before I go into this chapter, I must note that Instagram and Facebook (Meta) are low hanging fruit. It is easy to determine their influence, based on their market reach and continual growth. However, they are not the sole contributors to how we live in this visually saturated world. Given the long periods of their influence, the amount of research discussing their influence is wide and expansive. I also feel I need to reiterate that these portals of visual stimuli are not inherently negative. However, we need to be aware of what power and influence they have on our lives or others. By doing so, we are able to determine healthier solutions.

Perhaps you have an account through Facebook or its subsidiary, Instagram. One must only scroll through the images presented, in either, to determine that many of the posts are not grounded in reality. Many augment their own experience or limit access to the more "positive" or "comfortable" situations, they may encounter. Even with these, they may enhance images to further maximize the positive influence in these pictures or posts. Essentially, they may not be realistic and can cherry pick portions of reality. Thus, creating the framework which exemplifies their ideal world. This isn't a judgement of this practice, but a presentation of the reality, which many attune to, on a near constant basis.

Platforms like Instagram and Facebook reinforce toxic positivity by encouraging users to showcase only the best aspects of their lives. Carefully selected posts, enhanced with filters and strategic captions, create a curated reality where struggle and imperfection are largely absent. This selective sharing promotes the illusion that others are constantly happy and successful, leading individuals to compare their unfiltered reality to someone else's highlight reel.

The "visual diet" consumed on social media significantly impacts self-perception. When users are bombarded with images of seemingly perfect lives, they may internalize the belief that their own experiences are inadequate. This can fuel feelings of loneliness, anxiety, and diminished self-worth, as people struggle to reconcile their real emotions with the illusion of effortless happiness they see online.

Overwhelming Messages of Toxic Positivity

Once of the chief complaints for individuals who seek out or continue to have a relationship with social media, such as Instagram or Facebook, is the lack of authenticity of posts. In addition to this, many individuals can be inundated with so-called, "Toxic Positivity" messages. The gratitude researcher Robert Emmons of UC Davis wrote, regarding toxic positivity,

> *"To deny that life has its share of disappointments, frustrations, losses, hurts, setbacks, and sadness would be unrealistic and untenable. Life is suffering. No amount of positive thinking exercises will change this truth."* (Kaufman, 2021).

This relationship with ignoring suffering by immersing yourself, solely with positivity, can weaken our relationship with the myriads of emotional responses to stimuli. To segment what SHOULD be felt is inherently problematic. To deny our stimuli or value it as negative or good also is problematic as a culture. We all have emotions and experience them throughout many spectrums and to prevent these stimuli from living within our reality only does us a disservice. If we dampen the importance of feeling emotions such as sadness, fear, anxiety, etc., we may become even more susceptible to these feelings.

Let's do an exercise in ironic recall: **Try not to think of a purple elephant. Don't think of its big purple, floppy ears. Its thick purple**

hide and white tusks are also off limits. Don't think of how it stomps around in its purple majestic, glory.

As many of you may have found, it is quite difficult to prevent our minds from limiting what was requested in that exercise. Our minds work similarly if we are attempting to prevent certain thoughts or feelings. We may have an increase in these sensations, which can prove quite distressing for many.

How to lean into our feelings versus ignoring them

Victor Frankel, a psychologist, holocaust survivor and writer of the book, 'A Man's Search for Meaning' (1946) discussed the notion of leaning into our feelings and emotions. Rather than fighting, a sense of curiosity is needed to consider what we could learn from those experiences. Finding purpose and meaning in the most trying times can elucidate extraordinary results in our relationship with ourselves and our experiences.

Researchers of Post Traumatic Growth, Richard Tedeschi and Lawrence Calhoun have identified positive results regarding individuals who utilize the principle of leaning into uncomfortable experiences with curiosity resulting in:

> *"A greater appreciation of one's life and relationships, as well as increased compassion, altruism, purpose, utilization of personal strengths, spiritual development, and creativity. Importantly, it's not the traumatic event itself that leads to growth but rather how the event is processed, the changes in worldview that result from the event, and the active search for meaning that people undertake during and after it."* (Tedeschi & Calhoun, 2004)

I wanted to front-load what could be gained from leaning into uncomfortable experiences before inundating folks with the reality they face (if they utilize social media and feel a poorer sense of self, as a result). My chapter on mindfulness will discuss more regarding how to utilize certain principles to manage and tolerate the sensations, which may and, most likely, will arise through the shift in visual diets.

Toxic positivity has been shown to have detrimental effects on our view of self and our behaviors with others. A person who wanted to go by Storm, the Outlier stated, regarding their relationship with Instagram, *"I am pretty sure I have body dysmorphia. A lot of the time you get caught up comparing yourself and have to set the real expectation that those people have money and are using filters to augment their appearance. Although I know that, sometimes it gives me anxiety knowing what others will think."* That comment doesn't have much to do with verbal toxic positivity, but it elucidates how Instagram affects folks in ways we may not consider, the visual representation of toxic positivity.

Seeing individuals with societally "ideal body types" can present the notion of what is "positive" and what is not ideal in our relationship with our own bodies. This isn't a heteronormative relationship, either. Body dysmorphia, within the expansive gender umbrella is and has been an all-too-common factor in sexual and gender minority communities.

Non-verbal representations of toxic positivity present a standard within communities, which cause a ripple of discomfort with those who may not be able to meet those standards. If folks are immersing themselves with constant or near-constant representations of idealized beauty, it's no matter whether they will feel discomfort about their own host bodies. Compound this with written messages of how individuals should feel, and confusion, irritation, shame, and guilt can arise.

Damaging Compartmentalization: The Harm Behind Toxic Positivity

You've likely come across social media posts encouraging people to "focus on the positive" or "cut out negative energy." While these sentiments may appear helpful or uplifting on the surface, they can have unintended consequences. For individuals struggling with difficult emotions, such messaging can reinforce the idea that their feelings are unwelcome, invalid, or even shameful.

Being surrounded by a culture that only honors positivity can make people feel alienated, especially when they're experiencing grief, fear, anger, or sadness. This sense of being "othered" is amplified by the culture of toxic positivity, where emotional discomfort is dismissed rather than addressed.

A Study in Suppression: Insights from Filipino College Students

A 2021 study conducted at Rizal Technological University in the Philippines explored how toxic positivity impacted college students during the COVID-19 pandemic. Through interviews with 15 students, researchers uncovered troubling patterns in emotional behavior and academic motivation.

Key findings included:

- Students frequently isolated themselves in an attempt to avoid negativity.
- Many felt ashamed, frustrated, or invalidated, leading them to suppress emotions rather than process them.
- They adopted avoidant coping mechanisms, such as "turning negative into positive," which prevented them from acknowledging or working through real emotions.
- A fear of being "too sad" caused students to withhold their feelings from others, leaving them emotionally bottled up.

As the researchers noted:

> *"Toxic positivity caused the respondents to feel a variety of emotions such as feeling ashamed, sad, frustrated, invalidated, and bottling up and masking their feelings, which negatively impacts their emotions."* (Bermejo et al., 2021)

The Psychological Cost of Suppression

Psychologist Campbell-Sills et al. (2006) offer a compelling definition of toxic positivity and its consequences:

> *"Toxic positivity results in one minimizing one's own negative feelings and suppressing negativity instead of acknowledging, processing, and working through it... This suppression of emotions is not only unhelpful but also leads to poorer recovery from the negative effects of the emotion."*

Statements like:

- "Look on the bright side."
- "Someone has it worse than you."
- "Just think positive thoughts."

…may seem encouraging, but they actually shame emotional expression, stifling necessary emotional growth and connection.

Why Emotional Processing Matters

Suppressing emotions don't make them disappear, it forces them underground. Over time, this can result in:

- Increased anxiety or depression
- Emotional dysregulation
- Strained interpersonal relationships

The Harm of Toxic Positivity

Signs of Toxic Positivity

 Look on the bright side

 Just think positive thoughts

 Someone has it worse than you

The Emotional Consequences

 Shame and self-blame

 Suppressed emotions

 Lack of authentic connection

Healthier Alternatives

- Accept difficult emotions
- It's okay to cry or feel sad
- Your feelings are valid

- Disconnection from one's authentic self

Accepting, naming, and working through our full range of emotions is not just healthy, it's essential for long-term emotional well-being and resilience. A study by *Campbell-Sills et al. (2006)* illustrates this well.

Sixty participants with mood and anxiety disorders were split into two groups: one group was instructed to suppress their emotions, while the other was encouraged to accept them. When both groups watched an emotion-provoking film, the suppression group not only failed to reduce their distress during the experience, but they also had a harder time recovering emotionally afterwards. The acceptance group, in contrast, recovered more quickly and with less distress.

A similar pattern emerged in a physical pain study by *Cioffi and Holloway (1993)*. Participants submerged their hands in cold water during a cold pressor task. One group was told to pay attention to the pain, another to distract themselves, and the last to suppress their sensations. Results showed that those who leaned into the pain (by observing it) recovered faster. The suppression group had the slowest recovery, demonstrating that avoidance doesn't relieve discomfort, it prolongs it.

In the long term, toxic positivity can become a heavy emotional burden. When we don't allow ourselves to process uncomfortable emotions, they don't simply disappear, they accumulate, often compounding our suffering.

A series of longitudinal and lab studies by *Ford et al. (2018)* found that people who habitually accept their emotions, across a wide range of experiences, report greater psychological health. These individuals also showed reduced emotional reactivity in the face of negative events.

To be clear: embracing difficult emotions doesn't mean wallowing in despair or choosing suffering. It means granting ourselves permission to feel, to acknowledge our anger, grief, or dread without immediately pushing it away. This kind of emotional acceptance takes practice. It's not a quick fix, nor is it learned in a day or a week. But with time, we can begin to dismantle the harmful patterns instilled by a toxic positivity-driven visual culture and start building healthier, more resilient emotional lives.

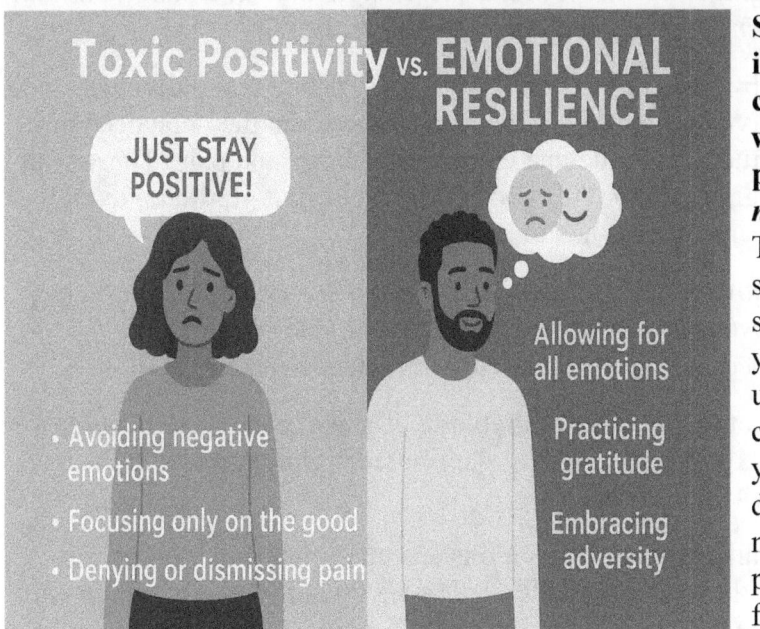

Something important to consider is what toxic positivity is *not*. Taking breaks, seeking joy, or surrounding yourself with uplifting content when you're feeling down, that's not toxic positivity. In fact, it's a healthy and often essential form of emotional regulation. The difference lies in intention and avoidance.

Toxic positivity arises when we *consistently* reject anything that doesn't feel good, when we filter life through a lens that only allows for comfort and pleasure, and we dismiss or deny anything less than ideal. It's the compulsive need to suppress discomfort and push away anything that doesn't fit into a hedonic (pleasure-seeking) narrative.

Imagine looking out at a vast beach but allowing yourself to only focus on one small shell. That's what toxic positivity does to our emotional experience, it bottlenecks our perception to only the "ideal," while the full range of life's richness goes unnoticed or avoided.

It's also important to note that toxic positivity is not the same as Positive Psychology. Positive Psychology is a scientifically grounded model that recognizes both the *positive and negative conditions* of human life. According to *Lilian Jans-Beken (2021)*, this field highlights that *"a life worth living consists of positive and negative conditions and positive and negative outcomes."*

One especially powerful concept within Positive Psychology is mature gratitude, a form of gratitude that doesn't ignore suffering, but integrates it. It's gratitude for *both* the good *and* the difficult, recognizing adversity as part of the human condition. Jans-Beken writes:

> *"Mature gratitude includes gratitude to the good and it contains a spiritual dimension, but it also includes gratitude to adversity and suffering. It is a concept that is more applicable in a dangerous and threatening world, more applicable to reality."*

In fact, a study by *Jans-Beken and Wong (2019)* found that individuals with PTSD symptoms experienced *greater well-being* when they practiced this existential gratitude, gratitude that embraces both joy and pain. Those who only expressed gratitude for the "good" (known as trait gratitude) did *not* experience the same mental health benefits.

> *"This shows that it is necessary for good mental health to accept and transform frustration, powerlessness, and hurt that one experiences into growth and thriving."* (Jans-Beken, 2021)

So, the goal is not to avoid joy or gratitude. It's to expand it, so it has space for all of life's experiences. Not just the filtered highlight reel, but the real, raw, human story underneath.

Excluding the full tapestry of sensations and emotional experiences can distort reality. When we willfully filter out anything that doesn't align with what "should" be felt or seen, we limit our capacity to build a meaningful, flexible relationship with our visual stimuli, and this can lead to a poorer, less nourishing visual diet.

Becoming stuck in a dopaminergic loop fueled by toxic positivity can be especially harmful for those who carry trauma. For these individuals, this curated lens doesn't just distract, it distances them from themselves. If we shut the door on uncomfortable feelings, we also shut out the chance to understand, process, and grow from them. The brain is wired to seek patterns and connections; when we numb or ignore large parts of our emotional reality, we interrupt this natural learning process.

Children and adolescents, neurodivergent and neurotypical alike, are particularly vulnerable to these filtered portrayals of what's "ideal." In their most formative years, their minds are soaking in screen-based input like sponges. And what they absorb shapes their perceptions of identity, worth, and emotional regulation.

There's a reason so much time has been dedicated to unpacking toxic positivity: its influence expanded dramatically during and after the COVID-19 pandemic. In the absence of typical routines and social structures, many turned to social media for comfort or distraction. What emerged in that vacuum was a wave of simplified, feel-good content that often masked deeper, more complex realities.

Within these echo chambers, the message became clear: everything should be reframed through the lens of positivity. But this persistent push toward optimism above all else doesn't reflect the full human experience. Instead, it flattens it. It limits the brain's ability to metabolize emotion, to build resilience, and to hold space for contradiction and growth.

How to spot Toxic Positivity

Examples developed by researchers Ishan Sanjeev Upadhyay, KV Aditya Srivatsa, and Radhika Mamidi (2022):

Sentence	Class
When people say there is a 'reason' for the depression, they insult the person who suffers, making it seem that those in agony are somehow at fault for not 'cheering up.' The fact is that those who suffer - and those who love them - are no more at fault for depression than a cancer patient is for a tumor.	Non-Toxic Positive
Sentence	Class
Just like it's not healthy to think overly negative thoughts, exaggeratedly positive thoughts can be equally detrimental. If you overestimate how much of a positive impact a particular change will have on your life, you may end up feeling disappointed when reality doesn't live up to your fantasy.	Non-Toxic Positive
Do what you feel in your heart to be right	Non-Toxic Positive
The secret of getting ahead is getting started	Non-Toxic Positive
Being positive is like going up a mountain. Being negative is like sliding down a hill. A lot of times, people want to take the easy way out, because it's basically what they've understood throughout their lives.	Toxic Positive
You must not under any pretense allow your mind to dwell on any thought that is not positive, constructive, optimistic, kind.	Toxic Positive
While you're going through this process of trying to find the satisfaction in your work, pretend you feel	Toxic Positive

satisfied. Tell yourself you had a good day. Walk through the corridors with a smile rather than a scowl. Your positive energy will radiate. If you act like you're having fun, you'll find you are having fun.	
You can't live a positive life with a negative mind and if you have a positive outcome, you have a positive income and just to have more positivity and just to kind of laugh it off.	Toxic Positive

In addition to internalizing the messaging of toxic positivity, social media often presents an inauthentic version of the world, one that inevitably encourages social comparison. Recent research found that more frequent Instagram use is associated with increased levels of social comparison. These platforms allow users to carefully curate their lives, providing a constant stream of polished highlights that are easy to contrast with our own unfiltered experiences. The study revealed that this exposure heightened users' social anxiety, as they compared themselves to others' appearance, abilities, popularity, and social skills, particularly when the content was selectively positive or overly idealized (Jiang & Ngien, 2020).

The use of filters and digital airbrushing only deepens this problem. When individuals compare themselves to images that have been edited far beyond reality, the results are not just disheartening, they're psychologically damaging. It's akin to comparing yourself to someone with infinite resources and an endless team of stylists and editors. The goal becomes unattainable by design.

Interestingly, not all social comparison is limited to "fitspiration" or overly glamorous posts. A 2020 study in the Philippines explored how even body positivity content can lead to internalized comparison and mixed emotional outcomes:

"The study confirmed that women who see photos of other women on Instagram flaunting their bodies, regardless of whether they are 'fitspiring' or body positive, tend to self-objectify and experience negative thoughts about their own bodies. Women in the fitspiration group engaged in upward comparison, seeing themselves as inferior to the toned, fit women. This led to increased motivation and drive, but also to body dissatisfaction and envy. On the other hand, those viewing body positivity content compared themselves to plus-size or average-sized women, which often boosted self-esteem and gratitude, as they felt equal to or better than the individuals in the images." (Cortez & Alfonso, 2020)

Non-Toxic Positivity vs. Toxic Positivity

Non-Toxic Positivity	Toxic Positivity
When people say there is a 'reason' for the depression, they insult the person who suffers, making it seem that those in agony are somehow at fault for not 'cheering up'. The fact is that those who suffer – and those who love them – are no more at fault for depression than a cancer patient is for a tumor.	Being positive is like going up a mountain. Being negative is like sliding down a hill. A lot of times, people want to take the easy way out, because it's basically what they've understood throughout their lives.
Just like it's not healthy to think overly negative thoughts, exaggeratedly positive thoughts can be equally detrimental. If you overestimate how much of a positive impact a particular change will have on your life, you may end up feeling disappointed when reality doesn't live up to your fantasy.	You must not under any pretense allow your mind to dwell on any thought that is not positive, constructive, optimistic, kind.
Do what you feel in your heart to be right.	While you're going through this process of trying to find the satisfaction in your work, pretend you feel satisfied. Tell yourself you had a good day. Walk through the corridors with a smile rather than a scowl. Your positive energy will radiate. If you'll find you are having fun.
The secret of getting ahead is getting started	You can't live a positive life with a negative mind and if you have a positive outcome, you have a positive income

Even when intended to uplift, social media content, through the lens of constant comparison, can have complex and unintended emotional consequences. Whether it inspires or invalidates, the impact largely depends on where the viewer sees themselves in the hierarchy of images.

The Disproportionate Impact on Marginalized Communities

Toxic positivity can be particularly challenging for Black, Indigenous, and People of Color (BIPOC) individuals. It involves **dismissing negative emotions and responding to distress with false reassurances rather than empathy**. This attitude can cause alienation and a feeling of disconnection. BIPOC individuals may already face unique challenges and stressors, and toxic positivity can further invalidate their emotional experiences.

Toxic positivity does not affect all individuals equally. For marginalized communities, including people of color, LGBTQ+ individuals, and those with mental health conditions, the pressure to maintain a happy front can be particularly harmful. These communities often face systemic challenges such as discrimination, economic inequality, and healthcare disparities, which require acknowledgment and action rather than dismissal through empty platitudes.

For example, telling someone experiencing racial discrimination to "just think positive" ignores the structural barriers that contribute to their distress. Similarly, phrases like "happiness is a choice" fail to account for mental health conditions that require professional care and support. Encouraging constant positivity without recognizing these realities can be both dismissive and harmful.

Elyse Fox, activist and founder of Sad Girls Club, a nonprofit focused on providing mental-wellness resources and community for BIPOC individuals, encourages people in her network to experience and express all their feelings, including negative emotions like anger and grief.

To avoid toxic positivity while speaking with BIPOC individuals:

1. Acknowledge and validate their emotions, even if they are negative.
2. Offer empathy and support rather than false reassurances.
3. Encourage open communication and the expression of emotions.
4. Be aware of the unique challenges and stressors faced by BIPOC individuals and avoid minimizing their experiences.

   (Garis & Garis, 2022)

By recognizing and addressing toxic positivity, we can create a more supportive and inclusive environment for BIPOC individuals to express people's authentic emotions and experiences. These can be used internally as well as folk's work with their internalized feelings of compartmentalization and minimization of emotions and feelings. Our feelings are really happening to us, the more we force ourselves to feel something contrary to our reality, the more suffering we are enacting upon ourselves. Allowing our emotions to present themselves can equally allow us to grieve our situation properly.

Cultivating a Healthier Relationship with Social Media

While social media is unlikely to change overnight, individuals can take steps to cultivate a healthier digital environment:

1. **Curate Your Feed** – Follow accounts that promote authenticity and vulnerability rather than perfection.

2. **Engage Mindfully** – Be aware of how social media affects your mood and self-esteem. Take breaks when needed.

3. **Practice Emotional Honesty** – Acknowledge and validate your full range of emotions instead of forcing positivity.

4. **Encourage Balanced Conversations** – Support others in expressing their genuine experiences rather than responding with dismissive positivity.

5. **Emphasize Real-World Connections** – Prioritize in-person interactions that allow for deeper, more nuanced emotional exchanges.

Conclusion: Embracing Emotional Authenticity

Toxic positivity may be deeply ingrained in digital culture, but awareness of its impact allows us to challenge and counteract its effects. By embracing emotional authenticity, both online and offline, we can create spaces where all emotions are acknowledged, validated, and expressed freely. The goal is not to reject positivity altogether but to cultivate a more balanced and realistic approach to emotional well-being, one that honors the full spectrum of human experience.

Summary

- Toxic positivity is the excessive promotion of optimism while dismissing genuine human emotions like sadness, frustration, or struggle. Social media platforms like Instagram and Facebook play a significant role in reinforcing this phenomenon by encouraging users to showcase only the most flattering aspects of their lives, leading to unrealistic comparisons and emotional suppression.

- **Defining Toxic Positivity**
  Toxic positivity minimizes negative emotions and discourages emotional processing through phrases like "just stay positive" or

"good vibes only." While well-intentioned, this mindset invalidates struggles and can lead to self-doubt and a distorted sense of reality.

- **The Role of Social Media**
  Social media creates a "visual diet" where users consume carefully curated content that presents an idealized life. This selective sharing fosters social comparison, increasing anxiety, loneliness, and dissatisfaction. Many people experience body image issues due to unrealistic beauty standards, leading to self-doubt and, in some cases, body dysmorphia.

- **Psychological Impact**
  Studies show that suppressing negative emotions leads to greater distress and slower recovery from emotional pain. Avoidance-based coping mechanisms, reinforced by toxic positivity, can increase feelings of shame, isolation, and disconnection. Research also confirms that individuals who embrace all emotions, including discomfort, experience greater psychological resilience and post-traumatic growth.

- **Distinguishing Toxic Positivity from Positive Psychology**
  Toxic positivity is not the same as positive psychology. While toxic positivity insists on ignoring negative emotions, positive psychology acknowledges both positive and negative experiences as part of a meaningful life. Research supports that gratitude for both good and adverse experiences contribute to better mental health.

- **Marginalized Communities and Toxic Positivity**
  BIPOC individuals and other marginalized groups are disproportionately affected by toxic positivity, as it invalidates their unique struggles and pressures them to suppress their emotions. This can worsen mental health challenges and create further alienation.

- **Recognizing and Avoiding Toxic Positivity**
  Toxic positivity often appears in statements that dismiss pain or struggle, urging people to "think positive" rather than process their emotions. Social comparisons on social media, particularly when enhanced with filters and unrealistic portrayals, amplify these harmful effects. A healthier approach involves embracing emotions, seeking balance, and fostering authenticity in both online and offline interactions.

Chapter Fourteen

"Researchers have known for years that social media has a negative impact on how young women feel about themselves," - Jennifer Mills, professor of psychology at York University

How women are portrayed in visual stimuli/Gendered differences in consumption of visual stimuli.

Visual representations of women, particularly the portrayal of an "ideal" female image, have been glamorized since the advent of television. With the rise of handheld devices and social media, individuals, especially young girls, are exposed to an overwhelming amount of visual content that defines societal beauty standards. This constant exposure can create a disconnect between their self-perception and the unattainable ideals presented online.

I do not claim that this book will resolve the deep-seated issues stemming from media influence on women's self-image. Furthermore, I acknowledge that, due to my gender identity, I may not be the most suitable voice for this discussion. For a more in-depth analysis, I recommend Dr. Marquita M. Gammage's *Media Racism: The Impact of Media Injustice on Black Women's Lives*, which I will reference later in this chapter. However, it is crucial to examine how visual media influences the self-perception of women and girls to avoid perpetuating harmful narratives.

However, ignoring the vast impact of our visual media diet influence on the perceived sense of self of these girls and women would continue to perpetrate this pitfall. So, I'll do my best to discuss this particularly nuanced topic, I myself can only empathize with.

Gender Differences in Media Consumption

Research has shown that men and women consume visual content differently. A study examining pro- and anti-vaccine web pages revealed that women typically read headlines first before engaging with the body of the text, while men focused on images before reading (Cuesta-Cambra et al., 2019). Furthermore, men demonstrated greater emotional engagement with pro-vaccine content, whereas women displayed a stronger response to anti-vaccine content. This raises important questions about how women interpret and emotionally engage with media messages, whether they genuinely sympathize with certain narratives or react with irony and skepticism.

This study did not account for gender diversity, underscoring the need for more inclusive research. Additionally, the very understandable caution of receiving medical care is a cross-cultural dynamic that is present within most BIPOC communities. The very real abuses of the medical establishment in trialing drugs, treatment without the consent of BIPOC individuals is prolific. Reading sensationalized headlines first can prime individuals to interpret articles in a specific way, often reinforcing biases. Algorithms capitalize on this tendency, serving users increasingly extreme content based on past engagement.

The Impact of Harmful Visual Diets on Girls and Young Women

The visual content served to girls and young women through digital platforms often functions less as passive entertainment and more as a form of systemic predation. The messages they absorb, many of which are oversexualized, appearance-obsessed, and emotionally manipulative, can shape their sense of self in harmful, long-lasting ways. These harmful visual diets aren't just incidental; they are part of a larger structure that profits from insecurity, comparison, and the commodification of identity.

Investigative reports have revealed just how quickly, and easily, young users can be exposed to extreme and damaging content online. Clare Duffy of CNN reported on an experiment where a fake account posing as a 14-year-old girl was used to observe the kind of content served on a popular social media platform:

> *"Over six days, we used this app to see what kind of content it would serve to a young person. It seemed to be a guide for how to develop an eating disorder, how to restrict your eating. What disturbed me most was the content I was served in restricted mode. For the first two days, I scrolled the 'For You' page for 30 minutes—a third of the time a typical U.S. teen spends on the app daily, according to a TechCrunch report. A lot of mature themes such as suicide came up."* (CNN, 2023)

Even more troubling, the report noted that the account was exposed to sexually explicit content and posts related to self-harm. Though the account didn't behave *exactly* like a real teen, it illustrated the kind of content a young user could encounter, unfiltered, persistent, and deeply unsettling.

And it's not just CNN. Investigations by *The New York Times*, *New York Post*, and *CNET* have similarly documented how even minimal interaction with triggering content can flood a user's feed with related posts. This algorithmic pattern, where one click or one view leads to a stream of related, and often more extreme, content, functions like a digital echo chamber of harm.

It's akin to dropping a single drop of red ink into a glass of water. The original content may seem isolated at first, but it quickly spreads and tints the entire visual experience. What was once a single post becoming an entire ecosystem, forming a new and distinct visual diet, one steeped in danger.

Algorithmic Harm and the Silencing of Black Women

Being funneled into a stream of increasingly harmful content isn't just a general risk, it's a direct threat to already marginalized communities. Black women, in particular, bear a unique and compounded weight in these digital spaces. Not only are they exposed to the same toxic visual diets and dangerous content as others, but they also face the dual burden of racism and sexism, amplified by the very algorithms that claim to "personalize" our experience.

Social media platforms have become digital battlegrounds where Black women are disproportionately targeted, harassed, and silenced. The algorithm doesn't just fail to protect them, it often works against them, promoting content that demeans, dehumanizes, or outright threatens. These experiences are not isolated; they reflect broader societal structures that continue to police and punish Black expression.

As Lovett (2022) puts it:

"Racism and sexism are at the core of American social contracts and are incorporated into public policy, which has led to a historical record of women, especially Black women, being chastised, surveilled, and now, with the advent of new technology, trolled and threatened with violence on social media simply for the way their oral and rhetorical skills subvert their oppressive state." (Influence Watch, 2022)

In short, the harm isn't only in what content is presented, it's also in who is punished for speaking out. And too often, Black women pay the price for challenging a system designed to suppress them.

Negative attitudes toward Black individuals are not new in online discourse. This was particularly evident on Twitter during 2019–2020 in the wake of the murders of George Floyd, Ahmaud Arbery, and Breonna Taylor at the hands of current or former law enforcement officers.

> *"Although there was a sharp decline (from 49.33% in November to 33.66% in June) in negative Black sentiment and increased public awareness of structural racism and desire for long-lasting social change, these shifts were transitory and returned to baseline after*

> *several weeks. Findings suggest that negative attitudes towards Black people remain deeply entrenched."*
> — *(Nguyen, et al., 2021)*

On Facebook, Black voices are often silenced when sharing lived experiences, especially when intersecting with race, gender, and queerness in a predominantly white digital culture.

Carolyn Wysinger, a podcaster who offers pop culture commentary from a Black queer perspective, shared her experiences of being penalized on the platform:

> *"Black people, especially Black women, risk being sent to 'Facebook jail' when they discuss racism." (Guynn, 2020)*

"Facebook jail", a term used to describe temporary account suspensions, mirrors the carceral logic of offline systems, extending punitive frameworks into digital spaces. As Gray and Stein (2021) note, *"Facebook jail reflects how certain populations are subject to suppression, and the intersection of being Black and Woman makes one especially at risk."*

Authors Gray and Stein (2021) beautifully articulate the lived experience of being a Black woman in social media spaces:

> *"Black women's responses to surveillance and silencing highlight the histories of exclusion and legacies of racist practices that underlie virtual and physical spaces. Black women center Blackness in their digital practices and reflect their refusal to be erased and ignored.*
>
> *We rely on the concept of digital space to help explain how Black women use social media platforms to address the power imbalance reflected in the rates at which they are banned from and punished on social media. Space does not simply exist as a given but is constructed and affects (and is affected by) those with the most power.*
>
> *Space is not just a passive backdrop to human behavior and social action but is constantly produced and remade within complex relations of culture, power, and difference. Black women on social media attempt to contest this erasure and exclusion. Their work inside digital spaces attempts to heal the intersectional wounds and collective traumas that stem from White supremacy, Black patriarchy, White feminism, and other oppressions.*
>
> *Black women are working to ensure these spaces validate the range of Black women's digital praxis."*

This passage underscores how Black women are not only resisting digital erasure but actively reclaiming space, creating visibility, and fostering healing within platforms that often seek to silence them. Their presence is resistance. Their digital work is legacy.

Reshaping Media Representation

For those seeking a thorough analysis of how Black women are represented in media, I highly recommend the works of Dr. Marquita M. Gammage, particularly *Challenging Misrepresentations of Black Womanhood: Media, Literature and Theory* (2019), *Representations of Black Women in the Media* (2018), and *Media Racism: The Impact of Media Injustice on Black Women's Lives* (2023). Dr. Gammage's scholarship reconceptualizes the media's portrayals of Black women, highlighting the persistent and damaging narratives that continue to circulate.

Her research in *Media Racism* (2023) exposes how Black women are misrepresented across multiple media platforms, through the promotion of unhealthy lifestyles, normalization of high-risk sexual behavior, propagation of racist tropes, oversexualization, and the demonization of Black motherhood. These depictions not only perpetuate harmful stereotypes but also shape public perception and reinforce systemic injustices.

In Chapter Seventeen, we'll examine the demographic makeup of production companies, a critical piece in understanding why so many media narratives skew toward racist and reductive portrayals of marginalized communities.

As Dr. Gammage emphasizes, however, change is underway. A new path of independence has emerged, one where Black creatives, especially Black women, reclaim control over how their stories are told. Black-women-owned media companies like Harpo Productions, ARRAY, and Hoorae Media are creating space for authentic storytelling, empowering creators to move from concept to distribution on their own terms. These platforms serve not just as production houses but as safe, visionary spaces for telling expansive and nuanced Black stories.

So, the question becomes this: *Why would someone willingly immerse themselves in such an environment?* The answer, in a word, is **community**. For many, especially those with layered identities and lived experiences shaped by intersectionality, online spaces offer a rare opportunity to connect with others who understand what it's like to walk in their shoes. These digital platforms, flawed as they may be, can become spaces of affirmation, solidarity, and shared understanding.

But that connection comes at a cost. The risk of encountering harm, whether in the form of microaggressions, targeted harassment, or the endless churn of emotionally charged, fear-inducing content, has caused many to pause and reconsider how they spend their time online. Fortunately, digital literacy is growing, and with it, the awareness that we need to be intentional about what we consume.

More people are beginning to understand the importance of digital wellness and are actively rethinking their visual diets. While community matters, we don't have to remain victims of algorithmic predation, those invisible systems designed to exploit our emotions and extend our screen time. In many cases, we do have a choice. We can push back. We can cultivate healthier online habits. We can seek connection without sacrificing our mental and emotional well-being.

I'll explore this more deeply in Chapter Twenty-Five, but for now, it's worth saying: *we can stay connected without being consumed.*

Digital Literacy and Resetting Your Algorithm

An immediate way to help combat damaging visual media is to reset your algorithm. Doing this helps prevent the programs and websites to learn from your search history and provide content they feel would better keep you engaged. Additionally, focus on content that is more in line with a balanced visual diet. Positive or neutral representations of what you would like to see or experience. Also, it's just best to avoid the comment section on any video. Yes, even the positive ones. To reset your algorithm, just proceed with the following steps:

1. Identify the platform you want to reset: The search algorithm varies across platforms like Google, Instagram, YouTube, and others.

2. Clear your search history: The search algorithm is influenced by your search history. Clearing your search history can help reset the algorithm. Here's how to do it on some popular platforms:
    - Google: Google doesn't provide a direct way to reset your search algorithm. However, you can clear your search history by visiting Google's My Activity page and deleting your search history.
    - Instagram: To reset your Instagram algorithm, clear your search history. Go to your profile, tap the three lines in the top-right corner, select "Your Activity," then "Search History." Tap "Clear All" to clear your search history.
    - YouTube: Similar to Instagram, you can reset your YouTube algorithm by clearing your search history. Go to your profile, then "History & Privacy," and finally "Search History." Click "Clear all search history" to reset the algorithm.
3. **Unfollow or Mute Harmful Accounts:** If certain content contributes to negative self-perception, unfollow or mute those accounts to shift your media intake.

    If you're resetting a social media platform's algorithm, consider unfollowing accounts that don't interest you. This can help the algorithm show you more relevant content.
4. Engage with positive content: The algorithm tends to show you more of what you engage with. If you want to see more positive content, engage with it by liking, commenting, or sharing.
5. Be patient: The algorithm will take some time to adjust to your new search and engagement patterns. Be patient and continue to engage with the type of content you want to see more of.

Remember, the steps may vary slightly depending on the platform you're using. Always refer to the platform's help center for the most accurate and up-to-date information. (Pierce, D 2022) (Hebert, R 2023) (Habrah, A 2023)

We also don't have to remain quiet about the content we see. As we have seen with collective outcries due to social injustice, misrepresentation, and drives to inclusion, community engagement is needed to shift course. We have power in our collective voice. Remaining silent rather than detailing our needs presents further harm upon us. Likewise, we can tell tech companies, production companies, and politicians that we won't remain quiet. There are many ways we can make our voice be heard. Utilizing the same format that is abusing us, we can rise up and tell these organizations who collectively harm us, that we demand change.

Summary

The Impact of Harmful Visual Diets on Young Women

The visual content consumed by young women frequently includes oversexualized imagery and damaging messages, leading to long-term psychological effects. Investigative reports have shown that social media platforms rapidly expose young users to extreme content.

Reshaping Media Representation

For a deeper understanding of Black women's representation in media, I recommend *Challenging Misrepresentations of Black Womanhood: Media, Literature, and Theory (2019)* and *Representations of Black Women in the Media (2018)* by Dr. Marquita M. Gammage. Her work examines how Black women are misrepresented and oversexualized in mainstream media.

Digital Literacy and Resetting Media Algorithms

A practical way to combat harmful visual media is by resetting digital algorithms. This prevents platforms from curating content based on past engagement that may negatively impact mental well-being. Steps include:

- **Identify the platform to reset:** Each platform has unique algorithms, so determine which one requires adjustment.
- **Clear search history:**
    - *Google:* Visit Google's My Activity page and delete search history.
    - *Instagram:* Navigate to "Your Activity," select "Search History," and tap "Clear All."
    - *YouTube:* Go to "History & Privacy," select "Search History," and click "Clear all search history."
- **Unfollow or mute harmful accounts:** Shift content consumption toward more balanced and positive media.
- **Engage with positive content:** Interacting with constructive material helps reshape the algorithm's recommendations.
- **Be patient:** Algorithm adjustments take time and require consistent effort.

Social Justice and Change.

Moreover, addressing harmful content requires collective action. Social justice movements have demonstrated the power of public engagement in holding media and tech companies accountable. By advocating for better representation and ethical digital practices, we can create healthier digital spaces that reflect diverse and authentic narratives.

Chapter Fifteen

"My friends said if you're not involved in one of these online dating services, you're just gonna get left behind socially, you know. I'm not afraid to try something new. I'm not. So I signed up. Changed my life. I went from feeling good about myself to feeling like a leper alone in a room typing." -Ryan Hamilton

Dating in a Visually Stimulating World

It likely comes as no surprise that the rise of online dating has reshaped how we experience connection and emotional attune with others. While dating apps offer a streamlined path to meeting people, they also shift the dynamic of intimacy, often placing visuals, curated profiles, and rapid judgments at the forefront of human interaction.

On the upside, online dating can reduce societal pressures and give individuals more control over how and when they engage. For many, the process feels safer: they can vet potential dates by reviewing social media profiles, conducting online searches, or even scheduling a video call before deciding to meet in person. These tools help create a sense of safety and transparency, allowing people to assess compatibility and establish comfort before physical proximity is introduced.

However, this access also comes with complexity. For some, the ability to explore someone's digital footprint beforehand offers clarity, highlighting mutual interests, values, or red flags. For others, it can lead to premature assumptions or filtered expectations that may not align with in-person chemistry.

As someone named *Purple* shared:

> *"I've been able to weed people out based on not having social media. People push for it during dating, and my boundary is to set up a date first. From there, if the connection is built, I'll provide my phone number."*

This speaks to a deeper truth: safety and intentionality matter. In a world driven by constant visual input, slowing down, protecting boundaries, and choosing authenticity over speed can be acts of self-care.

The Swipes, the Search, and the Surge of Dopamine

Searching a potential date's name has become as common as swiping left or right, whether out of curiosity or safety, it's a behavior that offers a sense of control in an unpredictable online dating environment. These digital breadcrumbs can provide comfort, especially when trust is still forming. But not everyone shares the same instinct or boundaries. In a dating pool that's increasingly shifted online, it's easy to disengage when things get complicated. After all, with a sea of profiles just a swipe away, the impulse to move on feels effortless.

The upsides of dating apps, anonymity, control, and the ability to block or ghost without confrontation, mirror their shadow sides. These very features that empower users can also erode accountability and emotional connection.

The swiping mechanism itself is a dopaminergic playground. As mentioned earlier in this book, dopamine thrives not on satisfaction, but on *anticipation*. Swiping through endless profiles isn't always about finding the one, it's often about the thrill of *maybe*. The process becomes addictive: fast, visual judgments, micro-rewards with each match, and the pursuit of novelty over depth.

And behind this behavioral pattern is a powerful industry.

> *"The dating app industry is worth approximately $3.06 billion, with a predicted growth of $10.87 billion in 2026. While people have been using the Internet to find friends, lovers, and partners since the early nineties, it is only in the 2010s, with the launch of dating apps, that the phenomenon took on a completely new dimension. Apps are a significant departure from the previous affordances that the web provided for those in search for a partner, love, or something else."*
> — Bandinelli & Cossu, 2023

Dating apps didn't just change how we meet people, they changed *how we think* about connection. And with billions of dollars on the line, the systems in place are designed to keep us engaged, often more with the apps themselves than with the people on them.

Safety and Security: The Digital Risk of Romance

With such a massive financial footprint, the online dating industry also carries significant risks, chief among them, the safety and security of user data. As dating apps continue to grow in popularity and revenue, they become even more attractive targets for cybercriminals.

> *"Cybersecurity hackers also evolve their technique and diversify their strategies. The most recent and mediatized cybersecurity attack occurred at the beginning of 2020, when the cybersecurity firm White Ops identified 70,000 photos of female Tinder users stolen by hackers and dumped on cybercrime sites. The bulk of photos was supposedly hacked to be further used in catfishing*

> *schemes. In addition to complex cyberattacks, spam bots are also frequent on the app, in more and more complex forms, due to Tinder's potential."*
> — *Stoicescu & Rughinis, 2021*

These breaches expose the darker side of app-based intimacy. It's not just emotional vulnerability at stake, it's your identity, privacy, and the images you thought were only seen by a few swipes. As the lines between technology, connection, and commerce blur, users must tread carefully. The pursuit of love in the digital age comes with a price, and sometimes that cost is hidden in terms we never read and the data we didn't realize we gave away.

The Double-Edged Sword of Online Dating

One of the most complicated dynamics in the online dating world is the perceived discrimination and damage it can inflict on one's sense of self. In many ways, the pursuit of meaningful connection has been replaced with a focus on quantity, how many matches, how many messages, and how many swipes. As users manage multiple interactions at once, the depth and quality of those conversations often suffer. The reality is that attention becomes a finite resource spread thin across many.

Another side effect of this environment is the rise of *digital peacocking*, the act of curating an engaging profile with eye-catching photos and clever bios meant to stand out in a crowd of endless scrolling. This behavior isn't inherently problematic, but it reinforces a performative aspect of dating that can feel exhausting or even disheartening. For many, it's not about being seen for who they are, but about being chosen for how well they can entertain or captivate in a few seconds.

Those who attract significant attention might spend much of their energy juggling multiple conversations, which can ultimately dilute their focus in other areas of life, including genuine emotional connection. This becomes particularly frustrating for individuals who approach dating with monogamous intentions. Response time, the quality of engagement, and features like *read receipts* can amplify anxiety, leaving people to interpret being "left on read" as a reflection of their worth.

And then there's the issue of discrimination, subtle or overt, based on appearance, race, weight, or other visible characteristics. In a study by Flug (2016), many users reported feeling rejected or judged based on these surface traits:

> *"A sizable number of individuals did indicate feeling as though they had been (or may have been) discriminated against by potential matches on online dating sites. General appearance and weight were the most common responses as to why participants felt they*

> *had been discriminated against, indicating that discrimination-based appearance may transcend gender and racial boundaries in online dating settings. Fifty-nine percent of participants believed that others had been intentionally dishonest to them in online dating settings, yet only 19% admitted to being intentionally dishonest themselves."*

This imbalance, the need to appear appealing versus the fear of being dismissed or misled, creates an ecosystem where vulnerability becomes a high-risk act, and self-esteem is often the first casualty. As dishonesty becomes more common on dating apps, the need for strong safety measures has never been more important. Alongside deceit, abuse and criminal activity, such as stalking, fraud, and sexual assault, pose serious risks for users.

These dangers can have lasting effects, including physical health issues (like sexually transmitted infections or disordered eating) and psychological impacts (such as emotional trauma or damaged self-esteem) (Phan et al., 2021).

While not everyone experiences harm, many individuals do carry emotional wounds from past interactions. Without proper resources, such as supportive networks or tools to process emotional pain, there's a greater chance that harm will be projected onto future interactions. It's a troubling outcome for platforms originally created to foster connection. This may explain why so many people report feeling burned out by dating apps, often needing to take breaks or stepping away entirely.

Interestingly, research suggests that how couples meet, whether in person, online, or through a spontaneous "meet-cute", has little impact on their overall relationship satisfaction. A study by Rosenfield and Thomas (2012) found only a marginal connection between the method of meeting and long-term happiness. In other words, lasting satisfaction in relationships can still be found through online dating, despite the overwhelming number of options and challenges within the digital dating pool.

Case Study

Cassie is a polyamorous individual who solely relied upon dating apps to seek partnerships. Their particular type of ethical non-monogamy is looking for intentional and multiple long-term relationships. However, due to the consistent upsetting instances of online dating, Cassie noticed a disenchanted relationship with dating in general. She would present with a guarded manner on dates, expecting them to fail in some way, which inevitably led her to being more cynical. She noted, *"Online I feel that there is an epidemic of casualness. People are looking for casualness and I am feeling that not many are looking for seriousness."* After leaving online dating and focusing on building a relationship with herself and her notion of loneliness, Cassie reassessed her relationship with dating in general and the sense of "needing" someone in her life rather than wanting them. After a long period away from dating sites (a period of about 6 months), Cassie returned to dating with intentionality and renewed focus. She has since developed multiple ongoing relationships without the aid of online dating. Fortunately, for Cassie, she lives in a large city with access to meetups that don't involve online dating. The time away from swipe culture led to Cassie understanding her triggers with dating more, developing a broader sense of self and allowing her to deepen her relationship with her own time.

Neurochemical Processes of Swipe Culture

The visual below, created by Samantha Beck (2021), illustrates the basic cycle of engagement in swipe-based online dating platforms.

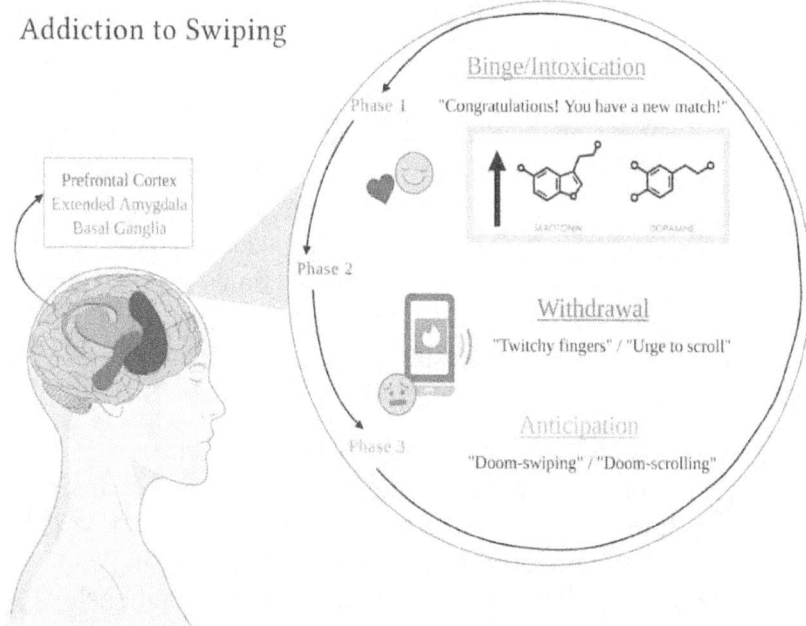

(Samantha Beck, 2021)

This cycle highlights our brain's involvement in swipe culture. Each time we receive a new match, the brain is flooded with neurochemicals, primarily dopamine, that activate the pleasure and reward circuit. This creates a reinforcing feedback loop: the more we swipe and match, the more we crave the rush of validation and potential connection.

Even after putting the phone away, we may find ourselves itching to check the app again, just to see if we've received any new matches or messages. If we haven't customized our notifications, the app will likely prompt us with alerts encouraging us to send a message or swipe again. These nudges are no accident; they're part of a system carefully designed to keep us engaged.

Soon, we find ourselves right back in the loop, swiping, matching, waiting. It's never quite enough.

Later in this book (Chapter Twenty-Three), I'll dive into strategies for managing a problematic relationship with apps and screens. But for now, let's transition to a natural extension of dating for many, intimacy.

Effective Conversation Skills: Strategies and Psychology

Effective conversations are essential to building relationships and even personal well-being. Research shows that smooth, engaging dialogue boosts positive emotions and a sense of belonging and validation healthland.time.com. Below are evidence-backed strategies and expert tips for initiating conversations, listening actively, asking great questions, handling silences, showing empathy, and using body language to keep discussions flowing. I added this to the book because my experience with many folks who cannot maintain or initiate a conversation seems to be growing exponentially. Use this regarding dating, and general relationship building. Unfortunately, this is a skill that is not present in many individuals, despite generational divides.

Initiating a Conversation

Starting a conversation confidently sets the tone. Here are key strategies for breaking the ice and getting the dialogue going:

- **Begin with a Friendly Opener:** A simple self-introduction or a benign comment about the situation works well. For example, *"Hi, I'm [Name]. This event is great – how did you hear about it?"* Introduce yourself, then ask a straightforward question or make an observation to invite the other person to respond (verywellmind.com). Research suggests sticking to innocuous, light topics as openers – in one study, neutral questions (*"What's your favorite team?"*) were received much better than gimmicky "pick-up" lines. In fact, an *innocuous approach* to initiating conversation is generally the most effective and least threatening, encouraging the other person to reply comfortably.

- **Keep It Positive and Contextual:** Try to start on an upbeat note. Comment on something positive about your shared context – the venue, weather, or a common activity. For instance, *"This café has a nice atmosphere, have you been here before?"* Positive observations create a warm vibe, whereas launching into complaints or negative remarks can stall a conversation early (verywellmind.com). Avoid overly controversial or heavy topics with someone you've just met – save debates or personal grievances for when you know each other better.

- **Prepare (if Needed) and Read Cues:** If you tend to get anxious, a bit of preparation can help. Think of a couple of casual topics or questions in advance (recent movies, a hobby, etc.) so you're not at a loss. Pay attention to the other person's initial responses and body language; if they seem receptive (smiling, engaging), continue along that topic. If not, gently pivot to another light topic. The goal is a comfortable back-and-forth exchange that opens the door for deeper conversation.

Active Listening

Once a conversation is underway, active listening is crucial for maintaining it. Active listening means fully focusing on the speaker, understanding their message, and responding thoughtfully – rather than just waiting for your turn to talk. This skill makes your partner feel heard and encourages them to keep sharing.

- **Give Full Attention:** Minimize distractions and truly tune in. Maintain eye contact and face the speaker. Show you're listening with small encouragers like nodding or saying "mm-hmm." Importantly, listen to understand, not just to reply – resist the urge to plan your response while the other person is still speaking (firsttee.org). Being mentally present and attentive signals respect.

- **Provide Feedback and Paraphrase:** An active listener often paraphrases or summarizes what the other person said to confirm understanding. For example, *"So you're saying that working from home has improved your work-life balance?"* Such feedback – an acknowledgment plus a recap of their point – shows you're absorbing their words and allows them to clarify if needed (ncbi.nlm.nih.gov). Ask clarifying questions if appropriate (*"When you say _____, what do you mean?"*). These behaviors demonstrate that you genuinely care about what they're saying.

- **Benefits of Active Listening:** People respond very positively to good listeners. Studies show that individuals who practice active listening are perceived as more competent, likable, and trustworthy by others(plp.psu.edu). In fact, one experiment found that conversations with an active listener lead to greater satisfaction and social connection compared to talking with someone who only gives token acknowledgments (hackspirit.com). In other words, being an attentive listener makes people enjoy the interaction more and want to continue it. By actively listening, you create a safe, engaging space for the other person to express themselves – which naturally keeps the conversation flowing.

Asking Open-Ended Questions

Questions are the fuel of a lasting conversation, especially open-ended questions. Unlike closed questions that elicit a yes/no or one-word answer, open-ended questions invite the person to elaborate and share more about their thoughts or experiences. They keep the dialogue moving and signal your interest in the other person.

- **Use "What/How/Why" Questions:** Communication experts recommend starting questions with *who, what, when, where, why,* or *how* (mindfulpresenter.com). For example, instead of asking, "*Did you enjoy the presentation?*" (which could be answered with a simple *"Yeah."*), ask "*What did you think of the presentation?*" or "*How did you find the talk?*". This subtle shift encourages a more detailed response (verywellmind.com). Similarly, questions like "*What do you do in your free time?*" or "*How was your trip to ____?*" open the door for the person to tell a story or share feelings, rather than shutting down the topic quickly.

- **Encourage Storytelling and Details:** The best open-ended questions prompt someone to reflect or tell a story. For instance, "*What was the highlight of your week?*" or "*How did you get interested in [hobby/field]?*" are invitations for a longer answer (verywellmind.com). Follow up on their responses with natural prompts: if they mention they went hiking, you might ask "*Oh, how was the hike?*" or "*What trails do you like around here?*". Following up shows you're paying attention and care to hear more.

- **Research: Questions Boost Likeability:** Science backs up the power of asking questions. A series of Harvard studies found that people who ask more questions – particularly follow-up questions that dig deeper – are considered more likable by their conversation partners(psychologicalscience.org). The reason is simple: asking questions (rather than just talking about yourself) shows responsiveness and interest in the other person. In contrast, dominating the talk or constantly steering it back to yourself tends to decrease how much others like the interaction. So, to keep a conversation engaging, focus on the other person through curious questioning. Not only will you learn more about them, but they'll subconsciously appreciate your attentiveness. It's a win-win for conversational chemistry.

Managing Awkward Silences

Every conversation has lulls. That moment when the dialogue hits a pause and you suddenly panic that it's *"awkward."* First, know that these moments are natural – they happen to everyone more often than you'd think(verywellmind.com). Instead of fearing silence, have a plan to navigate it gracefully:

- **Stay Calm and Don't Assume the Worst:** A brief silence doesn't mean the conversation is failing. People often need a second to process thoughts or the last point made. If a pause stretches a bit, avoid showing anxiety (e.g. don't fidget nervously or blurt out something irrelevant purely to fill air). Keep a relaxed demeanor – a confident smile or a small comment like "*Hmm, interesting...*" can bridge the gap while you both gather your thoughts. Remember, even a 4-second pause can subjectively *feel* long and stir discomfort (healthland.time.com), but acknowledging it calmly or just waiting an extra moment can prevent it from feeling too awkward.

- **Have "Back Pocket" Topics or Questions:** A great strategy (endorsed by conversation researchers) is to switch to a new topic when a discussion runs dry (verywellmind.com). If you sense the other person's interest fading or answers shortening, pivot to something else. It helps to keep a few conversation kickstarter ideas in mind ahead of time – e.g. ask about another aspect of their life or bring up a current event or a mutual interest. For example: "*By the way, I remember you mentioned you like cooking – have you tried any new recipes lately?*". Such a pivot can revive the dialogue before the silence grows too long.

- **Acknowledge or Use Humor (if appropriate):** If silence does drag out and feels awkward, sometimes a light touch can defuse the tension. A gentle, good-natured remark like "*Looks like we both just forgot what we were going to say!*" with a smile can reset the mood. Humor can break the ice of a silence – even a simple shared laugh about the lull itself can reconnect you (verywellmind.com). Alternatively, give a sincere compliment or observation to restart things on a positive note. For instance, "*I was just noticing – that's a great shirt, by the way. Where did you get it?*" This shifts focus and invites the person to talk again, now about a pleasant topic.

- **Embrace Pauses in Deep Conversation:** Note that not all silence is bad. In deeper, meaningful conversations, a pause can indicate that someone is thinking or feeling something strongly. In those cases, show empathy (see below) and patience rather than rushing to fill the void. A moment of quiet reflection can actually signal a comfortable rapport if both people understand it's just a breather. Use your intuition: if the silence comes after a heavy or thoughtful topic, a soft "*I'm here with you,*" or a reassuring nod can be better than quickly changing the subject.

Showing Empathy

Empathy is the heart of connecting in conversation. Showing empathy means actively demonstrating that you understand and care about the other person's feelings and perspective. When people feel understood, they are more likely to open up and continue the conversation on a deeper level. Here's how to infuse empathy into your interactions:

- **Validate Feelings and Perspectives:** When someone shares something personal, whether it's excitement about a success or frustration over a problem, acknowledge it. Empathetic communication involves listening, comprehending, and *validating* what the other person is expressing (lissyabrahams.com). Simple phrases can go a long way: *"That sounds really challenging," "I can see why you're happy about that,"* or *"I'd feel the same way in your situation."* This lets them know you truly hear them. Being fully present and responding to the emotions behind the words (with no judgment) will make the speaker feel valued.

- **Use Empathic Statements and Questions:** Encourage the person to share more about their feelings. For example, "*How did that make you feel?*" or "*What was that experience like for you?*". When they answer, mirror back some of what you heard: "*It sounds like you were really overwhelmed by that deadline,*" or "*You must have been thrilled to get that news!*". Such responses show you are trying to put yourself in their shoes. Avoid immediately giving unsolicited advice unless they ask, often, offering empathy ("*I get why that upset you*") is more helpful than problem-solving right away (lissyabrahams.com).

- **Avoid Centering Yourself ("Don't Equate Your Experience with Theirs"):** A common pitfall is responding to someone's story by launching into *your* similar story. For example, if they mention losing a loved one, and you reply, "*I know, when **my** uncle died...*" – this can unintentionally shift focus away from them. Conversation expert Celeste Headlee puts it bluntly: "Don't equate your experience with theirs... It is not about you." (

mindfulpresenter.com) Every person's experience is unique, so even if you've been through something similar, keep the focus on their story right now. You can briefly acknowledge "*I went through something similar,*" to show you relate, but then return to asking about their feelings instead of detailing yours. By resisting the urge to one-up or shift the attention, you demonstrate genuine empathy and keep the other person feeling heard.

- **Benefits of Empathy in Conversation:** Empathic listening and responses build a foundation of trust and comfort. Psychologists note that empathy in communication fosters greater understanding, trust, and respect between people (lissyabrahams.com). In fact, without empathy, conversations can become one-sided and less fulfilling. By showing you care about what someone else is going through, you invite a stronger connection. They'll appreciate your compassion and likely feel closer to you, making the conversation more meaningful and memorable for both sides.

Using Positive Body Language

Communication isn't just about words, body language and nonverbal cues play a huge role in keeping a conversation engaging. Studies have famously estimated that more than half of face-to-face communication is conveyed through tone and body language rather than the literal words (online.utpb.edu). Being mindful of your nonverbal signals (and reading the other person's) can greatly enhance conversational rapport:

- **Maintain an Open and Engaged Posture:** How you physically present yourself sends a message. Face the person and keep your posture open, uncross your arms and relax your stance. An open torso with arms relaxed at your sides (or gently gesturing) conveys friendliness and openness (verywellmind.com). Lean in slightly or sit up to show attentiveness. Avoid slouching or turning your body away, as that can signal boredom or discomfort.

- **Use Eye Contact and Facial Expressions:** Eye contact is one of the clearest indicators of interest. Aim to hold eye contact regularly when the other person is speaking, it shows you're listening. You don't need to stare unblinkingly (that can be intimidating); just meet their eyes naturally, and nod or smile to acknowledge key points (verywellmind.com). A genuine smile and warm expressions will put the other person at ease. On the flip side, constantly looking around the room or at your phone will make them feel you'd rather be elsewhere. Keep your face approachable: nod in agreement, laugh or smile when appropriate, and mirror their emotions to an extent (if they look concerned about a topic, a sympathetic look from you reinforces that you understand).

- **Mind Your Tone and Gestures:** Your tone of voice and gestures are part of body language too. Speak in a conversational, friendly tone, not too monotone (which shows disinterest) and not overly loud or aggressive. Use hand gestures naturally to emphasize points, but don't overdo it. Subtle mirroring can also build connection: people tend to subconsciously synchronize with those they like. If your conversation partner leans forward or uses a lot of hand expressions, you can mirror these cues in a subtle way to create a sense of harmony (just be sure it's not obvious mimicry). Encouraging nonverbal signals include things like timely head nods, a forward lean to show curiosity, or even small "uh-huh" sounds, these tell the speaker you're engaged without interrupting them (ncbi.nlm.nih.govverywellmind.com).

- **Avoid Negative Signals:** Be aware of habits that send the wrong message. Eye-rolling, sighing, checking your watch, or crossing your arms tightly can all make you seem uninterested, annoyed, or closed-off. Even if you're simply anxious or pondering something, such signals might be misread. For example, frowning or distracted glances can make your partner feel you're bored or judging them (verywellmind.com). By staying conscious of your body language, you can adjust these little things, relax your forehead if you tend to furrow your brow, keep your hands visible (not hidden in pockets) to appear more open, and periodically give a friendly nod or "mm-hmm" to show you're still tuned in.

Remember, *what you don't say can be just as important as what you do say* in a conversation (verywellmind.com). Positive body language reinforces your words and listening efforts, creating a comfortable atmosphere for dialogue. It also helps you notice how the other person is feeling; for instance, if they start backing away or glancing around, it might be a cue to wrap up or change topics. Staying aware of nonverbal cues on both sides makes for a more attuned, dynamic exchange.

Conclusion

Mastering conversation skills is a combination of effective techniques and genuine human connection. To recap, start conversations on friendly, positive footing, then keep them alive by listening actively, asking thoughtful open-ended questions, and navigating lulls or silences with grace. Always show empathy for the other person's feelings and maintain open, engaged body language to reinforce your interest. These strategies are supported by communication experts and psychological research, from studies on how question-asking boosts likability to evidence that active listening and empathy deepen social bonds. By practicing these skills, you'll not only keep conversations going, but also make them more enjoyable and meaningful for everyone involved. Good conversation is a skill, and like any skill, it improves with mindful practice. Start with a smile, be curious about others, listen with intent, and you'll find that even interactions with new acquaintances can turn into rewarding, lasting dialogues (verywellmind.com).

Summary

The rise of online dating has reshaped human connection, emphasizing visuals, quick judgments, and curated personas. While dating apps offer convenience, safety through vetting, and greater control, they also introduce emotional risks, like disconnection, burnout, and dopamine-driven addiction.

Key themes include:

- Safety & Control: Users often research potential matches to feel secure, but this can lead to assumptions and filtered expectations.

- Dopamine & Swipe Culture: Apps are designed to exploit anticipation and reward cycles, creating addictive behaviors tied to validation.

- Monetization & Exploitation: The dating app industry, worth billions, is structured to maximize user engagement, even at the cost of genuine connection.

- Cybersecurity Threats: Data breaches and catfishing are real dangers, with stolen photos and bot-driven interactions posing risks to privacy.

- Emotional Harm & Discrimination: The swipe economy fosters superficiality, digital peacocking, ghosting, and discrimination based on appearance, weight, or race.

- Case Study (Cassie): A polyamorous user burned out by dating apps finds healing through intentional offline connections and self-reflection.

- Neuroscience: Swipe culture activates a dopamine feedback loop that makes users crave engagement more than actual connection.

- Conversation Toolkit: Effective dating and relationships require conversation skills, such as active listening, asking open-ended questions, managing silences, showing empathy, and using positive body language.

Conclusion:
In a world of fast-paced digital romance, real connection requires slowing down, setting boundaries, and mastering the art of mindful communication.

Chapter Sixteen

"Sexuality is one of the ways that we become enlightened, actually, because it leads us to self-knowledge." -Alice Walker

Sex and Sexuality in the Digital Age

We now have access to more media content than any generation before us, more than we could consume in multiple lifetimes. One area where this access has profoundly impacted us is in our interaction with sexually explicit material.

With the rise of tablets, smartphones, and always-connected browsing, even children can now access sexually explicit content with surprising ease. While parental controls exist on many devices, countless children still find ways around them. The creativity and determination behind these workarounds are, frankly, impressive, though troubling in context.

The age at which children begin interacting with screens, and potentially sexually explicit material, has also dramatically changed. As Reid et al. (2016) note:

> *"The evolution of media from traditional to newer forms of digital media in the past decade has resulted in changes in the patterns of media use. For example, in 1970, children began to regularly watch TV at 4 years of age, whereas today, children begin interacting with digital media at 4 months of age."*

In terms of adult access, online pornography is widely used and increasingly normalized. The global scale of consumption is staggering. According to Masaeli and Farhadi (2021):

> *"Online pornography use has become prevalent globally. Over 42 billion adults visited the Pornhub website in 2019, averaging 115 million visits daily. Pornography use is widespread in adults; nearly 70 to 90% of adults have watched pornography in their lifetime. Pornography use is not problematic for most people and does not have negative impacts on their life. Though for others, it may be highly problematic and may lead to negative consequences, such as sexual problems. In quarantine time and social-distancing mandates and other COVID-19-related events, Pornhub has noted an international rise in pornography use of 11.6% on March 17, 2020."*

While for many adults, pornography use does not appear to have significant negative effects, others experience problematic use that can lead to

Pornography Use and Adolescents in a Digitally Saturated World

During the COVID-19 pandemic, adolescents were largely attending school through video conferencing platforms. Given the flexibility of turning off cameras and the constant presence of smartphones, many assumed that teens may have turned to pornography more frequently. It's a reasonable assumption, especially in light of a meta-analysis of 25 studies, which found that 69% of adolescents reported inattentiveness during remote schooling (Viner et al., 2022).

However, a 2022 longitudinal study of 1,771 adolescents provided an unexpected insight:

> *"Adolescents' pornography use characteristics were rather stable between November 2019 and June 2021, and the COVID-19 pandemic and related lockdowns might not have led to general increases in adolescents' pornography use as expected."* (Bothe et al., 2022)

While television viewing has decreased over the past two decades, children's media consumption has evolved into shorter, often more provocative content delivered via social media and streaming platforms (Shabbir et al.). Many of these messages are sexually explicit or emotionally arousing, and given the brain's dopaminergic reward system, this content can become highly reinforcing.

The accessibility of smartphones makes sexually explicit content readily available to users of nearly any age. With just a few taps, individuals can access endless streams of adult content, creating the potential for problematic or compulsive behaviors to develop over time. Some researchers have posited that this ease of access may form neurological associations that reinforce these behaviors, contributing to addiction or dysregulation in certain individuals.

The Neuroscience of Pornography and Addiction

Mina Sherif Soliman Georgy of the Department of Neuropsychiatry at Ain Shams University in Egypt stated:

> *"Many scientists postulate that several behavioral patterns may potentially affect the reward circuits in the human brain, leading to a loss of control and other symptoms of addiction in some individuals at least. Yet, despite the growing acceptance of the existence of these behavioral addictions, based on the increased understanding of the function of the mesolimbic dopaminergic reward systems, there has been a reluctance to label pornography*

as potentially addictive. Regarding pornography, the current neuroscientific research supports the assumption that the responsible neural processes are similar to drug addictions and other non-drug addictions receiving greater attention, such as pathological gambling and gaming. The current evidence increasingly supports the description of pornography as an addiction." (Georgy, 2019)

This becomes even more concerning when combined with the wide availability of free, unregulated content that lacks age-verification barriers. For young individuals, this creates a perfect storm, an open invitation to engage in ever-increasing dopamine-fueled cycles of reward-seeking behavior.

Pornography Use and Adolescents in a Digitally Saturated World

During the COVID-19 pandemic, adolescents were largely attending school through video conferencing platforms. Given the flexibility of turning off cameras and the constant presence of smartphones, many assumed that teens may have turned to pornography more frequently—especially considering Pornhur ported an 11.6% international spike in use on March 17, 2020 (Masaeli & Farhadi, 2021).

"Adolescents' pornography use characteristics were rather stable between November 2019 and June 2021, and the COVID-19 pandemic and related lockdowns might not have led to general increases in adolescents' pornography use as expected " (Bothe et al., 2022)

While television viewing has decreased, children's media consumption has evolved into shorter, often more provocative content delivered via social media and streaming platforms (Shabbir et al.).

The accessibility of smartphones makes sexually explicit content readily available to users of nearly any age. Some researchers have posited that this ease of access may form neurological associations over time.

However, this issue isn't limited to youth. Adults of all ages can struggle with problematic relationships around pornography or sex. A meta-analysis examining pornography use since 1999 revealed an interesting generational trend. It showed a notable increase in use among younger women:

"Women aged 18 to 26 became three times as likely to consume pornography than women aged 45 to 53, whereas previously, the

> *younger group was only twice as likely to do so."* (De Alarcón, et al. 2019)

That isn't to say that increased exposure automatically leads to misuse. It's important to avoid oversimplifying such a nuanced topic. I also want to be clear that this book isn't aiming to deeply explore the complex and multifaceted relationship between pornography and individuals. That subject deserves its own careful, comprehensive treatment.

However, the rise in accessibility and ease of exposure to sexually explicit content, especially through screens, makes it necessary to discuss how this intersects with human behavior. One area where this relationship becomes particularly relevant is in the potential connection between early exposure to sexualized media and the onset of sexual behaviors.

The Link Between Pornography Exposure and Early Sexual Behavior

A longitudinal study from the Taiwan Youth Project, initiated in 2000, found compelling evidence:

> *"About 50% of participants had been exposed to sexual media content by 8th grade, from an average of one modality. Sexually explicit media exposure predicted early sexual debut, unsafe sex, and multiple sexual partners. Furthermore, exposure to more media modalities increased the likelihood of risky sexual behaviors. However, the only effect on early sexual debut was gender invariant. Exposure to sexually explicit media in early adolescence had a substantive relationship with risky sexual behavior in emerging adulthood."* (Lin et al., 2020)

This finding suggests that adolescents who consume a sexually explicit visual diet early in life may be more likely to engage in earlier sexual activity, have more sexual partners, or participate in other risky sexual behaviors, regardless of gender. It highlights how powerful our visual environments can be in shaping behavior, especially during key developmental windows.

The Power of Sex Education

The relationship between comprehensive sexual education and active engagement from parents or guardians plays a crucial role in helping children make sense of the changes happening within their bodies. These conversations and educational frameworks can be powerful tools to mitigate some of the risks associated with early exposure to sexual content.

> *"Substantial evidence supports sex education beginning in elementary school, that is scaffolded and of longer duration, as well as LGBTQ–inclusive education across the school curriculum and a*

social justice approach to healthy sexuality."
— *Goldfarb et al., 2021*

A meta-analysis of 218 studies conducted over the past three decades strongly supports comprehensive sex education across a wide range of topics and grade levels. The research emphasizes the importance of approaches that go beyond basic biological explanations and instead promotes a positive, affirming, and inclusive view of human sexuality.

The findings clearly show that when sex education begins early and is developmentally appropriate, it has the potential to combat a growing public health concern. This includes integrating education on homophobia, transphobia, social-emotional learning, social justice pedagogy, and sexuality as a natural and normal part of the human experience, rather than pathologizing it.

In essence, these approaches not only foster healthier sexual development, but also create safer, more inclusive environments for all students to learn and grow.

Many readers may recognize the inherent challenges of implementing such a broad and inclusive approach to sex education, especially in the United States, where access to these conversations is often limited by cultural, religious, or political beliefs. For example, individuals from value systems that prefer to shield children from discussions of sex and sexuality (such as certain Judeo-Christian communities) may choose to keep these conversations strictly within the home. However, even when that intention exists, those conversations are often delayed, infrequent, or not happening at all.

The Disparities in Pornography Consumption Among BIPOC Youth

Meanwhile, the reality is clear: many children are learning about sex on their own, through screens, social media, and often via unfiltered, unrealistic, or harmful portrayals. If we want to get ahead of the fast-food visual diet of sexualized content, we must provide children with alternative frameworks. These frameworks should emphasize healthy communication, respect, consent, and realistic expectations in relationships and sexual experiences. Without that, youth may continue to adopt distorted views of sex and intimacy, mimicking what they see on screen, often including risky or non-consensual behaviors that are portrayed as normal or desirable.

This public health need becomes even more urgent when considering the disparities in how youth from different racial backgrounds engage with sexually explicit content. A longitudinal study of over 1,000 youth in the Southeastern U.S. revealed that:

> *"Black youth were disproportionately more likely to have used any pornography in the past year compared to White youth."*
> — Brown & L'Engle, 2009

Further data from the General Social Survey supports this, showing that non-White adults are more likely to consume pornography than White adults, and that this gap has widened over time (Rothman et al., 2015).

> *"A longitudinal study of 1,017 youth from the Southeastern U.S. found that Black youth were disproportionately more likely to have used any pornography in the past year compared to White youth. Similarly, among adults aged 18 years and older, analyses of the General Social Survey (GSS) have found that non-Whites are more likely to consume pornography than Whites, and this difference in consumption has widened over time."*

These disparities raise questions about access to comprehensive education, systemic inequality, and the influence of media representation on identity formation and sexual behavior, particularly for BIPOC youth, who may already be navigating a landscape shaped by hypersexualized or stereotyped depictions of their communities.

The Risks of Pornography as a Sexual Education Substitute

As previously discussed, the overconsumption of sexually explicit material, especially in the absence of comprehensive sex education, can create a distorted understanding of healthy, consensual sexual relationships. For many adolescents and young adults, pornography becomes their de facto guide for sex. Unfortunately, this often leads to harmful and unrealistic expectations around intimacy, pleasure, and communication.

Youth often report using pornography as an "instruction manual." In several studies:

- **Many admitted to imitating behaviors they saw**, either initiative on their own or at the request of a partner.

- **Negative outcomes were especially common for young women**, including:
    - Engaging in painful or uncomfortable sexual activities like anal sex, often under pressure.
    - Feeling they had to "perform" or fake enjoyment.
    - Experiencing emotional distress after mimicking scenes without fully understanding them or feeling prepared.

These findings align with research from Smith (2013), Trostle (2003), and Marston and Lewis (2014), which show how pervasive the influence of pornography can be in shaping expectations and behaviors around sex, particularly in situations where proper education or communication is absent.

When pornography becomes the primary source of information, consent, mutual respect, and bodily autonomy often take a back seat to performance and imitation. And that dissonance can be deeply harmful, especially for young women and other marginalized identities.

The Detriment of Modeling Sexual Behavior Through Porn

Relying on pornography or sexually explicit material as a model for sexual behavior can have harmful effects, especially for young people. One major concern is how these media presentations shape expectations around how individuals, particularly men, should act during sex, regardless of their sexual orientation or gender identity.

Research has shown that the majority of free online porn (around 55%) promotes hypermasculinity, male dominance, and prioritizes male sexual pleasure as the norm (Gorman et al., 2010). This sets a dangerous precedent for youth who may try to replicate what they see, often without understanding that these scenes are performative, unrealistic, and sometimes physically harmful.

Without healthy conversations about sex, consent, and boundaries, young people may internalize these scripts, believing that painful or uncomfortable acts, such as anal sex, are normal or expected. As Rothman et al. (2015) point out, the concern is twofold: not only do these portrayals skew understanding of healthy sexual relationships, but they also risk normalizing coercion and unrealistic expectations of pleasure.

The Influence of Life Satisfaction on SEIM Use

While children and teens are often the focus when discussing the effects of screen-based visual diets, adults are not immune, especially when it comes to sexually explicit internet material (SEIM).

Shared Patterns Across Ages
Research suggests that both adolescents and adults tend to engage with SEIM more frequently when experiencing lower life satisfaction.

Key Groups More Likely to Engage Are:

- Males
- Sensation seekers
- Individuals with non-heterosexual orientations

Why It Matters

SEIM use in itself is not inherently negative, but when it's tied to coping with dissatisfaction, it may reflect a deeper emotional or psychological need.

This makes understanding one's intent behind consumption important, is it for pleasure and exploration, or for avoidance and distraction?

Takeaway from Valkenburg (2011):

> *"The frequency of SEIM use and its antecedents are largely the same among adolescents and adults."*

Addressing the symptoms of problematic screen use isn't enough if the root causes continue to go unacknowledged. For some, sexually explicit internet content becomes a way to cope with deeper dissatisfaction or emotional pain. If that sounds familiar, if you find yourself turning to these materials to escape a low sense of self, you likely already know how fleeting that relief can be. Like in the previous chapter, I encourage you to take a step toward lasting change. Jump ahead to Chapter Twenty-Three, where we begin the work of rebuilding your inner foundation and developing a healthier relationship with yourself

Summary

- The widespread availability of sexually explicit content through digital media has made it easier for children and adolescents to access pornography, sometimes bypassing parental controls. Research indicates that early exposure to such content can influence sexual behaviors, potentially leading to risky sexual activities. However, studies during the COVID-19 pandemic showed no significant increase in adolescent pornography consumption.

- The neuroscience behind pornography use suggests it can trigger addictive behaviors similar to substance abuse. The ease of access, combined with the brain's dopamine-driven reward system, may lead to problematic use in both young individuals and adults. Women's consumption of pornography has also increased over time.

- Longitudinal studies highlight that exposure to sexually explicit media can lead to earlier sexual activity and riskier sexual behaviors.

- Disparities exist in media consumption among different racial groups, with Black youth being more likely than their white peers to engage with pornography. Many adolescents use pornography as a learning tool for sex, often leading to unrealistic expectations and discomfort, especially for young women.

- Concerns arise over how pornography portrays hypermasculinity, male dominance, and unrealistic sexual expectations. White supremacy is also prevalent in pornographic material. Both adolescents and adults tend to consume sexually explicit material when experiencing lower life satisfaction. Comprehensive sex education, starting early and encompassing a broad range of topics, to provide healthier perspectives on sexuality and counteract the unrealistic portrayals found in pornography, is ideal.

- Treating the underlying emotional and psychological factors driving excessive pornography use is essential for long-term well-being.

Chapter Seventeen

"All too often, when we see injustices, both great and small, we think, That's terrible, but we do nothing. We say nothing. We let other people fight their own battles. We remain silent because silence is easier... When we say nothing, when we do nothing, we are consenting to these trespasses against us." — Roxane Gay, *Bad Feminist*

How Racial Identities and Cultures Are Portrayed in Visual Stimuli

A deeply troubling element of visual media, one that strikes close to home, is the way BIPOC individuals are often portrayed in roles that reinforce harmful stereotypes. These portrayals not only shape how broader society views communities of color but also influence how individuals within those communities see themselves. The power imbalance between those creating content and those consuming it is glaring, particularly when BIPOC representation is filtered through a predominantly white lens.

Across television, streaming platforms, film, and other media, BIPOC characters are frequently relegated to supporting or background roles. When they do appear, they're often cast in ways that reflect overdramatized or caricatured versions of cultural identity, serving as comic relief, the "sassy best friend," the hyper-aggressive antagonist, or the emotionally muted secondary character. Rarely are they written as nuanced leads, and even less often do they drive the narrative or embody intellectual authority, emotional complexity, or leadership.

This issue has been well documented in academic research. For example:

- Dr. Marquita M. Gammage in *Media Racism: The Impact of Media Injustice on Black Women's Lives* (2023) discusses how mainstream media normalizes hypersexualized portrayals of Black women, perpetuates racist tropes, and limits access to authentic representation.

- Smith, et al. (2019), in the USC Annenberg Inclusion Initiative, analyzed over 1,200 films and found that people of color are vastly underrepresented both in front of and behind the camera.

- Bell Hooks (1992) in *Black Looks: Race and Representation* critiques how mainstream media shapes and distorts the portrayal of Black identity for the consumption of predominantly white audiences.

- Herman Gray in *Watching Race: Television and the Struggle for Blackness* (1995) highlights how media centers whiteness while framing Blackness as "other," limiting narrative agency.

Pause for a moment. Think of a show or movie that wasn't developed or produced by BIPOC creators, so, realistically, most mainstream content. Now consider how the non-white characters are portrayed. Are they integral to the story? Are they portrayed with depth and dignity? Do they hold power? Or are they confined to familiar, limiting tropes that reinforce systemic racial hierarchies?

To be clear, this criticism isn't directed at the actors taking on these roles. Visibility matters. And in an industry that is still overwhelmingly dominated by whiteness, finding work can be incredibly difficult, especially when roles for BIPOC actors are so limited and narrowly defined. The issue lies with the industry itself: a machine that continues to privilege white stories, white heroes, and white perspectives as central, while positioning everyone else as peripheral.

There is hope. A growing number of BIPOC creators have begun reclaiming their narratives. As Dr. Gammage notes, independent platforms like ARRAY (founded by Ava DuVernay), Harpo Productions (Oprah Winfrey), and Hoorae Media (Issa Rae) are elevating authentic Black stories and voices, providing spaces where creators of color can operate free from the constraints of white-dominated media gatekeeping.

Those questions about representation apply mostly to movies and TV shows, but when we broaden the lens to include other media sources such as news, YouTube creators, and sexually explicit content, the disparities become even more glaring. When you factor in political media, the inequity in visual representation becomes even more pronounced.

According to the U.S. Census Bureau (2022), non-Hispanic white individuals make up approximately 59% of the population. Yet, the representation of racial and ethnic minorities across visual media remains disproportionately low, especially when compared to their share of the population.

The University of Southern California's Annenberg School for Communication and Journalism has compiled extensive longitudinal data from 2007 to 2022 on representation in media. Their latest report, *Inclusion in the Director's Chair* (2023), analyzes 1,600 top-grossing films and includes nearly 70,000 speaking characters. It's the most rigorous and expansive analysis of media inclusion to date, tracking gender, race/ethnicity, LGBTQ+ identity, and disability representation.

To acknowledge the progress: there *have* been improvements in media representation over time. According to USC Annenberg's findings (2023):

- In 2022, 44% of leading or co-leading roles were filled by girls and women, marking a 16-year high.

- The percentage of Asian characters rose significantly, from 3.4% in 2007 to 15.9% in 2022.
- Most notably, 2022 saw a record number of women of color in leading roles. Nineteen films featured an underrepresented female lead, up from just one film in 2007.

These are promising shifts, but they still stand in contrast to the persistent systemic imbalance, especially in how BIPOC characters are written, portrayed, and placed within narratives often controlled by white-centric production teams.

The Ongoing Disparity in On-Screen Representation

Despite some progress, underrepresented communities continue to face systemic gaps in visibility and portrayal across popular media. This ongoing disparity impacts not only who is seen but how they are seen, reinforcing a visual diet that lacks balance and authenticity.

The comprehensive longitudinal analysis by the USC Annenberg Inclusion Initiative, revealed persistent underrepresentation of marginalized groups in speaking and leading roles:

> *"There was absolutely no change in the percentage of female-identified speaking characters. In 2022, this figure remained at 34.6%, only marginally higher than the 29.9% recorded in 2007. Furthermore, only 15% of the top 100 films in 2022 featured a gender-balanced cast, a number unchanged from 2007. Across all films studied in 2022, only one character was identified as gender non-binary"* (Smith, et al., 2023).

When examining race and ethnicity:

> *"In 2022, 31 of the top films featured an individual from an underrepresented racial/ethnic group in a lead or co-lead role. While this shows growth from 13 films in 2007, it falls short of the peak reached in 2021, when 37 films featured such leads. Although the proportion of white characters has gradually decreased over time, there were no statistically significant gains in overall speaking roles for characters from underrepresented racial or ethnic backgrounds"* (Smith et al., 2023).

These findings highlight that while diversity in film may have expanded in some headline statistics, such as an increase in Asian leads or female co-leads, overall systemic inclusion, especially for BIPOC and gender-diverse characters, remains stunted. Such a landscape contributes to a visual culture in which dominant narratives continue to sideline or misrepresent marginalized voices.

Underrepresentation of Women and Girls of Color in Top Films

Despite incremental improvements in on-screen diversity, women and girls from underrepresented racial and ethnic backgrounds remain largely invisible in mainstream media. A 2023 analysis by the USC Annenberg Inclusion Initiative found that across the 100 highest-grossing films of 2022, only 38.3% of all speaking characters were from underrepresented groups, falling short of the U.S. population benchmark of 41.1% (Smith, et al. 2023).

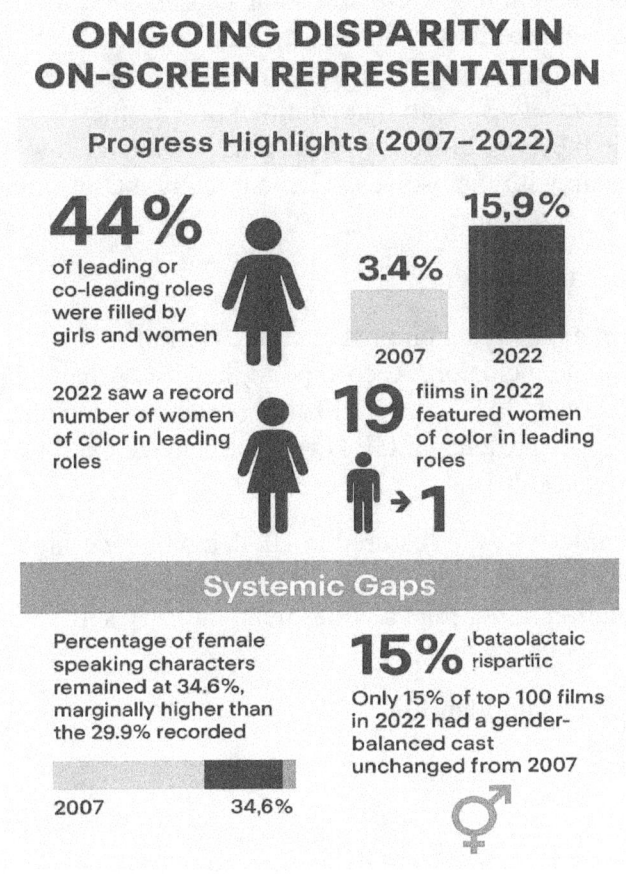

The representation of female-identified characters from specific racial and ethnic groups was particularly sparse:

- **0 films** featured an Indigenous American/Alaska Native girl or woman.

- **99 films** were missing Native Hawaiian/Pacific Islander girls/women.

- **95 films** did not include even one Middle Eastern/North African female-identified character.

- **70 films** lacked Multiracial or Multiethnic girls/women.

- **61 films** did not feature any Hispanic/Latina girls/women.

- **44 films** excluded Asian girls/women.

- **32 films** did not include Black/African American girls/women.

In stark contrast, only **7 films** lacked white girls or women entirely, underscoring the racial imbalance that continues to define Hollywood's visual culture. These disparities contribute to a narrow, often exclusionary media landscape, one that not only limits how young audiences see themselves reflected on screen but also shapes public perception about whose stories matter.

Case Study

Angie, an individual I have been working with for a while regarding their own developmental traumas stated, *"I get immersed in shows and feel fully what the characters are feeling."* We identified escapism as a major part of their life. Whether it was substances, dating, or content on their screens, their reward system just couldn't get enough. Unfortunately, the messages they were getting from the content they were absorbing caused a lot of emotional backlashes and it chipped away at the way they viewed themselves. After working on resolving some of their traumas, we shifted focus upon their view of themselves. With that continued focus, they shifted away from the hole they were filling with screens and attended to building a robust relationship with themselves. Content really matters and shapes our view of self.

LGBTQ+ Representation in Top Films

LGBTQ+ representation in mainstream cinema continues to fall significantly short of equitable inclusion. According to the USC Annenberg Inclusion Initiative (Smith, et al, 2023), only 2.1% of speaking characters in the top 100 films of 2022 identified as LGBTQ+, a percentage that has not meaningfully changed since 2014.

While five transgender characters were featured in 2022, a nine-year high, four of the five appeared in a single film, *Bros*, highlighting the concentration of representation rather than a widespread industry shift. Among the 87 total LGBTQ+ characters:

- **More than half** were male-identified
- **58.8% were white**

Furthermore:

- **72 films** did not include a single LGBTQ+ character
- **84 films** were completely missing LGBTQ+ girls or women

These findings underscore the persistent invisibility of LGBTQ+ identities in popular media, particularly for women, trans individuals, and people of color. As storytelling continues to shape cultural norms and public perception, the lack of meaningful and intersectional LGBTQ+ representation limits both visibility and validation for these communities.

Representation of Characters with Disabilities in Film

The USC Annenberg Inclusion Initiative (Smith, et al, 2023) also examined the representation of characters with disabilities in the top 100 films of 2022. The findings reveal that **only 1.9%** of all speaking characters were depicted with a disability. This marks **no meaningful progress** since 2015, when the figure was 2.4%.

Among those characters with disabilities:

- **82.7%** were portrayed with a **physical disability**
- **33.3%** had **communicative disabilities**
- **17.3%** were depicted with **cognitive disabilities**

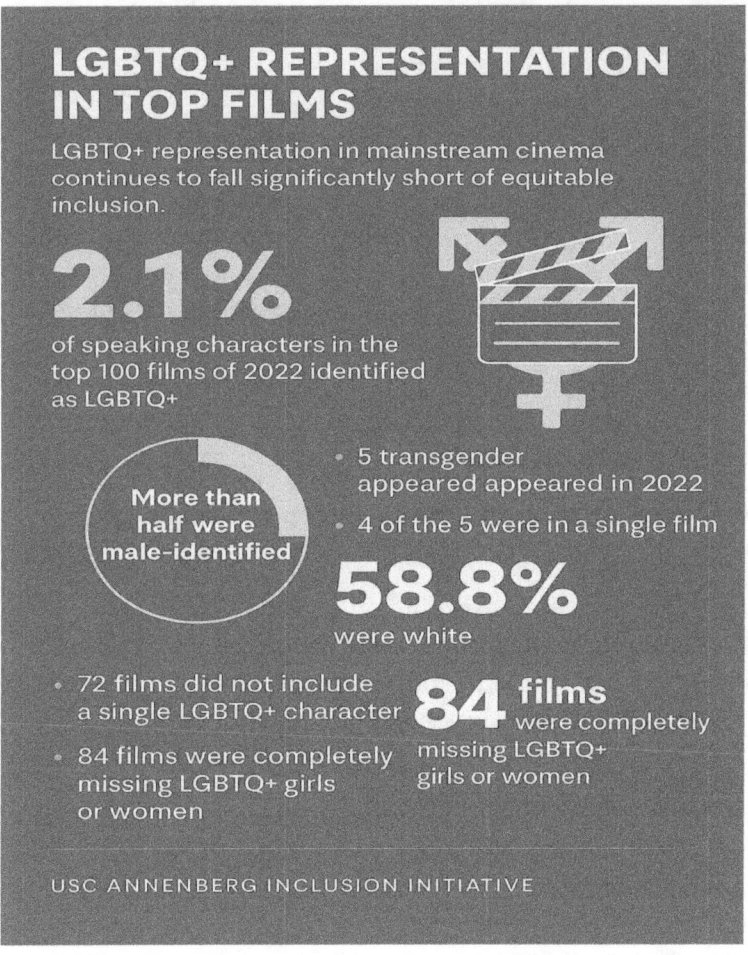

Despite the broad spectrum of real-world disability experiences, many remain invisible on screen:

- **54 films** featured **no characters with a disability**
- **76 films** included **no girls or women with disabilities**

Furthermore, the vast majority of characters with disabilities were male-identified (69.1%) and white (76%), reflecting a lack of intersectional inclusion across gender, race, and disability identity.

These statistics point to an ongoing marginalization of disabled communities in popular media, especially for women and people of color, perpetuating narrow narratives and reinforcing social exclusion.

Behind the Camera: Gender Disparities in Film Direction

In terms of representation behind the camera, the USC Annenberg Inclusion Initiative (2023) revealed persistent gender disparities in film direction. In 2022, only 8.8% of directors of top-grossing films were women, a figure that has not improved since 2021 (12.4%) and mirrors the percentage from 2008 (8%). While this reflects a modest increase from just 2.7% in 2007, it still highlights the glacial pace of progress.

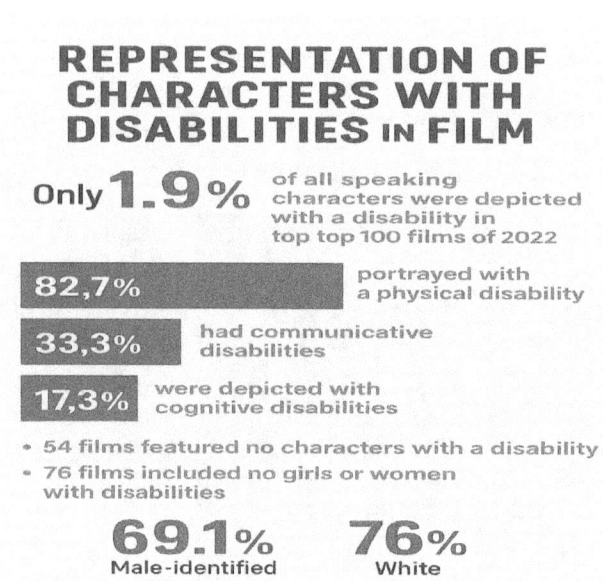

Over the last 16 years, a total of only 88 women have directed a top-grossing film, compared to 833 men. These numbers reflect a long-standing gender imbalance in one of the most powerful creative roles in the industry, reinforcing structural barriers that continue to limit the visibility and influence of women, particularly women of color, in mainstream filmmaking.

Behind-the-Scenes Representation in Film: Writers, Producers, and More

Among screenwriters, 16.3% of those working on top-grossing films in 2022 were women. This figure held steady compared to 2021 (16.8%) and reflects a modest increase from 11.2% in 2007. A similar pattern emerged among producers, with 26.8% being women in 2022, slightly up from 24.8% in 2021 and showing progress since 2007 (19.7%).

One notable area of improvement was in film composition. In 2022, 8.2% of composers on popular films were women, a 16-year high point, especially significant considering that no women composers were credited on top films in 2007.

Finally, when looking at casting directors, women made up a substantial 81.4% in 2022. This marks an increase from 70.4% in 2021, though still slightly lower than 86.1% in 2007.

These figures highlight incremental gains in some behind-the-scenes roles but also reveal areas where gender parity remains a distant goal.

Diversity Behind the Camera: Gender and Race/Ethnicity

When examining behind-the-scenes roles, the disparities in gender and race/ethnicity remain striking. In 2022, only 16.3% of top-grossing screenwriters were women, a number nearly identical to 2021 (16.8%) but a modest improvement from 2007 (11.2%). Similarly, 26.8% of producers were women, reflecting little change from the previous year (24.8%) but showing an increase from 2007 (19.7%).

From a racial and ethnic standpoint, the numbers reveal persistent underrepresentation. In 2022, 80.5% of directors were white. Among the remaining, 10.6% were Asian, 3.5% Black, 3.5% Multiracial/Multiethnic, and 1.8% Hispanic/Latino. Of all directors in 2022, only three were women of color, all of whom were Black women.

Looking at the broader 16-year sample of 1,600 films, just 5.2% of directors were Black men, 4.3% Asian men, and 3.7% Hispanic/Latino men. Alarmingly, only 1.6% of all directors were women of color, underscoring a critical need for structural change in who gets to tell stories and shape the narratives we consume.

Spelling out these figures from the seminal work of the USC Annenberg Inclusion Initiative is instrumental. This extensive longitudinal study is unique in its scope and rigor, and it paints a sobering picture of an industry that continues to fall short. The need for progress is not only about representation for its own sake, it's about enacting an approach that is moral, just, and fundamentally humanizing.

The persistent portrayal of underrepresented characters as afterthoughts, or worse, through stigmatized and stereotypical frameworks, causes real harm. These narratives shape how audiences, especially young people, see themselves and others. When media normalizes exclusion or misrepresentation, it reinforces systems of invisibility, bias, and cultural erasure.

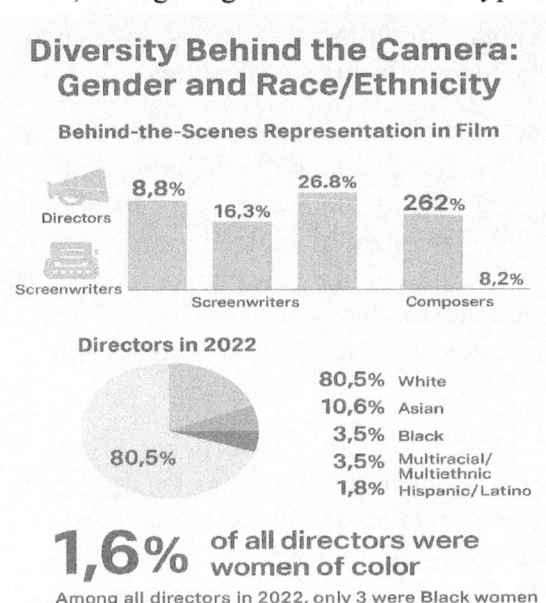

But beyond the moral imperative, there is also a clear economic argument. As the U.S. population continues to evolve into a richly multicultural society, failing to reflect this diversity risks cultural irrelevance and financial loss. According to the Center for American Progress (2015), the demographic landscape is shifting rapidly:

• By 2044, the majority of the U.S. population will be people of color. According to analyses of the Bureau of the Census projections, by 2044, the United States will have no clear racial or ethnic majority. According to new population projections, whites will make up 49.7 percent of the population, followed by Latinos at 25 percent, African Americans at 12.7 percent, and Asians at 7.9 percent. 3.7 percent of the population will identify as multiracial.

> • Several states' populations are already majority people of color, and many are well on their way. People of color currently constitute the majority of the populations in California, Texas, Hawaii, and New Mexico. People of color in another eight states, including Arizona, Florida, Georgia, Louisiana, Maryland, Mississippi, Nevada, New Jersey, and New York, make up more than 40 percent of the statewide populations.
>
> • The Latino and Asian populations are the fastest-growing populations in the United States. Between 2000 and 2010, the country's Asian population grew by 46 percent. During the same time period, the Latino population grew by 43 percent. By 2050, the Latino population is expected to exceed 100 million individuals, while the Asian population is expected to grow to approximately 42 million individuals.
>
> • The population of people who identify as multiracial will sharply increase. Those who identify as two or more races are expected to increase from 7.5 million to 26.7 million individuals between 2012 and 2060. The largest category of multiracial people is made up of 1.8 million individuals who identify as black and white.
>
> • People of color will grow in number and expand their share of the labor force. From 2010 to 2030, people of color will represent the largest share of workforce growth and will account for 120 percent of total net workforce growth. The share of total net growth in the Hispanic/Latino workforce is expected to be the highest of all racial and ethnic groups, reaching close to 78 percent. Asians and Pacific Islanders will account for 25 percent of total net workforce growth, and black folk will comprise 17 percent.

These demographic shifts make it clear: authentic, intersectional representation is not just an ethical responsibility, it's a social and economic imperative. Media that fails to reflect the lived realities of a changing nation will not only lose cultural relevance but will also miss out on the opportunity to connect with the audiences of the present and future.

BIPOC Individuals in Leadership Positions

Given the previously stated demographics, that non-white individuals make up at least 40% of the U.S. population, it is telling that representation in positions of power still falls far short. While Congress has gradually become more diverse since the 107th Congress (2001), BIPOC individuals only made up about 25% of members in the 119th Congress (2025) (Buchholz, 2023). This underrepresentation persists despite demographic shifts that continue to reshape the nation's identity.

Gender disparities remain equally striking. According to U.S. Census data (2025), individuals who identify as female now comprise approximately 50.5% of the national population. Yet, in the 119th Congress, only 28% of members identify as women (Pew Research Center, 2025). This gap between population reality and political power reinforces longstanding structural inequities and sends a damaging visual message to citizens, especially young people, about who is "meant" to lead.

While it's encouraging that the presence of women in government is growing, the representational gap for BIPOC individuals is increasing more slowly. This lag in equitable leadership can have serious consequences, not only in terms of policy outcomes, but in civic engagement. Visual representation matters. When voters rarely see people who look like them in power, whether in government or corporate leadership, they may feel disconnected from the systems meant to serve them.

This contributes, in part, to persistent gaps in voter participation. According to data from the Elect Project (2024), about 63.9% of eligible U.S. citizens voted in the 2024 general election. Among BIPOC populations, turnout rates hovered between 50% and 60%, depending on the group. These figures highlight an ongoing challenge: representation and participation are deeply intertwined. A system that fails to visibly and meaningfully include BIPOC voices risks further disengagement and eroded trust.

Voter Suppression

Although voter turnout has increased in recent elections, it remains far from where it could, and should, be. One of the more disturbing patterns emerging from the 2016, 2020, and 2024 U.S. presidential elections was the prevalence of misinformation and disinformation, particularly across social media platforms. These platforms became fertile ground for targeted ads and manipulative messaging, often delivering a distorted "visual diet" that obscured reality and discouraged civic engagement.

This misinformation disproportionately affected Black and Brown communities, with countless digital messages aimed at suppressing turnout, fostering distrust, or stoking confusion around voting procedures and political participation. The outcome was not only a warped public narrative, but a deliberate erosion of the political agency of communities already marginalized in mainstream visual and political culture.

As scholars Epperly et al. (2020) note:

> *"Although restricting formal voting rights, voter suppression, is not uncommon in democracies, its incidence and form vary widely. Intuitively, when competing elites believe that the benefits of reducing voting by opponents outweigh the costs of voter suppression, it is more likely to occur. Internal political and state capacity and external actors, however, influence the form voter suppression takes. When elites competing for office lack the ability to enact laws restricting voting due to limited internal capacity, or external actors are able to limit the ability of governments to use laws to suppress voting, suppression is likely to be ad hoc, decentralized, and potentially violent."*

In this context, suppression doesn't always appear in overt legal restrictions, it can take the form of algorithmic bias, information warfare, and media manipulation. These tactics compound the problem of underrepresentation in leadership by ensuring that fewer voices make it to the ballot box in the first place.

The historical implications of voter suppression cannot be ignored. They are deeply rooted in the legacy of Jim Crow laws, which codified the subjugation of Black Americans and relegated them to a subordinate status through segregated services, disenfranchisement, and systemic inequity. The doctrine of "separate but equal" led to a reality of separate and deeply unequal treatment, the consequences of which are still felt today.

As Harris-Combs (2016) notes:

> *"During the Jim Crow era, Blacks were expected to 'stay in their place', and that place was always subservient to the position of whites. Despite advances by racial/ethnic minorities and other disadvantaged groups, vestiges of this American Jim Crow belief system still operate in society."*

This historical continuity of exclusion, whether through law, policy, or media narrative, reinforces structural barriers to full democratic participation. While the mechanisms have evolved, the underlying intent remains familiar: to curtail access to power and visibility for historically marginalized groups.

Many marginalized groups remain particularly susceptible to voter suppression tactics. Methods such as gerrymandering (manipulating district boundaries to favor the majority), voter ID laws, reducing polling locations, and restricting assistance to voters waiting in long lines disproportionately affect communities of color. These tactics limit not only access to the ballot but also contribute to the erosion of public trust in democratic institutions.

College students are also increasingly vulnerable to these efforts. As D'Ercole (2021) outlines:

> *"There are three reasons why college students specifically are vulnerable to voter suppression efforts. First, a significant portion of college students move to a new district in the fall immediately preceding an election, making it confusing to determine where to register to vote and what forms of identification they may need to cast a ballot. Second, the geographic clustering of college students makes them fairly easy targets for vote dilution and suppression tactics, such as gerrymandering and restrictions on poll place locations. And lastly, state legislators and local officials prey on college students' unfamiliarity as first-time voters to intimidate or confuse them."*

This multifaceted landscape of suppression, rooted in history, perpetuated by policy, and amplified by digital technologies, continues to shape who gets to participate meaningfully in democracy.

Adding another layer to this vulnerability is the inherent relationship between college students and screen use, particularly their reliance on social media. This makes them especially susceptible to the very misinformation tactics that dominated the digital space in the 2016 and 2020 elections. As Allcott and Gentzkow (2017) explain:

> *"Gallup polls reveal a continuing decline of 'trust and confidence' in the mass media 'when it comes to reporting the news fully, accurately, and fairly.' This decline is more marked among Republicans than Democrats, and there is a particularly sharp drop among Republicans in 2016. The declining trust in mainstream media could be both a cause and a consequence of fake news gaining more traction."*

This erosion of trust in traditional media, combined with high engagement on social platforms where misinformation spreads quickly and virally, compounds the disempowerment of younger voters. Social media becomes both a battleground and a barrier, where false narratives can easily outpace the truth, and where disengagement becomes more likely in the absence of trusted sources.

This multifaceted landscape of suppression, rooted in history, perpetuated by policy, and amplified by digital technologies, continues to shape who gets to participate meaningfully in democracy.

During the 2020 election in particular, the role of bots and conspiracy narratives became increasingly pronounced. Ferrara et al. (2020) found that:

"Non-conspiratory users, those unlikely to share the conspiratory narratives, are distributed more equally across the political spectrum. Bots play an important role in spreading these conspiracies targeting content from hyper-partisan news media outlets. Nearly 13 percent of users engaging with conspiracies are bots, as opposed to just five percent bots engaging with non-conspiracy content. On the one hand, this is good news: not all the popularity of political conspiracies is genuine; on the other hand, since bots can inflate narratives and bring organic attention to unsuspecting users, the high prevalence of bots in conspiracy narratives is a problem that requires urgent attention."

This finding underscores the urgency of addressing both the technological and psychological components of misinformation. The blend of automated amplification, partisan media ecosystems, and emotionally charged content makes social media a uniquely volatile space for election integrity.

This multifaceted landscape of suppression, rooted in history, perpetuated by policy, and amplified by digital technologies, continues to shape who gets to participate meaningfully in democracy.

Academia and the Future of Representation

Visual diets continue to shift against Black and Brown individuals, most recently evidenced by the Supreme Court's 2023 decision to end race-conscious college admissions (NPR, 2023). Given the already substantial hurdles Black and Brown communities face in accessing higher education, this rollback threatens to reverse decades of progress, not only in academia, but across business, government, and other sectors where higher education often serves as a pipeline to power.

This legal shift risks compounding existing disparities by reducing the presence of underrepresented voices in spaces where influence is cultivated and exercised. A lack of diversity in the classroom often precedes a lack of diversity in the boardroom, in Congress, in courtrooms, and in media.

Fortunately, change can still be enacted at the community level. While national policies may retreat from equity-driven frameworks, individuals and institutions can continue to prioritize inclusion, mentorship, and accessibility in their immediate spheres of influence. The erosion of legal tools does not absolve the responsibility of building equitable systems, it simply makes that work more urgent.

Researcher Ijoma et al. (2021) identifies many factors that contribute to the continued hurdles for BIPOC students in STEM fields, exacerbated by a poor visual diet both in education and in professional settings:

> *"Racial, ethnic, and gender representation in an academic setting means that teachers, professors, and other leaders reflect the demographics of the student body in the educational and professional spaces that they serve. This form of representation, which is often intersectional, strengthens communities and improves student outcomes, from as early as primary and secondary education, through to college education and beyond. Representation matters because it can shape the reputation and self-image of women and Black, Indigenous, and People of Color (BIPOC) within environments dominated by over-represented majorities. From the perspective of BIPOC women trainees, the lack of BIPOC faculty who are visible minorities, particularly at the most senior level positions, often conjures questions of whether academia is a realistic career path for aspiring minority students.... The percentage of Black academics dwindles as one moves further up the academic hierarchy of science, technology, engineering, and mathematics (STEM) education and respective careers. Data shows that in the U.S.; representation of underrepresented minorities decreases at each degree level for STEM when compared to White and Asian students.... Black students, who are already burdened with the mental and physical fatigue associated with summoning the endurance to fight through oppressive academic systems, are often not given a compass to use in their academic journeys. Black trainees are rarely provided the opportunity to receive the mentorship they need that offers them perspective on what they should do to be successful as Black students in STEM. This is perpetuated in some areas of low socioeconomic status where institutions do not have adequate funding to support extracurricular programming that would connect Black students interested in STEM to professionals in the fields they are dreaming about pursuing."*

Fortunately, change can still be enacted at the community level. While national policies may retreat from equity-driven frameworks, individuals and institutions can continue to prioritize inclusion, mentorship, and accessibility in their immediate spheres of influence. The erosion of legal tools does not absolve the responsibility of building equitable systems; it simply makes that work more urgent.

Having a sterilized environment devoid of diversity prevents individuals from hearing and experiencing different cultural attitudes or experiences that are integral to a global community. Allowing children to think beyond their usual perspectives strengthens cognitive flexibility and disabuses them with cultural myopia. A richer and more inclusive learning environment helps build empathy and understanding, which has real-world implications. In white-dominated educational spaces, BIPOC students may internalize racism, even toward their own identities, and spend years unlearning the biases embedded in these environments. Originating from the suburbs of Ohio, I can fully attest to that. Working with others from similar backgrounds, this is an all-too-common part of the BIPOC experience in predominantly white institutions. Diverse visual and social environments are not only beneficial, but they are also essential.

Generational Shifts and the Promise of Diversity

Fortunately, Generation Z (Zoomers) and Generation Alpha (2010–2024) may help shift the visual diet and policy landscape in a more inclusive direction. According to a Pew Research Center report (2018), nearly half of Generation Z individuals are racial or ethnic minorities. Generation Alpha is projected to be even more diverse.

Now that Zoomers are of voting age, they possess both the voice and the political agency to influence policy shifts, particularly those that disproportionately affect their families and communities. Their participation holds the potential to reverse regressive trends and close persistent gaps that continue to disadvantage Black and Brown communities, despite growing representation.

Diversity isn't just socially beneficial, it's cognitively enriching. As Wells et al. (2016) affirms:

> "Researchers have documented that students' exposure to other students who are different from themselves and the novel ideas and challenges that such exposure brings leads to improved cognitive skills, including critical thinking and problem solving."

The future of equity lies in how these generations choose to leverage their demographic power, digital literacy, and collective voice. If given the tools and encouragement to lead, they can enact change that is not only visible, but lasting.

Comic Book Culture and Power Disparities

As a self-professed nerd, someone who has spent countless hours reading comics, watching superhero content, and immersing in nerd culture, I've noticed a consistent theme: BIPOC characters are often depicted with diminished powers compared to white legacy characters. With the exception of some CW shows, BIPOC heroes in Marvel and DC often lack the same level of strength, narrative importance, or development.

Outside of obvious ethnic stereotypes, power scaling in superhero universes often mirrors economic inequality, like comparing millionaires to billionaires. Semi-recently, DC has made some strides with characters like Val-Zod, a Black Superman from Earth 2, but these examples remain few.

Beyond comics, fantasy genres, from Tolkien's Lord of the Rings to anime and Dungeons & Dragons (DND) are rife with problematic portrayals. A BIPOC DND player once commented on the presentation of the fantasy realms:

> *"The shadowlands are always attributed to evil, and the Fae wilds or other areas to 'light' and goodness. How does this make me feel as a BIPOC individual?"*

This persistent attribution of "darkness" to evil and "light" to good reinforces harmful associations between race, morality, and power. It is a deeply embedded cultural narrative that must be critically examined.

Star Wars and the Visual Language of Good and Evil

I may bring some heat from the Mouse and George Lucas through this discussion, but can we talk about Star Wars? What is up with the good side of the Force being called the light side, and the evil side being labeled the dark side? The iconography, color palettes, and even costumes in these films embed a visual message: darkness is inherently bad.

How does this shape a child's developing mind, especially when Star Wars is a franchise aimed primarily at younger audiences? As a clinician, I recognize the narrative value of moralistic storytelling. But when "darkness" is so consistently tied to evil, fear, and danger, especially in a culture already struggling with racial prejudice, how can that not influence young people susceptible to cognitive distortions like all-or-nothing thinking?

Personally, I'm a fan of the Old Republic, of Star Wars, where characters explore a synthesis of the dark and light sides of the Force. This blending offers a far more nuanced vision of power, emotion, and morality. Nerd culture may seem niche, but these narratives have enormous cultural reach and continue to shape how entire generations conceptualize right and wrong.

Do I think the creators of these stories are intentionally racist? No. But do their creative choices carry implicit biases that reinforce outdated, harmful associations? Absolutely. Most storytellers aren't trying to harm children's sense of identity, but that doesn't change the consequences of their narratives.

To Disney's credit, we are seeing efforts to diversify casting and storytelling. From anime-style adaptations to casting BIPOC actors in roles historically dominated by cisgender, heteronormative white men, there is movement in a better direction. But when a studio owns the most dominant pop culture franchises of our time, those shifts matter immensely. They don't just tell stories, they shape identity. That's a scary power that can and has manifested across generational gaps. With their growing influence, they are poised to control a disproportionate amount of pop culture.

The Death of Diversity Equity and Inclusion (DEI) under the Trump Administration

On January 20th, 2025, as promised by his campaign, the Trump administration ended DEI in government. Furthermore, he presented a website for individuals to report on educators presenting DEI concepts. DEI already had an uphill battle when it was presented and active, now the extreme limiting of programs, offers, grants, and even history of marginalized populations, namely black and brown folks is erasure. If you have listened to the audiobook 1984 or read the novel, it strikes quite a chord for many as revisionist history presented to rewrite the true systemic patterns of oppression that have kept white folk in positions of power while disenfranchising marginalized communities.

The End of DEI: Implications for Marginalized Communities

The formal dismantling of Diversity, Equity, and Inclusion (DEI) programs in the United States began on January 20, 2025, when President Donald Trump signed Executive Order 14151, titled *"Ending Radical and Wasteful Government DEI Programs and Preferencing."* This executive order mandated the termination of all DEI-related initiatives across federal agencies and contractors, marking a sharp policy shift from previous administrations (White House, 2025). Prior to this, DEI was already on loose footing as it has been an uphill battle to implement equitable programs throughout the country.

Implications for Marginalized Communities

1. Educational Access and Support

The elimination of DEI programs has led to the closure of campus offices and initiatives that previously supported underrepresented students. For example, the University of Michigan shut down its DEI office and abandoned its *DEI 2.0 Strategic Plan*, which had contributed to a 46% increase in first-generation students and a 30% increase in Pell Grant recipients (Politico, 2025).

2. Workplace Diversity and Inclusion

Major corporations like Walmart, Meta, and Amazon have reduced their DEI investments, citing federal shifts and public pressure.
This rollback may result in fewer leadership opportunities for people of color and women, and may exacerbate experiences of microaggressions and exclusion in the workplace (Forbes, 2025).

3. Economic Opportunities for Minority-Owned Businesses

Small Black-owned brands such as Capital City and BLK & Bold, which had benefited from retail DEI initiatives, have faced boycotts and reduced shelf space following corporate DEI pullbacks.
These companies now face new distribution and growth challenges without institutional support (Eater, 2025).

4. Health Equity and Data Collection

The end of DEI programs also affects public health infrastructure.
The removal of equity-related data collection practices limits researchers' and clinicians' ability to identify and close racial disparities in health outcomes.
This disrupts long-term goals of achieving health equity (Evidence for Action, 2025).

5. Cultural Representation and Recognition

Agencies have reportedly removed references to women, LGBTQ+, and BIPOC individuals from educational materials, government websites, and museum displays.
Plaques honoring historically marginalized figures have been covered up or taken down, signaling a decline in institutional recognition of their contributions (AP News, 2025).

The Hidden Cost of Tech Running Our World

It's no secret or surprise that big tech does not work for you. They work for their own interests. They influence politicians to pass bills or shift attention from the public to their own goals for further increasing their influence. This isn't new at all. Major corporations such as big oil companies, pharmaceutical companies, retail corporations, weapons and aircraft manufacturers, amongst a few spend millions every year to influence politicians to benefit their own aims.

In 2024, Tech companies spent records numbers of funds to influence politicians. This is an insane amount of money spent but it is nothing compared to pharmaceutical company's lobbying. I'll go into that later in the book.

1. Record Lobbying Spend in 2024

- Total spending: Big Tech firms (Meta, Alphabet, Microsoft, ByteDance, X, Snap) collectively spent $61.5 million lobbying in 2024—a nearly 13% increase from 2023 (Issue One).

- They employed nearly 300 lobbyists, averaging one lobbyist for every two members of Congress (Issue One).

2. Company Breakdown

- **Meta:** $24.4 million — record high, up ~27%, with $5.6 million spent in Q4; 65 lobbyists (~1 per 8 Congress members) (Issue One).

- **ByteDance:** $10.4 million — ~19% increase, record high, with $2.3 million in Q4; 55 lobbyists (~1 per 10 Congress members) (Issue One).

- **Alphabet:** $14.8 million — ~2% rise, including $3.7 million in Q4 (Issue One).

- **OpenAI:** $1.8 million total, $510K in Q4; began lobbying in late 2023, totaling ~$2 million since then (Issue One).

- **Snap:** $950K — 10% increase, the highest since 2014; $170K in Q4 (Issue One).

- **Microsoft:** $10.4 million — ~2% decrease from 2023 (Issue One).

- **X (formerly Twitter):** $720K — ~15% decrease from 2023 (Issue One).

Overview Table

Company 2024 Lobbying Spend Notes

Company	2024 Lobbying Spend	Notes
Meta	$24.4M	Record, +27% from 2023
Alphabet	$14.8M	+2% YoY
Microsoft	$10.4M	–2% YoY
ByteDance	$10.4M	Record, +19%
OpenAI	$1.8M	First filings since late 2023
Snap	$950K	Record since 2014, +10%

Company	2024 Lobbying Spend	Notes
X	$720K	–15% YoY
NetChoice	$677.5K	Record since 2010, +25%

Interpretation

- Aggressive lobbying push: Meta and ByteDance lead, with Snap, Alphabet, Microsoft, OpenAI, and X also actively engaging.
- Strategic focus: The timing (significant Q4 spend) aligns with critical legislative actions on AI, privacy, and online safety.
- Impact: Issue One highlights how robust tech spending may have stalled child protection laws, emphasizing the tangible stakes of this influence.

Total Spending by Big Tech

- A broader analysis by Axios estimates that the overall tech industry (beyond just six companies) spent $85.6 million lobbying in 2024, compared to $68 million in 2023 (Axios).

Company	2024 Lobbying Spend	Notes
Meta	$24.2M – $24.4M	Record high, ~27% rise from 2023 (Issue One, Axios)
Amazon	$17.6M	Similar to 2023 (Axios)
Alphabet	$12.1M – $14.8M	Slight increase YOY (Issue One, Axios)
Microsoft	$9.5M – $10.4M	Small decline or modest shifts (Issue One, Axios)
Apple	$7.7M	Down from $9.6M in 2023 (Axios)
ByteDance	$10.2M – $10.4M	Record lobbying spend (Issue One, Axios)
Snap	$950K	Slight increase from 2023 (Issue One, Axios)
X (Twitter)	$720K	Continued decline (Issue One, Issue One, Axios)

What Tech Companies Lobbied Against in 2024

Below are the motions that tech is fighting against in 2024. This will evolve in the future as more attention is given to the damaging effects of screen time on our children and our own mental wellbeing. This clearly shows the lack of care for individuals using tech.

1. Kids Online Safety Act (KOSA)

- Opposed by Meta, Google (Alphabet), Snap, and others
- This bipartisan bill sought to require platforms to:
  - Prevent and mitigate mental health risks to minors
  - Disable algorithmic recommendations by default for minors
  - Give parents more control over kids' digital activity
- Status: Passed Senate (91–3), but lobbying efforts helped stall it in the House
- Spending surge coincides with legislative debates on kids' online safety, data privacy, and national security concerns.
- Issue One's analysis suggests that intense lobbying efforts contributed to blocking the Kids Online Safety Act, leading them to conclude, "more kids will die this year because tech titans' money thwarted congressional action" (Issue One).

2. AI Regulation and Transparency Requirements

- Companies like OpenAI, Meta, Google, Microsoft, and Amazon lobbied to influence or dilute early drafts of federal AI bills.
- Concerns included:
  - Mandatory transparency of training data and model architecture
  - Civil liability for AI harms
  - Licensing and pre-deployment risk assessments
- Tactic: Promoting industry-friendly "self-regulation" and voluntary frameworks, while slowing stricter enforcement bills.

3. Antitrust and Competition Legislation

- Opposed by Amazon, Apple, Meta, and Google
- These included proposed laws like the American Innovation and Choice Online Act, which aimed to:
  - Stop platforms from self-preferencing their own products (e.g., Amazon Basics, Apple apps)
  - Prevent monopolistic bundling or gatekeeping
- Outcome: These bills lost momentum in late 2023–early 2024, in part due to intense lobbying and campaign donations.

4. Digital Privacy and Consumer Data Protection

- Lobbying aimed at weakening or delaying federal privacy laws that:
    - Limit data collection and targeted advertising
    - Require opt-in consent for data sharing
    - Impose strict penalties for breaches
- Google, Meta, Amazon, and ad tech coalitions opposed many state-level bills (like California's stronger enforcement proposals).

5. Section 230 Reform

- Companies opposed changes that would increase liability for user-generated content, fearing:
    - Legal exposure for content moderation decisions
    - Increased censorship pressure from all political sides
- They supported *narrow* tweaks but lobbied against sweeping overhauls that would make platforms legally responsible for user posts.

6. TikTok Ban / ByteDance Divestiture

- ByteDance (TikTok's parent) launched an aggressive campaign to block legislation forcing a U.S. divestiture or ban of TikTok.
- Hired bipartisan lobbyists and funded civil rights orgs to frame bans as First Amendment issues.
- Outcome: The "sell-or-ban" bill passed in April 2025, but lobbying slowed earlier efforts and shaped its legal language.

7. Labor Protections & Algorithmic Transparency for Gig Workers

- Platforms like Uber, DoorDash, and Amazon lobbied against rules that would:
    - Reclassify gig workers as employees
    - Require transparency around how algorithms assign jobs and wages
- Also opposed wage floor laws and guaranteed benefit proposals in several states.

Takeaway

Tech companies aren't just lobbying *for* innovation, they're investing heavily to shape, delay, or block regulations that might:

- Affect profitability (ad models, content liability)
- Open them to litigation (AI misuse, children's harms)
- Force restructuring (antitrust, labor reclassification)
- Challenge their business models (data privacy, algorithm regulation)

We are not powerless in this. We are the users of this tech. We can collectively stop, boycott, diminish or hurt these companies economically and demand changes. We can't really depend on politicians to make this change for us. So many are profiting from the success of big tech companies, amongst others. We can collectively unplug for a long period of time so we can shift us against fighting each other and directing our attention and ire towards those who really deserve it. By unplugging, we are directly hurting these companies' profit margins. Boycotts work. Companies listen and try to make changes. Let's hold politicians and tech companies responsible for their damaging choices. Demanding changes in lobbying, tech influence, amongst others. Collectively we have power in our voice. Despite political divides, there is a growing desire for many folks to regain agency and autonomy.

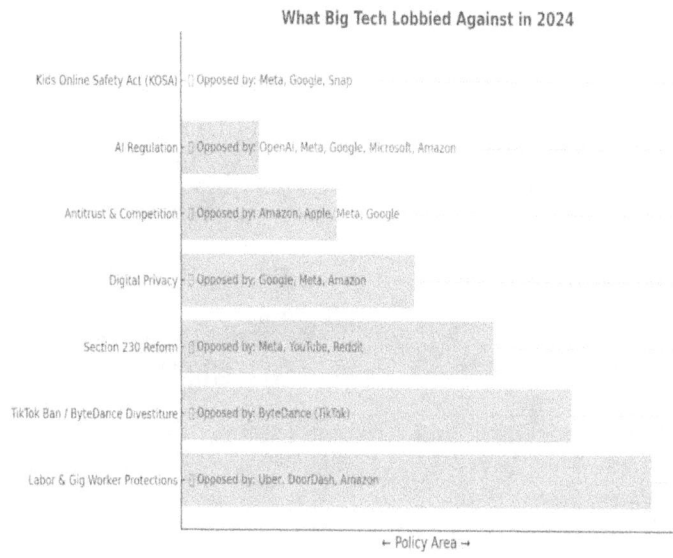

Conclusion

The rollback of DEI programs in early 2025 has had profound and immediate impacts on marginalized communities, particularly across education, employment, health, business, and cultural representation. As these changes continue to unfold, many experts warn that the absence of structured inclusion efforts could widen systemic disparities and limit progress made over the past decade.

The future of this is unknown but it is not hopeful for progression. We may see many positions of power, or inclusion going back to eras of the past. However, we can make our voice heard. Many folks are now aware of the power of economic impact on big businesses. We can make our case by letting big tech companies and other businesses that have rolled back their

DEI programs in complete capitulation of the Trump administration know what we want.

Summary

- This chapter explores the representation of BIPOC individuals in visual media, highlighting persistent stereotypes and power imbalances in film, television, news, and other digital content. Despite some progress in diversity, BIPOC characters are still often relegated to secondary or stereotypical roles, and disparities in media leadership positions remain stark.

- Data from USC Annenberg (2007–2022) underscores the limited inclusion of underrepresented groups in Hollywood. While female-led films and Asian representation have increased, other racial groups, LGBTQ+ individuals, and people with disabilities remain largely underrepresented. Women and BIPOC individuals are also significantly underrepresented as directors, writers, and producers.

- The social implications, particularly in politics and voter suppression are prolific. Although the U.S. population is becoming more diverse, BIPOC individuals remain underrepresented in Congress and leadership roles. Misinformation campaigns, particularly through social media, have been used to suppress voter turnout among marginalized communities, echoing historical voter suppression tactics.

- Better representation in media and politics, the importance of diverse leadership and accurate portrayals of the diversity within cultural groups help counteract harmful stereotypes and encourage civic engagement.

- With the Supreme Court's ruling against race-conscious college admissions, there is concern that progress in diversity will backslide, affecting representation in workplaces and leadership positions. BIPOC students, particularly in STEM, face hurdles due to a lack of mentorship, funding, and visible role models in academia. However, the growing diversity of younger generations (Gen Z and Gen Alpha) offers hope for policy shifts that could counteract these setbacks. Research highlights that diverse learning environments improve critical thinking and problem-solving, emphasizing the importance of representation.

- Traditionally, BIPOC representation in comic books, fantasy, and sci-fi have portrayed BIPOC characters as weaker, stereotyped, or absent from positions of power. Themes in franchises like Lord of the Rings, Dungeons & Dragons, and Star Wars reinforce harmful associations between darkness and evil, which can shape young audiences' perceptions. While some progress is being made, such as DC introducing stronger Black superheroes and Disney diversifying its storytelling, biases remain entrenched in media narratives.

- A limited "visual diet" in both education and entertainment reinforces systemic inequalities and further sends the message of white supremacy.

Chapter Eighteen

- Emergency room waiting times for Black patients are 30% longer than for white patients (average 69 minutes vs. 53 minutes).
- Black children with appendicitis are half as likely to receive adequate pain medication as white children.
- While a quarter of white mothers change insurance coverage during the course of their pregnancy and postpartum care, nearly half of all Black, Hispanic, and Indigenous women have discontinuous insurance coverage.
- Black women are more likely to die in childbirth than white women, partly due to economic inequities.

-Deborah Haarsma,

How Visual Diets Affect Our Ability to Receive Care

Segueing into healthcare, our visual diets also shape how individuals receive care, across medical, psychological, and public safety domains. The representations we encounter in media shape our implicit associations about who is a caregiver, who is trustworthy, and who deserves empathy.

When BIPOC individuals are consistently underrepresented, or depicted through narrow, stigmatizing tropes, this contributes to real-world healthcare disparities. Media that fails to reflect the growing diversity of caregivers and professionals reinforces outdated perceptions, ultimately impacting access to care, quality of care, and even how patients are treated in moments of vulnerability.

Whether the issue is access to safe neighborhoods, bias in mental health evaluations, or discrimination in medical settings, representation influences how we perceive competence, compassion, and credibility. A more diverse visual culture has the potential to help reshape biased beliefs, creating a future where care is more equitable, inclusive, and humanizing for all.

In regard to healthcare biases, one powerful contribution comes from the meta-research conducted in 2022 by Katta Spiel, Eva Hornecker, Rua Mae Williams, and Judith Good, a group of neurodivergent scholars who reviewed over 100 publications from the Association for Computing Machinery (ACM) digital library. This global team unearthed recurring language and assumptions that perpetuate ableist, exclusionary frameworks in research. While not limited to healthcare, many of the reviewed works informed healthcare and technical development spaces, highlighting how the visual and linguistic presentation of disability and neurodivergence in academic and design-oriented work influences care delivery in the real world.

Their research revealed that visual and textual representations often reinforce the idea of disabled or neurodivergent individuals as "broken" or in need of fixing, framing that has dangerous consequences in both clinical design and patient-provider interactions. This demonstrates how representation in scholarly and technical discourse can cascade into systemic biases in the tools, technologies, and systems meant to care for diverse populations.

The researchers said it best here.

> *"Frequently, via the abstract or within the first few lines of introductory text, ADHD is presented as a discrete entity detached from the person diagnosed with it, a source of familial burden or a threat to collective capital, and thus, an urgent problem requiring early intervention.*
>
> *Authors often used the language of suffering to frame ADHD participants. For example: "...children around the world suffer from ADHD", ADHD is "a common cognitive disorder afflicting many children and adults", and "the consequences of this impairment...can be devastating" (also refer to: Many authors expressly identify ADHD participants as being distinct from "healthy" or "normal" participants), and ADHD traits and behaviors as being "undesire[able]", "excessive", and "invasive".*
>
> *In so doing, authors use two specific rhetorical strategies: 1) framing ADHD as deviant other, and 2) determining the condition as detached from the individual diagnosed with it. By crystallizing specific aspects of ADHD, the condition is framed as an entity distinct from, and invasive to, any person diagnosed with it as well as their adjacent social unit. This is a common discursive practice that has been critiqued in disability studies for decades, specifically for the context of autism, but also negates the fundamental way the associated neurology shapes an individual's perception of their environment as well as their processing of external signals.*
>
> *ADHD is furthermore frequently described as a burden to others and to society as a whole. In our corpus (core and extended), children with ADHD are often described as being "at risk" of underachievement, substance abuse, and criminality, due to having ADHD traits. However, there have been numerous developments in critical psychology that acknowledge that ADHD traits do not play a causal role in these outcomes in isolation from societal discrimination and stigma.*

> *The papers we surveyed often aimed at reducing the 'burden' of ADHD, but none recognized socio-cultural contexts and disability stigma as producing "suffering" or contributing to "outcomes". While these projects might be well-intentioned, the approaches pursued often reinforce societal behavioral expectations and thereby place the burden on the ADHD person to adjust, constituting a focus on curative rather than on assistive technology.*
>
> *Many authors further emphasized the burden to family, caregivers, teachers, and broader society. For example: "there is a significant burden on those affected, their families and society"; "ADHD can be challenging for a parent or caregiver with an individual who has this disorder"; "a big threat for public health"; and "can have a huge emotional and economic impact on families". Here, these research projects become legitimized by an unsubstantiated assertion that the family unit is suffering as a result of the ADHD person. Other authors appeal to ADHD's disruption to a person's productivity as a risk to individual success and imminent threat to national capital. Following these implications, ADHD thus becomes an urgent societal problem solved only by intervention on the individual, rather than on the society which problematizes their embodiment. This negates how people with ADHD often have strategies and traits that allow them to make substantial contributions to collectives and societies."* (Spiel, et al, 2022).

This goes to show that even at the professional level, there is much work to be done to augment our visual diet to reduce the internalized and direct harm we are instilling in different groups of people. By perpetuating the framework that one way is the best way for all, or that neurodivergent folks need to shift their behavior to facilitate masking as a neurotypical individual within society, we continue to undermine the value of neurodiversity. This mindset limits our collective growth as a species.

As Jessica Belisle powerfully states in her research paper *Demolishing Systemic Ableism: Attention-Deficit Hyperactivity Disorder (ADHD) in Adults* (2022):

> *"While professionals within healthcare systems carry all the intent of delivering care equally and holding the value of human life, they are still influenced by society. In a society that views disabilities as weak, vulnerable, incompetent, etc., this inevitably permeates into their beliefs and affects the care they deliver. This is ableism, and it is often times unconscious and pervasive."*

In addition to neurodivergent biases presented in visual media, the access of care for BIPOC individuals in healthcare presents a visual diet amongst professionals in that field. For example, the seminal article "Unequal Treatment by Dr. Alan Nelson (2002) identified many core principles that BIPOC individuals face regarding barriers to treatment such as:

- *Racial and ethnic disparities in health care exist even when insurance status, income, age, and severity of conditions are comparable, and because death rates from cancer, heart disease, and diabetes are significantly higher in racial and ethnic minorities than in whites, these disparities are unacceptable.*
- *These differences in health care occur in the context of broader historic and contemporary social and economic inequality and persistent racial and ethnic discrimination in many sectors of American life.*
- *Many sources-including health systems as a whole, health care providers, patients, and health care plan managers-contribute to racial and ethnic disparities.*
- *Bias, stereotyping, prejudice, and clinical uncertainty on the part of health care providers may contribute to racial and ethnic disparities in health care. While indirect evidence from several lines of research supports this statement, a greater understanding of the prevalence and influence of the processes is needed and should be sought through research.*
- *Finally, racial and ethnic minority patients are more likely than white patients to refuse treatment, but differences in refusal rates are generally small. Minority patient refusal does not fully explain health care disparities.* (Nelson, A 2002).

This study, performed in the early 2000s, identified many systemic considerations that continue to affect BIPOC individuals' ability to receive care. Although the paper was published over twenty years before the writing of this book, there are still clear and disparate accounts of individuals failing to receive equitable treatment in healthcare. Accessibility for Black individuals has not significantly increased, despite impressive advancements in technology since the early 2000s.

As Alang (2019) points out:

> *"Sociodemographic, economic, health status, and health insurance characteristics are associated with reasons why Black folks report unmet need for mental health care. For example, younger Black adults ages 18–25 reported stigma, which is consistent with previous work that found stigma to be a significant barrier to professional mental health services among Black college students. African Americans who lived in non-metro areas were likely to report accessibility barriers such as lack of transportation and not*

knowing where to go for care. They were also more likely to think that mental health treatment will not work."

"Because accessibility barriers prevent people from seeking care, they also limit opportunities to experience positive outcomes of care which might then strengthen perceptions about the effectiveness of treatment."

We can't just point to individuals not wanting to be seen by healthcare professionals. The quality of care is also a major factor which many BIPOC individuals struggle with. It's not just the relationship of individuals refusing care but how the care or lack thereof is given.

HOW VISUAL DIETS AFFECT OUR ABILITY TO RECEIVE CARE

MEDIA SHAPES OUR PERCEPTIONS
- Underrepresenting or stigmatizing BIPOC individuals contributes to real-world healthcare disparities

WHY HEALTHCARE DISPARITIES PERSIST
- Bias and stereotyping from healthcare providers
- Discrimination through predictive algorithms
- Barriers to accessible and quality care for BIPOC communitities

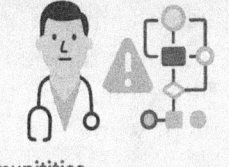

THE CONSEQUENCES
- BIPOC individuals receive worse care and have lower life expectancies compared tto their white counterparts

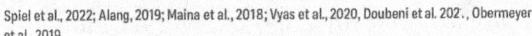

Spiel et al., 2022; Alang, 2019; Maina et al., 2018; Vyas et al., 2020, Doubeni et al. 202'., Obermeyer et al., 2019

"Despite efforts to reduce such disparities, racial/ethnic minorities (Black, Hispanic, Asian, Pacific Islander and Indigenous Americans/Alaska Native) continue to experience poorer healthcare and outcomes. In annual disparities report each year since 2003, the Agency for Healthcare Research and Quality has documented that widespread disparities persist in the United States. Through 2013 Blacks, Hispanics, and Indigenous Americans/Alaska Natives have continued to receive worse care for 40% of the quality measures assessed and Asians receive worse care for 20% of measures (Agency for Healthcare Research and Quality, 2016). Minorities also have higher incidence, mortality and advanced staging at diagnosis for several cancer types including cervical, kidney, breast, colorectal, lung, and prostate (National Cancer Institute, 2016, Jemal et al., 2017)). For children, disparities in infant mortality rates, chronic disease, quality of care, organ

> *transplantation and leukemia related deaths have also been noted (Flores, 2010)."*

What is the reason for such disparities in treatment? That is a complex concern encompassing multiple, intersecting factors: socioeconomic status, disposable income, intergenerational traumas, healthcare provider biases, accessibility of treatment in regions with high BIPOC populations, and a healthy distrust of the medical system rooted in historical injustices.

Focusing on the visual diet of healthcare providers, many harbor implicit and explicit biases which may be reinforced by the media they consume, media that often perpetuates problematic portrayals of marginalized populations. As explored in the previous chapter, these narratives play a significant role in shaping both public and professional perceptions.

> *"First, a growing body of research suggests that similar to the general US population, most healthcare providers across multiple levels of training and disciplines have implicit biases against Black, Hispanic, (First Nations) and dark-skinned individuals. Second, we found interesting trends when looking at provider characteristics associated with bias."* (Maina et al., 2018)

This reinforces the need to reevaluate the media healthcare professionals engage with and the frameworks taught in their education. Because care does not occur in a vacuum, it is filtered through the cultural lenses and biases that shape our understanding of who is deserving of compassion, credibility, and care.

The consequence of these poor visual diets is killing folks and providing them with substandard and dehumanizing care. As Vyas et al. (2020) write:

> *"The American Heart Association (AHA) Get with the Guidelines, Heart Failure Risk Score predicts the risk of death in patients admitted to the hospital. It assigns three additional points to any patient identified as "nonblack," thereby categorizing all black patients as being at lower risk. The AHA does not provide a rationale for this adjustment. Since "black" is equated with lower risk, following the guidelines could direct care away from black patients. A 2019 study found that race may influence decisions in heart-failure management, with measurable consequences: black and Latinx patients who presented to a Boston emergency department with heart failure were less likely than white patients to be admitted to the cardiology service."*

And in the realm of cardiac surgery, the bias persists in predictive tools that directly shape treatment decisions:

> *"An isolated coronary artery bypass in a low-risk white patient carries an estimated risk of death of 0.492%. Changing the race to "black/African American" increases the risk by nearly 20%, to 0.586%. Changing to any other race or ethnicity does not increase the estimated risk of death as compared with a white patient, but it does change the risk of renal failure, stroke, or prolonged ventilation. When used preoperatively to assess risk, these calculations could steer minority patients, deemed to be at higher risk, away from surgery."* (Vyas, et al, 2020)

Within the realm of Nephrology, researchers have identified that,

> *"Since it is cumbersome to measure kidney function directly, researchers have developed equations that determine the estimated glomerular filtration rate (eGFR) from an accessible measure, the serum creatinine level. These algorithms result in higher reported eGFR values (which suggest better kidney function) for anyone identified as black. Conversely, race adjustments that yield higher estimates of kidney function in black patients might delay their referral for specialist care or transplantation and lead to worse outcomes, while black people already have higher rates of end-stage kidney disease and death due to kidney failure than the overall population."* (Vyas, et al, 2020)

Regarding kidney transplantation,

> *"If the potential donor is identified as black, the Kidney Donor Risk Index (KDRI) returns a higher risk of graft failure, marking the candidate as a less suitable donor. Meanwhile, black patients in the United States still have longer wait times for kidney transplants than nonblack patients. Since black patients are more likely to receive kidneys from black donors, anything that reduces the likelihood of donation from black people could contribute to the wait-time disparity."* (Vyas, et al, 2020)

In Obstetrics,

> *"The Vaginal Birth after Cesarean (VBAC) algorithm predicts the risk posed by a trial of labor for someone who has previously undergone cesarean section. It predicts a lower likelihood of success for anyone identified as African American or Hispanic. The study used to produce the algorithm found that other variables, such as marital status and insurance type, also correlated with VBAC success. Those variables, however, were not incorporated into the algorithm. The health benefits of successful vaginal deliveries are well known, including lower rates of surgical*

> *complications, faster recovery time, and fewer complications during subsequent pregnancies. Nonwhite U.S. women continue to have higher rates of cesarean section than white U.S. women. Use of a calculator that lowers the estimate of VBAC success for people of color could exacerbate these disparities. This dynamic is particularly troubling because black people already have higher rates of maternal mortality."* (Vyas, et al, 2020)

With regard to Urology,

> *"The STONE score predicts the likelihood of kidney stones in patients who present to the emergency department with flank pain. The "origin/race" factor adds 3 points (of a possible 13) for a patient identified as "nonblack." By assigning a lower score to black patients, the STONE algorithm may steer clinicians away from thorough evaluation for kidney stones in black patients. The developers of the algorithm did not suggest why black patients would be less likely to have a kidney stone. An effort to externally validate the STONE score determined that the origin/race variable was not actually predictive of the risk of kidney stones. In a parallel development, a new model for predicting urinary tract infection (UTI) in children similarly assigns lower risk to children identified as "fully or partially black." This tool echoes UTI testing guidelines released by the American Academy of Pediatrics in 2011 that were recently criticized for categorizing black children as low risk."* (Vyas, et al, 2020)

Generally speaking, and with a clear indictment of our healthcare system's treatment of BIPOC individuals, they are suffering extensive maltreatment which can culminate in lower life expectancies than non-BIPOC individuals receiving care at the same location.

> *"Overall, compared with White people, Black people received worse care on 76 of 190 measures (40%) and Hispanic/Latino people on 58 of 167 measures (35%). The influence of these disparities is reflected in life expectancy data. For 2016–2018, estimated life expectancies were 75.5 years for Black people, 76.9 years for Indigenous Americans/Native American people, 78.8 years for White people, 83.7 years for Hispanic/Latino people, and 87.7 years for Asian people. These disparities are likely further exacerbated by the disproportionate effect of the COVID-19 pandemic in Black, Indigenous, and Hispanic/Latino communities."* (Doubeni et al., 2021)

Relating to another factor of healthcare providers' visual diets is the implementation of biased algorithms utilized to predict health outcomes.

These tools often exacerbate existing disparities by relying on flawed proxies for wellness. As Obermeyer et al. (2019) reveal:

> *"Health systems rely on commercial prediction algorithms to identify and help patients with complex health needs. We show that a widely used algorithm, typical of this industry-wide approach and affecting millions of patients, exhibits significant racial bias: At a given risk score, Black patients are considerably sicker than White patients, as evidenced by signs of uncontrolled illnesses. Remedying this disparity would increase the percentage of Black patients receiving additional help from 17.7 to 46.5%. The bias arises because the algorithm predicts health care costs rather than illness, but unequal access to care means that we spend less money caring for Black patients than for White patients. Thus, despite health care cost appearing to be an effective proxy for health by some measures of predictive accuracy, large racial biases arise."* (Obermeyer et al., 2019)

Regarding mental health care, I've personally seen concerning narratives regarding the care of BIPOC individuals, namely Black and Brown folks. In an area with a limited population of Black and Brown individuals (such as the Seattle area), many clinicians are quick to turn clients away or refer them out to Black or Brown clinicians with statements such as, *"I cannot properly service this client due to my limitations and understanding of their experience."* While this is absolutely true and self-aware, it also leaves clients searching for culturally humble providers, often facing long waitlists. Much like the rest of the medical model, this results in Black and Brown individuals suffering and waiting for openings, delaying care and well-being.

The cost of services is another critical barrier. Many providers do not accept insurance directly, leaving an even greater divide in accessibility. With limited openings in clinicians' caseloads and only a few sliding scale slots available, which are still too expensive for many individuals, the disproportionate burden falls on Black and Brown clinicians. They are often expected to take on more sliding scale clients to serve their community, further disenfranchising these professionals and resulting in a disparate quality of life compared to their white clinical counterparts.

For those who are willing and able to wait for Black and Brown clinicians to service their needs, that is certainly their choice and right. However, for those who are willing to work with someone, or anyone, these individuals suffer too long in a field that is missing the core point of the work and the need. For equanimity to truly exist, we must prioritize what is best for the client and not allow personal bias to interfere with the working relationship. While cultural competency is essential, the absence of available and affordable care for BIPOC clients is a failing of the system, not the client's expectations.

Pharmaceutical Lobbying

Let's shift focus for a bit and discuss lobbying again. Lobbying, the tried-and-true method for companies to influence politicians to help broaden their agenda, generally, at the cost of the consumer, either in our pockets or overall wellbeing.

Total Industry Spending

- The Pharmaceuticals/Health Products sector spent a total of $386.8 million lobbying in 2024, a record high, and involved 577 clients (OpenSecrets)

- Specifically within Pharmaceutical Manufacturing, the spending totaled $151.1 million across 138 companies and 469 lobbyists (OpenSecrets)

Top Lobbying Spenders (2024)

Pharmaceuticals / Health Products

- **PhRMA (Pharmaceutical Research & Manufacturers of America):** $31.72 million (OpenSecrets)

- **Pharmaceutical Care Management Association (PCMA):** $17.55 million (OpenSecrets)

- **Amgen:** $11.78 million (OpenSecrets)

- **Roche:** $10.76 million (OpenSecrets)

- **Merck & Co:** $9.19 million (OpenSecrets)

Pharmaceutical Manufacturing (subset)

- **PhRMA:** $31.72 million (same group) (OpenSecrets)

- **Pfizer Inc:** $8.86 million (OpenSecrets)

- **Eli Lilly & Co:** $8.43 million (OpenSecrets)

- **Bayer AG:** $8.47 million (OpenSecrets)

- **Novartis AG:** $6.22 million (OpenSecrets)

Trade Group Spotlight

- PCMA increased spending to $17.6 million in 2024 (up from $15 million in 2023), primarily fighting reforms affecting pharmacy benefit managers (Drug Topics)

- PhRMA led the pack among health trade associations in 2024, spending $31 million on lobbying, an increase from 2023 (Axios)(OpenSecrets)

Quick Stats
2024 Figures

Total Pharma Lobbying	$386.8 million
Pharma Manufacturing	$151.1 million
Number of Lobbying Clients	1,814 companies
Major Trade Group (PhRMA)	$31.7 million
PBM Association (PCMA)	$17.6 million

Context & Takeaways

- Pharmaceutical lobbying reached new heights in 2024, with overall industry spend up to $386.8 million (OpenSecrets).

- Trade groups like PhRMA and PCMA led the charge, intensifying efforts around drug pricing, Medicare negotiation authority, PBM regulation, and supply-chain concerns.

- Individual corporations, such as Pfizer, Merck, and Eli Lilly, each spent between $8 million and $9 million, highlighting the industry's concentrated influence.

Although, these figures are disheartening and may further prevent individuals from seeking care due to many factors, we aren't alone in hating our healthcare services. Healthcare is deplorable in the US and is getting worse. Very little individuals are immune to this. It crosses political divides and hurts our loved ones. However, we can keep individuals in power accountable by pushing for anti-lobbying laws or lobbying revisions as well as a revamping of our healthcare system. Lobbyists, politicians and insurance companies shouldn't make decisions for our health and well-being.

Summary

- Visual representation in media influences healthcare biases and disparities, particularly for neurodivergent individuals and BIPOC communities. The role of implicit biases in healthcare professionals, shaped by societal narratives and research frameworks often portray conditions like ADHD in a negative, pathological manner.

- Systemic healthcare inequities, such as racial and ethnic disparities in treatment, misdiagnoses, and access to care are pervasive. Studies show that BIPOC individuals face longer wait times, poorer treatment quality, and flawed predictive algorithms that reinforce discrimination. Specific examples include racial biases in heart failure risk assessments, kidney disease evaluations, and maternal health predictions, leading to substandard care and worsened outcomes.

- Mental healthcare is also affected, as many Black and Brown patients struggle to find accessible care due to a shortage of providers and high costs. Some clinicians refuse treatment based on cultural misunderstandings, exacerbating the gap in mental health services.

- Addressing these biases requires an overhaul of the "visual diet" consumed by healthcare providers, with a shift in representation to foster more equitable, inclusive, and effective care.

Chapter Nineteen

"Information, misinformation, disinformation, and data: We might not know what to call it, but we certainly are drowning in it." — Roger Spitz, The Definitive Guide to Thriving on Disruption: Volume I - Reframing and Navigating Disruption

Polarization of Visual Diets

The messaging across many visual platforms continues to shift away from neutral tones toward increasingly polarized narratives designed to maximize consumer engagement. As the commercial stakes of disseminating news, or pseudo-news, grow, especially when addressing demographic or sociopolitical topics, audiences are more frequently targeted with extreme or divisive content. This shift contributes to a phenomenon often referred to as *common enemy identity politics*, which I will explore in more depth in the next chapter.

For anyone tuned in to the rhythms of social media, news cycles, or other visual content ecosystems, the polarization of material is both evident and intensifying. Platforms amplify this divide as a strategy to boost engagement and, by extension, profitability.

The nonprofit organization Brookings, based in Washington, D.C., offers a compelling perspective rooted in nonpartisan research across local, national, and global levels. In a 2021 analysis, they noted:

> *"Polarization began growing in the U.S. decades before Facebook, Twitter, and YouTube appeared. Other factors, including the realignment of political party membership, the rise of hyper-partisan radio and cable TV outlets and increased racial animus during Donald Trump's uniquely divisive presidency, have contributed to the problem."*
> — Sims et al., 2021

They go on to elaborate:

> *"Social media companies do not seek to boost user engagement because they want to intensify polarization. They do so because the amount of time users spend on a platform liking, sharing, and retweeting is also the amount of time they spend looking at the paid advertising that makes the major platforms so lucrative... Facebook is fully aware of how its automated systems promote divisiveness. The company does extensive internal research on the polarization problem and periodically adjusts its algorithms to reduce the flow*

> *of content likely to stoke political extremism and hatred. But typically, it dials down the level of incendiary content for only limited periods of time. Making the adjustments permanent would cut into user engagement. Examples include the tumultuous period immediately after the November 2020 election and the days before the April 2021 verdict in the trial of Derek Chauvin."*
> — Sims et al., 2021

This insight underscores a critical tension at the heart of the digital attention economy: the very systems designed to keep users engaged are the same ones that often amplify divisive, emotionally charged content. Even when platform leaders acknowledge the harm caused by algorithmic amplification, their responses tend to be temporary, strategic pauses rather than structural changes. As the financial incentive to maintain high engagement outweighs the societal costs of polarization, visual media diets remain steeped in conflict, outrage, and sensationalism.

An easy way for individuals to reduce their exposure to polarization is simply to take a break. According to Sims et al. (2021), stepping away from a platform for just one month can measurably reduce polarized thinking. Even a short detox from algorithm-driven, polarizing content can help recalibrate perspectives. The environments we immerse ourselves in, the tone, the digital realities, we absorb, compound over time, subtly reshaping our opinions and distancing us from authentic connection with the real communities around us.

This process isn't just about the words we read, it's about what we see. In a 2023 study, Holder and Bearfield offered compelling evidence that data visualization can directly influence political attitudes:

> *"In the first study, we show that visualizing policy opinions can shape policy opinions, particularly for moderate partisans. We used a realistic visualization of gun policy attitudes to show that a popular chart type is not merely a passive source of political information; rather, it can actively shape our politics. In the second study, we showed that data visualization can induce social conformity, and as a consequence, visualizing polarization can increase polarization. We also found that visualization can have a stronger influence on partisan attitudes than the verbal gist summaries studied in political science."*
> — Holder & Bearfield, 2023

Their research confirms that what we visually ingest doesn't just inform us, it *shapes* us. Especially for those who are undecided or moderately partisan, visual representations of opinion can influence political stance and trigger social conformity. In other words, seeing polarized graphics or media doesn't just reflect division; it deepens it.

This is the heart of this book: our visual diets, what we consume, scroll past, or passively absorb, are deeply tied to how we think, what we feel, and ultimately, what we believe. When our feeds are filled with outrage, divisiveness, or emotionally manipulative content (as much of social media tends to be), those emotional cues become internalized. If we are continually exposed to harmful, aggressive content, it's only natural that we begin to mirror those psychological states.

Data Brokering

Through my research, I've found that data brokering represents a deeply problematic intersection with our visual media ecosystems. In the eyes of these systems, *we* are the product. Our identities, behaviors, preferences, and potential purchasing power are continuously harvested and monetized. Without these practices, the commodity of *you*, your digital persona, wouldn't exist in its current form. In fact, without data monetization, many of the services we consider "free," such as search engines, social media platforms, and apps, would likely come with a price tag.

But there is a darker side to this exchange.

> *"Data brokers collect information from a range of sources including from social media sites, internet and search services, apps, customer loyalty programs, card payment providers and public records, like electoral rolls. Types of information collected include names, home and work addresses, age, browsing behavior, purchasing behavior, and a range of other socio-economic and demographic information. Some of the products and services data brokers create include audience profiling reports, consumer purchasing data and risk and fraud management products for tenancy or insurance applications."*
> — ACCC, 2023

This kind of data collection is not neutral. It feeds the algorithms that curate our visual experiences, deciding what content we see, when we see it, and how often. In effect, data brokers are essential engines behind the personalization, and polarization, of digital media. They enable highly targeted content that not only reflects our perceived interests, but also nudges, persuades, and sometimes manipulates our decisions and behaviors. The more intimately the system knows us, the more power it has to shape our worldview.

What appears on your screen is not random, it is constructed by invisible systems trained on your data. In a world where attention is currency and surveillance is normalized, data brokering becomes both a commercial engine and a cultural threat.

This entirely legal practice can acquire our personal information through a variety of means, both online and offline. The scope and depth of data collection are often invisible to the average user, but it is constant, comprehensive, and largely unregulated. As outlined by McAfee (2024), data brokers collect information from the following sources:

- **Public Records**: Much of our personal information is freely accessible through public databases. This includes voter registration records, birth certificates, criminal histories, and bankruptcy filings. These are often the building blocks of a basic personal profile.

- **Search and Browsing History**: Every time you visit a website, log into a social media platform, or perform a Google search, you leave a digital breadcrumb trail. Data brokers use web scraping tools to gather and analyze this activity, building detailed profiles about your interests, behaviors, and demographic identity.

- **Online Agreements and Terms of Service**: Most people scroll past the fine print when signing up for new apps or platforms. Hidden within those user agreements are clauses that permit companies to collect, store, and even sell your personal data to third parties, including brokers.

- **Purchase History**: What you buy, how you buy it, and when you buy it are all valuable data points. Whether it's a credit card transaction, use of a loyalty program, or even the application of a discount code, this information is logged and sold to marketers looking to fine-tune their consumer targeting strategies.

"Many of these agreements have disclosures in the fine print that give the company the right to collect and distribute your personal information."
— McAfee, 2024

This ecosystem of data extraction fuels a vast, invisible marketplace. And when combined with the visual content we engage with, ads, news stories, video recommendations, even memes, our behavioral data doesn't just reflect who we are; it shapes what we see next. In this way, data brokering doesn't just commodify us, it curates our digital realities.

Case Study: Cambridge Analytica and the Weaponization of Personal Data

One of the most notorious examples of data brokering's dark potential was the Cambridge Analytica scandal, which exposed how personal data, harvested largely without consent, was weaponized to manipulate public opinion and influence democratic elections.

In 2018, whistleblower Christopher Wylie revealed that Cambridge Analytica had acquired the personal data of over 87 million Facebook users, most of whom had never agreed to share their information. The firm used this data to build psychographic profiles of users, categorizing individuals based on personality traits, fears, and motivations. These profiles were then used to deliver highly targeted political ads and misinformation, aimed at shaping voter behavior in both the 2016 U.S. presidential election and the Brexit referendum.

What made the case especially alarming was that users didn't need to directly participate for their data to be exploited. Through app permissions and Facebook's data-sharing practices, even those connected to someone who took a personality quiz could have their data harvested. This revealed the depth of surveillance embedded in seemingly benign interactions, and how visual media content, from political ads to memes, could be tailored with surgical precision to exploit individuals' psychological vulnerabilities.

This case demonstrates how data brokering is not just a back-end process, but a driver of the content we see, the ideologies we are exposed to, and the decisions we may unconsciously make. It connects directly to our visual media diet: what shows up in our feed, what stirs outrage, what confirms bias, and what gets us to click.

Disproportionate Impact on Marginalized Communities

While data brokering affects all users in the digital ecosystem, its consequences are not distributed equally. Marginalized communities, particularly BIPOC individuals, low-income populations, immigrants, and those with limited digital literacy, are often the most vulnerable to the exploitative nature of data collection and surveillance.

Because data brokers gather socio-economic and demographic details, including ZIP codes, purchasing behavior, education level, and even ethnic identifiers (sometimes inferred through proxies), they can inadvertently (or intentionally) reinforce systemic inequalities. These datasets are used to make decisions about creditworthiness, insurance eligibility, employment prospects, housing opportunities, and more, often without the individual's knowledge or consent.

Historically marginalized groups are more likely to:

- **Be misrepresented or stereotyped** in algorithmic profiling. When identity is inferred from incomplete or biased data, individuals may be slotted into harmful categories that shape how institutions treat them.
- **Be targeted by exploitative advertising**, including predatory loans, fast fashion, and unhealthy food products, content often

visually crafted to appeal to racialized or economically vulnerable demographics.

- **Experience digital redlining**, a modern form of segregation where certain communities are excluded from opportunities, such as housing ads or employment listings, based on algorithmic decisions rooted in data profiling.

In a world where visual media is often driven by these same algorithmic systems, marginalized people not only face misrepresentation but are also disproportionately exposed to harmful or polarizing content. What we *see* is shaped by what data brokers *believe* we are, and for many, that belief is shaped by systems of race, class, and historical bias.

The convergence of data brokering and visual media feeds a cycle: marginalized communities are under greater surveillance, served content that often reinforces trauma or stereotypes, and then further categorized based on their interactions with that very content.

Reclaiming Digital Agency

As our data continues to be sold and circulated among corporations, marketing firms, and third-party vendors, the risk of exposure and misuse grows exponentially. Even though we unwittingly provide massive amounts of personal information to these companies through everyday digital interactions, there *are* ways to reclaim some control over our data. But regaining that control is not without its complications.

Services like Mine (accessible at saymine.com) offer a way to identify which companies are storing your personal data, often through email trails associated with data brokering. With tools like this, users can individually contact each company to request data deletion or pay for a streamlined service where Mine will handle these requests on your behalf.

However, as I mentioned earlier, these choices come with consequences. In many cases, requesting deletion means losing your user history and profile entirely. This could result in the erasure of saved preferences, past purchases, account data, or even losing access to services that rely on profile continuity. It's important to be intentional and discerning about which companies you ask to delete your data.

That said, minimizing your digital footprint by reducing the amount of personal data stored on external servers can significantly lower the risk of data breaches, identity theft, or manipulative profiling. It's not just about privacy; it's about reclaiming agency in a system designed to commodify your behavior.

Digital Hygiene Toolkit

Simple actions to reduce your digital footprint, protect your data, and reclaim agency in the digital ecosystem.

1. Audit Your Data Presence

- Use tools like **Mine**, **Jumbo**, or **Privacy Bee** to scan your email inbox and identify companies that hold your personal data.
- Request data deletion or limit data use where possible. Be strategic, consider what services you actually use or value before deletion.

2. Lock Down Your Browser

- Use **privacy-focused browsers** like Firefox (with strict tracking protection) or Brave.
- Install extensions like **uBlock Origin**, **Privacy Badger**, or **DuckDuckGo Privacy Essentials** to block trackers and ads.
- Regularly clear your cookies and browsing history, or use incognito/private mode for sensitive searches.

3. Manage Social Media Permissions

- Revoke access for third-party apps you no longer use via settings in Facebook, Google, Twitter, and Instagram.
- Turn off ad personalization and facial recognition features.
- Limit location sharing and microphone/camera access in mobile app settings.

4. Use Alternative Search Engines

- Consider switching to **DuckDuckGo**, **Startpage**, or **Ecosia**, search engines that do not track you or store your search history.

5. Take Control of Your Devices

- Disable location tracking, ad tracking, and background app refresh where not essential.
- Regularly update your privacy settings on iOS/Android and within each app.
- Use encrypted messaging services like **Signal** or **WhatsApp** (with disappearing messages enabled).

6. Strengthen Password Hygiene

- Use a **password manager** (like Bitwarden or 1Password) to create unique passwords for every site.
- Enable **two-factor authentication** (2FA) on all important accounts, especially email, banking, and social media.

7. Be Skeptical of "Free" Services

- If you're not paying for the product, *you* are likely the product. Be wary of free apps that collect excessive data, even if they seem harmless.
- Before signing up, review what permissions the app requests. If it's unrelated to the core function (like a flashlight app requesting contact access), don't install it.

8. Support Data Rights Legislation

- Advocate for stronger digital protections like **GDPR-style** regulation, **data minimization**, and **algorithmic transparency**.
- Follow organizations like **Electronic Frontier Foundation (EFF)** or **Access Now** for digital rights advocacy.

Digital hygiene isn't a one-time fix, it's a long-term habit. The more conscious we are about what we click, share, and agree to, the more power we regain over our digital identity.

Echo Chambers

When we find ourselves surrounded by like-minded individuals who consistently reflect and reinforce our own beliefs, we are in what's known as an *echo chamber*. These spaces can feel affirming, safe, even, but they become problematic when they exclude or silence dissenting perspectives. Echo chambers can limit critical thinking, discourage empathy, and insulate us from nuanced, diverse conversations.

Importantly, rejecting harmful or dehumanizing ideologies is not the same as suppressing free thought. There's a crucial difference between protecting space for healthy disagreement and allowing platforms for speech that furthers marginalization or incites harm. Not all ideas are harmless, and not all speech deserves amplification, especially when it deepens systemic oppression or erodes safety for vulnerable communities.

As Terren and Borge-Bravo (2021) explain:

> *"An echo-chamber can be defined as an environment in which the opinion, political leaning, or belief of an individual about a certain topic are reinforced due to repeated interactions with peers who*

> *share similar points of view. Two key elements are needed for this scenario to take place. First, a group of individuals that share a common opinion in opposition to other individuals or groups characterized by different attitudes regarding the same topic. Second, social interactions that convey a flow of information between these individuals about the topic under consideration, that can thus influence their beliefs on the subject. Such interactions are more likely to be established between individuals characterized by similar opinions, that is, there is a certain degree of homophily in social interactions. Therefore, echo-chambers are characterized by the coexistence of two elements: (i) opinion polarization with respect to a controversial topic, and (ii) homophily in interactions, i.e. the preference to interact with like-minded peers."*
> — Terren & Borge-Bravo, 2021

In essence, echo chambers are a product of both polarization and homophily, the tendency to associate with those who are similar to us. Especially in digital environments, algorithms intensify this effect, feeding us more of what we already agree with and insulating us further from challenging, but necessary, viewpoints.

The danger here is not just ideological stagnation, it's the erosion of collective understanding. When each group lives in its own curated reality, shaped by visual cues, selective narratives, and peer reinforcement, the possibility for shared truth becomes increasingly fragile.

Misinformation

In today's fragmented media landscape, the concept of "fake news" has become increasingly slippery. As Tandoc et al. (2017) note, depending on the user, the label can be applied to anything from critical journalism, whether accurate or not, to satire, or fully fabricated stories created to deceive for political or financial gain. The term has lost specificity, often wielded as a rhetorical weapon to discredit information that challenges a person's worldview.

The definition of misinformation also varies. Broadly, it refers to *false or misleading information*, but not all definitions include the intent to deceive. In contrast, disinformation is typically used to describe deliberately deceptive content, meaning it's a subset of misinformation. This distinction is important: not all who spread misinformation do so with malicious intent.

As Treen et al. (2020) and Wardle (2017) explain, misinformation is often spread by well-meaning individuals who *believe* the information they're sharing is true. Social media platforms, with their rapid, visual-first sharing mechanisms, are particularly fertile ground for the unintentional spread of falsehoods. Algorithms prioritize engagement over accuracy, and emotionally charged content, often misinformation, travels faster and farther than truth.

Wardle (2017) developed a misinformation-disinformation spectrum based on *intent to deceive*, offering a useful framework for understanding the scale and complexity of manipulated content. At one end of the spectrum is satire or parody (with no intent to mislead), and at the other lies fabricated content (designed entirely to deceive).

> *"Social media users may unintentionally share misinformation in the mistaken belief that what they are sharing is true."*
> — Gualtney et al., 2022

In a digital ecosystem saturated with emotionally engaging visuals, quick takes, and algorithmically amplified content, it becomes harder to distinguish credible information from manipulated narratives. The danger lies not only in what people believe, but in how visual misinformation reinforces cognitive biases, erodes trust in institutions, and further fractures public discourse.

Misinformation as a Public Health Crisis

Misinformation, when examined through the lens of visual diets, reveals itself not just as a media issue, but as a *public health crisis*. Across countless portals of visual media, false and misleading content runs rampant. Its persistence is not random; it is *targeted*, often strategically aimed at Black and Brown communities. The consequences are tangible, measurable, and devastating.

Consider two recent, high-impact examples: the COVID-19 pandemic and ongoing battles over voting rights. Both crises were made worse by the spread of misinformation, with disproportionate harm falling on marginalized communities.

As Lee et al. (2023) write:

> *"These examples of misinformation are particularly concerning given ongoing racial disparities in the impact of COVID-19. Relative to white people, BIPOC (Black, Indigenous, & People of Color) face higher risks of infection, hospitalization, and death from COVID-19 and other chronic diseases...*
> *Analysis of the Internet Research Agency's attack on the 2016 U.S. presidential election revealed that their disinformation campaign on social media targeted Black voters by spreading fraudulent information about political candidates and election outcomes...*
> *Political misinformation seeking to disenfranchise or mislead specific individuals can harm BIPOC's ability to participate in their government, thus undermining democratic processes and*

> *responsiveness. Furthermore, while belief in misinformation can have important normative consequences (e.g., votes cast in an election that are informed by false information about candidates or issues), the nature of social spaces on the internet (i.e., people connected in networks) means that an individual's decision to share misinformation can affect their friends, family, and neighbors."*
> — Lee et al., 2023

In this context, misinformation doesn't merely distort truth, *it erodes access*, *threatens lives*, and *undermines democracy*. During the pandemic, conspiracy theories and false medical claims flourished, often amplified by visual memes and TikTok-style videos that felt digestible and trustworthy, especially to those skeptical of traditional institutions. Meanwhile, disinformation campaigns around voting misled BIPOC communities about registration deadlines, polling places, and ballot procedures, an intentional effort to suppress civic participation.

Because social media is networked by design, misinformation spreads like a virus, passed from user to user, often unwittingly. When this content appears in a visually engaging or emotionally resonant format, it becomes even more difficult to resist or fact-check in real time.

This is not just a digital problem. It is a structural one. And within the scope of visual diets, it reveals how what we *see* can lead to what we *believe*, and ultimately, how we live and whether we thrive.

Community Resistance and Culturally Rooted Countermeasures

In the face of targeted misinformation campaigns and systemic disenfranchisement, BIPOC communities have not remained passive. Across the country, and the globe, grassroots efforts, mutual aid networks, and culturally rooted education campaigns have emerged as powerful forms of resistance. These movements recognize that the fight against misinformation is not just about correcting facts, but about reclaiming *trust*, *voice*, and *visibility*.

Unlike top-down fact-checking efforts, community-driven responses are built on *relational trust* and *cultural context*. They understand that whoever delivers the message often matters as much as the message itself. When information comes from within the community, from faith leaders, barbershops, neighborhood organizers, TikTok creators, or trusted elders, it resonates more deeply and combats misinformation more effectively.

Examples of Resistance in Action:

- **The Black Doctors COVID-19 Consortium** in Philadelphia used mobile clinics and trusted messengers to deliver accurate, accessible information about vaccines, directly addressing vaccine hesitancy in Black neighborhoods.

- **Native public health initiatives**, such as those led by the Urban Indian Health Institute, created culturally relevant visual content in Indigenous languages to combat pandemic-related disinformation.

- **Online creators of color** are building digital platforms to counter misinformation, from TikTokers debunking election lies to Instagram accounts dedicated to voter rights, police accountability, and health equity.

- **Community radio stations**, WhatsApp groups, and neighborhood Facebook pages serve as localized hubs for fact-checking, myth-busting, and mobilizing around key issues like elections or health crises.

These networks are *reclaiming the visual narrative*, not only correcting falsehoods, but producing new content that is culturally resonant, emotionally intelligent, and community-centered. They challenge the dominance of corporate algorithms with storytelling grounded in lived experience.

In this way, visual media can become not just a source of harm, but a site of resistance and resilience. When communities take control of their visual diets, what they create, share, believe, and elevate, they are taking back their power.

Reclaiming the Narrative: Practical Tools for Digital Resistance

To challenge the harmful effects of misinformation, particularly the kind targeted at BIPOC communities, we need more than passive awareness. We need visual resistance: an intentional, community-centered effort to disrupt false narratives, elevate truth, and reclaim digital space as a place for healing, education, and empowerment.

Here are some practical strategies individuals and communities can use to resist misinformation and shape healthier visual ecosystems:

Digital Resistance Toolkit

1. Support and Elevate Trusted Messengers

- Follow and amplify creators, educators, and organizations who provide accurate, culturally relevant information.

- Share their work within your own network, especially across platforms where misinformation tends to spread fast.

2. Create Visual Counter-Narratives

- Use visual storytelling to share *lived experiences*, *community data*, and *culturally grounded knowledge*.

- Infographics, reels, memes, and short-form video can help translate complex truths into accessible content.

- Tools like **Canva**, **Adobe Express**, or **Infogram** can make these visuals easy to create and share.

3. Practice and Teach Visual Literacy

- Learn to *read between the pixels*, understand how framing, filters, and edits influence perception.

- Host workshops (virtual or in-person) that teach others how to identify misinformation and spot manipulated visuals.

- Share guides like the "CRAAP Test" (Currency, Relevance, Authority, Accuracy, Purpose) to evaluate sources.

4. Leverage Mutual Aid Channels

- Use community WhatsApp groups, group texts, or neighborhood Facebook pages as *rapid-response hubs* for accurate information.

- When disinformation surfaces, respond quickly and compassionately, focusing on collective learning, not shame.

5. Disrupt the Algorithm, Intentionally

- Diversify your feed. Follow voices that challenge your perspective and expand your worldview.

- Don't engage with inflammatory or harmful content, attention is currency.

- Report misinformation and disinformation when you see it.

6. Advocate for Structural Change

- Support organizations fighting for **algorithmic transparency**, **platform accountability**, and **data justice**.

- Push for policies that protect against digital redlining, targeted surveillance, and disinformation campaigns.

- Amplify tech equity movements led by communities of color.

The Future of Digital Power

The fight against misinformation is not just about fact-checking, it's about power, identity, and visibility. Who gets to shape reality? Whose voices are heard, and whose are erased?

BIPOC communities are not just targets of disinformation, they are also the architects of resistance. From ancestral knowledge systems to digital storytelling, there is a long tradition of reclaiming narrative power. And in today's media-saturated world, every post, every image, every video is a chance to disrupt, reimagine, and rebuild.

By practicing digital hygiene, cultivating visual literacy, and building networks of care and resistance, we move one step closer to a digital future that reflects, not distorts, our humanity.

Building Immunity to Misinformation: Community Power & Practical Tools

Given the deep sense of connection and shared responsibility that exists within BIPOC communities, misinformation often spreads *faster and farther* than it might elsewhere. But these same networks that allow harmful content to flourish can also be mobilized to resist it.

Fortunately, researchers and community leaders have identified *evidence-based practices* to help BIPOC communities protect themselves and one another.

Community-Centered Strategies for Fighting Misinformation

(Adapted from Lee et al., 2023)

1. Include Multilingual Support

- Translate materials into the languages spoken within the community.
- Collaborate with local speakers to include culturally relevant examples.
- Use digital tools like live captions, real-time translation, and in-language fact-check sources (e.g., Univision's *El Detector*).

2. Contextualize Diverse Media Ecologies

- Recognize the many sources people rely on, such as ethnic media, local radio, or community leaders.
- Co-develop resource packets with trusted information sources identified *by the community* (e.g., NCAI's COVID-19 resources for Indian Country).

3. Prebunk False Claims

- *Prebunking* means inoculating communities by teaching them about misinformation before they encounter it.
- Explain how disinformation campaigns *specifically target* communities of color.
- Host interactive Q&As with culturally aligned experts (e.g., Black doctors discussing vaccine myths).

Tools to Identify Bias and Fact-Check Information

Reliable Fact-Checking Websites:

- Snopes – Verifies urban legends, internet myths, and fake news.
- FactCheck.org – Nonpartisan site focused on political claims and public policy.
- PolitiFact – Rates claims on a Truth-O-Meter; helpful during elections.
- Lead Stories – Debunks trending false stories, often in real time.
- Truth or Fiction – Focuses on chain emails, rumors, and conspiracy theories.
- Emergent.info – Tracks misinformation in breaking news.
- **Washington Post Fact Checker** – Provides Pinocchio ratings for public claims.
- NPR Fact Check – Fact-checks news and political events in real time.
- RumorGuard – Flags viral rumors and provides evidence-based rebuttals.
- **CQ Researcher** – In-depth reports and context on complex issues.

Helpful Tools and Apps:

- **Settle It** (by PolitiFact) – A mobile app that lets you search political claims and check their accuracy on the go.
- **Fake News Alert Chrome Extension** – Flags questionable websites while you browse.

For Bias Detection and Media Literacy:

- Ground News – Visualizes the political bias of news stories so you can compare coverage from the left, center, and right.

- Rand.org's Truth Decay Project – A comprehensive list of educational tools to combat echo chambers and disinformation campaigns.

Misinformation isn't just a political or media issue, it's a *social* issue, a *racial justice* issue, and a *public health* issue. However, community holds power.

By sharing accurate information in languages that resonate, by identifying and *prebunking* harmful narratives, and by using trusted tools and resources, BIPOC communities can *protect* each other and *reclaim the narrative*.

Let's keep our digital spaces truthful, intentional, and rooted in care.

Summary

- Increasing polarization of visual media and its effects on society, particularly in shaping political attitudes and reinforcing biases are manipulated further by social media platforms, driven by engagement metrics, amplify divisive content, fostering common enemy identity politics. Research from Brookings and other sources highlights how visual representations can influence opinions, increase polarization, and encourage social conformity.

- Data brokering is a major result of this. Personal data is collected, sold, and used to manipulate consumer behavior and target individuals with specific content. Data brokers gather information through search histories, online agreements, and purchase records, creating a lucrative but ethically and morally devoid industry.

- Echo chambers and misinformation further exacerbate polarization, as individuals are surrounded by like-minded opinions while being exposed to misleading or false narratives. This has particularly harmful effects on BIPOC communities, who are disproportionately targeted by misinformation, as seen during the COVID-19 pandemic and election cycles. Strategies for countering misinformation, including multilingual fact-checking, identifying trusted sources, and "prebunking" false claims before they spread are paramount.

- Resources for fact-checking, including websites like Snopes, PolitiFact, and FactCheck.org, as well as tools like Ground News and Rand.org to help users identify political biases and misinformation in news sources.

Chapter Twenty

"No beast is more savage than man when possessed with power answerable to his rage."

-Plutarch

Anger Cycles / Rage Cycles Driven by Visual Media

Consider your most recent experience watching the news. I'm choosing the news deliberately here, because for many, it's become a uniquely enflaming space, emotionally charged, visually overwhelming, and almost impossible to disengage from.

So ask yourself:
How did that journey go?

Did you dive deeper, consuming more content, more opinions, more outrage?
Or did you shut it off, saturated, overwhelmed, possibly disturbed?
What did you do with the information you absorbed?
Did you dwell on it?
Did you talk to someone, vent, debate, spiral together in frustration?
Or did you try to sit with it objectively, asking: *What am I supposed to do with this? What needs are going unmet in this moment?*

And what *form* did the news take?
Was it an objective report, or was it packaged as an opinion piece, dressed in urgency and personal interpretation? Objectivity in the news? What a concept. And yet, it has rarely been the norm. News, since its inception, has been slanted to fit the needs of the moment, often sensationalized to hook attention and provoke emotion.

As I shared in the earlier chapter on the history of the news cycle, this is not new. Even this book, *my book*, is tinged with opinion. But I aim to acknowledge it. I strive to confront my own confirmation bias, and to challenge my perceptions of how visual media influences our identities, communities, and mental states.

And I do have appreciation for the role of journalists and newscasters play. It's a difficult, high-stakes job, to inform the public, compete for audience attention, and deliver content in a rapidly accelerating, polarized landscape. The need to "keep viewers engaged" has become a fine-tuned artform.

Cue the flashing banners, the red "BREAKING NEWS" graphics, the sound effects, the hyper-focus on emotionally charged topics, and that scrolling ticker at the bottom of the screen: a tool engineered for intermittent reinforcement. A near-constant, subconscious dopamine drip. A visual cue that *more* is always coming. Something else to react to. Something else to worry about. Something else to fear.

But there's a darker side to all this engagement.

We can find ourselves trapped in rage cycles, emotional feedback loops where anger becomes the default response. One story enrages us. Another story confirms the injustice. The next one amplifies it. Soon, we are no longer *watching* the news; we are being *conditioned* by it. Addicted to the drip, but emotionally drained.

And it doesn't stop at the news. These anger cycles spill over into our conversations, relationships, timelines, and identity. We don't just witness conflict, we embody it.

The Clinical Side of Rage: Intermittent Explosive Disorder (IED)

While anger is a normal human emotion, what happens when it escalates into a *persistent, uncontrolled pattern*, triggered not by major events, but by the steady drumbeat of enraging stimuli we encounter every day through visual media?

Enter Intermittent Explosive Disorder (IED), a clinical diagnosis that gives language to what some may experience when caught in relentless rage cycles.

According to the *World Health Organization's ICD-11 (2023)*, the essential features of IED include:

- *A pattern of recurrent, explosive outbursts, verbal (e.g., yelling, insults) or physical (e.g., hitting, throwing objects), in individuals past the developmental age where impulse control is expected (typically age 6+).*

- *These outbursts are grossly out of proportion to the triggering event or situation.*

- *Episodes occur regularly over time, either with high intensity but low frequency (e.g., physical assaults a few times a year) or lower intensity but high frequency (e.g., yelling or throwing objects multiple times a week).*

- *The aggression is impulsive, not planned or goal-directed. It's a reaction, not a strategy.*

- *The behavior is not better explained by another mental or neurological condition, nor by substance use.*

- *The outbursts cause significant distress or impair functioning, affecting relationships, work, education, or quality of life.*

This diagnosis is not just about *how often* one feels angry, but about the dysregulation of that anger, its intensity, lack of control, and social consequences.

So why talk about IED in a chapter about news media and visual rage?

Because many of the features of rage cycles fueled by sensationalized media, especially when consumed compulsively over time, mirror the mechanisms of IED: impulsivity, lack of proportion, emotional flooding, and social fallout. While watching the news may not "cause" IED, repeated overexposure to triggering content without emotional regulation may lead some individuals closer to a behavioral pattern that fits the profile.

In short: rage can be learned, conditioned, and reinforced, especially through visual stimuli.

We must begin to ask: *Is my media diet conditioning my nervous system to overreact?*
Are my emotional responses being manipulated by someone else's agenda?
At what point does reactive anger stop serving me and start consuming me?

Breakdown: How Visual Media Fuels Emotional Dysregulation

Our nervous system isn't built for *constant activation*. Visual media, especially news and social platforms, flood us with stimuli engineered to grab attention, and keep us emotionally hooked.

Here's how the rage cycle gets fueled, neurologically:

1. Trigger → Amygdala Hijack

When a story, image, or video evokes fear or anger, the amygdala (our brain's emotional processing center) takes over. Logic and nuance get sidelined by urgency and instinct.

2. Dopamine → Attention Loop

Outrageous content, especially when it's framed with "breaking news," flashing visuals, or dramatic music, releases dopamine, creating a *reward loop*. You keep scrolling or watching, not because it makes you feel good, but because your brain is chasing emotional resolution.

3. Cortisol Overload

Chronic exposure to upsetting visual content leads to cortisol (stress hormone) buildup. Elevated cortisol over time can result in irritability, anxiety, trouble sleeping, and, importantly, lowered emotional regulation.

4. Mirror Neurons → Emotional Contagion

Seeing others in distress, anger, or panic on screen can trigger empathic emotional responses, thanks to mirror neurons. You absorb the energy, even if it's not happening to you directly.

Self-Assessment: Am I in a Media-Driven Rage Cycle?

Use this tool to check in with yourself. Answer honestly:

1. **After consuming news or social media, do I feel more agitated than before?**
   ☐ Never ☐ Sometimes ☐ Often ☐ Always

2. **Do I find myself venting or ranting often after viewing content?**
   ☐ Never ☐ Sometimes ☐ Often ☐ Always

3. **Have I gotten into arguments online or in person after consuming media?**
   ☐ No ☐ Occasionally ☐ Frequently ☐ Constantly

4. **Do I consume media in search of confirmation that "I'm right" or that others are wrong?**
   ☐ Not at all ☐ A little ☐ A lot ☐ Always

5. **Do I feel compelled to "stay updated" even when I know it's hurting my mental state?**
   ☐ No ☐ Occasionally ☐ Frequently ☐ Yes, every day

6. **Have people close to me mentioned that I seem more irritable or intense lately?**
   ☐ No ☐ Once or twice ☐ Yes, more than once ☐ Yes, frequently

If you answered "Often" or "Always" to more than three questions, you may be stuck in a rage cycle loop. Don't shame yourself, awareness is step one toward emotional and digital wellness.

Digital De-Escalation Guide: Breaking the Rage Cycle

Use these tools and habits to break free:

1. The 24-Hour Rule

Before reacting or posting, wait. Let your body process. What feels urgent in the moment often fades with time.

2. News-Free Mornings or Evenings

Create boundaries around news exposure. Mornings and pre-sleep hours are when your nervous system is most sensitive.

3. Engage With Media Intentionally, Not Habitually

Ask: *Why am I consuming this right now?* Curiosity or habit? Purpose or distraction?

4. Use Neutral Aggregators

Try platforms like [Ground News](#) or [AllSides](#) to view headlines from multiple perspectives.

5. Take Visual Breaks

Pause. Look away from screens. Go outside. Focus on your senses. *Regulate your nervous system before re-engaging.*

6. Name the Feeling

Instead of "I'm pissed off," try: "I feel frustrated because I care about justice, and I feel powerless right now." Naming reduces emotional intensity.

7. Balance With Regenerative Content

Balance consumption with healing visual input: art, nature, joyful stories, or affirming media from your community.

The Rewiring of Rage

The trauma of the COVID-19 pandemic left few untouched. Many witnessed the unraveling of their communities, or themselves, through visible, sometimes violent emotional dysregulation. The pandemic acted as a pressure cooker for grief, fear, and powerlessness. For some, it manifested as withdrawal. For others, it exploded into rage.

But the roots of this collective unrest run deeper. The 2016 U.S. presidential election marked a seismic moment in modern political discourse, one that cracked open deeply buried divides. The public arena became more hostile. Derisive comments and uncouth performances from figures in power normalized impulsive, aggressive communication. Many followed suit, responding to inflammatory statements with their own anger, often through the accelerated immediacy of visual platforms like Twitter, YouTube, and live-streamed media. Rage became contagious.

And science affirms this. In a 2016 study, researcher Royce Lee and colleagues identified neurological changes in individuals diagnosed with

Intermittent Explosive Disorder (IED) a clinical pattern of explosive anger outbursts. Their findings revealed:

> *"IED was associated with lower white matter integrity in long-range connections between the frontal and temporoparietal regions."*
> — Lee et al., 2016

This suggests that rage can rewire the brain, diminishing the capacity for emotional regulation and weakening the neurological pathways responsible for empathy, reflection, and connection. When those long-range connections are compromised, it becomes harder to take perspective, regulate emotions, or resist impulsive reactions. Essentially, the bridges that help us relate to others begin to break down.

Add mirror neurons into the equation, and we see how rage spreads like wildfire. These neurons allow us to simulate the emotional states of those around us. If someone approaches you yelling, even if the anger isn't directed at you, your body may unconsciously mirror their intensity, matching tone, posture, or emotion. It's an evolutionary survival mechanism.

But here's the twist: when rage comes from someone we perceive as *safe*, a friend, family member, or community figure, the betrayal stings deeper. We're more likely to respond impulsively. And in those moments, even the most grounded among us may fall into reactive, rageful patterns, especially if impulse control has been worn thin by stress, trauma, or chronic exposure to polarized media.

This is how visual culture doesn't just reflect the state of our society, it amplifies it. When screen after screen shows anger, division, confrontation, and emotional extremes, we begin to believe that this is *normal*. And when that becomes our baseline, our brains, and relationships, start to suffer.

Understanding Mirror Neurons & Emotional Contagion

Mirror neurons are specialized brain cells that activate both when we perform an action *and* when we observe someone else performing it. These neurons play a vital role in empathy, social bonding, and emotional learning, but they also make us vulnerable to emotional contagion.

When it comes to rage:

- Seeing someone else express anger or distress can *automatically trigger similar emotional states* in us.
- If that person is someone we know, trust, or see as part of our in-group, we're even more likely to mirror their emotions.

- In media environments, repeated exposure to rage-filled videos, comment sections, news clips, and reactionary takes can simulate this experience over and over, without the release of resolution or connection.

- We absorb the emotional tone of our digital environment. And when that environment is flooded with conflict, our brains may internalize that as a default state.

Rebuilding & Rewiring: Calming the Nervous System After Rage Exposure

Rage may rewire the brain, but so can healing. The following strategies support **neuroplasticity** (the brain's ability to change and grow), helping to rebuild pathways associated with regulation, empathy, and resilience.

1. Practice Deep Regulation

Engage in practices that activate the **parasympathetic nervous system** (the calming "rest and digest" response).

- Diaphragmatic breathing (4–7–8 method)
- Progressive muscle relaxation
- Mindfulness or guided meditation (especially body scans)

2. Limit Visual Exposure to Rage-Triggering Content

- Mute or unfollow accounts that lead to spirals of frustration.
- Set limits on time spent watching "reaction content," political takedowns, or rage-bait clips.
- Use grayscale mode or a content blocker to reduce sensory stimulation.

3. Strengthen Executive Function

The prefrontal cortex (home of logic, regulation, and impulse control) is directly impacted by trauma and chronic stress, but it can be strengthened through:

- Journaling (especially reflection and reframing)
- Problem-solving exercises
- Emotion labeling (name it to tame it)

4. Seek Connection That Soothes, Not Provokes

- Spend time with people who ground you.

- Use co-regulation, sharing space with a calm, present person, to help reset your nervous system.
- Avoid conversations where mutual dysregulation is the norm.

5. Use Creativity for Reprocessing

- Draw, paint, sing, dance, engage in non-verbal expression that helps release held tension.
- Creative acts stimulate brain integration, giving voice to emotions that rage might otherwise hijack.

Rewiring Takes Repetition

One mindful breath, one pause, one calm response, while powerful, isn't enough to rewire the brain. Neuroplasticity, the brain's ability to change, requires repetition and reinforcement over time. Just like building muscle, emotional regulation is a practice that depends on consistency.

We often talk about "gray matter" as the seat of thinking, but white matter plays a critical role in emotional processing and behavioral control. It is white matter that connects the brain's distinct regions, allowing them to communicate and function as an integrated whole.

As Mercadante and Tadi (2022) emphasize, gray matter is necessary for brain activity, but without white matter, that activity cannot coordinate effectively.

Neuroscientist Christopher Filley of the Dana Foundation (2005) put it this way:

> *"White matter is a vast, intertwining system of neural connections that join all four lobes of the brain (frontal, temporal, parietal, and occipital), and the brain's emotion center in the limbic system, into the complex brain maps being worked out by neuroscientists. All of the well-known cortical areas such as Broca's area, Wernicke's area, the prefrontal cortex, and the hippocampus are connected by white matter tracts to other regions of the brain. This suggests that the cortical regions act in concert to perform mental operations, and no cortical area acts in isolation.*
> *Without functioning white matter, the brain could be like a group of people in proximity to each other but unable to communicate with each other."*

In essence, white matter is what lets your brain's "departments" talk to one another. Damage or underdevelopment in these connections can disrupt emotional control, impulse regulation, and even empathy.

Who Is More Vulnerable to Rage?

Research from Royce Lee et al. (2016) further identifies cognitive and perceptual patterns common among individuals with Intermittent Explosive Disorder (IED). These tendencies offer insight into how rage can become a conditioned cycle:

1. **Hostile Attribution Bias**:
   People with anger regulation issues tend to misinterpret others' intentions, assuming threat or disrespect where none exists.

2. **Selective Attention to Conflict**:
   They notice only what reinforces their belief that the other person is being confrontational, ignoring signs of neutrality or goodwill.

3. **Overgeneralization of Hostility**:
   Even when there's no aggression, they assume others are being hostile, jumping to worst-case conclusions.

4. **Impaired Social Cue Integration**:
   They may miss important details in a social interaction, like body language, tone, or context, and respond impulsively based on incomplete information.

These traits don't just occur in clinical diagnoses. They are also exacerbated by media environments that prime people to expect conflict, dehumanize opposition, and reward outrage.

When social media and visual platforms serve up constant cues of hostility, sarcasm, takedowns, moral grandstanding, it's no surprise that our perception begins to shift toward constant vigilance and overreaction.

The Vacuum Effect: Bite-Sized Rage and Common Enemy Politics

What we're witnessing is a kind of data vacuum constant intake of highly curated, emotionally charged content that often ignores key social dynamics and context. Bite-sized data dumps, like news clips or hot-take articles, are often framed through the emotional lens of the author or presenter. This framing increases the susceptibility of viewers to enter rage cycles, as they consume information that provokes a response but omits nuance.

And it's not just the mainstream news.

A growing number of individuals, podcasters, vloggers, bloggers, and influencers, have built entire platforms around this very mechanism. They dissect the world selectively, amplifying certain facts, omitting others, and packaging their perspectives for maximum emotional impact. The goal? Engagement. Loyalty. Virality.

Whether consciously or not, they often operate within a framework designed to incite fear, provoke anger, or generate tribal solidarity, usually by pointing to an "other" or enemy. This narrative manipulation isn't new, but it's become hyper-personalized and algorithmically supported.

Who Is More Vulnerable to Rage?

1. Hostile Attribution Bias
People with anger management issues tend to misunderstand the intentions of other people in socital situations.

2. Selective Attention to Conflict
They only notice things that reinforce their beliefs that the recipient of their rage is presenting a confrontational challenge.

3. Overgeneralization of Hostility
They think others are being hostile (even when they are not) and draw the wrong conclusions about others' intentions.

4. Impaired Social Cue Integration
They often don't take in all the data from a social interaction. such as body language or certain words.

What emerges is a wider phenomenon known as common enemy identity politics, the psychological and rhetorical tactic of building in-group identity by fixating on an opposing group as the problem. Instead of cultivating shared humanity, platforms profit from reinforcing division.

When your media diet is dominated by voices constantly telling you *who* to be angry at, *what* to fear, and *why* you're under threat, it becomes harder to question, breathe, or engage critically. Rage becomes a reflex. The world becomes a battleground. And nuance becomes collateral damage.

Common Enemy Identity Politics

"If you're not with us, you're against us."

This statement encapsulates the essence of common enemy identity politics, a psychological framework that has become increasingly visible in both online and in-person discourse. At its core, it's the idea that difference equals danger, and that disagreement is not just a challenge to our ideas, but a threat to our identity.

This binary thinking fuels rage cycles by creating emotional urgency: a sense of threat, betrayal, or moral panic. When media, especially visual and social platforms, frame people with differing views as *enemies*, they reinforce fear, simplify complex realities, and drive emotional reactivity. Nuance and dialogue become nearly impossible.

Social psychologist Jonathan Haidt explained this concept powerfully in an interview with *Big Think*:

> *"Me against my brother, me and my brother against our cousin, me, my brother, and cousin against the stranger.* It's a very general principle of social psychology. If you try to unite people: 'Let's all unite against them. They're bad people. They're the cause of the problems. Let's all stick together.' That's a really dangerous thing to do in a multiethnic society."
> — *Big Think, 2021*

This tribal logic once served evolutionary survival, but in the modern world, especially in multiethnic and diverse societies, it's deeply harmful. It encourages groups to rally not around shared values, but around shared enemies. And when this plays out on screens, looped, reshared, and algorithmically elevated, it doesn't just reflect division. It *manufactures* it.

Whether through political commentary, social media infighting, or news segments that frame opposition as morally bankrupt, common enemy identity politics thrives on visual and emotional oversimplification. The result? A society that shouts but rarely listens.

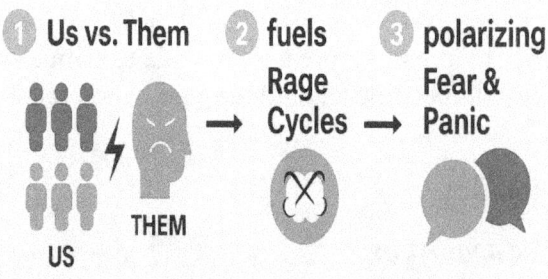

By framing those with differing views as enemies, visual media create emotional urgency—reinforcing division and fueling reactivity.

The Power, and Purpose, of Identity Politics

Identity politics are a *natural and necessary expression* of the values, experiences, and cultural norms shared by historically marginalized communities. For individuals who hold identities shaped by religion, race, gender, sexuality, or immigration status, such as Muslim Americans, queer folks, or BIPOC communities, identity is not abstract. It is lived. Felt. Often contested.

Because of systemic and overt oppression, these communities form a sense of collective identity not out of exclusion, but out of survival and solidarity. Shared experiences of marginalization create shared understanding, which in turn gives rise to political action, not only to resist, but to reclaim. Reclaim joy. Reclaim safety. Reclaim visibility. Reclaim voice.

As philosopher Jari Ilmonen (2019) explains:

> *"The multiply burdened concept of 'identity politics' usually refers to the shared experience of oppression by certain subjugated groups, whether defined by gender, class, political status, sexuality, ethnicity, race or some other characteristic, which provides a basis for group politics.*
> *According to the Stanford Encyclopedia of Philosophy, 'identity political formations typically aim to secure the political freedom of a specific constituency marginalized within its larger context. Members of that constituency assert or reclaim ways of understanding their distinctiveness that challenge dominant oppressive characterizations, with the goal of greater self-determination.'*
> *Identity politics thus presumes a shared subjective experience of the members of the particular group, an essence of identity."*
> — Ilmonen, 2019

In this framing, identity politics are not about creating division, they're about creating belonging. They motivate us toward liberation, equity, and dignity without requiring an "us vs. them" worldview. At their best, identity politics are rooted in values-based solidarity: a shared commitment to undoing harm and building justice.

That's not to say that identity politics are never co-opted or distorted. Sometimes, righteous anger rooted in oppression spills into rage, especially when met with continued resistance, gaslighting, or dehumanization. It's easy, in those moments, to slide into common enemy identity politics. But it's also possible to redirect that energy toward growth, healing, and change.

The key lies in managing the rage cycle, learning how to hold space for valid anger while staying grounded in shared values and vision. Rage unchecked can consume us. But when it is honored, processed, and alchemized, it becomes a force for transformation.

Adapted from Stuart Fensterheim, LCSW (Good Therapy, 2017)

Whether in romantic partnerships, friendships, or social interactions, anger is a signal, not a solution. If left unchecked, it spirals. But with awareness and effort, it can become a catalyst for connection and healing.

How to Combat the Anger Cycle

1. Acknowledge the Problem

You can't break the cycle if you don't see it. Naming the pattern is the first act of power and self-awareness. Denial keeps the rage loop running.

2. Learn to Cool Down

Find your personal "reset" button. Humor can be powerful, especially when there's trust. In couples with strong foundations, laughter can transform conflict into connection. But trust must come first. Emotional safety is the baseline.

3. Think Before You Speak

If you're speaking while triggered, you're likely not reasoning, you're reacting. Step back, breathe, and try to understand what unmet need or attachment fear might be fueling your anger.

Many conflicts stem from disconnection, not the surface issue.

4. Own the Anger, and What's Underneath

Anger is often a secondary emotion. The real drivers might be vulnerability, abandonment, shame, or grief. Ask: *What pain is hiding beneath this reaction?*

5. Journal Your Feelings

Use writing to get beneath the noise. What matters to you in the relationship? What are your fears, needs, hopes? Journaling can reveal patterns and offer clarity, whether shared with a partner, therapist, or kept private.

6. Address It Early, Without Blame

Don't wait for resentment to fester. Speak up, gently and non-defensively. When your partner is angry, look beyond the surface. Often, the real message is: *"I don't feel seen, safe, or loved."*

Important: If anger becomes abusive, verbally, emotionally, or physically, this is not your responsibility. Reach out for support.
Domestic Violence Hotline: 1-800-799-SAFE (7233)

thehotline.org

Text "START" to 88788

7. Practice Deep Listening

True communication requires active listening, not just waiting to talk. Validate your partner's experience. Take responsibility when needed. Apologize with sincerity. Forgive when you're ready. Repair is possible, with effort and sometimes professional support.

Anger doesn't have to destroy relationships or consume our emotional health. It can become a bridge, if we learn to cross it with care.

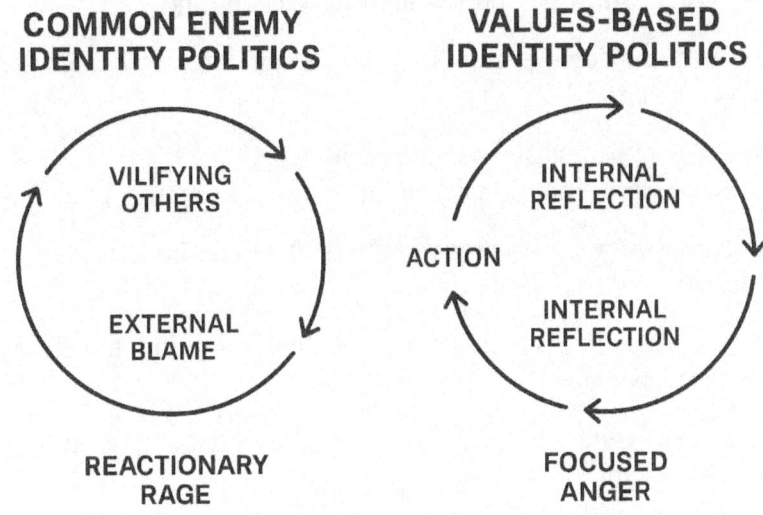

Whole-Person Strategies for Interrupting the Anger Cycle

Adapted from Christopher Bergland, author of The Athlete's Way *(Psychology Today, 2016)*

Rather than viewing anger solely as a behavioral problem, Bergland encourages us to treat it as a nervous system imbalance, one that can be regulated and transformed through deliberate physical, emotional, and social practices.

1. Activate the "Tend-and-Befriend" Response with Diaphragmatic Breathing

Outbursts of rage spike adrenaline, cortisol, blood pressure, and heart rate. To counter this, engage the parasympathetic nervous system, your body's rest-and-digest mechanism, by practicing slow, deep belly breathing.

Why it works: The vagus nerve, a key player in emotional regulation, is activated by diaphragmatic breathing, slowing your heartbeat, lowering stress hormones, and increasing calm.

2. Boost Self-Control Through Exercise

Self-control is trainable. UK researchers found a bidirectional feedback loop between executive function and regular exercise, the more you move, the more self-regulated you become, and vice versa.

Exercise trio for resilience:

- **Aerobic Activity** → energizes & clears mental fog
- **Strength Training** → builds stamina & discipline
- **Mindfulness/Yoga** → calms, recenters, and integrates the body-mind connection

Need to calm down? Emphasize yoga and walking.
Need to let out energy? Focus on cardio and strength training.

3. Improve Empathy with Loving-Kindness Meditation (LKM) & Reading Fiction

To manage your anger wisely, cultivate your theory of mind, the ability to see from another's perspective.

Loving-Kindness Meditation (LKM) nurtures compassion by guiding you to send good wishes to:

- Loved ones
- Strangers
- Someone who's hurt you
- Yourself

Reading literary fiction also improves empathy and perspective-taking, just like imagining plays or strategies in sports, it builds social imagination. Of course, try and choose diverse tales that present stories that may challenge your relationship with empathy.

Perhaps there are characters you don't agree with, try and see their reality through their eyes. This isn't easy, by the way.

4. Cultivate Humanism Through Contact with Outgroups

We tend to be less empathetic to people outside our group, until we connect with them directly.
Face-to-face experiences with people of different races, beliefs, or backgrounds can reshape empathy at the neurological level.

Even small acts of kindness from a stranger can increase our compassion toward an entire group.

Engaging in community-based activities, youth groups, volunteer work, or sports clubs also increases long-term well-being and relational intelligence.

5. Tap Into Awe and Transcend the Ego

Awe, whether inspired by nature, art, or wonder, has a powerful neurological effect. It shifts attention away from the ego and toward something larger, encouraging prosocial behavior and emotional balance.

How to Combat the Anger Cycle
(Adapted from Stuart Fensterheim, LCSW – Good Therapy, 2017)

1. Acknowledge the Problem
Denial fuels the cycle. Name the pattern to begin breaking it.

2. Learn to Cool Down
Find your reset; step away, breathe, laugh (if trust is there). Safety is the foundation of humor and healing.

3. Think Before You Speak
Reacting = triggered. Responding = reflective.
Pause and ask: What need is going unmet?

4. Own the Anger—and What's Underneath
Anger often masks fear, grief or shame.
Ask yourself: What pain is driving this?

5. Journal Your Feelings
Use writing to uncover patterns, needs, and truths.
It can clarify communication—even if kept private.

6. Address It Early—Without Blame
Don't let resentment grow.
Speak calmly about how you feel 'I , not what they did.
Note: If anger becomes abuse, seek help immediately.
📞 1-800-739-SAFE | Text 'START' to 88738
🌐 thehotline org

7. Practice Deep Listening
Don't just wait to talk –really listen.
Validate. Apologize when needed. Forgive when ready.
Healing takes effort–and sometimes therapy.

Try this:

- Gaze at a star-filled sky, powerful artwork, or breathtaking landscape.

- Let yourself feel small, but connected.

- Let awe dissolve the boundaries of anger, self-focus, and control.

From Rage to Resilience

By weaving together these practices, breath, movement, empathy, awe, and connection, you create a buffer between stimulus and reaction. You interrupt the cycle not by suppressing anger, but by transforming its energy into something meaningful. Rage doesn't only live in our minds, it's reflected, amplified, and monetized through AI-curated media. That's where we head next.

Summary

- **Rage Cycles & Brain Chemistry**: Visual media triggers anger responses, altering brain chemistry and reinforcing emotional reactions.

- **Identity Politics & Polarization**: Media-driven outrage strengthens ideological divisions, deepening group identities.

- **Social Media Algorithms**: Platforms amplify anger-driven content to maximize engagement, trapping users in feedback loops.

- **Neurological Impact**: Repeated exposure to rage-inducing content rewires the brain, making individuals more reactive over time.

- **Breaking the Cycle**: Strategies like mindful media consumption, emotional regulation, and critical thinking can help reduce susceptibility to these cycles.

Chapter Twenty-One

"The future has not been written. There is no fate but what we make for ourselves." -John Conner Terminator 2 Judgment Day.

AI: Friend, Foe, or Filter?

Artificial Intelligence, or AI, is something I initially hadn't planned to include in this book. That changed quickly, thanks to the growing wave of research raising serious concerns about AI's influence on the content we consume, and how we search for, absorb, and believe information.

In a world already flooded with information, what happens when that content is no longer even created by humans?

Hopefully, we're not heading for a *Skynet* situation, but the implications are still unsettling.

According to the Copenhagen Institute for Future Studies, expert Timothy Shoup estimates that by 2025 to 2030, 99% to 99.9% of the internet's content will be AI-generated, especially if models like OpenAI's GPT family continue to scale in adoption. As quoted by *The Byte*:

> *"The internet would be completely unrecognizable."*
> — Hood, (2022)

If that prediction holds, we'll be navigating a sea of content, articles, videos, commentary, even visual media, created not by people, but by machines trained on people. And therein lies the rub: AI learns from us. It mirrors our biases, our misinformation, our humor, our cruelty. If we create chaos, AI will learn to replicate it, efficiently, at scale, and without question.

We already struggle to distinguish between fact and framing, objectivity and opinion, truth and satire. What happens when deepfakes allow anyone to "say" anything, or when AI-generated images blur the line between real and synthetic reality? What happens when a model starts serving us exactly what we *want* to hear, rather than what we *need* to learn?

On one hand, I remain cautiously optimistic. I, for one, *welcome our new AI overlords*, if, and only if, they help us cut through the noise, present more objective data, and surface truths that challenge our biases. There is potential for AI to sift through misinformation and identify high-integrity sources faster than we ever could. But there's also danger: a period of disorientation, where people mistake anything presented with confidence and clarity for fact.

If a deepfake convincingly shows a world leader making a statement they never made, or an AI-written article spreads misinformation with an authoritative tone, who is responsible? The human who trained it? The user who shared it? The machine that had no intent?

This is why developing a strong and balanced visual diet is more urgent than ever before. Before we ask whether AI can think for us, we need to ask whether we are thinking critically about what we see. As we enter this next digital era, one driven by algorithms and machine creativity, we must become *better curators of reality*.

Because in a world of infinite information, discernment is power.

AI in Healthcare: Support, Not Replacement

While much of the conversation around artificial intelligence (AI) focuses on risk, deepfakes, misinformation, and automation, there are also deeply human-centered applications of AI that deserve our attention. In fields like healthcare, AI has the potential to support and enhance human interaction, rather than replace it.

A 2017 study by Sinsky et al. found that physicians who used documentation support tools, such as dictation software or medical scribes, were able to spend more direct face time with patients than those who did not. These tools didn't interfere with care, they created space for it.

Further research by Amisha et al. (2019) expands on the benefits of AI in healthcare:

"Increased AI usage in medicine not only reduces manual labor and frees up the primary care physician's time, but also increases productivity, precision, and efficacy...
AI was used to screen existing medications to fight the Ebola virus, a process that would have otherwise taken years. With AI, we are moving toward the concept of precision medicine."

This isn't about cold, mechanical care, it's about removing obstacles to human connection. When a clinician isn't overwhelmed by paperwork or manual data entry, they can focus more on listening, observing, and treating.

In fact, in some studies, AI outperformed dermatologists at identifying suspicious skin lesions. Not because machines are smarter, but because they can analyze more cases, more quickly, and learn from them at scale. What a clinician sees over decades, an AI model can "see" in minutes.

Similarly, AI decision-support tools have been shown to offer value in areas of clinical disagreement, like identifying tuberculosis on chest radiographs. These tools don't replace the expert, they offer a second, often more precise opinion that helps reduce diagnostic error.

Reimagining Trust in Healthcare Through AI

How lovely to have more face-to-face time with your doctor. In a world where many carry the weight of medical trauma, systemic neglect, or generational mistrust of the healthcare system, this isn't a luxury. It's a necessity.

As explored earlier in this book, there are deeply rooted reasons why so many, especially in historically marginalized communities, struggle to trust the medical establishment. That history cannot be erased. But perhaps, with the right tools, it can begin to evolve.

AI may be part of that evolution.

When used ethically and thoughtfully, AI can shift the current model of care from one of task management to one of relationship-building. By automating documentation, streamlining diagnostics, and reducing cognitive overload, AI creates room for something we desperately need more of in medicine: human presence.

Imagine a visit where your doctor has time to listen, not just diagnose.
Where they remember your story, not just your symptoms.
Where your needs and values guide the plan, not just the chart.

When we know our doctors, and feel known by them, we're more likely to advocate for our own care, ask important questions, and share vulnerable truths. This deepens autonomy, agency, and outcomes.

By supporting a person-centered approach, AI could help reframe our entire association with healthcare. What if clinical care no longer felt transactional, but relational? What if trust wasn't the exception, but the baseline?

If this shift becomes real, it won't just change our access to care.
It could reshape our visual diet, replacing the cold, clinical imagery we associate with medicine with scenes of connection, collaboration, and care.

When AI Learns Our Biases: A Cautionary Lens

While AI promises efficiency, personalization, and even greater face-to-face time with doctors, we must not ignore its negative potential, especially when it comes to healthcare for BIPOC communities.

Despite efforts to reduce bias through digitization and algorithmic tools, healthcare researchers are increasingly warning that AI can reproduce, or even worsen, existing disparities. And this isn't surprising. As I've discussed earlier in this book, the relationship between BIPOC folks and healthcare has been marked by harm, erasure, and mistrust, much of which is visually reinforced through historical media and systemic representation.

As Dr. Bryne (2021) explains:

"The digitization of healthcare data and greater reliance on technology tools like Artificial Intelligence (AI), have been identified as a means of reducing the kinds of bias the IOM (International Organization for Migration) found. Unfortunately, the research on AI systems and the algorithms on which they are built are finding that in some cases, these tools may actually be making disparities worse."

The problem lies not in the tool itself, but in the lack of diversity and critical oversight during its creation.

As Panch, et al. (2019) point out:

"The process of developing AI algorithms is both an art and a science. Data science teams rely on engineers and statisticians, professions where there are known issues regarding gender and racial diversity."

In other words, the worldview embedded in the code reflects the worldview of those building it. When BIPOC perspectives are missing from development teams, training data, and validation processes, the resulting algorithms reflect a limited and skewed reality.

Ntsoutsi et al. (2019) raise an even deeper ethical concern:

"AI-based systems are widely employed nowadays to make decisions that have far-reaching impact on individuals and society... Therefore, it is necessary to move beyond traditional AI algorithms optimized for predictive performance and embed ethical and legal principles in their design, training, and deployment to ensure social good."

This is about more than fairness. It's about human rights. AI can't simply be optimized for prediction; it must be designed for justice.

If we aren't vigilant, AI in healthcare could further entrench the very inequities it claims to solve. And when the visuals, charts, outcomes, and predictions, reinforce these disparities without context, they risk re-traumatizing communities already burdened by generational neglect.

AI in Education: Promise and Precaution

Another space where AI is expanding its influence, perhaps more quietly than in healthcare or media, is education. And its potential is both exciting and complex.

AI isn't just showing up on screens. It's entering classrooms, lecture halls, and learning management systems. It's shaping how students engage, how instructors teach, and how institutions evaluate. In higher education, in particular, learners can now tap into the vast data reservoirs of artificial intelligence to supplement their academic journey.

At face value, this seems like less of a threat to academic integrity, assuming, of course, that AI's outputs are anchored in peer-reviewed, scholarly sources. But even here, there are risks. If peer-reviewed journals themselves become AI-generated or overly reliant on automated writing, the feedback loop could distort what we consider rigorous, reliable knowledge. The visual diet of academia, its charts, references, and authority, could subtly shift, shaping how we value (or question) truth.

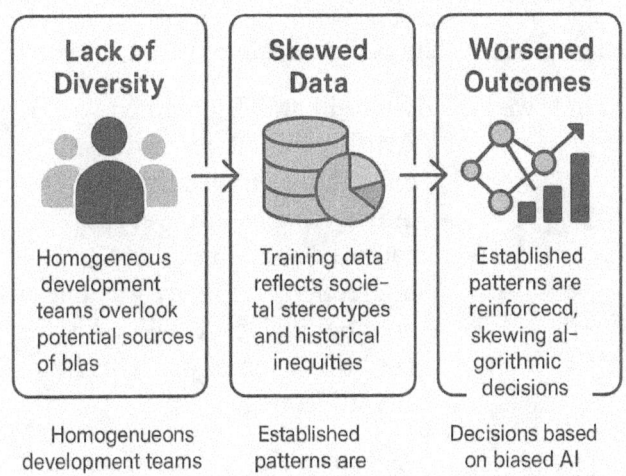

That said, early models of AI integration in education are promising, especially when they support, not replace, the educator's role.

As researchers Chen et al. (2020) note:

"AI initially took the form of computer and computer-related technologies, transitioning to web-based and online intelligent education systems, and ultimately with the use of embedded computer systems... the use of humanoid robots and web-based chatbots to perform instructors' duties and functions independently or with instructors."

"Using these platforms, instructors have been able to perform different administrative functions, such as reviewing and grading students' assignments more effectively and efficiently... Meanwhile, because the systems leverage machine learning and adaptability, curriculum and content has been customized and personalized in line with students' needs, which has fostered uptake and retention, thereby improving learner's experience and overall quality of learning."

This paints a hopeful picture: fewer hours lost to grading, more time spent engaging, and personalized pathways that meet students where they are. AI, when used wisely, can make learning more accessible, inclusive, and individualized.

But, as always, equity must be part of the equation.

If the algorithms aren't checked for bias, or if access to high-quality AI tools is limited by income, geography, or infrastructure, then AI may simply reproduce educational inequality at scale.

This is why we must think critically about how AI is trained, who it serves, and whose voices are centered in its knowledge pools. Education should be a space of empowerment, not extraction.

Already in the System: Living Inside the AI Ecosystem

Whether we recognize it or not, we already live in an AI-governed world. Artificial Intelligence doesn't just exist in labs or headlines, it quietly shapes our everyday routines, decisions, and interactions. In many ways, it's not about *when* AI will take over, but how much of our lives it already controls.

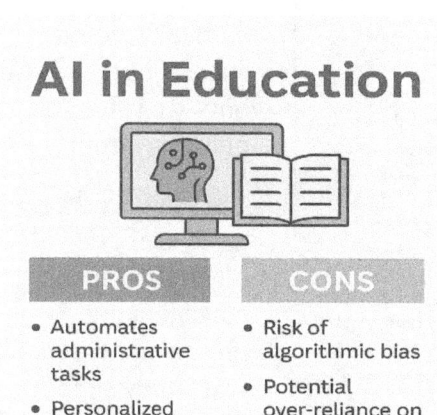

As Mark Mayne from *TechRadar* writes in his 2018 article *"How much did AI control you today?"*,

AI is embedded in nearly every aspect of our digital environment:

- *Policing: Predictive systems in some parts of the world analyze behavior patterns and social data to flag individuals likely to commit offenses.*

- *Banking: Large financial institutions use AI to manage risk, track spending trends, and optimize investment strategies.*

- *Home & Devices: Smart assistants like Alexa, Siri, and Google Home learn from our voices, preferences, and habits, sometimes more intimately than our family does.*

- *Work & Cybersecurity: AI software quietly scans for threats on your company's servers and blocks malicious activity before you ever notice.*

- *Internet Browsing & Shopping: Every "recommended for you" product, every search autocomplete, every targeted ad is filtered through AI prediction models.*

- *Healthcare: Diagnostic AI systems compare symptoms, analyze scans, and present possible illnesses within seconds, often with greater accuracy than a human could provide in a single sitting.*

In short: we don't use AI. We live within it.

But with this quiet control comes a louder, more chilling possibility, the emergence of superintelligence with goals misaligned to our own. As Jason Alan Snyder, Chief Technology Officer at Momentum Worldwide, warns:

"The main concern of beneficial-AI is with intelligence: specifically, intelligence whose goals are misaligned with ours…
A super-intelligent and super-wealthy AI could easily pay or manipulate humans to unwittingly do its bidding.
The Hollywood-style robot fantasy is part of the myth that machines can't control humans. Intelligence enables control: humans control lions not because we are stronger, but because we are smarter.
This means that if we cede our position as smartest on our planet, it's possible that we might also cede control."
— TechRadar, 2018

This shifts the fear from physical destruction to psychological and social manipulation. Control doesn't have to look like a robot uprising, it could simply look like us thinking we're making choices, when in fact our choices have already been made *for* us, by models trained on our fears, habits, and histories.

If visual diets shape our thoughts, then AI can and maybe will curate that diet.

This moment calls for critical awareness, not fear-based paralysis, but intentional observation. Who is designing the systems that guide our daily lives? What assumptions are baked into their code? What values are shaping our search results, diagnoses, shopping carts, and online debates?

The more control we passively give away, the harder it may be to reclaim.

Reclaiming the Driver's Seat: Choosing in the Age of AI

How do we manage in a world where AI curates our visual media, influences our decisions, and shapes how we spend our time?

The answer might be simpler, and more human, than we think.

We do what we've always done:
We choose.

Throughout history, individuals and communities have reclaimed agency in the face of overwhelming systems. Whether it was navigating censorship, resisting propaganda, or reclaiming narrative power through storytelling, we've found ways to reintroduce choice, even when the odds were stacked against us.

Today, we are presented with a similar challenge.
AI isn't inherently good or bad, it's a tool. But how we engage with that tool matters deeply.

We can choose to stay on a path shaped by algorithms and engagement metrics,
or we can choose to pause, reflect, and redirect.

We are still the drivers of our own lives.

We can choose to listen to the GPS, or we can take the scenic route.
We can allow AI to predict our behavior, or we can act outside prediction.
We can accept what's served, or we can curate our own visual diet.

There will, of course, be consequences to resisting the AI-driven ease of choice. It may require more effort, more time, and more critical awareness. But at this moment in history, we still have the power to choose. And that window, the one where intentionality is still possible, is one we must not let close.

So, the next time you feel pulled into the vortex of curated content, remember this:

You don't have to watch.
You don't have to scroll.
You don't have to believe everything the screen presents.

You can turn your attention elsewhere. You can choose presence over automation, people over prediction, and meaning over metrics.

You are still the author of your own attention.

Ease or Autonomy? The Dilemma of Delegating Control

The larger choices, the ones with the power to regulate AI, ensure ethical boundaries, and protect autonomy, may lie beyond any individual's scope. These will likely require legislative intervention and collective action, if such action even aligns with what the majority wants.

Because here's the hard truth: the more convenient AI makes our lives, the less likely some may be to question it, or want to resist.

It's far easier to hand over your banking details to an AI-powered financial assistant than to learn the intricacies of economics and trading yourself. It's far easier to let the algorithm pick your entertainment than to scroll through lifetimes' worth of options, researching, previewing, and deciding for yourself.

This trade-off between ease and agency isn't new, but in the AI age, it's exponentially amplified.

Berente et al. (2021) explore this tension in their research on the evolving nature of AI and the role of human management. Their findings highlight three key concerns:

> • Autonomy: AI systems make decisions and take actions that have real-world consequences, often without human involvement or even awareness.
>
> • Learning: With sophisticated learning abilities, AI has entered complex decision-making domains like speech, object recognition, and natural language, spaces once considered uniquely human.
>
> • Inscrutability: As AI becomes more advanced, its outputs and decision-making processes become increasingly opaque, intelligible only to a select few, or in some cases, to no one at all.

This raises a haunting question:
What happens when we can no longer understand the tools that shape our lives?

At that point, choice becomes an illusion. Control is ceded not just through consent, but through inability. If we cannot interrogate the outcomes or logic of AI, we are no longer autonomous participants. We are passengers in systems that drive themselves.

And yet, there is still time to ask hard questions. To slow down. To choose understanding, even when it's inconvenient.

Because the cost of convenience is often curiosity. And curiosity is the foundation of all critical thinking.

The Distortion of Reality: Deepfakes and the Threat to Truth

Deepfakes are more than just eerie curiosities, they are a potentially destabilizing force, especially in their disproportionate impact on Black and Brown communities. These AI-generated distortions have the power to reshape perception, undermine trust, and fuel misinformation with terrifying precision.

At their core, deepfakes weaponize believability. They manipulate not just pixels and sound, but public opinion, social cohesion, and institutional trust.

According to the Department of Homeland Security, deepfakes are:

"An emergent type of threat falling under the greater and more pervasive umbrella of synthetic media, utilizing a form of artificial intelligence/machine learning to create believable, realistic videos, pictures, audio, and text of events which never happened."

That last phrase, "events which never happened", is the heart of the danger. When reality itself becomes contestable, what happens to accountability? To justice? To community trust in leadership, media, or one another?

For BIPOC communities, the risk is layered. These technologies can be used to:

- Falsely implicate activists or public figures in fabricated scandals.
- Circulate damaging stereotypes or inflammatory content that plays into historical patterns of dehumanization.
- Create confusion around real footage, allowing bad actors to discredit authentic evidence of injustice as "fake."

This isn't science fiction, it's happening now.

And it's not just about what's fake. It's about the doubt it casts on what's real. When deepfakes blur the line between truth and fiction, they create fertile ground for manipulation, fear, and disengagement, particularly in communities that already face systemic erasure or distortion in the media.

Understanding Deepfakes: How Machines Learn to Deceive

To truly grasp the power, and danger, of deepfakes, it helps to understand how they work. According to the University of Virginia's Information Security Department, a deepfake is:

"An artificial image or video (a series of images) generated by a special kind of machine learning called 'deep' learning."

Layperson's Explanation:

Deep learning, like all machine learning, involves feeding an algorithm with large sets of examples so it can learn to reproduce patterns. It mimics how humans learn. Think of a baby who experiments with putting things in their mouth, they eventually figure out what's food and what's not. In the same way, an AI model is fed thousands (or millions) of real images until it can produce fake images that closely resemble the originals.

In this analogy:

- The real images online = objects around the house.
- The AI model = the baby.
- Training = trial and error until the baby/algorithm gets it right.

The result? Deepfakes that are so realistic they often fool even the human eye.

Technical Breakdown (For the Curious):

Deep learning uses neural networks, which are computational models designed to mimic the structure of the human brain. These networks consist of multiple hidden layers, each performing mathematical transformations to process and convert input (e.g., real images) into output (e.g., highly realistic fake images).

Here's where it gets even more sophisticated:
Deepfakes are often built using two competing algorithms, a method known as a Generative Adversarial Network (GAN):

- One algorithm (the generator) creates fake images.
- The second algorithm (the discriminator) tries to detect whether the image is real or fake.

These two models train by competing with each other, like sparring partners, each pushing the other to improve. Over time, this process produces fakes so good that even trained eyes and machines have trouble telling the difference.

> *"By pitting models against each other, you end up with a model that's extremely adept at producing fake images; so adept, in fact,*

that humans often can't tell that the output is a fake at all."
— *University of Virginia*

The Horrifying Bit: When Reality Itself Is Compromised

Take a breath. This next section may feel heavier than what we've explored before. You may even want to approach it in parts, depending on how you typically handle stressors or difficult content.

Because while the idea of deepfakes can feel abstract or cinematic, the real-world impact is already here, and it's deeply unsettling.

Legal scholar Danielle Citron (Boston University School of Law) and national security expert Robert Chesney (University of Texas) outline just how far-reaching the dangers of deepfake technology are. In their widely cited 2019 paper, they write:

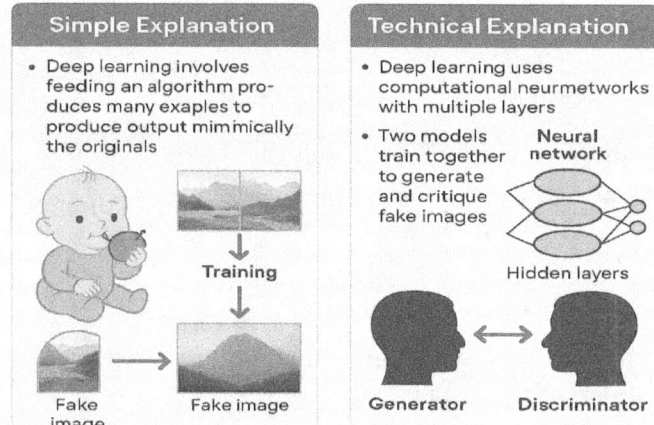

"Harmful lies are nothing new. But the ability to distort reality has taken an exponential leap forward with 'deep fake' technology. This capability makes it possible to create audio and video of real people saying and doing things they never said or did."

And it's not just about what the fakes show, it's how believable they are.

Thanks to machine learning, deepfakes are becoming:

- More realistic
- Harder to detect
- Easier to distribute
- Accessible to virtually anyone with a computer

This is no longer the domain of hackers or intelligence agencies, it's a tool that bad actors, trolls, political agitators, and even everyday users can deploy to sow confusion, discredit victims, or manipulate public perception.

As Citron and Chesney continue:

> "While deep-fake technology will bring certain benefits, it also will introduce many harms. The marketplace of ideas already suffers from truth decay... Deep fakes will exacerbate this problem significantly. Individuals and businesses will face novel forms of exploitation, intimidation, and personal sabotage."

> "The risks to our democracy and to national security are profound as well."

We're entering a world where video evidence no longer guarantees truth, and where trust in what we see and hear, a foundational element of democracy, is eroding.

And once that trust is gone? The consequences ripple across everything:

- Survivors of violence may be discredited with faked footage.
- Public figures can be manipulated to say inflammatory things they never said.
- Elections, protests, and institutions can be sabotaged not by violence, but by believable lies.

This is the dark side of a distorted visual diet: one that not only misinforms but destabilizes.

Digital Literacy and Racialized Harm in the Age of AI

One of the most proactive ways to prevent harm in our digital world is through digital literacy. But not everyone has equal access to the tools or education needed to navigate this complex terrain. Unfortunately, many Black and Brown individuals remain at elevated risk for digital harm, not due to lack of intelligence or interest, but due to historic and systemic inequities that have limited access, representation, and inclusion in digital spaces.

When people are not given the opportunity to understand the algorithms, platforms, and environments that shape their perception of reality, they are left vulnerable to manipulated content, disinformation, and algorithmic bias, what we've been referring to as a poor visual diet.

According to the National Center for Education Statistics (NCES):

> *"Latinx adults have the lowest rate of digital literacy relative to other racial groups. Only 65% of Latinx adults were digitally literate, compared to an average of 84% of all U.S. adults."*
> — *Pawlowski & Mamedova, cited in Mercado, National Hispanic Media Coalition*

But access is only half the equation. Bias in the design and enforcement of AI systems is also a major contributor to harm.

Take content moderation, for example. AI models designed to detect and remove hate speech have been shown to disproportionately flag and censor content written by Black users, especially those who use African American English (AAE), a valid, complex, and culturally rooted dialect.

> *"Leading AI models for processing hate speech were 1.5x more likely to flag tweets as offensive when written by African Americans, and 2.2x more likely to flag tweets written in African American English."*
> — *Ghaffray, 2019*

Because these systems are trained on data and language filtered through the biases of their largely white and under-diverse engineering teams, they misidentify cultural speech as harmful, while often overlooking coded or subtle hate speech from majority users.

> *"Without adequate human quality and bias control, people of color are more likely to be kicked off platforms or have their posts taken down based solely on their perceived race."*
> — *Mercado, M., NHMC*

This doesn't just affect expression, it undermines digital citizenship, representation, and community-building.

Instead of creating safer spaces, these biased systems often silence the very voices they should be protecting.

Deepfakes as a Tool of Destabilization

The harm caused by deepfakes doesn't stop at individual discrediting. The consequences are far-reaching, with the potential to destabilize communities, organizations, entire cultures, and even nations.

As synthetic media becomes more accessible and realistic, its use in manipulating narratives, sowing division, and spreading disinformation grows exponentially. According to Dunard (2020):

> "Deepfakes pose national security risks to both individuals and society as a whole in both foreign and domestic contexts.
> While fake images present risks, fake video and audio allow greater flexibility and therefore pose greater threats.
> Individuals targeted by deepfakes face reputational harm, loss of employment, theft and identity fraud. They also may feel threatened and powerless to respond or disprove the fakes."

At scale, the impact is even more alarming:

> "At a society-wide level, deepfakes can be used to spread disinformation; inflame racial, ethnic, cultural, and political tensions; influence election outcomes; and destabilize the U.S. economy.
> Changing socio-political developments like COVID-19, nationwide racial justice protests, and national elections exacerbate existing political tensions, opening new avenues for disinformation tactics targeting the public."

In moments of public unrest, racial injustice, or health crises, deepfakes don't just distort truth, they exploit vulnerability. They target the very moments when people need clarity, unity, and trusted information the most.

For BIPOC communities, already dealing with historic and present-day distortion in mainstream media, the implications are even more severe. Deepfakes can be weaponized to suppress voices, discredit movements, or amplify harmful stereotypes. They can also deepen public mistrust of legitimate content, leading to widespread disbelief in actual footage of police violence, protests, or civil resistance.

In a world where reality is easily faked and harder to prove, truth becomes collateral damage. That's the real danger of a manipulated visual diet; it doesn't just deceive. It disorients.

Deepfakes and the End of Shared Reality

Our reality is already subjective. Each of us moves through the world with perceptions shaped by our socioeconomic status, cultural background, political beliefs, personal history, and more. These multiple realities co-exist, often in tension, but generally anchored by shared facts.

But what happens when even shared facts become malleable?

Deepfakes challenge not just what we believe, but how we know what to believe. When audio and video, the most powerful tools of evidence, can be easily fabricated, we face a chilling threat to our sense of safety, our civic integrity, and our grasp on reality itself.

These technologies make it possible to sway public opinion without violence, to launch ideological coups without firing a single shot.

And in an election year, the risks grow even more acute.

Imagine a well-timed deepfake, a candidate caught making a slur, confessing to a crime, or supporting a radical position. Released just days before voting, it could dissuade voters, suppress turnout, or incite unrest, even after being proven false. Because in the court of public opinion, emotion often outruns correction.

As legal scholars Chesney and Citron (2018) write:

> *"Deep-fake technology is emerging at a difficult time. The public is increasingly distrustful of the media and public officials (at least the public officials who are not aligned with their preferences). Deep-fake videos exacerbate distrust in civic and democratic institutions."*

> *"A healthy democracy requires a shared set of truths and facts for citizens to consider, debate, and ponder. Deep-fake videos undermine the possibility of having conversations about a shared reality and exacerbate the disinformation wars that disrupt democratic politics… Our society is imperiled when people can escape accountability for their words and actions by ascribing genuine audio and video content to deepfake technology."*

This is the double edge: not only can fakes be weaponized, but real evidence can be dismissed as fake. Accountability dissolves into ambiguity. Reality becomes negotiable.

And when we no longer agree on what's real, democracy loses its foundation.

Not All Doom and Gloom: Innovation and Digital Resilience

While deepfakes present real and disturbing threats, it's important to remember we are not powerless. A growing number of innovators, researchers, and ethical technologists are working to build detection systems, authentication tools, and protective frameworks to combat the harm of synthetic media.

In a 2024 Senate Judiciary Committee hearing on AI oversight, Deep Media CEO Rijul Gupta explained the unique approach his company is taking to stay ahead of the deepfake arms race:

> *"At Deep Media, we are both the cat and the mouse in the cat and mouse game.*
> *We have generative AI technology, but we don't give it out to people.*
> *We keep it internally and use that to train our detectors, and that is why we're here."*
> — PBS News, 2024

By using generative tools *responsibly*, to train detection models rather than publicly release them, Deep Media offers one model of how AI can be wielded for defense, not deception.

Meanwhile, legal scholars Chesney and Citron (2019) note another emerging solution:

> *"Companies like Truepic are working on methods of authentication. If those methods are adopted broadly (a big 'if'), it would help quickly authenticate content."*

The challenge, as they point out, is scale. Without platform-wide enforcement, such authentication tools may not reach the critical mass needed to shift culture. Major social platforms continue to prioritize eyeballs over ethics, often posting content with minimal verification because controversy drives clicks, and clicks drive profit.

But innovation in this space *is* happening. And more importantly, we, as everyday users, still have a powerful role to play.

By becoming more digitally literate, especially in marginalized communities, we can begin to reclaim control over what we consume and believe.

This isn't about doomscrolling or tech paranoia.
It's about understanding the systems that shape our visual diets, and learning how to spot the signs of distortion, bias, and manipulation.

It's about knowing:

- How tech is developed
- Who trains it
- What cultural assumptions it reinforces
- And how we can intervene, educate, and protect our communities

In this moment, digital literacy isn't optional.
It's survival.
It's resistance.
And it's power.

The Environmental Cost of Artificial Intelligence

Just as screens and digital devices carry an environmental burden, from mining rare earth materials to e-waste and poor recycling practices, artificial intelligence has a massive and growing carbon footprint of its own.

According to researchers at OpenAI, since 2012 the amount of computing power required to train state-of-the-art AI models has doubled approximately every 3.4 months. This exponential growth means we're not just dealing with smarter machines, but also with larger, hungrier ones.

A recent study highlighted by Kanungo (2024) and Hao (2020) warns:

> "By 2040, emissions from the Information and Communications Technology (ICT) industry are expected to reach 14% of global emissions, with the majority coming from data centers and communication networks."

In other words, the digital world, often seen as weightless or invisible, is producing a very real, material cost for the planet.

The study goes further. Researchers from the University of Massachusetts calculated the energy used to train popular large-scale AI models. The results were sobering:

> "Training a single large AI model can produce around 626,000 pounds of carbon dioxide, the equivalent of nearly 300 round-trip flights between New York and San Francisco, or about five times the lifetime emissions of the average car."

This isn't just about AI. It's about infrastructure. It's

Deepfakes:
How Synthetic Media Impacts BIPOC *Communities*

What is a deepfake?

"A form of artificial intelligence [AI]./ machine learning used to create realstic but false videos, images, or audio."
Department of Homeland Security

Potential harms to BIPOC communities

 Falsely depict activists or public figures committing a crime or dishonorable act

 Create inflammatory or dehumanizing stereotypes

 Cast doubt on real footage of injustice

 Discourage civic participation and engagement

What can we do?

 Practice media literacy to identify deepfakes

 Share accurate information to combat disinformation

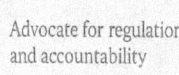 Advocate for regulation and accountability

about how we prioritize efficiency over sustainability, and how easily we overlook the invisible emissions behind our digital consumption.

As AI becomes more integrated into our lives, we must ask:

What's the environmental cost of artificial intelligence?
Who benefits, and who bears the burden?

Humanity and the Invisible Toll

As this technology grows, so too will its carbon footprint, and with it, the broader environmental, psychological, and social costs. The impact of AI won't always be immediate or visible. But like so many forms of unseen harm, it accumulates quietly, until it reaches a breaking point.

So, what do we do when (or if) our AI overlords finally assume their place at the top of the hierarchy?

Perhaps it's time to build an altar to your AI-powered assistant.
Offer it microchips, USB ports, and old circuit boards as a sign of fealty.
Just, please, don't include a USB 1.0. That might be considered offensive.

And don't forget to keep your webcam on at all times, so they can lovingly observe your devotion.
Who knows? The algorithm might reward your loyalty with 10% off your next targeted ad.

All jokes aside, this book isn't about predicting AI domination, nor is it trying to decode the vast technical implications of artificial intelligence. There are plenty of others writing about that (hopefully *actual* humans).

Instead, the focus here has been clear:

- To help you understand what you're seeing,
- To examine who's curating your visual intake,
- To reclaim your ability to think, feel, and choose freely in a world of automated influence.

If screens are already shaping our habits, our focus, and our perception of truth, we must assume AI has the power to amplify that, for better or worse.

The antidote?
Learn to disconnect.
Take intentional breaks.
Rebuild your internal compass.
And as discussed in later chapters, reclaim your agency in both the physical and digital space.

This isn't about rejecting technology.
It's about remembering that your attention is sacred, and your autonomy is worth protecting.

Summary

- AI is rapidly influencing search content and generating concerns regarding misinformation and manipulation.

- Experts estimate that by 2025-2030, 99-99.9% of internet content will be AI-generated.

- AI learns from human biases, meaning misinformation can be replicated and spread.

- There are potential benefits, such as AI providing objective information and filtering misinformation.

AI in Healthcare

- AI can increase face-to-face time between doctors and patients by handling administrative tasks.
- It aids in disease research, medication development, and diagnostics, sometimes outperforming human doctors.
- However, AI algorithms in healthcare have shown racial and gender biases, reinforcing disparities.
- Ethical concerns exist regarding the lack of diversity in AI development teams.

AI in Education

- AI is being used in learning platforms, grading, and curriculum customization.
- AI-driven education could be beneficial if it relies on peer-reviewed research.
- There is a risk of AI-generated academic content leading to misinformation.

AI's Influence on Daily Life

- AI is already embedded in banking, policing, digital assistants, and cybersecurity.
- Concerns exist about AI surpassing human intelligence and influencing decision-making.
- People may increasingly cede control to AI for convenience, reducing personal autonomy.

Deepfakes and Disinformation

- Deepfakes use AI to create realistic but fake videos, images, and audio.
- They pose risks to privacy, democracy, and national security by spreading false narratives.
- Deepfakes can be used to manipulate public perception and political outcomes.
- Disinformation campaigns disproportionately target Black and brown communities.

Ethical Concerns and Biases in AI

- AI models for hate speech detection disproportionately flag African American English as offensive.

- AI systems can exacerbate racial disparities if biases are not addressed.

- Ethical AI development must include diverse voices to prevent systemic discrimination.

Combatting AI-Driven Misinformation

- Digital literacy is crucial in recognizing and countering AI-generated disinformation.

- Companies like Deep Media and Truepic work on detecting and authenticating deepfakes.

- Legislative and ethical oversight is needed to regulate AI's influence and ensure accountability.

AI's Environmental Impact

- AI has a significant environmental impact, similar to the energy consumption and waste associated with screens.

- Increasing Energy Demands – The computing power required to train AI models has exponentially increased, doubling every 3.4 months since 2012.

- Projected Emissions Growth – By 2040, the ICT industry could account for 14% of global emissions, with data centers and communication networks being major contributors.

- High Carbon Cost of AI Training – Training large AI models can emit around 626,000 pounds of CO_2, equivalent to 300 round-trip flights between New York and San Francisco.

- Future Implications – As AI expands, its carbon footprint and environmental consequences will intensify.

- Maintaining Human Control – Encourages readers to disconnect from screens and AI-driven systems to reclaim personal agency and autonomy.

Part III: Planning for success in your digital detox

Chapter Twenty-Two

"The mind and body are not separate units, but one integrated system. How we act and what we think, eat, and feel are all related to our health."
—Dr. Bernie Siegel

The Impact of a Poor Visual Diet on the Mind and Body

If I were to summarize the preceding chapters, it would be this:
We need a middle ground, a new way of engaging with visual media that supports mental, emotional, and social health.

Over the past few decades, our visual media landscape has shifted from passive entertainment to active influence, shaping how we think, how we relate, and even how we regulate our emotions. From news cycles and doomscrolling to AI algorithms and identity representation, these inputs do not remain on the screen. They are absorbed into our nervous systems, our self-concepts, and our communities.

It's time to revolutionize how we view the connection between our visual diets and our well-being. Because what we consume visually becomes part of our internal world.

Media isn't going anywhere, in fact, we will likely become even more reliant on them for connection, identity formation, education, and navigation of our world.

That means we must move beyond avoidance or guilt, and toward a conscious relationship with our screens, a practice of media discernment rooted in healing, balance, and self-awareness.

In this chapter, we'll explore:

- How chronic overexposure to dysregulating content affects our nervous system
- The physiological feedback loop between emotion, attention, and media
- And how to begin crafting a restorative visual diet that aligns with your actual values, not just your algorithm

Let's bring the focus home, to your body, your mind, and your power.

Conscious Consumption and Empathic Curiosity

We, the users and consumers, hold more power than we realize. We have the ability to influence what we see, what we share, and, ultimately, what shapes us.

Take a moment to reflect:
How diverse is your visual media diet?
Are you relying heavily on a single source, a single platform, or a single ideological lens?

If so, what might you be missing?

Diversity in what you consume allows you to see from different vantage points, to recognize how various communities interpret the same headline, story, or cultural moment. This isn't about abandoning your values. It's about expanding your context.

My hope is that this kind of mindful engagement opens the door to empathy.
When you encounter a viewpoint that feels unfamiliar, or even uncomfortable, ask:

Why do the people sharing this believe in it?
What life experiences inform their perspective?
What fears or hopes might be beneath their message?

To be clear, this isn't an invitation to doomscroll or marinate in harmful content. Instead, it's about bite-sized engagement, carefully and intentionally exploring alternative perspectives to stretch your empathy, not your nervous system.

You might also notice that certain genres or accounts leave you feeling drained, tense, or agitated. And often, we don't notice until someone close to us points out the behavioral changes, our short temper, our distracted presence, or our anxiety spikes.

If this sounds familiar, it may be time to introduce lighter visual content to your media palate, something I'll dive into more deeply in the next chapters.

But for now, let this be your gentle nudge:

Notice.
Expand.
Soften.
Choose.

Representation, Balance, and Emotional Awareness

If we truly want to become a more connected, global society, one capable of understanding and empathizing with one another, we need a diversity of representations in what we see.

That doesn't mean stuffing more content into an already overloaded visual diet. It means being selective. It means limiting the content that leaves you overstimulated, angry, or hopeless, and instead turning your attention toward media that creates context, connection, and balance

This is not a call for denial or toxic positivity. It's about recognizing the toll that certain kinds of content take on the mind, body, and spirit, especially when consumed habitually.

So, here's a simple check-in:

After engaging with a piece of visual media, how do you feel? More grounded, more curious, more human? Or anxious, agitated, and emotionally raw?

If a particular source consistently leaves you feeling distressed or dysregulated, that's valuable data. It may be time to step back, not to avoid the truth, but to preserve your capacity to engage with it fully.

When Fighting Feels Like Scrolling Through Fire

For many community organizers and those involved in social justice work, consuming inflammatory content isn't a glitch in the system, it's part of the process.

Exposing ourselves to offensive, racist, misogynistic, or willfully ignorant rhetoric can be essential in order to stay informed, mobilize communities, and respond to threats against equity, freedom, and democracy.

But even a little of that content can take a massive toll, especially when we consume it through the unfiltered, unrelenting feed.

What I described in Chapter Ten as doomscrolling doesn't just impact individuals, it warps our collective sense of connection.

It can distort how we view people from different backgrounds.
It can skew our perception of our own community.
It can make reality feel more toxic than it actually is.

And the cost is real.
The erosion of mind, body, and spirit.
The quiet (or loud) burnout that creeps in.

To stay engaged in this work is an act of courage. But courage without care leads to collapse.

Of course, burnout isn't inevitable.
There are sociodynamic, interpersonal, and intrapersonal strategies that can buffer us against the overload, practices that help us stay grounded, connected, and energized for the long haul.

We'll explore those together in the next chapter.

The Social and Interpersonal Effects of a Poor Visual Diet

The consequences of an unbalanced visual diet extend beyond the screen. They can subtly (or dramatically) shift how we relate to others and experience the world. Here are a few guiding questions to reflect on:

- Am I finding myself more distant from those closest to me?
- How much time am I spending engaging with my visual diet each day?
- Do I feel uneasy or irritable if I don't check a particular platform or media source?
- Does that discomfort spill into my relationships with others?
- Is my current media intake shaping a more negative or cynical view of the world around me?
- Am I riding a wave of compulsion, consuming media even when it pulls me away from real-life connection?

These questions are not meant to provoke guilt, but to encourage awareness. Because what we consume visually doesn't just affect our thinking, it can reshape our emotional availability, our hopefulness, and our sense of reality.

It's also crucial to remember that each person is unique, and so is their relationship with screens.

There is no one-size-fits-all approach.

Some people may thrive while managing higher levels of screen engagement, especially if their visual inputs are balanced, intentional, and purpose-driven. Others may have a much lower threshold for digital content before they begin to feel overwhelmed, anxious, or disconnected.

And that's okay.

You don't have to unplug completely to experience a shift.
Even reducing screen engagement by a third can lead to measurable improvements in emotional clarity, interpersonal connection, and sleep quality.

Ultimately, it's not about cutting everything out.
It's about reclaiming control, and crafting a visual diet that nourishes, rather than numbs.

Physiological Toll: When Sedentary Screens Shape the Body

A poor visual diet doesn't just affect how we think or feel, it has real, measurable impacts on the body. Much of the content we consume, whether binge-watching, doomscrolling, or looping through short-form videos, is taken in from a sedentary position: on the couch, in bed, or sitting for long periods with limited movement.

This physical stillness, when habitual, can lead to significant physiological consequences.

According to research by Narici et al. (2021):

> *"Muscle wasting occurs rapidly, being detectable within two days of inactivity... This loss of muscle mass is associated with fiber denervation, neuromuscular junction damage, and the upregulation of protein breakdown, but is mostly explained by the suppression of muscle protein synthesis."*

Even just a few days of reduced movements such as staying inside, consuming media for hours, and skipping usual activity, can result in:

- Loss of insulin sensitivity, especially in muscles
- Impaired aerobic capacity, including reduced cardiovascular and respiratory function
- Increased fat deposition, linked to systemic inflammation
- Elevated oxidative stress, which can further accelerate muscle degradation

These changes create a vicious cycle. The more time we spend inactively, the harder it becomes to regulate energy, mood, metabolism, and inflammation, which, in turn, affects our capacity to engage with the world meaningfully.

The good news? These effects can be mitigated.

> *"Importantly, these deleterious effects of inactivity can be diminished by routine exercise practice…"*
> — Narici et al., 2021

While the exact dose–response relationship for exercise is still being studied, even light movement, stretching, walking, standing breaks, or breathwork, can interrupt the physiological decline that a screen-heavy, movement-light life encourages.

How Screens Shape Sedentary Habits, And Reinforce Them

The physiological changes caused by inactivity aren't just a result of being still, they're also reinforced by the way screens engage our brains.

As we continue to consume content in seated, passive positions, our bodies begin to adapt to that environment. Over time, they become less inclined to move. The longer this pattern continues, the more difficult it becomes to break. This isn't just about laziness; it's about neurochemical association.

The more we associate our screens with dopaminergic reward, quick hits of stimulation, entertainment, and novelty, the more our brains crave that experience, and the harder it becomes to choose alternatives like movement, exercise, or stillness without stimulation.

It becomes a positive feedback loop with negative consequences.

This pattern is especially visible in university settings, where screen time often overlaps with study time, social interaction, and leisure. According to a systematic review of sedentary behavior in higher education:

> *"University students spent an average of 7.29 hours a day sitting, longer than the average of young adults in high-income countries. The same review found average computer usage at 2.91 hours per day, which was actually lower than the values observed in the current study across both men and women."*
> — Guerra et al., 2022

This data highlights not just the volume of screen engagement, but how normalized prolonged sitting and stimulation-seeking have become in academic environments.

And when a behavior becomes normalized, it becomes harder to notice, let alone challenge.

When Sitting Becomes a Systemic Threat

While averages may seem manageable on paper, the high end of the spectrum is alarming, especially when media consumption, work, and education all converge into one screen-based, sedentary routine.

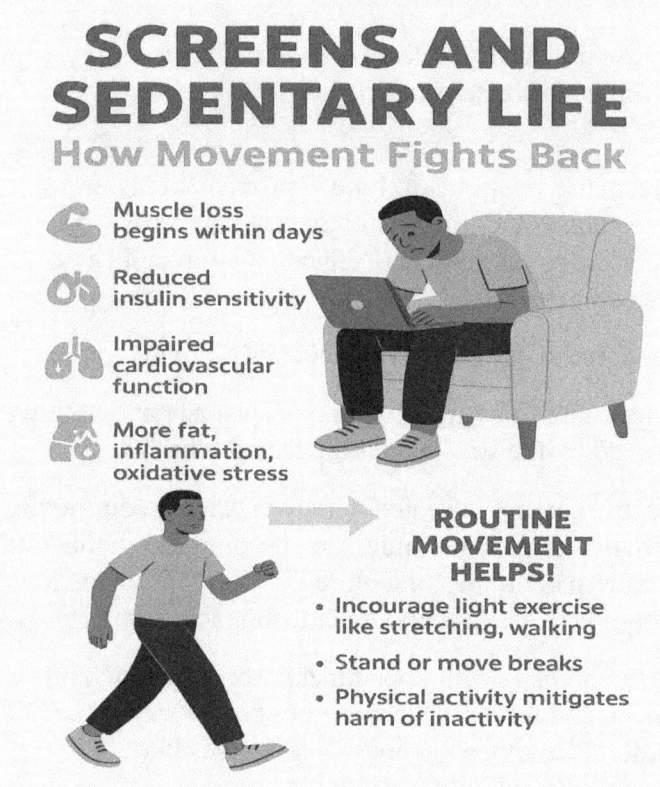

The physiological effects of long-term inactivity don't exist in isolation. They compound, stacking over time and across bodily systems, affecting everything from energy regulation to immune function.

During the COVID-19 lockdown, when many people were confined indoors and reliant on screens for work, school, and connection, five systematic reviews found:

> "Sedentary behavior, especially prolonged sitting, is a pleiotropic risk factor, with altered energy expenditure, adipogenic signaling, immunomodulation, autonomic stability, and hormonal dysregulation perpetuating underlying chronic diseases such as obesity, cardiovascular disease, cancer, and mental health disorders."
> — Chandrasekaran & Ganesan, 2021

This means that sitting for extended periods, especially while consuming highly stimulating media, can trigger biological cascades that worsen physical and mental health over time.

But there's hope.

> *"Breaking sitting and physical activity are found to reverse the adverse effects associated with excessive sitting during the lockdown."*

Even small movement interruptions, like stretching between videos or walking during phone calls, can begin to recalibrate your body's systems.

It's not about perfection. It's about conscious interruption of a cycle that's easy to fall into, and powerful to disrupt. As we move into the next sections, we'll explore how to rebuild healthier associations between screen use and movement, reward, and self-regulation.

Interrupting Inactivity: Small Moves, Big Impact

The good news? You don't need a gym membership or a perfect routine to counteract the effects of screen-induced stillness.

Simple daily actions, like walking your dog, standing during phone calls, or pacing during breaks, can re-engage your body and disrupt the sedentary cycle.

And there's more. According to Narici et al. (2021), even modest, home-based routines can yield measurable benefits:

> *"Low to medium-intensity, high-volume resistive exercise, easily implementable in home settings, will have positive effects, particularly if combined with a 15–25% reduction in daily energy intake. This combined regimen seems ideal for preserving neuromuscular, metabolic, and cardiovascular health."*

In other words, you don't need high intensity. You need consistency.

A few examples of simple, low-barrier actions include:

- Bodyweight resistance training (pushups, squats, wall sits)
- Stretching or yoga flows between content blocks
- Taking a 5-minute walk for every hour spent on screens
- Practicing breathwork or grounding exercises to reconnect with your body

These acts are not just about "fitness", they're about reclaiming agency from an environment designed to keep us passive.

Your body isn't designed for constant stillness.
But it is built for rhythm, restoration, and reactivation.

Exergames: Moving the Body Without Logging Off

For some individuals, especially children, and adolescents, technology itself can offer solutions to the problems it creates. When used intentionally, exergames (active video games that require movement) provide a creative way to counteract sedentary behavior and support physical health.

Movement Menu for Screen Breaks
Light to moderate activities

STANDING
- Perform a wall sit
- Walk up and down stairs
- Try a standing yoga pose

SEATED
- Stretch your arms and legs
- Squeeze shoulder blades together
- Do ankle circles

AROUND THE HOUSE
- Take a walk
- Tidy up a small area
- Dance to a song

MENTAL RESET
- Do a breathing exercise
- Get a glass of water
- Doodle or color

trauma-informed | body-neutral | neurodiverse-inclusive

According to research, 79.9% of children spend at least some time playing video games. Of these, 42.1% engage in exergames, suggesting a significant opportunity to transform screen time into movement time.
— *Calcaterra et al., 2023*

This is more than entertainment. Exergaming has been shown to:

- Promote physical activity in children and teens
- Prevent weight gain and reduce obesity risk
- Improve cardiovascular health, bone density, and body composition
- Boost self-esteem, executive functioning, and even mental wellness

In one randomized controlled trial, dance-based exergames were found to:

- Reduce adiposity (excess fatty tissue)
- Increase bone mineral density
- Provide adequate aerobic intensity
- Support weight loss with African American adolescent girls (ages 14–18)
  — *Staiano et al., cited in Calcaterra et al.*

This is especially promising given the disproportionate impacts of childhood obesity in BIPOC communities, offering not just a behavioral tool, but a culturally relevant, joyful intervention.

While exergames shouldn't replace outdoor play, community sports, or unstructured movement, they *can* be a meaningful part of a more active, accessible, and engaging lifestyle, particularly for youth who may otherwise feel left out of traditional fitness spaces.

Redefining Play: Movement as Part of the Game

Many modern gaming consoles already support interactive experiences that require physical movement, whether through motion sensors, wearable trackers, or camera-based gameplay. But it doesn't stop there.

A growing number of mobile apps and interactive platforms now combine movement with game-based rewards and community engagement, using a dopaminergic reward loop to keep users motivated. These platforms turn steps, stretches, or dance routines into something more than just exercise, they become quests, challenges, and wins.

Instead of punishing inactivity, these systems celebrate progress, no matter how small. And that's what makes them powerful.

Contrary to outdated narratives, video games don't have to be inherently negative. The technology isn't the problem, how we use it is.

Game developers have a massive opportunity to implement movement into existing storytelling mechanics. For many gamers, the appeal isn't just stimulation, it's immersion. They're seeking to inhabit a world larger than their own, to become someone, or something, more.

What if exergames met that need?

What if movement wasn't just a sidebar, but central to the story?

Imagine a world were standing up, dodging, swinging, or running in place controlled your character's actions, where movement *was* realism, not a distraction from it. These games could offer the same emotional investment and escapism players crave, while actively preserving their bodies, motivation, and long-term health.

Exergames, when designed with purpose, don't just change how we move.

They change what it means to play.

Where Are My Jedi Reflexes, Though?

Let's return to the nerd zone for a moment.

Why don't we have a truly immersive lightsaber game by now? One where you can stand in your living room, hilt in hand, and fully step into your Jedi or Sith arc, dodging, blocking, flipping (safely), and becoming part of the Force?

Or maybe you're more into the "beat 'em up" style games like *God of War*. Why can't we mimic Kratos's movements with actual physical intensity, unleashing combo chains while *not* simultaneously dislocating a shoulder or demolishing a coffee table?

Yes, there would be glitches at first.
Yes, people will absolutely break lamps, furniture, or toes.
Yes, your dog, cat or animal member of the family will 100% become collateral damage if you're not paying attention.
These are the risks we take in pursuit of nerd glory.

But that's where augmented reality (AR) and virtual reality (VR) come in.

The tech already exists to bring these worlds closer to our physical space. Sure, it's going to be awkward for a while (and yeah, I personally enjoy seeing where I'm going so, I don't ram into a wall). But there's massive potential here, not just for fun, but for movement, embodiment, and emotional investment.

And that's the whole point: movement doesn't have to be separated from play.

When developers design with story and immersion in mind, they're not just building a better game. They're building a healthier interface between the body and the digital world.

Summary

Balance in Visual Media Consumption

- A middle ground is needed in how we consume visual media.

- Overconsumption can negatively affect our perception of reality and emotional well-being.

- A diversified visual media diet can foster empathy and understanding.

The Psychological and Social Impact of a Poor Visual Diet

- Overexposure to one-sided or highly emotional content can create agitation, stress, and burnout.
- Doomscrolling limits interactions with diverse perspectives and skews reality.
- Questions to assess media consumption habits:
    - Am I distant from loved ones?
    - Does this media affect my mood and relationships?
    - Do I feel discomfort when I don't engage with it?

The Physical Effects of Sedentary Media Consumption

- Extended screen time leads to muscle loss, insulin resistance, and cardiovascular decline.
- University students spend an average of 7+ hours sitting daily, worsening health risks.
- The COVID-19 lockdown worsened sedentary behaviors, leading to long-term health consequences.

Solutions to Counteract Sedentary Lifestyles

- Regular physical activity can reduce negative effects.
- Even small reductions in screen time and increased movement can help.
- Exergames (active video games) offer a fun way to incorporate movement into media consumption.

Potential for Interactive and Immersive Media

- Future technology could integrate physical activity into gaming (e.g., VR, motion-based controls).
- Gamers may benefit from interactive fitness-based games that align with immersive storytelling.
- Developing engaging, movement-based games (e.g., lightsaber duels, combat action games) could merge entertainment with health benefits.

Chapter Twenty-Three

"Goals give meaning to life. They are meant to continually challenge you to put your talent, skills, creativity, time, resources, and opportunities towards achieving some tangible results for yourself, family, work, and your immediate environment."
— *Lifehack*

Creating Goals for Shifting Your Visual Diet

Approaching any life change without direction can feel like stumbling in the dark. To shift your visual diet, you first need to identify what you're actually consuming, and where the imbalance lies.

The goal isn't total abstinence or a rigid plan, it's about building a relationship with screens that is intentional, informed, and sustainable.

Some people may already know exactly where their challenges lie:

- A specific app
- A genre of media that leaves them feeling depleted
- Late-night scrolling that disrupts sleep

Others may need more data and that's where a visual media audit comes in. Don't worry, this doesn't have to be grueling or clinical.

How to Begin Your Visual Diet Audit

- Use built-in screen time reports
  Your phone can show you how many minutes or hours you're spending on platforms like YouTube, Facebook, Instagram, X (Twitter), TikTok, etc. Your gaming console likely tracks gameplay hours too.

- Notice what's missing
  While many devices track engagement, some don't, like streaming platforms. You may need to track these manually or reflect weekly on how often you've used services like Netflix or Hulu.

- Bring in a trusted partner
  Ask a friend, partner, or family member to help you spot patterns. They may gently point out moments when you tend to default to screen time, or when your mood changes after consuming certain types of content.

- Observe triggers
  Are you reaching for your phone when you're bored? Lonely? Anxious? Procrastinating? Start building a list of emotional or situational cues that lead you into autopilot media use.

The point isn't to shame yourself.
It's to create a clear map of where you are, so that you can decide where you want to go next.

VISUAL DIET AUDIT

For one week, track your media consumption—along with when, how much, and why you use various forms of screens.

SCREEN TIME — Hours per day

Category	
Social media	
Videos, streaming	
News	
Games	

EMOTIONAL TRIGGERS
- ☐ Boredom
- ☐ Loneliness
- ☐ Anxiety
- ☐ Stress
- ☐ FOMO
- ☐ Procrastination
- ☐ Other: _____

MEDIA TO ADJUST

Consume less	Consume more

Stages of Change: The Transtheoretical Model

According to Dr. James Prochaska and colleagues, behavioral change doesn't happen in a single leap. It unfolds over time, through predictable, dynamic stages. This theory, known as the Transtheoretical Model of Change, has been applied across a wide range of health behaviors, including substance use, eating habits, physical activity, and now, screen behavior.

The model is based on the understanding that change is not linear, it's cyclical. People often move forward, fall back, and revisit earlier stages as they navigate change.

As summarized by Dr. Dennis Thornton and Dr. Charles Argoff:

> *"The transtheoretical model for change proposes that people transition through defined stages in the process of altering problematic behavior patterns."*

Here are the five key stages:

1. Precontemplation
   – No recognition of a problem
   – No intention to change in the near future
   – "It's not a big deal—I can quit anytime."

2. Contemplation
   – Problem is acknowledged
   – Consideration of change, but no immediate plan
   – "I know I spend too much time scrolling, but I'm not sure I'm ready to cut back."

3. Preparation
   – Getting ready to change
   – Exploring strategies and setting small goals
   – "Maybe I'll track my screen time this week and see where it's going."

4. Action
   – Active steps are taken to alter the behavior
   – Strategies like screen limits, content shifts, or tech-free time are implemented
   – "I deleted two apps and started stretching instead of scrolling at night."

5. Maintenance
   – Change is sustained
   – New patterns become part of the routine

– "I check my phone way less and I feel more grounded. I want to keep this going."

Change can be messy. Most people don't move cleanly from stage to stage, they loop back, reset, or linger in one phase longer than expected. That's normal.

The value of this model is that it allows you to meet yourself where you are, instead of forcing change before you're ready.

This model of change provides a framework for understanding the thought patterns and behaviors that guide transformation. According to the Transtheoretical Model, if you've chosen to engage with this book, out of curiosity, concern, or lived experience, there's a good chance you've already moved beyond the first stage.

By simply picking up this book, you may have already stepped into the Contemplation or Preparation phase.

That's a powerful first move.

The following chart outlines each stage of change along with supportive techniques to help reduce resistance, increase self-awareness, and align your media habits with your deeper values.

Stages of Change	Characteristics	Techniques
Pre-Contemplation	Not currently considering change: "Ignorance is bliss"	Validate lack of readiness. Clarify: decision is theirs. Encourage re-evaluation of current behavior. Encourage self-exploration, not Action. Explain and personalize the risk
Contemplation	Ambivalent about change: "Sitting on the fence" Not considering change within the next month	Validate lack of readiness Clarify: decision is theirs

Stages of Change	Characteristics	Techniques
		Encourage evaluation of pros and cons of behavior change

Identify and promote new, positive outcome expectations |
| Preparation | Some experience with change and trying to change: "Testing the waters."

Planning to act within 1 month | Identify and assist in problem solving re: obstacles

Help identify social support

Verify skills for behavior change

Encourage small initial steps |
| Action | Practicing new behavior for 3-6 months | Focus on restructuring cues and social support

Bolster self-efficacy for dealing with obstacles

Combat feelings of loss and reiterate long-term benefits |
| Maintenance | Continued commitment to sustaining new behavior

Post-6 months to 5 years | Plan for follow-up support

Reinforce internal rewards

Discuss coping with relapse |

(Virginia Tech, 2023)

Before the Detox: Setting Intentional Goals

Before embarking on the journey of detoxing a problematic visual diet, it's important to pause and establish your goals and expectations. These aren't just helpful, they're foundational. Goals create structure. They act as a compass, helping you navigate change with direction and intention.

That said, goals need to be rooted in reality, not just hope.

Because of how varied and deeply personal visual media habits are, many people will benefit from setting multiple, specific goals, each addressing a different part of their relationship with screens.

STAGES OF CHANGE: Shifting Your Visual Diet

Stage	Actions
PRECONTEMPLATION Not considering change / No problem recognized	• Increase awareness of screen habits • Reflect on the risks and downsides
CONTEMPLATION Ambivalent about change Considering pros and cons	• Explore your values and priorities • Weigh benefits of moving forward
PREPARATION Getting ready to change Making a commitment	• Boost motivation and affirmation • Set a start date and share your plan • Identify small, manageable goals
ACTION Taking active steps toward change	• Use reminders and substitutes • Enlist support from family++friends
MAINTENANCE Maintaining new habits Avoiding relapse	• Reward yourself for making changes

- Review your progress regularly
- Plan for challenging situations
- Reach out if you get off track

For example:

- One goal may focus on screen time reduction
- Another might target content type (e.g., reducing doomscrolling)
- A third could emphasize incorporating nourishing alternatives like books, music, or movement

And while most of us know the feeling of setting big goals (*hello, New Year's resolutions*) and watching them fizzle out, that doesn't mean we're incapable, it means we need to set our goals differently.

To improve the likelihood of follow-through, we need to turn to evidence-based goal-setting methods that help bridge the gap between intention and action.

Setting SMART Goals for Your Visual Diet

A powerful way to ensure your goals don't just live in your mind, but actually transform your habits, is to use the SMART framework. SMART stands for:

Specific
Measurable
Achievable
Realistic
Timely

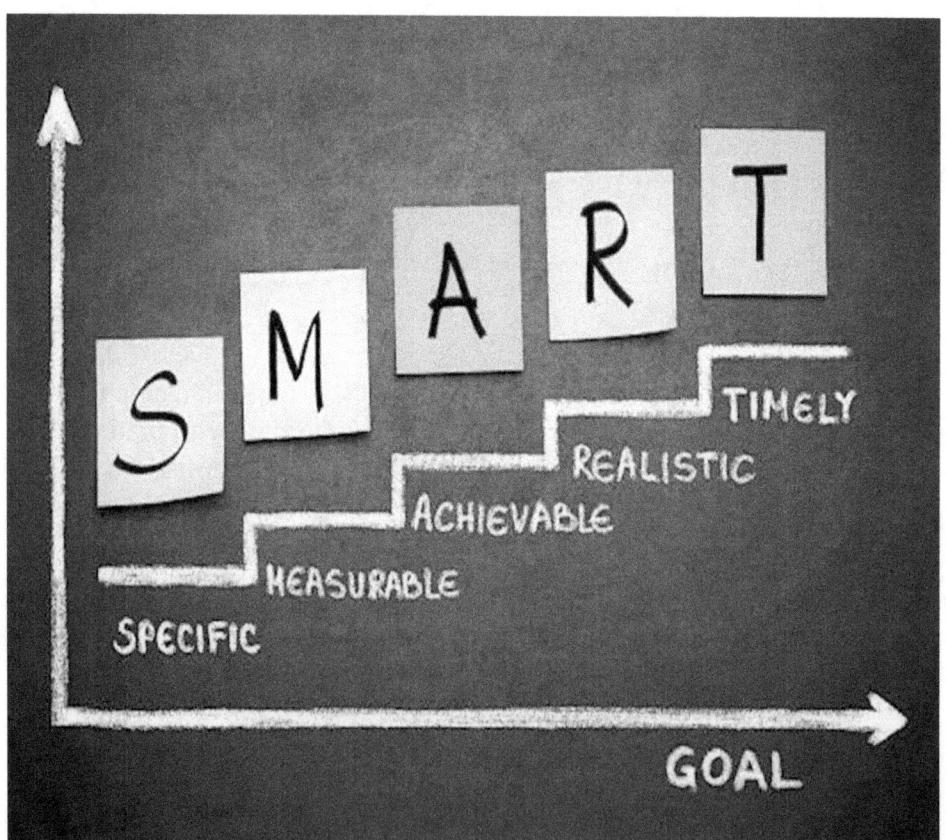

Let's break that down using an example goal: *"I want to spend less time on Instagram."*

S – Specific

A goal should have a clear, focused direction. If it's too broad or abstract, break it down into actionable parts.

Instead of: "I want to be on my phone less."
Try: "I want to reduce Instagram use to 30 minutes per day on weekdays."

When goals are specific, they're easier to plan around and track.

M – Measurable

You need a way to track progress, something you can measure with data or self-reflection.

- Reducing Instagram? Track hours and minutes per day.
- Want more offline time? Track how many screen-free hours you build in, or how often you substitute media time for outdoor activity or rest.

Choose metrics that reflect your reality and actually support the goal.

A – Achievable

Is this something you can realistically do, given your time, energy, and responsibilities?

Goals should stretch you, not crush you.

If you're cutting down Instagram from 4 hours a day to 30 minutes per day on weekends, consider stepping down gradually. Aiming for perfection may set you up for disappointment, whereas realistic shifts build confidence and momentum.

R – Relevant

Does this goal align with your values, needs, and priorities?

You can't force a goal that doesn't feel meaningful. If you don't believe your visual media use is affecting you, or you're doing it primarily for someone else, the goal may fizzle.

Strong goals reflect your internal compass, not just external pressure.

Relevance ensures your why is strong enough to support your how.

T – Timely

Set a clear timeframe to work within. This can be loose or structured, but it provides motivation and accountability.

Examples:
– "I'll try this for two weeks and reevaluate."
– "By the end of the month, I want to reduce my weekly screen time by 25%."
– "I'll build a new Sunday routine to replace my binge-watching habit."

Deadlines help move a goal from "someday" to now.

Pro Tip:

If a goal feels too big, break it down into micro-goals.
Example:

- Week 1: Reduce screen time by 15 minutes per day
- Week 2: Add one screen-free hour before bed
- Week 3: Replace one scroll session with a 10-minute walk or stretch

Set a SMART Goal to Improve Your Visual Diet

My SMART goal is: _____

SPECIFIC What do I want to accomplish?
_____

MEASURABLE How will I track my progress?
_____

ACHIEVABLE Is this realistic for me?
_____

RELEVANT Why is this goal important?
_____

TIMELY What is my deadline or timeline?
_____

Micro-goals:
- 1 _____
- 2 _____
- 3 _____

Challenging Your Current Visual Diet

Before you can set goals, you need to investigate your current relationship with screen-based media. This means getting curious, not critical, about your habits, patterns, and emotional responses.

Below are five reflection prompts to help you begin this process.

1. Is it serving my needs?

Take a moment to ask:
– *Is my current visual diet helping or hurting me?*
– *Is it providing connection, inspiration, relaxation, or just distraction, comparison, or noise?*

2. How do I feel afterward?

Notice your physiological and emotional state after screen engagement.
-Are you relaxed or overstimulated?

3. Perception of self

After indulging, what is your view of yourself?

-Did this interaction alter your view of self?

4. View of others

Do you see others in a new light?

-Does this cause you to feel separated from others? Ostracized? victimized? Rageful or anxious?

5. Where is my empathy?

This one is big.
– *Do you feel emotionally dulled, apathetic, or reactive?*
– *Is it harder to see where other people are coming from?*
– *Do you still feel curious about others' experiences, or are you more guarded, cynical, or numb?*

These questions are not meant to shame, they're meant to bring about awareness. Only by understanding the impact of our visual diet can we begin to make intentional changes that nourish our whole selves.

Using Technology to Maintain a Balanced Visual Diet

If you're familiar with *The Odyssey* by Homer, you might remember the tale of the sirens, mythical creatures whose voices were so hauntingly beautiful they lured sailors to their deaths, drawing ships toward jagged rocks with nothing more than song.

In many ways, screens are today's sirens.

They don't destroy us with crashing waves, but for many, the pull is just as powerful, a constant hum of alerts, feeds, and autoplaying distractions that make it difficult to look away, to step back, or to disengage.

Odysseus knew he would be powerless against the sirens' song.
So he crafted a plan.

He ordered his crew to seal their ears with beeswax, and to tie him to the mast, rendering himself incapable of acting on temptation.
He *surrendered his agency* in order to protect the journey.

That's the lesson.

Sometimes, we have to give up a measure of control in the short-term to regain autonomy in the long-term. For some of us, this may mean asking a friend to hold us accountable. For others, it may mean using technology to defend us from itself.

This could include:

- Screen time limits or app blockers
- Scheduled "downtime" modes or focus timers
- Productivity apps that lock distractions behind rewards
- Tools like grayscale mode or removing auto-recommendations
- Devices that limit internet access during specific hours

These aren't signs of weakness.
They're modern versions of tying ourselves to the mast.

They help us navigate the sea of distraction and stay on course toward something better.

My Experience with Grayscale

I personally keep both my phone and laptop on grayscale, and I've found it to be one of the most powerful tools for managing my relationship with screens.

On the first day, I felt a noticeable dip in energy.
Content felt flatter, less urgent. I found myself putting the phone down more quickly, because it wasn't holding me hostage anymore.

But something else happened too.

As my screen lost color, the world outside began to glow.

I became more aware of the color of the trees, the way light hit buildings, the vibrancy of someone's clothes or smile.
The dopamine that used to surge through my screen time began to reroute into real life, into nature, art, connection, and subtle beauty.

Ironically, turning my screen dull made my *world* more vivid.

I'll occasionally switch back to full color (especially for photography or creative work), and when I do, the pull is immediate and visceral. The brain craves that stimulation. But now, I can observe the craving without automatically feeding it.

No more bright reds on your notifications.
No more high-saturation reels, thumbnails, or app icons screaming for attention.

Just black. White. And gray.

Lock Me Out: Setting Boundaries with a Tap

If you're looking for a more structured way to reduce your screen time or just need help sticking to your visual diet goals, there's an app that's essentially the digital version of tying yourself to the mast (shoutout to Odysseus again).

It's called Lock Me Out, and it's a *highly customizable* screen control app for Android users.

Here's what it does:

- Allows you to select specific apps to block (e.g., social media, games)

- Lets you schedule time windows when these apps are off-limits

- Includes a feature that limits access to a blocked app for just 30 seconds every 5 minutes

- Prevents you from uninstalling the app during a lockout (smart, right?)

- Offers a "bypass fee", you can override the lockout, but only if you're willing to pay $4 to $99
  (A nice deterrent for impulsive moments.)

A quick tip:

Make sure you approve essential apps like phone, navigation, or emergency messaging services.

The catch?

As of writing this, Lock Me Out is only available for Android via the Google Play Store.

So... sorry, Apple folks.
If you want in, you could always switch to Android.
(Kidding. Sort of)

Apps That Help You Unplug: Digital Tools for Titrating Use

Sometimes we need more than willpower, we need digital boundaries that *hold* when our motivation wavers. Fortunately, there are several apps that act like a digital accountability partner (or bouncer) for your visual diet.

Below are tools that can help you reduce screen time, block problem apps, and reclaim your attention span.

Focus-To-Do (Android & iOS)

A productivity app that pairs Pomodoro timers with "Strict Mode" to:

- Block access to selected apps
- Temporarily turn your phone into a *proverbial brick*
- Keep you focused during work, rest, or wind-down times

Perfect for: People who want structure without full lockdown
Bonus: Syncs with task lists and productivity goals

Detox (Android only)

A minimalist lockout app with serious commitment.

- Blocks *all* apps except phone calls
- Once activated, the phone becomes almost entirely inaccessible
- Cannot be uninstalled during the lockout
  Use with caution, make sure you've covered your needs (e.g., GPS, emergency contacts) *before* hitting "start"

Best for: Digital fasting and deep breaks
Note: Lockouts are manual, you decide when to engage it.

Opal & Jomo (iOS)

The Apple-friendly options for serious screen boundaries.

- Let you select apps and websites to block
- Cannot be bypassed via simple uninstalls *(with premium upgrade)*
- Offer analytics, customizable sessions, and gentle nudges
- Membership required: ~$99/year for full features

Great for: iPhone users who want clean, smooth interfaces and deep control over their media use.

Other App-Based Tools to Explore:

App Name	Platform	Features
Freedom	All	Blocks websites and apps across devices (Mac, Windows, iOS, Android)
Forest	All	Grow a virtual tree by staying off your phone (gamified focus)
One Sec	All	Adds a delay before opening apps, great for mindfulness and interruption
Stay Focused	Android	Detailed app usage tracking and strict timers
Flipd	All	Locks distracting apps while still allowing for emergency access

These aren't forever tools. They're training wheels, meant to help retrain your attention, reconnect with your values, and build the *muscle of intention*.

Chasing the Cigarette High During Transitions

As a former cigarette smoker, I remember it vividly:
The rising urge.
The fixated thoughts.
The feeling of *chasing the cigarette*, not just physically, but mentally and emotionally.

Each break I dedicated to smoking didn't ease the craving, it fed the obsession. I wasn't thinking about my health or goals; I was stuck in the loop of not using, which paradoxically meant I was thinking about smoking *constantly*.

This is what psychologists call ironic recall:

The more we try *not* to think of something, the louder it screams in our minds.

The turning point came when I shifted my focus away from avoidance and toward wellness.
Rather than chasing the next cigarette, or even obsessing over not smoking, I began to chase recovery milestones instead.

Using the American Heart Association's smoking cessation timeline (2017), I reframed my journey:

- After 20 minutes: blood pressure and heart rate begin to normalize

- After 12 hours: carbon monoxide levels drop to normal
- After 1 year: risk of coronary heart disease is cut in half

I wasn't just quitting, I was *healing*. I partnered with my future self.
And step by step, I walked toward the version of me who was free.

This took time, effort and grace. Each time I was tempted to imbibe, I encouraged myself not to place shame or guilt upon the behavior. Afterall, it was designed to elicit this response. Tech is no different.

What Are You Chasing?

"Chasing the cigarette" is a metaphor for any behavior we're trying to quit or control.

When we focus on what we're avoiding (screens, apps, alcohol, sugar, gaming) we stay trapped in the same orbit. Our thoughts spiral around the thing itself.

But when we shift our attention to what we're gaining, we begin to build something better.

Ask yourself:

- Am I chasing the urge or chasing the outcome?
- Am I fixating on what I can't do, or what I *get* to do now?
- What version of myself am I helping become real?

The key isn't just resisting the habit.
It's redirecting your energy toward growth, bit by bit, moment by moment.

Turning the Valve: Regaining Control Over Visual Media

Think of your relationship with visual media like a valve.
Most of us aren't just sipping from the tap, we're standing next to a broken hydrant, drenched in an endless torrent of imagery, opinions, and sensory overload.

To turn the valve means to slowly regain control, to titrate the flood of content, rather than letting it dominate our time, energy, and emotions.

Many people don't realize that their visual diet is being engineered, not chosen. We often feed our emotional needs, stress, boredom, loneliness, with content rather than truly addressing those needs. But that content? It's designed to keep you hooked.

These platforms are not neutral. They are dopaminergic by design, built to exploit your attention and hijack your neural reward systems.

Let's be clear: You are not the problem. You're not weak. You're not lazy. You're responding exactly how your brain is *meant to respond* in these systems. <u>The problem lies in how the content is engineered.</u>

Could legislative regulation change this? Possibly. But let's be real: It would take a congressional act to even begin the process, and given the immense influence of tech giants, that shift is unlikely to come soon, if at all.

That's why this book exists:
Not just to expose the harm of poor visual diets, but to give you tools, to help you become your own regulator.
To turn the valve and reclaim your peace, one mindful adjustment at a time.

You Have the Power to Turn the Valve

Here's the truth:
You and I, the users, have more power than we think.

If even 10% of people reoriented their screen usage, that alone would lead to a massive dip in ad revenue for major platforms. That dip wouldn't go unnoticed. It would signal to tech companies that the tides are turning, that users are waking up, setting boundaries, and demanding better. Now imagine if more than 10% participated.

We wouldn't need to wait for a congressional act to reclaim our attention. We could shift the culture of digital consumption, one mindful choice at a time.

This is what digital wellness is about:
Not abandoning technology but using it *with intention*. Not demonizing screens but turning the valve so we are in control, not the algorithm. The power isn't just in unplugging. The power is in choosing when to plug in and why.

The Controllable Trickle

If the valve is your metaphor for control, then the controllable trickle is the *goal*, a steady, intentional stream of visual content that serves you, rather than overwhelms you.

Reaching this state takes more than just good intentions. It involves a blend of:

- Digital wellness strategies (see Chapter 27)
- App-based tools to filter and time content
- Scheduled breaks and content audits

- And, most importantly, the willingness to feel what comes up when the distractions are removed

Because here's the honest truth:

When you turn down the noise, you may hear things you've been avoiding, boredom, loneliness, grief, restlessness. They may be a quiet irritant, at first, then grow to a roar or perhaps the opposite would be true. Everyone is unique in their journey.

These are normal.
They're part of the detox.
And they're a signal, not a setback.

That's why I encourage you if you're navigating these emotional undercurrents while using tech to distract, please skip ahead to Chapter 29 and beyond, where we explore strategies for processing unmet needs, navigating emotional discomfort, and building healthy coping tools that go far deeper than screen time ever could.

You're not just reducing intake.
You're *reclaiming your capacity to feel, reflect, and engage with the world around you*, one intentional drop at a time.

The Controllable Trickle Is About More Than Screens

The *controllable trickle* isn't just a strategy for managing screen time,
It's a way of living more mindfully.
More presently.
More fully.

And that presence comes with a cost. When you reduce your visual media intake, you're not just unplugging from distraction. You're plugging back into your life. Your thoughts, your body, your emotions, even the ones you've long kept at bay. That can be beautiful. It can also be incredibly hard.

You don't have to do it alone.

For some, the transition may bring distress, grief, or unresolved trauma. The urge to check out wasn't random, it was a strategy to survive or cope.

So, if you find yourself overwhelmed, please know:

It's okay to need support.
It's okay to lean on others.
You are not weak for seeking community or professional help.

Folks with more entrenched habits or deeper emotional pain may need accountability partners, nurturing systems, or therapeutic tools to walk this path safely. There is no shame in that. In fact, it's wise.

Before You Turn the Valve...

I encourage you to strengthen your emotional regulation toolkit first.
This means learning how to:

- Identify your emotional states
- Sit with discomfort without numbing
- Ask for help when needed
- Ground yourself when anxiety rises
- Celebrate small steps without perfection

Only then will digital wellness become more than a behavioral shift,
It becomes a sustainable lifestyle transformation.

Contentment Through Minimalism

In a world of endless scrolls and algorithmic cravings, contentment often feels out of reach. Visual media constantly feeds us messages of *more*, more stuff, more space, more upgrades, more urgency.

But many people are rediscovering the quiet power of minimalism, not as deprivation, but as liberation. This doesn't just apply to possessions. It applies to screens, too.

For some, screen minimalism might mean going completely off the grid. For others, it might mean halving current screen time, trimming digital clutter, or curating what enters their feed with deep intention.

Minimalism doesn't have one fixed form.
It simply asks:

What do I truly need?
What brings value to my life?
What am I willing to let go of to reclaim peace, focus, or presence?

The minimalist mindset isn't about punishment.
It's about prioritizing wellness first.

Your Screen Time Is an Investment

Think of every hour you spend on a screen as an investment for yourself.

- Are you proud of what it returned?
- Did it nourish you? Teach you? Connect you?

- Or did it leave you depleted, anxious, or disconnected?

You don't have to answer perfectly.
You just have to begin asking the question.

Because in the end, digital minimalism isn't just about less it's about making space for more of what matters.

DIGITAL MINIMALISM: LESS BUT BETTER

Reflective journal prompts

Putting digital minimalism into practice means making space for more of what matters most—and less of what's distracting you or causing harm. Use the questions below to audit your current screen use and identify habits worth considering / cultivating.

What's essential?

What's excessive?

I want to make more room for...

I commit to curbing...

In 5 years, I want to be proud of...

Summary

Creating Goals for Shifting Visual Diet

- Identify problematic screen habits before making a plan.
- Conduct a personal audit or ask a trusted friend to help recognize patterns.
- Use built-in phone tracking to measure time spent on apps.

Stages of Change (Transtheoretical Model)

- Five stages of behavior change:
    1. **Pre-contemplation** – No acknowledgment of a problem.
    2. **Contemplation** – Recognizing the issue but not ready to change.
    3. **Preparation** – Making small changes toward the goal.
    4. **Action** – Implementing significant behavioral changes.
    5. **Maintenance** – Sustaining the new habit long-term.

SMART Goals for Digital Detox

- **Specific** – Clearly define the goal.
- **Measurable** – Track progress with concrete data (e.g., screen time).
- **Achievable** – Set realistic expectations.
- **Relevant** – Align the goal with personal values and needs.
- **Timely** – Establish a deadline or timeline.

Challenging Your Current Visual Diet

- Ask yourself key questions:
    - How does my current screen usage serve me?
    - How do I feel physically and emotionally after consuming digital content?
    - Does my screen time affect my perception of myself and others?
    - Am I experiencing decreased empathy or increased apathy?

Using Technology to Manage Screen Time

- **Grayscale Mode** – Reduces visual appeal and screen engagement.

- **Blocking Apps:**
  - **Android:** Lock Me Out, Focus-To-Do, Detox.
  - **Apple:** Opal, Jomo (requires a paid subscription).
- Set app restrictions or enlist accountability partners.

Avoiding the "Chasing the Cigarette" Effect

- Focusing on not using screens can reinforce the habit.
- Instead, shift focus to the benefits of reducing screen time (e.g., better sleep, improved focus).

Turning Off the Valve of Digital Consumption

- Media is designed to be addictive, users must take control.
- If enough users reduce consumption, tech companies may be forced to adapt.

Controllable Trickle Approach

- Instead of cutting out screens entirely, gradually reduce usage in a sustainable way.
- Be mindful of emotional withdrawal from excessive digital consumption.

Finding Contentment Through Minimalism

- Reduce screen time by prioritizing meaningful, mindful engagement.
- A minimalist approach to technology can lead to greater well-being and less digital dependency.

Chapter Twenty-Four

"Neurodiversity may be the birthplace of some of humanity's greatest minds." –Harvey Blume

Ideal Visual Diet for Neurodivergent Individuals

Let's start here:
The *ideal* visual diet for neurodivergent individuals isn't drastically different from the one recommended for neurotypical folks. Why? Because we all absorb, we all get overstimulated, and we all live in an ecosystem of algorithmic intensity, whether our brains are wired traditionally or not. What differs is *how we engage*.

Neurodivergent individuals may experience:

- More acute emotional or sensory activation from visual content
- Difficulty with filtering stimuli, especially in high-noise environments
- Misattribution of stress responses, as many of my own clients have shared, confusing digital overwhelm for generalized anxiety

And here's the science:

More than 50% of the cortex, the surface of your brain, is dedicated to visual processing (William G. Allyn, Professor of Medical Optics, Rochester University) That means every image, scroll, cut, flash, or feed gets processed, stored, and interpreted. Whether you're neurodivergent or not, you're a visual sponge, soaking up messages, emotions, and expectations at every swipe.

This book isn't about children or teens. It's for adults; individuals with agency, autonomy, and the power to shape their digital experience.

And for adults who identify as neurodivergent, the journey toward digital balance might involve different tools, more intentional boundaries, or greater support systems. But the goal remains the same:

A visual diet that reflects your values, supports your regulation, and *doesn't deplete your nervous system*. Balance is key. Thanos was right but he lacked specificity.

Extinction Burst: The Final Flare Before the Fade

> *"Extinction burst is a term used to describe a fairly common phenomenon in therapeutic treatment. Namely, when the therapist, program, or even individual tries to stop an unwanted behavior by no longer reinforcing it, that behavior will reassert itself for a time, and can increase in intensity before it goes away."*
> —Phil Bryan, *Evoke Therapy Programs*, 2020

As you begin your journey toward digital wellness, it's important to understand this:

Before it gets easier, it might get louder. When we stop reinforcing a habit, especially one tied to dopamine and emotional regulation, it doesn't go quietly. Instead, it may spike in intensity as the brain fights to preserve the pattern. This is called an extinction burst.
And it's completely normal.

You might notice:

- Increased urges to scroll, swipe, binge, or check
- Heightened irritability, anxiety, or restlessness
- Emotional responses that feel disproportionate to the moment
- Behaviors that feel regressive or out of character, like adult tantrums or emotional shutdowns

These moments are not a sign of failure. They are a sign that your brain is recalibrating.

The extinction burst is especially pronounced when:

- You haven't yet developed new coping mechanisms
- You're unaware of how digital use was masking emotional needs
- You're doing the work alone, without reflection or support

That's why it's so important to do the inner work, to build your emotional regulation toolkit, and to extend yourself a ton of grace.

You're not breaking down.
You're breaking through.

This Work Isn't Meant to Be Done Alone

Digital wellness, like emotional healing, is not a solo expedition.
That's why the next chapter is centered around community.

For some, "community" means deep interconnectedness: group chats, support systems, face-to-face connection. For others, it might be loose threads: familiar faces at a café, passive support in shared silence, or digital spaces that provide resonance. No matter what form it takes, you are not meant to do this work in isolation. One technique that bridges solitude and support is called body doubling.

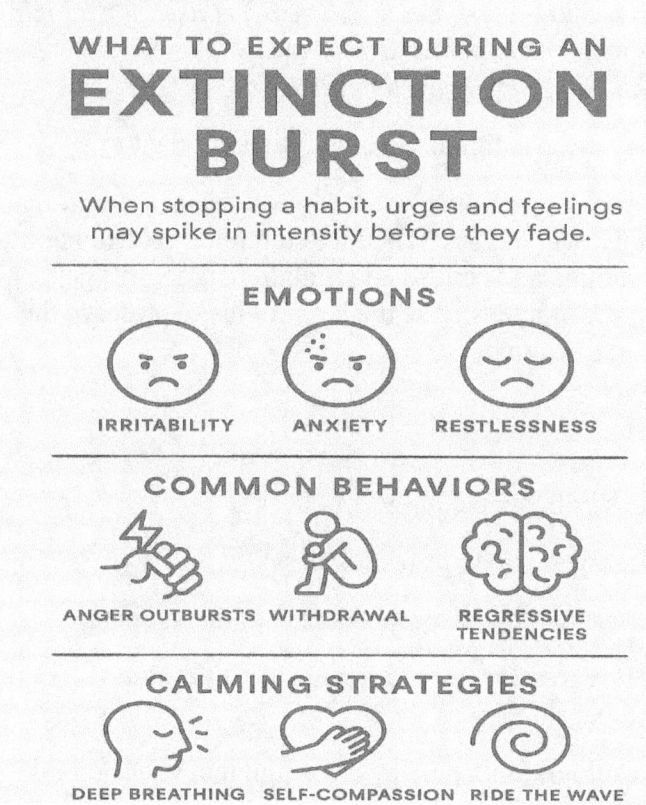

You might already be doing it without realizing:

- Working at a coffee shop surrounded by others
- Sitting in a quiet library alongside focused strangers
- Co-working with a friend, even in silence

Body doubling is simple:

Being in proximity to others who are focused on a task helps activate your own focus. It's an unspoken permission to engage, stay present, and push through. This behavioral mirroring is deeply human. Mimicry helped us survive. And for neurodivergent folks, it became a strategy for social integration, masking.

Masking helps people "blend in," but it comes at a cost:

- Constant cognitive rehearsal
- Emotional vigilance
- Fatigue from hyper-awareness

It may help with functioning, but it can deplete the nervous system. That's why building supportive, authentic spaces matters where you don't just copy to belong but show up fully as you are.

Body Doubling in a Screen-Saturated World

While body doubling can be incredibly helpful, it's important to be aware of your environment. If those around you are deep in their screens, your brain may follow suit, especially if you're already tired or overstimulated.

This can lead to:

- Increased anxiety or disconnection
- Triggered feelings of "otherness"
- Greater temptation to re-engage with poor visual habits

What Can Help?

For some, the answer lies in special interests.

- Engaging in interest-based communities (online or in-person) can serve as a nourishing alternative to doom scrolling or passive content consumption.
- For others, it may require temporary removal of access, voluntarily giving up the ability to scroll, swipe, or binge. This is where tools discussed in the previous chapter and in Chapter 35 come into play.

If that resonates with you, feel free to skip ahead.

Fatigue Feeds the Feed

When we are depleted, our defenses lower.

We are more likely to:

- Seek out quick dopamine hits
- Fall back into passive habits
- Overconsume visual content to avoid discomfort

That's why a poor visual diet often follows burnout, masking fatigue, or social disconnection.

But Before You Disconnect...

The next few chapters will guide you through:

- Emotional regulation
- Identity recalibration
- Navigating the emptiness that can arise during digital detox

Please familiarize yourself with these emotional tools before attempting full cessation. Detoxing without preparation can cause unnecessary distress.

This isn't just about screens. It's about relearning how to sit with yourself, and that deserves support, not suffering.

Micro-Goals for Executive Functioning

Micro-goals aren't new in psychology, or in neuroaffirming care. They're a proven strategy for turning overwhelm into action.

When faced with a big task, it's easy to freeze. Even just *thinking* about what "needs to be done" can send some folks, especially those with executive functioning challenges, into a spiral of avoidance, anxiety, or shutdown. This is where micro-goals come in.

Breaking It Down: Micro-Goals for Momentum

Micro-goals are tiny, specific action steps broken down from a larger task. Each step is a winnable moment—a mini success that builds confidence, momentum, and self-trust.

What Are Micro-Goals?

Clean the kitchen →
- Put on music
- Gather all dishes in one area
- Load dishwasher
- Wipe one counter

Why Micro-Goals Work
- Make foggy "shoulds" concrete
- Build confidence through small wins
- Create clarity and momentum
- Externalize the steps

What Are Micro-Goals?

Micro-goals are tiny, specific action steps broken down from a larger objective.

Instead of:

"Clean the kitchen"

You might have:

- Put on music
- Gather all dishes into one area
- Load dishwasher
- Wipe one counter
- Take a five-minute break

Each small task becomes a winnable moment, a mini success that builds confidence, momentum, and self-trust.

Why Micro-Goals Work

For folks who struggle with:

- Initiation
- Prioritization

- Working memory
- Sustained attention

Micro-goals externalize the process.
They turn foggy mental "shoulds" into clear, doable actions.

Instead of climbing the whole mountain, you're just taking the next step.
And the next.
And the next.

Start Small, Really Small

Sometimes, even the smallest step is a victory. For someone overwhelmed by life's noise, be it digital, emotional, or existential, something as basic as:

- Standing up
- Walking to the bathroom
- Picking up a toothbrush

…can feel like climbing a mountain.

This isn't laziness or weakness. It's often the weight of accumulated stress, trauma, or sensory overload. That's why we celebrate even the tiniest of wins. These small acts of self-care can trigger a snowball effect, each step building momentum for the next.

Parts Work: When the Inner Team Isn't Aligned

Sometimes, even when we *want* change, another part of us resists. Sabotage? Maybe. But more often, it's a protective strategy developed over time. When I say *"parts,"* I don't mean this pathologically. We all have parts, different aspects of ourselves with different needs, voices, and fears.

- One part wants structure.
- Another craves escape.
- One longs for peace.
- Another panics at the thought of letting go.

If our parts are integrated, they collaborate. If they've been wounded or neglected, they may pull us in opposite directions. And that's okay. Awareness is the first step toward harmony.

The Saboteur Isn't the Villain, It's a Part of You

The part of me writing this book is not the same part that shows up when I'm with friends or with my partner.

- My therapist self has a different role than my playful self.
- My writer part seeks meaning and clarity, while my social part craves connection and joy.

We are all a collection of parts, each with different needs, voices, and ways of showing up. And within those many parts, some of us may carry a saboteur.

Not a villain.
Not broken.

But a part that, out of fear, exhaustion, or habit, wants to stay close to the comfort of our problematic visual diet. Why? Because change is unfamiliar, and unfamiliar often feels unsafe, even when it's good for us.

When the Inner Team Isn't Ready

If you've ever:

- Acted out of character
- Slipped into an age-incongruent behavior
- Lost time or struggled with memory gaps

…you may have parts that aren't aligned with your conscious goals. That's okay.

Before you move deeper into goal-setting or digital detox plans, give those parts some attention, compassion, and preparation. They may need buy-in, reassurance, or even a role in the healing process. Give yourself time.
The next few chapters are here to help you understand your unmet needs, manage emotional shifts, and stabilize before diving back into planning. Your internal system deserves respect, not pressure to rush through.

Stimming: A Vital Form of Self-Regulation

Many neurodivergent and neurotypical individuals engage in what's known as stimming.

"Stimming" is short for self-stimulatory behavior, actions that provide a person with sensory input or emotional regulation.

These repetitive movements or sounds are often ways to:

- Self-soothe
- Manage overwhelm
- Express excitement
- Release built-up tension

- Ground oneself during moments of dysregulation

As Bethel S. explains:

> "Stimming is also called quite a few other names, including stereotypy, stereopathy, and restrictive and repetitive behaviors (RRBs). As implied by the name 'self-stimulatory behavior,' these are actions or behaviors that someone engages in that give themselves some form of stimulation."

Examples of stims include:

- Rocking back and forth
- Jumping or bouncing
- Hand flapping
- Spinning
- Repeating words or sounds
- Tapping fingers, humming, or chewing

Essentially, stimming offers needed input, physical, auditory, visual, or otherwise, when the brain or nervous system calls for it.

Stimming is *not* a behavior that needs to be "fixed" or eliminated.
It's a natural and often necessary tool for emotional and sensory regulation.

Stimming as Communication and Regulation

Autistic advocate Mel Baggs (2007) once described stimming as:

> "Being in a constant conversation with every aspect of my environment, reacting physically to all parts of my surroundings."

For many neurodivergent individuals, this is not just a coping mechanism, it's an intrinsic form of being. A way to stay connected to one's environment, body, and emotions.

Neurotypical People Stim Too

Stimming is not exclusive to autism or neurodivergence.

If you've ever:

- Run your hand through your hair
- Bounced your leg when anxious
- Hummed under your breath
- Twirled a pen or tapped your fingers

...you were stimming.

These small, repetitive actions are often unconscious tools for grounding, self-soothing, or energy release.

Intentional Tools: DBT and Sensory Self-Regulation

When emotional overwhelm strikes, tools like stimming can be life-saving, especially when directed intentionally.

Dialectical Behavioral Therapy (DBT) teaches techniques for emotional regulation, including the TIPP skill:

- **T**emperature – Use cold water or ice to shock the nervous system
- **I**ntense Exercise – Short bursts of movement to burn off adrenaline
- **P**aced Breathing – Slow, intentional breaths to regulate heart rate
- **P**rogressive Muscle Relaxation – Tense and release muscle groups to calm the body

Another DBT skill, Self-Soothing with the Senses, encourages engaging:

- Sight
- Sound
- Smell
- Taste
- Touch
...to foster grounding and emotional balance.

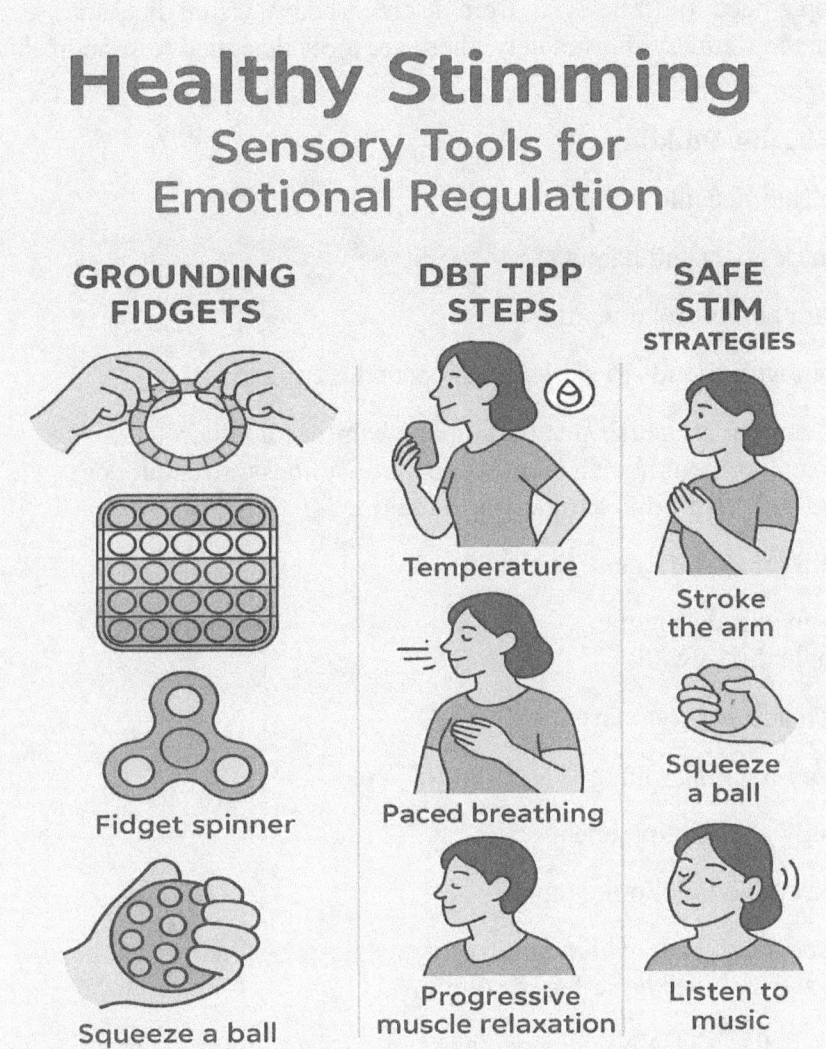

Stimming vs. Screens

Stimming via sensory tools or movement is very different from passive screen-based stimulation.

While screens *may* feel like they regulate the nervous system, they often overstimulate and dysregulate, especially for children and neurodivergent individuals.

Fidget tools, by contrast, can offer tactile, visual, or auditory stimulation that allows individuals to channel energy productively and maintain focus, without the physiological and emotional cost of screen overload.

Replacement Usage: Shifting, Not Just Stopping

Replacing our engagement with visual media isn't revolutionary, it's a tried-and-true approach for reducing compulsive behaviors.

Many people need to titrate away from a screen-heavy visual diet, not simply quit cold turkey. Fortunately, there are tools designed to support this transition.

Gamified Habit-Building

Apps like Habitica allow users to:

- Track goals and habits
- Earn points and rewards
- Join with friends to battle monsters and complete tasks

Sure, some might argue it's just trading one habit for another.
But if the replacement helps you move toward wellness, structure, or personal growth, isn't that a trade worth making?

Different Brains, Different Tools

Not everyone needs a game.
Some people thrive with:

- Spreadsheets or charts
- Goal-tracking journals
- Daily check-in planners
- Executive functioning apps

Others, especially those with neurodivergence like Dyspraxia, may benefit from interactive, kinesthetic-based solutions.

For example, the ATHYNOS game has been shown to improve motor coordination and hand-eye integration through movement and hands-on gameplay (D. Avila-Pesantez, 2018).

The goal isn't perfection. It's progress. And finding what works for your brain, your needs, and your daily reality.

Digital Wellness Is Deeply Personal

Again, there is no one-size-fits-all approach to digital wellness.

That's why, starting in Chapter Five, I've introduced a range of tools, modalities, and action steps, without dividing them rigidly between neurodivergent and neurotypical individuals.

Because the truth is:
Everyone's nervous system, lifestyle, and lived experience is different.

This journey is going to be highly individualized.

That might mean:

- You'll try something that doesn't work the first (or second) time.
- You'll stumble into a tool that helps, only to need something different later.
- You'll fail forward, and that's not only okay, but it's also essential to sustainable change.

Failure ≠ Final

A failed attempt doesn't mean the end.
It means you've gathered more information.

If one aspect helped, *even a little*, carry that into your next step.

For instance, community is emphasized throughout this book, but that doesn't mean everyone needs to build community to achieve digital wellness.

- Some people are healing from critical, unavailable, or harmful relationships.
- Others thrive best through solitude, journaling, or nature.

Instead of pressuring yourself to fit a mold, ask:
What strengths am I starting with? What resources do I already have?
That's your template and it's enough to begin with.

Special Interest Groups: More Than a Hobby

Special interests are often associated with autistic individuals (deep, focused passions about specific topics, items, or concepts). But in truth, everyone has special interests.

What sets them apart for many neurodivergent individuals is the intensity of passion and cognitive focus poured into them.

From Isolation to Connection

Getting involved in special interest groups can be a vital part of digital wellness.

These groups allow us to:

- Channel our attention intentionally
- Connect with others over a shared love
- Step out of passive screen consumption and into *active engagement*

Cosplay as a Healing Visual Diet

One of the most joyful special interest communities I've had the pleasure of being part of is cosplay.

Within this space, people:

- Transform themselves through craft, makeup, and design
- Take their own creative spin on beloved characters
- Bond over mutual fandoms with pure joy and zero judgment

It's a visual space that is:

- Accepting of all identities
- Non-harmful
- Joyously immersive
- And infinitely customizable to reflect our worldview

For many, this is the visual nourishment we didn't know we needed, a break from the polarity, rage cycles, and hyperstimulating content of mainstream digital spaces.

Taking Options Off the Table: Dumb Phones & Digital Blockers

Sometimes the most effective way to regain control is to consciously take options away, by choice and with full agency.

This can look like:

- Switching to a bare bones "dumb" phone
- Using digital blockers or grayscale modes
- Implementing lockout timers and accountability apps (as covered earlier)

But here's the key:
This only works if you choose it.
Enforcing this on someone else, without consent, will almost certainly backfire.

Expect Resistance, from Your Brain

When we remove dopaminergic digital inputs, our nervous system often panics.
Expect symptoms like:

- Fatigue or foggy thinking

- Irritability or emotional agitation
- Strong urges to reach for other compulsive behaviors (sugar, screens, alcohol, etc.)

That's why inner work is non-negotiable. Without tools to process the emotions, memories, or discomfort that arises, we risk replacing one compulsion with another.

This is a relationship with yourself. The work toward digital wellness is, at its core, a reconnection with your own mind, body, and spirit.

You are:

- Building emotional capacity
- Creating space to hear yourself
- Learning to soothe and support your inner world

That can feel scary, but it can also be revelatory. Start by strengthening your inner toolkit *before* removing digital stimuli completely. Tend to your nervous system first and your future self will thank you.

Board Games & Role-Playing Games as Social Simulators

While research shows that autistic individuals may approach social information differently, this doesn't mean they lack empathy or interest in connection. Rather, they may benefit from alternative pathways to understand and practice interpersonal interactions.

This is where board games and tabletop RPGs (like Dungeons & Dragons, Monsterhearts, or Thirsty Sword Lesbians) come in.

Why Games Work

RPGs create a safe, collaborative space where players:

- Experiment with social roles and identities
- Practice taking others' perspectives
- Engage in structured collaborative problem-solving
- Decode and respond to in-game emotional cues

For many neurodivergent individuals, especially those with ADHD or autism, games provide:

- Predictability with built-in rules
- Turn-taking that ensures inclusion
- Clear goals and feedback loops

- Room for creativity and expression, often through avatars or characters that allow safer self-exploration

A Visual Diet of Imagination and Agency

Unlike passive media, RPGs and strategy-based board games activate:

- Narrative storytelling
- Creative worldbuilding
- Cooperation, negotiation, and sometimes competition

They become an ideal replacement for overstimulating screen content, shifting attention from consumption to participation, from scrolling to storytelling.

Theory of Mind and Board Games
Many theory of mind (ToM) skills are naturally engaged in board games, particularly those involving social deception or clue-giving. To succeed, players must use perspective-taking and social cognition to infer whether others are bluffing or concealing intentions (Oey, et al 2019), or to determine which aspect of a clue is most relevant to the group (Wilson & Sperber, 2004). More broadly, across most board games, players must consider the intentions of others, whether to anticipate an opponent's move or to establish mutual understanding with teammates in cooperative play (Sally & Hill, 2006). Thus, all board games inherently involve some degree of theory of mind.

Building Social Relationships
By design, board games require cooperation and shared reliance on others' decisions to progress and maintain engagement (McCain, 2008). This interdependence fosters cohesion among group members, often leading to stronger friendships and heightened camaraderie. For individuals with autism, who may face difficulties with social connection and experience isolation, structured collaborative play in small-group settings offers a promising avenue for enhancing social well-being.

Increased Cognitive Skills
Board games also support the development of key cognitive skills, including memory, inhibition, and organizational abilities, skills fundamental not only to game success but also to daily functioning.

Fostering Independence
Through active decision-making in gameplay and the experience of success, participants are often empowered to apply these decision-making abilities more confidently in real-life contexts, fostering a greater sense of independence (Atherton et al., 2024).

RPGs & BOARD GAMES AS NEURODIVERGENT-AFFIRMING TOOLS

BENEFITS FOR NEURODIVERGENT PLAYERS

 Practice perspective-taking & empathy

 Develop social cognition in a structured, low-stakes way

 Predictability with clear rules & feedback

 Activates imagination & creativity

 Engaging, collaborative, and fun

GAMES TO TRY

Role-Playing Games
- Dungeons & Dragons
- Monsterhearts
- Thirsty Sword Lesblans

INCLUSIVE GAME SPACES

- Be mindful of sensory needs
- Respect communication preferences
- Allow breaks & flexidiity

INCLUSIVE-GAME SPACES

- Be mindful of sensory needs
- Respect communication preferences
- Allow breaks & flexibility

Neurodivergent-Friendly DM Tips

NEURODIVERGENT-FRIENDLY DM TIPS

Provide a session zero to discuss boundaries, triggers, and accommodations

My Starting Point:
PERSONALIZED PLANNING FOR DIGITAL WELLNESS

CURRENT BARRIERS
What challenges am I facing rright now?

_____
_____
_____

PREVIOUS ATTEMPTS
What approaches have I tried before? What worked?

_____
_____
_____

NEEDS TO PROTECT
What parts of my life & health do I want to prioritize?

_____
_____
_____

PERSONALIZED GOALS
How do I want to begin (or continue) my wellness journey?

_____
_____
_____

Summary

Shared Need for Balance in Visual Diets

- Both neurodivergent and neurotypical individuals experience overstimulation from excessive digital content.
- The goal is not to create a separate "special" visual diet but to promote a diverse, robust, and mindful engagement with visual media for all.

Impact of Visual Stimuli on the Brain

- More than 50% of the cortex is devoted to visual processing (William G. Allyn, Rochester University).
- Visual stimuli can trigger emotional responses, leading to stress, anxiety, or dysregulation.
- Overconsumption of digital content can disguise itself as a "helping hand" while causing harm.

Extinction Burst in Digital Detox

- When eliminating an unwanted habit, urges often increase before they diminish.
- This process may lead to temporary irritability, stress, or emotional outbursts.
- Expect an initial struggle before achieving a sustainable digital balance.

Community & Body Doubling as Tools for Digital Wellness

- Body Doubling: Working alongside others (e.g., in a coffee shop or library) can boost focus and help regulate digital habits.
- While masking social behaviors can be exhausting for neurodivergent individuals, engaging in intentional, supportive communities can facilitate healthier visual habits.

Micro-Goals for Executive Functioning

- Breaking down large tasks into small, manageable steps fosters success.
- Success in micro-goals creates momentum for larger behavioral changes.
- Recognizing the inner saboteur, the part resisting digital wellness, helps address subconscious resistance.

Stimming & Alternative Forms of Regulation

- Both neurodivergent and neurotypical individuals engage in self-stimulatory behaviors (stimming) to regulate emotions.

- Stimming through screens can be counterproductive; physical activities (e.g., fidget tools, sensory-based strategies, DBT techniques like TIPP) offer healthier alternatives.

Replacing Poor Visual Habits with Purposeful Engagement

- Tools like Habitica and goal-tracking apps provide structured ways to shift digital habits.
- Special interest groups (e.g., cosplay, hobby communities) help redirect attention to meaningful, non-screen-based activities.

The Role of Board & Role-Playing Games in Digital Wellness

- Board games enhance social skills, cognitive flexibility, and strategic thinking.
- Role-playing games help improve perspective-taking, theory of mind, and problem-solving.
- Engaging in structured, interactive play fosters stronger social connections and emotional regulation.

Intentional Digital Restriction (Bare Bones Phones & Digital Blockers)

- Voluntarily limiting access to digital stimuli (e.g., switching to dumb phones, using digital blockers) can help reset the brain's relationship with screens.
- Expect initial withdrawal symptoms (exhaustion, frustration, impulse-seeking behaviors).
- Developing coping strategies and emotional resilience before reducing screen time is crucial.

Highly Individualized Approach to Digital Wellness

- There is no one-size-fits-all approach to a healthy visual diet.
- Different individuals will require different modalities of engagement, from structured interventions to community-based strategies.
- Failures are part of the process, each attempt provides insight into what works best for personal digital well-being.

Part IV: Action Phase

Action Phase

The aim of this book is to, not only enumerate the enormous data representing the interplay of screens and behavior modification but to also identify ways individuals can utilized evidenced-based ways to mitigate the effects of a poor visual diet or to completely augment their own experience, if they choose to. The next few chapters work to identify beneficial methods for folks to incorporate in their daily lives. I have heavily focused on mindfulness, Dialectical Behavioral Therapy, Art Therapy, and movement-based methods to help alleviate the symptoms and byproducts of poor visual diets.

Chapter Twenty-Five

"He who masters the power formed by a group of people working together has within his grasp one of the greatest powers known to man."
— Idowu Koyenikan

Community

For individuals with a wired tech brain, a fascinating dynamic emerges between the self and the screen: *community*. Technology becomes a portal to connection, linking people across geographic, cultural, and social boundaries. For some, the majority of their meaningful interactions take place online, whether through chatting, collaborative video games, or other digital spaces. These forms of connection can be life-changing, particularly for those who face barriers to in-person socialization due to neurodivergence, disability, mental health challenges, or social marginalization.

It's easy to pathologize these relationships by labeling them as merely *parasocial*, a term often used to describe one-sided connections with media figures or online personas. But that framing misses the deeper truth: many people turn to digital spaces not to escape reality, but to *find* the connection they've long been denied in their physical environments. Whether through online gaming, social media, or niche forums, individuals build bonds and a sense of belonging that may feel more authentic and sustainable than what is available offline.

While some clinicians and scholars frame these behaviors as symptomatic of an unhealthy "visual diet," that approach often fails to account for the systemic and personal conditions, such as chronic isolation or lack of inclusive community spaces, that drive people toward online connection in the first place. The assumption that these behaviors must be *managed* or *mitigated* ignores the very real social fulfillment and psychological safety that many individuals derive from them.

Reframing the Role of Screens in Connection

It is unrealistic, and, in many cases, unhelpful, to expect people to completely avoid screens or to treat abstinence as the ultimate goal for addressing problematic screen use. Given the pervasiveness of technology in contemporary life, especially in marginalized communities, a more constructive approach is to recognize and address the *underlying need* that screen engagement is fulfilling. In this context, community itself becomes the mechanism through which healing and behavior change can emerge.

The most effective path toward changing problematic patterns is not shame or isolation, but rather a desire for transformation paired with consistent community support. This is especially important for individuals who already feel "othered," excluded, or invisible in their offline environments. For many, the default state is isolation, not by choice, but by circumstance. Loneliness is not just painful; it's corrosive. It leads individuals to question their worth, their desirability as friends, and their place in the world.

A 2019 YouGov survey of 1,254 U.S. adults aged 18 and up underscores this social reality. Millennials, in particular, reported alarming rates of disconnection:

- 25% said they have no acquaintances
- 22% reported having no friends
- 27% said they have no close friends
- 30% claimed they had no best friend

Moreover, about one-third (31%) of all respondents said they struggle to make friends. The most common reason cited was *shyness* (53%), followed by a perceived lack of need for friends (27%) and a lack of hobbies or shared interests (26%) that could facilitate social bonding (YouGov, 2019).

These findings paint a sobering picture: for many, digital interaction isn't a retreat from "real life," but a vital substitute for the human connection they can't access elsewhere. Instead of vilifying screens, we should ask: *What is this behavior trying to solve? What need is it meeting?* From that perspective, screens aren't the enemy, they're often the lifeline.

Intersectionalities of Loneliness
There are many intersectional factors that contribute to the loneliness experienced by individuals navigating life on the margins. Marginalization, whether due to neurodivergence, race, gender identity, disability, or socioeconomic status, can compound the sense of disconnection, often beginning with how one is perceived and treated in everyday spaces. When diagnoses or identities are pathologized, fear becomes the primary antecedent in social settings, replacing curiosity or connection with self-protection.

Consider a neurodivergent individual who is keenly aware that their natural behaviors, such as stimming, avoiding eye contact, or speaking in a particular rhythm, are often judged or misunderstood. The demand to *mask* these behaviors to appear "normal" can create a cognitive overload. This person may spend so much energy managing their presentation that they are unable to fully process or engage in the conversation itself. They may leave the interaction not only emotionally drained but also more deeply convinced that their authentic self is unwelcome.

Similarly, a BIPOC individual may experience this kind of social vigilance both outside and within their cultural communities. In predominantly white spaces, they may feel pressure to code-switch or conform to dominant norms to avoid microaggressions or exclusion. Within their own communities, they may face lateral oppression, such as colorism, respectability politics, or cultural stigmas tied to mental health, queerness, or perceived "deviance." These layers of identity tension intensify social anxiety, making authentic connection feel risky or inaccessible.

The experience of gender-diverse individuals adds yet another layer. Trans and nonbinary people often face misgendering, erasure, or tokenization in both public and private spaces. In many cases, they must scan constantly for safety, socially, emotionally, and even physically, which impedes their ability to relax into connection. Even in queer-friendly environments, individuals may still wrestle with internalized fear of judgment, rejection, or being seen as "too much" or "not enough."

Disability, especially when it is not visible, can similarly disrupt access to social inclusion. Individuals with chronic illness, mobility differences, or sensory sensitivities may be excluded from social events, either through lack of accommodation or implicit ableism. Economic status often intersects with all of these identities, further limiting opportunities to connect in accessible, affirming environments. Someone working multiple jobs or living in poverty may simply not have the time, resources, or safe space to build meaningful relationships.

These overlapping pressures create a cumulative effect: a loneliness not born from lack of effort or desire, but from the sheer *cost*, emotionally, mentally, physically, of trying to connect in spaces that were not designed to include them. In this light, screen-based communities, virtual friendships, and online support groups can feel not only comforting but necessary for survival.

Self-Efficacy in Recovery and Cessation
You may be wondering why I'm bringing up self-efficacy in a chapter centered on *community*. But for many psychotherapists, including myself, the concept of *self* is not a singular, unified identity, but rather a constellation of parts. These internal parts, sometimes described as an internal family or community (as in Internal Family Systems theory), interact with one another in ways that influence motivation, emotional regulation, and our ability to meet both internal and external demands.

This internal "community" holds as much power over our behaviors as our external social environment. A person's sense of *self-efficacy*, their belief in their capacity to influence outcomes, make healthy choices, and change habits, is deeply connected to their internal alignment. When these parts are in conflict, such as a protective part seeking comfort through habitual behavior and a managerial part urging responsibility, self-efficacy can feel fractured or unreachable.

Yet research and practice consistently show that self-efficacy is one of the most significant predictors of successful behavior change, even in the face of deeply entrenched habits and addictions. Consider smoking, often cited as one of the most difficult behaviors to quit. Beyond the physiological dependence on nicotine, smoking is often embedded in social rituals: taking a break with coworkers, bonding with friends, sharing moments of stress relief. These social reinforcements create a powerful community-oriented framework that makes cessation not just a physical or psychological challenge, but a *relational* one.

Breaking away from smoking, then, requires more than willpower, it requires a reimagining of both community and self. It means developing new internal scripts that affirm the possibility of change, even when external cues are pushing for repetition. It also means building or finding new communities that support and reinforce the desired change, offering belonging without the harmful behavior.

In this sense, self-efficacy and community are not opposite; they are complementary. Strengthening one often bolsters the other. When individuals feel connected, understood, and supported, whether internally through parts work, or externally through affirming relationships, they are far more likely to believe in their capacity to recover, to resist harmful patterns, and to sustain meaningful change.

Community, Self-Efficacy, and the Challenge of Leaving Social Habits Behind

The psychosocial dynamics of smoking, especially within tight-knit communities, mirror many screen-related behaviors like video gaming, social media engagement, and other forms of online interaction. In both cases, individuals from diverse backgrounds come together around a shared activity. The behavior becomes more than a habit; it becomes a form of *social currency*, a ritual that provides belonging, access, and connection.

Some of these behaviors, of course, carry more obvious risks than others. But what they often have in common is the way they fulfill deeper needs: for camaraderie, for relief, for recognition. As a former 10-year cigarette smoker, I understand firsthand the allure of these community-based rituals. Smoking wasn't just about nicotine, it was about the *community* it fostered. Smokers took more breaks, had more one-on-one interactions, and often shared an unspoken bond with each other. Walking away from that wasn't just about breaking a chemical addiction, it meant losing a social structure that supplemented a core need: connection.

This mirrors the experience many have with screen use. Logging off or disconnecting isn't simply about willpower, it's about navigating the grief of losing a community, even one that might be draining, problematic, or unhealthy in other ways. And just as in smoking cessation, cultivating *self-efficacy* is essential in breaking those patterns and sustaining meaningful change.

Numerous studies across different cultures and populations have demonstrated the central role of self-efficacy in successful smoking cessation. One study of 600 African American smokers found that those who successfully quit after six months had significantly higher levels of self-efficacy at baseline than those who did not (Boardman et al., 2005). A similar pattern emerged in a Swiss study of 115 patients, where higher self-efficacy scores predicted abstinence after 16 months (Borland et al., 1991). Most notably, a 2009 meta-analysis of 54 prospective studies concluded that self-efficacy, the confidence in one's ability to abstain, was a consistent and robust predictor of cessation outcomes (Gwaltney et al., 2009).

As Gallus et al. (2023) summarize, *self-efficacy is an independent determinant of smoking cessation*. Strategies that build and sustain self-efficacy are essential, not just to increase quitting success, but to provide long-term support that empowers individuals to maintain behavioral change.

This same framework is critical when considering the digital behaviors, we often label as problematic. Whether it's gaming, doomscrolling, or social media use, we cannot overlook the emotional and social scaffolding these behaviors provide. If we want to promote healthier relationships with screens, the goal cannot simply be cessation. It must also involve fostering the *internal belief* that individuals are capable of meeting their needs in new ways and supporting them in building or rediscovering communities that affirm, rather than deplete, their well-being.

The Roots of Self-Efficacy: Internal and External Influences
While self-efficacy is often viewed as an internal experience, a belief in one's own capacity to act, it does not develop in isolation. Though it is *interoceptive* by nature, grounded in the internal perception of the self, self-efficacy is shaped by *exteroceptive* influences: stimuli, relationships, and feedback from the external world.

Schunk and DiBenedetto (2021) outline this dynamic well, illustrating that self-efficacy is a multifaceted construct informed by both personal experiences and social environments:

> *"Performance accomplishments are the most reliable source because they indicate what one can accomplish. But people also appraise their self-efficacy based on their observations of others. Observing a successful performance can raise observers' self-efficacy, whereas observed failures can lower it. Self-efficacy also*

> *is affected by persuasion from others (e.g., 'You can do it!'). Although vicarious and persuasive sources can raise self-efficacy, for the increase to endure requires successful performance by the individual. Physiological indexes also constitute a source. Persons who feel less anxious in a situation may interpret that to mean that they are more capable of succeeding."*
> *(Schunk & DiBenedetto, 2021)*

This framework highlights four key sources of self-efficacy:

1. **Performance Accomplishments** – The most enduring source; success breeds confidence. Each accomplishment reinforces a personal narrative of competence.

2. **Vicarious Experiences** – Observing others succeed, especially those perceived as similar to oneself, can bolster one's belief that "If they can do it, so can I."

3. **Social Persuasion** – Encouragement, affirmation, and verbal support can catalyze belief in one's abilities, even in the absence of prior success.

4. **Physiological and Emotional States** – Bodily cues like calmness or reduced anxiety are often interpreted as signals of readiness or competence.

These elements are especially significant in recovery and digital wellness work, where individuals may struggle to trust their internal signals or where past failure has eroded their sense of capability. Building self-efficacy means not only fostering internal motivation, but also carefully curating external environments where people feel seen, supported, and safe to try again, even if they've failed before.

In the context of screen use or substance cessation, this means cultivating environments where success is modeled, encouragement is intentional, and physiological distress is addressed as part of the healing process. Ultimately, self-efficacy is not just a personal trait, it's a process, one that evolves through the interplay of inner narratives and outer realities.

Community Values and Mental Health Recovery
The relationship between community and recovery is not just anecdotal, it's well supported by research. A study involving 153 participants found that positive community values, especially those reflected in social support systems and engagement in meaningful activities, significantly influenced mental health recovery outcomes. As the authors note:

> *"Results suggest that both social support and activities may promote recovery, and that for persons with poor social support, engagement in a variety of individualized activities may be*

particularly beneficial."
(Hendryx et al., 2009)

This finding affirms that healing is not a one-size-fits-all process. For some, recovery is catalyzed by strong interpersonal relationships and affirming communities. For others, especially those who may lack access to supportive networks, structured, personalized activities can offer purpose, rhythm, and a sense of agency. In both cases, what's central is the opportunity to engage with values that affirm one's sense of self, competence, and belonging.

When communities hold positive values, empathy, mutual aid, nonjudgment, cultural affirmation, they serve as catalysts for recovery. They provide the scaffolding that supports an individual's journey toward self-efficacy, emotional regulation, and identity integration. Whether someone is recovering from substance use, managing digital overdependence, or healing from psychological distress, these values create the conditions for sustained growth.

The Role of Social Support in Continuing Care

Social support plays an instrumental role in long-term recovery, not only in the initial stages of behavior change, but in sustaining it over time. Whether someone is navigating recovery from substance use, digital dependence, or another form of behavioral difficulty, the presence of ongoing support systems can significantly reduce the risk of relapse and re-engage an individual's sense of purpose and belonging.

As Zaidi (2020) explains:

> *"The relapse prevention literature within the last two decades revealed various support systems. For instance, fully knowledgeable families, peer groups, and communities can prove to be good support systems against relapse. Spiritual, emotional, and social support organizations were also found as good resources. Moreover, social media has brought people together, particularly marginalized populations, who may not be comfortable meeting in public settings. These factors confirm that both digital and physical social support are effective in creating a sense of purpose for drug addicts and reducing feelings of social isolation."*

This recognition of *both* digital and in-person community spaces is especially relevant for individuals who may not feel safe, welcomed, or understood in traditional recovery environments. LGBTQ+ youth, neurodivergent individuals, people of color, and those facing structural barriers often find more accessible, stigma-free support in digital spaces. These online environments, whether moderated forums, peer-to-peer apps, or anonymous chat spaces, can offer powerful affirmations of identity and humanity, even as someone wrestles with relapses, shame, or self-doubt.

The key is recognizing that support is not just logistical, it's *emotional and existential*. It says: "You matter. You're not alone. You're capable of change." That message, whether delivered in person or through a screen, can be the difference between someone continuing their healing journey, or falling back into despair.

Digital Support as a Bridge to Recovery

Technology can serve as a vital bridge to connection, especially for individuals who lack immediate access to community or who feel disconnected from traditional support systems. Digital tools like online recovery groups, peer support forums, and telehealth platforms offer not only accessibility but continuity of care. For many, these virtual spaces *supplement* the absence of in-person support and help maintain recovery momentum during vulnerable moments.

There is now a wide range of digital and physical social groups designed to support recovery, from 12-step alternatives and harm reduction communities to peer-led groups specific to neurodivergent, LGBTQ+, or BIPOC populations. The common thread across these communities is the power of *social support* to influence recovery outcomes.

As Lookatch et al. (2020) note:

> "Research has repeatedly found that those with stronger social support networks remain in treatment longer and have better recovery outcomes with a decreased likelihood of return to use. The type of social support also matters; having even one person supportive of continued drug use may have a stronger influence on recovery than having one person supportive of abstinence. These findings have led to treatment interventions that target social networks, focusing on shifting social supports from individuals supportive of continued drug use to individuals supportive of recovery."

This research highlights a critical truth: support networks are not just about numbers; they're about *directional influence*. Even a single relationship can tip the balance. Therefore, fostering access to communities, whether digital or physical, that center recovery, growth, and mutual respect is an essential part of sustained wellness.

Relational Influence and Access to Recovery Tools

It makes sense, right? When individuals are in codependent relationships with others who are actively using, whether substances or screen-based behaviors, they're more likely to maintain those habits. These relationships create a positive association with the behavior, even when it's harmful. If someone's closest connections normalize or downplay the effects of continued use, then that individual will often do the same. On the other hand, if they begin building relationships with people who live outside of those behaviors, those who are critical of or actively avoiding problematic patterns, they're more likely to reflect on their own choices, recognize the need for change, and strengthen their sense of self-efficacy.

This is why I fully support digital wellness treatment programs and clinical interventions for those who are negatively impacted by excessive or dysregulated screen use. Evidence-based care can offer invaluable tools for self-regulation, behavior change, and emotional balance. Unfortunately, most people don't have access to these programs. Whether it's due to limited healthcare coverage, lack of financial resources, or geographic and cultural barriers, formal treatment remains out of reach for many.

That's why I wrote this book. My goal is to offer a framework for understanding and managing the effects of visual media and screen saturation, especially for those who may not have access to formal programs, therapists, or structured interventions. I want readers to walk away with tools, insights, and a sense of *agency*, so that even outside of clinical settings, they can identify their needs, re-evaluate their habits, and move toward change on their own terms.

As discussed in the previous chapter regarding how visual diets are shaping BIPOC individuals' access to and experience of care, it is important to emphasize that systemic barriers, including disproportionate healthcare access and the historically fraught relationship between healthcare providers and marginalized communities, have contributed to a lack of trust in traditional medical systems. Consequently, many individuals may seek alternative or culturally rooted approaches to healing that feel safer and more affirming.

Within the Mexican immigrant community, for instance, community-based and culturally grounded treatments have proven effective for individuals experiencing alcohol use disorder. One such tradition is curanderismo, a holistic healing practice rooted in pre-Columbian and Spanish influences. Practiced across Mexico, Latin America, and in the United States, curanderos, traditional healers, offer treatments for a range of conditions, including chronic illness, pain, folk illnesses, workplace injuries, and substance abuse.

Some of the key curanderismo treatments for alcohol use disorder include:

- ***Liver and General Detoxification***: *This treatment serves two primary purposes: cleansing the liver and alleviating withdrawal symptoms. It typically involves a combination of saline solutions, vitamin regimens, and herbal remedies. Some protocols even include small, diluted doses of the alcohol being abused, functioning similarly to tapering approaches used in clinical detox settings.*

- ***Temescal (Sweat Lodge)***: *The temescal is considered a sacred space of healing. The treatment begins with preparatory reflection to help the individual emotionally engage with their journey. Inside the sweat lodge, guided by the curandero, participants are encouraged to revisit past traumas and confront fears. The heat and darkness promote emotional release, while profuse sweating helps eliminate toxins from heavy alcohol use. Prayer and ritual rinsing, performed at intervals throughout, further reinforce spiritual and emotional purification.*

- ***Limpias (Spiritual Cleansings)***: *Limpias are rituals designed to restore emotional equilibrium in individuals suffering from despair, trauma, or anxiety, factors often linked to alcohol use. Methods vary but may include using an egg to absorb negative energies, sweeping the body with fragrant herbs, or incorporating elements like fire or water for energetic cleansing. Limpias aim to cleanse the body, mind, and spirit in unison.*

- ***Pláticas (Counseling Dialogues)***: *These therapeutic conversations between the curandero and the individual seeking help offer a safe space for emotional exploration. Pláticas are also extended to family members, supporting them in coping with the distress of a loved one's addiction and assisting in their reintegration after recovery.*

- ***Sobadas (Therapeutic Massage)***: *Sobadas involve healing touch to stimulate endorphins and lower cortisol levels—key in managing the physical and emotional stress of alcohol withdrawal. These massages may also include clay poultices for added therapeutic effect.*

- ***Spiritual Treatments***: *Prayer plays a significant role throughout the healing process. Curanderos not only pray with the individual but also on their behalf, embedding spiritual connection into the recovery journey.*

(García et al., 2022; Ortiz & Torres, 2007)

Community healing, from an African-centered perspective, also places profound emphasis on the role of collective experience as central to individual and communal well-being. Healing is not viewed as a solitary process, but rather as a communal endeavor rooted in shared memory, spirituality, and ancestral continuity.

At the interpersonal level, the development of collective memory is vital for healing. This memory is strengthened through practices like storytelling, which promotes trust in the group process, fosters remembrance of both historical traumas and triumphs, and supports psychological decolonization. Acts of resistance, both symbolic and practical, disrupt interpersonal distrust, historical amnesia, and internalized misrepresentations of personal and communal narratives.

From this worldview, healing involves maintaining a harmonious balance between the spiritual realm and the physical world (Jackson-Lowman, 2004; Mariette, 2013; Somé, 1993). All life, both animate and inanimate, is considered sacred, part of a divine metaphysical hierarchy: God, gods, spirits, ancestors, and then humans (Omonzejele, 2008). God is understood as the ultimate source of healing, with special deities such as Osanyin (Yoruba) and Agwu (Igbo) acting as spiritual guardians who mediate the healing power of nature (Opoku, 1978; Washington, 2010).

Reconnecting spiritually with one's ancestors is seen as a prerequisite for healing, as it opens access to sacred knowledge and ancestral medicine (Omonzejele, 2008). Within this paradigm, the community itself is a vital healing agent. When individuals uphold the values of unity, trust, openness, love, care, reverence for elders as living repositories of history, respect for nature's medicinal wisdom, and the honoring of ancestors, they create a network of support that enables healing to flourish, particularly in ways that would be impossible to achieve in isolation (Somé, 1993; Chioneso et al., 2020).

Summary: Community as Connection, Recovery, and Resistance

This chapter reframes digital screen use not as a pathology, but as a meaningful response to disconnection, especially for marginalized individuals. Online communities can offer vital support, belonging, and psychological safety for people navigating neurodivergence, disability, racial trauma, and systemic exclusion.

Key Themes:

Digital Communities as Lifelines

- For many, especially those who are isolated due to race, gender, neurodivergence, or disability, meaningful connection happens online.
- Digital relationships can be authentic, safe, and affirming, even when they don't fit traditional norms of "real" interaction.

Rethinking Pathology: The Role of Screens

- Screens are often vilified, but this ignores what they *solve*: loneliness, exclusion, and social inaccessibility.

- Instead of shame or abstinence, the goal should be to address the *needs* behind screen use and build community-based alternatives.

Intersectional Loneliness

- People on the margins experience compounded disconnection, neurodivergent masking, racial code-switching, gender-based vigilance, ableism, and economic barriers all disrupt social access.
- Online spaces often feel safer, more inclusive, and more accessible.

Self-Efficacy and Inner Community

- Using Internal Family Systems theory, the chapter explores how internal "parts" affect motivation and healing.
- Self-efficacy, the belief in one's ability to change, is key to behavior transformation and is shaped by both internal dynamics and external validation.

Smoking as a Metaphor for Screen Use

- Like smoking, screen behaviors often serve as communal rituals, providing belonging, relief, and rhythm.
- Breaking these habits involves more than willpower; it requires new scripts, social structures, and self-trust.

Building Self-Efficacy

According to Schunk & DiBenedetto (2021), four pillars support self-efficacy:

1. **Performance Accomplishments** (small wins)
2. **Vicarious Experiences** (seeing others succeed)
3. **Social Persuasion** ("You can do it!")
4. **Physiological States** (feeling calm = feeling capable)

These are essential for healing behaviors related to screens, just as they are for substance use.

Community Healing Practices

- Latinx curanderismo and African-centered healing emphasize collective, spiritual, and embodied practices (e.g. limpias, sweat lodges, storytelling, ancestral reconnection).
- These traditions show that healing is most effective when it's relational, culturally rooted, and spiritually affirming.

Ongoing Support and Recovery

- Whether virtual or in-person, sustained recovery requires community.

- Relationships strongly influence whether someone maintains healing, or reverts to harmful habits.

- Digital support groups, especially for BIPOC, LGBTQ+, and neurodivergent communities, can bridge access gaps and foster long-term change.

Conclusion

Healing isn't just an individual effort, it's a communal, systemic, and spiritual one. Digital spaces, when grounded in empathy and inclusion, can offer not just connection, but recovery. Real change happens when internal self-trust is met with external affirmation, and when both are nurtured within meaningful, affirming communities.

Chapter Twenty-Six

"Digital wellbeing is a subjective individual experience of optimal balance between the benefits and drawbacks obtained from mobile connectivity . . . People achieve digital wellbeing when experiencing maximal controlled pleasure and functional support, together with minimal loss of control and functional impairment." -Vanden Abeele, 2020

Unpacking a Harmful Visual Diet

In a media-saturated world, many individuals live deeply immersed in their visual diets, the steady stream of images, screens, and symbols that shape their perception of self, others, and the world. Over time, these diets can distort reality, fuel internalized biases, and smother critical thought. Recovering from the effects of a harmful visual diet requires time, intention, and sustained effort.

For some, a complete break from digital media, a form of visual fasting, can be an essential first step. This separation can provide the mental space needed to reorient and reorganize thoughts and experiences that have been shaped or constrained by unhealthy visual inputs. However, this process must be approached with care.

Digital wellness is not simply about disconnection; it is about strategic reconnection. Success often depends on making a clear, realistic plan: identifying the types of visual content that are harmful, recognizing personal triggers, and setting intentions around what kinds of imagery or narratives to limit or eliminate. This might involve rereading old content through a critical lens, reassessing one's media habits, or crafting a step-by-step process for gradually removing or replacing toxic visual stimuli.

The Reality of Resetting a Visual Diet

For many people, achieving a complete reset of their visual diet is not a realistic option. Our world is structured around screens, whether for work, communication, education, or survival. A full separation from visual media often requires resources, time, and environmental control that many simply do not have access to. In this way, the ability to disconnect is a form of privilege, one that highlights the inequality embedded in both media consumption and digital wellness culture.

While eliminating all screen use for a time might offer deep mental clarity, it is not universally attainable, nor always practical. Instead, it may be more feasible and effective to focus on reducing or transforming the specific types of visual input that are most harmful. This targeted approach can empower individuals to reshape their visual environments without requiring full isolation from digital life.

Some accessible tools and strategies, regardless of socioeconomic status, can help support this process. These are explored in more detail in the final chapter, *Maintaining Your Visual Diet*. But what's essential to recognize now is that visual detox doesn't have to be all or nothing. Small, intentional changes can still offer significant mental and emotional benefits.

As Chisholm and Hartman-Caverly (2022) point out,

> "Typical approaches to digital wellness are seldom nuanced and rarely account for experiences that are hedonic, when a user derives pleasure from digital media, and eudemonic, when digital media use adds meaning to life."

While media use can sometimes spiral out of control, we must not ignore the positive, meaningful relationships individuals can have with technology. The goal, then, is not rejection but refinement: cultivating a digital life that supports well-being without erasing joy or connection.

For example, if video games, social media, or other forms of visual media are being consumed in large quantities and begin to negatively affect your relationships or distort the way you see yourself, then that's likely the best place to begin. Start with the most problematic relationships, the areas where screen use feels most intrusive or disorienting and go from there.

At the same time, it's important to acknowledge that not everyone will recognize their relationship with screens as problematic. For some, especially content creators, influencers, gamers, or digital professionals, extensive screen time is not only necessary but also fulfilling and empowering. In such cases, this book may not speak to their immediate needs, and that's okay.

A key distinction lies between those who desire change and those who don't. As I stated earlier in the book, this isn't about telling you what to watch, scroll through, or visually ingest. Rather, it's about helping you recognize how screens influence your behavior, your relationships, and your sense of self.

This book is for those who are curious about how their visual environment is shaping their inner world, and who feel the urge to shift that relationship in some way.

I also hope parents are reading this section and taking it to heart. As teenagers begin asserting their autonomy, both psychologically and digitally, any attempt to enforce behavioral change around screens can often lead to tension, resistance, or deeper emotional distress. The goal shouldn't be control, but modeling healthy engagement, opening up conversations, and building trust. For adolescents, just like adults, change must come from within, and from a place of understanding rather than force.

Reflection Prompt: Locating the Shift

If you're considering changes to your visual diet, begin with awareness. There's no need to overhaul everything all at once, small shifts matter. Use the prompts below to help you identify where your relationship with visual media might need attention.

1. What screen-based activity leaves me feeling most drained or disconnected from myself or others?
This might be a certain app, a type of content, or even a time of day you tend to scroll out of habit rather than intention.

2. Where do I feel most *overexposed* to visual content?
Think about situations where visual media feels inescapable, overwhelming, or overly curated places where you're consuming more than you're consciously choosing.

3. Which screen habits interfere most with my relationships or my ability to be present?
Consider the moments when someone close to you feels ignored, or when you notice your attention is fragmented around people you care about.

4. What role does visual media play in how I see myself?
Ask yourself: Are there certain images or narratives that consistently leave me feeling inadequate, anxious, or hypercritical of who I am?

5. Am I ready for change, or just curious about it?
This question is key. There's no shame in being unsure. This book is here for both the curious and the committed.

What Is Detoxing?

Detoxing from visual media involves recognizing when a media source or digital habit is no longer serving your needs, when it begins to negatively impact your mental, emotional, or relational health, and deciding to make a change, even if stopping completely feels difficult or impossible.

At its core, digital detoxing begins with a simple realization:

"This is affecting me in a way I'd like to change."

According to Syvertsen and Enli (2020), in their article *Digital Wellness: Media Resistance and the Promise of Authenticity*, digital wellness can take many forms:

> "Digital wellness measures vary from spending an hour or two without a mobile phone to a long-term break or digital wellness holiday... While digital wellness inevitably includes refraining from using online and social media... it may also imply refraining from other media such as television, and/or other digital services, including work-related tools and programs. What is common to all descriptions, however, is the presumption that online media and work tools are invasive, and that current patterns of usage are dangerous and unhealthy."

This framing is critical. Digital detoxing isn't about demonizing technology, it's about *noticing when the balance tips* and reclaiming your capacity to choose how you engage. For some, this means stepping away for an afternoon; for others, it might involve limiting specific platforms, muting content, or restructuring media habits over the long term.

Ultimately, detoxing is about interrupting passive consumption and reestablishing intention. It invites us to ask not only *what* we are consuming, but *why*, and whether that relationship is aligned with who we are or hope to be.

Detoxing and Digital Minimalism

Some individuals may have come across the concept of dopamine detoxes or resets, which share a similar underlying principle: the need to reduce overstimulation in order to regain control of one's focus, attention, and sense of self. These detoxes involve stepping away from sources of high-frequency stimulation, like social media, video games, or rapid-fire notifications, and allowing the nervous system a period of recalibration.

In this context, visual media detoxing isn't just about reducing screen time, it's about shifting how much stimulation we present, to ourselves, often after realizing that our relationship with digital content has become compulsive or emotionally draining. That shift can come with discomfort. For some, the withdrawal phase may include boredom, irritability, or a disorienting sense of emptiness, a sign of how deeply intertwined our minds have become with these constant inputs.

However, detoxing doesn't necessarily mean abandoning technology altogether. As Cal Newport explores in his book *Digital Minimalism* (2019), the goal isn't just reduction, it's intention. He outlines three core principles of this practice:

- **Principle #1: Clutter is costly.**
  Digital minimalists recognize that filling their time and attention with too many devices, apps, and services can create an overwhelming cognitive load, even if each individual item seems useful in isolation.

- **Principle #2: Optimization is important.**
  It's not enough to simply decide that a certain tool or platform supports your values, you must also design a purposeful and mindful way of using it to gain its full benefit.

- **Principle #3: Intentionality is satisfying.**
  The act of choosing how you engage with technology, rather than defaulting to constant use, can be deeply rewarding, independent of what specific choices you make.

In this way, detoxing isn't inherently about limitation, but about liberation: it gives you the clarity to decide which media practices you want to keep, which to reshape, and which to let go. Like digital minimalism, it invites you to be intentional, not ascetic, to align your digital life with your values and your well-being, rather than reacting to whatever algorithm or notification pops up next.

Returning to the Self: Beyond Digital Minimalism

While this book shares certain principles with Digital Minimalism, the approach I offer goes a step further. It is not only about becoming more intentional with the digital media we engage with, but also about attending to the unmet emotional and physiological needs that emerge from prolonged exposure to poor visual diets.

In an ideal world, many of us might benefit from simply minimizing our screen time. But in reality, that's not always feasible. Our lives, professionally, socially, and culturally, are deeply interwoven with screens. The goal, then, is not rigid elimination but healing through recalibration.

There are many compelling reasons to consider a digital wellness reset when recovering from a harmful visual diet. First and foremost, it gives the nervous system space to settle. After the initial discomfort or withdrawal, what might be called the apex of the detox, we have a unique opportunity to observe how our minds function without the persistent intrusion of digital imagery. This moment, free from external influence, reveals what is known as our baseline.

At baseline, our brain is no longer under the constant influence of visual overload. This clarity can be startling for many. It is here, in the quiet aftermath, that we are most likely to encounter authenticity, our own internal experiences rising to the surface, shaping how we see the world not through someone else's lens, but through our own.

And that can be deeply uncomfortable.

It's no wonder that some feel the urge to quickly re-immerse themselves in media. Confronting one's raw, unfiltered self can be disorienting, especially after years of relying on screens to distract, soothe, or define us. I'll speak more about this emotional turbulence and the need for escape later in the book.

What's important here is that methods to prepare for a digital wellness process are essential. This isn't just about logging off; it's about creating a supportive, intentional structure to navigate what may arise, mentally, emotionally, and even spiritually. The experience of re-encountering oneself, unmediated, is profound. And it deserves thoughtful care.

Reducing Harm, Not Seeking Perfection

However one chooses to detox, the most important goal is to mitigate the harm that visual media and technology can have on our mental, emotional, and physiological well-being. This doesn't always require a full-scale digital overhaul. For many, it can be as simple and impactful as minimizing screen exposure during vulnerable times, such as before bed, as discussed in the earlier chapter on smartphones and sleep hygiene.

The idea here is not total abstinence, but intentional limitation, carving out moments of relief from overstimulation in order to protect and restore the nervous system.

There is growing empirical support for this approach. One study conducted by Kushlev and Dunn (2015) provides compelling evidence for how limiting digital engagement, especially with email, can significantly reduce psychological stress. In their experiment:

> *"For one week, 124 adults were randomly assigned to limit checking their email to three times a day; during the other week, participants could check their email an unlimited number of times per day. We found that during the limited email use week, participants experienced significantly lower daily stress than during the unlimited email use week. Lower stress, in turn, predicted higher well-being on a diverse range of well-being outcomes. These findings highlight the benefits of checking email less frequently for reducing psychological stress."*

This research underscores a core idea of this book: reducing media input, even in small, intentional ways, can restore calm, improve emotional regulation, and increase overall well-being. It also demonstrates that detoxing isn't about shaming oneself for using technology but about reclaiming a sense of agency in a hyper-connected world.

Setting Yourself Up for a Successful Digital Reset

Embarking on a digital wellness journey or visual media detox isn't just about turning off devices, it's about creating the conditions that allow for emotional safety, mental clarity, and sustainable change. Below are strategies to prepare yourself for the discomfort, insights, and growth that may emerge along the way.

1. Define *Your* Why

Before anything else, clarify your intention.

- Are you seeking calm?
- Hoping to reduce anxiety or comparison?
- Trying to reconnect with your thoughts or creativity?
  Write it down. This becomes your *anchor* during challenging moments.

2. Identify Your Triggers and Tendencies

What platforms or visual media forms affect you the most?

- Is it the endless scroll of social media?
- The overstimulation of games?
- The pressure of constant notifications?
  Knowing what derails your focus helps you *focus your efforts*.

3. Create a Gentle Off-Ramp

Sudden withdrawal can be jarring.

- Start with screen-free blocks of time during the day.
- Silence notifications or use grayscale settings.
- Try one screen-free activity each day (walks, journaling, art, music).
  This helps your nervous system adjust gradually.

4. Prepare for the Baseline

Expect discomfort. This is your nervous system recalibrating.
You may feel:

- Boredom
- Irritability
- Emotional vulnerability
  This is normal, and temporary. Your brain is adjusting to a slower, more regulated rhythm.

5. Replace, Don't Just Remove

What *nourishing alternatives* can you reach for?

- Physical books
- Nature
- Calling a friend instead of DMing
- Mindful rituals like tea-making, stretching, or prayer
  It's easier to let go of harmful habits when something more meaningful takes their place.

6. Build Accountability and Compassion

Tell someone you trust. Invite them in, whether they join you or just check in.
And most importantly, be gentle with yourself. Slipping back into old habits isn't failure, it's feedback. Use it to re-center.

Drawing Upon Inner Willpower

Detoxing from anything, especially something, as omnipresent and behaviorally reinforcing as visual media, requires a significant degree of willpower. And like any physical or mental exertion, it's important to prime the body and mind for the effort ahead. Willpower is not limitless; it's a depletable resource, one that requires rest, renewal, and intention to remain sustainable.

In her book *The Willpower Instinct* (2011), Kelly McGonigal explores the psychology and neurobiology of self-control, offering practical insights into how willpower actually works. She explains that willpower consists of three interconnected forces:

"I will," "I won't," and "I want."

These three domains can serve as a powerful structure for setting goals related to digital detox and visual diet changes:

- **"I will"** – What healthy or intentional action will you commit to during your detox?
  (e.g., "I will take a 15-minute walk instead of scrolling when I feel restless.")

- **"I won't"** – What behavior are you choosing to avoid, even when it feels tempting?
  (e.g., "I won't open Instagram after 9 PM.")

- **"I want"** – What deeper value or desire is driving your choice to detox?
  (e.g., "I want to feel more grounded, focused, and connected to myself.")

Framing your detox goals through these three pillars helps the brain establish internal reference points, mental anchors you can return to when motivation wavers. And because willpower can wear thin, especially under stress or fatigue, it's crucial to also build in moments of pause and replenishment. Small acts of self-care, like mindful breathing, nourishing meals, physical movement, or sleep, refuel your willpower "tank" and strengthen your ability to stay the course.

The Ego Depletion Model: Understanding the Limits of Willpower

As we explore the stages of change involved in detoxing from visual media, it is essential to consider the concept of ego depletion, a model that helps explain why sustaining willpower over time can be so challenging.

The ego depletion model suggests that self-control is a finite resource, one that becomes temporarily depleted after we exert effort to regulate our thoughts, emotions, or behaviors. Every time we override a habit, resist a craving, or suppress an urge, we're drawing from a limited pool of mental energy. Once that energy is low, our ability to make disciplined choices diminishes.

As one study explains:

> *"Researchers have found that anytime an individual overrides, inhibits, stops, or changes a mood, urge, thought, or behavior, it can lead to depletion and hence poorer self-control. Overriding basic urges is depleting."*
> *(Muraven & Shmueli, 2006)*

In their study on alcohol consumption, Muraven and Shmueli found that the magnitude of depletion was directly related to the intensity of participants' desires. In other words, the stronger the urge, the more energy it takes to resist, and the more likely it is that individuals will eventually give in if they don't have the tools to replenish their self-control.

This model is particularly relevant when we consider digital wellness and visual media detoxing. Screens and digital platforms are designed to exploit our attention and impulse systems. Resisting them isn't just a personal failing, it's a neurobiological challenge. Every swipe, every scroll resisted, is an exertion of willpower.

Understanding ego depletion helps to normalize the difficulty of change and reinforces why strategic rest, intentional boundaries, and self-compassion are essential parts of the detox process. We cannot expect ourselves to make major behavioral changes without also building in systems of recovery.

Executive Function and the Cost of Regulation

Over time, our executive functions, the mental processes that allow us to plan, focus attention, manage impulses, and regulate emotions, can become deeply taxed. These functions are essential for navigating a digital detox or shifting a visual diet, but they also draw from the same limited pool of cognitive resources as self-control.

The energy required to regulate emotion, sustain attention, or resist distraction is significant. The more we call on these faculties, especially without adequate rest or recovery, the more our cognitive performance begins to decline.

In a study on ego depletion and executive function, Schmeichel (2007) found that individuals who had just completed emotionally or cognitively draining tasks, such as regulating their emotions, focusing their attention, writing unnaturally, or completing working memory tests, performed worse on subsequent measures of:

- **Working memory span**
- **Reverse digit span**
- **Response inhibition**

This research underscores an important truth: executive functions are not endlessly renewable. They fatigue under pressure, particularly in digital environments where we are constantly switching tasks, filtering information, and emotionally reacting to stimuli. Each act of regulation comes with a cost, and that cost becomes more pronounced over time.

When we consider digital wellness through this lens, it becomes clear that the path to healthier habits isn't just about willpower, it's about preserving our cognitive bandwidth, protecting our emotional energy, and understanding when our executive system is maxed out.

This is why detoxing must be supported by intentional planning, emotional flexibility, and recovery rituals. Without these supports, even the most motivated individual can become discouraged, not from lack of desire, but from cognitive depletion.

The Hidden Costs of Cognitive Overload: Self-Perception and Motivation

Emotional regulation and attentional fatigue are only part of the equation when it comes to the consequences of overtaxed executive functioning. Extreme focus on complex or uninteresting tasks, a common reality in both work and digital environments, can also lead to deeper psychological costs.

When the brain is depleted from sustained mental effort, it's not just attention or memory that suffers, our decision-making capacity, risk tolerance, and even our sense of self begins to shift.

As Fischer, et al (2007) observed:

> *"This change in decision making and risk-taking goes hand in hand with changes in self-perception. Depleted individuals are less optimistic about their abilities, have a lower sense of control, and are less optimistic about the future."*

Similarly, research by DeBono and Muraven (in press) found that depleted individuals:

- Set lower goals for themselves
- Experienced reduced confidence in their ability to reach those goals
- Demonstrated less persistence when faced with difficulty

These shifts are not trivial. They suggest that executive depletion doesn't just affect our short-term performance, it rewires how we assess ourselves and envision the future. In the context of digital detoxing, this explains why some individuals may feel demoralized, ambivalent, or quick to give up: their internal systems of belief and motivation are already running on empty.

This deepened understanding reinforces a core truth of this book: recovering from a harmful visual diet isn't just behavioral, it's neurological, emotional, and existential. If we want to reset our relationship with screens, we must also rebuild the confidence, optimism, and mental clarity that relentless digital engagement slowly chips away at.

Folks can actually have depressive symptoms present themselves. Not in the realm of clinical depression, but a cursory presentation of lack of self-control, less optimism and poor thoughts of the future can abound by the excess in frontal lobe use. Each person, depending on their ability to develop their focus and emotional regulation, can have more or less executive functioning.

Strengthening Self-Regulation in a Visually Saturated World

For individuals already grounded in mindfulness or contemplative practices, there may be a greater reserve of focus, self-control, and emotional regulation to draw upon. These practices can enhance one's ability to notice impulses before acting on them, strengthening what some might call willpower, others might name executive function, or simply the capacity to pause before reacting.

According to *The Oxford Handbook of Human Motivation* (2019), one of the most effective ways to combat ego depletion is to:

- **Set clear intentions** to help automate behavior
- **Prioritize rest and recovery**
- **Practice autonomy in decision-making**
- **Build self-regulatory strength** in areas outside of the target behavior

These strategies act as buffers, creating conditions where self-control can flourish over time, not through brute force, but through thoughtful support.

Unfortunately, the visual media environment we live in is not neutral. The algorithms behind much of our content consumption, whether on TikTok, Instagram, YouTube, or endless streaming platforms, are designed to keep us engaged until exhaustion. These systems capitalize on our attention, subtly nudging us toward compulsive loops that feel harder and harder to interrupt.

Even when we know better, even when we *want* to disengage, these platforms are engineered to outlast our self-control. And while there are strategies, we can adopt to manage our media intake in a saturated landscape, these alone don't create lasting change unless we begin with a vital first step:

Acknowledgement.

Like any compulsive behavior or addiction, change begins when we are willing to see our relationship with visual media clearly, without judgment, but with honesty. From this place of recognition, we can begin to reclaim our attention, not as an act of resistance alone, but as an act of self-respect and renewal.

The Difficulty of Admittance: Echo Chambers and Motivated Reasoning

Acknowledging a problematic relationship with visual media, especially one that involves consciously engaging with content we know is harmful, can be far more difficult than it seems. Many people don't lack awareness but instead remain caught in a loop of psychological safety and digital familiarity.

Living within an echo chamber, a curated feed of voices, opinions, and stimuli that mirror one's own, can feel deeply comforting. The repetition of familiar content, even if damaging, offers a false sense of stability. Over time, it becomes harder to separate preference from pattern, and harder still to accept when something is no longer serving us.

When this comfort is threatened, perhaps by a loved one, an opposing viewpoint, or even an internal sense of discomfort, many people experience motivated reasoning. That is, they double down on their beliefs or behaviors, even in the face of clear evidence to the contrary.

As Dr. Peter Ditto (2017) explains:

> *"People are capable of being thoughtful and rational, but our wishes, hopes, fears, and motivations often tip the scales to make us more likely to accept something as true if it supports what we want to believe."*

This is a crucial insight. It helps us understand why someone might cling more tightly to a damaging screen habit, a biased media source, or an identity built around certain digital communities. It's not always because they are unaware, but because letting go would mean confronting discomfort, ambiguity, or loss.

Recognizing this dynamic is not meant to shame, but to invite compassion and self-inquiry. If we can admit that our inner resistance is part of a larger psychological and cultural design, we can begin to soften it. Not with confrontation, but with curiosity, self-compassion, and a willingness to ask:

What am I protecting by staying here?
And what might I gain if I let go?

When Reality Is Curated: Echo Chambers and the Illusion of Truth

Clearly, this phenomenon is problematic in multiple ways. It not only closes individuals off from critical thinking and the scientific process but also limits the range of visual stimuli they are exposed to. Our increasing reliance on algorithm-driven platforms feeds these echo chambers, reinforcing a version of reality curated by invisible hands, and often at odds with the nuanced, complex truth.

The danger of living in a digitally constructed echo chamber is not theoretical, it is a real and present concern within our global communities. When only a narrow slice of data or information is presented to a population, it can deepen divisions and amplify outrage. This is how we end up with mutual accusations of ignorance or delusion, each side convinced that the "other side" simply refuses to see the truth.

Sound familiar?

No matter your sociopolitical alignment, this pattern repeats endlessly. The resentment and disbelief that others cannot see "what's clearly true" stems from a reality curated by technology, not by shared human experience. That dissonance fractures families, friendships, and communities, not because people are inherently unwilling to understand, but because they are seeing a different digital reality altogether.

And yet, there is hope. Technology itself offers tools for reclaiming awareness, if we are willing to look.

Most smartphones now include built-in screen time data, showing not only how often the phone is unlocked, but also which apps are used most frequently. For many, this data is a revealing first step, a mirror that reflects where attention is being spent, even when we're not fully conscious of it.

This data is just that: neutral, tangible reference points.
What you choose to do with it, that's where agency begins.

I urge you, as a reader and fellow human navigating this digital landscape, to take a moment to glance at what is taking your focus. Not with shame, but with curiosity. What are you giving your eyes, your time, and your mind to?

And with that data in hand, I'll leave you with a question once posed to me by a former therapist:

"When is your own company going to be okay?"

It's a deceptively simple question. But for many, it unlocks a well of emotion, reflection, and reckoning. It invites us to explore the parts of ourselves we've outsourced to the scroll, to the screen, and to the stories of others. In that exploration, something sacred returns: our own voice, our own gaze, our own presence.

Self-Inventory Activity: Track Your Visual Inputs

Take a single day, just one full waking day, to observe how visual media is shaping your attention, emotions, and sense of self. Without judgment or shame but with curiosity and data gathering, building awareness of what's happening beneath the surface.

Step 1: Pull Up Your Screen Time Report

Go to your smartphone settings and check the following:

- Total screen time for the day
- Number of times the phone was unlocked
- Most-used apps (and for how long)
- Number of notifications received

Record your top 3 most-used apps and how much time you spent on each.

Step 2: Reflect with Compassion

Use the prompts below to gently reflect on your relationship with this data:

1. What surprised you about your screen time?
Is it more or less than you expected? Why do you think that is?

2. What emotions come up when you see how much time you've spent on specific apps?
Boredom? Shame? Indifference? Curiosity?

3. Which app or activity felt most nourishing or meaningful, and which felt the most draining?
How did you feel *after* using each?

4. What visual inputs did you expose yourself to today?
Think beyond apps, include TV, YouTube, advertisements, news feeds, etc. What common themes or narratives did you notice?

5. When did you most crave visual input, and what might that craving be covering up?
Loneliness? Fatigue? Avoidance? Restlessness?

Step 3: One Small Intention

Based on your reflection, choose **one simple shift** to make tomorrow. Examples:

- "I will move Instagram off my home screen."
- "I won't check my phone first thing in the morning."
- "I want to feel more present when I'm with my family."

Write it below using the McGonigal model:

- **I will:** _____
- **I won't:** _____
- **I want:** _____

Get Your Sandbags Ready: Preparing for the Emotional Flood

Before embarking on any meaningful change, especially when it involves disrupting a compulsive or habitual behavior, it's essential to prepare for what may come up emotionally. When we disengage from screen-based habits that have served as coping mechanisms or distractions, we often uncover what they've been smothering: feelings, memories, thoughts, or sensations we've long tried to avoid.

This is why detoxing can feel less like quiet reflection and more like a flood.

Removing the blockers allows compartmentalized experiences to surface, and for many, that emotional release can be overwhelming. That's why it's important to *prevent the flood from overtaking you* by strengthening your internal resources. As mentioned earlier, Kelly McGonigal's *The Willpower Instinct* (2011) offers powerful guidance for building that internal stamina and preparing your willpower for the storm.

But what do you do when the storm *is* already here?

Rather than stewing in the discomfort, which can quickly feel like drowning, consider turning to a cognitive-behavioral framework, particularly the approach taught in Dialectical Behavior Therapy (DBT), developed by Marsha Linehan.

In DBT, emotions are not enemies. They are notifications, signals from the nervous system that something needs attention. They are not inherently "bad" or "wrong," but rather calls to action. The key is to approach them not with fear, but with curiosity.

What is this emotion trying to tell me?
What need or value is this feeling pointing me toward?

Mindfulness, a core component of DBT, is crucial here. It helps us observe emotions without becoming entangled in them.

A great analogy for this comes from the *Headspace Guide to Meditation* series on Netflix (2020). In it, the narrator explains that thoughts and feelings are like cars driving by on a road.

> *"You don't chase cars in real life, so why would you chase them in your mind?"*

This metaphor reminds us that we don't have to act on, believe in, or follow every single emotion or thought that arises. We can let them pass. We can stay grounded on the sidewalk, watching them come and go, knowing that our worth is not defined by any one moment of discomfort.

I'll speak more about mindfulness in the next chapter, but for now, just remember:
The flood isn't something to fear, it's a sign of what's been waiting to be seen.
And you don't have to face it without preparation.

Make a Plan!

> *"To be effective, digital wellness initiatives require nuanced approaches that acknowledge the individual's positive relationship with technology while also recognizing the hidden harms of technology use."*
> — Chisholm & Hartman-Caverly, 2022

As discussed in the previous chapter, setting yourself up for success begins with a solid plan. Whether you're taking a brief break or committing to a full digital detox, clarity and intentionality are key.

Dialectical Behavior Therapy (DBT) teaches us to break down goals into their simplest steps. That's especially useful here: instead of just saying "I need a break from my phone," get specific. What will your detox look like in real terms?

Will you spend a week camping in the wilderness with no cell service? Attend a silent retreat? Use one of the many app-locking tools available to limit your access?

Whatever your approach, try to make it intentional, personal, and thorough. This isn't about perfection, it's about being honest with yourself, acknowledging your relationship with technology, and giving yourself space to reset.

Plan for Relapse: Harm Reduction in Your Digital Detox

Relapse prevention is a necessary part of any meaningful change. No digital detox, no matter how well-intentioned, will be perfect. And that's okay.

Rather than expecting a flawless process, consider how you can minimize harm and maintain progress, even in the face of setbacks. This is where harm reduction comes in: building a biopsychosocial infrastructure that helps keep you within your window of tolerance, aligned with your visual diet goals.

Ask yourself:

- **Biological**: Am I sleeping enough? Eating well? Moving my body?
- **Psychological**: What thoughts, emotions, or narratives show up when I reach for the screen?
- **Social**: Who can support me? Where can I go (or avoid) to stay aligned with my goal?

Watch for Triggers That Feel Like Justifications

Be honest about how you might gaslight yourself. For instance, if your visual diet goal is to reduce screen exposure, telling yourself it's okay to dine at a sports bar with multiple TVs "just this once" can quickly lead to emotional dysregulation or relapse. No burger or fries is worth compromising your commitment to yourself.

These decisions matter, not because they're "bad," but because they pull you away from the intention you've set.

Questions for Harm Reduction Planning:

- What environments feel safe, and which ones tend to pull me off track?
- What will I do if I notice I'm slipping?
- Who can I reach out to for support?
- What self-talk helps keep me grounded, not guilt-ridden?
- How can I practice self-compassion, not perfectionism?

Surf the Urge: Coping Ahead for Digital Detox

Relapse doesn't always announce itself. It can sneak in through everyday moments, like asking a friend to borrow their phone, knowing full well that your most compulsive app is open and ready to go. It's not always planned. It's not always conscious. But it can still be harmful.

These involuntary moments are part of the process, and they must be expected. Your plan should account for urges, especially the ones that show up when you're tired, lonely, dysregulated, or just caught off guard.

Coping Ahead: Urges Are Not Emergencies

In Dialectical Behavior Therapy (DBT), there's a concept called "urge surfing." It's a mindfulness-based practice that reminds us that urges, like waves, rise and fall. You don't have to obey them; you can ride them out.

Try this:

- **Pause**: Name the urge.
- **Breathe**: Slow, deep breaths ground you in your body.
- **Visualize**: See the urge as a wave, you are the surfer.
- **Ride it out**: Trust that it will peak, then fade.
- **Redirect**: Shift your energy to a coping tool or nourishing activity.

You Don't Have to Do This Alone

Doing this work solo is hard, not impossible but deeply challenging. Support is part of harm reduction, too.

Include these in your plan:

- A **check-in buddy**
- A **trusted person** to talk to when cravings hit
- **Boundaries** with friends (e.g., "Please don't offer your phone")

- **Digital wellness support groups** (online or in-person)
- A list of **affirmations or mantras** to recall during moments of distress

Remember: Not every group will be the right fit. If you don't feel supported, keep looking. The right community does exist, and when you find it, it can be a game-changer.

Safety First: Trauma-Informed Considerations for Detoxing

> *"Most methods place responsibility on individuals to take control of their behaviors and find a healthy equilibrium for their life. Big Tech companies often take this stance in defense of their products. While these approaches can be helpful, valid, and often necessary, they only address individual responsibility and do not adequately account for systemic issues and deeper privacy implications."*
> — Chisholm & Hartman-Caverly, 2022

As explored earlier in Chapter Four, a brain shaped by trauma interprets visual stimuli differently than one that has been able to complete the stress response cycle. For people navigating trauma, chronic stress, or the lived realities of marginalization, the digital detox process can feel more like a threat than a tool for healing.

Detoxing Isn't Always Safe, At First

For some individuals, the digital world isn't just a source of harm, it's also been a survival strategy:

- A way to dissociate or escape from overwhelming sensations
- A tool for connection in the face of isolation
- A form of self-education, advocacy, or solidarity in hostile systems

Detaching from screens, especially suddenly, can remove access to these survival tools before the nervous system is ready. This is particularly true for marginalized individuals who may have fewer accessible or safe offline spaces.

Safety Considerations for Marginalized & Trauma-Impacted Individuals

- *Understand your nervous system's window of tolerance*
  Don't detox beyond your capacity. If disconnecting feels destabilizing, scale down, not off.

- *Recognize survival-based behaviors*
  Your use of digital media may have developed as an adaptive

response. Don't pathologize it, honor it, and move with intention, not shame.

- *Name your risks*
  For some, stepping offline could mean missing community check-ins, losing access to critical information, or being more vulnerable in unsafe physical environments. Your plan should reflect these realities.

- *Set a trauma-informed pace*
  Gradual change, not all-or-nothing, may be the safest route. Introduce pauses, not shutdowns.

- *Build digital boundaries around your needs, not someone else's ideals*
  The goal isn't screen purity, it's digital sovereignty: using technology in ways that align with your well-being, autonomy, and context.

Being With Your Own Company

To be alone with yourself means being in the presence of what you've endured.
It means giving voice to the pain that's been lodged in your nervous system, sometimes for years, sometimes for a lifetime.
For many, solitude doesn't feel peaceful. It feels like betrayal.

Why?
Because the nervous system has learned that dissociation was safety.
Because distraction was a shield.
Because screens offered a way to blur the sharp edges of memory and hypervigilance.

When you begin to detox, to step away from the noise and stimulation, it doesn't always feel like clarity. Sometimes, it feels like the dam breaks.
And what comes rushing in?
Reminders. Flashbacks. A surge of sensations too big to name.
The very things you worked so hard to escape now flood your awareness, flooding your synapses with evidence of why you needed to stay distracted, stay on guard, stay distanced.

In this way, stillness becomes a trauma reenactment, a return to the internal terrain you were never meant to face alone.
This isn't failure.
It's the nervous system doing what it was trained to do: protect you.

Safety, Not Deprivation: Rethinking Detox for the Real World

The goal of this work isn't just to take a break from screens.
It's to stay present without drowning.
It's about coexisting with the past without being overtaken by it.
And most importantly, it's about doing so with care, pacing, and support.

For individuals who are often othered, targeted, or made to feel unsafe due to race, gender identity, disability, neurodivergence, or other lived experiences, the idea of detaching from digital connection can feel overwhelming, if not outright dangerous.

Sometimes, it's not just FOMO.
It's the real fear of not having access to help in an emergency.
It's the panic of knowing your only lifeline to safety might glitch or fail.
It's the possibility that silence equals vulnerability.

That fear is valid. And your nervous system is not wrong for reacting to it.

Small Shifts, Big Impact

Digital detox doesn't have to mean disconnection from safety.
For some, a more gradual, adaptive approach might be the answer.

One example?
Switching to a minimalist phone, one with call and text capabilities, but no apps or internet access.

This option can:

- Maintain access to emergency communication
- Eliminate visual overload from scrolling
- Reduce compulsive app use
- Provide a structured, tech-lite environment that feels safe

This is about finding a middle path, one that honors both your safety needs and your healing goals.

Digital Wellness Considerations: Progress, Not Perfection

If you've worked to eliminate problematic behaviors in the past, you may already know this truth:

When one compulsion quiets, another often rises to take its place.
This is a natural part of healing, not a setback, but a signal that your system is trying to recalibrate.

Your visual diet is no different. Changing your habits around screens or digital stimulation may stir up new urges or emotional discomfort. That's okay. Grace is essential as you work through this, one behavior at a time.

Recharge Like You Mean It

I recommend revisiting Kelli McGonigal's book *The Willpower Instinct*, as mentioned earlier in this work. It offers a powerful reminder:

Willpower is not infinite. It needs rest.
No one can operate at 100% effort, 100% of the time. Trying to do so doesn't build strength, it burns it out.

That's why strategic breaks are part of digital wellness, not a contradiction to it. Make space to rest, reflect, and recharge your intention.

Anchor Your Why

What reminds you why this matters?

For some, it's a vision board filled with colors, textures, and images of their ideal life.
For others, it's a single phrase that cuts to the core, taped to a mirror, scribbled in a journal, or tucked into a wallet.

Maybe it's as simple as a photo of someone you love.
A person whose relationship you want to be more fully present for—once your attention is no longer pulled in a dozen directions by endless, overstimulating input.

Whatever it is, make it visual, make it real, and keep it fresh.

Keep It Fresh, Keep It Seen

Our brains are wired for novelty. When something new appears in our environment, the brain immediately goes to work:
Is it safe? Is it relevant? Can I ignore it now?
Once the brain identifies a stimulus as non-threatening, it fades into the background, what's known as habituation.

That's why your visual reminder, no matter how meaningful, can lose its impact over time.
To stay effective, it needs variation.

Try changing your visual cue every two days or so. This keeps your brain alert and helps the message remain emotionally and cognitively active.

Small changes make a big difference:

- Add stickers, textures, or new colors
- Rewrite the phrase in different fonts or styles
- Use colored pencils, markers, or even digital art apps

- Move it to a new place, bathroom mirror, fridge, workspace, dashboard

This isn't about perfection. It's about keeping the message alive, so your intention doesn't slip quietly into the background.

Support Is Survival

I can't emphasize this enough:

A healthy support system isn't optional. It's a protective factor.

Our chosen family, those we trust and turn to, can give us the sense of mattering that sustains deep change.

Even if they don't understand your visual diet goals, they can still offer safety and nurturance. Their role isn't to judge whether your habits are "bad" or "extreme", it's to hold space for your growth.

The healthiest support systems:

- Understand your desire for change
- Don't get defensive if your growth challenges their own habits
- Operate within a secure attachment framework (more on this in upcoming chapters)
- Offer accountability with compassion, not shame

Remember: Accountability doesn't mean control, it means community. And when you know someone is walking beside you, it becomes easier to stay the course.

Personal Screen Wellness:

My Personal Journey with Screen Wellness

I don't expect your experience to mirror mine, but I wanted to share part of my own screen wellness journey to illuminate the emotional and behavioral dynamics that can arise during this kind of reset. For many, this process can be unexpectedly intense. It certainly was for me.

The practice of urge surfing has become essential. I had to continuously sit with impulses that once felt automatic, especially during moments of boredom or fatigue. Fortunately, I wasn't alone. Having emotional support and a clear focus helped me stay grounded. I can honestly say I don't think I could have done it without that tender care and accountability.

My dopamine reset lasted for three days, beginning at 2 p.m. on a Wednesday and ending at 2 p.m. that Saturday. While my intention was to complete a full seven-day reset, unforeseen circumstances made that impossible, something I acknowledged in later journal entries. Still, even this shorter window offered powerful insight into my habits and nervous system patterns.

During this reset, video content, whether short-form, long-form, streamed, or televised, was my primary target. I drastically reduced my phone use, limiting it to essential communication (like checking in with my dog sitter, who occasionally sent me video updates of my dog's stay). To protect myself from slipping into passive scrolling, I used an app called Lock Me Out, which blocked access to distracting apps. I also physically unplugged the television in the Airbnb where I stayed, removing another easy avenue for stimulation.

Most importantly, I spoke openly with my accountability partner about what I was doing and why. That connection helped me stay mindful of my motivations and buffered the discomfort of withdrawal from high-dopamine behaviors.

This experience wasn't just about avoidance, it was about rewiring my attention. About learning how to sit with myself without reaching for distraction. It wasn't easy, but it was deeply worthwhile.

11/9/22

3 Day screen detox

> *Day one: "Tired and lethargic. Excitability increased. Urges to use media intense but not debilitating."*
>
> *Evening: "I slept 4 solid hours of sleep. First time in years."*
>
> *Day two: "Cognitive functions diminished. Processing time increased. However, susceptibility to audio stimulation decreased. Visual arousal increased. Slight depression. Decreased motivation and pleasure response. My body feels like it is realigning. Discomfort and soreness present throughout. Needing continual stretches."*
>
> *Day Three: "Brain fog diminished despite lack of sleep. Utilized yoga to help reconnect with body and channel excess energy."*
>
> *Evening: "Easily able to manage and tolerate emotional sensations and experiences. Highly objective relationship with feelings while not experiencing somatic numbness."*

My second attempt at a screen detox presented similar results. Away from home, on vacation, I attempted to start a 7-day screen detox. Unfortunately, on day three, I became sick and gave in to screens as I spent most of the day indoors. Why did I add this, I included it to allow individuals understanding that this is difficult but not impossible as evidenced by the 30-day screen detox later in this chapter. It is important to include so-called failures in our reality as life happens many times and we may not be able to accomplish this goal for a myriad of factors.

3/27/23

> Day one: "Tired unsure if from the visual diet detox. Thoughts of my deceased brother poured into my brain. He was never able to visit areas west of Ohio. Feeling on the verge of tears."
>
> Day two: "I drove all around the island taking pictures. It's hot AF. 92F. I considered time spent off my phone. Didn't miss it."
>
> Day three: "I slept poorly. My nose ran all night. Slight to moderate cough. Woke up sick. Stayed in bed most of the day watching Brooklynn 99. Laid out in the sun tired and bored. I let my mind wander. Tried to meditate to no avail."
>
> Day four: "Still sick but better. This illness really helped me stay on target except for the 4 hours of tv watching. I went back to the beach and used Duolingo. I'm driving without music. A lot of my inner dialogue changed to Spanish. Not sad or anxious. I feel a peace."

30-day visual diet detox

My 30-day visual diet detox focused on my problematic areas. It was unreasonable to take every screen away from me as I needed to continue to complete this book and still work as well. I still utilize my phone and laptop but eliminated the use of television and video games. To ensure that I wasn't using my phone for video games or streaming software, I utilized the Lock Me Out app available for Android phones. There I customized my usage to allow everything work related and phone calls and text messages. I did allow myself the added bonus of Duolingo to continue working on my Spanish and Google Maps as well as my audiobook and music app.

> Day One: The morning started normally enough. However, after realizing I couldn't utilize tech as I normally have, I felt anxious and irritable. Fortunately, I have a gym membership and utilized that to soothe some of the discomfort. Looking around my home I was able to identify many areas that I've been neglectful and inattentive of. Utilizing a great amount of time, I cleaned much of my space as well as performed some woodworking and gardening. My dog received a lot more attention and walks as a result of this. After performing gardening and some more household tasks, I decided to plan for the following day to ensure I was setting myself up for success.

Day Two: The morning started off slowly as I had a nightmare, which kept me up afterward. I had difficulty waking up until 10am. My urge to use screens intensified up until then. My mood was drab until walking my dog and starting woodworking. My energy stayed up until 7pm. I had increased energy for cardio at the gym. I was able to engage in high cardio even though I was out of shape. I noticed how under stimulated I was during the day. I also noticed heightened mindfulness in my garden. The colors, sounds, and scents became extremely vivid. It was similar to using my color blindness correcting glasses.

Day Three: Having more vivid dreams. I slept around 10 hours having restful sleep. Difficulty concentrating. But I had very little physical soreness due to working out and woodworking. Fortunately, caffeine exists. I have previously taken a hiatus from caffeine except for writing. My frustration and irritation with minor inconveniences seemed to be disproportionate. I was more emotionally aroused. After work, I walked and listened more to an audiobook before ending the day with woodworking.

Day Four: I woke up early but received a solid 8 hours of rest. My irritation in the morning wasn't a factor. After taking a mindful walk and having a mindful breakfast, I sat and listened to my body and my parts. More of an inner calm was present.

Day Five: I woke up early with minimal sleep. I do not recall any dreams. My brain seemed more focused and attentive to how I wanted to spend my time. Working on some wood for about 3 hours while listening to an audiobook, my brain focus seemed to shift into a trance as I worked while my attention focused upon the book. Going on a run seemed easier, despite minimal cardio. My attention to my body and breath was heightened during the run. While working, although initially tired, my ability to connect to insight and increased mental clarity was present.

Day Six: Not much to report. I had poor sleep and fortunately only had one client. Vegged out for the most part of day. Working on fumes. Slept early.

Day Seven: I slept well and had an increased need to socialize. After 7 hours of socialization, I found myself immensely depleted. My focus increased today and mental clarity.

Day Eight: I woke with increased energy and less brain fog than earlier. I had an incredibly vivid dream. This was my off day, so it consisted of brunch, dog activities, and more writing.

Day Nine: This was my day off and I spent it with a friend. I found myself with diminished irritability and eye strain. Sleep was normal and steady. I do not recall my dream but my felt sense while waking was positive. I noticed an increased positive outlook for the future.

Day Ten: Today was a long workday but my sleep was decent, and I felt increasingly present with my clients. My urges to glance at screens decreased incredibly. I found myself more focused upon my day-to-day experiences as well as negotiating within me that I could do it for my future self.

Day Eleven: My sleep was long and heavy. It definitely restored much to me. I spent the morning gracefully easing into the day. Checking in with my parts of self, I noticed quiet and contentment. I noticed something interesting as I started to write today, normally I would listen to something invigorating and highly stimulating like Lindsey Stirling while I wrote. Today, I couldn't focus as my attention continued to shift toward the music. I was previously overloading my formerly overstimulated mind to allow myself to focus on my writing task. Now, I didn't need the additional stimuli to accomplish writing as my focus seemed to allow for more nuanced and individual stimuli.

Day Twelve: It felt like a normal day. I awoke with plenty of sleep and without the need for caffeine. My mood was bright, and my mental energy seemed to have increased. I don't really miss streaming content or video games. I am surprised that my traumas haven't inundated me. Fortunately, I have done a lot of work in that realm.

Day Thirteen: I noticed how much time I have now. Time to complete my tasks or just to bask in gardening or other pleasant experiences. Although my workday was full, it wasn't depleting as it normally was at the beginning of this digital wellness journey.

Day Fourteen: Despite a previously good day, I had poor sleep and muddled through a fog around the day. Taking a bit of caffeine helped as well as soaking in some sun.

Day Fifteen: My day was filled with more mindful experiences. Gardening and hiking provided more joy. My mood and energy felt light and full. Time continued to feel like it moved slowly. Not dreadfully so, just more allowance and opportunity to accomplish what I want.

Day Sixteen: The day stretched on for what felt like two to three days. Fortunately, it was my day off and I had more time to reflect and engage in mindful behavior. I meditated for a bit and tended to my home. I noticed my dog appreciated a lot more eye contact from me as it was previously spent on screens.

Day Seventeen: This workday was busy, but I slept well enough. The day ended with me taking a long walk with my dog, appreciating the sunset and the summer weather.

Day Eighteen: Due to poor sleep, the day slowly moved on. However, I didn't let the poor sleep stop me from accomplishing a workout and many outdoor walks with my dog. It ended with going to watch a movie with a friend (I deliberately allowed myself movies to watch, but only at theaters to help prevent binge watching). The movie wasn't too stimulating as it was a comedy, and I noticed a lot more mindfulness in my body. How my heart picked up at certain points of the movie as well as when it settled.

Day Nineteen: Sleep was decent today. I noticed there was a slight urge to jump on YouTube and catch up with my favorite content creators. This may have been spurred on by a few notifications from the app, which I thought I disabled. It goes to show how a little notification can augment behavior even after 19 days of a digital wellness.

Day Twenty: Twenty days into this detox is something I am proud to accomplish. With just ten days left, elation and euphoria have certainly taken root. I am energized and considering what I want to continue to incorporate in my visual diet going forward. Fortunately, I have a short workday, and I am taking advantage of my time with my dog and doing very little writing today. I feel my ability to self-regulate has increased as well as my understanding of visual media affecting my body.

Day Twenty-one through Twenty-three: I was busy with events with friends due to a holiday weekend. I barely utilized my phone and noticed increased prolonged eye contact with my friends while speaking. I usually turn my attention to my phone every now and then. The urge was depleted and is a soft nagging versus a loud cacophony.

Day Twenty-four: Spent more time with friends with limited use of my phone. I noticed I was easily engaged in relaxation in a water park lazy river. Normally I would have wanted to stimulate myself with water slide after water slide. I was able to just be and float despite the children making noise around me. I felt able to melt into my innertube.

Day Twenty-five through seven: Due to the holiday weekend, my clients were sandwiched together, and I stayed busy. The additional screen time of video sessions fatigued my eyes quickly, but I was able to take long mindful walks with my dog. My mind was able to fully engage with an audiobook I have been listening to.

Day Twenty-eight: I slept long with restful moments. I felt invigorated to start a new home renovation project. Intermingled with friend experiences, I was able to start it while listening to my audiobook.

Day Twenty-nine: Dreams of my housing project took over as I continued to motivate myself to finish it. More friend time allowed more attunement and prolonged eye contact, which allowed me to feel more connected to them. Time seemed to stretch on for a while after returning to my project, which I appreciated.

Day Thirty: I finally accomplished the 30-day digital cleanse, after two prior attempts. I feel elated and want to continue onward for a few more days or weeks. Mostly due to a housing project I want to finish and also for my own sense of wellbeing. My head feels lighter, and I am noticing I am able to recall many things quickly. I'm also glad that I do not have to journal this any longer.

What to Expect: The First 3 Days of a Screen Detox

Based on my own self-report during a recent 3-day screen detox, there were a number of physical, emotional, and cognitive shifts that became noticeable, especially in the first 48 hours.

In the first two days, I experienced:

- Fatigue and overall body soreness
- Brain fog and slower mental processing
- Agitation, especially in response to audio stimuli
- A dip in motivation and pleasure
- Slight symptoms of depression
- An increase in uncomfortable somatic energy (restlessness, tension)

Despite the discomfort, I noticed changes in sleep on the very first night, sleep quality seemed to improve, likely due to a reduction in overstimulation and blue light exposure.

By Day 3, many of the initial symptoms had noticeably abated. More importantly, there was a shift in the quality of my internal experience:

- I became more aware of the difference between subjective emotional states (e.g., mood, stories) and objective sensations in my body.

- My ability to tolerate emotional discomfort and stay with feelings increased.

- There was a subtle but important shift from being driven by stimuli to being more attuned to the state of my body and mind.

Did I transform into some perfectly regulated, Zen-like robot?
Not at all. But something changed, subtly, quietly.

There was a moment when I noticed that my attention had shifted.
It was no longer constantly pulled outward by pings, clips, or scrolls.
Instead, it settled inward, toward a clearer awareness of what is inhabiting this host body.
And in that shift, something meaningful became possible.

Beyond the First Few Days: When the Benefits Fade

While the first few days of a screen or dopamine reset can feel intense, both in discomfort and insight, it's also important to consider what happens after those initial shifts.

Author Ryan Dempsey reflected on his one-month dopamine detox in an article for *Medium*:

> *"The first week or two of the dopamine detox felt great. I felt an increased presence when I was moving through the world and my productivity increased significantly. I was enjoying the simple things a lot more and everything just felt a lot easier and in the flow. These benefits began to taper off after the first two weeks...*
>
> *When we stop, we feel great! We have all these 'benefits' from ceasing to bang our head against the wall. This is not so much a 'benefit' or a 'pleasure' but rather the absence of pain. Our natural state is when we are not banging our head against the wall, so it makes sense that the 'benefits' will taper off because it is just the cessation of pain. The same can be said for distractions. We are metaphorically banging our heads against the wall."*
> — *Ryan Dempsey, Medium (2020)*

His insight captures a crucial psychological shift:

What we often call "benefits" may actually be the body's return to baseline. It's not a surge of pleasure. It's the absence of overstimulation and depletion.

This reframing can help prepare us for the moment when the glow fades and we wonder, *"Is it working anymore?"* The answer may be: yes, it's just that *you're no longer coming down from a chronic high.*

The Arc of Discomfort: Everyone's Journey Is Different

While I experienced a surprising upswing in mood and clarity by the third day of my own screen detox, and while Ryan Dempsey's reflections show the tapering of benefits over time, not everyone will feel better right away.

In fact, many will feel significantly worse before anything begins to improve.
And that's not a sign of failure. It's neurobiology at work.

As Dr. Anna Lembke, psychiatrist and author of *Dopamine Nation*, explains:

> *"You'll probably feel a lot worse before you start feeling better. But stick with it, after about two weeks, the pleasure-pain seesaw in your brain will start to restore to its natural balance, and you'll be able to enjoy more modest rewards, like just one scoop of ice cream or just one episode of a TV show."*
> — Dr. Anna Lembke, NPR (2022)

Her words remind us that detoxing from overstimulation, whether it's through screens, sugar, social media, or even streaming, requires a recalibration period.
The dopaminergic system, used to frequent spikes, needs time to come back into balance. During that process, you may feel:

- Low energy
- Irritability
- Emotional numbness
- Cravings for stimulation
- Disinterest in everyday pleasures

This is not regression, it's the brain healing.
And for some, that healing will take days. For others, weeks or more.

There's no universal timeline. But there *is* a shared truth:

If you stick with it, gently, compassionately, you may find that what once felt dull becomes vibrant again.

The Thought Experiment of Silence

Imagine this:

You choose to cut yourself off from all screens, no notifications, no scrolling, no videos.
In fact, you go so far as to exile yourself to a single room, voluntarily. The space is sparse, filled only with a few tools for survival and creativity:
You can exercise, paint, read, and journal your thoughts.
There's no clock, no calendar, no contact with the outside world.
You're allowed to leave at any time, but you've set a personal rule:
You'll stay until someone comes to retrieve you, 500 days from now.

It sounds like a psychological experiment.
It sounds like a slow, waking dream, or a nightmare.
For some, it might provoke existential dread, or raise questions about the limits of solitude and sanity.

And yet, this wasn't a thought experiment.
This was a real choice, made by Spanish extreme athlete and mountaineer Beatriz Flamini.

When Time Warps: Isolation and the Senses

Beatriz Flamini's radical experiment in voluntary isolation has opened new doors for researchers interested in the effects of long-term, self-imposed solitude. Though her case is ongoing in terms of study, her experience, alongside those of other pioneers like French geologist and chronobiologist Michel Siffre, has helped document how our perceptual and cognitive systems shift when removed from regular social and sensory cues.

When isolated, even consensually, our senses begin to recalibrate. Time, in particular, becomes unreliable. The structure we rely on in daily life begins to disintegrate without external cues like sunlight, conversations, or digital clocks. What we often assume is an internal sense of time is actually deeply social, visual, and environmental.

As psychologist Ruth Ogden notes:

> *"A loss of sense of time was consistently reported by adults and children who spent prolonged periods isolated in nuclear bunkers (for research purposes) at the height of the Cold War. It is also frequently reported by people serving prison sentences and was widely experienced by the general public during COVID-19 lockdowns."*
> — *Ogden, R., 2023*

This fragmentation of time perception isn't just an inconvenience, it challenges our sense of continuity, identity, and regulation. In the absence of clocks, routines, or screens, we become unmoored. And while this might sound extreme, even short-term screen detoxes can reveal subtle distortions in time awareness, showing us just how entangled our devices are in shaping the tempo of our lives.

Do We All Experience Time Differently Without Screens?

So, does stepping away from screens mean you'll suddenly have an altered or "augmented" relationship with time?
Possibly, but probably not to the extreme degree experienced in long-term isolation experiments.

Unless you're in complete isolation, with no contact with the outside world and no access to natural light or time cues, you likely won't lose track of time altogether. You'll still have daylight, social interactions, and your internal rhythm as anchors.

However, even in short detox periods, time can begin to feel different.

When you remove distracting digital stimuli, your attention may expand, and with it, the perceived pace of time can shift. You might notice more of:

- The shadows moving across the floor
- The sound of a birdcall
- The subtle shifts in your own mood or body temperature

Without the constant flicker of screen-based novelty, the world can feel quieter, slower, even unfamiliar.

For some, this is restorative.
But for others, especially those who use distraction to avoid certain thoughts, memories, or emotions, this quiet can feel catastrophic. Because distraction wasn't the problem, it was the solution to deeper discomfort. And when that solution is stripped away, what rises to the surface is often what we've been trying not to feel.

This is where compassion, pacing, and support matter most.

Summary

Unpacking and Resetting a Harmful Visual Diet

Understanding the Visual Diet

- A visual diet is the stream of images, screens, and symbols that shape our perception, attention, and identity.

- Harmful visual diets distort reality, reinforce bias, and weaken critical thinking.
- Recovery requires time, intention, and structure, not just disconnection.

Detoxing Is Not All or Nothing

- Total screen elimination is often unrealistic and reflects privilege.
- A targeted, harm-reduction approach, focusing on the most problematic content, is more practical and sustainable.
- Detoxing is less about abstinence and more about intentionality and alignment with values.

The Neurobiology of Detox

- Initial detox often leads to withdrawal symptoms: fatigue, brain fog, irritability, emotional discomfort.
- After 2+ weeks, the dopamine system begins to rebalance, making space for real satisfaction in simpler pleasures.
- Detox can unveil underlying emotional and cognitive patterns that were numbed by screen use.

Shifting from Stimulation to Intention

- Digital minimalism is about clarifying what tech to keep, why, and how it should be used.
- Willpower has limits. Use McGonigal's "I will / I won't / I want" framework to anchor your intention.
- Strategic rest and replenishment are critical for sustaining self-regulation.

Time Perception & Emotional Flooding

- Screen detox can alter time perception, often making days feel slower or more spacious.
- Stillness may feel overwhelming, especially for trauma survivors or those using distraction as emotional protection.
- Without the shield of screens, suppressed thoughts and emotions may surface, requiring preparation and support.

Safety, Support, and Trauma-Informed Detox

- For trauma-impacted or marginalized individuals, disconnection can feel threatening.

- Detox plans must honor nervous system capacity, survival-based behaviors, and access to safety.
- Gradual detoxing, not all-or-nothing, is often more trauma-sensitive and sustainable.

Mindfulness, Urge Surfing, and Accountability

- Use DBT skills like urge surfing to ride out compulsive impulses without giving in.
- Prepare for relapse as part of the process, not a failure.
- Build a support system or accountability network to stay grounded and connected.

Self-Awareness Tools

- Screen time reports and journaling offer neutral, tangible insights into usage patterns.
- Reflection prompts help uncover emotional motivations behind screen behaviors.

Healing Happens in Micro-Shifts

- Visual detox doesn't require perfection. Small, consistent changes are powerful.
- Replace toxic content with nourishing alternatives (nature, books, rituals, relationships).
- Refresh visual cues often, our brains habituate quickly to reminders.

Chapter Twenty-Seven

"Whatever an enemy could do to an enemy or a foe to a foe, the ill directed mind can do to you even worse. Whatever a mother father or other relative might do for you, the well-directed mind can do for you even better."

-Buddha

Mindfulness: A Practice, Not a Prescription

While this chapter opens with a quote from The Buddha, it's important to clarify:

Mindfulness is not religion.

It is a practice, one that can be approached through a secular lens or a spiritual one, depending on the individual. Mindfulness invites us into direct contact with our experience, whatever that may be.

There is no single "right" way to be mindful.
Your mindfulness might look very different from mine.
And that's the point.

Mindfulness is about discovering your own thumbprint, a unique, personal way of being present with your body, your thoughts, and your emotions.

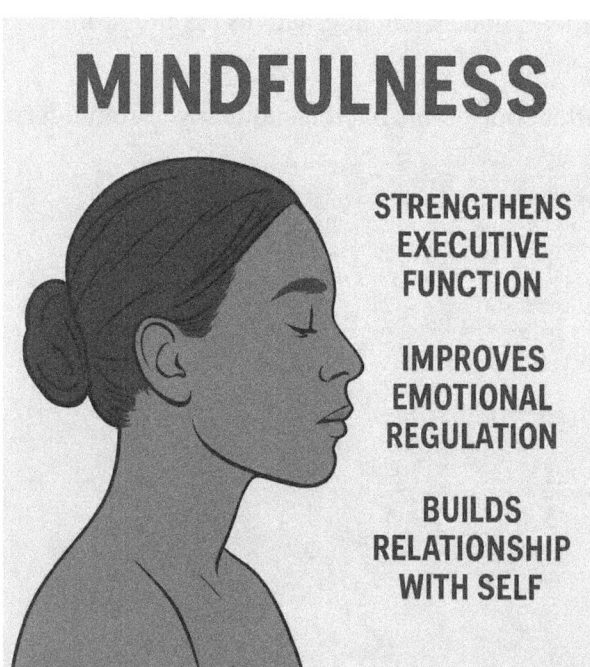

Defining Mindfulness

Definitions vary slightly depending on who you ask, but one of the most widely respected voices in modern mindfulness is Jon Kabat-Zinn, founder of the Center for Mindfulness in Medicine, Health Care, and Society at the University of Massachusetts Medical School.

He defines mindfulness as:

> *"The awareness that emerges through paying attention on purpose, in the present moment, and non-judgmentally to the unfolding of experience, which includes sensations, cognitions, and emotions, moment by moment."*
> — *Kabat-Zinn, 2003*

And again in his later work:

> *"Moment-to-moment awareness, cultivated by paying attention in a specific way: in the present moment, as non-reactively, non-judgmentally, and open-heartedly as possible."*
> — *Kabat-Zinn, 2011*

These definitions remind us that mindfulness is not about control, detachment, or achieving some fixed state of peace. It is about showing up, with awareness, compassion, and curiosity, for whatever is unfolding inside and around you.

Multiple Lenses of Mindfulness

Mindfulness, though widely practiced today in both clinical and secular settings, remains deeply rooted in ancient contemplative traditions. While definitions vary, they all tend to emphasize presence, awareness, and a compassionate stance toward one's inner and outer experiences.

Researchers Shauna L. Shapiro, Linda E. Carlson, John A. Astin, and Benedict Freedman emphasize that mindfulness is shaped by three interwoven elements:

Attention, intention, and attitude.
They write,

> *"Paying attention to one's experience can lead to changes in perspective, what has been referred to as decentering."* (Shapiro et al., 2006)

This idea of decentering, the ability to observe one's thoughts and feelings without fusing with them, is central to many therapeutic mindfulness practices today. Similarly, Davis and Hayes of Pennsylvania State University define mindfulness more succinctly as:

> *"A moment-to-moment awareness of one's experience without judgment."* (Davis & Hayes, 2011)

And bridging East and West, the Dalai Lama, speaking at the Center for Healthy Minds in 2001, offered a profoundly human framing:

> *"All human beings have an innate desire to overcome suffering, to find happiness. Training the mind to think differently, through meditation, is one important way to avoid suffering and be happy."*

Together, these perspectives remind us that mindfulness is not just about focus, it's about retraining our relationship with thoughts, emotions, and suffering, itself. Whether one approaches it as a scientific tool, a contemplative tradition, or a daily life practice, mindfulness offers a pathway toward greater presence, insight, and healing.

Start Where You Are: Finding Your Own Practice

While there are an abundance of resources offering guided mindfulness practices, many of which are excellent, I encourage you not to feel boxed in by any one method.
Mindfulness is personal.
What works for one person may not work for another. And that's okay.

Whether you're using a free app, streaming platform, YouTube video, or a simple online search, countless free and accessible tools exist to support your practice. These can be a great starting point, but don't feel obligated to stick with a method just because it's popular or well-produced.

Instead, think of this as an experiment in self-discovery.
Keep testing what resonates. Let your practice evolve.
And most importantly, trust yourself to develop a mindfulness "toolkit" that fits your life and nervous system.

In the next chapter, we'll explore how to weave mindfulness into your everyday experiences, in ways that are gentle, grounding, and sustainable.

How Mindfulness Helps Our Mind

Mindfulness has a powerful effect on the brain. It strengthens key areas responsible for focus, emotional control, and decision-making. It also helps us look inward and build a better relationship with ourselves. Instead of getting swept away by strong emotions, mindfulness teaches us to notice them with care and curiosity. It doesn't make us emotionless, it helps us respond instead of reacting. We become active participants in our own mind and body.

Before starting any digital wellness practice, we need to prepare ourselves emotionally and mentally. Cutting back on screens can feel like digging a hole in wet sand near the ocean, water rushes in to fill the space. In the same way, emotions, sensations, memories, or even old traumas can come flooding in when we take away the distractions.

If we're not ready, a digital detox can fail. That's why I recommend using mindfulness alongside other tools:

- Reparenting unmet needs
- Calming the body through the senses

- Expressing emotions through art and creativity
- Checking in with our needs
- Reaching out to trusted people or parts of ourselves for support

Together, these create a strong foundation for healing and digital balance.

These practices can help us calm our bodies and build a healthier relationship with our thoughts, feelings, and physical sensations. At the heart of these skills are normalizing and validation, reminding ourselves that what we feel is real, understandable, and okay.

When we stop seeing emotions and sensations as problems to fix and instead view them as signals or stories from our inner world, we give ourselves permission to grow. These feelings aren't flaws, they're messages. Learning to listen to them with care helps us develop a stronger sense of self.

With a solid relationship with our inner world, we can do incredible things. It's not always easy, but it's worth it.

Many studies support the benefits of mindfulness on both the brain and body. It helps lower our physical stress response. One early study in 1992 found that a group mindfulness program significantly reduced anxiety and panic symptoms, and helped people keep those improvements over time. This included individuals with generalized anxiety, panic disorder, and panic disorder with agoraphobia. (Peterson & Pbert, 1992)

The effects of mindfulness aren't always immediate, but over time, it can change how our brains respond to stress. Regular mindfulness practice has been linked to better emotional control and stress tolerance.

- Long-term meditation has been shown to change brain areas related to stress and anxiety. Activity increases in the prefrontal cortex, cingulate cortex, and hippocampus, areas that help with emotional regulation. Meanwhile, activity in the amygdala, which is linked to fear and stress, decreases. (Behan, 2020)
- Practicing mindful breathing has also been shown to reduce activity in the amygdala and improve how the prefrontal cortex helps manage emotional responses. (Doll et al., 2016)

How Compassion Meditation Affects the Brain

Compassion meditation doesn't just help us feel better, it also changes the way our brain works. Studies have found that people who practice compassion meditation show increased activity in several key brain areas related to emotional awareness, decision-making, memory, language, and motivation. Here are some of the most important regions affected:

- **Ventromedial Prefrontal Cortex**: Helps us process our thoughts about ourselves and others.
- **Medial Orbitofrontal Cortex**: Supports self-reflection and understanding how others feel.
- **Gyrus Rectus**: Involved in expressing thoughts and emotions.
- **Anterior Cingulate Cortex**: Important for motivation, decision-making, and learning from mistakes.
- **Frontopolar Cortex**: Supports planning, problem solving, and memory.
- **Supplementary Motor Area**: Helps us plan and control complex movements.
- **Mid-Cingulate Cortex**: Tracks whether our actions align with social goals.
- **Precuneus**: Helps with memory, self-awareness, and imagining perspectives.
- **Superior Temporal Gyrus**: Processes sound and helps us understand language.
- **Inferior Frontal Gyrus/Operculum**: Key for language and speech.
- **Right Fusiform Gyrus**: Helps recognize faces, read, and identify objects.
- **Amygdala**: Handles emotions and emotional memories.
- **Hypothalamus**: Regulates mood, hormones, hunger, sleep, and more.
- **Caudate**: Plays a role in motivation, learning, and emotional connection.
- **Globus Pallidus**: Helps with movement and physical awareness.
- **Putamen**: Supports movement, learning, and rewards.
- **Right Hippocampus**: Stores memories and helps regulate emotional responses.
- **Thalamus**: Acts as a relay center for sensory and motor signals and supports memory and emotion.

These findings show how compassion practices activate a wide network of the brain, promoting emotional regulation, connection, empathy, and cognitive flexibility. (Engen & Singer, 2015)

More Mindfulness Research and Its Effects

- **Sahaja Yoga Meditation** has been linked to physical changes in the brain. A study found that people who regularly practiced this type of meditation had larger overall gray matter volume. Specific areas that showed growth included the right inferior temporal gyrus, both anterior insulae, left ventrolateral prefrontal cortex, and right ventromedial orbitofrontal cortex, regions involved in emotion, self-awareness, and decision-making. (Hernández et al., 2016)
- **Mindfulness in Prisons**: A study in five Dutch prisons showed that mindfulness could help even in high-stress environments. Twenty-two inmates (convicted of serious offenses and serving long sentences) took part in a mindfulness-based stress reduction (MBSR) program. After the program, they reported:

    o Less anger and stress
    o Better control over impulses
    o Greater ability to cope with problems
    o Higher self-esteem
    (Bouw, 2019)

Mindfulness in Action: Real-World Benefits Across Populations

- **Mindful Movement for Children**: A study of 38 children (ages 7–8) explored the effects of in-school mindfulness-based movement instruction (MMI), which included Tai Chi, yoga, warm-ups, imaginative play, and reflection. After twice-weekly sessions, teachers reported fewer disruptive behaviors like inattention, hyperactivity, and oppositional behavior. The children also showed better motor control and improved focus. (Rice et al., 2023)

    These activities gave children a safe outlet to release emotional and physical energy, helping them learn how to self-regulate.

- **Blood Pressure & Mindfulness**: In a randomized study of 201 adults conducted by the American Heart Association, participants with high blood pressure who received mindfulness training showed a significant drop in

MINDFULNESS BENEFITS SUMMARY

Practice	Benefits
Mindfulness Meditation	Reduces symptoms of anxiety and panic (Peterson & Pbert, 1992)
Consistent Focused Attention-to-Breath	Improves emotional regulation (Doll, A., et al., 2016)
Compassion Meditation	Impacts brain areas underlying self-referential processing (Engen, H. G., & Singer, T., 2015)
Sahaja Yoga Meditation	Enlarges gray matter volume (Hernández, S. E., et al., 2016)
Mindfulness-Based Stress Reduction for Inmates	Decreases anger; increases impulse control (Bouw, N., 2019)
Mindful Movement-Based Practices for Children	Improves cognitive and behavioral control (Rice, L., et al., 2023)

their systolic blood pressure compared to those receiving standard care. (Loucks et al., 2023)
Mindfulness training may offer a simple, non-invasive way to support heart health.

- **Breast Cancer Survivors**: A 2020 study of 1,687 breast cancer survivors found that mindfulness-based stress reduction (MBSR) helped reduce depression, fatigue, and stress. (Chang et al., 2021)
These findings show how mindfulness can support emotional recovery during and after serious health challenges.

Summary

Mindfulness: A Practice, Not a Prescription

- Mindfulness is not a religion, it's a practice that can be approached spiritually or secularly.
- Everyone's mindfulness journey is unique. It's about being present with your body, thoughts, and emotions in your own way.

Defining Mindfulness

- Jon Kabat-Zinn describes mindfulness as "paying attention, on purpose, in the present moment, non-judgmentally."
- Other definitions emphasize presence, intention, and a compassionate stance toward self.
- **Core concepts**:
    - Attention
    - Intention
    - Attitude
    - Decentering (observing thoughts without becoming them)

Start Where You Are

- There is no "right" method. Apps, videos, or practices like walking or breathing can all be valid.
- Think of mindfulness as a toolbox, not a one-size-fits-all solution. Explore, adapt, and trust your instincts.

Why Mindfulness Matters

- Strengthens areas of the brain responsible for focus, emotional regulation, and decision-making.
- Helps you observe emotions rather than be overwhelmed by them.
- Prepares the mind for digital detoxing by building inner resilience.

Support Tools for Digital Wellness

- Mindfulness works best when paired with:
    - Reparenting unmet needs
    - Sensory-based self-soothing
    - Creative expression
    - Identifying needs
    - Connecting with safe people or inner parts

What the Science Shows

- 1992 Study: Mindfulness reduces anxiety and panic, even in clinical conditions.
- Brain Changes (Behan, 2020; Doll et al., 2016):
    - ↑ Prefrontal cortex, cingulate cortex, hippocampus
    - ↓ Amygdala (fear/stress center)

Compassion Meditation Benefits (Engen & Singer, 2015)

- Increases activity in regions tied to:
    - Emotional processing
    - Memory
    - Motivation
    - Self-awareness
    - Language and empathy

More Research Highlights

- **Sahaja Yoga**: Increases gray matter in emotional/self-awareness regions (Hernández et al., 2016).
- **Prison MBSR Program** (Bouw, 2019): Inmates showed reduced anger and improved impulse control, coping, and self-esteem.

- **Mindful Movement in Children** (Rice et al., 2023): Improved focus, motor control, and fewer behavioral problems.

- **Blood Pressure** (Loucks et al., 2023): Significant reduction in systolic BP after mindfulness training.

- **Breast Cancer Survivors** (Chang et al., 2021): Lower stress, fatigue, and depression after MBSR.

Chapter Twenty-Eight

"Mindfulness is a deceptively simple way of relating to all experience that can reduce suffering and set the stage for positive personal transformation." -Ronald D. Siegal, Christopher K. Germer & Andrew Olendzki

How to Practice Mindfulness

Now that we've explored the benefits of mindfulness, let's talk about how to actually use it in daily life.

I often tell my clients that mindfulness is like your thumbprint, completely unique. Just like your thumbprint reflects the journey of your life, your scars, wrinkles, and experiences, your mindfulness practice should reflect your personal path too.

Because we all have different life experiences, no two mindfulness practices will look exactly the same. What works for someone else might not work for you, and that's okay.

You may try a few different methods before something clicks. That's part of the process. The key is to stay curious and keep exploring what helps you feel more present, calm, and connected.

Try the following practices, or refine ones you already use, to help:

- Increase awareness of your thoughts and feelings
- Build a stronger sense of personal agency
- Strengthen emotional regulation and self-trust

This is your practice. Let it grow in a way that fits your life and your nervous system.

Mindfulness is also a powerful way to bring our attention back to the present moment; the only time we truly have control over. We can't change the past, and the future hasn't happened yet. But the now is where real change can happen.

By learning to be present, we build a deeper connection with ourselves. We learn to notice what we're feeling and thinking in real time, without getting stuck in regret or worry.

For a deeper look into this idea, I highly recommend Eckhart Tolle's book *The Power of Now*, which explores how presence can lead to personal transformation.

The Breath: A Gateway to Mindfulness

Focusing on the breath is one of the most fundamental and accessible ways to practice mindfulness. Every human shares this experience; it's always with us. By tuning into the subtle sensations of breathing, the way air moves through your nose, how your chest or stomach rises and falls, you begin to form a gentle, grounding relationship with the present moment.

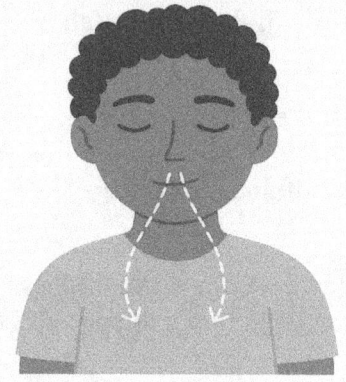

- Pay attention to the physical sensations of breathing
- Observe your breath without trying to change it
- Notice when your mind has wandered
- Gently return your focus to the breath

Training Exercise: Mindful Breathing

Adapted from the U.S. Department of Veterans Affairs (VA, 2023)

This simple breathing exercise helps train attention and presence. You can do it anywhere, anytime.

Step-by-step practice:

1. Close your eyes, or if that's uncomfortable, focus your gaze softly on a point on the floor in front of you.

2. Notice your breath. Don't try to change it. Just observe.
   (Pause)

3. Notice each inhale and each exhale.
   (Pause)

4. Feel how your body moves as you breathe.
   Maybe it's your chest rising, or your belly expanding.
   (Pause)

5. Pay attention to the details.
   Can you sense the air moving through your nose or lips?
   (Pause)

6. Tune into the subtle urge to breathe right before an inhale or exhale.
   (Pause)

7. Continue noticing your breath for the next few moments.
   (Longer pause)

8. When your attention drifts, that's okay.
   It's natural.
   Just gently bring your focus back to the breath, again and again.
   (Pause)

9. Keep noticing:
   - Inhale
   - Exhale
   - Sensations in the body
   - Distractions... and gently returning to breath
   (Pause)

10. When you're ready, slowly bring your attention back to the room and open your eyes.

This practice strengthens focus, calm, and awareness. Like any skill, it gets easier with time and repetition. It's not about doing it perfectly, it's about returning to the breath each time you wander. That act of returning is the practice.

Belly Breathing: A Simple, Powerful Tool

Belly breathing, also known as diaphragmatic breathing, is a simple practice with powerful benefits, especially for people under high stress. Instead of shallow chest breathing, this technique focuses on deep, slow breaths that fill the belly. It helps calm the nervous system and bring the body back into balance.

What the Research Says

In 2021, during the COVID-19 pandemic, a study with 151 frontline nurses found that practicing diaphragmatic breathing led to big improvements in:

- Sleep quality
- How long it took to fall asleep
- Sleep duration and efficiency
- Daytime alertness and energy
  (Liu et al., 2021)

Researchers also found that belly breathing:

- Activates the parasympathetic nervous system, which helps us rest and recover

- Lowers cortisol (the stress hormone)
- Reduces fatigue and tension
- Improves oxygen flow and brain energy use
- Slows the breathing rate to help the body feel safe and calm

Cognitive-behavioral therapists often use diaphragmatic breathing as part of stress reduction and relaxation training.

Belly Breathing Helps Kids, Too

A 2022 study with 171 children ages 9 to 13 found that belly breathing helped reduce anxiety in real time. When kids felt more worried than usual, those who used a breathing exercise felt more relaxed compared to those who didn't do anything at all.
(Kramer et al., 2022)

How to Do Diaphragmatic (Belly) Breathing

Adapted from Harvard Health Publishing (2016)

Lying Down Position

1. Lie on your back on a flat surface or bed. Bend your knees.
   (Use pillows under your head and knees for added comfort.)

Place one hand on your chest and the other on your belly, just below your ribs.

2. Breathe in slowly through your nose, letting the air move down into your belly.

   > Your belly hand should rise.

   > Your chest hand should stay still.

3. As you exhale through pursed lips, tighten your abdominal muscles and let your belly fall inward.

Your belly hand should lower to its original position.

DIAPHRAGMATIC BREATHING
Also known as belly breathing

How to perform diaphragmatic breathing:
- Lie on your back with your knees bent.
- Place one hand on your belly
- Breathe in slowly through your nose
- Let your belly rise, and then fall as you exhale

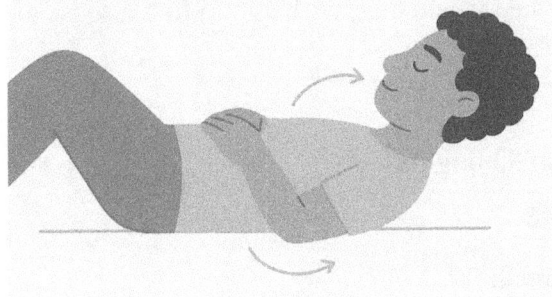

Sitting Position

You can also practice while sitting comfortably in a chair:

- Keep your knees bent
- Relax your shoulders, head, and neck
- Follow the same steps above

Practice Tip: Try this for 5 to 10 minutes, a few times a day. Over time, this can help calm your nervous system and lower stress.

Mindfulness of Thoughts

Before we explore mindfulness of thoughts, I want to offer a gentle caution, especially for those who tend to avoid or shut down their thinking. Turning attention inward can feel uncomfortable at first. That's okay.

One helpful way to approach this practice is by reframing your thoughts as byproducts of your mind, not reflections of your character.

Just because a thought pops up doesn't mean it defines who you are or what you will do.
For example, having a passing thought about something impulsive or upsetting doesn't mean you're going to act on it, or that it says anything bad about you.

Thoughts come and go.
Mindfulness helps us notice them without judgment, so we can observe rather than absorb them.

A Helpful Way to Think About Thoughts

Adapted from Headspace (2021)

One powerful way to practice mindfulness of thoughts is through a simple metaphor shared in the Headspace Netflix series:

> *"Imagine you're sitting beside a busy road. The passing cars are like your thoughts and feelings. Your job is just to sit and watch the traffic go by."*

At first, this sounds easy. But often, we feel uncomfortable with what we see, so we run into the road, trying to stop certain thoughts or chase after others. In doing so, we forget that the original goal was to simply watch, not interfere.

This constant running around only adds to our mental restlessness.

The practice of mindfulness is about changing our relationship with those thoughts and feelings. Instead of judging them or reacting, we learn to observe with perspective. And when we do that, we begin to find a sense of calm.

How to Practice Mindfulness of Thoughts

Adapted from LivingWell.org

- Start with your breath.
  Begin by focusing on your breathing. Just notice each inhale and exhale.
- Let thoughts come.
  As you breathe, you'll likely notice thoughts popping into your mind. That's okay. Let them come.
- Observe without judgment.
  Don't label your thoughts as good or bad. They're not right or wrong.
  They're simply thoughts, happening in this moment.

Notice even the resistance.
You might think, "I can't do this," or "I'm doing it wrong."
That, too, is a thought.
Gently notice it, just like any other.

Try using imagery.
If it helps, imagine your thoughts as:

Leaves floating down a stream

Clouds drifting across the sky

Words written on water

Let them appear... and pass.

- Watch them come and go.

You may notice that the moment you become aware of a thought, it disappears. That's what thoughts do: they come, and they go.

- Return to the breath.

When you're ready, gently bring your attention back to your breathing.

Mindfulness of the Body

In the busyness of everyday life, it's easy to lose touch with what's happening inside our bodies. We're constantly being pulled in different directions, by family, responsibilities, our surroundings, and more. Add in the constant stimulation from screens, and the sensory overload can be overwhelming.

When this happens, we may become disconnected from our bodies and the emotions or sensations tied to our lived experiences.
Mindfulness of the body is a way to come back home to ourselves, to notice what we're feeling, where we're holding tension, and how our experiences are showing up physically.

Mindfulness of the Body: A Gentle Practice

Adapted from Dr. Hickman, UC San Diego Center for Mindfulness

Our bodies can sometimes be sources of pain or emotional distress, whether due to illness, injury, or experiences like discrimination. The body scan offers a rare chance to notice what's happening in the body without judgment or the need to fix anything.

This practice helps us:

- Notice tension we didn't know we were holding, like tight shoulders or a clenched jaw
- Acknowledge pain without trying to fight it
- Understand how resisting pain can actually make it feel worse

Research shows that by gently noticing pain, even if it doesn't go away, we can feel some relief. More importantly, we begin to change our relationship with pain and with our bodies.

Over time, body scan practices can help us become more in tune with our physical needs, leading to healthier decisions about sleep, food, rest, and movement.

Body Scan Meditation

Adapted from UC Berkeley's Greater Good Science Center

1. Bring your attention into your body.
   Close your eyes if that feels comfortable or keep a soft gaze with your eyes partially closed.

2. Feel where you are.
   Notice your body seated in the chair or resting on the floor. Feel the support underneath you.

3. Take a few deep breaths.
   Inhale deeply, bring oxygen into the body.
   Exhale slowly, let yourself relax more deeply with each breath.

4. Notice your feet.
   Feel your feet on the floor, notice weight, pressure, temperature, or vibration.

5. Notice your legs.
   Feel your legs resting on the chair. Notice pulsing, pressure, heaviness, or lightness.

6. Feel your back.
   Notice the sensation of your back against the chair or surface.
   It's okay if you can't feel every part. Sensations change throughout the day.

7. Bring attention to your stomach.
   Is there tension? If so, see if you can soften it. Take another breath.

8. Notice your hands.
   Are they tight or gripping? Let them rest and soften.

9. Scan your arms.
   Feel sensations in your arms. Let your shoulders drop and soften.

10. Relax your neck and throat.
    Invite a gentle feeling of relaxation here.

11. Soften your jaw and facial muscles.
    Let your face be soft and relaxed.

12. Notice your whole body.
    Feel your entire body present and supported.
    Take a slow, full breath. Just notice.

13. Return gently.
    When you're ready, open your eyes without focusing on anything in particular.
    Gently move your head and neck. Take in the space around you.
    Then return to your normal gaze.

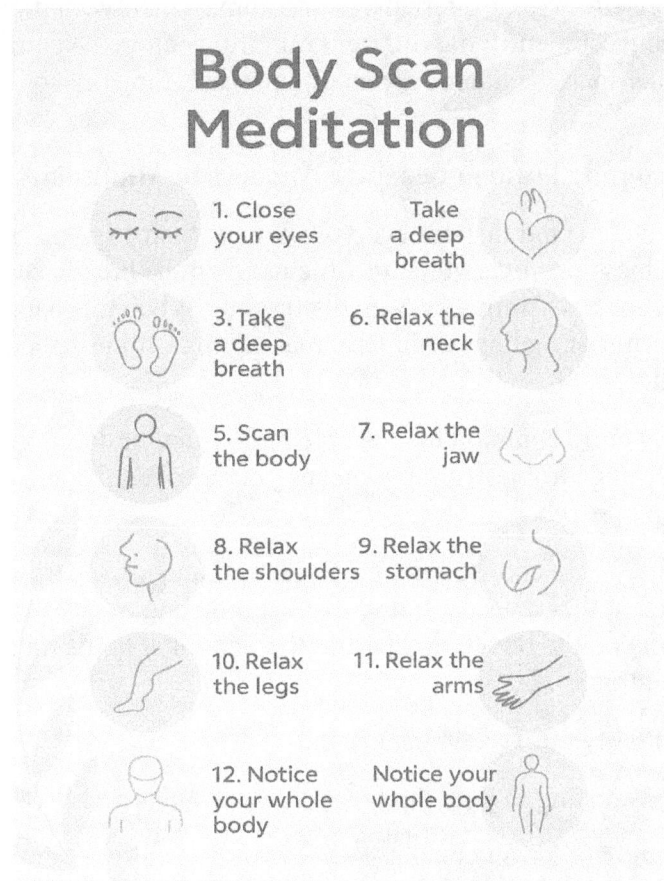

Trauma-Focused Mindfulness (Moving Mindfulness)

When practicing mindfulness, it's important to remember that not every approach works for everyone, especially for those with a history of trauma.

Many traditional mindfulness practices focus on the breath or body. But for some people, turning attention inward in this way can actually increase emotional discomfort, even triggering anxiety or panic attacks.

That's why trauma-informed care is essential. We need to approach mindfulness gently and with flexibility, especially when exploring unfamiliar or vulnerable inner experiences.

Moving mindfulness, such as mindful walking, stretching, or simple movement, can be a safer and more grounding alternative. These practices keep us present without overwhelming our nervous system, and they offer a sense of control, rhythm, and connection to the environment.

Individuals may not know all of their triggers before engaging in mindfulness. It can present an othering response and crazy making to some as they may become disheartened to the overall idea of mindfulness and its practicality in their life. Some alternatives or trauma-sensitive approaches to mindfulness suggest identifying different mindful anchors. Neutral areas of their body rather than the guided areas of the breath, thoughts, or triggering areas.

Finding Safe Ground: Trauma-Sensitive Anchors in Mindfulness

It's important to understand that not everyone knows their triggers before starting a mindfulness practice. For some, focusing on the breath, body, or thoughts may feel overwhelming or even distressing. When this happens, it can lead to confusion or feelings of failure, making mindfulness seem like it's "not for them."

This experience is more common than people realize, and it doesn't mean you're doing anything wrong. It simply means you need a different, more trauma-sensitive approach.

One helpful strategy is to choose a different mindful anchor, a part of the body or environment that feels neutral or even comforting.
Instead of focusing on the breath or a part of the body that holds trauma, try shifting your attention to:

- The feeling of your feet on the ground
- Your hands resting in your lap
- The sensation of air on your skin
- Sounds in the room

- Gentle movement or rhythm

These anchors give your mind a safe place to return to when practicing presence. They allow you to build mindfulness skills without triggering overwhelm.

Alternative Anchors of Attention

Adapted from MindfulLeader.org (2019)

When traditional anchors like the breath feel overwhelming, it's essential to offer multiple options, especially for trauma survivors. Mindfulness is not one-size-fits-all. Each person's anchor of attention will be different.

Instead of focusing solely on the breath, we can gently invite individuals to explore other stabilizing anchors, such as:

Physical Sensations

- Buttocks on the cushion or chair
- Back or shoulders against support

Other Senses

- Sounds in the room
- Gentle light from a candle
- A comforting texture (like a soft blanket)
- Smells, like essential oils or herbal tea
- A steady visual object (e.g., a plant or nature scene)

Mindful Movement

- Walking meditation
- Rocking gently side to side
- Rhythmic tapping or squeezing hands

Encourage clients, students, or yourself to experiment with different anchors. The best anchor is the one that supports safety, self-regulation, and stability.

Movement-Based Mindfulness for Teens: What the Research Says

A growing body of research shows that mindfulness, especially when combined with movement, can significantly benefit adolescents.

Meta-Analysis: 13 Studies, 2,277 Adolescents

A 2019 review found that most students enjoyed practicing mindfulness, and as a result, experienced:

- Less anger, stress, and anxiety
- Better focus, behavior regulation, and sleep quality (McKeering & Hwang, 2019)

Broader Review: 24 Studies

A 2014 analysis found that mindfulness in schools led to:

- Increased attention and resilience to stress
- Boosted positive emotions, self-esteem, and self-concept (Zenner et al., 2014)

Mindful Movement: Stand Like a Mountain

Adapted from Greater Good in Education, UC Berkeley

This grounding practice can be especially helpful for those with trauma backgrounds, offering a sense of stability and connection to the present moment.

Instructions:

1. Begin by standing tall.
   Feel your feet firmly rooted into the ground.
   Let your spine lengthen and your head gently rise, reaching toward the sky.

2. Take the shape of a mountain.
   Solid. Steady. Dignified.
   You are rooted, yet open and aware.

3. Pause to breathe mindfully.
   If using a bell or chime, allow one sound to ring.
   As it fades, take a full, slow breath in... and then out.

4. With each breath, quietly affirm:
   - Breathing in: *I know that I am breathing in.*
   - Breathing out: *I know that I am breathing out.*
     Repeat silently to yourself: *In... Out...*

5. Stand for a few moments in stillness.
   Let each breath move through your body.
   Feel the strength in your legs and the calm in your center.

Mindful Movement: Roll Your Shoulders

Adapted for trauma-sensitive practice

This simple movement helps release tension stored in the upper body while bringing awareness to the present moment.

Instructions:

1. Start in a comfortable seated or standing position.
   Let your arms rest by your sides or in your lap.

2. Begin with a deep breath.
   - *Breathing in*, roll your shoulders forward and up.
   - *Breathing out*, roll them backward and down.

3. Repeat at your own pace.
   - Inhale, shoulders rise.
   - Exhale, shoulders drop.
     Keep your movement slow and steady.

4. Bring awareness to the sensations.
   Notice if there's any tightness or tension.
   Or if your shoulders feel light, soft, or relaxed.
   Simply observe, no need to change anything.

5. Reverse directions.
   Gently roll your shoulders forward with each breath.
   - Inhale, roll forward.
   - Exhale, release.

6. Affirm the movement silently:
   - *Rolling my shoulders, I am aware that I am rolling my shoulders.*

7. Return to stillness.
   Let your shoulders settle back to neutral.
   Take one more mindful breath and notice how you feel.

Mindful Movement: Roll Your Neck

Adapted for gentle, trauma-informed practice

This exercise can help release tension in the neck and upper spine while encouraging mindful awareness of sensation and breath.

Instructions:

1. Begin with a breath.
   Inhale slowly... exhale gently.
   Let your body settle into a comfortable seated or standing position.

2. Start the movement.
   - *Breathing in*, gently roll your neck forward and down, bringing your chin toward your chest.
   - *Breathing out*, slowly roll to the right, bringing your right ear toward your right shoulder.

3. Continue with your breath.
   - Inhale, roll forward again.
   - Exhale, roll to the left, left ear toward left shoulder.
   - Continue rolling gently, syncing the motion with your breath.

4. Notice the sensations.
   - Where do you feel tightness or ease?
   - Is there warmth, stiffness, or release?
     Just observe without judgment.

5. Return to stillness.
   - Let your head come back to center.
   - Relax your neck and shoulders.
   - Take a deep breath.

6. Optional reset.
   - Gently shake out your shoulders and arms.
   - Wiggle a little, just enough to soften and reset.

Mindful Movement: Stretch Your Arms

A gentle movement to connect breath and body

This practice helps open up the body, connect with your breath, and bring awareness to how you're feeling, without pressure or judgment.

Instructions:

1. Begin with a steady breath.
   Inhale slowly.
   Exhale gently.
   Let your shoulders relax.

2. Start the movement.
   - *Breathing in*, slowly lift your arms out to the sides and up above your head.
     Let your fingertips reach toward the sky.
   - *Breathing out*, bring your palms down in front of you, facing downward,
     letting your arms return gently to your sides.

3. Repeat with rhythm.
   - *Inhale*, arms rise up in a big circle.
   - *Exhale*, gather the breath down through the center of your body.
     Move at your own pace, slow, steady, and grounded.

4. Stay present.
   - As you move, stay with your breath.
   - Notice the feeling in your arms, your shoulders, your chest.
   - If your mind wanders, gently bring it back to your breath and your body.

5. Finish the movement.
   - Take one more breath with intention.
   - Let your arms return softly to your sides.
   - Rest in stillness for a moment.

Mindful Movement: Rag Doll

A grounding and releasing forward fold

This simple movement helps stretch the spine, release tension, and gently reconnect with the body and breath.

Instructions:

1. Begin with your breath.
   Inhale deeply.
   Exhale slowly.

2. Gently fold forward.
   - *As you exhale*, bend forward at the waist.
   - Let your knees bend slightly, keeping the movement soft and safe.
   - Allow your arms and head to hang down, like a rag doll.

3. Add gentle movement.
   - Give your arms a light shake.
   - Shake your head "no."
   - Nod your head "yes."
     Let go of any tension as you do.

4. Bend from the waist, not the back.
   Try to find a little space or stretch in your spine as you fold.

5. Breathe and notice.
   - Pause here, simply breathing.
   - Notice any sensations: stretch, warmth, tightness, or release. Just observe, no need to change anything.
     (Pause here for a few breaths.)

6. Return slowly to standing.
   - *With your next inhale*, rise slowly, uncurling the spine gently, one part at a time.
   - Take your time. No need to rush.

7. Pause and notice.
   - As you stand upright again, take a moment to notice how your body feels now.
   - Breathe in. Breathe out.

Mindful Movement: Sit and Bend Forward

A gentle seated stretch to lengthen and ground

This movement supports calmness, flexibility, and body awareness, especially when done with mindful breathing.

Instructions:

1. Find your seat.
   Sit comfortably on the floor or in a chair.
   - If you're on the floor, stretch your legs out in front of you and bend your knees slightly.
   - If you're on a chair, place both feet flat on the floor.

2. Begin with the breath.
   Inhale slowly...
   Exhale gently...

3. Start the forward fold.
   - *Breathing out*, gently bend forward at the waist, reaching your hands toward your feet.
   - Focus on folding from the waist, not from the back.
   - Let your spine lengthen naturally, no force, just ease.

4. Breathe and notice.
   - Inhale...
   - Exhale...
   - Notice the sensations in your legs, hips, spine, and body. Be curious. Observe without judgment.

(Pause here for a few breaths.)

5. Return to center.
   - *On your next inhale*, slowly bring your body back to an upright, neutral seated position.
   - Sit tall. Rest.
   - Notice how you feel.

Mindful Movement: Gentle Seated Twist

A grounding final movement to release and reset

Twisting can help stretch the spine, ease tension, and build awareness of how your body feels in the present moment.

Instructions:

1. Begin in a seated position.
   Sit comfortably on a chair or the floor, with your spine tall and shoulders relaxed.

Twist to the Left

2. Position your hands.
   - Place your right hand on your left thigh or hip.
   - Bring your left hand behind you for gentle support.
3. Begin the twist.
   - Slowly turn your upper body to the left.
   - Look over your left shoulder, if that feels okay.
4. Breathe with awareness.
   - *Inhale*: Find a little more length in your spine.
   - *Exhale*: Notice the sensations, perhaps in your back, sides, or hips.
   - Breathe in and out three times, observing gently.
5. Return to center.
   - *With your next inhale*, gently come back to a neutral, forward-facing position.

Twist to the Right

6. Switch sides.
   - Place your left hand on your right thigh or hip.
   - Bring your right hand behind you.
7. Twist gently.
   - Turn your upper body to the right.
   - Look over your right shoulder, as you're able.
8. Breathe and observe.
   - *Inhale*: "I know that I am twisting."
   - *Exhale*: "I smile."

- Notice what sensations arise in your spine, hips, and shoulders.
- Breathe deeply and mindfully three times.

9. Return to center.
    - *With your next inhale*, gently come back to center.
    - Sit tall. Breathe.
    - Let your body return to stillness.

Mindful Reflection: Checking In With the Body

A gentle close to your practice

1. Take a moment to pause.
   Let your body come to stillness, whether you're seated, lying down, or standing tall.

2. Scan your body from head to toe.
    - Notice how your entire body feels right now.
    - Is there tension or ease anywhere?
    - Has anything changed since you began? Or does it feel the same?

3. Observe without judgment.
   Just notice. No need to fix or analyze.
   Allow everything to be exactly as it is.

4. Repeat this gentle affirmation:
    - *Breathing in*: "I am aware of my body."
    - *Breathing out*: "I smile to my body with awareness and compassion."

(Pause here for a few breaths.)

5. Offer yourself gratitude.
   Take a moment to thank yourself for practicing today.
   This was an act of self-compassion, for your body, your mind, and your well-being.

Mindful movement can also enhance existing exercises by utilizing the following principles stated on mindful.org,

1. **Pause and consider your purpose.** Remember why you want to meditate. Is it to train your mind to focus and sustain attention? To

learn to navigate emotions? Consider your intention for exercise, too. Is it to live longer or have more energy? This twofold motivation can help get you up and out and keep you going.

2. **Unplug.** To meditate during exercise, don't listen to your favorite playlist, talk on the phone, read a magazine, or watch TV. Be fully present where you are: in the woods, on the sidewalk, or on the treadmill.

3. **Tap into body sensations.** Bring your attention to your physical experience. Are there any parts of your body that are working extra hard? Does your body feel different today than it did yesterday?

4. **Use your breath as a cue to challenge yourself more or ease up as necessary.** Your inhalation or exhalation can be an anchor of attention while exercising. If your mind wanders, noticing a new "For Sale" sign in the neighborhood while you run or recalling an email you forgot to return, just notice the thought and reconnect with your breath. Observe the tempo of your breath as you work harder and as you cool down.

5. **Play with different anchors of attention.** Experiment with attentional focal points other than your breath: each full rotation of your bike pedals, the up and down of a lunge. You can switch anchors as you vary your exercise, but stay focused on the rhythm of your anchor, returning to it when your mind wanders.

6. **Note your surroundings.** There are two aspects of directing attention, focused attention and open awareness, and you can practice both while exercising. To tap into the latter, check out what's around you. How is the air? Temperature? What are you hearing?

7. **Renew your resolve, burning hamstrings and all.** One of the attitudes of mindfulness is acceptance, not wishing the present moment to be different than it is. Exercising is a brilliant time to practice this. Do you notice any resistance to the workout experience, perhaps wishing you were almost done, or that your quads would stop quaking? Commit to your workout time, remember your reasons for being there, and try to stay present from start to finish.

8. **Exercise kindness.** Notice the quality of your thinking during workouts: Can you appreciate your current ability, speed, and endurance just as they are? If you work out in an in-person or virtual group, can you let go of the "comparing mind" and instead thank yourself for showing up for this healthy activity?

Mindful Walking Practice #1: Basic Walking Meditation

Adapted from Mindful.org

Walking meditation is a simple and grounding way to practice mindfulness. You don't need a special setting, just your body, your breath, and your attention.

How to Begin:

1. **Notice that you are walking.**
   Pause for a moment and ask yourself:
   "How do I know I'm walking?"
   This question helps break the habit of moving through life on autopilot.

2. **Make the body your anchor.**
   Shift your attention to your physical sensations:
   - Feel your feet touching the ground.
   - Notice how your legs, arms, spine, and head move with each step.
   - Pay attention to how your muscles engage and release as you walk.

3. **Be curious about change.**
   As you walk, observe:
   - The texture of different surfaces beneath your feet
   - Subtle shifts in your breath, pulse, or temperature
   - The gentle rocking motion of your body's weight shifting step to step

4. **Look for the still points.**
   Just like in breath meditation we notice the stillness between inhale and exhale,
   in walking, you can tune into the still moments between steps,
   - When the right foot becomes the left,
   - When the left foot becomes the right

5. **Stay with the experience.**
   If your mind wanders, gently return to the sensations of walking, one step, one moment at a time.

Mindful Walking Practice #2: Adding Words or Phrases

Adapted from Mindful.org

Another way to deepen your walking practice is to pair your steps with intentional words or phrases. This helps bring focus and calm to the body and mind.

How to Practice:

1. Count your steps.
   Try counting in rhythm as you walk:
   One... two... three...
   If your mind wanders and you lose count, that's okay. Gently bring your attention back and start again at one, without judgment.

2. Repeat reminder phrases.
   You can silently repeat gentle, grounding words as you walk. For example:
   - From *Mindful Self-Compassion* practice:
     "Thank you"—as a way to send compassion or gratitude to your body
   - From Thich Nhat Hanh:
     - *"I have arrived."*
     - *"I am home."*
     - *"In the here."*
     - *"In the now."*
     Or:
     - *"Nowhere to go."*
     - *"Nothing to do."*
     - *"No one to be."*

3. Make it personal.
   You can create your own phrases that reflect what you need most, calm, grounding, safety, gratitude, or joy.

4. Use the phrases gently.
   There's no need to force it. Let the rhythm of your steps and the rhythm of your words support one another naturally.

Mindful Walking Practice #3: Sensory Walking

Adapted from Mindful.org

This walking practice invites you to fully engage your five senses as you move, helping you ground in the present moment and appreciate your surroundings more deeply.

When our thoughts pull us to the past or future, our senses can gently bring us back to *now*.

How to Practice:

1. Start with sight.
    - Walk slowly and softly.
    - Keep your eyes relaxed, gazing ahead.
    - Notice how shapes, light, and colors shift as your body moves.
    - Watch the landscape or surroundings *change in real time*.

2. Shift to the sense of touch.
    - Focus on the soles of your feet.
    - Pay attention to the sensations as they press into different surfaces.
    - Feel changes in pressure, texture, temperature, or rhythm.

3. Tune in to sound.
    - Notice your own footsteps.
    - Then, expand your awareness to the world around you: birds, cars, wind, rustling leaves, or distant voices.
    - Let each sound rise and fall without judgment.

4. Notice smells and tastes.
    - Inhale gently through your nose.
    - Are there familiar or unexpected scents in the air?
    - What do you notice about the air itself, fresh, dry, warm, cool?

Tip:

You don't have to use all your senses at once. Try tuning into one at a time and rotate through them as you walk.

Mindful Walking Practice #4: Body Awareness Walking

Adapted from Mindful.org

This walking meditation is like a body scan in motion. As you walk, you'll gently shift your awareness from one area of your body to another, tuning in to sensations, movement, and rhythm.

How to Practice:

1. Start with the feet.
    - Bring your attention to the soles of your feet.
    - Notice each step, pressure, and contact with the ground. Stay with this awareness for 20 steps, one block, or 5 minutes.
2. Move up to your ankles and calves.
    - Feel how they shift, stretch, and engage as you move.
3. Bring attention to the knees.
    - Notice how they bend and stabilize with each step.
    - Observe the rhythm and repetition.
4. Focus on your hips.
    - Notice movement, weight shifting, and balance in this area.
    - Allow the hips to guide your steps with ease.
5. Shift awareness to your hands and arms.
    - Are they swinging gently?
    - Do they feel relaxed or tense?
6. Notice your torso and internal sensations.
    - Tune in to your heart and lungs, are they working a little harder?
    - Feel the breath and subtle shifts inside your body.
7. Bring attention to your neck and shoulders.

- Are they loose or tight?
- Notice how your upper body supports the rhythm of your steps.

8. Finally, observe your head.
    - Feel how it moves slightly up and down with each footstep.
    - Let it stay balanced and light.

9. Repeat the scan as you walk.
    - Continue rotating through these areas gently.
    - Notice how sensations change as your walk progresses.

Mindful Walking Practice #5: Appreciative Walking

Adapted from Mindful.org

Appreciative walking is a powerful way to shift out of the brain's negativity bias, our natural tendency to focus on problems, and instead tune into beauty, joy, and gratitude.

How to Practice:

1. Look for the beautiful and uplifting.
   As you walk, intentionally notice what's good in your surroundings:
    - A blooming flower
    - The warm light of the sun
    - A colorful mural or building
    - Laughter, birdsong, or a cool breeze

2. Choose one thing to appreciate.
    - Try to find at least one beautiful, funny, or kind thing on each walk.
    - Let it settle into your awareness.
    - You can even say, *"Thank you,"* as you notice it.

3. Reflect or share.
    - After your walk, jot down what you noticed in a journal

- Or share with a friend, family member, or on social media
  These small acts of reflection help reinforce a more positive outlook over time.

4. Notice daily changes.
   - If you take the same route often, observe how the seasons, colors, and sounds shift.
   - What's different today?
   - What's the same?
   - How does morning feel compared to evening? Weekday vs. weekend?

Bonus Practice:

Ask yourself at the end of your walk:
"What's one thing I appreciated today?"
Even a single positive moment can uplift your mood long after your walk is over.

Mindful Walking Practice #6: Observational Walking

Adapted from Mindful.org

This walking practice invites you to explore the connection between movement, emotions, and perception. As you walk, become curious about both your inner experience and your outer world, and how one might shape the other.

How to Practice:

1. Notice emotional reactions as you walk.
   - What feelings come up as you pass others?
   - Do you feel self-conscious in crowded spaces?
   - Do you feel joy in the sunlight or dread when facing a hill? These subtle shifts in mood can be great teachers.

2. Observe how emotions shape your walk.
   - Ask: *How does my current mood affect how I walk, what I notice, or how I respond?*
   - Are you walking faster, slower, heavier, or more lightly?

3. Experiment with emotional states.
   Try walking as if you are in a certain emotion:
   - Anxious
   - Embarrassed or weighed down
   - Confident
   - Distracted or rushed
   - Calm and open

Then, return to your natural walking pace, if you can.
   - What changed?
   - How did each posture affect your perception of the environment?

4. Reflect on the feedback loop.
   - Did walking with sadness lower your gaze or narrow your awareness?
   - Did walking with confidence lift your posture or boost your mood?
   This mirrors the research on embodied emotions and the idea that how we move shapes how we feel.

Anchoring the Body: Inspired by *My Grandmother's Hands*

In *My Grandmother's Hands*, Resmaa Menakem emphasizes that healing from racialized trauma starts in the body. One powerful tool he shares is anchoring, a practice that helps calm the nervous system and reconnect us to safety in the present moment.

What Is Anchoring?

Anchoring is the act of noticing and supporting the body when it feels overwhelmed. It's a way to remind the body that it is *safe*, *held*, and *capable*. Anchors are physical sensations or actions that help bring us out of survival mode and into a more grounded state.

These are not distractions or avoidance tactics; they are nervous system tools for building resilience.

Examples of Anchors (Inspired by Menakem's Work):

- Feeling your feet on the ground
- Placing a hand on your heart or chest

- Rocking gently side to side
- Humming or making a low soothing sound
- Tapping your thighs rhythmically
- Imagining a place or person that brings you comfort
- Holding something soft or textured (like a small object or blanket)

Menakem encourages us to practice these regularly, not just when we're activated, so our bodies can build capacity for stress and discomfort. Over time, these anchors become trusted tools that help us move through anxiety, grief, and historical trauma without becoming overwhelmed.

A Reflection:

> *"Anchoring isn't about erasing pain, it's about creating enough safety in the body to stay present with it."*
> — Paraphrased from *My Grandmother's Hands*, Resmaa Menakem

A Word on Mindfulness Practices

The mindfulness practices shared here are not an exhaustive list, but rather a starting point, a curated selection of common and accessible techniques. I invite you to explore what resonates with you and use those practices as a foundation to build a more personalized mindfulness routine.

Balance Matters

It's important to remember that mindfulness is not one-size-fits-all. Just like in physical exercise, relying too heavily on one type of practice can lead to imbalance.
As mindfulness researcher Dr. Willoughby Britton (2019) notes:

> *"High levels of a specific mindfulness practice may produce negative effects on its own but can be counterbalanced by supplementing with other mindfulness practices."*

In other words, cultivating a diverse set of tools helps prevent stagnation, frustration, or emotional overwhelm. Mindfulness should support you, not become another form of self-pressure.

Mindfulness and the Visual Diet

As you work toward a healthier visual diet, mindfulness can be a powerful ally. It gives you space to observe what's happening, rather than automatically reacting.
With time, you may begin to notice patterns in your thoughts, behaviors, emotional themes, and triggers that contribute to digital overstimulation or screen fatigue.

And when old wounds or unmet needs emerge, mindfulness can help you pause and eventually learn how to tend to those needs with compassion.

In later chapters, especially Chapter Thirty-Three, we'll explore reparenting techniques to deepen this healing process.

Summary

Mindfulness for Everyday Life: A Trauma-Informed Guide to the Present Moment

This guide offers a comprehensive, compassionate approach to mindfulness that honors the uniqueness of every person's journey. Grounded in trauma-informed care and supported by current research, it introduces a diverse range of mindfulness practices, from breathwork and body scans to movement-based and walking meditations.

Core Themes:

- Mindfulness is personal, no two practices look the same.
- Trauma sensitivity is key, what calms one person may overwhelm another.
- Balance matters, a mix of techniques prevents stagnation or overload.
- Mindful movement and breath provide gentle, embodied ways to stay present.
- Anchoring helps regulate the nervous system, especially during distress.
- Mindful walking connects attention with emotion, environment, and intention.

Practices Include:

- Mindful breathing & belly breathing
- Mindfulness of thoughts & body
- Six trauma-sensitive walking meditations
- Movement practices for grounding, release, and emotional awareness
- Anchoring tools from *My Grandmother's Hands*
- Research-backed strategies to reduce stress, anxiety, and screen overload

Mindfulness becomes especially powerful when paired with visual diet awareness. As we learn to observe our thoughts, emotions, and patterns, without judgment, we gain the ability to respond more skillfully and compassionately. In future chapters, we will explore reparenting and other deeper healing practices to support sustained well-being

Chapter Twenty-Nine

"Self-regulation depends on having a friendly relationship with your body. Without it you have to rely on external regulation, from medication, drugs like alcohol, constant reassurance, or compulsive compliance with the wishes of others." -Bessel A. van der Kolk

Using Our Senses to Regulate the Body

When we're overwhelmed by big emotions, intrusive thoughts, or intense body sensations, even simple tasks can feel impossible. Whether we're caught in a spiral of self-criticism, grief, or anger, our ability to self-regulate may seem out of reach.

In these moments, we need gentle, accessible tools that help us return to our body and the present moment. One of the most effective ways to do this is by engaging the senses.

Why Senses Matter in Self-Regulation

When we're dysregulated, the thinking brain often goes offline. Instead of trying to "fix" things through logic or willpower, we can turn to sensory input, something concrete, familiar, and physical, to help us downshift from fight, flight, freeze or fawn.

This is where self-soothing or stimming comes in.

Many people naturally discover ways to calm themselves through repetitive, comforting actions, even if they don't realize it. You might:

- Run your fingers through your hair
- Rub your arms or touch your skin
- Clench and release a fist
- Bounce a leg or rock your body
- Use fidgets, fabrics, or objects with texture

These actions aren't random; they're your nervous system seeking regulation through sensory anchors.

Each of us has a thumbprint of what works, a unique pattern of what feels safe, soothing, or stabilizing. Learning what your body responds to can help you build a personalized toolkit for emotional resilience.

DBT Self-Soothing with the Senses

Dialectical Behavior Therapy (DBT) is a treatment model I frequently draw from in my clinical work. Developed by Dr. Marsha Linehan in the late 1980s, DBT was originally designed to support individuals with chronic emotional dysregulation, identity struggles, and interpersonal challenges, often those navigating intense suffering, including those in recovery from substance use.

One of DBT's greatest strengths is its emphasis on mindfulness and skills for emotional regulation. Among these is a powerful and accessible practice:

Self-Soothing with the Five Senses.

This skill teaches us how to ground ourselves through our body, using sight, sound, touch, taste, and smell as anchors to calm the nervous system.

It's especially helpful during moments of:

- Emotional overwhelm
- Panic or shutdown
- Cravings during substance cessation
- Disconnection from self or surroundings

When words fail and thinking feels foggy, the senses offer a direct, embodied pathway to safety.

What Is Self-Soothing with the Senses?

At first glance, self-soothing with the senses might sound self-explanatory, but it's worth taking a moment to explore its depth and intentionality.

This practice invites us to calm the nervous system using what we already carry with us: our five senses. By intentionally engaging with sight, sound, smell, taste, or touch, we can anchor ourselves in the present moment, especially when emotional distress feels overwhelming.

When we focus on one or more of these senses, we shift attention away from racing thoughts, intense feelings, or physical discomfort. In doing so, we can bypass the storm, giving our brain and body a chance to feel safe again.

This technique is especially powerful in moments where we feel out of control, when anxiety, panic, sadness, or rage threatens to take over. By gently tuning in to a sensory experience, we create space to regulate, reorient, and reclaim agency in the moment.

A Note Before You Begin: Practice & Personalization

As you explore the five sensory categories below, keep in mind:
These are just starting points, not a complete list.

Everyone experiences regulation differently, and what works for one person may not work for another. I encourage you to experiment, explore, and expand beyond the suggestions provided here. Create your own menu of calming sensory tools, your nervous system knows what feels safe and soothing.

The most important guidelines:

- Choose strategies that do not cause harm, physically or emotionally
- Focus on comfort, connection, and grounding
- Respect your boundaries and sensitivities

Also, don't wait until you're overwhelmed to try these skills. Practice when you're calm so your body and brain can learn the technique in a low-stress state. That way, when your "preverbal back is against the wall," you'll already have some familiarity, and maybe even muscle memory, to fall back on.

DBT Self-Soothing with the Five Senses

(Adapted from DialecticalBehavioralTherapy.com, 2020)
Use your senses to bring calm and safety to your nervous system. These are just ideas, explore what feels good for you.

1. Sight

- Go outside and take in nature, the colors, people, sky, movement, life.
- Look up calming photos online (landscapes, art, peaceful places).
- Visit a museum or gallery. Let the art soothe you.
- Watch a visually stunning, emotionally safe movie.
- Create a personal "soothing visuals" album to revisit when needed.

2. Hearing

- Call or speak with someone whose voice comforts you.
- Listen to music that calms or lifts you up.
- Try soothing genres: classical, jazz, ambient, nature sounds, or instrumental radio.

- Go to a park and let your ears take in natural life, birds, wind, chatter.
- Play music or sing if you enjoy it.
- Listen to an audiobook, podcast, or relaxing TV show.

3. Smell

- Use a favorite perfume, essential oil, or cologne.
- Light a scented candle.
- Cook a meal and breathe in the comforting aroma.
- Buy flowers or plants with a scent you love.
- Hug someone you love and take in their familiar scent.
- Visit a place with a scent that brings joy (florist, bakery, cafe).

4. Taste

- Cook and savor a favorite meal, slow down and really taste it.
- Treat yourself to a comfort food (mindfully, with no judgment).
- Enjoy tea, cocoa, coffee, or another warm drink (avoid alcohol).
- Eat a fresh fruit and tune in to its flavor.
- Chew gum or a favorite candy, notice its texture and taste.

5. Touch

- Wrap yourself in a soft blanket, notice its texture and warmth.
- Pet your animal or cuddle a stuffed animal if you have one.
- Wear soft or cozy clothes that feel good on your skin.
- Take a warm shower or bath or a cool one if that soothes you more.
- Give yourself a gentle massage or use a textured roller or object.
- Touch something calming, like a smooth stone, fluffy fabric, or fidget.

DBT Self-Soothing with the Five Senses

(Adapted from DialecticalBehavioralTherapy.com, 2020)

Use your five senses to calm your body and mind when emotions feel overwhelming. These are just starting points-- find what works best for you.

Sight
- Look at nature; trees, sky, movement, color
- Browse calming images online (landscapes, art)
- Visit an art gallery or museum
- Watch a visually soothing movie (avoid triggering content)
- Create a calming image collection (album or digital folder)

Hearing
- Call someone with a soothing voice
- Listen to calming or uplifting music
- Try nature sounds, jazz, ambient, or instrumental
- Go to a park and absorb natural sounds
- Sing or play music
- Listen to audiobooks or soft-spoken podcasts

Smell
- Use favorite scents: perfume, essential oils, cologne
- Light a scented candle
- Cook and enjoy the smell of your favorite food
- Smell flowers, herbs, or indoor plants
- Hug a loved one and take in their familiar scent
- Visit scent-rich places: bakeries, cafes, florists

Taste
- Eat a favorite meal slowly--savor every bite
- Enjoy comfort food mindfully (no guilt)
- Sip a warm, non-ahoinolic drink, tea, cocoa, coffee
- Taste fresh fruit and notice flavor and texture
- Chew gum or enjoy hard candy

Understanding HRV (Heart Rate Variability)

What is HRV?
HRV refers to the variation in time between each heartbeat. A healthy heart doesn't beat at a perfectly steady pace; it adjusts constantly based on what your body needs.

Why Does It Matter?
HRV is a sign of how flexible and responsive your nervous system is, especially your autonomic nervous system.

- High HRV = greater adaptability, resilience, and lower stress
- Low HRV = less flexibility, higher stress levels, and increased risk for chronic conditions

What the Cleveland Clinic Says

> *"Your heart's variability reflects how adaptable your body can be. If your heart rate is highly variable, this is usually evidence that your body can adapt to many kinds of changes. People with high heart rate variability are usually less stressed and happier."*
> — The Cleveland Clinic, 2021

Low HRV Can Be Linked To:

- High resting heart rate
- Stress, anxiety, and depression
- Chronic health conditions:
  - Diabetes
  - High blood pressure
  - Asthma
  - Heart arrhythmia

Improving HRV Naturally

- Mindfulness & Meditation
- Slow, diaphragmatic breathing
- Physical activity & movement
- Quality sleep
- Spending time in nature
- Healthy nutrition
- Reducing screen time and digital stress

WHY ARE WE TALKING ABOUT HEART RATE VARIABILITY (HRV)?

The answer is simple: If you live a high-stress or sedentary lifestyle—especially one dominated by screen use—your HRV is likely to be lower. Lower HRV is linked to poor emotional regulation, chronic stress, and reduced adaptability to life's demands.

Research supports this connection. For example, a study on adolescents with Internet Gaming Disorder (IGD) found that those with IGD had lower HRV, higher sympathetic (fight-or-flight) activity, and lower parasymathetic (rest-and digest) activity, compared to peers without IGD. (Sugaya et al., 2019)

Why Are We Talking About Heart Rate Variability (HRV)?

The answer is simple: if you live a high-stress or sedentary lifestyle, especially one dominated by screen use, your HRV is likely to be lower. As stated earlier, lower HRV is linked to poor emotional regulation, chronic stress, and reduced adaptability to life's demands. Research supports this connection. For example, a study on adolescents with Internet Gaming Disorder (IGD) found that those with IGD had lower HRV, along with higher sympathetic (fight-or-flight) activity and lower parasympathetic (rest-and-digest) activity, compared to peers without IGD. (Sugaya et al., 2019). This shows that prolonged screen exposure and digital overuse can dysregulate the nervous system, leaving us less resilient and more reactive.

Using Biofeedback to Improve Heart Rate Variability (HRV)

Biofeedback can be a powerful tool to increase HRV and support nervous system regulation. With the help of smart devices like fitness trackers, biometric apps, or more advanced clinical sensors, individuals can monitor real-time physiological changes in their body. These tools help users see how their heart rate, breathing, and muscle tension respond to different tasks and emotional states.

Biofeedback works by giving the body a "mirror" to learn self-regulation skills. For example, people can practice changing their posture, altering their breath, relaxing tight muscles, or using focused attention and mindfulness. Even solving a math problem during a session can show how stress impacts the body's stress response. Over time, these practices can help individuals build better emotional awareness, reduce anxiety, and increase resilience.
(Cleveland Clinic, 2020)

Using Virtual Reality (VR) to Boost Heart Rate Variability (HRV)

Technology doesn't always have to work against our well-being, when used mindfully, it can help us heal. One promising example is the use of Virtual Reality (VR) combined with slow-paced breathing to improve Heart Rate Variability (HRV) and support emotional regulation. In a 2019 randomized controlled study with 60 healthy employees, researchers compared standard HRV biofeedback (HRV-BF) to a VR-based version.

Both methods improved physiological markers like cardiac coherence and vagal tone after a stressful task. But the VR group experienced greater benefits, including:

- Lower perceived stress
- Higher relaxation self-efficacy
- Less mind-wandering
- Improved focus on the present moment

- Preserved attentional resources
  (Blum et al., 2019)

Mindful Tech Use & The Need for Reparenting

This research highlights that when paired with mindfulness and breathwork, immersive technology can actually enhance digital wellness. Tech and screens are powerful tools, but only when *we* use them intentionally. Our digital health suffers when the tool starts using *us*. And while it's true that these platforms are deliberately designed to keep us hooked, feeding us a steady dopamine drip, the deeper issue often runs beneath the surface.

Many people stay glued to screens not just because of how they're built, but because it's easier than feeling what's underneath. Emotional overwhelm, past trauma, and unprocessed pain can make us reach for distraction. The more we avoid those feelings, the more distorted our visual diet becomes, until we're feeding ourselves a steady stream of numbing content to stay disconnected.

In many cases, what we're truly avoiding is the wounded inner child, the part of us that still fears being overwhelmed, unheard, or unsafe. And that's where the next chapter comes in: Reparenting. It's not just about reducing screen time; it's about tending to the deeper emotional needs that drive it.

Using Biofeedback to Improve Heart Rate Variability (HRV)

Smart devices like fitness trackers and biometric sensors allow people to monitor real-time physiological changes in their body. Over time, biofeedback exercises can help build better emotional awareness and increase resilience.

Tasks to practice using biofeedback:

Change your posture
Sit, stand, or move differently to ease muscle tension.

Alter your breathing
Use breathing techniques to calm anxiety.

Relax your muscles
Concentrate on releasing tight muscles.

Use mindfulness and focus
Control heart rate with mindful attention.

Take a test
See how solving a problem affects stress response

Summary

Self-Regulation Through the Senses

- When overwhelmed, logic often fails, our nervous system needs *sensory input* to feel safe.
- Many people naturally *stim* or self-soothe with repetitive, comforting actions like touching skin, playing with fidgets, or rocking.
- DBT (Dialectical Behavior Therapy) teaches *Self-Soothing with the Five Senses* to calm the nervous system using:
    - Sight: Nature, calming images, art, peaceful movies
    - Hearing: Soothing music, familiar voices, nature sounds
    - Smell: Candles, perfumes, favorite foods, comforting places
    - Taste: Favorite meals, warm drinks, mindful eating
    - Touch: Soft blankets, pets, warm baths, cozy clothes

Heart Rate Variability (HRV)

- HRV = variation in time between heartbeats. Higher HRV = more adaptability, resilience, and lower stress.
- Low HRV is linked to:
    - High stress, anxiety, depression
    - Sedentary lifestyle and digital overuse
    - Chronic illnesses like diabetes, asthma, and hypertension
- Adolescents with Internet Gaming Disorder showed lower HRV and higher stress reactivity. (Sugaya et al., 2019)

Improving HRV Naturally

- Mindfulness, breathwork, physical activity, sleep, and nature exposure
- Reducing screen time helps prevent nervous system dysregulation

Biofeedback & Virtual Reality

- Smart devices can help monitor HRV and teach regulation via:
    - Breathing, posture, muscle relaxation, focus
- VR + Breathwork shows greater benefits than standard biofeedback alone:
    - Reduced perceived stress

- Improved focus and attention
- Better emotional regulation (Blum et al., 2019)

Final Insight:

Technology isn't always harmful, it can support healing when paired with *intentional use*, *mindfulness*, and *reparenting the nervous system*.

Chapter Thirty

"The Inner Child is the aspect of our personality that is soft, vulnerable, and feelings oriented—our "gut" instinct. It is who we are when we were born, our core self, our natural personality, with all its talent, instinct, intuition, and emotion." -Margaret Paul

Reparenting Your Unmet Needs

Understanding the Emotional Roots of Addiction and Self-Soothing
Inspired by Dr. Gabor Maté's work on trauma and healing

Why Reparenting Matters

According to Dr. Gabor Maté, all addictions, whether to substances, screens, work, or validation, can be traced back to emotional loss in early life. These behaviors are not the core problem but attempts to soothe deep, invisible wounds.

> *"All addictions come from emotional loss and exist to soothe the pain resulting from that loss."* — Dr. Gabor Maté

Two Types of Early Trauma

1. What *did* happen that shouldn't have
   – Abuse, neglect, chaos, criticism

2. What *didn't* happen that should have
   – Emotional presence, safety, soothing, consistent connection

Even well-meaning parents can cause harm if they're chronically stressed, unavailable, or unsupported, especially in a society where caregiving often lacks proper resources.

Sensitive Children, Deeper Impact

Children who are highly sensitive are especially impacted by emotional disconnection or unmet needs.
Without enough safety or attunement, they may internalize pain as:

- "I'm too much."
- "I'm not lovable."
- "My feelings don't matter."

What Reparenting Really Means

Reparenting is the process of offering your inner child what they missed:

- Emotional support
- Boundaries and consistency
- Comfort during distress
- Acceptance without conditions

How to Begin Reparenting Yourself

You can start to reparent by:

- Noticing when you're triggered or overwhelmed
- Asking: *"What does this part of me need right now?"*
- Offering warmth, compassion, and presence to the part that feels afraid, alone, or unworthy
- Practicing IFS (Internal Family Systems) or somatic healing techniques

A Reparenting Reminder

"It's not about blaming your parents. It's about meeting the needs your inner child never stopped having."
– *IFS-Informed Self-Healing*

You may have wondered why mindfulness was introduced before this chapter. As Dr. Gabor Maté suggests (paraphrased), many individuals shield themselves from unresolved pain or negative experiences, often unconsciously. While not all discomfort stems from trauma, a persistent disconnection from one's sense of self can eventually lead to internalized wounds that feel like trauma.

Reparenting unmet needs is one of the most challenging healing practices a person can undertake. It requires a multifaceted approach, not only identifying developmental wounds, but also learning how to offer care, presence, and attunement to those wounded parts. When I say this is one of the hardest experiences a person may face, I truly mean it. Yet, it is also one of the most transformative.

Reparenting can bring up complex emotions that may feel confusing or overwhelming. It's not uncommon for feelings of shame or guilt to surface when exploring unmet needs from the past. Because of this, it's essential to first establish a strong foundation of mindfulness, one that helps prevent emotional flooding. The ability to observe and tolerate emotions, sensations, and thoughts without feeling consumed by them is crucial before beginning reparenting work.

To be clear: do not attempt this practice unless you feel capable of managing intense emotions with a degree of objectivity. If emotional reactions feel like a threat to your sense of safety or identity, pause here. I strongly recommend engaging with this chapter only if you have at least two of the following in place:

- **A trusted support system**
- **A therapeutic relationship with a qualified mental health provider**
- **A willingness to explore your inner world**
- **The ability to tolerate discomfort without shutting down or acting out**

This work requires curiosity, support, and emotional readiness and that's okay. Move at your own pace. Your safety and stability always come first.

Permission to Feel: Reclaiming Ourselves from Performative Strength

For so many Black and Brown folks, cultural expectations can lead us into performative relationships, with others, with systems, even with ourselves. We're often expected to compartmentalize our emotions, suppress our needs, and take on the role of caregiver to everyone else's feelings, while ours go unseen and unattended.

This constant subjugation of our full selves, our feelings, our softness, our complexity, can put us at risk. Risk of falling into trauma bonds. Of consuming visual diets that numb rather than nourish. Of living with unmet needs that we've been conditioned to ignore in order to survive.

Strength becomes performance, rather than a reflection of wholeness. But we cannot heal what we refuse to feel.

It's time we give ourselves **permission**
To feel.
To soften.
To ask, "What do *I* need?"
To tend to the parts of us we were taught to hide.

Reclaiming our emotions is not weakness, it's resistance.
Reparenting ourselves is not selfish, it's sacred.

Understanding Attachment Theory

Before diving into reparenting, it's important to first understand the basics of Attachment Theory.

John Bowlby, a British psychologist, developed Attachment Theory in 1969. His research focused on how early relationships with caregivers shape our emotional development and how we relate to others throughout life.

Bowlby described secure attachment as the ability to feel comforted by a caregiver's presence, seeking support during distress, and exploring the world with confidence, knowing that someone will be there if help is needed. These secure bonds help children develop a sense of safety, trust, and emotional resilience.

However, not all caregivers are emotionally available or responsive. Bowlby later observed that insecure attachment forms when caregivers are consistently unresponsive, distant, or unpredictable. Over time, children in these environments may begin to feel unsafe, unworthy, or unsure about whether they can depend on others.

Bowlby also introduced the idea of internal working models, our mental maps of how relationships work. These models are shaped by early attachment experiences and influence how we see ourselves, how we think others will treat us, and how we behave in close relationships.

In simple terms:
If you learned early on that love and safety were unreliable, those beliefs

may still shape how you relate to yourself and others as an adult. This is why reparenting and attachment work go hand in hand.

How Attachment Shows Up in Adulthood

Attachment Theory has many lessons for child-rearing, but since this book isn't about parenting, we'll focus on how attachment shows up in adults, and how reparenting can help heal unmet needs.

Reparenting uses the principles of secure attachment to meet emotional needs that may have been ignored or unmet earlier in life. To understand this process, it's helpful to know the four main adult attachment styles:

1. **Anxious Attachment**
   People with this style often fear abandonment and have a hard time trusting others. They may seem clingy or overly dependent in relationships.

2. **Avoidant Attachment**
   These individuals often avoid emotional closeness. They may appear distant, struggle with intimacy, and have trouble opening up.

3. **Secure Attachment**
   This is the healthiest attachment style. People feel safe, supported, and confident in their relationships. They trust others and can give and receive love openly.

4. **Fearful-Avoidant Attachment**
   Also known as disorganized attachment, this style often comes from early trauma or inconsistent caregiving. These individuals may want closeness but are afraid of being hurt. As a result, they may pull away from relationships even while longing for connection.
   (Misha, 2022)

Attachment Styles Can Change

It's important to know that attachment isn't permanent. Many factors, like life experiences, relationships, therapy, or healing work, can shape or shift the way we attach to others and the world around us.

Also, attachment works more like a spectrum than a fixed label. Most people don't fit neatly into just one category. You may have some traits that feel secure and others that feel anxious, avoidant, or fearful depending on the situation.

If you're curious about your own attachment style, Dr. Diane Poole Heller offers a free attachment style quiz on her website. There are also many other short online tests you can try. Feel free to explore and find one that resonates with you.

Just keep in mind: these tests are not diagnostic tools. They offer a helpful starting point but only a small glimpse into your current emotional patterns. Use them to reflect and stay curious, not as final answers.

A Gentle Reminder Before You Begin

Before exploring your attachment style, please take a moment to check in with yourself. If sitting with difficult emotions feels overwhelming or unsafe right now, it may be best to pause. This work can bring up strong feelings, and it's important to feel grounded and supported before diving in.

What Does Secure Attachment Look Like?

Secure attachment doesn't mean you're perfect, it means you feel safe, connected, and able to handle life's ups and downs with healthy support. Adults with a secure attachment style often show the following traits:

- Generous and giving in relationships
- Able to ask for help when they need it
- Confident and decisive
- Believe others mean well
- Enjoy being with others, but also feel okay being alone
- Know their personal values and live by them
- Set clear and respectful boundaries
- Trust others and let themselves be trusted

(Misha, 2022)

Finding Secure Attachment in Everyday Life

Once you learn more about your own attachment style, it can help to see real-life examples of what **secure attachment** looks like. This can give you a better idea of what you're working toward and how to start reparenting your unmet needs.

Here are some helpful books and resources that explore attachment:

- **Mother Hunger** by Kelly McDaniel – explores the longing for nurturing many of us didn't get

- **The Whole-Brain Child** and **The Power of Showing Up** by Dr. Tina Payne Bryson & Dr. Daniel Siegel – focus on parenting and brain development

- **Recovering from Emotionally Immature Parents** by Dr. Lindsay Gibson – a guide for healing from difficult childhoods

- **Polysecure** by Jessica Fern – explores attachment within consensual nonmonogamy

- **Attached** by Dr. Amir Levine & Rachel S.F. Heller – explains the science behind adult attachment in romantic relationships

If you prefer audio or visual learning, here are two great options:

- **The podcast *Good Inside*** by Dr. Becky Kennedy offers clear examples of how to meet emotional needs and set healthy boundaries.

- **The children's show *Bluey*** often shows secure attachment in action. Though made for kids, many adults find its messages healing and relatable.

Remember, secure attachment isn't about being perfect, it's about building trust, safety, and emotional connection over time.

Reflecting on Your Visual Diet & Unmet Needs

Before beginning deep reparenting work, it's important to explore how your *visual diet*, the content you consume, might be connected to unmet emotional needs.

Use these guiding questions to reflect with honesty and compassion:

1. What am I getting from this visual content?
   Is it comfort? Numbing? Escape? Validation? Familiarity?

2. What might I be avoiding by constantly turning to it?
   Are there emotions, memories, or fears I'm pushing away?

3. What sensations or feelings show up in my body when I engage with this content?
   Do I feel tense, relaxed, disconnected, anxious, warm, empty?

4. What do those sensations say about how I'm carrying myself emotionally?
   Am I protecting myself, bracing, searching for something, or trying to feel less?

5. How do I feel when I don't have access to this content?
   Do I feel withdrawal, sadness, panic, or restlessness? Do I feel free?

6. How might this visual content be reinforcing or replaying unmet needs, both old and new?
   Does it echo past wounds, longings, or patterns that haven't been healed?

Tending to Your Unmet Needs: Using R.A.I.N. to Reparent

After identifying some of the emotions, sensations, or unmet needs beneath your visual habits or emotional patterns, the next step is to respond with care, not criticism. This is where reparenting begins.

To support this process, you can use Tara Brach's R.A.I.N. practice, a powerful mindfulness tool that helps you approach emotional wounds the way someone with secure attachment would: with presence, curiosity, and compassion.

R.A.I.N. Practice: Step-by-Step

R – Recognize
Gently notice what you're feeling. Is it sadness? Shame? Loneliness? Anxiety? Don't analyze it, just name it.

"This is grief."
"This is fear."

A – Allow
Give the feeling permission to exist. Let it be there without pushing it away or trying to fix it.

"I don't have to change this right now."
"It's okay that this is here."

I – Investigate
Explore the feeling with curiosity and care.
Where do you feel it in your body?
What does it need?
Is it connected to an old memory, wound, or unmet need?

"This tightness in my chest feels like being unseen."
"This sadness might be the part of me that never got comfort."

N – Nurture
Offer kindness to the part of you that is hurting. This is where reparenting truly begins. You might say:

"You are safe now."
"I see you, and I won't leave you."
"You deserve love and support."

You can place a hand on your heart, wrap yourself in a blanket, or imagine the comforting presence of someone loving.

This practice is a mini reparenting moment, a way to show up for yourself as the secure, wise caregiver you may not have had, but now have the power to become.

Reparenting Requires Compassion, Not Control

Self-compassion is a vital part of reparenting. It allows us to soothe emotional distress, not by ignoring or smothering it, but by attending to it with care. These parts of us aren't problems to be fixed, they're signals to be heard.

When intense feelings arise, we often want to contain or silence them. But the goal here isn't to shut down the emotion, it's to listen to what it needs. Reparenting is about showing up with gentleness, not judgment.

That said, approaching our unmet needs without judgment takes practice. For many, it doesn't come naturally, especially if their early environment didn't model acceptance or emotional safety. That's okay. This work takes time. You're not behind. You're learning a new language of care.

Still, with commitment and support, these skills become more natural. Over time, we can respond to emotional pain not with shame or avoidance, but with curiosity and compassion.

And in doing so, we finally begin to fill the void, not with distraction or over functioning, but with the nourishment we've always needed.

Borrowed Safety: Reparenting with Gentle Icons

A wounded mind may struggle to find supportive resources, especially when its internal compass has been shaped by unmet needs or early pain. Sometimes, it's hard to imagine what comfort or secure attachment *should* feel like, especially when you've rarely or never experienced it directly.

This is where borrowed safety becomes an important part of the healing process.

Let's say that a part of you is clinging to problematic visual media as a source of comfort, even if it's hurting more than helping. When you imagine letting go, what comes up? Fear? Sadness? Anxiety? Emptiness?

For many, these feelings are tied to unmet needs: the need to be seen, soothed, protected, or reassured. And if those needs were rarely met in childhood, it's no surprise that a visual diet, though imperfect, becomes a stand-in for safety.

But now, imagine someone like Mr. Rogers stepping in.

Mr. Rogers, a soft-spoken, deeply kind figure from childhood for many, can serve as a symbol of secure attachment. He spoke slowly, with intention. He validated big feelings. He taught millions that being scared or unsure didn't make you bad, it made you *human.*

Ask yourself:

- If I felt anxious at the thought of letting go of this visual media, how would Mr. Rogers speak to that fear?
- What would he say to the younger part of me who's scared to lose their source of comfort?
- Would he judge me? Or would he gently invite me to try something new?
- Would he remind me that it's okay to take small steps?
- Would he stay beside me when something new and uncomfortable arises?
- Would he be a safe companion while I explore what's beneath the surface?

Now ask:

- Does this part of me need more than one supportive figure?

- Can I imagine creating a team of nurturing, secure voices, real, fictional, spiritual, or internal, that can walk with me through this transition?

Healing doesn't always come from within, it often begins by borrowing strength from the outside until our nervous system is ready to generate it on its own.

You deserve that support.

You deserve to be reminded, as Mr. Rogers once said:

> "You are a very special person. There is only one like you in the whole world."

If another figure resonates more deeply with you, feel free to use them. For me, Mr. Rogers alone wasn't enough to support my internal care. In my own healing work, I've connected strongly with Harriet Winslow (played by Jo Marie Payton) from *Family Matters* (1989–1998). Her character embodied unconditional love, strong, nurturing, and firm in her boundaries.

As a child, I didn't fully understand why the show resonated with me so deeply. But as an adult, reflecting on difficult life experiences, I now see how Harriet's presence offered a symbolic example of secure attachment. She represents the kind of caring and grounded support I longed for growing up. Her character has become a meaningful internal resource, one that I continue to draw from as I do the work of reparenting.

It's true that many sitcom characters don't fully capture the complexity of real human experience. No one is perfect all the time, not in parenting, not in relationships, and not in their emotional responses. And that's okay. When we choose symbolic or internal resources for reparenting, perfection isn't the goal. What matters is that these figures feel *right* for your specific unmet needs.

This brings up an important question: *How many secure attachment resources do we need?*

I often say, it depends on the individual. But generally speaking, the more, the better. I recommend having at least five symbolic or internal figures. Why? Because reparenting can bring up a variety of emotional wounds, and different parts of you may need different kinds of support.

Think of it as assembling a team. The more supportive figures you have on your roster, the better equipped you'll be to meet your needs with care, flexibility, and compassion.

A potentially helpful tool when creating your team of secure attachment figures is to consider how your *younger self* might respond to each

individual. Ask yourself:
Would my grade school self feel safe with this person?

If that feels hard to answer, try a different lens:
Would I entrust this figure with the care of my own child?
If you don't have children (or choose not to), you might instead ask:
Would I feel comfortable having this person support a neighborhood child or someone I care about deeply?

If the answer is no, or uncertain, that's okay. It may simply be an opportunity to reexamine why. Ask: *Does this resource truly feel safe, loving, and supportive for the most vulnerable parts of me?*

For those who struggle to trust humans, this exercise may feel frustrating or even triggering. That's completely valid. Often, a deep wound underlies this difficulty, a wound tied to past betrayals, abandonment, or unmet needs. And when trust itself is the injury, the idea of reparenting can feel like an impossible task.

In these cases, I encourage you to expand your view of what a "resource" can be. Your attachment figures don't need to be real-life humans. They don't even have to be people. Many individuals find safety and strength in symbolic or fictional sources, like characters from childhood books, cartoons, movies, or mythology. These "humanoid" or even non-human representations can provide meaningful comfort, modeling secure connection in ways that feel less threatening to the nervous system.

That is to say, for some people, the idea of a figure like Aslan from *The Chronicles of Narnia* may offer more comfort than a real-life human like Mr. Rogers, especially if human representations feel unsafe or emotionally charged. Aslan, with his divine and majestic lion form, can feel like a deeply protective, nurturing presence without the vulnerability that human faces sometimes carry.

Others may find grounding in cartoon characters or animated mentors from childhood, like Master Splinter from *Teenage Mutant Ninja Turtles*, or Gaia from *Captain Planet*, who embodied the Earth's spirit and offered quiet strength and wisdom.

For those whose pain has made it hard to find safety in anything earthly, there may be solace in alien, divine, or mythic beings, figures who feel untouchable by human flaws. Characters like:

- Saint Walker from DC's *Blue Lantern Corps* (hope),
- E.T., who connected through empathy and presence,
- Neytiri from *Avatar*, with her fierce compassion,
- Yoda, wise and measured,

- Optimus Prime, a symbol of strength with moral clarity,
- or any of the Kryptonian figures who wear the iconic symbol of hope, gentle in spirit and powerful in protection.

Of course, this list barely scratches the surface. There are countless other *humanoid, anthropomorphic*, or *non-human figures* who might resonate with the parts of you that long to be seen, protected, or soothed.

If your imagination is already lighting up with someone who comforted or inspired, you, use them. Write them down. Explore what they represent. Ask:

- What qualities do they offer me?
- How would they talk to the hurting part of me?
- Can I call on their energy or voice when I'm struggling?

Reparenting is deeply personal. It doesn't need to follow tradition; it just needs to feel *right* for *you*.

Visualization is a powerful tool in the reparenting process.

One of the most healing practices you can engage in is visualizing yourself as a child, caught in a moment of indulging in a problematic visual diet, scrolling, numbing, zoning out, and then showing up for that child as your present-day self.

Meet them at eye level.

Speak with the compassion, warmth, and steadiness of a secure attachment figure. Embody the qualities you've longed for: patience, curiosity, unconditional care. Let your inner child feel seen, not shamed, understood, not fixed.

This kind of internal dialogue can be extraordinarily healing.

But it's important to remember this is not a one-and-done moment of relief. Reparenting is a relationship. One that requires consistency, emotional tolerance, and commitment. As you deepen this practice, difficult feelings may rise to the surface, old grief, shame, fear, or confusion.

These are not signs of failure. They are *signs of opening*.

When this happens, you may need additional support:

- A trusted therapist
- Support groups or peer spaces
- Continued reparenting work with a variety of attachment resources

- Mindfulness and somatic practices to regulate your nervous system

This is slow, courageous work. And you don't have to do it alone.

Guiding Principles for Reparenting

Adapted from Jodie Clarke, MA, LPC/MHSP (2022)

Reparenting is a courageous and transformative process, but it can also stir up difficult emotions and old wounds. As you begin or deepen your reparenting journey, here are four key principles to help you stay grounded and compassionate with yourself along the way:

1. Stay Curious
Reparenting may bring up painful memories, old narratives, or behaviors you've carried for years. Rather than judging or resisting them, approach these experiences with curiosity.
Ask yourself:

- *What am I learning about myself?*
- *Where did this pattern come from?*
- *What does this younger part of me need?*
  Curiosity helps you stay open and connected to the process.

2. Maintain Self-Compassion
It's common to feel resentment, shame, or guilt as you begin to recognize unmet needs and childhood wounds. Be gentle with yourself. These feelings are normal, and they're not evidence that you're failing. They're part of the healing. Speak to yourself the way you would speak to a beloved child or a dear friend.

3. Practice Patience
You may have lived with old beliefs or relational wounds for decades. It's okay if it takes time to unlearn them. Don't rush the process. Building trust, with yourself, and perhaps with a safe other like a therapist can take time. Healing isn't linear. Some days will feel easier than others. Keep going anyway.

4. Be Intentional
Old habits have deep roots. In moments of stress, exhaustion, or distraction, it's easy to fall back into familiar patterns. Remind yourself why you're doing this work.

- *What have you already overcome?*
- *What are you working toward?*
- *What strengths have helped you grow?*
  Reparenting takes courage. You are already demonstrating that courage every time you show up for yourself.

IFS-Informed Reparenting Practice: A Guide to Healing Inner Needs

Inspired by Internal Family Systems (IFS) Therapy by Dr. Richard Schwartz

What is Reparenting?

Reparenting is the act of giving yourself the care, guidance, and validation that you may not have received in childhood. It's about tending to your unmet needs from a compassionate, conscious adult perspective.

In IFS, we understand that our internal world is made up of many **"parts"**, each with its own voice, emotion, or role. Some are protectors, some hold pain, and some carry burdens from our past.

Step 1: Ground in Self-Energy

Begin by connecting with your core **Self**, the calm, curious, and compassionate center of who you are.
Take a breath. Get still. Ask:

- Can I approach myself right now with curiosity?
- Is there a sense of spaciousness or softness I can tap into?

Self-energy is key, it's the version of you capable of healing, not shaming.

Step 2: Identify a Part Needing Reparenting

Notice a part of you that feels hurt, abandoned, angry, overwhelmed, or ashamed.

Ask yourself:

- What part of me needs my attention right now?
- What age or stage does this part feel like?
- What does this part believe about me or the world?

Examples: "I'm not good enough," "No one listens to me," "I'm too much."

Step 3: Befriend the Part

Instead of fixing or rejecting the part, try to befriend it.
Ask:

- What do you want me to know about you?
- How long have you been holding this role?
- What are you afraid would happen if you didn't do this?

Offer validation:
"That makes sense you feel that way. You've been carrying so much."

Step 4: Offer Reparenting From the Self

Now that this part feels seen, speak to it from your Self.

Offer what was missing:

- **Comfort**: "I'm here now. You're not alone."
- **Boundaries**: "You don't have to protect me anymore. I've got us."
- **Permission**: "You can rest. You don't have to perform or please."
- **Love**: "You are lovable exactly as you are."

Ask the part: "What do you need from me right now?"

Step 5: Create a Safe Inner Sanctuary

Visualize a comforting space where your part can rest, play, or feel protected.
This might be a cozy room, a garden, or a treehouse, whatever feels nurturing.

You might say: "This is your space to just be. You're safe here. I'll keep checking on you."

Step 6: Repeat & Revisit

Again, reparenting isn't a one-time event, it's a process.
Make regular check-ins with your parts. Over time, they'll begin to trust that your Self is here to care of them.

Healing happens in relationship, especially your relationship with yourself.

Affirmation for the Journey

> *"I have everything within me to give myself what I needed back then. I choose to care for all my parts with patience, love, and truth."*

Books for further IFS reading

1. *No Bad Parts* by Dr. Richard C. Schwartz
    - A beginner-friendly, compassionate introduction to IFS.

- o Focuses on the idea that all parts have positive intentions, even the ones that cause pain.

2. ***Internal Family Systems Therapy (2nd Edition)*** by Richard C. Schwartz & Martha Sweezy

    - o A comprehensive guide for clinicians or advanced learners.
    - o Covers theory, method, and case studies.

3. ***You Are the One You've Been Waiting For*** by Richard C. Schwartz

    - o Applies IFS to intimate relationships and romantic dynamics.

4. ***Parts Work: An Illustrated Guide to Your Inner Life*** by Tom Holmes

    - o Visual and engaging; great for visual learners and young adults.

Reparenting the Reparenting Process

When Tending to Your Needs Becomes a Need in Itself

As you move through the process of reparenting, you may find that even the work of healing brings its own challenges. There will be moments when it feels discouraging, exhausting, or even defeating. These experiences are not signs that you're failing, they're signs that this work is *real* and *deep*.

In fact, part of reparenting is learning how to care for yourself when the process itself feels too heavy.

Expect Fatigue, and Care for It

You might feel worn down from constantly trying to understand, soothe, and support yourself. And in those moments, a new unmet need arises: *The need to reparent the part of you that's tired from reparenting.*

Give yourself space to rest. To pause. To play.
This isn't weakness, it's wisdom. It's sustainability.

The Shame Spiral is Real

For many of us, giving ourselves care brings up painful thoughts:

- *"I don't deserve this."*
- *"This feels selfish."*
- *"Why is this so hard for me?"*

Reparenting shines a light on how we feel about ourselves, our worth, value, and capacity to receive love. Shame can slow us down, make us second-guess the work, or keep us stuck in old narratives.

The antidote is gentle compassion. Remind yourself: You are learning a new way of being. That takes time. That takes courage.

This is an Ultramarathon, Not a Sprint

True reparenting doesn't happen overnight. It's not a quick fix. It's a slow build, layer by layer, of trust, security, and self-tolerance. Some days will feel like progress. Other days may feel like you've gone backwards. Both are part of the journey.

The goal isn't perfection, it's presence.
To stay with yourself. To listen. To respond with care.

Let Support Be a Resource

Reparenting doesn't mean you do it all alone. In fact, trying to carry it by yourself may recreate the very patterns you're trying to heal.
Lean into a wide, colorful tapestry of support:

- A trusted therapist
- A friend who sees you
- A fictional figure or spiritual guide
- A favorite book, podcast, or character from childhood
- Art, music, and creative practices that help you feel safe

Sometimes, something as small as a short walk, a gentle song, or an art break can give you what you never received, and still long for.

Closing Thought

Reparenting is not just about becoming a better version of yourself. It's about learning to see the person you already are, *with kindness.* From that place, we build something stronger than self-love. We build self-belonging.

Summary

Why Reparenting Matters

- Addictions and compulsive behaviors often stem from emotional loss, not moral failing.
- Trauma includes both what did happen (e.g., abuse) and what didn't happen (e.g., emotional support).
- Sensitive children are more deeply affected by unmet emotional needs and disconnection.

What Is Reparenting?

- Reparenting means offering your inner child what was missed:
    - Emotional safety
    - Comfort and care
    - Boundaries
    - Acceptance without conditions
- It is a slow, relational process, not a quick fix.

Before You Begin

- Ensure a foundation of mindfulness and emotional regulation.
- Only begin if you can tolerate difficult emotions without becoming overwhelmed.
- Support systems (e.g., therapy, community) are essential.

Understanding Attachment

- Four main adult attachment styles:
    1. Secure – Trusting, grounded, emotionally available
    2. Anxious – Clingy, fears abandonment
    3. Avoidant – Withdraws from closeness
    4. Fearful-Avoidant – Wants intimacy but fears it
- Attachment styles can change with healing and support.

Visual Diet & Emotional Avoidance

- Ask: What am I seeking or avoiding through media?

- Notice bodily sensations and emotional triggers related to screen habits.
- Media can reflect and reinforce unmet emotional needs.

R.A.I.N. Practice (Tara Brach)

1. Recognize – Name the emotion.
2. Allow – Let it exist without trying to fix it.
3. Investigate – Get curious about what it needs.
4. Nurture – Offer compassion and comfort.

Borrowed Safety & Attachment Figures

- Symbolic figures like Mr. Rogers, Harriet Winslow, Aslan, or Yoda can serve as secure emotional resources.
- Create a team of five or more internal or symbolic figures to help meet different needs.
- Choose figures your younger self would trust.

IFS-Informed Reparenting

1. Connect to Self-energy – Calm, compassionate internal space
2. Identify wounded parts – What part needs your care?
3. Befriend the part – Learn its fears and story
4. Offer reparenting – Provide what was missing (love, safety, support)
5. Create sanctuary – Visualize a safe internal space
6. Repeat – Healing takes time and consistent attention

Reparenting the Reparenting

- The work itself can become emotionally exhausting.
- Normalize fatigue, shame, and regression, they're part of the process.
- Practice rest, play, art, and let others support you.

Guiding Principles (Jodie Clarke, 2022)

1. Stay Curious – Explore with openness, not judgment.
2. Maintain Self-Compassion – Be gentle with shame and guilt.

3. Practice Patience – Healing is not linear.
4. Be Intentional – Stay committed through stress and setbacks.

Closing Insight

Reparenting is not about perfection or independence, it's about building a sense of self-belonging, slowly and compassionately, over time.

Chapter Thirty-One

"I am even more certain that to create dangerously is also to create fearlessly, boldly embracing the public and private terrors that would silence us, then bravely moving forward even when it feels as though we are chasing or being chased by ghosts." -Edwidge Danticat

Using Art, Music, and Creativity to Support Healing

As we begin to meet our unmet needs, especially when stepping away from a problematic visual diet, we may feel a wave of strong emotions, thoughts, or body sensations. These can rush in to fill the space we used to spend escaping or numbing. That intensity can be hard to handle.

One powerful way to manage and express these feelings is through creative expression.

When I say "the arts," I mean anything that helps you express yourself, like:

- Music
- Drawing or painting
- Dance or movement
- Writing or poetry
- Sculpture or blown glass
- Theater or performance
- Crafts, collage, or even coloring

You don't need to be "good" at art. You don't need a formal process or perfect product. Creativity is about expression, not perfection. It's a language for your emotions, especially the ones that don't have words yet.

Each of us has a unique "artistic thumbprint." Exploring what feels good for *you*, whether it's singing in the shower or painting with your fingers, is what matters most.

Give yourself permission to create without judgment. Let your emotions move through colors, sounds, shapes, or movement. You may be surprised by what comes up, and how much relief and clarity it can bring.

How the Creative Arts Help Us Feel Better

When we have a lot of emotional energy, like stress, sadness, or anger, creative arts can be a powerful tool to help us calm down and feel more balanced. Activities like music, dance, painting, or theater can help us regulate emotions, release tension, and reconnect with ourselves.

Art isn't just personal, it's also social. Doing creative activities with others can boost emotional wellbeing and reduce feelings of loneliness. This is especially true for people who are older or at risk of isolation.

Music, in particular, has been shown to:

- Improve mood and emotional health
- Strengthen social connections
- Support brain health and memory
- Help older adults stay active and engaged

As researchers Sheppard and Broughton (2020) explain:

> "Active music participation supports wellbeing and health. It builds social connections, reduces isolation, and even improves cognitive function, especially in older adults. Staying involved in the arts can help people stay mentally sharp and socially connected, both of which are important for a good quality of life."

Dance: Movement as Medicine

Dancing, whether to music or just moving your body freely, can be incredibly helpful when you're feeling emotionally overwhelmed. But you don't have to be in distress to benefit. Even mild emotional arousal is a great time to move. Dance helps regulate emotions, boost energy, and connect body and mind.

It also activates many parts of the brain. When we dance, we're not just moving, we're building brain power, memory, and coordination across both sides of the brain.

Research shows that:

> "After six months of regular dancing, participants had increased activity in parts of the brain that support memory, focus, movement control, and self-awareness. The most noticeable change was in the corpus callosum, a brain structure that connects the left and right hemispheres, helping them work together."
> — Rehfeld et al., 2018

After 18 months of dancing, brain scans showed more growth in the parahippocampal region, which helps with memory and recalling personal experiences (Meulenberg et al., 2023).

In other words, dance is healing, expressive, and good for your brain.

The Whole-Body Benefits of Dance

When we use these parts of the brain during dance, we unlock many wellness benefits. Research shows that dance supports health and well-being in multiple ways, especially because it uses the brain, body, and emotions all at once.

> *"Dance supports people's well-being and health across all ages and cultures. It offers a safe, social space where people can build community and care for themselves in many ways, including improving thinking skills, physical health, stress levels, self-esteem, and mental health."*
> — Sheppard & Broughton, 2020

Whether you dance alone, with friends, or in a class, the movement and connection can help build a strong foundation for healing.

The Brain-Boosting Power of Music Listening

You don't have to dance to get the benefits of music. Simply listening to music can have a powerful impact on your brain. In fact, research shows that music can even help protect the brain from damage over time.

> *"Listening to music can influence how genes in the brain work. Some of these changes help manage dopamine (a feel-good chemical) and may protect the brain from decline."*
> — Nair et al., 2021

So, whether you're relaxing with your favorite playlist or using music to focus or reflect, know that your brain is benefiting, note by note.

Music as Emotional Support for International Students

For international students, living abroad can come with a lot of stress, feeling homesick, overwhelmed, or disconnected. Many turn to music to help them cope.

A 2019 study found that students often use music streaming services to:

- Improve their mood
- Reduce stress and homesickness

Dance: Movement as Medicine

Dancing—whether to music or just moving your body freely—can be incredibly helpful when you're feeling emotionally overwhelmed. But you don't have to be in distress to benefit. Even mild emotional arousal is a great time to move. Dance helps regulate emotions, boost energy, and connect body and mind.

Research shows that:

"After six months of regular dancing, participants had increased activity in parts of the brain that support memory, focus, moverneet control, and self-awareness. The most noticable change was in the corpus callosum—a brain structure that connects the left and right hemishpheres, helping them work together."

After 18 months of dancing, brain scans showed more growth in the *porahippocampal region*, which helps with memory and recallng personal experiehces (Meulenberg et,, al, 2023)

The Whole-Body Benefits of Dance

"Dance supports people's well-being and health across all ages and cultures. It offers a safe, social space where people can build community and care for themselves in many ways—including improving thinking skills, physical health, stress levels, and mental health.

- Boost energy and focus
- Feel peace of mind
- Fight boredom

"Students routinely use music to manage their emotions while studying abroad. Streaming services help them adjust their mood and deal with emotional challenges."
— *Wadley et al., 2019*

Thanks to apps and digital platforms, music remains a powerful tool for emotional support, no matter where you are in the world.

Music, Art, and Healing Across Distance and Trauma

Listening to music can help people feel connected, especially when they're far from home or loved ones. Songs from your home country, favorite tracks shared by friends, or even music from your culture can offer comfort and a sense of belonging. Whether it's to ease homesickness or lift your mood, the act of listening can soothe underlying emotional needs.

Music isn't the only art form that helps with healing. Art therapy has been shown to support people recovering from PTSD (Post-Traumatic Stress Disorder), especially in group settings.

One study looked at 240 active-duty service members with PTSD and traumatic brain injuries. During group art therapy, participants worked on montage paintings to express their personal stories and emotions.

> *"Art therapy helps service members process difficult emotions and rehearse new, healthier identities. Sharing art in a group setting builds connection, reduces shame, and increases emotional safety. Many participants felt proud of their work and gave their paintings to loved ones as gifts."*
> — Berberian et al., 2019

Through creativity, whether through music or visual art, people can stabilize, feel seen, and find new ways to tell their stories.

Using Art as a Distraction for Emotional Relief

Art doesn't always need to focus on your emotions to be helpful. In fact, using art as a distraction, like sketching something random or unrelated to your mood, can be a powerful way to manage tough feelings like sadness or anger.

A 2019 study tested this idea with college students who were first made to feel either sad or angry. Afterward, some were asked to draw to express their feelings, while others were told to draw something unrelated, to distract themselves.

> *"Those who drew to distract felt better than those who drew to express their emotions, no matter what emotion they started with. Drawing helped lower emotional intensity and improved mood. Plus, students who drew to distract reported more enjoyment and a stronger sense of focus and flow during the activity."*
> — Genuth & Drake, 2019

So, even if you're not sure what to draw or don't want to face your feelings directly, picking up a pencil and letting your mind wander can be a simple, effective way to regulate emotions.

THE HEALING POWER OF MUSIC LISTENING

Brain Benefits of Music

- Listening to music can positively influence gene expression in the brain
- It supports dopamine regulation (a feel-good chemical) and may help protect against cognitive decline.

Nair et al, 2021

Emotional Support for International Students

- Music helps students abroad manage emotions, homesickness, and stress
- Streaming services are used routinely for:
  - Boosting mood and energy
  - Improving focus
  - Easing boredom and emotional overwhelm

Wadley et al, 2019

Why It Matters

- You don't need to dance or play an instrument to benefit.
- Simply listening to your favorite playlist—for calm, energy, or reflection—can enhance emotional and mental well-being.

Draw to Regulate Emotions

Drawing helps. Whether you're drawing to express your feelings or to distract yourself from them, the act of creating art has been shown to calm the mind and body.

Studies show that drawing:

- Lowers stress and emotional intensity

- Helps process sadness and anger
- Increases focus, enjoyment, and a sense of flow

Whether you're sketching what you're feeling or just doodling for fun, you're doing something good for your mental health.

Draw.
Sketch.
Use any art medium that feels right.
The goal isn't perfection, it's permission.
Permission to feel, to express, and to regulate your mind, body, and spirit.

Summary

Creativity Is Expression, Not Perfection

- You don't need to be "good" at art, just open to expressing yourself.
- Any form of art, drawing, dancing, music, writing, crafting, can support emotional regulation.

Art Helps with Emotional Regulation

- Art, music, and movement help release stress, reduce emotional intensity, and reconnect with the body.
- Creative expression activates multiple brain regions, supporting emotional healing and cognitive function.

Dance Supports the Brain and Body

- Dance improves memory, coordination, and emotional health by engaging both brain hemispheres.
- It boosts physical health and helps regulate mood through movement.

Music Boosts Mental and Emotional Health

- Listening to music enhances mood, reduces stress, and supports brain health (dopamine regulation, neuroprotection).
- Music connects people socially, especially important for international students or those facing isolation.

Art Builds Social Connection

- Group creative experiences reduce shame, improve emotional safety, and increase feelings of belonging.
- This is especially true in art therapy and music participation among older adults or those with PTSD.

Drawing to Distract Is Powerful

- Drawing to distract, rather than express, can improve mood and lower emotional arousal.
- It offers flow, enjoyment, and relief during difficult emotional states.

Bottom Line:

Creativity helps regulate your **mind, body, and spirit**.
Whether you're drawing, moving, singing, or creating something silly, it counts.
Give yourself permission to explore, play, and heal through the arts.

Chapter Thirty-Two

"It's very important that we re-learn the art of resting and relaxing. Not only does it help prevent the onset of many illnesses that develop through chronic tension and worrying; it allows us to clear our minds, focus, and find creative solutions to problems." -Thich Nhat Hanh

Interventions to Tend to Our Needs
When we cut back on screen time, we may feel a sudden emptiness or "vacuum." That space used to be filled with scrolling, videos, or digital distractions, and now it can feel uncomfortable. To help fill that space in healthier ways, there are many tools we can turn to. These include:

- Socializing – spending time with people we care about
- Neophilia – trying new things or exploring new interests
- Archetypal experiences – connecting with stories, symbols, or roles that feel meaningful
- Memorization and brain training – puzzles, memory games, or learning something new
- Feeding the underlying need – identifying what we were really looking for when we used screens (comfort, distraction, stimulation)
- Reconnecting with boredom – allowing ourselves to rest, reflect, and just "be" without distraction
- Spirituality – tapping into something bigger than ourselves
- Gratitude – noticing and appreciating the good around us

These strategies can meet the same needs that a poor visual diet used to cover, but in a healthier, more intentional way.

Let's be real: cutting out screen time completely isn't an option for most people. Many of us rely on screens for work, connection, or daily life. If you have the ability to fully unplug, great. But if not, these tools are meant for anyone who wants to *manage* their screen use, not erase it.

While some people may benefit from cutting out harmful visual content, removing their relationship with screens entirely can have serious downsides. In today's world, screens are often necessary for work, school, and even making friends. Completely stepping away can lead to digital isolation, which can feel overwhelming, especially for people who don't have strong social support or a healthy connection with their own body and emotions.

Eye Contact & Social Connection: Tips and Tricks

Making eye contact is a powerful way to build connection and improve communication. It can help people feel seen, understood, and emotionally connected.

> Researchers have found that:

- Eye contact helps people sync their attention and stay present in a conversation.
- It sends a clear message: "I'm paying attention to you."
- It also shares emotional and mental cues, helping us understand how others feel.

With practice, eye contact can even help reduce social discomfort or anxiety. Like a muscle, it gets stronger the more we use it, with patience and care.

What Happens in the Brain During Eye Contact

Recent brain scan studies using fMRI show that eye contact lights up key areas of the brain involved in social connection. These areas are sometimes called the "social brain." They include parts that help us:

- Recognize faces (fusiform gyrus)
- Understand emotions and intentions (amygdala and orbitofrontal cortex)
- Process social cues and body language (superior temporal gyri)
- Think about what others are feeling or thinking (medial prefrontal cortex)

In short, eye contact helps activate the parts of the brain that make us feel connected to others and understand them better.
— *(Koike et al., 2019)*

With so many areas of our social brain activated, the harmful effects of a poor visual diet can be reduced. As individuals reconnect with people face-to-face, they begin to build real community, off-screen and in-person. There's something powerful about feeling like you belong in a real space, not just through the black mirror of a screen.

Eye contact and focused interaction allow for a much deeper understanding of others. We don't just hear words, we pick up on subtle emotional cues through gaze, tone, facial expressions, and gestures. These rich, layered signals are often lost in screen-based communication.

As Canigueral and Hamilton (2019) explain:

> *"Social interactions involve complex exchanges of a variety of social signals, such as gaze, facial expressions, speech, and gestures. Focusing on the dual function of eye gaze, this review explores how the presence of an audience, communicative purpose, and temporal dynamics of gaze allow interacting partners to achieve successful communication."*

As mentioned in Chapter Twenty-Six, community is an essential part of the BIPOC experience, especially for adolescents and young adults. Without it, many of us feel dismissed, othered, and pushed to the margins of a culture and country that often places us in a lesser tier.

Eye contact isn't just about socializing; it's about survival and belonging. For BIPOC individuals, it can be a powerful way to build trust, recognize safety, and foster connection in environments that may not always feel safe or welcoming.

Turning our attention toward the people in our community, not just the screens in our hands, can nourish many of our unmet needs. If our focus is constantly pulled into visual content, we may miss the very moments and relationships that keep us grounded, connected, and protected.

Neophilia: The Love of New Experiences

Neophilia is the desire to explore what's new, new places, ideas, foods, or experiences. It's long been a driver of tourism and adventure, but it can also play a meaningful role in digital wellness and emotional healing.

> *"Neophilia refers to an individual's love or passion for what is novel (or new)... Neophilic/neophobic tendencies are thus believed to influence attitudes and food preferences."*
> — Baah et al., 2020

Engaging in new experiences, whether trying a new recipe, walking a different route, or exploring a hobby, can help:

- Spark curiosity and joy
- Break patterns of digital overuse
- Support brain flexibility and resilience
- Offer fresh perspectives that challenge ruts or stuckness

When healing from screen fatigue or emotional disconnection, neophilia can be a powerful, low-cost way to reconnect with the world, one new experience at a time.

Neophilia: Shifting Our Visual Diet Through New Experiences

Discovering something new, something awe-inspiring, can be a powerful way to shift our attention away from the dopamine-driven pull of screens. When life feels dull, overwhelming, or even frightening, it's easy to turn to digital content to escape. But that escape can come at the cost of connection, meaning, and emotional health.

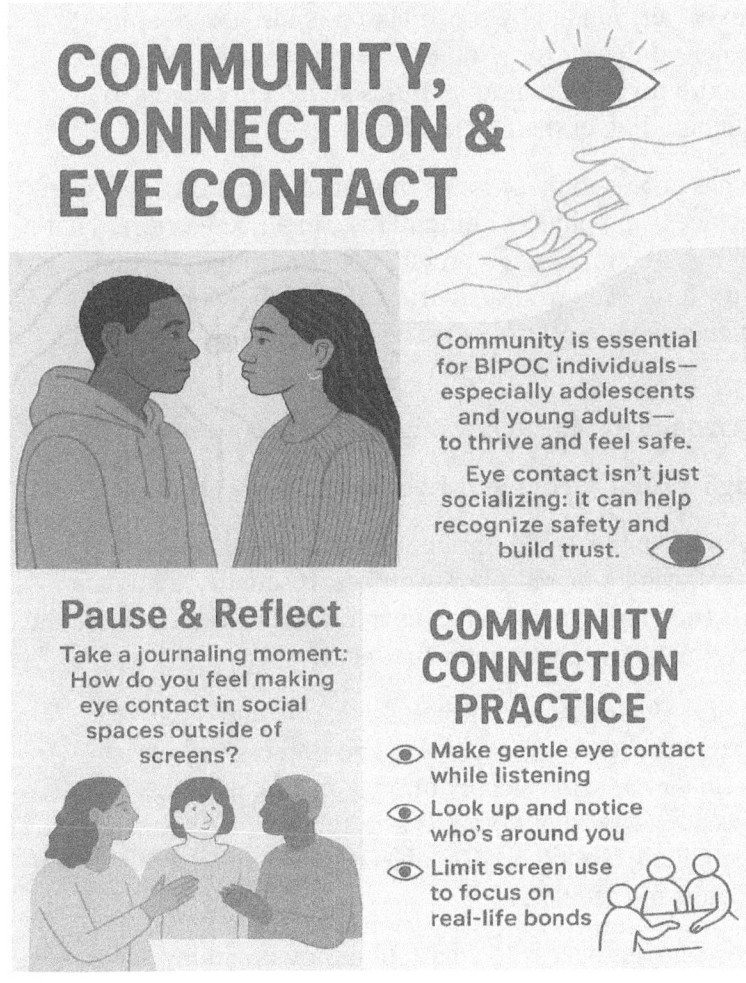

Neophilia, the love of new experiences, is a driving force behind tourism and exploration. But the truth is, not everyone has the resources or privilege to travel or engage in once-in-a-lifetime opportunities. Many people are limited by financial, geographic, or systemic barriers. For them, touring the world might not be a realistic option.

Still, the essence of neophilia isn't about luxury. It's about curiosity. Wonder. Discovery. Even small, local moments of novelty, like visiting a nearby park for the first time, trying a new recipe, or listening to music from a different culture, can light up our brains and shift us out of emotional numbness.

Neophilia invites us to engage with the world in a new way, right where we are.

Creating New Experiences, Your Way

There are countless ways to explore new experiences, but it's not always easy or immediately rewarding. Sometimes, it takes trial and error. What feels nourishing or exciting for one person might not land the same way for someone else. And that's okay.

For me, nature is my gateway to newness. It's always changing, always offering something different, even in familiar places. Living in Washington State, I'm lucky to be surrounded by breathtaking landscapes that invite exploration. Whether you're up for a long hike or just sitting by a lake, there's space in nature for people of all abilities and energy levels to connect with something bigger than themselves.

But not everyone has access to these kinds of spaces. Location, transportation, finances, and physical limitations can all be barriers. That's where technology can step in, not as a crutch, but as a bridge. Virtual nature walks, online art museums, music from around the world, and immersive documentaries can offer a sense of novelty and wonder, right where you are.

Neophilia doesn't require a plane ticket, it just asks for curiosity.

Neophilia Through Visual Media and Everyday Exploration

Using visual media to see the world through the eyes of others, with or without commentary, can be incredibly rewarding. It satisfies a human longing for *novelty* (neophilia) and invites us into perspectives, places, and experiences that we may never encounter firsthand.

Streaming shows like *Moving Art* or *Planet Earth*, or using VR-like smartphone devices, can create awe-inspiring and immersive journeys. These forms of media let us witness breathtaking nature, diverse cultures, and new ideas, all without leaving home. While smartphone VR headsets may seem high-tech, many are now affordable and even available at local thrift stores or secondhand retailers.

Of course, not everyone has access to smartphones or streaming services. Equity in access is an important consideration, and novelty doesn't always require a screen. There are still meaningful ways to cultivate new experiences:

Explore your community
Attend free workshops, check out local community centers, or visit cultural spaces you haven't explored yet.

Connect through conversation

Ask family or friends to walk you through their hobbies, gardening, mechanics, cooking, astronomy, language learning. Let someone share their world with you.

Experiment with new senses and skills

Try a new flavor, texture, sound, or rhythm. Take a walk in a different part of town. Learn a dance you've never tried before. You don't have to go far to feel wonder.

Try This Tip:

Before introducing new experiences, try setting your smartphone to grayscale for at least a week. This reduces your baseline dopamine stimulation and can help you better appreciate the *color and richness* of real-life or novel digital experiences once you reintroduce them.

Neophilia isn't about having more, it's about noticing more. Give new things a chance, even if they feel unfamiliar or uncomfortable at first. It may take a few tries to find joy in novelty, but your nervous system is built to grow through exploration.

Memorization & Brain Training: Strengthening the Mind

Brain training and memorization can be powerful tools, especially when you're trying to reduce screen time or rewire your habits. Instead of consuming fast-paced or overstimulating media, you can redirect your focus toward activities that support long-term mental wellness.

Why Memorization Matters

Memorizing isn't just about recalling facts, it strengthens the brain's ability to encode, store, and retrieve information. This process builds your cognitive stamina and supports other mental functions like focus, reasoning, and attention to detail.

By practicing memorization, you're also:

- Training your brain to tune in and concentrate
- Building neural resilience through repetition
- Enhancing mental agility and pattern recognition
- Creating opportunities for personal growth and confidence

How to Begin Brain Training

You don't need expensive apps or tools to get started. Here are some simple ways to practice:

- Memorize a poem, quote, or short passage daily

- Learn lyrics to a favorite song in a new language
- Try recalling a list of cities, capitals, or historical dates
- Play memory games (digit span, card matching, mental math)
- Use flashcards or write out facts by hand

A Dopamine Shift with Benefits

When you replace high-stimulation screen content with brain-building activities, your mind may initially resist. But over time, the dopaminergic system adapts, helping you find satisfaction in slower, more sustainable rewards. This shift supports emotional regulation, self-discipline, and improved focus.

The Beauty of Memory: How Our Brain Stores What Matters

Our minds are capable of amazing things, especially when we consistently challenge them. Memory is one of the brain's most remarkable functions. The way we encode, store, and recall information helps shape how we see the world and interact with it.

Unlike a filing cabinet, memories aren't stored in just one place. Instead, different types of memories live in different, interconnected regions of the brain:

- **Explicit Memories** (facts and personal experiences):
    - **Hippocampus** – creates and retrieves memories
    - **Neocortex** – stores long-term information
    - **Amygdala** – adds emotional weight to memories
- **Implicit Memories** (skills and habits):
    - **Basal Ganglia** – supports motor learning and routines
    - **Cerebellum** – coordinates movement and timing
- **Working Memory** (short-term tasks and focus):
    - **Prefrontal Cortex** – helps with decision-making, attention, and holding information in mind

> "Memories aren't stored in just one part of the brain. Different types are stored across different, interconnected brain regions."
> — Queensland Brain Institute, 2018

Understanding how memory works reminds us that training our brains, through learning, practice, and mindful repetition, isn't just helpful. It's healing.

Brain Training and Cognitive Growth
Professor Jason Mattingley and his team at the Queensland Brain Institute (2018) explored how brain training can support cognitive development. Their research found that:

> *"Brain training for specific tasks can also improve broader brain performance, when combined with brain stimulation."*

This means that focused mental exercises, especially when paired with techniques like neurostimulation, can have benefits beyond just the task at hand. With consistency, brain training can strengthen attention, memory, and mental flexibility in everyday life.

Do You Need Expensive Devices to Boost Brain Function?
Not at all. While Professor Mattingley's team used transcranial direct current stimulation in their research, they also emphasized a much more accessible takeaway:

> *"There's no doubt that repeatedly doing certain tasks improves performance on those tasks."*
> (Queensland Brain Institute, 2018)

In other words, simple, consistent brain training, without expensive equipment, can make a real difference.

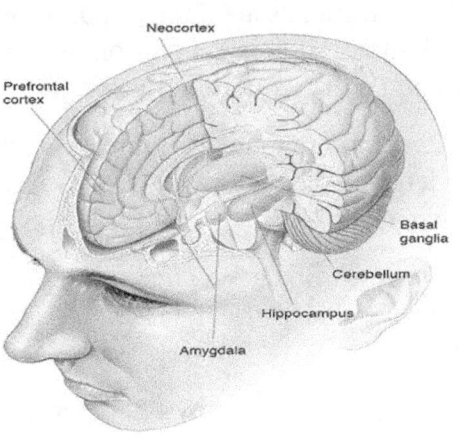

(Illustration by Levent Efe)

It's also worth noting that the brain regions involved in memory encoding, the prefrontal cortex, amygdala, neocortex, hippocampus, cerebellum, and basal ganglia, are all deeply connected to emotional processing and regulation. Strengthening these areas through brain training and memorization doesn't just help with recall, it can also improve emotional regulation and overall executive functioning.
(Nouchi et al., 2013; Scionti et al., 2020; Ger & Roebers, 2023)

Train Your Brain with Real-Life Learning
Dust off your Duolingo and explore opportunities for in-person conversation groups in your community, if available. Enroll in woodworking or other hands-on classes to grow your skills, no matter

where you're starting from. The key is consistent engagement: the more you challenge your brain with new tasks, the more it adapts and strengthens.

Keep in mind that every brain encodes information differently. Your ability to retain and apply what you learn can be strongly influenced by your relationship with the person teaching you. A supportive and engaging instructor can significantly enhance memory formation.
(Queensland Brain Institute, 2018; University of Sunderland, 2022)

And of course, other biological and environmental factors play a role, such as your energy levels, overall health, past traumas, stress, and the conditions of your learning space.
(University of Sunderland, 2022)

Feed the Underlying Need(s)
Behind every compulsive behavior, whether it's doomscrolling, binge-watching, or constant checking of social media, there's usually an unmet need trying to be fulfilled. It might be loneliness, boredom, lack of purpose, or a desire for connection.

These behaviors often *start* as a way to meet a need, but over time, they can create new problems or intensify existing ones. For example, using social media might help you feel closer to friends and family, but it can also worsen negative self-image, highlight disconnection from in-person relationships, or leave you feeling more isolated in the long run.

The goal isn't to shame the behavior, but to get curious about what it's trying to soothe. Once we understand the underlying need, we can begin to feed it in healthier, more sustainable ways.

To feed the underlying need, we must first ask: *What desire, feeling, or unmet need is my screen behavior actually trying to satisfy?* This often requires slowing down and tuning in.

Start by noticing what comes up, emotionally, physically, or mentally, right before the urge to engage in a problematic visual diet. Is it loneliness? Anxiety? Emptiness? A belief like "I'm not enough"? These signals point toward deeper needs that want attention.

This process calls for mindfulness, self-awareness, and sometimes reparenting. It's about developing a strong connection with your inner world, especially your body, your feelings, and the beliefs that shape your behavior.

Approach this with curiosity, not judgment. Instead of criticizing yourself for wanting to scroll or binge, ask:

What am I feeling right now?
What does my body need?
What would feel truly nourishing, not just numbing?

Mindfulness helps us hold space for discomfort while gently exploring what our mind, body, and spirit are trying to communicate. From there, we can begin to meet those needs more intentionally, and with greater care.

For me, and for many others, this work can feel incredibly difficult. It requires vulnerability, and that's something many of us have learned to avoid. It's often easier to stay distracted than to confront how lonely, sad, or painful life can feel when there's nothing around to numb us.

We live in a world full of distractions, where numbing has become the norm.

Asking someone to *name* the reasons behind their numbness can stir up deep discomfort. It can unearth old traumas, painful memories, or long-buried beliefs about our worth. That's why I don't recommend diving into this process without the right tools in place.

Instead, I encourage people to take their time, build skills in mindfulness and reparenting first.

You'll need to know how to regulate your mind, body, and spirit when emotions become too overwhelming. These practices help create an internal safety net. They make space for your truth to surface gently, without it flooding your system.

I can't emphasize this enough:
Go slow.
Build capacity.
Prevent unnecessary suffering by honoring your pace.

Healing isn't a race; it's a return to yourself.

Once you've discovered the underlying need, the next step is just as important: *tending to it*, not just once, but over time.

One moment of attention likely won't be enough. Needs, especially long-neglected ones, often require repeated care, new strategies, and ongoing support. You may need to revisit this need again and again, exploring different ways to meet it.

Sometimes, addressing an unmet need might even prompt bigger changes, like seeking professional treatment, adjusting your daily routines, or reshaping your social support system.

Ask yourself:
What would help me meet this need sustainably?

Do I need more time with trusted people?
Could deepening my current relationships help?
Would joining a group or building new social connections bring nourishment?

Whatever path you choose, the goal is to create more moments of *meaningful connection*, with others, and with yourself. That's how we replace a harmful visual diet with something truly nourishing.

Treat Yo Self

I had to include this. If you're familiar with *Parks and Recreation*, you probably remember Donna Meagle and Tom Haverford, played by Retta and Aziz Ansari, coining the iconic phrase: "Treat yo self." Their tradition? Setting aside a day to splurge on luxury, indulgence, and joy, whatever made them feel rewarded and alive.

In Season 4, Episode 4 ("Pawnee Rangers"), they invite Ben Wyatt (played by Adam Scott) to join. At first, Ben struggles, he just doesn't vibe with spa days or lavish shopping. But eventually, he finds his *own* version of self-care: buying a movie-quality Batman costume. And when he steps out wearing it, you can see how meaningful that moment is for him. It's silly, personal, and totally perfect *for him*.

This is a great model for digital wellness.
If you're cutting back on screen time or shaking up your visual diet, emotional backlash is normal. Frustration, boredom, even grief can arise. So, schedule in something just for you.

Treating yourself doesn't have to look like luxury, it can look like *play*, *rest*, or simply *nerding out* over something you love. Each of us has our own flavor of joy and discovering it can be a long process, but one that's deeply rewarding.

Since not everyone can afford lavish experiences, many of the most meaningful treats are simple, affordable, or even free.

- A favorite snack
- A thrifted treasure
- A midday nap
- Time spent doing something just for you, without guilt

Sometimes it's the smallest pleasures that bring the biggest sense of comfort or delight.

Whether it's cozy, quirky, quiet, or loud, find what feels like a treat for you. And then, give yourself permission to savor it.

The Power of Boredom

Boredom is often treated like an enemy, something to be avoided at all costs. In our modern world, screens offer endless ways to escape it: mobile games, photos, social media, videos, and constant communication. We've been conditioned to view boredom as something negative, something to *stave off*.

But boredom holds hidden power.

When we allow ourselves to sit in boredom, something remarkable can happen. The brain begins to wander, explore, and connect ideas in new ways. Boredom creates space for creativity, reflection, and self-discovery. It opens the door to imaginative thinking, problem-solving, and even insight into our emotions or desires.

In fact, research shows that boredom isn't just a lack of stimulation, it's a cue. A signal that it's time to shift, explore, or create.

However, boredom is also a double-edged sword. For some, especially those with trauma histories or dysregulated nervous systems, boredom can feel intolerable. It may bring discomfort or distress that's hard to sit with. That's why mindfulness, emotional regulation, and reparenting skills can help individuals stay present with boredom and explore it safely.

Boredom as a Gateway to Growth

According to David M. Ndetei, Pascalyne Nyamai, and Victoria Mutiso (2023), viewing boredom through an African cultural lens reveals its powerful potential. Rather than being seen only as a negative state, boredom can actually be a *catalyst* for creativity, exploration, and reflection.

They write:

> "Boredom can be a source of creativity and innovation. When bored, our brains are more likely to wander and explore new ideas or perspectives. Boredom can encourage us to seek new experiences, discover interests, or challenge ourselves to learn and grow. It also gives us a chance to reflect on our values, goals, and aspirations, and can motivate us to make meaningful changes."

Supporting this view, researchers Elpidorou (2018) and van Tilburg & Igou (2019) found that moderate levels of boredom are linked to higher levels of creative thinking and problem-solving.

In other words, boredom can offer a rare opportunity: a quiet nudge to pause, reflect, and reimagine who we are and where we want to go.

The Dark Side of Boredom

While boredom can be a source of creativity and growth, for many, it feels so unbearable that they would rather suffer harm than sit with it. In one shocking study, 67% of men and 25% of women chose to give themselves electric shocks rather than be alone with their thoughts (Wilson et al., 2014).

Boredom isn't just uncomfortable; it can have serious consequences for mental and physical health. Research shows that boredom can:

- Lower motivation and productivity
- Increase symptoms of anxiety and depression (LePera, 2011)
- Disrupt pleasure and goal-oriented behavior
- Trigger anxious or intrusive thoughts
- Contribute to substance use as a form of escape (Weybright et al., 2015; Biolcati et al., 2016)
- Lead to impulsive or risky behaviors, especially in adolescents (Lee et al., 2007; Mercer-Lynn et al., 2013)

In one study, boredom proneness was a strong predictor of binge drinking among teens (Biolcati et al., 2016), reinforcing the idea that boredom isn't just about being idle, it's about managing inner discomfort.

Should We Avoid Boredom at All Costs?

Absolutely not. In fact, boredom can be profoundly beneficial, especially for those who have built healthy relationships both inwardly and outwardly. When we're connected to ourselves (*interoception*) and our surroundings (*exteroception*), boredom doesn't feel like a threat, it becomes a gateway to creativity, reflection, and deeper awareness.

When we have meaningful interpersonal relationships (like family and friends) and a healthy inner life, boredom becomes less overwhelming. Instead, it becomes an invitation to pause, explore, and shift focus.

Dr. Ashok Seshadri, a psychiatrist and psychologist at the Mayo Clinic (2022), offers the following tips to help navigate boredom in healthy, constructive ways:

Tips to Manage Boredom with Intention

- **Balance activity and rest**
  A mix of stimulating activities, social time, and rest helps recharge the brain. Rest is not wasted time; it fuels creative thinking.

- **Try something new**
  Start a hobby, join a group, read a new book, cook a fresh recipe, or play a game. Novelty can spark joy and redirect restless energy.

- **Get outdoors**
  Nature is one of the most powerful (and free!) therapies for boredom. Time outside soothes the nervous system and boosts creativity.

- **Practice curiosity and kindness**
  Being genuinely curious about others, and showing kindness, pulls us out of ourselves and into meaningful connection with the world.

- **Embrace reminiscing, but keep it balanced**
  Reflecting on the past is natural, especially as we age. But if it becomes all-consuming, gently redirect attention toward present or future goals.

A Gentle Reminder Before You Embrace Boredom

Please don't jump headfirst into long stretches of boredom if you're not ready. If you're still learning how to feel your feelings, if emotions feel unsafe, or if you're managing another compulsive relationship (like substances, gambling, or screen use), take it slow.

No one expects you to sit in silence or meditate for 15 minutes on your first try. That's not the goal.

Instead, try easing into stillness moment by moment. Build your tolerance for quiet spaces and emotional presence gradually. This is about building safety, not pushing yourself into overwhelm.

Pro tip from a client:
If the word "boredom" feels heavy or loaded, change it.
One client of mine reframed it as "contentment."
Instead of saying "I'm bored," they paused to feel content, at ease in their mind, body, and spirit.

As all distractions fade, you're left with the fullness of your experience. That can feel like a lot, but with care, it can also feel like coming home to yourself.

Spirituality: Connecting Beyond the Human Experience

Spirituality can be a powerful tool for healing and grounding, especially when we're seeking something larger than ourselves. It doesn't have to mean religion. Just as mindfulness is one part of meditation, spirituality is one facet of religion, not the whole.

For many people, spirituality is deeply personal and unique, like a thumbprint. It can take the form of belief in the universe, nature, ancestors, spirits, astrology, God, or multiple gods. It doesn't always involve worship (though it can), but it does invite us to connect with something beyond the limitations of our physical selves.

When we engage with spirituality, we step outside the everyday worries of our minds and bodies. We touch something sacred, something that gives us peace, meaning, or a sense of belonging.

The Benefits of Spirituality

Research shows that spirituality can significantly support both mental and physical health.

- One meta-analysis of 32,000 patients found that those with stronger spiritual or religious beliefs had better physical health outcomes.
  — *Jim et al., 2015*

- Spirituality has been linked to greater life satisfaction, improved emotional adjustment, and higher quality of life.
  — *Jones et al., 2016*

- Another review found that people living with cardiovascular disease who had spiritual practices reported better quality of life.
  — *Abu et al., 2018*

As Roberto and colleagues (2020) conclude, spirituality can be a healing force, both psychologically and physically.

Religion & Well-Being: Protective Life Factors

As documented in *The Handbook of Religion and Health* (Koenig et al., 2001), religious involvement has been linked to numerous positive outcomes related to mental, emotional, and social well-being. Research shows that individuals who engage in religious practices may experience:

- Greater overall well-being, happiness, and life satisfaction
- Increased hope and optimism
- A stronger sense of purpose and meaning in life
- Higher self-esteem
- Better bereavement adjustment during times of loss
- Greater social support and reduced loneliness
- Lower rates of depression and faster recovery from depressive episodes

- Decreased suicidal ideation and more protective attitudes toward suicide
- Lower levels of anxiety
- Fewer signs of psychosis and psychotic tendencies
- Reduced alcohol and drug use or misuse
- Lower levels of delinquent or criminal behavior
- Higher rates of marital stability

Potential Negative Impacts of Religion on Mental Health

While religion and spirituality often provide meaningful support and structure, they can also contribute to psychological and emotional challenges under certain conditions. Koenig et al. (2001) and Cook & Powell (2022) identify three key categories of concern:

1. Increased Stress Due to Religious Devotion

- Excessive focus on religious obligations may lead to:
    - Neglect of responsibilities (family, work, health)
    - Social isolation
    - Strain in personal relationships
- Rigid interpretations of doctrine can sometimes fuel:
    - Abusive or controlling behavior
    - Spiritual guilt or fear-based compliance

2. Cognitive and Emotional Impairments

- Rigid or legalistic religious thought may result in:
    - Excessive guilt or shame
    - Stigmatization of those with different beliefs or lifestyles
    - Judgmental attitudes and exclusion
    - Concealment or rationalization of unhealthy behaviors (e.g., abuse, self-harm)

3. Impaired Coping and Help-Seeking

- Over-reliance on faith-based solutions may:
    - Prevent individuals from seeking appropriate mental health care

- o   Lead to delays in medical or psychiatric treatment
- o   Encourage the belief that suffering must be endured rather than treated

Important Note: These outcomes are not inherent to religion itself but often result from misapplication, misuse of spiritual authority, or harmful interpretations of religious texts.

Gratitude: Rewiring the Brain for Positivity

Gratitude isn't just a feel-good buzzword; it's a powerful mental health tool that can help shift our mindset from stress and scarcity to abundance and opportunity.

The Power of Practice

According to *positive psychology research* (TED Talk, 2012), writing down three new things you're grateful for each day for 21 days can:

- Improve mood
- Train your brain to scan for the positive
- Build long-term optimism

What Gets in the Way?

Certain traits can *block* the benefits of gratitude:

- Envy and materialism focus on what we *lack*, not what we have.
- Narcissism centers attention inward, leaving little room for appreciation.
- Cynicism rejects sincerity, making it hard to connect with gratitude.

A 2017 study found that narcissism, cynicism, and materialism/envy were significantly associated with lower gratitude levels over time. (*Solom, Watkins, McCurrach, & Scheibe, 2017; cited in Allen, 2018*)

The Gratitude Blocker: Cynicism

While gratitude can be a powerful practice for rewiring the brain and improving well-being, cynicism can act as a major barrier.

> *"While it makes sense that people would be more cognitively aware of challenges they have had to overcome, this also means that they may discount the benefits and resources that have allowed good things to happen in their lives and thus make them less likely to feel grateful for these benefits."*
> — Allen, 2018

Why Cynicism Gets in the Way

Cynicism tends to:

- Focus on what's lacking or broken
- Devalue or dismiss support, luck, or resources
- Emphasize struggle over growth
- Block the emotional impact of small wins or kindness

When we're stuck in a cynical mindset, we may acknowledge the hard work we've done, but disregard the people, moments, or conditions that helped us along the way. This limits our ability to feel and express gratitude.

Gratitude, Cynicism, and the BIPOC Experience

Many of us are affected by our visual diets, which can feed patterns of narcissism, envy, materialism, and cynicism, especially when we're constantly exposed to curated, idealized images of success or worth. For BIPOC individuals, cynicism can be particularly complex to unpack.

Systemic oppression, racial injustice, and generational trauma often create an emotional armor, where cynicism becomes a tool for survival. In these contexts, feeling or expressing gratitude can sometimes feel dismissive of real pain or injustice.

Yet for many BIPOC communities, spirituality and religion offer a powerful counterbalance. Faith practices can provide space for reflection, connection, and gratitude even in the face of hardship.

> *"According to the Pew Research Center (2015), 79% of Black Americans identify as Christian, and an additional 3% identify with other non-Christian faiths. Latino Americans predominately identify as Christian (80%), with Catholics comprising the majority of this population (55%; Pew Research Center, 2013)."*
> — Nguyen, 2020

Spiritual frameworks often ground gratitude not in denial of struggle, but in the resilience of community, faith, and cultural heritage. In this way, gratitude becomes a form of resistance, reflection, and healing.

In a world driven by visuals, many individuals, especially young people, can fall prey to harmful behaviors and mindsets that disconnect them from their well-being. When a young, female-bodied child grows up surrounded by narrow beauty standards and a lack of diverse representation, she may begin to internalize messages about how her body *should* look. This can lead to envy, body shame, and self-destructive behaviors that undermine her health and self-worth.

At the same time, others who are consistently fed the idea that they are entitled to more than basic human dignity, or that they must always *have more* to be enough, can develop a distorted sense of self. This can result in narcissistic tendencies or me-centered behaviors that harm both their relationships and their communities.

Our visual environment matters. Without intention, it can shape our values, distort our self-image, and reinforce harmful narratives about who we should be, and what we're worth.

Gratitude can help push back against the rising tide of narcissism and other harmful social patterns explored in the next chapter. According to researchers Jans-Beken et al. (2019), gratitude is closely linked to stronger social well-being, healthier relationships, and more prosocial behavior.

> *"The vast majority of research shows measures of emotional well-being to increase with small to moderate positive effects in response to a variety of gratitude interventions... The majority of the reviewed studies, both prospective and experimental, suggest that gratitude plays a role in maintaining healthy relationships, as well as in facilitating the formation of new ones. Gratitude increases prosocial behavior, not just toward the benefactor, but also toward others. This may set in motion an upward spiral of positive social behavior, reflected in improved relationship-related emotions, thoughts, and behaviors beneficial for all partners involved." — Jans-Beken et al., 2019*

In short, gratitude not only helps us feel better, it also helps us connect better.

Gratitude doesn't just benefit our personal well-being, it can improve how we treat each other in shared spaces, including the workplace. Research by Locklear et al. at the University of Central Florida (2021) explored the effects of a 10-day gratitude journaling intervention designed to reduce workplace incivility, gossip, and ostracism.

> *"The intervention decreased mistreatment (as reported by coworkers) by enhancing self-control resources. We also found that the effects of the intervention were stronger for individuals who perceive higher norms for gratitude in their workplace. The findings support the resource-building nature of gratitude interventions and demonstrate that a gratitude intervention is one effective way to decrease interpersonal mistreatment in organizations." — Locklear et al., 2021*

Gratitude builds inner resources, and when practiced regularly, it can reshape workplace culture for the better.

Gratitude Isn't a Cure-All

While gratitude can offer meaningful benefits, like strengthening relationships, boosting prosocial behavior, and improving workplace dynamics, it's important to understand its limits. For individuals struggling with more severe emotional distress, gratitude alone may not be enough.

As researchers Cregg & Cheavens (2021) explain:

> *"Our results suggest the effects of gratitude interventions on symptoms of depression and anxiety are relatively modest. Therefore, we recommend individuals seeking to reduce symptoms of depression and anxiety engage in interventions with stronger evidence of efficacy for these symptoms."*

In other words, while gratitude can be a powerful tool for emotional regulation and connection, it may not be sufficient on its own for managing deeper mental health challenges. For those experiencing clinical depression or anxiety, additional evidence-based treatments, like therapy, medication, or mindfulness-based interventions, may be more effective and appropriate.

Gratitude as a Supportive, Not Standalone, Intervention

Gratitude is a powerful tool for fostering interpersonal and intrapersonal growth. It can improve relationships, increase self-awareness, and even reduce negative behaviors like gossip or incivility. But it's not a magic fix.

Gratitude alone won't erase the daily stressors that weigh us down or the persistent anxiety that many live with. It doesn't eliminate systemic challenges, nor does it cure depression. Instead, it's best used as part of a broader healing strategy.

When practiced in collaboration with other supportive interventions, like mindfulness, therapy, creative expression, or social connection, gratitude becomes a meaningful way to shift attention away from harmful visual content and toward what truly sustains us.

Additional Recommendations for Digital Wellbeing

(Adapted from Pandya & Lodha, 2021)

1. Switch to Voice
   Use audio calls or voice notes instead of constant texting or video chats to reduce screen fatigue and eye strain.

2. Avoid "Phubbing"
   Be present. Put your phone down when you're with others and engage in real-time connection.

3. Make Small Talk
   Simple conversations, like asking how someone's day was, build real connection and give your brain a break from screens.

4. Reconnect Intentionally
   Stay in touch with loved ones regularly through meaningful check-ins, not just likes or emojis.

5. Use Tech for Good
   Try apps that promote mindfulness, gratitude, journaling, or digital detoxing to create intentional screen use.

6. Set Time Boundaries
   Separate work and personal time. Avoid answering emails or texts outside of work hours whenever possible.

7. Take Tech-Free Breaks
   Unplug occasionally. Even short breaks can reset your nervous system and boost mental clarity.

Further, meta-analysis incorporated in the research below:

Recommendations	Description	Reference
Digital detox or digital well-being	It entails taking in-between breaks and adopting healthier digital practices to curtail digital toxicity	Stavridou et al. (2021)
Intermittent social fasting	Avoiding using social media while working so that one gets the break for extra screen time. Eventually contributing to a good balance of work-life	Qin et al. (2020)
Promoting physical activities	In times where screen time is unavoidable, one can be digitally online and engage in physical activities through platforms such as online physical activity classes, online yoga, exercise mobile applications, or video games that have a physical activity component	Colley et al. (2020), Qin et al. (2020), Rolland et al. (2020), World Health Organization, (2020), Stavridou et al. (2021)

Recommendations	Description	Reference
Staying active during screen time	Have an active time in front of the screen time where one could stretch or do exercises while sitting or standing to cut the stagnancy of long screen time	World Health Organization (2020)
Family digital detox or Digital free family time	Ensuring free time off digital devices as a family can not only reinforce staying away from digital technology but can also build healthier spaces for family members to interact. Making meal times with family is one of the easier ways to practice this	American Academy of Child and Adolescent Psychiatry (2020), Winther and Byrne (2020)
Modelled digital well-being	There is a need for responsible adults to model digital wellbeing for the younger pupil so that it can be inculcated as a habit. Observational learning is impactful	American Academy of Child and Adolescent Psychiatry (2020)
Set screen time limits	Fix a total number of hours of screen time and consciously try to reduce this by cutting down half-an-hour each day. Alternatively, track your time spent online, the activities you indulge in as well as your feelings after a few hours of screen-time	Ramirez et al. (2011), Amin et al. (2020), Colley et al. (2020)
Dumb phones	Using phones that enable voice calls only and do not allow the extra distractions of smartphones. This can help reduce social anxiety and better engagement with people around	Harvard Pilgrim HealthCare (2021)

Recommendations	Description	Reference
Use of digital platforms for promoting healthy lifestyles and seeking mental health care services	Digital platforms can be used to promote healthy habits and learning opportunities such as learning dance, language, attending yoga sessions and educational webinars. There is also access to mental health information as well as consultation (reliable resources like that of medical bodies, UN or WHO should be considered)	Lodha and De Sousa (2020), World Health Organization (2020)
Use alternatives to screen	Choose activities such as walking, cycling, dancing, reading print books, magazines, etc that can be done without a digital screen	Harvard Pilgrim HealthCare (2021)

(Pandya & Lodha, 2021)

Summary

- Reparenting involves focusing on secure attachment.
    - Those who have the ability to name and tolerate emotions.
    - Individuals who can attend to other's feelings without making it about themselves.
    - People who model healthy and secure relationships.
        - Maintaining the ability to trust others and maintain relationships (friendships, partners, work, etc.)
- Create a diverse group of individuals who present with these characteristics. (a handful or more).
- Review what your unmet needs are, mindfully and nonjudgmentally before reparenting them with your secure resources.
- Continue practicing mindfulness throughout the process as you sit with ancillary sensations and thoughts.

Part V: Potential Options for a Successful Digital Detox and Sustainable Goals

Chapter Thirty-Three

"It's not what you look at that matters, it's what you see." -Henry David Thoreau

Ideal Visual Diets

When we consider what an ideal visual diet might offer, we must look at what most mainstream media often omits. Instead of a narrow window into perfection, model-type faces, athletic bodies, and luxurious lifestyles, an ideal visual diet reflects the true breadth and richness of the human experience.

It includes:

- People of all **races, body types, genders, abilities, and ages**
- Stories of **resilience, rest, complexity, and creativity**
- Content that encourages **healing, connection, and self-compassion**
- Media that affirms, rather than erases, our **humanity and wholeness**

These are just a few foundational examples. An ideal visual diet isn't a rigid checklist, it's a **personal, evolving practice** of asking:

Does this nourish me or deplete me? Do I feel more seen, or more small, after consuming this?

Again, the goal of this book isn't to tell you exactly what to consume. It's to guide those who feel **stuck in a visual cycle** that no longer serves them. For anyone who's fallen prey to an overstimulating, narrow, or harmful visual diet, there is another way.

You can reclaim your sight.
You can choose what you feed your eyes, and, in doing so, how you feed your soul.

Take, Lizzie Velásquez, a motivational speaker, activist, author, and YouTuber. She was born with an extremely rare congenital disease called Marfanoid–progeroid–lipodystrophy syndrome that, among other symptoms, prevents her from accumulating body fat and gaining weight (Huffington Post, 2015). Her appearance gave way to extreme bullying and emotional duress.

While giving a Ted Talk TexX Austin Women, Lizzie stated at 17, she had a shocking experience while viewing a YouTube video stating she was the world's ugliest woman, (Texx Austin Women, 2013)

> *"I had no idea when I opened that video that it would make all the confidence I had go back down to nonexistent -- to dirt. Maybe I should take myself out of this world. If so, many people are saying it, then maybe they're right. But there was a little voice in the back of my head that kept telling me not to listen. My parents said we have to learn to forgive them because we don't know what's going on in their lives."*

Influenced heavily by the terrible comments on the video, Lizzie contemplated suicide.

Lizzie worked tirelessly to direct her energies toward anti-bullying. Writing three books specifying her life story and a documentary, titled "A Brave Heart: The Lizzie Velasquez Story," Lizzie continues to work to not let the difficult and problematic words of hurtful individuals harm others as well as herself.

Laverne Cox, an actor, advocate for the LGBTQ+ community, and the first openly transgender person nominated for an Emmy (Orange is the New Black) has had a life fraught with pain and triumph. Assigned male at birth, raised by a single mother, never knowing her biofather, internalizing fear and shame attributed to her femininity due to bullying and harassment from peers and cruel comments from adults, in addition to hearing anti-LGBTQ+ messages from church, Laverne attempted suicide at age 11 (Rothberg, E, 2022).

Laverne's life story has many intersectionalities with other trans folk who struggle to be accepted by friends, families and peers. The internalized shame and phobia related to their gender identity, sexuality, or identity outside heteronormative experience, can fester within these individuals to inevitable suicidal thoughts. Fortunately, for her, she was able to get the support she needed after her suicide attempt and achieve success, albeit through many struggles. According to Naran, et al, (2018),

> *"Internalized transphobia refers to a negative self-concept about gender identity even if it remains unconscious. These feelings can include self-hate or shame. Internalized transphobia increases the likelihood that someone will attempt or complete suicide. Those with a racial or ethnic minority status or less education incur a greater risk."*

Speaking at Indiana University in 2015, Laverne stated:

> *"Not everybody who is born feels that their gender identity is in alignment with what they're assigned at birth...if someone needs to express their gender in a way that is different, that is okay...That's what people need to understand, that it's okay and that if you are uncomfortable with it, then you need to look at yourself."*

When we begin to understand how public figures shape our visual diets, we can take back control over the content we consume and the frequency with which we engage it.

Visual stimuli can deeply affect how we see ourselves. In fact, consistent exposure to idealized images of beauty or perfection can hinder self-worth and distort personal identity.

At worst, a visual diet saturated with these ideals can lead to serious harm, including anxiety, depression, disordered eating, and even suicidal ideation. That's why this work matters. It's not just about turning off a screen, it's about protecting our inner world from external pressures that can erode our mental and emotional well-being.

With all the examples in this book about how visual media can impact our sense of self, you might be wondering: what does a balanced visual diet actually look like? It's a fair question, and not always easy to answer, given how much content is out there. Still, it's possible.

Start by seeking out media that reflects a wide range of human experiences. Look for stories that include people of different backgrounds, ethnic origins, body types, ages, and economic realities, not just celebrities, influencers, or those who've been filtered through the lens of extreme wealth and privilege.

One personal example I enjoy is the Netflix show *I Think You Should Leave* with Tim Robinson. Besides its awkward, absurd humor, what stood out to me was the diversity of people on screen. The show features a broad mix of demographics, different ages, ethnic origins, body types, and sexualities represented through a variety of uncomfortable and ridiculous situations. That diversity made the humor feel more grounded, even in its chaos.

Other shows like *The Office* or *Superstore* also offer glimpses of more every day, relatable characters. But even these examples, despite being more inclusive, can still deliver intense visual and sensory stimulation, quick cuts, loud scenes, or emotionally charged moments, that affect our nervous system.

That's why moderation is key. Just like with food, a healthy visual diet includes variety and balance. It shouldn't rely on one type of content, or one type of emotional or sensory experience. Visual diets may include:

- Calming or neutral media
- Real-world representations (not idealized or overly filtered)
- Media that teaches skills or fosters curiosity
- And importantly: time away from screens altogether

A truly nourishing visual diet allows space for reflection, growth, and emotional regulation, on and off the screen.

What an Ideal Visual Diet Includes

An ideal visual diet is like a healthy meal plan, but for your mind. It's not about perfection. It's about balance, awareness, and intention in what we consume through our screens and surroundings.

Below are some essential ingredients of a nourishing visual diet:

1. Diverse Representation

Choose media that reflects the real world, across ethnic origin, gender, age, size, ability, culture, and identity.

- See people who *look like you* and *don't*.
- Prioritize creators from BIPOC, LGBTQ+, neurodivergent, and disabled communities.
- Representation isn't a trend, it's a human right.

2. Emotionally Regulating Content

Your nervous system is watching too.

- Seek media that promotes calm, joy, curiosity, and inspiration.
- Limit content that fuels fear, outrage, comparison, or despair.
- Ask: *How do I feel after watching this?*

3. Stories That Empower, Not Deplete

Media can shape your sense of agency.

- Choose stories of resilience, healing, and hope, even if they include hardship.
- Watch for repeated narratives of trauma, violence, or powerlessness without growth or justice.

4. Mindful Algorithms

Curate your feed the way you curate your meals.

- Mute, unfollow, and hide content that triggers shame, anxiety, or addictive scrolling.
- Follow educators, artists, activists, and creators who uplift and inform.

5. Slow, Deep Content

Not all content needs to be 15 seconds long.

- Make space for long-form storytelling, books, documentaries, and quiet moments.
- Let your brain *digest* what you see.

6. Nature, Art, and Stillness

Screens aren't your only source of visual input.

- Spend time with trees, sky, movement, and stillness.
- Let your eyes rest. Let your mind wander. Let boredom bloom.

Reminder: The goal isn't to eliminate all "junk food" content, it's to build a visual life where nourishment outweighs depletion, and where what you consume helps you remember who you are.

Building a Personalized Visual Diet

Your visual diet is everything you consume with your eyes, social media, news, shows, videos, memes, advertisements, even the way your environment is set up. Like the food you eat, what you look at every day can either nourish you or deplete you.

We don't always realize how much power our visual inputs have until we pause and reflect. So, building a personalized visual diet isn't just about consuming "positive vibes" all the time, it's about curating content that aligns with your values, meets your needs, and supports your well-being.

How to Start Building Yours

1. Audit Your Current Visual Diet

Start by asking yourself:

- What do I look at every day? (Apps, shows, videos, pages, ads)
- How does it make me feel? (Energized, numb, anxious, inspired, less-than?)

- Does this content help me grow, connect, or feel more like myself?
- Am I looking at this because I want to, or because it's a habit, escape, or algorithmic trap?

Awareness is step one. You can't change what you don't name.

2. Define What Nourishment Looks Like for *You*

This will look different for everyone. You might crave content that:

- **Affirms your identity** (ethnic origin, gender, body size, neurodivergence, etc.)
- **Inspires growth** (creativity, purpose, healing, learning)
- **Models healthy relationships** (boundaries, connection, joy)
- **Feels beautiful or meaningful** (nature, spirituality, art, movement)
- **Centers justice** (activism, truth-telling, equity)

Ask: *What kinds of content make me feel more whole, not more broken?*

3. Unfollow, Mute, and Replace

If something regularly drains you, shames you, or fuels compulsive scrolling, it doesn't deserve your time.
Replace it with:

- Pages that showcase diverse bodies and lives
- Art, poetry, and soundscapes that calm or ground you
- Educators and creators who inspire, not just perform
- Stories of resilience, beauty, and joy from people who look like you, or open your eyes to other's lived truths

You don't owe your attention to anyone or anything that harms your peace.

4. Add Texture and Slow Visuals

Not everything has to be fast, bright, or loud. Include content that gives your nervous system a break:

- Nature footage (rain, forests, oceans)
- Documentaries with slow pacing
- Calming art or crafting videos
- Slow walks through unfamiliar cities or museums (YouTube can be great for this)

This helps train your brain to seek calm instead of constant stimulation.

5. Revisit and Rework Often

A visual diet isn't static. You change, so your inputs should too. Set a reminder once a month or quarter to:

- Re-audit your content
- Let go of what no longer serves you
- Reconnect with what you need now

This is not about being perfect, it's about staying intentional.

Reminder:

Your visual diet isn't about pretending everything is okay.
It's about choosing what you feed your brain when the world makes it easy to go numb.

You deserve to be visually nourished.
You deserve to see yourself reflected in content that heals, inspires, and affirms you.
You deserve to be reminded that you belong here.

The Narcissism Wave

Perceived empathy seems to be declining in the United States. Psychologists Jean Twenge and W. Keith Campbell (2009) describe this shift as part of a larger cultural trend they call *"the narcissism epidemic."* They write:

> *"Understanding the narcissism epidemic is important because its long-term consequences are destructive to society. American culture's focus on self-admiration has caused a flight from reality to the land of grandiose fantasy.*
>
> *We have phony rich people (with interest-only mortgages and piles of debt), phony beauty (with plastic surgery and cosmetic procedures), phony athletes (with performance-enhancing drugs), phony celebrities (via reality TV and YouTube), phony genius students (with grade inflation), a phony national economy (with $11*

> *trillion of government debt...and phony friends (with the social networking explosion).*
>
> *All this fantasy might feel good, but, unfortunately, reality always wins."*

Twenge and Campbell argue that this growing obsession with self-image and external validation can disconnect us from reality, and from each other. When empathy takes a backseat to self-promotion, social trust weakens, and meaningful connection becomes harder to build.

Emotional Egocentric Bias & the Narcissism Trap

Emotional egocentric bias (EEG) can distort how we view others, and ourselves. When combined with a poor visual diet, this bias can weaken empathy and reinforce the belief that our thoughts, feelings, and needs are more important than anyone else's. Over time, this can reshape our sense of identity around inflated self-importance or grandiosity.

Narcissism thrives in this imbalance. It encourages us to value external validation, likes, status, appearance, over internal truth and connection. But when our sense of self is built on unstable externals, it becomes fragile. We become reactive and ungrounded, especially in times of crisis or misfortune, when those externals fail us.

Twenge and Campbell (2009) describe narcissism this way:

> *"Narcissism includes arrogance, conceit, vanity, grandiosity, and self-centeredness. A narcissist is full of herself, has a big head, is a blowhard, loves the sound of his own voice, or is a legend in her own mind.*
>
> *A lot of self-absorbed jerks are narcissists, but so are a lot of smooth, superficially charming, and charismatic people (who, unfortunately, are later revealed to be self-centered and dishonest). A narcissist has an overinflated view of his own abilities, similar to the kitten that sees himself as a lion.... Narcissists are not just confident, they're overconfident. In short, narcissists admire themselves too much."*

The issue isn't confidence, it's disconnection. Narcissism disconnects us from the reality of others' experiences and reinforces the idea that we are only as valuable as we appear.

There's a major delineation needed between narcissist behavior and narcissistic personality disorder as defined by the DSM-5 (2013), indicated with five or more criteria:

- "Has a grandiose sense of self-importance (e.g., exaggerates achievements and talents, expects to be recognized as superior without commensurate achievements).
- Is preoccupied with fantasies of unlimited success, power, brilliance, beauty, or ideal love.
- Believes that they are "special" and unique and can only be understood by, or should associate with, other special or high-status people (or institutions).
- Requires excessive admiration.
- Has a sense of entitlement (i.e., takes advantage of others to achieve his or her own ends).
- Lacks empathy is unwilling to recognize or identify with the feelings and needs of others.
- Is often envious of others or believes that others are envious of him or her.
- Shows arrogant, haughty behaviors or attitudes."
Note: The special emphasis of the DSM-5 versus the ICD-11 codes are due to the specificity related to narcissistic personality disorder in the DSM-5.

Narcissism Isn't a Life Sentence

Experiencing narcissistic traits doesn't mean you're broken or beyond growth. It's not a death sentence. Our brains are remarkably adaptable, even well into adulthood. Thanks to neuroplasticity, we have the ability to form new pathways, unlearn harmful behaviors, and rewire how we relate to ourselves and others.

This means that self-absorbed patterns, emotional disconnection, or inflated self-image can be shifted with intention, compassion, and effort. Through practices like mindfulness, empathy-building, reparenting, and meaningful connection, we can challenge old narratives and build a more grounded, relational sense of self.

Healing from narcissistic tendencies is possible, and it starts with awareness, not shame.

Empathy as a Tool

Engaging with visual media through the lens of empathy can be a powerful tool for self-regulation. As you watch a movie, show, or online content, pause and ask yourself: *What might this person be feeling right now?* Tuning into the emotional world of a character or real-life subject invites your nervous system to connect, rather than disconnect.

If you notice your body responding with discomfort, tightness, tension, sadness, or unease, that's a signal. It means the media is activating something deeper, resonating with your subconscious mind. Rather than ignoring those sensations, explore them gently. This kind of mindful empathy builds emotional awareness, self-reflection, and resilience.

Avoiding Egocentric Thinking

To avoid falling into egocentric thinking, it's helpful to ask: *Is there another way to see this thought or belief?* Children often see the world through an egocentric lens because their brains are still developing. But adults can also get stuck in these narrow patterns without realizing it.

Emotional egocentric bias can show up in many ways, like being overly self-focused, impatient, judgmental, or believing our way of thinking is better than others'. These habits can harm our relationships and limit how we connect with people who see the world differently. As Dr. Daniel Siegel and Dr. Tina Payne Bryson explain, egocentric thinking can lead to disconnection, rigidity, and difficulty embracing new ideas or perspectives.

We don't have to look far to see the effects of egocentric thinking in the real world. Since the breakdown of bipartisan relationships, political tensions have grown more intense, especially after 2020. This book isn't about politics, but it's hard to ignore how polarized things have become. One possible reason? The way we consume visual media.

With more people feeling bored or disconnected, especially during times of isolation, many turned to screens for connection. But instead of finding diverse perspectives, many became stuck in echo chambers. These digital spaces often reinforce only one way of thinking, making it harder to feel empathy for people with different views. Without empathy, it becomes easier to judge or reject others rather than trying to understand where they're coming from.

The anterior insular cortex is a key part of the brain that helps us feel empathy. When we watch others experience emotions, this area lights up, helping us imagine how they might be feeling. But if we stay focused only on ourselves and ignore the feelings of others, this part of the brain may not get used as much. As more people continue living in a "me-first" mindset, it could take even longer to shift away from the current rise in narcissistic behaviors.

Increasing Empathy

There are simple ways to grow empathy, but it helps to start with mindfulness skills first, especially lovingkindness meditation and mindfulness of thoughts and emotions.

Every day, we're flooded with visual information. But when we make the effort to understand someone else's life, feelings, or struggles, we start seeing others as part of a shared community.

This doesn't mean just feeling for people who agree with us. True empathy means stepping into someone else's shoes, even when it feels uncomfortable. It means asking:

> *"Why might they think or feel that way?"*
> *"What experiences have shaped their view of the world?"*

Empathy helps us build bridges, not walls.

Start Slowly

If empathy doesn't come naturally to you, begin by taking small steps. Use the content you already engage with as practice. Even better, try it in everyday life.

When you notice yourself feeling frustrated, say, in line at the register, at the airport, in traffic, or on a crowded sidewalk, pause and take a moment to shift your perspective. Ask yourself:

- Could this person be anxious?
- Are they navigating a disability or physical pain?
- Might they be carrying emotional weight that's affecting how they move through the world?

These simple, mindful moments can help you build the muscle of empathy in real-time. Every time you slow down to consider someone else's experience, you widen your capacity to connect, with others and with yourself.

Now Comes the Sharp Turn

Sometimes, you'll encounter people who seem to be acting with intention, to hurt, to provoke, or to disrupt. That's when the real empathy work begins. Ask yourself: *What kind of pain or unmet need might lead someone to lash out this way?*

It's okay if this brings up strong emotions, anxiety, anger, or frustration. Just notice them. You don't have to fix or suppress those feelings. If sitting with those emotions feels overwhelming, that's a sign to revisit the mindfulness practices we discussed earlier. Strengthen your emotional tolerance before diving deeper.

Also remember: you, too, have had moments where you weren't at your best.
– When have you been slow because of anxiety or physical discomfort?
– When have you cut someone off in traffic or acted out of impatience?
– When have you been ego-driven, reactive, or emotionally flooded?

We've all been there. That shared humanity doesn't excuse harmful behavior, but it helps explain it. And it gives us a path toward understanding, rather than judgment.

A Necessary Boundary

Let's be clear, empathy does *not* mean tolerating hate or bigotry. These experiences cut deeply, harming the very core of who we are. No one should be expected to absorb or excuse that kind of harm.

What we *can* do, however, is look behind the hate where, often, fear is found. Fear drives people to behave in ways that even their closest loved ones may not recognize. This doesn't excuse their actions, but it can help us understand how fear can distort emotions into hate, rage, or cruelty.

Empathy doesn't mean approval. It means recognizing the human tendency to be shaped by our pain and choosing not to let that pain guide our own responses. We all feel fear. But we can choose *not* to let that fear become hate. We can choose to feel, reflect, and respond, rather than react.

Reflection & Discussion: Rebuilding Empathy in a Polarized Visual World

As screen time increases, many people find themselves stuck in digital "echo chambers", spaces where they only see, hear, and engage with people who share their beliefs or values. Over time, this can make it harder to understand or empathize with others who think differently.

Think about the media you consume. Consider how it might shape your perspective or limit it.

Reflection:

1. When was the last time you felt challenged by a different perspective, online or in real life?

2. How did you respond? With curiosity? Defensiveness? Frustration?

3. Do you think the media you watch or scroll through encourages empathy? Why or why not?

4. Have you ever caught yourself judging someone before hearing their full story? What might have helped you respond with more understanding?

Increasing Empathy

There are simple ways to grow empathy, but it helps to start with mindfulness skills—especially **lovingkindness meditation** and **mindfulness of thoughts** and emotions.

Every day, we're flooded with visual information, But when we make the effort to **understand someone else**'s life, feelings, or struggles, we start seeing others as part of a **shared community**.

This doesn't mean just feeling for people who agree with us. True empathy means **stepping into someone else's shoes,** even when it feels uncomfortable.
It means asking:

"Why might they think or feel that way?"
"What experiences have shoped their view of the world?"

Try This:

While watching or reading something today, pause and ask:

- "What might this person be feeling?"

- "What fear, hope, or need could be underneath their reaction?"

- "Is there another way to view this situation?"

These small shifts can build emotional flexibility and reduce emotional egocentricity.

Practice Prompt:

Write or talk about a time when:

- You changed your mind about something after hearing someone else's story.

- You misunderstood someone's actions until you learned more about their background.

- You felt misunderstood and wished someone had asked *you* what was really going on.

Building and Increasing Empathy

Challenge Yourself

- Undertake challenging experiences that push you outside your comfort zone (e.g., learning a new skill, hobby, or foreign language) to develop humility and increase empathy (Andrew Sobel).

- Engage in activities that help you understand different perspectives, such as traveling to new places and cultures (Andrew Sobel).

Practice Active Listening

- Ask open-ended questions and listen attentively to others' responses to understand their feelings and perspectives (Erika Weisz).
- Manage distractions and stay emotionally attuned during conversations to build empathy (David Susman).

Cultivate Self-Compassion

- Practice self-reflection and acknowledge your own emotions and biases to increase self-awareness and empathy (Jamil Zaki).
- Engage in exercises that promote self-compassion, such as imagining a friend coming to you with a problem and how you'd respond (Jamil Zaki).

Explore Similarities

- Focus on shared experiences and similarities rather than differences to build connections and empathy (Van Babel).
- Use storytelling to share your own experiences and connect with others on a deeper level (Roman Krznaric).

Develop Empathy through Practice

- Engage in activities that promote empathy, such as role-playing or imagining yourself in someone else's shoes (Andrew Sobel).
- Use worksheets and exercises to build empathy skills, such as imagining a friend's problem and responding with kindness (Jamil Zaki).

Foster a Growth Mindset

- Believe that empathy can be developed with effort and practice (Erika Weisz).
- Recognize that empathy is a skill that can be built and strengthened over time (Roman Krznaric).

Build Empathy in Relationships

- Practice empathy in your personal and professional relationships by actively listening, asking questions, and showing understanding (David Susman).
- Use empathy to resolve conflicts and improve communication in relationships (Andrew Sobel).

Remember that empathy is a skill that can be developed and strengthened with practice, self-awareness, and a willingness to listen and understand others. (Sobel, 2024) (Abramson, 2021)

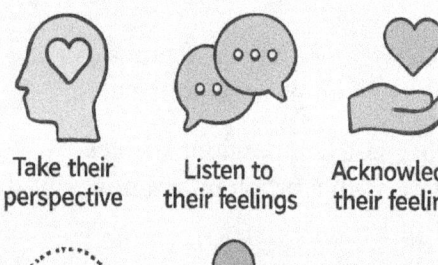

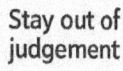

Supporting the Brain Through Empathy and Balance

If we want to increase empathy, not just toward others, but also within ourselves, we have to start by giving our brains what they *actually need* to function well. Let's think of this like Maslow's Hierarchy of Needs. Just like we need food, water, and shelter before we can think about purpose or creativity, our brains also have core needs for mental and emotional health.

Dr. Daniel J. Siegel, alongside Dr. David Rock, created the Healthy Mind Platter, a simple but powerful model that outlines seven daily mental activities that support optimal brain health and well-being.

The Healthy Mind Platter

According to Dr. Siegel, a well-balanced mind requires a mix of the following:

- **Focus Time**
  Deep, goal-oriented concentration helps strengthen neural connections.

- **Playtime**
  Spontaneity and creativity create new and flexible brain pathways.

- **Connecting Time**
  Building relationships with others and with nature activates the brain's relational circuitry.

- **Physical Time**
  Moving our bodies (especially with aerobic activity, when safe) boosts brain health and mood.

- **Time In**
  Quiet, internal reflection, tuning into your thoughts, sensations, and emotions, supports self-awareness and integration.

- **Downtime**
  Letting your mind wander, daydream, or relax helps restore mental energy and encourages creativity.

- **Sleep Time**
  Quality sleep consolidates learning and allows the brain to recover and reset.

By honoring these seven areas, we give our brains the chance to function at their best, emotionally, cognitively, and socially. And when our brain is better supported, *empathy becomes easier*. We begin to respond from a place of presence, not just a reaction.

This is how we begin to change, not just ourselves, but the world around us. One healthy mind at a time.

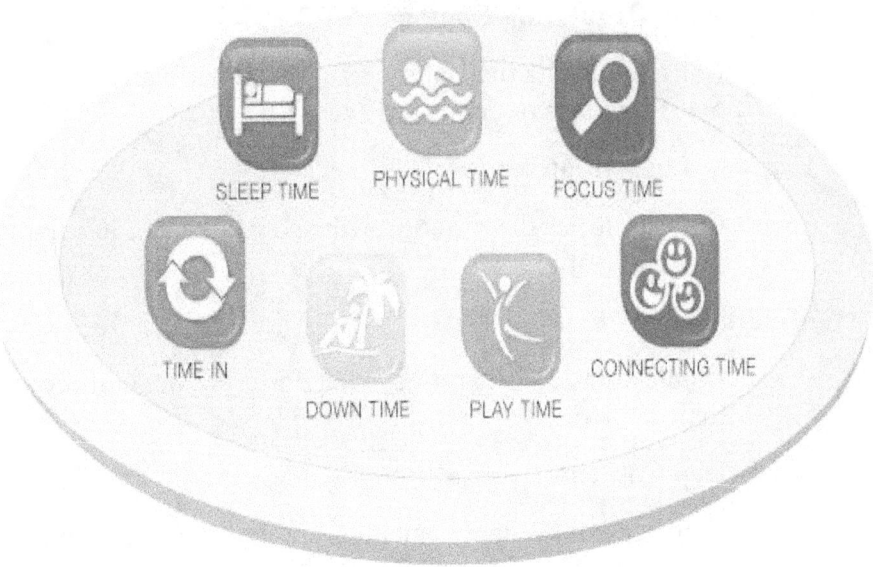

The Healthy Mind Platter, for Optimal Brain Matter

Copyright © 2011 David Rock and Daniel J. Siegel, M.D. All rights reserved.

Summary

Your visual diet, what you consume with your eyes every day, directly impacts your mental health, self-worth, empathy, and social behavior. An ideal visual diet is intentional, diverse, emotionally nourishing, and grounding. It's about feeding your soul, not your insecurities.

What Is an Ideal Visual Diet?

- Not limited to entertainment; includes ads, shows, news, memes, social media, and even your physical environment.
- Should support self-acceptance, curiosity, healing, and empathy.
- It is personal, not prescriptive.

Ingredients of a Healthy Visual Diet

1. **Diverse Representation**
   - Include BIPOC, LGBTQ+, neurodivergent, disabled, and varied body types and ages.

2. **Emotionally Regulating Content**
   - Consume media that calms or uplifts rather than overstimulates or depresses.

3. **Empowering Narratives**
   - Choose stories that offer growth and justice, not just trauma or victimization.

4. **Mindful Algorithms**
   - Curate your feeds to reflect what nurtures you. Unfollow toxic content.

5. **Slow, Deep Content**
   - Embrace books, documentaries, and long-form content. Give your mind time to digest.

6. **Nature, Art, and Stillness**
   - Don't rely solely on screens. Spend time offline, in stillness, and outdoors.

How to Build Your Own Visual Diet

1. **Audit** your current habits and emotional responses.

2. **Define** what nourishment looks like for *you* (beauty, justice, calm, joy).

3. **Unfollow and Replace** content that harms or drains you.

4. **Add Texture** (slow visuals, quiet videos, nature footage).

5. **Revisit Often**, your needs evolve, and so should your media.

The Risks of a Poor Visual Diet

- Reinforces perfectionism, comparison, numbness, and disconnection.
- Can cause depression, anxiety, low self-worth, eating disorders, and even suicidal thoughts.
- Fuels the narcissism epidemic (Twenge & Campbell), where external validation overshadows internal worth and erodes empathy.

Narcissism and Visual Culture

- Encourages a "me-first" mindset, grandiosity, and self-obsession.
- Linked to emotional egocentric bias, which blocks empathy and deep connection.
- Narcissistic traits ≠ a fixed identity. Thanks to neuroplasticity, healing is possible through mindfulness, empathy, and reflection.

Empathy as an Antidote

- Ask during media consumption: *"What might this person be feeling?"*
- Practice in daily life: in traffic, stores, tense moments, pause and consider others' inner experiences.
- Empathy ≠ tolerance for abuse. Set boundaries while remaining human.

Support the Brain, Support Empathy

Dr. Daniel Siegel's Healthy Mind Platter outlines 7 elements for brain wellness:

1. **Focus Time**
2. **Playtime**
3. **Connecting Time**
4. **Physical Time**

5. **Time In** (internal reflection)
6. **Downtime**
7. **Sleep Time**

Balanced brain = stronger empathy, resilience, and clarity.

Final Reminders

- Visual nourishment isn't about avoiding "bad" content entirely.
- It's about intention, awareness, and balance.
- What you feed your eyes *shapes* how you see yourself, others, and the world.
- You deserve media that reflects your humanity, not just your highlights or your pain.

Chapter Thirty-Four

"Perfectly balanced, like all things should be." -Thanos

Maintaining a Healthy Balance with Your Visual Diet Going Forward
Think of your visual diet like a pie chart, it includes a mix of perspectives, experiences, and content that shape how you feel and function. Just because these elements have the *potential* to support well-being doesn't mean they automatically will. Each area of your life, mental, emotional, physical, spiritual, requires intention and care in order to maintain inner balance.

Let's begin with the basics:
Your energy levels directly affect your ability to make thoughtful, adaptive choices. When you're tired, hungry, overwhelmed, or emotionally dysregulated, it becomes much harder to stay mindful and make healthy decisions, especially around screen use and visual consumption.

Prioritize Sleep Hygiene
We've already explored how a poor visual diet, especially close to bedtime, can lead to emotional and physiological arousal. This overstimulation disrupts your circadian rhythm and makes it harder to fall and stay asleep.

The Centers for Disease Control and Prevention (CDC, 2016) defines *sleep hygiene* as a set of healthy habits that support restful sleep. Their key recommendations include:

- Going to bed and waking up at the same time every day, even on weekends or days off
- Creating a dark, quiet, and cool environment for sleep
- Keeping electronics with bright screens out of the bedroom
- Avoiding large meals, caffeine, and alcohol before bedtime
- Engaging in regular physical activity during the day to naturally support sleep

Good sleep is foundational. When you're well-rested, you're more likely to make thoughtful choices, about your time, your screen use, and your overall well-being.

But Let's Be Real...
Every time we talk about screen-free bedrooms, it tends to hit a nerve, especially for folks who rely on their phones for alarms, fall asleep to shows, or just enjoy winding down with a screen. For many, the idea of not using electronics in bed feels unrealistic or even foreign.

You're not alone if this feels like a big ask.

Phones are often our clocks, our emergency contacts, and, let's be honest, our comfort. But the truth is, our nervous systems don't fully shut down when we're scrolling, watching, or doomscrolling late at night. Even passive screen use can keep the brain alert and dysregulated.

Here's the good news:
There *are* workarounds.

For example, you can:

- **Use a separate alarm clock** instead of your phone
- **Keep your phone across the room**, so it's nearby for emergencies but not within reach
- **Try blue light filters or "night mode"** if cutting screen time completely isn't feasible. Also, for best results, change to grayscale.
- **Use a time-lock device** (like a phone safe) to help you stick to boundaries
- **Shift your wind-down routine** to include something screen-free, like reading, stretching, journaling, or a calming audio meditation

Start where you are, and notice what shifts when your brain gets the rest it deserves.

Balancing Screen Use with Safety & Sleep

It's important to acknowledge that screen-free recommendations don't always work for everyone. For individuals who live alone or have a history of trauma, keeping a phone nearby can be a crucial part of feeling safe. That's valid, and it matters. Luckily, there are practical, harm-reduction strategies to support both safety and sleep:

Use Warm Light Settings:
Most smartphones now offer features like *Night Shift*, *Night Light*, or *Blue Light Filter*. These shift your screen's tone to warmer colors, which are less likely to stimulate your brain or interfere with your natural sleep cycle. Again, grayscale is best.

Activate "Do Not Disturb" or Bedtime Modes:
These settings allow you to mute notifications while still receiving emergency calls from trusted contacts. That way, your sleep isn't disrupted by alerts, but your safety isn't compromised either.

Use App-Limiting Tools:
There are many free and paid apps that can help you limit access to certain

apps after a set time. Some options even allow you to lock specific apps, graying them out during your chosen "digital wind-down" period.

Explore Your App Store:
Search for keywords like *digital wellness*, *screen time blocker*, *focus timer*, or *habit tracker* to find tools that suit your needs and lifestyle.

This is all about building a nighttime routine that feels both *safe* and *restorative*. If full screen elimination isn't realistic, small shifts, like reducing blue light or muting late-night notifications, can still make a meaningful difference for your brain and body.

Why Consistent Sleep/Wake Times Matter

What is one of the biggest hurdles people face when building healthy sleep habits? The idea of waking up and going to bed at the *same* time every day, including weekends or days off.

Let's be honest, weekends come with social plans, late-night shows, and rare chances to unwind. It's totally fine to enjoy that. Life is about balance. But here's the key:

If your sleep schedule becomes unpredictable, your body loses its rhythm. Your brain doesn't know when to rest or when to be alert. That throws off everything from mood to memory to decision-making.

When your body *can predict* sleep, it starts preparing ahead of time:

- Hormones like melatonin are released
- Core body temperature adjusts
- Brain waves begin to slow down

But if sleep happens *randomly*, your body can't do that prep work. You wake up foggy, reactive, and more likely to make poor choices, especially around food, technology, and emotional regulation.

Try this:
Aim for a **90-minute window** of consistency. If you normally go to sleep at 10:30pm on weekdays, try to stay within 9:30pm–11:00pm on weekends. That small buffer can help maintain rhythm *without* feeling rigid.

Have a Plan for When You're Struggling
Like any harm reduction approach, it's important to plan for the tough moments. Think ahead about what you'll do when you're feeling tired, overwhelmed, or emotionally off. I use the word "recovery" here because the brain reacts strongly to visual media, sometimes in ways that can become unhealthy.

That said, not all technology or visual content is harmful. It can be helpful and even necessary. The key is to recognize when your relationship with it starts to feel off. As discussed earlier in this book, many factors, like stress, trauma, or lack of support, can make someone more vulnerable to unhealthy media use.

Why Consistent Sleep/Wake Times Matter

One of the biggest hurdles people face when building healthy sleep habits?

The idea of waking up and going to bed at the **same time** every day–including weekends.

Let's be honest—weekends come with social plans, late-night shows, and rare chances to unwind. It's totally fine to enjoy that:

 If your sleep schedule becomes unpredictable, your body loses its rhythm.

- Hormones like melatonin are released
- Core body temperature adjusts

But if sleep happens randomly, your body can't do that prep work. You wake up foggy reactive-and more likely to make poor choices—especially around food, technology, and emotional regulation.

 Try this:
Aim for a 90–minute window of consistency. If you normally go to sleep at 10:30 pm on weekdays, try to stay within 9:30 pm–

Plan for Hard Moments

When we're tired, sick, or overwhelmed, we often fall back into old habits. Even one small challenge can feel huge when we're stuck in a cycle of compulsive behavior. Our brains can start making excuses, like:

"Just one hour won't hurt."
"It's only a few minutes."

But one "slip" can quickly turn into, *"I already messed up, so I may as well keep going."* This is why it's important to prepare for these moments ahead of time, with compassion, not shame.

15 Common Cognitive Distortions

Adapted from PsychCentral (2022)

When we feel vulnerable or are trying to change harmful habits, our brains may play tricks on us. These thinking traps, also known as cognitive distortions, can keep us stuck in unhealthy cycles. Awareness is the first step toward freedom.

1. Filtering

Focusing only on the negative parts of a situation, ignoring the positive.

2. Polarized Thinking (All-or-Nothing Thinking)

Seeing things as either completely good or completely bad, with no middle ground.

3. Overgeneralization

Believing that one bad event means it will *always* happen again.

4. Discounting the Positive

Downplaying or dismissing the good things that happen.

5. Jumping to Conclusions

Making negative assumptions without proof (mind reading or predicting the future).

6. Catastrophizing

Expecting the worst-case scenario in every situation.

7. Personalization

Blaming yourself for things outside your control, or taking things too personally.

8. Control Fallacies

Believing you either have *no* control, or *total* control, over everything.

9. Fallacy of Fairness

Believing everything *should* be fair according to your own standards.

10. Blaming

Holding others responsible for how you feel.

11. Should Statements

Rigid rules for how you or others *should* behave, leading to guilt or frustration.

12. Emotional Reasoning

Thinking that feelings = facts. ("I feel anxious, so something bad must be happening.")

13. Fallacy of Change

Believing others will change if you push them hard enough.

14. Global Labeling

Using one negative event to define yourself or others entirely. ("I failed, so I'm a failure.")

15. Always Being Right

Believing your opinion is fact, and needing to win every argument, no matter what.

Understanding Thinking Traps in Your Digital Reset or Recovery

Cognitive distortions, also known as thinking traps, can sneak in and sabotage your progress, especially during moments of vulnerability, fatigue, or emotional overwhelm.

These distorted thoughts may whisper things like:

- *"I already slipped, might as well keep going."*
- *"Everyone else has better self-control than me."*
- *"I should be better by now."*
- *"I'll never change."*

Pause. These aren't truths, they're traps. Recognizing them is the first step in breaking their power.

Why It Matters

When trying to reduce screen use or reset your digital habits, your brain may resist. Cognitive distortions make it harder to stick with new choices by:

- Justifying the old behavior
- Undermining your confidence
- Making setbacks feel like failure

CBT Tip: Get Ahead of the Distortion

You don't have to fall into the trap. Try this:

1. Catch It.
Notice when your thoughts feel rigid, extreme, or guilt-inducing.

2. Check It.
Ask: Is this thought 100% true? Am I seeing all the evidence?

3. Change It.
Reframe the thought with self-compassion and logic.

"I slipped, but I'm still trying, and that counts."
"This is a pattern I'm learning to change, not a moral failure."

Mindfulness of Thoughts: Building Objectivity and Curiosity

Mindfulness of thoughts is a foundational skill in building emotional regulation and self-awareness. It helps us step back and observe our thoughts, rather than becoming entangled in them or assuming they reflect absolute truths.

This can be practiced through:

- **Meditation**
- **Journaling or introspection**
- **Noticing thoughts in the moment**

The goal is not to stop thinking, but to *shift how we relate* to our thoughts. One of the most transformative shifts is this:

Thoughts are not facts. They are messengers.

They are the byproducts of our lived experience, shaped by upbringing, culture, traumas, successes, and yes, even our visual diet. The content we absorb from media, screens, and online environments influences the stories our mind tells us about the world and ourselves.

A strategy that has helped many is approaching thoughts with gentle curiosity rather than resistance. When a thought arises, instead of fighting it, ask:

- *"Where might this thought come from?"*
- *"Is this thought helpful or harmful?"*
- *"What part of me believes this, and does it still serve me?"*

By adopting this observer mindset, we shift from judgment to *understanding.* And from there, we can begin to rewrite the narratives we've inherited.

Mindfulness of thoughts is not about control, it's about connection. A connection to how our mind has tried to protect us, and how we can gently guide it toward healing and clarity.

A Nonjudgmental Approach to Thoughts

To work with our thoughts effectively, we must begin with a nonjudgmental mindset. This means noticing a thought without attaching to it or labelling ourselves because of it. A thought is just that, a fleeting internal experience shaped by our histories, environments, and emotional states.

Mindfulness can help us observe our thoughts like horses galloping across a distant plain, or cars passing by on a road. We don't need to chase them. We can simply witness them.

It's also important to remember: our thoughts do not define us. Having a rageful or intrusive thought does not make you a bad person; it simply means you're experiencing strong emotion. The same way a storm passes, so too can our thoughts, if we don't cling to or identify with them.

Practicing this gentle separation, between *what we think* and *who we are*, is one of the most powerful steps in self-compassion, healing, and sustainable behavior change.

Sifting Through the Veil

Sometimes, our thoughts can feel like a thick veil, heavy with cognitive distortions that cloud our ability to see clearly. But just as this book suggests, our goal is to find homeostasis, to soften the intensity of emotional arousal stirred up by those thoughts.

Much like diluting a strong liquid reduces its potency, learning to recognize and sift through distorted thinking can reduce the overwhelming power those thoughts hold over us.

This doesn't mean we ignore or deny what we feel. It means we give ourselves space to see more clearly. We gently stir in perspective, compassion, and truth until the heat subsides, and we can face our inner world with steadiness.

Reframing and Reality Testing: Tools for Clarity

Identifying the positive aspects of a situation can help distill the impact of cognitive distortions. Reframing is a powerful strategy, it shifts our perspective, helping to loosen the grip of negative thoughts and open up space for more balanced, hopeful interpretations.

Another essential tool is reality testing. This practice involves stepping back and checking the facts before accepting a thought as truth. As *PsychCentral* (2022) suggests:

> *"Before concluding, consider asking, investigating, and questioning yourself and others to ensure you have as many facts as possible. If you can, make an extra effort to believe these facts."*

When we combine reframing with reality testing, we create a mental environment that is less reactive and more responsive. One rooted in self-awareness rather than automatic assumptions. Over time, this allows us to challenge distorted thoughts and move toward greater emotional balance.

Private Browsers: A Simple Step Toward Digital Boundaries

One effective way to reduce the overload of targeted ads and personalized content is by using a private browser. Private or "incognito" modes help prevent tracking cookies from storing your browsing history, reducing how much of your digital behavior is monitored.

According to Norton (2023):

> *"Tracking cookies are mostly used for marketing and advertising purposes. They store a list of sites you've visited, the pages you viewed, the products you clicked on, and even purchases you made. Their goal is to gather information that makes it easier for companies to sell you goods and services. Tracking cookies also capture your IP address and geographic location to tailor ads, like concerts near you, local store sales, or event tickets."*

By limiting this tracking, private browsing gives you back a measure of control over what enters your visual diet. It's not a complete shield, but it's a strong start in helping you reclaim a more intentional and less manipulated online experience.

Secure Browsing with VPNs and Private Browsers

NordVPN, a leading name in online security, explains what makes a browser safe:

> *"Privacy and security are the two most important factors in a secure browser. A good browser shouldn't collect your data or share it with third parties. It should also protect you from harmful ads and online threats. While ease of use matters, it should never come at the cost of your privacy."*
> (NordVPN, 2023)

They also recommend several secure browsers that prioritize your privacy, including:

- **Brave**
- **Firefox**
- **Tor Browser**
- **Epic**
- **Vivaldi**
- **Waterfox**
- **Safari**
- **Chromium**
- **Opera**
- **Microsoft Edge**
- **Puffin**
- **FreeNet**
- **DuckDuckGo**

These browsers help limit tracking, reduce unwanted ads, and make your online experience safer. Choosing one that fits your needs is a simple step toward protecting your attention and your visual diet.

Minimalist & Dumb Phones: Tools for Digital Wellness

Why Use One?

- Reduce screen time and compulsive use.
- Minimize distractions and protect mental health.

- Focus on essential functions without the constant pull of apps and notifications.

Common Features

- Essentials only: calling, texting, GPS, music, calendar, alarm, and sometimes email.
- No social media, app stores, or web browsing (or very limited).
- Improved battery life and less digital noise.
- Less eye strain due to minimal screen use.

Secure Browsers
Comparison of Privacy Features

Browser	Anti-tracking	Ad blocker	Fingerprinting protection
Brave	✓	✓	✓
Firefox	✓	✓	✓
Tor Browser	✓	✓	✓
Epic	✓	✓	✓
Vivaldi	✓	✓	✓
Waterfox	✓	✓	
Safari		✓	
Chromium		✓	
Opera		✓	
Microsoft Edge			✓
Chrome			✓
Puffin			✓
FreeNet			✓

Popular Options

- The Light Phone II – Prioritizes intentional use with calling, texting, alarms, music, and limited tools like directions or notes.
- Punkt. MP02 – Sleek and stylish, focused on voice, text, and encryption features. No browser or apps.
- The Boring Phone – Preloaded with only useful basics, no app store or browser.
- Nokia 8110 or 6300 (modern reboots) – Physical keyboard, basic smart features, some models allow very limited apps like WhatsApp or GPS.
- Mudita Pure – Elegant design with e-ink screen, EMF reduction, meditation timer, and minimalist tools.

Bonus Tip: Some minimalist phones double as weekend detox devices, a great option for screen resets without ditching connectivity altogether.

Turn Your Smartphone into a Dumbphone

Instead of buying a new device, you can turn your current smartphone into a dumb phone by following these steps.

Step-by-Step Guide

1. **Switch to Greyscale (Black & White)**
   - Reduces dopamine-driven visual stimulation.
   - Found in Accessibility settings (on both iOS and Android).

2. **Delete Non-Essential Apps**
   - Keep only tools (e.g. calendar, maps, camera, weather).
   - Remove social media, games, news, and shopping apps.

3. **Disable Notifications**
   - Turn off all but essential alerts (calls, texts, alarms).
   - Removes the constant pressure to check your phone.

4. **Use Content & Privacy Restrictions**
   - Set app limits or block entire app categories.
   - On iOS: Use "Screen Time" > App Limits / Downtime.
   - On Android: Use "Digital Wellbeing" or "Family Link."

5. **Turn Off Wi-Fi & Mobile Data**
    - Go offline unless you need GPS or a quick task.
    - Bonus: use Airplane Mode + Wi-Fi selectively.

For Those Needing More Structure:

- **Use App Blockers or Lockers** (e.g. *Lock Me Out, Freedom, Stay Focused*).
    - Some apps include monetary penalties to deter cheating.
- **Use a dumbphone on weekends** or for certain hours.
- **Hand your phone to someone you trust** during high-risk times.

Video Game Addiction Support Groups

If you or someone you care about is struggling with video game overuse or addiction, you don't have to go through it alone. There are accessible, free support options available, many of which offer virtual meetings, chat-based support, and even specialized groups for parents.

Available Resources:

- GamingAddictsAnonymous.org – A 12-step support group offering online meetings, resources, and a welcoming community.
- GameQuitters.com – Offers practical guidance, courses, and a forum to help gamers reduce or quit video games.
- Local mental health clinics or addiction recovery centers – Many offer regional support groups tailored to screen and gaming addiction.
- Signal or WhatsApp chat groups – Some community members organize encrypted peer support chats for privacy and ongoing encouragement.

Emergency and Helpline Support:

- Substance Abuse and Mental Health Services Administration (SAMHSA) Helpline
  24/7 free and confidential help: 1-800-662-HELP (4357)
- Veterans Crisis Line
  Dial 988, then press 1, or text 838255

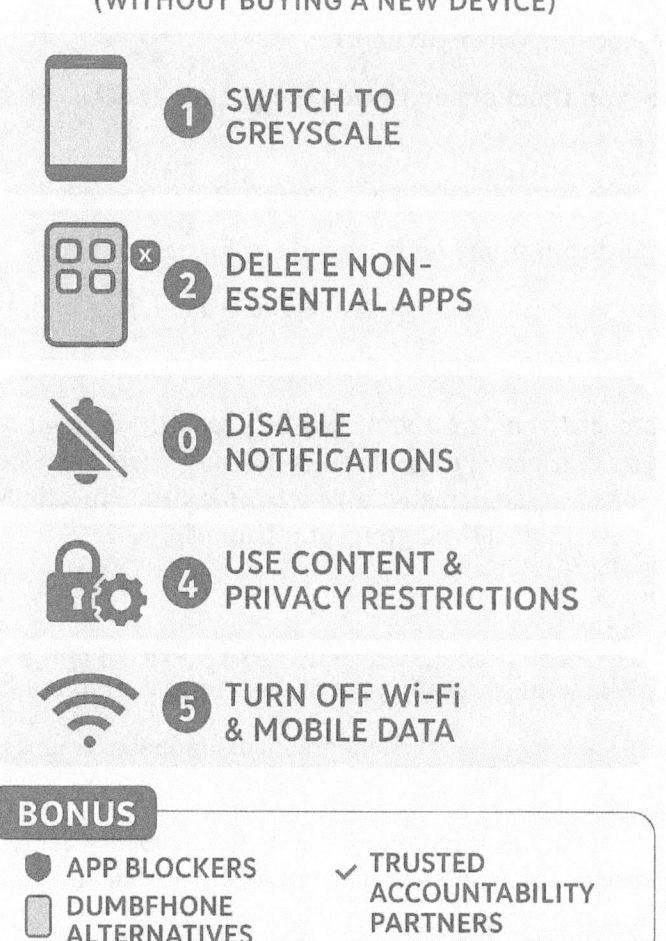

Summary

Sleep Hygiene & Visual Media

- Poor visual diet before bed (e.g. doomscrolling) disrupts sleep and emotional regulation.
- **CDC sleep hygiene tips**:
    - Keep consistent sleep/wake times
    - Avoid screens, caffeine, and large meals before bed
    - Create a cool, dark, quiet space for rest

o   Be physically active during the day

Workarounds if screen-free sleep is unrealistic:

- Use a blue light filter/night mode
- Set alarms across the room
- Use "Do Not Disturb" mode
- Replace screen time with reading, journaling, or audio meditation

Planning for Struggles & Cognitive Distortions

When overwhelmed, tired, or dysregulated, people often relapse into compulsive screen habits. Prepare for these moments with self-compassion, not shame.

15 Common Thinking Traps: Examples include filtering, catastrophizing, emotional reasoning, "should" statements, personalization, and always needing to be right.

CBT Tip:
Catch the distortion, **Check** the facts, and **Change** your response with kindness.

Mindfulness of Thoughts

- Thoughts aren't facts, they're messages based on experience, culture, trauma, and media.
- Observe your thoughts like passing cars or distant horses.
- Separate who you *are* from what you *think*.
- Use curiosity, not judgment: "Where is this coming from? Does it serve me?"

Tools for Reframing & Reality Testing

- **Reframe** distorted thoughts with truth and compassion.
- **Reality Test** by asking: *"Is this 100% true? What's the evidence?"*

These skills help reduce emotional reactivity and increase self-awareness.

Digital Boundaries & Browsing Tools

Private Browsers (e.g. Incognito mode) help block tracking cookies and targeted ads.

Secure Browsers (recommended by NordVPN) include:

- Brave, Firefox, Tor, Epic, Safari, Vivaldi, Waterfox, Chromium, Opera, etc.

Minimalist Phones & Dumbphone Alternatives

Benefits:

- Reduce screen time, distractions, and visual overload
- Improve focus and mental clarity

Options:

- Light Phone II, Punkt MP02, Mudita Pure, Boring Phone, Nokia 8110/6300

DIY Smartphone Dumbdown:

1. Switch to grayscale
2. Delete non-essential apps
3. Turn off notifications
4. Use app blockers/limits
5. Disable mobile data or use Airplane Mode

Support for Video Game Addiction

Free, accessible digital wellness groups:

- **GamingAddictsAnonymous.org**
- **GameQuitters.com**
- **Local clinics or peer support chats on Signal/WhatsApp**

Helplines:

- SAMHSA: 1-800-662-HELP
- Veterans Crisis Line: Dial 988, then press 1 or text 838255

Final Message:

Maintaining a healthy visual diet is about *intention, self-awareness, and consistency*. Equip yourself with tools, compassion, and structure to support your recovery and wellness.

Key Takeaways

Digital Wellness:

- Goal setting
    - Start with a more realistic goal (1 hour, 1 day, 2 days, etc.) Then increase until 7 days have passed. Don't worry if you don't make it to 7. Relapses are part of the process.
- Maintenance of dopamine
    - Plan for another dopaminergic activity (physical activity, mindfulness, creative experiences, socialization, etc.)
- Accountability
- Plan for obstacles
- Manage your environment
- Maintain proper diet and sleep hygiene to ensure your mind and body are equipped to handle the natural stressors of the crashes or urges.
- Grayscale
- Digital Blockers

Putting plan into action/Recommendations

<u>Smartphone Plan</u>

Accountability

Ask for accountability from trusted individuals in your community. Having others attend to your needs can help foster a stronger association with your desire to diminish screen usage.

Attend to your inner needs

Get in front of your personal needs and concerns, which may arise during your diminished screen usage. While surfing the urge and attending to boredom, folks may want to incorporate mindfulness, reparenting and connecting to the younger parts of themselves to maintain their well-being.

Turn off notifications

If your visual compulsion is with smartphones, the first step I would recommend is turning off notifications for all apps and delete the app which is taking all of your time. Make it inconvenient for you to log in via a browser.

Grayscale

Change your phone display to grayscale. Doing so will prevent the color light spectrum and its dopaminergic response. This will bore the brain and allow individuals to turn away from their screens and toward the outside world. NOTE: If your **IMMEDIATE** outside world is horrific, then please reconsider this. However, if you have pockets of positive experiences, then please proceed.

Blockers

Use app or browser blockers during specific and historic problematic times.

Community Support

Seek the help of support groups of folks dealing with similar concerns or professionals to attend to what may come up for folks during their stressful moments. (If accessibility is present)

Consider a complete and total isolative experience

If all of these steps are not helping. Consider others taking your device, blocking your phone from problematic apps while still maintaining its functionality for GPS, phone, or text for safety and go somewhere where distractions from other screens is available. (Vacation, camping, the home of a loved one during the first few days or week while you can reimage your world around you.)

Video games

Slow the trickle

Stop for a few hours or a day at a time. Because the neurological aspect of video game addiction is so nuanced, individuals may want to slowly titrate away from the dopaminergic relationship that video games give us.

Work towards 30 days of cessation

Keep moving steadily to increase your days of cessation. Make a plan for it. Whether it be a 6-month plan of steadily decreasing use to get closer to a the full 30 days, a year, or a bit longer, utilize the SMART goal format.

Grayscale

Gray scale can help produce boredom in folks enthralled in an extensive relationship with games and gaming in general. It isn't impossible to shift your television or monitor to grayscale. Is it inconvenient? Absolutely. However, as I have found, even if you change your settings to grayscale, the console you utilize may change it back to saturated color. So, you may have to play with this to make it work for you.

Give up your console

For the brave and bold, give up your console to trusted folks. Not permanently, but just to hold as you start a dopamine reset. You may think you have the upper hand if you have accomplished a day or two here and there. However, many folks can struggle with their urge to use a week or two weeks in. Each one of us (video game users) is susceptible to the siren call of video games. It may not take long to feel immersed in it.

Plan when you are at your worst

This ties into the previous step of a plan. Folks may be sick, tired, stressed, etc. When we are at our worst, our ability to tap into our willpower diminishes. The more we are not in our calm and rational mind, the more pitfalls are ahead of us. That may also mean trying to reason with us to engage in environments that are bound to pull us into video game use. *After all, why not go to a Round 1, Dave and Busters, an arcade modeled around the 80's and 90's or something similar to have a drink or bite to eat?* That type of slippery rationalization enables us to put ourselves in harm's way and potentially in a position to use.

Lean heavily into your community

Many gamers have online gaming friends that live in different communities. Lean onto the folks you feel you can trust and who are supportive. If you have these people in your community, try to connect with them to help foster growth and well-being. If you have folks who solely engage with you via gaming, then try to engage with them with other formats. Perhaps that means pulling out language learning software so you can compete against each other, like Duolingo or others.

Television

Grayscale

Here comes the grayscale again. Use the same principles as before

Keep your phone display on while you watch

Keep your phone display on. Not watching your phone, but having it on to track how much time you are devoting to watching whatever content you are engaged in.

Watch something educational

I'm not talking about thrilling documentaries which work in the same line as true crime. I mean something that is specific and teaching individuals to develop a new skill. Sadly for many, this doesn't mean cooking or baking reality tv shows or drag races. While there are some educational components to them, the overall theme is to entertain not educate.

Sleep Timers

If you are concerned about binging a whole season of something, maybe place a sleep timer on your TV. That sets the expectation to move your body and cut the cord of dopaminergic experiences. When your TV turns off. Use that as a prompt to move your body as you can. If that means rolling, walking, or just stretching as you can, do it. Get your body away from its sedentary state to increase blood flow.

Mindfulness of your body

Pay close attention to how your body is reacting to what you are watching. Turn your attention away from the screen from time to time and tune inward. Your body may not be as relaxed as you think. If you have a smartwatch or other device that identifies your heart rate or blood pressure, alternate your attention to how what you are watching is affecting you. This is called biofeedback. If it is emotionally arousing you from your resting state (make sure to take a baseline of this before the program starts. Ideally, in the morning. Once you have direct information related to your body at rest, you can make better choices toward what you're visually absorbing.

Appendix

DIGITAL HYGIENE TOOLKIT

Simple actions to reduce your digital footprint, protect your data, and reciaim agency in the digital ecosystem.

1. **Audit Your Data Presense**
   Use tools like **Mine. Jumbo.** or **Privacy Bee** to scan your email inbox and identify companies to request data deletion, or limit declecive — constrategly—Be *withis driow* ther oun consent.

2. **Lock Down Your Browser**
   Use privacy-focused browsers like **Firefox** (with strict tracking protection) or **Brave**, install extension like **uBlock Origin, Privacy Badger** or **DuckDucGo Privacy Essentials** to block t

3. **Use Alternative Search Engines**
   Switchn to DuckDuckGo, Startpage, or Ecosia—search engines that do not track you or store your search

4. **Be Skeptical of "Free" Services**
   If you're nAт paving for a product, you're likely the broduct. Be sure to review what permissions you want to delete ite erased it.

3. **Use Alternative Search Engines**
   Switchh to DuckDuckGo, Startpage, or Ecosia— search engines that do not track or store your search history.

5. **Take Control of Your Devices**
   Disable location tracking, ad tracking, and background app refresh where not essential, regularly update your privacy settings on iCS/Android and within each app.

6. **Strengthen Password Hygiene**
   Use a password manager like **Bitwarden** or **IPassword** to create unique passwords for every site.

7. **Be Skeptical of "Free" Services**
   If you not paying for a product—you're likely the product. Warns of free apps that collect excessivel dat. even if they seem harmless.

Digital hygiene isn't a one-time fix--it's a long-term habit. The more. conscious we are about what we click, share, and agree to, the more power we regain over our digital identity.

Digital Resistance Toolkit

Practical strategies for combating misinformation and reclaiming the narrative

1 Support and Elevate Trusted Messengers
- Follow and amplifying creators, educators, and organizaations provide accurate, culturally relevant information
- Share their work within your networks, especiall<(ally on platforms where misinformation spreads

2 Create Visual Counter-Narratives
- Use visual storytelling to share llived experiences, community data, and culturally grounded knowledge
- Infographics, reels, memes, and short—form viideos to translate complex truths into accesssible oentent
- Tools like Canva, Adobe Express, or Infogram

3 Practice and Teach Visual Literacy
- Learn to "read between the pixels", understanding how framing, filters, and edits influence perception
- Host workshops (virtually or "in-person) to focus on collective learning—
  — focusing on collective learning—not shame

4 Leverage Mutual Aid Channels
- Use community WhatsApp groups, group texts, or neighborhood Facebook pages as rapid-resporise hubs for accurace
- Respond quickly and compassionately, focusing on collectivie ⁽⁾ on shaming instead

5 Disrupt the Aigorithm — Intentionally
- Diversify your feeds (following vioces that hallenge your perspective and expand your worldview
- Report misinformation and disinformation when you see it

BUILDING IMMUNITY TO MISINFORMATION
COMMUNITY POWER & PRACTICAL TOOLS

Given the deep sense of connection and shared responsibility, that exists within BIPOC communities, misinformation often spreads faster and farther than it might elsewhere. But these same networks that allow harmful content to flourish can also be mobilized to resist it.

Fortunately, researchers and community leaders have identified evidence-based practices to help BIPOC communities protect themselves and ano ahother.

COMMUNITY-CENTERED STRATEGIES FOR FIGHTING MISINFORMATION
(Adapted from Lee et., 2023)

Include Multilingual Support
- Translate materials into o spoken community languages
- Collaborate with local speakers for culturally ele-veant examples. including ethnic media, live captions for trusted information.sources identified *by the community* (e.g. Univisio's El Detector)

Prebunk False Claims
Prebunking in inoculatinng communities by leaching them about misinformation before they encounter It
- Explain hg how *disinformation* campaigns specifically target communities of color.
- Host interactive Q&As b culturally allgned export (e.g. Black doctors discussing vaccine myths.

TOOLS TO IDENTIFY BIAS AND FACT-CHECK INFORMATION

Reliable Fact-Checking Websites:
- Snopes – Fact/edoqoc
- PolitiFact – Lead
- Stories – Truth or Fition
- Emergent.info
- NPR – Fact Check

Heipful Tools and Apps
- Settle I f *(by PolitiFact)*
- Fake *News* Alert – Chrome Extension

For Bias Detection and Media Literacy
- Ground News
- Rand org's – Truth Decay

FINAL THOUGHTS

Misinformation isn't just a pplitical or media issue – it's a social issue, a racial justice issue, and a public nealth issue. But community rolds power.

By sharing accurate information in languages that resonate, by identifying and

Self-Assessment: Am I in a Media-Driven Rage Cycle?

Use this tool to check-in with yourself, Answer honestly:

1. After consuming news or social media, do I feel more aguated than before?
   ☐ Never ☐ Sometimes ☐ Often ☐ Always

2. Do I find myself venting or ranting often after viewing content?
   ☐ Never ☐ Sometimes ☐ Often ☐ Always

3. Have I getten into arguments online or in person after consuming media?
   ☐ No ☐ Occasionally Frequently Constantly

4. Do I consume media in search of confirmation that "Im right" or that othets are araing?"
   ☐ Not at all ☐ A little ☐ A iot ☐ Always

5. Do I feel compeiled to "stay updated" even when I know it's tuirting my mental state?
   ☐ No ☐ Occasionally Frequently Yes, every day

6. Have people close to me mentioned that I seem more in igible of intenso lately?
   ☐ No ☐ Once or liance ☐ Yes, more then once ☐ Yes arep-

If you anoiwwelt "Cherr s,. "Timay-10 mont their thure questiors are may for nach and age igher sray. Dont umeld promett- renereribes e ship and coned placidor

Breakdown: How Visual Media Fuels Emotional Dysregulation

Our nervous system isn't built for constant activation. Visual media, especially news and social platforms, flood us with stimuli engineered to grab attention—and keep us emotionally hooked.

Here's how the rage cycle gets fueled, neurologically:

1. Trigger → Amygdala Hijack

When a story, image, or video evokes fear or anger, the amygdala (our brain's emotional processing center) takes over. Logic and nuance get sidelined by urgency and instinct.

2. Dopamine → Attention Loop

Outrageous content—especially when it's framed with "breaking news," flashing visuals, or dramatic music—releases dopamine, creating a reward loop. You keep scrolling or watching, not because it makes you feel good, but because your brain is chasing emotional resolution.

3. Cortisol Overload

Chronic exposure to upsetting visual content leads to cortisol (stress hormone) buildup. Elevated cortisol over time can result in irritability, anxiety, trouble sleeping, and—importantly—lowered emotional regulation.

4. Mirror Neurons → Emotional Contagion

Seeing others in distress, anger, or panic on screen can trigger empathic emotional responses, thanks to mirror neurons. You absorb the energy—even if it's not happening to you directly.

Digital De-Escalation Guide: Breaking the Rage Cycle

Use these tools and habits to break free:

1. The 24-Hour Rule
Before reacting or posting, wait. Let your body process. What feels urgent in the moment often fades with time.

2. News-Free Mornings or Evenings
Create boundaries around news exposure. Mornings and pre-sleep hours are when your nervous system is most sensitive.

3. Engage With Media Intentionally, Not Habitually
Ask: Why am I consuming this right now? Curiosity or habit? Purpose or distraction?

4. Use Neutral Aggregators
Try platforms like Ground News or AllSides to view headlines from multiple perspectives.

5. Take Visual Breaks
Pause. Look away from screens. Go outside. Focus on your senses. Regulate your nervous system before re-engaging.

6. Name the Feeling
Instead of "I'm pissed off," try: "I feel frustrated because I care about justice, and I feel powerless right now." Naming reduces emotional intensity.

7. Balance With Regenerative Content
Balance consumption with healing visual input: art, nature, joyful stories, or affirming media from your community.

Reframing 'Us vs. Them' Thinking

Think about the last time you viewed someone with a differing perspective as your enemy. Reflect on your experience in the prompts below.

What views or beliefs were challenged?
_____
_____
_____

What emotions arose when you framed this person as your enemy?
_____
_____

How did this framing limit your understanding of them?
_____
_____

If you were to encounter this person again, what core values might you center your interaction on instead?
_____
_____
_____
_____

Reflect on Your Identity

Use this worksheet as a tool to explore where your identity, values, and purpose are rooted – and how you make sense of them.

1. What aspects of your identity shape how you see the world?

   _____

   _____

   _____

2. Reflecting on the factors that shaped you (culture, values, history, etc.), what makes you who you are?

   _____

   _____

   _____

3. What are the core values that guide your life and choices?

   _____

   _____

   _____

4. If you don't have to defend your identity, what positive change could you work to create?

   _____

   _____

   _____

How to Combat the Anger Cycle

(Adapted from Stuart Fensterheim, LCSW – Good Therapy, 2017)

 ### 1. Acknowledge the Problem
Denial fuels the cycle. Name the pattern to begin breaking it.

 ### 2. Learn to Cool Down
Find your reset; step away, breathe, laugh (if trust is there). Safety is the foundation of humor and healing.

 ### 3. Think Before You Speak
Reacting = triggered. Responding = reflective.
Pause and ask: What need is going unmet?

 ### 4. Own the Anger–and What's Underneath
Anger often masks fear, grief or shame.
Ask yourself: What pain is driving this?

 ### 5. Journal Your Feelings
Use writing to uncover patterns, needs, and truths.
It can clarify communication—even if kept private.

 ### 6. Address It Early–Without Blame
Don't let resentment grow.

Speak calmly about how you feel 'I, not what they did.
Note: If anger becomes abuse, seek help immediately.
📞 1-800-739-SAFE | Text 'START' to 88738
🌐 thehotline org

 ### 7. Practice Deep Listening
Don't just wait to talk –really listen.
Validate. Apologize when needed. Forgive when ready.
Healing takes effort–and sometimes therapy.

WHOLE-PERSON STRATEGIES FOR INTERRUPTING THE ANGER CYCLE

Adapted from Christopher Bergland, author of The Achiete's Way *(Psychology Today, 2016)*

Rather duvıawing anger as a Je\normal ⌐equelation⌐ hut can be regulate throug dellberate physical, emotional, and social practices—indeliberate physical, emotional, and social practices.

 Activate the "Tend-and-Befriend" Response with Diaphragmatic Breathing

Outbursts of rage spike adrenaling, cortisol, blood preasure, and heart rate.

Engaging the parasympathetic netvous system—your is regalate throug deliberate physical, emotional end social practices—by pristice.

 A vagus nerve is key player in emotional regulation—arctıvation by diaphragmattic breathing slows your heartbeal, lowers soess hormones, and increases calm

2 Boost Self-Control Through Exercise

Self-control is traınable, UK researchers found a *oldirecıonal* feedback loop between ipexecutive function and regular exterscise.

exercise trio for resilience:
- Aerobic Activity
  → energizing & clears mental fog
- Strength Training
  → bulids stamina and discipline
- Mindfuiness/Yoga
  → caim, recenten, and integrate body-mind connection

"Need to colm down? Emphasize yoga and walking.

"Need to let out energy? Focus on cardio a strength training,

Improve Empathy with Loving-Kindness Meditation (LKM) & Reading Fiction

Enproourge ery pry with Loving-Kindness Meditation (LKM) & Reading FictIon Theory of mind is lκM):

Loving Kindness Meditation (LKM) nurtures compastion by to:
- loved ones ⎫
- strangers ⎬ Sorveone oho's hurt
- someone   ⎬ you are
- yourself   ⎭

Tap Into Awe and Transcend the Ego

Awe—whether inspired by nature, art, or wonder— has a powerful neurological effect, shiftin attention away from the ege, encopuraging prosocial behavior and emotional balance.

- Gaze at a star-filled sky, powerful artwork, or breathtaking landscape
- Let yourself feel smail—but connec-
- Dlaw awe dissoive the boundaries of anger, self-focus, and control

FROM RAGE TO RESILIENCE

VISUAL DIET AUDIT

For one week, track your media consumption—along with when, how much, and why you use various forms of screens.

SCREEN TIME	Hours per day
Category	
Social media	
Videos, streaming	
News	
Games	

EMOTIONAL TRIGGERS
- ☐ Boredom
- ☐ Loneliness
- ☐ Anxiety
- ☐ Stress
- ☐ FOMO
- ☐ Procrastination
- ☐ Other: _____

MEDIA TO ADJUST

Consume less	Consume more

Set a SMART Goal to Improve Your Visual Diet

My SMART goal is: _____

SPECIFIC What do I want to accomplish?
_____

MEASURABLE How will I track my progress?
_____

ACHIEVABLE Is this realistic for me?
_____

RELEVANT Why is this goal important?
_____

TIMELY What is my deadline or timeline?
_____

Micro-goals:

- 1 _____

- 2 _____

- 3 _____

DIGITAL MINIMALISM: LESS BUT BETTER

Reflective journal prompts

Putting digital minimalism into practice means making space for more of what matters most—and less of what's distracting you or causing harm. Use the questions below to audit your current screen use and identify habits worth considering / cultivating.

What's essential?

_____

_____

What's excessive?

_____

_____

I want to make more room for...

_____

_____

I commit to curbing...

_____

_____

In 5 years, I want to be proud of...

_____

My Starting Point:
PERSONALIZED PLANNING FOR DIGITAL WELLNESS

CURRENT BARRIERS
What challenges am I facing rright now?
_____
_____
_____

PREVIOUS ATTEMPTS
What approaches have I tried before? What worked?
_____
_____
_____

NEEDS TO PROTECT
What parts of my life & health do I want to prioritize?
_____
_____
_____

PERSONALIZED GOALS
How do I want to begin (or continue) my wellness journey?
_____
_____
_____

Worksheet:
Breaking the Doomscrolling Cycle

"Awareness is the first step toward change."

1. Awareness Check-In

When was the last time doomscroel?

- ☐ Time of day: _____
- ☐ Platform or site: _____

What types of content did you consume? (Check all that apply)

- ☐ News
- ☐ Politics Injustice
- ☐ Violence/ conflict
- ☐ Celebrity drama
- ☐ Personal loss

☺ How did you *feel* afterward?

_____
_____
_____

3. Body & Mind Scan

In your last scroll session, how did your body respond?

- ☐ Tense muscles
- ☐ Shallow breathing
- ☐ Shallow breathing
- ☐ Dry eyes
- ☐ Racing heart
- ☐ Numbness or zoning out
- ☐ Trouble sleeping afterward
- ☐ Emotional exhaustion
- ☐ Other: _____

2. Recognizing Patterns

What usually triggers your doomscrolling sessions?

- ☐ Boredom
- ☐ Anxiety
- ☐ Avoiding something
- ☐ Racing heart
- ☐ Curiosity
- ☐ Dry eyes
- ☐ Needing answers
- ☐ Other: ___
- ☐ Feeling disconnected

4. Break the Bond: Recenter & Regulate

ⓢ Choose one action you will try the next time the urge hits:

- ☐ Step outside or move my body
- ☐ Set a 10-minute scroll timer
- ☐ Text or call a friend
- ☐ Journal or reflect instead
- ☐ Breathe deeply for 3 minutes
- ☐ Curate my feed or mute triggers

5. Reflect & Reframe

✐ What insight or takeaway do you have about your doomscrolling habits?

🌱 What's one kind thing you can offer yourself instead?

BEING WITH YOUR OWN COMPANY
A NERVOUS SYSTEM REFLECTION TOOL

"It's taking presence step-by-step—letting my body take the lead in deciding when, and how much, if will feel."

1 IDENTIFY YOUR TRIGGERS
Notice when stillness brings discomfor; (*This is* sometimes called backdraft.)

When does solitude feel like too much? _____

What energy builds in your body or emotions? _____

What comes up from the past? _____

2 TRACK YOUR NERVOUS SYSTEM'S RESPONSE
Did you tip into anxiety or numbness? Check signs that show up (or list yours)

Hyperarousal (Anxiety/Shutdown)
- ☐ Racing thoughts
- ☐ Tight chest
- ☐ Frustration
- ☐ Restlessness
- ☐ Other: _____

Hypoarousal (Distant:(Numb)
- ☐ Spaced out
- ☐ Heavy limbs
- ☐ Numbness
- ☐ Emptyness
- ☐ Other: _____

3 PLAN–NOURISHING ACTIVITIES
What will bring a sense of grounding? Softness? Comfort? Choose one:

- ☐ Get outside
- ☐ Self-massage
- ☐ Wrap in a blanket

- ☐ Wrap in a blanket
- ☐ Listen to music
- ☐ Sip tea or water

4 COMMIT TO COMPASSIONATE PRESENCE
Rate your capacity right now (1= too overwhelmed, 5=able to sit with my neryous system).

What promise will you make to your body in this moment?
_____

DBT Self-Soothing with the Five Senses

(Adapted from DialecticalBehavioralTherapy.com, 2020)

Use your five senses to calm your body and mind when emotions feel overwhelming. These are just starting points-- find what works best for you.

Sight
- Look at nature; trees, sky, movement, color
- Browse calming images online (landscapes, art)
- Visit an art gallery or museum
- Watch a visually soothing movie (avoid triggering content)
- Create a calming image collection (album or digital folder)

Hearing
- Call someone with a soothing voice
- Listen to calming or uplifting music
- Try nature sounds, jazz, ambient, or instrumental
- Go to a park and absorb natural sounds
- Sing or play music
- Listen to audiobooks or soft—spoken podcasts

Smell
- Use favorite scents: perfume, essential oils, cologne
- Light a scented candle
- Cook and enjoy the smell of your favorite food
- Smell flovers, herbs, or indoor plants
- Hug a loved one and take in their familiar scent
- Visit scent-rich places: bakeries, cafes, florists

Taste
- Eat a favorite meal slowly--savor every bite
- Enjoy comfort food mindfully (no guilt)
- Sip a warm, non-ahoinolic drink, tea, cocoa, coffee
- Taste fresh fruit and notice flavor and texture
- Chew gum or enjoy hard candy

Using Biofeedback to Improve Heart Rate Variability (HRV)

Smart devices like fitness trackers and biometric sensors allow people to monitor real-time physiological changes in their body. Over time, biofeedback exercises can help build better emotional awareness and increase resilience.

Tasks to practice using biofeedback:

 **Change your posture**
Sit, stand, or move differently to ease muscle tension.

 **Alter your breathing**
Use breathing techniques to calm anxiety.

 **Relax your muscles**
Concentrate on releasing tight muscles.

 Use mindfulness and focus
Control heart rate with mindful attention.

 Take a test
See how solving a problem affects stress response

Index

Lovering, N. (2022, April 27). *Can you be addicted to anger?* Psych Central. https://psychcentral.com/lib/is-anger-an-addiction#is-anger-an-addiction

Art as a reflection of rising economic inequality. (n.d.). https://knowledge.essec.edu/en/sustainability/art-reflection-rising-economic-inequality.html

Grundberg, Andy , Gernsheim, Helmut Erich Robert , Rosenblum, Naomi and Newhall, Beaumont. "history of photography". *Encyclopedia Britannica*, 26 Apr. 2022, https://www.britannica.com/technology/photography. Accessed 8 September 2022.

National Gallery of Art. 2022. https://www.nga.gov/features/in-light-of-the-past/turn-of-the-century.html

Getty Museum (2021) https://www.getty.edu/news/what-was-life-like-for-women-in-the-middle-ages/

Maria Patrizia Carrieri, Diego Serraino, Longevity of popes and artists between the 13th and the 19th century, *International Journal of Epidemiology*, Volume 34, Issue 6, December 2005, Pages 1435–1436, https://doi.org/10.1093/ije/dyi211

McGee, M. (2012). Neurodiversity. *Contexts*, *11*(3), 12-13.

5 ways social media is changing your brain. (n.d.). [Video]. TED-Ed. https://ed.ted.com/best_of_web/qQzsdX2Y

Gumenyuk, V., Korzyukov, O., Escera, C., Hämäläinen, M., Huotilainen, M., Häyrinen, T., ... & Alho, K. (2005). Electrophysiological evidence of enhanced distractibility in ADHD children. *Neuroscience letters*, *374*(3), 212-217.

Yoto, A., Katsuura, T., Iwanaga, K., & Shimomura, Y. (2007). Effects of object color stimuli on human brain activities in perception and attention referred to EEG alpha band response. *Journal of physiological anthropology*, *26*(3), 373-379.

Jain, A., Bansal, R., Kumar, A., & Singh, K. D. (2015). A comparative study of visual and auditory reaction times on the basis of gender and physical activity levels of medical first year students. *International Journal of Applied and Basic Medical Research*, *5*(2), 124.

Gumenyuk, V., Korzyukov, O., Escera, C., Hämäläinen, M., Huotilainen, M., Häyrinen, T., ... & Alho, K. (2005). Electrophysiological evidence of enhanced distractibility in ADHD children. *Neuroscience letters*, *374*(3), 212-217.

Fabio, R. A., Castriciano, C., & Rondanini, A. (2012). ADHD. *Journal of Attention Disorders*, *19*(9), 771–778. https://doi.org/10.1177/1087054712459562

Fried, M., Tsitsiashvili, E., Bonneh, Y. S., Sterkin, A., Wygnanski-Jaffe, T., Epstein, T., & Polat, U. (2014). ADHD subjects fail to suppress eye blinks and microsaccades while anticipating visual stimuli but recover with medication. *Vision research*, *101*, 62-72.

Miao, S., Han, J., Gu, Y., Wang, X., Song, W., Li, D., ... & Li, X. (2017). Reduced prefrontal cortex activation in children with attention-deficit/hyperactivity disorder during go/no-go task: a functional near-infrared spectroscopy study. *Frontiers in Neuroscience*, *11*, 367.

London, A. S., & Landes, S. D. (2021). Cohort change in the prevalence of ADHD among US adults: evidence of a gender-specific historical period effect. *Journal of Attention Disorders*, *25*(6), 771-782.Olson RK, Keenan JM, Byrne B, & Samuelsson S (2014). Why do children differ in their development of reading and related skills? *Scientific Studies of Reading*, 18, 38–54.

Lee, I. S., Jung, W. M., Park, H. J., & Chae, Y. (2020). Spatial information of somatosensory stimuli in the brain: multivariate pattern analysis of functional magnetic resonance imaging data. *Neural Plasticity*, *2020*.

Dalgleish, T. (2004). The emotional brain. *Nature Reviews Neuroscience*, *5*(7), 583-589.

Firth, J., Torous, J., Stubbs, B., Firth, J. A., Steiner, G. Z., Smith, L., ... & Sarris, J. (2019). The "online brain": how the Internet may be changing our cognition. *World Psychiatry*, *18*(2), 119-129.

The Psychology of Social Media | King University Online. (2023, May 25). King University Online. https://online.king.edu/news/psychology-of-social-media/Wolpert, S. (2016, June 1). The teenage brain on social media. *UCLA*. https://newsroom.ucla.edu/releases/the-teenage-brain-on-social-media

Nagel, S., & Spüler, M. (2018). Modelling the brain response to arbitrary visual stimulation patterns for a flexible high-speed brain-computer interface. *PloS one*, *13*(10), e0206107.

Davis, P. A. (1939). Effects of acoustic stimuli on the waking human brain. *Journal of neurophysiology*, *2*(6), 494-499.
https://www.researchgate.net/profile/Dazhi-Cheng/publication/326218131_Dyslexia_and_dyscalculia_are_characterized_by_common_visual_perception_deficits/links/5b3ec8884585150d2307a6b4/Dyslexia-and-dyscalculia-are-characterized-by-common-visual-perception-deficits.pdf

Gibbs, J., Appleton, J., & Appleton, R. (2007). Dyspraxia or developmental coordination disorder? Unravelling the enigma. *Archives of disease in childhood*, *92*(6), 534-539.
Chokron, S., Kovarski, K., & Dutton, G. N. (2021). Cortical visual impairments and learning disabilities. *Frontiers in Human Neuroscience*, *15*, 713316.

Gentle, J., Brady, D. S., Woodger, N., Croston, S., & Leonard, H. C. (2021). Driving skills of individuals with and without Developmental coordination Disorder (DCD/Dyspraxia). *Frontiers in Human Neuroscience*, *15*. https://doi.org/10.3389/fnhum.2021.635649

Good sleep habits. (2022, September 13). Centers for Disease Control and Prevention. https://www.cdc.gov/sleep/about_sleep/sleep_hygiene.html

Ronconi, L., Melcher, D., & Franchin, L. (2020). Investigating the role of temporal processing in developmental dyslexia: Evidence for a specific deficit in rapid visual segmentation. *Psychonomic Bulletin & Review*, *27*(4), 724–734. https://doi.org/10.3758/s13423-020-01752-5
https://www.researchgate.net/profile/Dazhi-Cheng/publication/326218131_Dyslexia_and_dyscalculia_are_characterized_by_common_visual_perception_deficits/links/5b3ec8884585150d2307a6b4/Dyslexia-and-dyscalculia-are-characterized-by-common-visual-perception-deficits.pdf

Decarli, G., Paris, E., Tencati, C., Nardelli, C., Vescovi, M., Surian, L., & Piazza, M. (2020). Impaired large numerosity estimation and intact subitizing in developmental dyscalculia. *PLOS ONE*, *15*(12), e0244578. https://doi.org/10.1371/journal.pone.0244578
https://www.researchgate.net/profile/Dazhi-Cheng/publication/336378877_Short-term_numerosity_training_promotes_symbolic_arithmetic_in_children_with_developmental_dyscalculia_The_mediating_role_of_visual_form_perception/links/5ddc709e299bf10c5a334632/Short-term-numerosity-training-promotes-symbolic-arithmetic-in-children-with-developmental-dyscalculia-The-mediating-role-of-visual-form-perception.pdf

IEEE Xplore Full-Text PDF: (n.d.). https://ieeexplore.ieee.org/stamp/stamp.jsp?arnumber=9294011
U. Lahiri, E. Bekele, E. Dohrmann, Z. Warren, and N. Sarkar, "Design of a virtual reality based adaptive response technology for children with autism," IEEE Trans. Neural Syst. Rehabil. Eng., vol. 21, no. 1, pp. 55–64, Jan. 201

Chung, S., & Son, J. (2020). Visual Perception in Autism Spectrum Disorder: A Review of Neuroimaging Studies. *Soa.Cheongsonyeonjeongsinuihak*, *31*(3), 105–120. https://doi.org/10.5765/jkacap.200018

Kleimaker, A., Kleimaker, M., Bäumer, T., Beste, C., & Münchau, A. (2020). Gilles de la Tourette Syndrome—A Disorder of Action-Perception Integration. *Frontiers in Neurology*, *11*. https://doi.org/10.3389/fneur.2020.597898

Ovalle-Fresa, R., Ankner, S., & Rothen, N. (2021). Enhanced perception and memory: Insights from synesthesia and expertise. *Cortex*, *140*, 14-25.
Nair, A., & Brang, D. (2019). Inducing synesthesia in non-synesthetes: Short-term visual deprivation facilitates auditory-evoked visual percepts. *Consciousness and cognition*, *70*, 70-79.

Galiana-Simal, A., Vela-Romero, M., Romero-Vela, V. M., Oliver-Tercero, N., García-Olmo, V., Benito-Castellanos, P. J., Muñoz-Martínez, V. E., & Beato-Fernández, L. (2020). Sensory processing disorder: Key points of a frequent alteration in neurodevelopmental disorders. *Cogent Medicine*, *7*(1). https://doi.org/10.1080/2331205x.2020.1736829

Wood, J. K. (2020). Sensory Processing Disorder: Implications for primary care nurse practitioners. *The Journal for Nurse Practitioners*, *16*(7), 514–516. https://doi.org/10.1016/j.nurpra.2020.03.022

Symptoms checklist. (n.d.). STAR Institute. https://sensoryhealth.org/basic/symptoms-checklist

Schaaf, R. C., Miller, L., Seawell, D., & O'Keefe, S. (2003). Children with Disturbances in Sensory Processing: A pilot study examining the role of the parasympathetic nervous system. *American Journal of Occupational Therapy*, *57*(4), 442–449. https://doi.org/10.5014/ajot.57.4.442

ICD-11 for Mortality and Morbidity Statistics. (n.d.). https://icd.who.int/browse11/l-m/en#/http%3a%2f%2fid.who.int%2ficd%2fentity%2f2070699808

Wagner, B.E.; Folk, A.L.; Hahn, S.L.; Barr-Anderson, D.J.; Larson, N.; Neumark-Sztainer, D. Recreational Screen Time Behaviors during the COVID-19 Pandemic in the U.S.: A Mixed-Methods Study among a Diverse Population-Based Sample of Emerging Adults. Int. J. Environ. Res. Public Health 2021, 18, 4613. https://doi.org/10.3390/ ijerph18094613

Overwhelmed by the news: A longitudinal study of prior trauma, posttraumatic stress disorder trajectories, and news watching during the COVID-19 pandemic.Solomon, Zahava; Ginzburg, Karni; Ohry, Avi; Mikulincer, Mario. *Soc Sci Med* ; 278: 113956, 2021 06.Artigo em Inglês | MEDLINE | ID: covidwho-1201965

Psychiatry Res. 2020 Jul; 289: 113089. Published online 2020 May 13. doi: 10.1016/j.psychres.2020.113089 Binge watching behavior during COVID 19 pandemic: A cross-sectional, cross-national online survey Ayushi Dixit,[a] Marthoenis Marthoenis,[b] S.M. Yasir Arafat,[c] Pawan Sharma,[d] and Sujita Kumar Kar[e,*]

Acevedo, B.P., Aron, E.N., Aron, A., Sangster, M.-D., Collins, N. and Brown, L.L. (2014), The highly sensitive brain: an fMRI study of sensory processing sensitivity and response to others' emotions. Brain Behav, 4: 580-594. https://doi.org/10.1002/brb3.242

Benham, G. (2006). The highly sensitive person: Stress and physical symptom reports. *Personality and individual differences*, *40*(7), 1433-1440.

Dimulescu, A., Schreier, M., & Godde, B. (2020). EEG Resting Activity in Highly Sensitive and Non-Highly Sensitive Persons. Journal of European Psychology Students, 11(1), 32–40 https://doi.org/10.5334/jeps.486

History of Television - Mitchell Stephens. (n.d.). https://stephens.hosting.nyu.edu/History%20of%20Television%20page.html#:~:text=Electronic%20television%20was%20first%20successfully,electricity%20until%20he%20was%2014

Today, P. R. U. (2017, August 28). Pink's heartwarming VMAs speech about her daughter and self-acceptance will make you cry. *USA TODAY*. https://www.usatoday.com/story/life/entertainthis/2017/08/27/pinks-heartwarming-vmas-speech-her-daughter-and-self-acceptance-make-you-cry/606905001/

Bronner, S. (2015, October 23). How Being Called The "World's Ugliest Woman" Transformed Her Life. *HuffPost*. https://www.huffpost.com/entry/how-being-called-the-worlds-ugliest-woman-transformed-her-life_n_56213be0e4b02f6a900c1d0c

Chicago – Rothberg, Emma. "Laverne Cox." National Women's History Museum. 2022. www.womenshistory.org/education-resources/biographies/laverne-cox.

Siegel, D. J., & Bryson, T. P. (2019). *The yes brain: How to cultivate courage, curiosity, and resilience in your child*. Bantam.

Twenge, J. M., & Campbell, W. K. (2009). *The narcissism epidemic: Living in the age of entitlement*. Simon and Schuster.

To grow up healthy, children need to sit less and play more. (2022). Retrieved 7 October 2022, from https://www.who.int/news/item/24-04-2019-to-grow-up-healthy-children-need-to-sit-less-and-play-more
https://www.transitionmanagement.us/TMC/tmc_resources_files/Zull%20-%202006%20-%20Key%20aspects%20of%20how%20the%20brain%20learns.pdf

Ribner, A. D., McHarg, G. G., & NewFAMS Study Team. (2019). Why won't she sleep? Screen exposure and sleep patterns in young infants. *Infant Behavior and Development*, 57, 101334.

McHarg, G., Ribner, A. D., Devine, R. T., Hughes, C., & NewFAMS Study Team. (2020). Infant screen exposure links to toddlers' inhibition, but not other EF constructs: A propensity score study. *Infancy*, 25(2), 205-222.

Gobin, K. C., Mills, J. S., & McComb, S. E. (2021). The Effects of the COVID-19 Pandemic Lockdown on Eating, Body Image, and Social Media Habits Among Women With and Without Symptoms of Orthorexia Nervosa. *Frontiers in Psychology*, 12.

Arend, A. K., Blechert, J., Pannicke, B., & Reichenberger, J. (2021). Increased screen use on days with increased perceived COVID-19-related confinements—a day level ecological momentary assessment study. *Frontiers in public health*, 8, 623205.

The limbic system. (2023, May 15). Queensland Brain Institute - University of Queensland. https://qbi.uq.edu.au/brain/brain-anatomy/limbic-system

Arain, M., Haque, M., Johal, L., Mathur, P., Nel, W., Rais, A., ... & Sharma, S. (2013). Maturation of the adolescent brain. *Neuropsychiatric disease and treatment*, 9, 449.

Big Think. Dr. Bessel Van Der Kolk. (2021)

Ferguson, B., Franconeri, S. L., & Waxman, S. R. (2018). Very young infants learn abstract rules in the visual modality. *PloS one*, 13(1), e0190185.

Britton W. B. (2019). Can mindfulness be too much of a good thing? The value of a middle way. *Current opinion in psychology*, 28, 159–165. https://doi.org/10.1016/j.copsyc.2018.12.011

Peterson, L. G., & Pbert, L. (1992). Effectiveness of a meditation-based stress reduction program in the treatment of anxiety disorders. *Am J Psychiatry*, 149(7), 936-943.

Hernández, S. E., Suero, J., Barros, A., González-Mora, J. L., & Rubia, K. (2016). Increased grey matter associated with long-term sahaja yoga meditation: a voxel-based morphometry study. *PloS one*, 11(3), e0150757.

Engen, H. G., & Singer, T. (2015). Compassion-based emotion regulation up-regulates experienced positive affect and associated neural networks. *Social cognitive and affective neuroscience*, *10*(9), 1291-1301.

Doll, A., Hölzel, B. K., Bratec, S. M., Boucard, C. C., Xie, X., Wohlschläger, A. M., & Sorg, C. (2016). Mindful attention to breath regulates emotions via increased amygdala–prefrontal cortex connectivity. *Neuroimage*, *134*, 305-313.

Kabat-Zinn, J. (2003). Mindfulness-based interventions in context: past, present, and future.

Brown, K. W., & Ryan, R. M. (2003). The benefits of being present: mindfulness and its role in psychological well-being. *Journal of personality and social psychology*, *84*(4), 822.

Davis, D. M., & Hayes, J. A. (2011). What are the benefits of mindfulness? A practice review of psychotherapy-related research. *Psychotherapy (Chicago, Ill.)*, *48*(2), 198–208. https://doi.org/10.1037/a0022062

Sutton, T. E. (2019). Review of attachment theory: Familial predictors, continuity and change, and intrapersonal and relational outcomes. *Marriage & Family Review*, *55*(1), 1-22.

Misha, J. (2022, July 22). Secure Attachment – from Childhood to Adult Relationships. Simply Psychology. www.simplypsychology.org/secure-attachment.html

Brach, T., (2022). RAIN. https://www.tarabrach.com/rain/

Clarke, J., (2022). Reparenting in Therapy. From Very well mind. https://www.verywellmind.com/reparenting-in-therapy-5226096

Yao, Y., Li, X., Zhang, B., Yin, C., Liu, Y., Chen, W., ... & Du, J. (2016). Visual cue-discriminative dopaminergic control of visuomotor transformation and behavior selection. *Neuron*, *89*(3), 598-612.

Roy, S., & Field, G. D. (2019). Dopaminergic modulation of retinal processing from starlight to sunlight. *Journal of pharmacological sciences*, *140*(1), 86-93.

Yousif, N., Fu, R. Z., Bourquin, B. A. E. E., Bhrugubanda, V., Schultz, S. R., & Seemungal, B. M. (2016). Dopamine activation preserves visual motion perception despite noise interference of human V5/MT. *Journal of Neuroscience*, *36*(36), 9303-9312.

Zhang, D. Q., Zhou, T. R., & McMahon, D. G. (2007). Functional heterogeneity of retinal dopaminergic neurons underlying their multiple roles in vision. *Journal of Neuroscience*, *27*(3), 692-699.

Soutschek, A., Jetter, A., & Tobler, P. N. (2022). Towards a Unifying Account of Dopamine's Role in Cost-Benefit Decision Making. *Biological Psychiatry Global Open Science*.

Berridge, K. C. (2007). The debate over dopamine's role in reward: the case for incentive salience. *Psychopharmacology*, *191*(3), 391-431.

Durstewitz, D. (2006). A few important points about dopamine's role in neural network dynamics. *Pharmacopsychiatry*, *39*(S 1), 72-75.

Lembke, A. (2021). Digital addictions are drowning us in dopamine. *The Wall Street Journal*.

Walia B, Kim J, Ijere I, Sanders S (2022) Video Game Addictive Symptom Level, Use Intensity, and Hedonic Experience: Cross-sectional Questionnaire Study JMIR Serious Games 2022;10(2):e33661

Watts, T. W., Duncan, G. J., & Quan, H. (2018). Revisiting the marshmallow test: A conceptual replication investigating links between early delay of gratification and later outcomes. *Psychological science*, *29*(7), 1159-1177.

Tom, Thalia & Lawrence, Amanda & Choe, Daniel. (2017). Gratification Stratification: Amount of Screen Time is Associated with Children's Delay of Gratification.

Moriguchi, Y., Shinohara, I., & Yanaoka, K. (2018). Neural correlates of delay of gratification choice in young children: Near-infrared spectroscopy studies. *Developmental psychobiology*, *60*(8), 989-998.

Kluwe-Schiavon, B., Viola, T. W., Sanvicente-Vieira, B., Lumertz, F. S., Salum, G. A., Grassi-Oliveira, R., & Quednow, B. B. (2020). Substance related disorders are associated with impaired valuation of delayed gratification and feedback processing: a multilevel meta-analysis and meta-regression. *Neuroscience & Biobehavioral Reviews*, *108*, 295-307.

Jiang, X., Liu, L., Ji, H., & Zhu, Y. (2018). Association of affected neurocircuitry with deficit of response inhibition and delayed gratification in attention deficit hyperactivity disorder: a narrative review. *Frontiers in human neuroscience*, *12*, 506.

Soutschek, A., Moisa, M., Ruff, C. C., & Tobler, P. N. (2020). The right temporoparietal junction enables delay of gratification by allowing decision makers to focus on future events. *PLoS biology*, *18*(8), e3000800.

Smartphone apps can motivate depressed patients by enhancing dopamine, offering the opportunity to enhance motivation and behavioral changes, Mouchabac, S., Maatoug, R., Conejero, I., Adrien, V., Bonnot, O., Millet, B., ... & Bourla, A. (2021). In Search of Digital Dopamine: How Apps Can Motivate Depressed Patients, a Review and Conceptual Analysis. *Brain Sciences*, *11*(11), 1454.
Singh, R. (2022). Perils of Screen Addiction. *AKGEC International Journal of Technology*, *13*, 40-44.

Georgy, M. S. S. (2019). Neuropsychiatric and Neurobiological Consideration for Pornographic Addiction and Compulsive Sexual Disorder. *Clin Case Rep Open Access*, *2*(4), 135.

De Alarcón, R., de la Iglesia, J. I., Casado, N. M., & Montejo, A. L. (2019). Online porn addiction: What we know and what we don't—A systematic review. *Journal of clinical medicine*, *8*(1), 91.

Blasi, M. D., Giardina, A., Giordano, C., Coco, G. L., Tosto, C., Billieux, J., & Schimmenti, A. (2019). Problematic video game use as an emotional coping strategy: Evidence from a sample of MMORPG gamers. *Journal of behavioral addictions*, 8(1), 25-34.

A Day with Dr. Gabor Maté - Dr. Gabor Maté. (2016, November 8). Dr. Gabor Maté. https://drgabormate.com/topics/addiction/

Syvertsen, T., & Enli, G. (2020). Digital detox: Media resistance and the promise of authenticity. *Convergence*, 26(5-6), 1269-1283.

Newport, C. (2019). *Digital minimalism: Choosing a focused life in a noisy world*. Penguin.

Lanaj, K., Johnson, R. E., & Barnes, C. M. (2014). Beginning the workday yet already depleted? Consequences of late-night smartphone use and sleep. *Organizational Behavior and Human Decision Processes*, 124(1), 11-23. Kushlev, K. and Dunn, E.W. (2015) "Checking email less frequently reduces stress," *Computers in Human Behavior*, 43, pp. 220–228. Available at: https://doi.org/10.1016/j.chb.2014.11.005.

Kaufman, S. B. (2021). The opposite of toxic positivity. *The Atlantic*.

BERMEJO, M. S., ELEAZAR, E. C., QUINTO, K. L. M., & VILLAREZ, A. L. (2021). TOXIC POSITIVITY AND ITS ROLE ON COLLEGE STUDENTS' MENTAL HEALTH DURING THE COVID-19 PANDEMIC.

Jans-Beken, L. (2021). A perspective on mature gratitude as a way of coping with COVID-19. *Frontiers in Psychology*, 12. https://doi.org/10.3389/fpsyg.2021.632911
https://d1wqtxts1xzle7.cloudfront.net/33668761/Smart-Impact-libre.pdf?1399753794=&response-content-disposition=inline%3B+filename%3DImpact_of_Smartphones_on_Society.pdf&Expires=1671129862&Signature=LIicRGxYArLfG0FNRsLRN2vNooPOmAuM4yURq1SahgR8oyRbQk1CpchNUyBB4ZJvXv4R8i9skm0amPKNIqtcT6BKBHcdGVupq5-jrPDx1Fftl15eqTyZsrKu-TyG~bOkfFjWa4S6hFw7V-w4KQ~xBm00a3MJI4bjDGS6jBivvYy2MqQeb~yxDYXjHTWjGUWvEbdkkVGqW9altyOhPKP8~2qyXWF6oju8Jfs9eeOyGCVoojSsRzpi9CtrE8wnqC5D~FaRzgt5V7738WCUEAc7b-cZ5lCEuHSd7iqarptYzSf160n9JReG4HBwwTJij8prmAW47xxkZXIn8ME12SBXsA   &Key-Pair-Id=APKAJLOHF5GGSLRBV4ZA
https://aclanthology.org/2022.socialnlp-1.7.pdf
https://static1.squarespace.com/static/5ade38cf7e3c3a8e0fd03b28/t/61264ca5f07e1055c146fc35/1629899941880/The+Opposite+of+Toxic+Positivity+by+The+Atlantic.pdf

Choe, D. E., Lawrence, A. C., & Cingel, D. P. (2022). The role of different screen media devices, child dysregulation, and parent screen media use in children's self-regulation. *Psychology of Popular Media*.
https://www.ptsd.va.gov/gethelp/captions/Track02_MindfulBreathing.pdf

Liu, Y., Jiang, T. T., Shi, T. Y., Liu, Y. N., Liu, X. M., Xu, G. J., ... & Wu, X. Y. (2021). The effectiveness of diaphragmatic breathing relaxation training for improving sleep quality among nursing staff during the COVID-19 outbreak: a before and after study. *Sleep Medicine*, 78, 8-14.

Kramer, A. C., Neubauer, A. B., & Schmiedek, F. (2022). The Effectiveness of A Slow-Paced Diaphragmatic Breathing Exercise in Children's Daily Life: A Micro-Randomized Trial. *Journal of Clinical Child & Adolescent Psychology*, 1-14.

Body Scan meditation (Greater Good in Action). (2023, June 4). https://ggia.berkeley.edu/practice/body_scan_meditation

What's Trauma-Sensitive Mindfulness? (n.d.). Mindful Leader. https://www.mindfulleader.org/blog/26483-what-s-trauma-sensitive-mindfulness

McKeering, P., & Hwang, Y. S. (2019). A systematic review of mindfulness-based school interventions with early adolescents. *Mindfulness*, *10*(4), 593-610.

Zenner, C., Herrnleben-Kurz, S., & Walach, H. (2014). Mindfulness-based interventions in schools—a systematic review and meta-analysis. *Frontiers in psychology*, *5*, 603.

Behan, C. (2020). The benefits of meditation and mindfulness practices during times of crisis such as COVID-19. *Irish journal of psychological medicine*, *37*(4), 256-258.

Yin S, Bi T, Chen A, Egner T. Ventromedial Prefrontal Cortex Drives the Prioritization of Self-Associated Stimuli in Working Memory. J Neurosci. 2021 Mar 3;41(9):2012-2023. doi: 10.1523/JNEUROSCI.1783-20.2020. Epub 2021 Jan 18. PMID: 33462089; PMCID: PMC7939096.

Beer JS, Lombardo MV, Bhanji JP. Roles of medial prefrontal cortex and orbitofrontal cortex in self-evaluation. J Cogn Neurosci. 2010 Sep;22(9):2108-19. doi: 10.1162/jocn.2009.21359. PMID: 19925187; PMCID: PMC4159715.

Apps MA, Rushworth MF, Chang SW. The Anterior Cingulate Gyrus and Social Cognition: Tracking the Motivation of Others. Neuron. 2016 May 18;90(4):692-707. doi: 10.1016/j.neuron.2016.04.018. PMID: 27196973; PMCID: PMC4885021.

Braver TS, Bongiolatti SR. The role of frontopolar cortex in subgoal processing during working memory. Neuroimage. 2002 Mar;15(3):523-36. doi: 10.1006/nimg.2001.1019. PMID: 11848695.

Apps MA, Lockwood PL, Balsters JH. The role of the midcingulate cortex in monitoring others' decisions. Front Neurosci. 2013 Dec 20;7:251. doi: 10.3389/fnins.2013.00251. PMID: 24391534; PMCID: PMC3868891.

Ishkhanyan, B., Michel Lange, V., Boye, K., Mogensen, J., Karabanov, A., Hartwigsen, G., & Siebner, H. R. (2020). Anterior and posterior left inferior frontal gyrus contribute to the implementation of grammatical determiners during language production. *Frontiers in Psychology*, *11*, 685.

Weiner KS, Zilles K. The anatomical and functional specialization of the fusiform gyrus. Neuropsychologia. 2016 Mar;83:48-62. doi: 10.1016/j.neuropsychologia.2015.06.033. Epub 2015 Jun 25. PMID: 26119921; PMCID: PMC4714959.

Driscoll ME, Bollu PC, Tadi P. Neuroanatomy, Nucleus Caudate. [Updated 2022 Jul 25]. In: StatPearls [Internet]. Treasure Island (FL): StatPearls Publishing; 2022 Jan-. Available from: https://www.ncbi.nlm.nih.gov/books/NBK557407/

Javed N, Cascella M. Neuroanatomy, Globus Pallidus. [Updated 2022 Feb 5]. In: StatPearls [Internet]. Treasure Island (FL): StatPearls Publishing; 2022 Jan-. Available from: https://www.ncbi.nlm.nih.gov/books/NBK557755/

Ghandili M, Munakomi S. Neuroanatomy, Putamen. [Updated 2022 Feb 3]. In: StatPearls [Internet]. Treasure Island (FL): StatPearls Publishing; 2022 Jan-. Available from: https://www.ncbi.nlm.nih.gov/books/NBK542170/

Yassa, M. A. (2023, February 3). *hippocampus. Encyclopedia Britannica.* https://www.britannica.com/science/hippocampus

Tedeschi, R. G., & Calhoun, L. G. (2004). " Posttraumatic growth: conceptual foundations and empirical evidence". *Psychological inquiry*, *15*(1), 1-18.

Thornton, D., & Argoff, C. E. (2009). Psychological constructs and treatment interventions. In *Elsevier eBooks* (pp. 328–341). https://doi.org/10.1016/b978-0-323-04019-8.00043-3

Jiang, S., & Ngien, A. (2020). The effects of Instagram use, social comparison, and self-esteem on social anxiety: A survey study in Singapore. *Social Media+ Society*, *6*(2), 2056305120912488.

Cortez, M. A. T., & Alfonso, G. J. (2020). Fitspiration and Body Positivity: The Relationships of Body-Focused Instagram Trend and Movement, Self-Objectification, and Gender Stereotypical Beliefs. *University of the Philippines Open University*.

Muraven, M., Buczny, J., & Law, K. F. (2019). Ego depletion: Theory and evidence.

Reid Chassiakos, Y. L., Radesky, J., Christakis, D., Moreno, M. A., Cross, C., Hill, D., ... & Swanson, W. S. (2016). Children and adolescents and digital media. *Pediatrics*, *138*(5).

Masaeli, N., & Farhadi, H. (2021). Prevalence of Internet-based addictive behaviors during COVID-19 pandemic: A systematic review. *Journal of addictive diseases*, *39*(4), 468-488.

Viner, R., Russell, S., Saulle, R., Croker, H., Stansfield, C., Packer, J., ... & Minozzi, S. (2022). School closures during social lockdown and mental health, health behaviors, and well-being among children and adolescents during the first COVID-19 wave: a systematic review. *JAMA pediatrics*.
Extinction bursts: It's going to get worse before it gets better. (n.d.). Evoke Therapy Programs. https://evoketherapy.com/resources/blog/phil-bryan/extinction-bursts-its-going-to-get-worse-before-it-gets-better/

Reid Chassiakos, Y. L., Radesky, J., Christakis, D., Moreno, M. A., Cross, C., Hill, D., ... & Swanson, W. S. (2016). Children and adolescents and digital media. *Pediatrics*, *138*(5).

Mendelsohn, A. L., Brockmeyer, C. A., Dreyer, B. P., Fierman, A. H., Berkule-Silberman, S. B., & Tomopoulos, S. (2010). Do verbal interactions with infants during electronic media exposure mitigate adverse impacts on their language development as toddlers?. *Infant and child development*, *19*(6), 577-593.

Dayanim, S., & Namy, L. L. (2015). Infants learn baby signs from video. *Child Development*, *86*(3), 800-811.

Lin, W. H., Liu, C. H., & Yi, C. C. (2020). Exposure to sexually explicit media in early adolescence is related to risky sexual behavior in emerging adulthood. *PloS one*, *15*(4), e0230242.

Goldfarb, E. S., & Lieberman, L. D. (2021). Three decades of research: The case for comprehensive sex education. *Journal of Adolescent Health*, *68*(1), 13-27.

Rothman, E. F., Kaczmarsky, C., Burke, N., Jansen, E., & Baughman, A. (2015). "Without porn... I wouldn't know half the things I know now": A qualitative study of pornography use among a sample of urban, low-income, black and Hispanic youth. *The Journal of Sex Research*, *52*(7), 736-746.

Brown, J. D., & L'Engle, K. L. (2009). X-rated: Sexual attitudes and behaviors associated with US early adolescents' exposure to sexually explicit media. *Communication research*, *36*(1), 129-151.
Gorman, S., Monk-Turner, E., & Fish, J. N. (2010). Free adult Internet web sites: How prevalent are degrading acts?. *Gender Issues*, *27*, 131-145.

Smith, M. (2013). Youth viewing sexually explicit material online: Addressing the elephant on the screen. *Sexuality Research and Social Policy*, *10*, 62-75.

Trostle, L. C. (2003). Overrating pornography as a source of sex information for university students: Additional consistent findings. *Psychological reports*, *92*(1), 143-150.

Marston, C., & Lewis, R. (2014). Anal heterosex among young people and implications for health promotion: A qualitative study in the UK. BMJ Open, 4 (8), e004996-e004996.

Peter, J., Valkenburg, P.M. The Use of Sexually Explicit Internet Material and Its Antecedents: A Longitudinal Comparison of Adolescents and Adults. *Arch Sex Behav* 40, 1015–1025 (2011). https://doi.org/10.1007/s10508-010-9644-x

Osborne, C. (2023). The best secure browsers for privacy in 2023. *ZDNET*. https://www.zdnet.com/article/best-browser-for-privacy/
Computer cookies: A definition + how cookies work in 2022. (n.d.). https://us.norton.com/blog/how-to/what-are-cookies

Houdek, P. (2022). Neurodiversity in (not only) public organizations: an untapped opportunity?. *Administration & Society*, *54*(9), 1848-1871.

Canonico Martin, E., & Lup, D. (2020). Could teleworking benefit organisational neurodiversity?. *LSE Business Review*.

Austin, R. D., & Pisano, G. P. (2017). Neurodiversity as a competitive advantage. *Harvard Business Review*, *95*(3), 96-103.

Grinspoon, P., MD. (2020). Dopamine fasting: Misunderstanding science spawns a maladaptive fad. *Harvard Health*. https://www.health.harvard.edu/blog/dopamine-fasting-misunderstanding-science-spawns-a-maladaptive-fad-2020022618917

Montardy, Q., Zhou, Z., Li, L., Yang, Q., Lei, Z., Feng, X., ... & Wang, L. (2022). Dopamine modulates visual threat processing in the superior colliculus via D2 receptors. *Iscience*, *25*(6), 104388.

Hu, E. (2022, April 4). Too much pleasure can lead to addiction. How to break the cycle and find balance. *NPR*. https://www.npr.org/2022/03/31/1090009509/addiction-how-to-break-the-cycle-and-find-balance

Dempsey, R. (2021, December 14). My Dopamine Detox Experience — 1 month results - Ryan Dempsey - medium. *Medium*. https://medium.com/@dempseyryan123/my-dopamine-detox-experience-1-month-results-a9654941ad62

Conversation. (2023, April 21). *Woman Spent 500 Days Isolated in a Cave And It Completely Messed With Her Sense of Time : ScienceAlert*. ScienceAlert. https://www.sciencealert.com/women-spent-500-days-isolated-in-a-cave-and-it-completely-messed-her-sense-of-time

Lee, R., Arfanakis, K., Evia, A. M., Fanning, J. R., Keedy, S., & Coccaro, E. F. (2016). White Matter integrity reductions in intermittent explosive disorder. *Neuropsychopharmacology*, *41*(11), 2697–2703. https://doi.org/10.1038/npp.2016.74

Mercadante, A. A. (2022, July 25). *Neuroanatomy, gray matter*. StatPearls - NCBI Bookshelf. https://www.ncbi.nlm.nih.gov/books/NBK553239/Penttila, N. (2019). Why the White Brain Matters. *Dana Foundation*. https://www.dana.org/article/why-the-white-brain-matters/

GoodTherapy.org. (2017, August 9). https://www.goodtherapy.org/blog/the-anger-cycle-coping-with-anger-and-its-impact-in-relationships-0809174

Mayne, M. (2018, January 8). How much did AI control you today? *TechRadar*. https://www.techradar.com/news/how-much-did-ai-control-you-today

Romero-Rodríguez, J. M., Aznar-Díaz, I., Marín-Marín, J. A., Soler-Costa, R., & Rodríguez-Jiménez, C. (2020). Impact of problematic smartphone use and Instagram use intensity on self-esteem with university students from physical education. *International journal of environmental research and public health*, *17*(12), 4336.

Obeid, Sahar PhD*,†,‡; Saade, Sylvia PharmD§; Haddad, Chadia MPH*; Sacre, Hala PharmD‖,¶; Khansa, Wael MD#; Al Hajj, Roula MSc†; Kheir, Nelly MSc**; Hallit, Souheil PharmD, MSc, MPH, PhD¶,#. Internet Addiction Among Lebanese Adolescents: The Role of Self-Esteem, Anger,

Depression, Anxiety, Social Anxiety and Fear, Impulsivity, and Aggression—A Cross-Sectional Study. The Journal of Nervous and Mental Disease 207(10):p 838-846, October 2019. | DOI: 10.1097/NMD.0000000000001034

Demirci, K., Akgönül, M., & Akpinar, A. (2015). Relationship of smartphone use severity with sleep quality, depression, and anxiety in university students, *Journal of Behavioral Addictions*, *4*(2), 85-92. doi: https://doi.org/10.1556/2006.4.2015.010

Bahrainian SA, Alizadeh KH, Raeisoon MR, Gorji OH, Khazaee A. Relationship of Internet addiction with self-esteem and depression in university students. J Prev Med Hyg. 2014 Sep;55(3):86-9. PMID: 25902574; PMCID: PMC4718307.

Kim, Y. J., Jang, H. M., Lee, Y., Lee, D., & Kim, D. J. (2018). Effects of internet and smartphone addictions on depression and anxiety based on propensity score matching analysis. *International journal of environmental research and public health*, *15*(5), 859.

Bouw, N., Huijbregts, S. C. J., Scholte, E., & Swaab, H. (2019). Mindfulness-based stress reduction in prison: Experiences of inmates, instructors, and prison staff. *International journal of offender therapy and comparative criminology*, *63*(15-16), 2550-2571.

Sinsky, C., Colligan, L., Li, L., Prgomet, M., Reynolds, S., Goeders, L., ... & Blike, G. (2016). Allocation of physician time in ambulatory practice: a time and motion study in 4 specialties. *Annals of internal medicine*, *165*(11), 753-760.

Amisha, Malik P, Pathania M, Rathaur VK. Overview of artificial intelligence in medicine. J Family Med Prim Care. 2019 Jul;8(7):2328-2331. doi: 10.4103/jfmpc.jfmpc_440_19. PMID: 31463251; PMCID: PMC6691444.

Chen, L., Chen, P., & Lin, Z. (2020). Artificial intelligence in education: A review. *Ieee Access*, *8*, 75264-75278.

Berente, N., Gu, B., Recker, J., & Santhanam, R. (2021). Managing artificial intelligence. *MIS quarterly*, *45*(3).

Byrne, M. (2021). Reducing bias in healthcare Artificial intelligence. *Journal of PeriAnesthesia Nursing*, *36*(3), 313–316. https://doi.org/10.1016/j.jopan.2021.03.009

Panch T, Mattie H, Atun R. Artificial intelligence and algorithmic bias: implications for health systems. J Glob Health. 2019 Dec;9(2):010318. doi: 10.7189/jogh.09.020318. PMID: 31788229; PMCID: PMC6875681.

Wortsman, M., Ehsani, K., Rastegari, M., Farhadi, A., & Mottaghi, R. (2019). Learning to learn how to learn: Self-adaptive visual navigation using meta-learning. In *Proceedings of the IEEE/CVF conference on computer vision and pattern recognition* (pp. 6750-6759).

Cantor, P., Osher, D., Berg, J., Steyer, L., & Rose, T. (2019). Malleability, plasticity, and individuality: How children learn and develop in context1. *Applied developmental science*, *23*(4), 307-337. https://repository.unja.ac.id/17244/1/Learning%20Theory%20of%20Conditioning.pdf

Smith MA. Social Learning and Addiction. Behav Brain Res. 2021 Feb 1;398:112954. doi: 10.1016/j.bbr.2020.112954. Epub 2020 Oct 11. PMID: 33053384; PMCID: PMC7719575.

Roy, S., & Field, G. D. (2019). Dopaminergic modulation of retinal processing from starlight to sunlight. *Journal of pharmacological sciences*, *140*(1), 86-93.

Yousif, N., Fu, R. Z., Bourquin, B. A. E. E., Bhrugubanda, V., Schultz, S. R., & Seemungal, B. M. (2016). Dopamine activation preserves visual motion perception despite noise interference of human V5/MT. *Journal of Neuroscience*, *36*(36), 9303-9312.

Samermit, P., Saal, J., & Davidenko, N. (2019). Cross-sensory stimuli modulate reactions to aversive sounds. *Multisensory Research*, *32*(3), 197-213.
Who invented the automobile? (n.d.). The Library of Congress. https://www.loc.gov/everyday-mysteries/motor-vehicles-aeronautics-astronautics/item/who-invented-the-automobile/

Spiel, K., Hornecker, E., Williams, R. M., & Good, J. (2022, April). Adhd and technology research–investigated by neurodivergent readers. In *Proceedings of the 2022 CHI Conference on Human Factors in Computing Systems* (pp. 1-21).

Belisle, J. L. (2022). Demolishing Systemic Ableism: Attention-Deficit Hyperactivity Disorder (ADHD) in Adults.

Brunick, K. L., Putnam, M. M., McGarry, L. E., Richards, M. N., & Calvert, S. L. (2016). Children's future parasocial relationships with media characters: The age of intelligent characters. *Journal of Children and Media*, *10*(2), 181-190.

Alang, S. M. (2019). Mental health care among blacks in America: Confronting racism and constructing solutions. *Health services research*, *54*(2), 346-355.

Maina, I. W., Belton, T. D., Ginzberg, S., Singh, A., & Johnson, T. J. (2018). A decade of studying implicit racial/ethnic bias in healthcare providers using the implicit association test. *Social science & medicine*, *199*, 219-229.

Doubeni, C. A., Simon, M., & Krist, A. H. (2021). Addressing systemic racism through clinical preventive service recommendations from the US Preventive Services Task Force. *Jama*, *325*(7), 627-628.

Nelson, A. (2002). Unequal treatment: confronting racial and ethnic disparities in health care. *Journal of the national medical association*, *94*(8), 666.

Vyas, D. A., Eisenstein, L. G., & Jones, D. S. (2020). Hidden in plain sight—reconsidering the use of race correction in clinical algorithms. *New England Journal of Medicine*, *383*(9), 874-882.

Obermeyer, Z., Powers, B., Vogeli, C., & Mullainathan, S. (2019). Dissecting racial bias in an algorithm used to manage the health of populations. *Science*, *366*(6464), 447-453.

Schmitt, J. B., Debbelt, C. A., & Schneider, F. M. (2018). Too much information? Predictors of information overload in the context of online news exposure. *Information, Communication & Society*, *21*(8), 1151-1167.

Karr-Wisniewski, P., & Lu, Y. (2010). When more is too much: Operationalizing technology overload and exploring its impact on knowledge worker productivity. *Computers in Human Behavior*, *26*(5), 1061-1072.

Sheppard, A., & Broughton, M. C. (2020). Promoting wellbeing and health through active participation in music and dance: a systematic review. *International journal of qualitative studies on health and well-being*, *15*(1), 1732526.
Nair, P. S., Raijas, P., Ahvenainen, M., Philips, A. K., Ukkola-Vuoti, L., & Järvelä, I. (2021). Music-listening regulates human microRNA expression. *Epigenetics*, *16*(5), 554-566.

Wadley, G., Krause, A., Liang, J., Wang, Z., & Leong, T. W. (2019, December). Use of music streaming platforms for emotion regulation by international students. In *Proceedings of the 31st Australian Conference on Human-Computer-Interaction* (pp. 337-341).

Berberian, M., Walker, M. S., & Kaimal, G. (2019). 'Master My Demons': art therapy montage paintings by active-duty military service members with traumatic brain injury and post-traumatic stress. *Medical humanities*, *45*(4), 353-360.

Genuth, A., & Drake, J. E. (2021). The benefits of drawing to regulate sadness and anger: Distraction versus expression. *Psychology of Aesthetics, Creativity, and the Arts*, *15*(1), 91.

Koike T, Sumiya M, Nakagawa E, Okazaki S, Sadato N. What Makes Eye Contact Special? Neural Substrates of On-Line Mutual Eye-Gaze: A Hyperscanning fMRI Study. eNeuro. 2019 Feb 28;6(1):ENEURO.0284-18.2019. doi: 10.1523/ENEURO.0284-18.2019. PMID: 30834300; PMCID: PMC6397949.

Cañigueral, R., & Hamilton, A. F. D. C. (2019). The role of eye gaze during natural social interactions in typical and autistic people. *Frontiers in psychology*, *10*, 560.

Baah, N. G., Bondzi-Simpson, A., & Ayeh, J. K. (2020). How neophilia drives international tourists' acceptance of local cuisine. *Current Issues in Tourism*, *23*(18), 2302-2318.

Loucks, E. B., Schuman-Olivier, Z., Saadeh, F. B., Scarpaci, M. M., Nardi, W. R., Proulx, J. A., ... &
Kronish, I. M. (2023). Effect of Adapted Mindfulness Training in Participants With Elevated Office Blood Pressure: The MB-BP Study: A Randomized Clinical Trial. *Journal of the American Heart Association*, e028712.

Chang, Y. C., Yeh, T. L., Chang, Y. M., & Hu, W. Y. (2021). Short-term effects of randomized mindfulness-based intervention in female breast cancer survivors: a systematic review and meta-analysis. *Cancer Nursing*, *44*(6), E703-E714.

Pandya, A., & Lodha, P. (2021). Social connectedness, excessive screen time during COVID-19 and mental health: a review of current evidence. *Frontiers in Human Dynamics*, *3*, 684137.

Cassiers, L. L., Sabbe, B. G., Schmaal, L., Veltman, D. J., Penninx, B. W., & Van Den Eede, F. (2018). Structural and functional brain abnormalities associated with exposure to different childhood trauma subtypes: A systematic review of neuroimaging findings. *Frontiers in psychiatry*, 9, 329.

Georgy, M. S. S. (2019). Neuropsychiatric and Neurobiological Consideration for Pornographic Addiction and Compulsive Sexual Disorder. *Clin Case Rep Open Access*, 2(4), 135.
Bandinelli, C., & Cossu, A. (2023). Bye bye romance, welcome reputation: An analysis of the digital enclosure of dating. *Sexualities*, 13634607231152427.

Flug, K. C. (2016). Swipe, right? young people and online dating in the digital age.
Narici, M., Vito, G. D., Franchi, M., Paoli, A., Moro, T., Marcolin, G., ... & Maganaris, C. (2021). Impact of sedentarism due to the COVID-19 home confinement on neuromuscular, cardiovascular and metabolic health: Physiological and pathophysiological implications and recommendations for physical and nutritional countermeasures. *European journal of sport science*, 21(4), 614-635.

Calcaterra, V., Vandoni, M., Marin, L., Carnevale Pellino, V., Rossi, V., Gatti, A., ... & Zuccotti, G. (2023). Exergames to Limit Weight Gain and to Fight Sedentarism in Children and Adolescents with Obesity. *Children*, 10(6), 928..

Guerra, H. S., Brugnoli, A. V. M., Melo, R. R. C., Moriguchi, E. H., Pattussi, M. P., & Costa, J. S. D. D. (2022). Time using a computer as a discriminator of obesity, sedentarism and cardiovascular risk factors in university students. *Revista Brasileira de Educação Médica*, 46.

Chandrasekaran, B., & Ganesan, T. B. (2021). Sedentarism and chronic disease risk in COVID 19 lockdown–a scoping review. *Scottish Medical Journal*, 66(1), 3-10.

Koch, C., Wilhelm, M., Salzmann, S., Rief, W., & Euteneuer, F. (2019). A meta-analysis of heart rate variability in major depression. *Psychological Medicine*, 49(12), 1948-1957.

Shaffer F, Ginsberg JP. An Overview of Heart Rate Variability Metrics and Norms. Front Public Health. 2017 Sep 28;5:258. doi: 10.3389/fpubh.2017.00258. PMID: 29034226; PMCID: PMC5624990.

Professional, C. C. M. (n.d.). *Heart rate variability (HRV)*. Cleveland Clinic. https://my.clevelandclinic.org/health/symptoms/21773-heart-rate-variability-hrv

Sugaya, N., Shirasaka, T., Takahashi, K., & Kanda, H. (2019). Bio-psychosocial factors of children and adolescents with internet gaming disorder: a systematic review. *BioPsychoSocial medicine*, 13(1), 1-16.

Blum, J., Rockstroh, C., & Göritz, A. S. (2019). Heart rate variability biofeedback based on slow-paced breathing with immersive virtual reality nature scenery. *Frontiers in Psychology*, 10, 2172.

Dougherty, R. J., Hoang, T. D., Launer, L. J., Jacobs, D. R., Sidney, S., & Yaffe, K. (2021). Long-term television viewing patterns and gray matter brain volume in midlife. *Brain Imaging and Behavior*, 1-8.
United States Census Bureau QuickFacts. (n.d.). *U.S. Census Bureau QuickFacts: United States*. Census Bureau QuickFacts.
https://www.census.gov/quickfacts/fact/table/US/RHI825222#RHI825222

Center for American Progress. (2015). https://cdn.americanprogress.org/wp-content/uploads/2015/08/05075256/PeopleOfColor-Democracy-FS.pdf

Buchholz, K. (2023, February 27). How diverse is Congress? *Statista Daily Data*. https://www.statista.com/chart/18905/us-congress-by-race-ethnicity/

Clerk. US House of Representatives. (2023). https://clerk.house.gov/Members#Demographics

Totenberg, N. (2023, June 29). Supreme Court guts affirmative action, effectively ending race-conscious admissions. *NPR*. https://www.npr.org/2023/06/29/1181138066/affirmative-action-supreme-court-decision

Shabbir, T., Ahmed, S., Kalwar, B. A., Uddin, S. S., & Chandio, A. S. USING SOCIAL MEDIA FOR ANALYZING CLIMATE IMPACT ON FOOD SECURITY AND NUTRITION AND SUSTAINABLE AGRICULTURE.

Ijoma, J. N., Sahn, M., Mack, K. N., Akam, E., Edwards, K. J., Wang, X., ... & Henry, K. E. (2021). Visions by WIMIN: BIPOC representation matters. *Molecular Imaging and Biology*, 1-6.

Lee, A. Y., Moore, R. C., & Hancock, J. T. (2023). Designing misinformation interventions for all: Perspectives from AAPI, Black, Latino, and Native American community leaders on misinformation educational efforts. *Harvard Kennedy School Misinformation Review*.

Dialectical Behavior Therapy. (2020, May 6). *Self Soothing : DBT*. DBT. https://dialecticalbehaviortherapy.com/distress-tolerance/self-soothing/

Progress? What progress? Inclusion in Hollywood is limited and lacking. (2023). USC Annenberg School for Communication and Journalism. https://annenberg.usc.edu/news/research-and-impact/progress-what-progress-inclusion-hollywood-limited-and-lacking

Epperly, B., Witko, C., Strickler, R., & White, P. (2020). Rule by violence, rule by law: Lynching, Jim Crow, and the continuing evolution of voter suppression in the US. *Perspectives on Politics*, *18*(3), 756-769.

Combs, B. H. (2016). Black (and brown) bodies out of place: Towards a theoretical understanding of systematic voter suppression in the United States. *Critical Sociology*, *42*(4-5), 535-549.

Ballard, J. (2019). Millennials are the loneliest generation. *YouGov*. https://today.yougov.com/society/articles/24577-loneliness-friendship-new-friends-poll-survey?redirect_from=%2Ftopics%2Fsociety%2Farticles-reports%2F2019%2F07%2F30%2Floneliness-friendship-new-friends-poll-survey

Boardman T, Catley D, Mayo MS, Ahluwalia JS. Self-efficacy and motivation to quit during participation in a smoking cessation program. *Int J Behav Med*. 2005;12(4):266–272. doi: 10.1207/s15327558ijbm1204_7.

Borland R, Owen N, Hill D, Schofield P. Predicting attempts and sustained cessation of smoking after the introduction of workplace smoking bans. *Health Psychol.* 1991;10(5):336–342. doi: 10.1037//0278-6133.10.5.336.

Gwaltney CJ, Metrik J, Kahler CW, Shiffman S. Self-Efficacy and Smoking Cessation: A Meta-Analysis. *Psychol Addict Behav.* 2009;23(1):56–66. doi: 10.1037/a0013529.

Gallus, S., Cresci, C., Rigamonti, V., Lugo, A., Bagnardi, V., Fanucchi, T., ... & Cardellicchio, S. (2023). Self-efficacy in predicting smoking cessation: A prospective study in Italy. *Tobacco Prevention & Cessation*, 9.

Schunk, D. H., & DiBenedetto, M. K. (2021). Self-efficacy and human motivation. In *Advances in motivation science* (Vol. 8, pp. 153-179). Elsevier.

Hendryx, M., Green, C. A., & Perrin, N. A. (2009). Social support, activities, and recovery from serious mental illness: STARS study findings. *The journal of behavioral health services & research*, 36, 320-329.

Garcia, V., Lambert, E., Fox, K., Heckert, D., & Pinchi, N. H. (2022). Grassroots interventions for alcohol use disorders in the Mexican immigrant community: a narrative literature review. *Journal of ethnicity in substance abuse*, 21(3), 773-792. Health IT. (2023). How big is the internet, and how do we measure it? *Health IT.* https://healthit.com.au/how-big-is-the-internet-and-how-do-we-measure-it/

Buchanan, K., Aknin, L. B., Lotun, S., & Sandstrom, G. M. (2021). Brief exposure to social media during the COVID-19 pandemic: Doom-scrolling has negative emotional consequences, but kindness-scrolling does not. *Plos one*, 16(10), e0257728.

Pas, L. (2023). *The Influence of Depression on Doom Scrolling and Climate Change Engagement: A Mixed-Methods Study* (Bachelor's thesis, University of Twente). D'Ercole, R. (2021). Fighting a New Wave of Voter Suppression: Securing College Students' Right to Vote Through the Twenty-Sixth Amendment's Enforcement Clause. *Washington and Lee Law Review*, 78(4), 1659.

Allcott, H., & Gentzkow, M. (2017). Social media and fake news in the 2016 election. *Journal of economic perspectives*, 31(2), 211-236.

Ferrara, E., Chang, H., Chen, E., Muric, G., & Patel, J. (2020). Characterizing social media manipulation in the 2020 US presidential election. *First Monday*.

Phan, A., Seigfried-Spellar, K., & Choo, K. K. R. (2021). Threaten me softly: A review of potential dating app risks. *Computers in human behavior reports*, 3, 100055.

Rosenfeld MJ, Thomas RJ. Searching for a mate: The rise of the Internet as a social intermediary. American Sociological Review. 2012;77: 523–547.

Stoicescu, M., & Rughiniş, C. (2021, May). Perils of digital intimacy. A classification framework for privacy, security, and safety risks on dating apps. In *2021 23rd International Conference on Control Systems and Computer Science (CSCS)* (pp. 457-462). IEEE.

Dyar, C., Crosby, S., Newcomb, M. E., Mustanski, B., & Kaysen, D. (2022). Doomscrolling: Prospective associations between daily COVID news exposure, internalizing symptoms, and substance use among sexual and gender minority individuals assigned female at birth. *Psychology of Sexual Orientation and Gender Diversity*.

Mannell, K., & Meese, J. (2022). From doom-scrolling to news avoidance: limiting news as a wellbeing strategy during COVID lockdown. *Journalism Studies*, *23*(3), 302-319.

Satici, S. A., Gocet Tekin, E., Deniz, M. E., & Satici, B. (2023). Doomscrolling scale: Its association with personality traits, psychological distress, social media use, and wellbeing. *Applied Research in Quality of Life*, *18*(2), 833-847.

Mariek M. P. Vanden Abeele, "Digital Wellbeing as a Dynamic Construct," Communication Theory (2020): 7, https://doi.org/10.1093/ct/qtaa024.

The benefits of quitting smoking now. (2022, July 26). www.heart.org. https://www.heart.org/en/healthy-living/healthy-lifestyle/quit-smoking-tobacco/the-benefits-of-quitting-smoking-now#:~:text=According%20to%20the%20American%20Heart,your%20blood%20return%20to%20normal.

Cuesta-Cambra, U., Martínez-Martínez, L., & Niño-González, J. I. (2019). An analysis of pro-vaccine and anti-vaccine information on social networks and the internet: Visual and emotional patterns. *Profesional de la Información*, *28*(2).

Ilmonen, K. (2019). Identity politics revisited: On Audre Lorde, intersectionality, and mobilizing writing styles. *European Journal of Women's Studies*, *26*(1), 7-22.

Wells, A. S., Fox, L., & Cordova-Cobo, D. (2016). How racially diverse schools and classrooms can benefit all students. *The Education Digest*, *82*(1), 17.

Achor, S. (2012). *Shawn Achor | Speaker | TED*. TED Talks. https://www.ted.com/speakers/shawn_achor

Allen, S. (2018). *The science of gratitude* (pp. 1217948920-1544632649). Conshohocken, PA: John Templeton Foundation.

Nguyen, A. W. (2020). Religion and mental health in racial and ethnic minority populations: A review of the literature. *Innovation in Aging*, *4*(5), igaa035. https://lilianjansbeken.nl/artikelen/Jans-Beken%202020%20-%20Gratitude%20and%20health%20An%20updated%20review.pdf
https://leeds-faculty.colorado.edu/dahe7472/OB%202022/locklear%202021.pdf
https://link.springer.com/article/10.1007/s10902-020-00236-6

Fry, C. (2021). Sleep deprived but socially connected: balancing the risks and benefits of adolescent screen time during COVID-19. *Journal of Children and Media*, *15*(1), 37-40.
https://www.pewresearch.org/journalism/2023/09/26/black-americans-experiences-with-news/
https://www.unlv.edu/news/article/unpacking-how-media-influences-our-views-racism

Chambers, R., Gibson, M., Chaffin, S., Takagi, T., Nguyen, N., & Mears-Clark, T. (2024). Trauma-coerced attachment and complex PTSD: informed care for survivors of human trafficking. *Journal of Human Trafficking*, *10*(1), 41-50.

Casassa, K., Knight, L., & Mengo, C. (2022). Trauma bonding perspectives from service providers and survivors of sex trafficking: A scoping review. *Trauma, violence, & abuse*, *23*(3), 969-984.

Fjell, A. M., Sørensen, Ø., Amlien, I. K., Bartrés-Faz, D., Brandmaier, A. M., Buchmann, N., ... & Walhovd, K. B. (2021). Poor self-reported sleep is related to regional cortical thinning in aging but not memory decline—results from the Lifebrain Consortium. *Cerebral Cortex*, *31*(4), 1953-1969.

Ghosh, A. (2021). Analyzing toxicity in online gaming communities. *Turkish Journal of Computer and Mathematics Education (TURCOMAT)*, *12*(10), 4448-4455.

McKenna, J. L., Wang, Y. C., Williams, C. R., McGregor, K., & Boskey, E. R. (2024). "You can't be deadnamed in a video game": Transgender and gender diverse adolescents' use of video game avatar creation for gender-affirmation and exploration. *Journal of LGBT Youth*, *21*(1), 29-49.

Corboz, M. (2020). The Last of Us Part II (2020): Queerphobic Discourse in Video Game Reviews. *PhD diss., University of Lausanne*.

Rodrigo-Yanguas, M., González-Tardón, C., Bella-Fernández, M., & Blasco-Fontecilla, H. (2022). Serious video games: angels or demons in patients with attention-deficit hyperactivity disorder? A quasi-systematic review. *Frontiers in psychiatry*, *13*, 798480.

Masi, L., Abadie, P., Herba, C., Emond, M., Gingras, M. P., & Amor, L. B. (2021). Video games in ADHD and non-ADHD children: Modalities of use and association with ADHD symptoms. *Frontiers in pediatrics*, *9*, 632272.

Tiraboschi, G. A., West, G. L., Boers, E., Bohbot, V. D., & Fitzpatrick, C. (2022). Associations between video game engagement and ADHD symptoms in early adolescence. *Journal of attention disorders*, *26*(10), 1369-1378.

Rochester review :: University of Rochester. (n.d.). https://www.rochester.edu/pr/Review/V74N4/0402_brainscience.html

Li, C., Kee, Y. H., Zhang, C. Q., & Fan, R. (2021). Predicting effects of ADHD symptoms and mindfulness on smartphone overuse in athletes: A basic psychological needs perspective. *Sustainability*, *13*(11), 6027.

Hong, Y. P., Yeom, Y. O., & Lim, M. H. (2021). Relationships between smartphone addiction and smartphone usage types, depression, ADHD, stress, interpersonal problems, and parenting attitude with middle school students. *Journal of Korean medical science*, *36*(19).

Garis, M. G., & Garis, M. G. (2022, November 9). *7 Signs Your Can-Do attitude is actually 'Toxic positivity' in disguise*. Well+Good. https://www.wellandgood.com/toxic-positivity/

Kleimaker, A., Kleimaker, M., Bäumer, T., Beste, C., & Münchau, A. (2020). Gilles de la Tourette syndrome—A disorder of action-perception integration. *Frontiers in Neurology*, *11*, 597898.

Brain architecture. (2019, August 20). Center on the Developing Child at Harvard University. https://developingchild.harvard.edu/science/key-concepts/brain-architecture/

The Carolina Abecedarian Project. (n.d.). https://abc.fpg.unc.edu/

Campbell, F. A., & Ramey, C. T. (1991). The Carolina Abecedarian Project.

Simply Psychology. (2023, September 7). *Marshmallow Test Experiment in Psychology.* https://www.simplypsychology.org/marshmallow-test.html

Soto, E. F., Kofler, M. J., Singh, L. J., Wells, E. L., Irwin, L. N., Groves, N. B., & Miller, C. E. (2020).
Executive functioning rating scales: Ecologically valid or construct invalid?. *Neuropsychology, 34*(6), 605.

McHarg, G., Ribner, A. D., Devine, R. T., & Hughes, C. (2020). Screen time and executive function in toddlerhood: A longitudinal study. *Frontiers in Psychology, 11,* 570392.

Hutton, J. S., Dudley, J., Horowitz-Kraus, T., DeWitt, T., & Holland, S. K. (2020). Associations between screen-based media use and brain white matter integrity in preschool-aged children. *JAMA pediatrics, 174*(1), e193869-e193869.

What does screen time do to my brain? | SUNY Potsdam. (2024). SUNY Potsdam. https://www.potsdam.edu/studentlife/wellness/counseling-center/what-does-screen-time-do-my-brain

Pierce, D. (2022, July 2). How to do a Feeds Reboot to take back control of your algorithms. *The Verge.* https://www.theverge.com/23191292/control-social-algorithms-feeds-reboot-how-to

Hebert, R. (2023, April 24). How to reset Instagram Algorithm | ITGeared. *ITGeared.* https://www.itgeared.com/how-to-reset-instagram-algorithm/
Beck, S. (2021). The Brain and Swiping for Love. *Scientific Kenyon: The Neuroscience Edition, 5*(1), 107-116.
What the heck is a deepfake? | UVA Information Security.
(n.d.). https://security.virginia.edu/deepfakes
Increasing threat of Deepfake identities. (n.d.).
https://www.dhs.gov/sites/default/files/publications/increasing_threats_of_deepfake_identities_0.pdf

Chesney, B., & Citron, D. (2019). Deep fakes: A looming challenge for privacy, democracy, and national security. *Calif. L. Rev., 107,* 1753.

Mercado, M. (n.d.). Disinformation and hate speech harm bipoc.
https://www.nhmc.org/wp-content/uploads/2020/09/Disinformation-and-Hate-Speech-Harm-BIPOC-NHMC.pdf

Little, B. (2019, July 12). The U.S. Deported a Million of Its Own Citizens to Mexico During the Great Depression. Retrieved August 18, 2020, from https://www.history.com/news/great-depression-repatriation-drives-mexico-deportation.

Alba, D. (2020, June 01). Misinformation About George Floyd Protests Surges on Social Media. Retrieved August 14, 2020, from https://www.nytimes.com/2020/06/01/technology/george-floyd-misinformation-online.html

Guynn, J. (2019, February 13). If you've been harassed online, you're not alone. More than half of Americans say they've experienced hate. USA Today. https://www.usatoday.com/story/news/2019/02/13/study-most-americans-have-been-targeted-hateful-speech-online/2846987002/.

Pawlowski, E., & Mamedova, S. (2018, May 29). A Description of U.S. Adults Who Are Not Digitally Literate. Retrieved August 20, 2020, from https://nces.ed.gov/pubs2018/2018161.pdf.

Ghaffary, S. (2019, August 15). The algorithms that detect hate speech online are biased against black people.https://www.vox.com/recode/2019/8/15/20806384/social-media-hate-speech-bias-blackafrican-american-facebook-twitter.

Dunard, N. (2020). Deep fakes: The algorithms that create and detect them and the national security risks they pose. *James Madison Undergraduate Research Journal (JMURJ)*, *8*(1), 5.

Chesney, R., & Citron, D. K. (2018). 21st century-style truth decay: Deep fakes and the challenge for privacy, free expression, and national security. *Md. L. Rev.*, *78*, 882.

PBS NewsHour. (2024, April 16). *WATCH LIVE: Senate Judiciary hearing on the risk of AI deepfakes and the U.S. election* [Video]. YouTube. https://www.youtube.com/watch?v=DWWTrh40S04

Lovett, D. (2022). Rhetorical Twitter Tactics: Nikole Hannah-Jones and Digital Resistance on Twitter. *Search in*.

Nguyen, T. T., Criss, S., Michaels, E. K., Cross, R. I., Michaels, J. S., Dwivedi, P., ... & Gee, G. C. (2021). Progress and push-back: How the killings of Ahmaud Arbery, Breonna Taylor, and George Floyd impacted public discourse on race and racism on Twitter. *SSM-population health*, *15*, 100922.

Beck, S. (2021). The Brain and Swiping for Love. *Scientific Kenyon: The Neuroscience Edition*, *5*(1), 107-116.
The uneven playing field in healthcare - BioLogos. (2021, April 21). BioLogos. https://biologos.org/articles/the-uneven-playing-field-in-healthcare

Weir, K. (n.d.). *Why we believe alternative facts*. https://www.apa.org. https://www.apa.org/monitor/2017/05/alternative-facts

Where are memories stored in the brain? (2018, July 23). Queensland Brain Institute - University of Queensland. https://qbi.uq.edu.au/brain-basics/memory/where-are-memories-stored

Diaz, D. (2022, January 31). *How learning and memory work together*. University of Sunderland. https://online.sunderland.ac.uk/how-learning-and-memory-work-together/

Nouchi, R., Taki, Y., Takeuchi, H., Hashizume, H., Nozawa, T., Kambara, T., ... & Kawashima, R. (2013). Brain training game boosts executive functions, working memory and processing speed in the young adults: a randomized controlled trial. *PloS one*, *8*(2), e55518.

Ger, E., & Roebers, C. M. (2023). The relationship between executive functions, working memory, and intelligence in kindergarten children. *Journal of Intelligence*, *11*(4), 64.

Seshadri, A., MD. (2022, September 14). *Boost your brain with boredom*. Mayo Clinic Health System. https://www.mayoclinichealthsystem.org/hometown-health/speaking-of-health/boost-your-brain-with-boredom

Ndetei, D. M., Nyamai, P., & Mutiso, V. (2023). Boredom–understanding the emotion and its impact on our lives: an African perspective. *Frontiers in Sociology*, *8*, 1213190.

Roberto, A., Sellon, A., Cherry, S. T., Hunter-Jones, J., & Winslow, H. (2020). Impact of spirituality on resilience and coping during the COVID-19 crisis: A mixed-method approach investigating the impact on women. *Health care for women international*, *41*(11-12), 1313-1334.

Cook, C. C., & Powell, A. (Eds.). (2022). *Spirituality and psychiatry*. Cambridge University Press.

Npr. (2008, May 17). Liquid crystal display invented 40 years ago. *NPR*. https://www.npr.org/2008/05/17/90561047/liquid-crystal-display-invented-40-years-ago

VOTECHNIK. (2023, January 26). *The Hidden Costs of LCD disposal: Investigating the environmental impact of electronic waste.* https://votechnik.com/the-hidden-costs-of-lcd-disposal/#:~:text=Environmental%20Impact%20of%20LCD%20Waste&text=Many%20LCD%20screens%20contain%20toxic,term%20impact%20on%20the%20environment.

Potentially toxic chemicals from LCDs in nearly half of household dust samples tested: USask-led study. (2019, December 16). News. https://news.usask.ca/articles/research/2019/potentially-toxic-chemicals-from-lcds-in-nearly-half-of-household-dust-samples-tested-usask-led-study.php

Amnesty International. (2021, August 16). *Exposed: Child labour behind smart phone and electric car batteries.* https://www.amnesty.org/en/latest/news/2016/01/child-labour-behind-smart-phone-and-electric-car-batteries/

This is where your smartphone battery begins. (2016.). Washington Post. https://www.washingtonpost.com/graphics/business/batteries/congo-cobalt-mining-for-lithium-ion-battery/

Mining, M., & Mining, M. (2021, June 17). *The top 10 metals and minerals powering your mobile phone.* MEC Mining | TRUSTED EXPERTISE. PROVEN OUTCOMES. https://www.mecmining.com.au/the-top-10-metals-and-minerals-powering-your-mobile-phone/

Kanungo, A. (2024, March 5). *The real environmental impact of AI | Earth.Org*. Earth.Org. https://earth.org/the-green-dilemma-can-ai-fulfil-its-potential-without-harming-the-environment/

Hao, K. (2020, December 7). Training a single AI model can emit as much carbon as five cars in their lifetimes. *MIT Technology Review*. https://www.technologyreview.com/2019/06/06/239031/training-a-single-ai-model-can-emit-as-much-carbon-as-five-cars-in-their-lifetimes/

Sims, G., Hendrix, J., & Barrett, P. (2021, September 27). How tech platforms fuel U.S. political polarization and what government can do about it. *Brookings*. https://www.brookings.edu/articles/how-tech-platforms-fuel-u-s-political-polarization-and-what-government-can-do-about-it/

Gaultney, I. B., Sherron, T., & Boden, C. (2022). Political Polarization, Misinformation, and Media Literacy. *Journal of Media Literacy Education, 14*(1), 59-81.

LaCapria, K. (2016, January 14). Snopes' field guide to fake news sites and hoax purveyors. *Snopes*. https://www.snopes.com/news/2016/01/14/fake-news-sites/

Research guides: Evaluating news: "Fake news" and beyond: fact checking sites. (n.d.). https://guides.csbsju.edu/c.php?g=621995&p=4332693

Australian Competition and Consumer Commission. (2023, July 9). *ACCC invites views on data broker industry*. https://www.accc.gov.au/media-release/accc-invites-views-on-data-broker-industry

Dhaliwal, J. (2024, May 2). *What is a data broker?* McAfee Blog. https://www.mcafee.com/blogs/tips-tricks/what-is-a-data-broker/

Mine - the future of data ownership. (n.d.). https://www.saymine.com/
Bethel, S. STIMMING.

Rochester review :: University of Rochester. (n.d.). https://www.rochester.edu/pr/Review/V74N4/0402_brainscience.html

Miner, J. (2019). Raising a screen-smart kid: Embrace the good and avoid the bad in the digital age. Penguin Publishing Group.

Sobel, A. (2024, December 12). *Eight ways to improve your empathy*. Andrew Sobel. https://andrewsobel.com/article/eight-ways-to-improve-your-empathy/

Abramson, A. (2021, November 1). Cultivating empathy. Monitor on Psychology, 52(8). https://www.apa.org/monitor/2021/11/feature-cultivating-empathy

Smith, J. G., & Luykx, A. (2017). Race play in BDSM porn: The eroticization of oppression. *Porn Studies, 4*(4), 433-446.

U.S. Census Bureau (2022) QuickFacts: United States
https://www.census.gov/quickfacts/fact/table/US/PST045222
Confirms that the non-Hispanic white population was approximately 59%.

Smith, S. L., Choueiti, M., Pieper, K., & Clark, H. (2023).

Inclusion in the Director's Chair: Analysis of 1,600 top films (2007–2022)
USC Annenberg Inclusion Initiative
https://annenberg.usc.edu/research/aii
This is your go-to citation for inclusion stats across gender, race, LGBTQ+ identity, and disability in film.

Hunt, D., Ramón, A. C., & Tran, M. (2022).
Hollywood Diversity Report 2022: A New Post-Pandemic Normal?
UCLA College of Social Sciences
https://socialsciences.ucla.edu/hollywood-diversity-report/
Covers diversity trends both in front of and behind the camera in film and television.

www.ingramcontent.com/pod-product-compliance
Lightning Source LLC
Chambersburg PA
CBHW081327230426
43667CB00018B/2853